PRAISE FOR *THE SHAMAN'S* *TO POWER ANIMALS*

"Soon to be a classic, this is truly the ultimate guide to spirit animals. Richly researched and written, the meanings and symbolism of animals pop off the pages, fulfilling your curiosity and enriching your connection. Shamanic perspectives from Mongolia to Machu Picchu are woven into this dynamic tapestry of wisdom by a powerful female shaman, who brings the voices of animals to humanity with surprising and enlightening messages. Certainly, a guide that I will refer to over and over to deepen my understanding of the animal kingdom and its superpowers."

—**Betsy Chasse**, author of *Tipping Sacred Cows* and cowriter/codirector/producer of *What the Bleep Do We Know!?* and producer of *Song of the New Earth*

"Lori Morrison has a profound connection to the spirit world that is evidenced in the contents of this book. She sees between the worlds and knows how to speak to the spirits of the animal nation. She then takes this gift and titrates it into usable form for the reader to glean insightful messages from the spirit world. Her book gives an analysis of the physical natures of numerous animals and interprets the meaning of the animal for persons who might encounter them in their spiritual journey. The encyclopedic nature of the work allows for easy reference to scientific fact and metaphysical attributes. As a reference guide it is a valuable assistance to the reader to discover deeper awareness of the messages that animals embody."

—**Jan Engels-Smith M.Ed., Sh.D.**, founder of LightSong School of Twenty-first-Century Shamanism and Energy Medicine, author of *Becoming Yourself* and *Through the Rabbit Hole*

"Between the covers of this book is a bounty of information from the voices of the animal spirit world. A treasure chest full of enlightenment and wisdom, this book will serve humanity in expanding a connection to the deeper meaning of spirit animals in our world. *The Shaman's Guide to Power Animals* will encourage our appreciation of Power Animals as mentors and wisdom keepers throughout our spiritual journey."

—**Stephanie Phelps,** intuitive spiritual guide, healer, teacher, and ceremonialist, owner of White Horse Journeys

"Lori Morrison's book is the ultimate shaman's handbook to Power Animals! I look forward to using this book as a go-to reference for my work."

—**Gogo Ekhaya Esima,** sangoma, traditional healer, and writer

"Lori is a gifted and powerful healer with the ability to see, hear, and communicate with alternative realities and the beings that reside there. Her unique skills bring forth vision, wisdom, clarity, and, ultimately, power and protection and healing for those that seek her services. She is a powerhouse, whose relationship with the spirit world is unequaled.

"What a fantastic departure from the basic facts and data that other totem animal books and websites typically regurgitate. This is not a carbon copy of anything else out there. This guide is authentic and refreshing, helping readers walk the mystical path with practical feet.

"While you will learn about animals in the Middle World you will also receive the channeled messages from the spirit animals themselves. This will allow you to have a deeper connection and understanding of the spirit world so that you can form your own relationship with these powerful allies."

—**Ashley Brothers**, shaman and founder of www.bonesoftheearth.org

THE SHAMAN'S GUIDE TO POWER ANIMALS

LORI MORRISON

Four Jaguars Press

Cover design: Caroline Maniere
CarolineManiere.com

Book Design: Gus Yoo

Editor: Stephanie Gunning
StephanieGunning.com

Library of Congress Control Number 2018965555

ISBN: 978-0-9987378-9-8

"Until one has loved an animal, a part of one's soul remains unawakened."
—Anatole France

AUTHOR'S NOTE

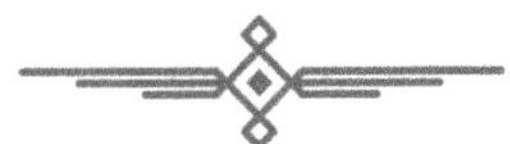

This book holds channeled messages from the spirits of almost 200 animals who came to support our earthly existence from their enlightened, power-animal perspective. The experience of connecting with these animal spirits revealed a lot to me about the intelligence of animals and their attunement with the world around them. They are ultrasensory, possessing a heightened awareness and perception of the natural environment that exceeds ours.

The relationships animals have with others of their own kind and other creatures are remarkable and distinctive. In the wild, they thrive on connectivity. The animals of the night have an extraordinary connection to the cosmos. They understand the cycles of the Moon and the other planets in our solar system, which guides them and supports their existence. Whether animals burrow in the soil or shelter above ground, nest in trees, or swim in the oceans, they carry an intelligence of our world's resources: They know what to gather for their food and in order to build their homes, and naturally return gifts in exchange for that which is taken. They are working in unison with Mother Earth, helping her to thrive, breathe, and ascend.

In my channeling of the animal spirits I learned that most animals on Earth live in a state of unconditional love and compassion for all things—including humankind. The complexity of the messages of the animal spirits often surprised me, especially the level of brilliance they have about human behavior. Earth's animal species—from the fish and insects, to the birds, reptiles, and mammals—are hard working in diverse ways. They live by instinct and have mastered the Earth walk. On a spiritual level, they are engaged in activities to sustain humanity that I did not anticipate.

Many of the animal spirits expressed deep empathy for us. Some struggled to understand our behaviors and perspectives and told me that they hoped more people would develop heightened awareness. Their generosity was astounding and beautiful. All the animal spirits came to me enthusiastically to share, demonstrating a willingness to offer their powers to all who would choose to work with them. They collectively hope that our relationship with them changes from domination to partnership. They ask that those who read this book protect their wisdom and commit to assuring them safe environments in which to thrive.

DEDICATION

To all animals who so graciously have shared their messages with us. We honor your awareness, powers, knowledge, and mastery of nature, which, through this book, will build a bridge between the world of animal spirits and humanity. May your sacred wisdom be a catalyst for shapeshifting the human soul, so it may love and feel deep appreciation for all creatures. We honor the sacred contribution of animals to our lives and our planet.

To the indigenous peoples of the world, the shamans, medicine men and women who have embraced the knowledge of Power Animals and kept its importance alive in the world so that others could learn and apply the practice of communicating with animal spirits. Your efforts to keep the fire of understanding the natural world burning is an enormous gift to the unconscious people of the world, children of the Great Creator, and to "all of our relations."

CONTENTS

Preface 1

PART ONE: THE WORLD OF SHAMANS AND THEIR POWER ANIMALS
The Tree of Life and the Symbolism of the Three Worlds 6
Nonordinary Reality 8
The Three Worlds 9
The Shaman 10
Power Animals 11
Types of Power Animals 12
Your Power Animal 14
Determining Your Power Animal 15
Calling in Your Power Animal 16
A Shamanic Journey 19
Indigenous Theories and Beliefs 21
Shape Shifting 22
Dreams 23
Power 24
Quantum Power Animal Retrieval 25
Energy Centers and Minerals 26
The Five Shamanic Elements 28
Summary 30

PART TWO: A TO Z GUIDE TO POWER ANIMALS
Aardvark 35
Albatross 36
Angelfish 37
Ant 38
Anteater 40
Antelope 41
Armadillo 42

Badger 43
Barracuda 44
Bat 45
Bear 46
Beaver 48
Bee 49
Beetle 51
Blackbird 52
Bluebird 53
Blue Jay 54
Boar 55
Bobcat 56
Buffalo 57
Butterfly 58
Caterpillar 60
Camel 61
Canary 62
Capybara 63
Cardinal 64
Caribou 65
Carp 66
Goldfish ⋆ Koi
Cat (Domestic) 67
Catfish 68
Cattle—Bull 69
Cattle—Cow 70
Centipede/Millipede 71
Chameleon 72
Cheetah 73
Chickadee 74
Chicken—Hen 75
Chicken—Rooster 76
Cicada 77
Condor 78
Vulture
Coral 79
Cormorant 80

Cougar 81
Puma
Coyote 82
Crab 83
Crane 84
Cricket 85
Crocodile 86
Alligator
Cuckoo. 87
Deer 88
Dingo 89
Dog (Domestic). 90
Dolphin 91
Porpoise
Donkey. 92
Ass ★ Burro
Dove. 93
Dragon 94
Dragonfly 95
Duck 96
Eagle. 97
Earthworm 99
Eel 100
Elephant 101
Elk 102
Emu 103
Falcon. 104
Firefly 105
Flea. 106
Fly 107
Fox 108
Frog 109
Giraffe 110
Goat 111
Goldfinch 112
Goose 113
Gopher 114

Gorilla 115
Grasshopper 117
Grouse 118
Groundhog 119
Guinea Pig 120
Hawk 121
Hedgehog 122
Heron 123
Egret
Hippopotamus 124
Horse 125
Hummingbird 127
Hyena 129
Ibis 130
Jackal 131
Jaguar 132
Javelina 133
Jellyfish 134
Kangaroo 135
Kingfisher 136
Kookaburra
Koala 137
Ladybug 138
Lark 139
Leech 140
Lemur 141
Leopard 142
Black Panther
Lion 143
Lizard 144
Chameleon ★ Gecko ★ Gila Monster ★ Iguana ★ Komodo Dragon
Llama 146
Alpaca ★ Guanaco ★ Vicuna
Manatee 147
Mockingbird 148
Thrasher
Mole 149

Mongoose 150
Meercat
Monkey 151
Baboon ★ Chimpanzee ★ Orangutan
Moose 153
Mosquito 154
Moth 155
Motmot 156
Mouse 157
Musk Ox 158
Nighthawk 159
Nuthatch 160
Octopus 161
Opossum 162
Ostrich 163
Otter 164
Owl 165
Panda 167
Parrot 168
Budgie ★ Cockatiel ★ Cockatoo ★ Love Bird ★ Macaw ★ Parakeet
Peafowl 170
Pelican 172
Penguin 173
Pheasant 174
Phoenix 175
Pig 176
Platypus 177
Porcupine 178
Prairie Dog 179
Praying Mantis 180
Puffin 181
Quail 182
Quetzal 183
Rabbit 185
Raccoon 187
Rat 188
Raven 189
Crow

Red Panda . . . 191
Rhinoceros . . . 192
Roadrunner . . . 193
Robin . . . 194
Salamander . . . 195
Salmon . . . 196
Sandpiper . . . 197
Scorpion . . . 198
Seagull . . . 199
Seahorse . . . 200
Seal . . . 201
Elephant Seal ★ Sea Lion ★ Walrus
Secretary Bird . . . 202
Shark . . . 203
Sheep/Ram . . . 205
Skunk . . . 207
Sloth . . . 208
Snail . . . 209
Conch ★ Slug
Snake . . . 210
Anaconda ★ Boa Constrictor ★ Cobra ★ Python ★ Rattlesnake
Sparrow . . . 212
Spider . . . 213
Black Widow ★ Daddy Long Leg ★ Recluse
Squirrel . . . 214
Starfish . . . 215
Starling . . . 216
Stingray . . . 217
Stork . . . 218
Swallow . . . 219
Swan . . . 220
Tasmanian Devil . . . 222
Thunderbird . . . 223
Tiger . . . 224
Toucan . . . 226
Turkey . . . 227
Turtle . . . 228
Tortoise

Unicorn 230
Wasp 231
Weasel 232
Ferret ⋆ Mink
Whale 233
Beluga ⋆ Humpback ⋆ Orca
Wolf 235
Wolverine 237
Wombat 238
Woodpecker 239
Sapsucker
Zebra 240

List of Endangered Animals 242
Table of Powers and Minerals 244
Acknowledgments 249
References 251
Art Credits 282
Resources 286
About Lori Morrison 288

THE SHAMAN'S GUIDE TO POWER ANIMALS

PREFACE

It was a rainy day in the Pacific Northwest. I lifted my five-year-old body into my father's delivery van. Our cargo was buttermilk pancake mix, maple syrup, bacon, potatoes, carrots, and canned goods. We were heading to my family's logging camp on the Olympic Peninsula in Washington State in the early 1960s. The road narrowed after we got to the Quinault Indian Reservation. Because over one hundred inches of rain fall there each year, the fir trees towered above us like a cathedral as we drove between them. Moss hung like lace from their branches. My father slowed the vehicle to allow a family of Elk to cross the road.

This trip is my first memory of being out in the woods far away from the bustle of civilization. Although dedicated to logging, my father's heart was so grateful for the forests that he was always proud of his efforts to ensure they were replenished after clearing the land. Many of the trees he planted on the Olympic Peninsula are mature and thriving fifty years later. His heart walked a tightrope between human development and preservation, a complicated balancing act in those early years of logging.

Continuing down the logging road with its rain-cut crevices, we soon arrived at the camp. Young and old loggers smiled as we pulled up to the makeshift kitchen ready to provide them the ingredients for their next meals. My father jumped out of the driver's side and called for some help to unload the van. After greeting us, the cooks checked items off the list of things they had ordered by radio a couple days before. Invited to sit down to a lumberjack breakfast, seven plate-size pancakes appeared on the table in front of me. I did my best to dig into them, but my stomach was swiftly overwhelmed. For his part, my father chowed down heartily. We'd been driving for several hours.

After breakfast my father took me by the hand and we walked along the banks of the Quinault River, me more successfully than him, as my weight was perfect to prevent me from sinking deeply into the clay and mud of the shoreline. Arriving at the edge, I was awestruck. Thousands of bright coral Salmon were in the water flip-flopping and struggling to make their way upstream to their spawning grounds. My father pointed upstream to a community of Bears engaged in a feeding frenzy. They had no interest in us as their focus was on the mass migration of fish that was taking place.

This was the first moment in which I realized that something greater and wiser than me existed beyond the walls of my colorful nursery full of stuffed animals. There was a natural power ready to be discovered out in the world.

On the way back home, we bounced down the same dirt road and this time we saw a Duckling that was alone on the side of the road. I remember my mind wondering if this fluffy creature was a sign from nature intended for us. My father stopped the van and got out and, after much searching for the Duckling's mother, he realized it had been abandoned. He picked up the tiny Duck, put it in an empty carton and handed it to me. I felt so blessed by this gift from the forest as I held the box with the Duckling on my lap all the way home.

During my childhood I often spent time in nature alone. In those days, a young girl could

venture about the bustling logging town of Aberdeen, Washington, on Grays Harbor in safety. Our neighbor had a large Koi pond where I would sit for hours watching pairs of Dragonfly dart about as several Koi peeked out from under the lotuses. Frogs would sit waiting for the next insect to land on their lily pads. The pond was a microcosmic world of its own, the world of the water spirits.

Life changed as I grew older. My connection to nature diminished as I embraced a more materialistic view of the world. Other than an occasional zoo visit, or a Sunday evening spent watching *Wild Kingdom* on television, the animal world was a distant thought or interest.

Moving to El Salvador in my late twenties changed that, as I became the keeper of eighty acres of land on the slopes of a dormant volcanic crater that held Lake Ilopango. I was handed my first machete and bought myself a good pair of sturdy boots, and with my civil engineer husband, Tino, started to open a road through the peninsula that we owned. Months of adventure ensued as we darted to avoid Snake, peeked at Panther and Fox, helped an Armadillo make its way, discovered an audience of Iguanas watching us from the trees, and enjoyed the curiosity of a multitude of tropical birds. In the late afternoon, Vultures would prepare for the hunt and Opossums would climb up the palm trees for the night. Agoutis would feed on the tender vegetation and Duck, Egret, Kingfisher, Owl, and other creatures abounded on and around the lake.

Many nights, Tino and I would drive our boat to a cliff where trees hung over the water to see the arrival of hundreds of birds who would sleep in its branches overnight. I was steeped in the circle of life; the animal kingdom was my neighborhood. Our dedication to the protection of this property evolved into maintaining a private sanctuary for many animals that were brought to us after being rescued from being offered for sale as pets in the central market.

Our love of wildlife took us on many other adventures. We traveled to Yellowstone National Park in the United States—another volcano! —and had thrilling experiences there with Bear and Buffalo. In Alaska, we flew by helicopter to the top of glaciers and spent time with Brown Bears that we discovered on Dog sleds as we ventured into the snowy banks near Juneau. We watched Whales in Prince Rupert Sound and enjoyed Seals floating on chunks of ice. More travels took us to Antarctica where we saw pods of Killer Whale and Leopard Seal, and I spent a day sitting on the beach in the Falkland Islands with a colony of Penguin.

Shortly after that, my husband and I took a trip that truly captivated me and deepened even more my perception of the animal world. We went to Africa. With local trackers for our guides, we went off the beaten path to find a male Leopard. Giraffe galloped alongside our jeep and Rhinoceros and Water Buffalo often stood only a few feet away. One day I sat for hours watching a female Leopard and her two cubs playing in the sunshine. During an outdoor lunch, my meal was stolen by a Baboon.

The moment that was most profound was when seven Lionesses joined us, moving stealthily alongside our open jeep as we moved along slowly. I could have reached out and touched them, although that would not have been a good idea. As the animals were in stalking mode, I sat insanely still. Suddenly one Lioness took off perpendicularly to us, while the others stopped in front of the jeep and waited. Moments later, a herd of Gazelle came running in front of us, right into the trap that had been set. One Gazelle couldn't escape the ambush and became the victim of a feeding frenzy that I reluctantly watched. When finished, the seven Lionesses all lifted their bloody faces from the carcass and walked off.

Our next stop was Botswana, where I enjoyed watching Elephant swimming across the river from us with their trunks like snorkels peeking out of the surface of the water. Staying in a tent, a

Hippopotamus decided to sleep next to us all evening, which made for a very nervous slumber party. We floated in a boat on the Okavango River for hours, watching the arrival of Zebra and observing how the massive Alligator in the river protected their babies, which would swim happily by our craft. The morning we arrived in Johannesburg for the return flight home, I got teary about leaving. I had just had three weeks of a major hakuna matata (no problems) moment and I would never be the same again. That trip was the ultimate immersion into another world, and I had the realization that there was so much more to the animal kingdom than I understood with my relative oblivion to the natural world beyond my garden walls.

I took home with me from Africa to El Salvador the sacred wisdom that when something dies it gives a new life to another and that, from the smallest insect to the largest mammal, each of us is participating in the balance of nature. We are all connected. The animals understood this, while we humans are the least aware of our role in this dynamic existence. The insight that everything is connected including the minerals, trees, and plants shook my human foundation. My ego shrunk, becoming small and insignificant. This was the first of many steps toward a spiritual awakening.

After a major shamanic initiation by ancestral spirits in 2010, I was able to see, hear, and experience animal spirits. At my home on the edge of Lake Ilopango my ordinary reality and perceptions cracked open and the spirits of four Jaguar became my teachers. After that, a Haitian shaman performed a Power Animal ceremony with me and blew a Lion spirit into my heart chakra, which, to this day, is my constant companion. This spiritual event was the accumulation of a journey into the Lower World, the place where the spirits of animals reside.

My experience with Lion has been more than remarkable. Its guidance and teachings have been beyond what any shaman or earthly being could have ever taught me. Lion is constantly teaching; I never leave her school. We have learned to merge, and I have come to accept her powers so that I may help people heal. This partnership continues to amaze me. Lion's eyes are like x-rays into the body of the sick. Lion's powerful spine supports me to take on negative energy, chewing it up and spitting it out of me and those who seek our healing powers. Lion completely wipes away fear, as if with the flip of a switch. I am never alone. Our relationship is one of great honor and respect for both of us. Lion has learned my hardiness and my weaknesses and uses everything she finds to our advantage.

At times, I have called in other animal spirits to help me, such as Condor to give me a wider view of the world, Snake to transform energy, Beetle to fine tune my psychic powers, and numerous birds that continue to arrive with messages from the deceased for their loved ones. I have had Hawk land on branches above my head, Fox appear after leaving a drumming circle, and Deer peer into my office window during a healing session. The spirit world is alive and well through the generosity and concern that the animals show for us as humans, even if we do not yet see our role in the natural order as they see theirs. By opening our hearts to Power Animals, we will come to know ourselves and our place in the dynamic circle of life.

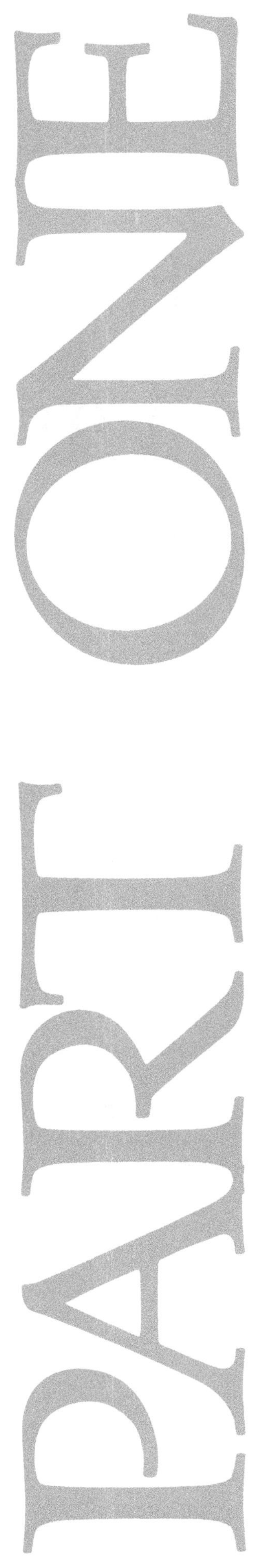

PART ONE

THE WORLD OF SHAMANS AND THEIR POWER ANIMALS

THE TREE OF LIFE AND THE SYMBOLISM OF THE THREE WORLDS

To visualize the world of the shaman it is helpful to use the symbol of the Tree of Life. This symbol has been found in almost every excavation of ruins abandoned by previous cultures and civilizations. The oldest Tree of Life was recently found in Göbekli Tepe in Turkey, an archaeological site thought to be 12,000 years old. The Tree of Life is a shamanic map to the landscape of all that exists. It has been carved in stone, written on papyrus scrolls, and orally transferred from shaman to shaman through thousands of generations. It illustrates the many dimensions that shamans travel to, in order to perceive and uncover information about the multiple layers of our existence. It also describes how to move through spiritual territories. Shamans have mastered the art of transcending the physical world by assuming a spiritual form that is able to travel the highways and byways of multidimensional reality.

The Tree of Life reminds us that we are connected, down from the roots and up through the branches, to the celestial world—that there is no separation between other dimensions of existence and ours. The separation is only a matter of perception. Unfortunately, after so many centuries of exposure to rhetoric and dogma that tells us otherwise, we have acquired a belief in separation between humanity and animals. The truth is that we are intimate partners on the planet. This sense of separation from the natural world has diminished us as human beings. But working with a Power Animal can be such an impressive experience that it reboots your personal power. You can create a relationship that enjoys the benefit of an unmeasurable spiritual experience.

Detail of world tree, sarcophagus cover, Temple of the Inscriptions, Palenque, Mexico. Drawn by Linda Schele. Rights were obtained from the Los Angeles County Museum of Art, Department of Rights and Reproductions.

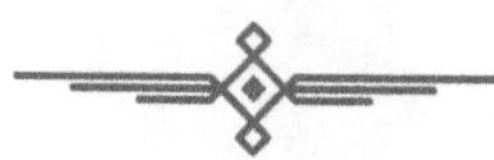

NONORDINARY REALITY

Non-ordinary reality lies beyond the seen world. It is a supernatural place (multiple dimensions, in fact) where we can connect to spirits and experience the past, present, and future simultaneously. Then we can return to ordinary reality with a wealth of information. This is a place of magic, miracles, and inexplicable experiences. Ancestors, spirits of the deceased, and helping guides—such as Power Animals—can be accessed in non-ordinary reality. Shamans shift into a trance-like state in order to move between realities with a certain level of awareness.

There are many places on earth with more easily accessible portals. Places like Egypt, Stonehenge, Sedona and Machu Picchu to mention a few, invigorate us and give us the opportunity to transcend from ordinary to nonordinary reality. In these places, the veil between the dimensions is thinner—meaning, there is a less defined separation between these realities.

Shamans take intentional journeys to contact spirits in the invisible realms. On these journeys, shamans will sense and intuitively capture what they experience. They will meet with Power Animals and spiritual teachers. The information is often downloaded into their understanding, or they will actually hear the voices of the spirits they encounter. Many shamans have extensive maps of nonordinary worlds, giving them knowledge of a clear path to where they may go to obtain the information they seek. Back in ordinary reality, they can share their experiences with others for the purpose of enlightenment.

THE THREE WORLDS

The Tree of Life represents three worlds: The Upper World, which is like the branches, the Middle World, which is like the trunk, and the Lower World, which is like the roots. Each World plays a role in the tapestry of life, death, and the in between. One cannot exist without the others. In each world, wisdom can be accessed by a shaman in an altered state of consciousness. Through chanting, drumming, dancing, or consuming medicinal plants, the shaman can travel to these three worlds to obtain information from elemental spirits and other beings who reside there. These three worlds are referred to as the shamanic cosmology. Bird spirits are important companions for shamans, as these beings can navigate the transition between the Upper World and Middle World with ease. Befriending bird spirits and learning their language can lead to receiving transformational messages.

The ***Upper World*** is normally accessed by traveling energetically through the branches of a tree with the intention of ascending upward toward the sky and then breaking through an interdimensional membrane. Beyond the membrane, you will find teachers and masters of higher vibrations. The experience here is of much light and angelic energy; it has a crystalline and etheric feeling. This world is a place of glistening trees and souls that look like bouquets of light orbs. You may find Power Animals here, although most of them are encountered in the Lower World. A Power Animal can help you reach this energetic plane.

With experience, shamans can journey to the Upper World for advice and consultation with those of a "higher vision." Spirits encountered here take on many recognizable forms. They show themselves to us as angels, archangels, ascended masters (such as Jesus and Buddha), and other teachers. The Upper World holds records of our many lifetimes—a blueprint of our total being. There is much to learn about ourselves from here.

The ***Middle World*** is where we spend our daily lives in survival mode, programed by the accumulation of our cultural conditioning and beliefs. This place is also called ordinary reality. Our ancestral spirits are found here, often still very attached to the lands in which they lived. We may also encounter the spirits of the deceased who have not transitioned. Because of our loss of connection to the natural world, many human beings can no longer see nature spirits, such as the elves, fairies, and dwarves who reside here with us. The Middle World can be a place of compassion, but also non-compassion, which is why only experienced shamans should engage with spirits who are stuck here.

The ***Lower World*** is the vast space of the natural spirit world. It may be accessed by traveling energetically through a tunnel, a cave, the root of a tree or bush, or a body of water. There is an unfortunate perception of this dimension in many cultures and religions that see it as a place of darkness and fire and where evil resides, a hell. This is untrue. It is really a beautiful landscape where Power Animals reside along with the elements of water, fire, air, earth; and plants, trees, rocks, and crystals. Here you will also find mythical animals, like Dragon and Unicorn, who have left the Middle World.

After transcending into the Lower World, you will encounter a variety of landscapes, such as deserts, mountains, lakes, or streams, with a multitude of ecosystems thriving side by side in a cosmic balance.

THE SHAMAN

"Healer and psychopomp, the shaman is these because he commands the techniques of ecstasy—that is, because his soul can safely abandon his body and roam at vast distances, can penetrate the underworld, and rise to the sky. Through his own ecstatic experience, he knows the roads of the extraterrestrial regions. He can go below or above because he has already been there. The danger of losing his way in these forbidden regions is still great; but sanctified by his initiation and furnished with his guardian spirit, a shaman is the only human being able to challenge the danger and venture into a mystical geography."

—Mircea Eliade

The term shaman comes from one tribe found in Siberia and Manchuria. Most other tribal people use different names for the role of the shaman in their communities. A shaman's craft is not a hobby or a self-improvement course. The use of Power Animals by indigenous shamans was to heal the sick, improve their crops, and contribute as spiritual counselors to their tribes on matters of life and death—including playing the role of a psychopomp, an escort for the souls of the dead to the realm of the ancestors.

For more than 40,000 years, shamans around the world have been practicing their craft of healing and divination with Power Animals. Shamans are a mystical combination of a healer, storyteller, doctor, priest, psychologist, and visionary. Shamans connect and merge with Power Animals as partners in accomplishing mystical tasks. Animal spirits are vital "medicine" for healing and protecting the shaman traveling in unknown territory and then guiding the shaman back to the third-dimensional world.

Very few modern people attain all aspects of the lifestyle of a shaman. A true shaman is chosen by spirits and it is considered to be a curse in most tribal societies. It is often bestowed abruptly, completely changing the direction of a person's life. It then requires decades of shamanic work and making the ultimate sacrifice of giving themselves to others. Many die in the course of doing their work. It requires great discipline, which is done for the sake of a community. The term *shaman* can seem seductive, but the lifestyle is not the glamorous or hipster, new age lifestyle that the label has come to imply. If there are no spirits, there is no shaman, as they live an intertwined existence.

If you have not been called to walk the ultimate shamanic path, it is not a missed opportunity; in fact, you have avoided being asked to carry a heavy load. What is very worthwhile and possible for everybody to learn from a shaman's lifestyle and practice is seeing the beauty in spiritual relationships—whether the relationship you cultivate is with a rainbow or a Butterfly. Integrating the concept of everything being connected will help you embrace the world you live in. Connecting with your personal Power Animal can be a rich and fulfilling personal experience.

POWER ANIMALS

Power Animals can be any living creature. From mammals to reptiles, insects, and sea creatures, they all bring much needed "power" into our lives. To partner with them and embody their energy, we must first be aware of them, and, second, form a relationship with them. You do not choose your Power Animal; your Power Animal chooses you. You may become aware of your Power Animal during meditation or a journey to the spirit world, or you may be introduced to it by a shaman. Beginning a relationship with a Power Animal comes with some responsibility. It is like adopting an animal into your life, with the only difference being that this animal is in spirit form. This partnership is a relationship whose foundations are trust, respect, and honor, qualities which go a long way toward ensuring a positive experience.

The terms *totem animal, animal messenger, spirit animal,* and *animal guide* are all used to describe Power Animals; however, these terms can refer to distinct roles a Power Animal may play. Often our encounters with these spirits can be the result of traits and skills we are seeking or in need of. These beings are more evolved than humans and come from an advanced spiritual dimension. Their purpose is to serve humanity and help us to raise our level of consciousness.

TYPES OF POWER ANIMALS

Totem Animal: An animal that is representative of a tribe or clan. Your connection to a totem remains with you throughout your life as a symbol of a collective power. If a person is lacking in power, the power of the totem animal can be brought in to strengthen a weakness. When a shaman names a child, the shaman often uses the name of an animal whose characteristics align with the child's life purpose and path. If the energy of the person changes as the child gets older, the person may identify and encounter his or her own Power Animal. This often happens on a vision quest or through a heroic act.

Personal Power Animal: This animal is your earthly spirit guide and you can partner with it when you go on shamanic journeys in non-ordinary reality. Any journey to the spirit world should be done while accompanied by a Power Animal, as Power Animals have the knowledge of the other worlds (especially the Lower World) and can keep you safe. The messages and support the Power Animals bring is a rewarding experience. The relationship you have with your Power Animal can become a lifelong partnership that fills you with the energy needed for your success and happiness. To go deeper into a relationship with your Power Animal think about your Power Animal as a great friend or mentor. The closer a Power Animal is to you the more knowledge you will receive.

Power Animal Messengers: Another type of Power Animal is the animal messenger that shows up in everyday life, not just in nonordinary reality. Many people are met by Bird, Butterfly, Hummingbird, and Dragonfly, to name a few common messengers. Often, we ignore the presence of the messengers, which is an error, as they can bring very profound messages and their visits have symbolic meanings. Each animal will carry a distinct message to you from the spirit world.

Shadow Power Animal: You may encounter a Power Animal in either ordinary reality or non-ordinary reality that has come to challenge you. This is your shadow animal. Its presence may seem scary or threatening, but its arrival likely indicates that the darker side of the spirit world is coming to shed light on the shadow side of your psyche and behavior. The seen world can dominate our sense of reality. In confrontations with shadow Power Animals, we need to go deeper within ourselves to discover the truth behind the mysteries we are being forced to expose. These animals often represent negative aspects of our psyche that we are ignoring.

People often ask if Power Animals have names and my experience has been that they do not have names, which is why they are referred to throughout this book by their description or label. Therefore when I talk about Power Animals, I use the terms Bear, Cardinal, and Snake, for example, as the language. Labels are not common in the spirit world. In fact, in the old times, Native Americans had no word for animals; they were called brothers and sisters.

Another question we are frequently asked is whether Power Animals come to us as male or female. Our experience has been that very rarely is gender a factor. The essence of the animal normally embodies both or one of its male and female aspects.

YOUR POWER ANIMAL

Indigenous shamans believe that every person has a Power Animal that is their protector. This Power Animal is given at birth. Although this concept may seem primitive, these ancient cultures believe that people are descended from members of other species- and are part of a lineage endowed with the power of the ancestral animal—therefore, meaning it is emblematic of our essential being; a totem animal. From the moment a child is born, a Power Animal is incorporated into their being with the hopes that their Earth walk will be calm and without fear. Should a child be faced with trauma or exorbitant fear, a shaman will intervene immediately to ensure that the child is reinforced with the energy of the Power Animal and is then strong enough to overcome the trauma. The concept of a Power Animal, in this sense, is similar to the meaning of a guardian angel.

Any Power Animal you connect with brings you wisdom derived from its own particular attributes to increase your awareness and power. Power Animals are wonderful helpers. For example, if you are lacking endurance, you may find working with Albatross helpful since it is an animal that travels great distances. If asked, Power Animals will show up to help you at intervals throughout your life. Each animal's characteristics can be called on, like calling in a specialist to manage different aspects of your journey.

Animals that have been domesticated are not considered Power Animals, since they are constantly in service to their humans in the Middle World where we all reside. I have, however, included them and their messages.

DETERMINING YOUR POWER ANIMAL

Your Power Animal is a living energy that resides in a nonordinary reality, a dimension that can be accessed through intentionality. Its wisdom is great, inspired by the millions of years of physical evolution that the animal and its ancestral lineage have undergone to master life on earth. In some cases, such as the case of reptiles and insects whose forebearers were dinosaurs, the animal species to which these animal spirits correspond have existed for many more epochs than the members of the ancestral lineage of human beings. Uniting with your Power Animal can be very rewarding. Power Animals are always around us and willing to deliver messages. Most communication from a Power Animal comes in the way of pictures, scenes, or images from that animal.

To discover your Power Animal on your own, you can ask the spirit world to show you and bring you this animal. You should not have any predisposed notion about which animal will be revealed to you. Do not be surprised if it does not fit with your ego's version of what you want. Sometimes people will feel disappointed that the Power Animal that comes to them is not what they believed it would be or what they wanted. Each animal holds distinctive knowledge that is important; it may just take you time to understand the depths of its wisdom and how it can benefit and teach you. From Flea to Elephant, the powers of Power Animals are great. Embrace the unexpected.

It has also been my experience that, when a Power Animal is revealed to someone, the person often has a subtle idea of its characteristics. People will mention that they collected artwork, trinkets, or stuffed animals of this animal throughout their lives, never previously knowing there was a spiritual connection.

CALLING IN POWER ANIMALS

Before you begin any work with the spirit world to call in your Power Animal, it is best to create a sacred and protective space around you. In creating this sanctuary, it is helpful to call in the spirits from the four cardinal directions (north, east, south, and west). This can be done with a small ceremony. You can expand or contract from the suggested outline I have provided of a ceremony to have it feel more like the essence of your beliefs and vernacular.

Some tribes teach us that our existence is a result of the marriage of Father Sky and Mother Earth. This is a common theory among the Lakota Sioux of North America. Father Sky is the chief of all spirits in the spirit world and Mother Earth is his counterpart, the feminine force of creativity, a goddess that gives life to all of us and is our foundation and balance. The most important thing for a strongly founded existence is having a sense of place. Call in your spiritual father and mother as well.

Your sanctuary is where you will experience your sacred connection to the spirit world. This connection builds a sense of safety, which comes from knowing that higher beings are protecting you and working with you in the unseen worlds, which, without a doubt, exist and are vibrant places to connect to and visit.

The medicine wheel or sacred hoop is an important ceremonial space created by Native Americans to perform rituals and prayers. It is often defined with a circle of stones on the land and represents the connection of humans to spirits of the natural world. This wheel contains the four directions, Father Sky, and Mother Earth. The medicine wheel is a portal to the spirit world. Here, with the support of your spirits, you can find your path of growth and self-realization.

Many shamans also carry a portable altar, or mesa. In Spanish, this means "table." The mesa is usually a textile bundle or pouch made of animal skin that contains sacred objects, such as healing stones and other things gifted from the natural world, such as leaves, shells, herbs, feathers, animal teeth or bones, and so forth. These are the shaman's tools for connecting to other dimensions and serve as their power packs for healing.

The following are shamanic protection prayers for the ritual of creating sacred space and to call in your higher self and the Power Animal spirits. This exercise is to create a circle of protection around you for the spiritual work you will be doing.

CALLING IN THE EAST

East is the place of the rising Sun and the element of air. In this direction of your circle you can place offerings of feathers, pumice, mint, incense, blades of lemongrass, and stalks of lavender. The color associated with this direction is yellow. Here you would also place stones that are yellow, like yellow calcite, sunstone, and amber or yellow Jasper.

Recite: Guardians of the East, Great Eagle *(if you are calling in from the Northern Hemisphere)* or Condor *(if you are calling in from the Southern Hemisphere)*, come to me from the place of new beginnings, open horizons, visions and inspiration of newness and fresh starts. Protect this corner of my circle and allow the air to flow in. Bless me with the music, melodies, and vibrations that ride the winds. Inspire me with new beginnings through the rising of the Sun. Bring clarity and perception from the eyes of Eagle/Condor and the right language for expression. Allow me to be the wind beneath your wings and to fly with the Creator and to see the unseen world from the perspective of the mountaintops. I bless you and request your infinite wisdom and blessing for this space. Join with me, spirits of the East.

CALLING IN THE SOUTH

South represents the element of fire and is the place of creation. In this direction of your circle you can place offerings such as stalks of rosemary, pomegranate seeds, cinnamon bark, sunflowers, marigolds, fresh tobacco, chunks of copal, frankincense, or Dragon's blood, and fruits like pineapples or tangerines. The color associated with this direction is red. You can also light a candle. Here you would put stones that are red, orange, and yellow, such as jasper, orange calcite and yellow moonstone.

Recite: Guardians of the South, Coyote/Mouse *(if you are calling in from the Northern Hemisphere)* or Great Serpent *(if you are calling in from the Southern Hemisphere)*, come to me from the place of the summer heat with strength and courage to ignite my heart with unconditional love. Protect this corner of my circle and allow the sacred fire to burn within it. Bless me with passion from the flames and allow them to burn away all that does not serve me. Inspire me to rise from the ashes into a higher place where I can speak my truth. Teach me to tread softly on the earth and bask in all the beauty here *(if you are speaking to Coyote/Mouse)*. Help me to shed the past the way you shed your skin *(if speaking to Serpent)*. I bless you and ask for your infinite wisdom and blessing for this space. Join me, spirits of the South.

CALLING IN THE WEST

West represents the element of water and is the place of the setting Sun. In this direction of your circle you can place offerings, such as shells, passion flowers, tamarind, morning glories, gardenias, avocados, aloe, hibiscus, sugar cane, papaya, and gourds. The color associated with this direction is black. You can also place luminescent stones here, such as moonstone and mother of pearl or obsidian and black tourmaline.

Recite: Guardians of the West, Bear or Whale *(if calling in from the Northern Hemisphere)* or Jaguar *(if you are calling in from the Southern Hemisphere)* come to me from the place of the harvest with community and sharing of the bounty of our efforts and purpose. Protect this corner of my circle and allow the water to flow into it. Bless me with cleansing from the sparkling streams and rivers, the powerful waterfalls, the mysterious oceans, and the serene lakes. Bring me the peace that comes from abundance and nurturing of Mother Earth and teach me to have a life that is fruitful and full. Help me to walk in the world with no fears and to live impeccably and love beyond the cycles of life and death. I bless you and ask for your infinite wisdom and blessing for this space. Join me, spirits of the West.

CALLING IN THE NORTH

North represents the element of Earth and is the place of sleeping and dreaming. Our ancestors come from here. In this corner of your circle you can place offerings of ferns, corn, cedar, sugar, tobacco, vetiver, squash, and items from your ancestors, like jewelry and photos. The color associated with the North is white. Here you can place quartz crystals, selenite, and coal.

Recite: Guardians of the North, White Buffalo or Wolf *(if you are calling in from the Northern Hemisphere)* or Great Hummingbird *(if you are calling in from the Southern Hemisphere)*, ancestors and ancient ones, come to me from the place of the night and winters that hold the wisdom of my elders. Protect this corner of my circle and allow the spirit that exists in all living things to support this space. Bless me with dreams, quiet, stillness, and introspection that take me deep into the reflection of my true self. Bring me the guidance of the wise ones and the knowledge of the Great Source for the understanding of my connection to all things. Help me to honor all who have come before and shower me with the light of crystals and plants that nourish my body and soul. I bless you and ask for your infinite wisdom and blessing for this space. Join me spirits of the North.

CALLING IN FATHER SKY

Recite: Spirit of Father Sky, come to me from the place of angels with the sparkle of stars in the night and the vast beyond that has no knowing. Bring a light to shine upon me and guide my steps into the unknown with confidence and connection to the cosmic world.

CALLING IN MOTHER EARTH

Recite: Spirit of Mother Earth, come to me from the place of the roots of my existence, the ever-changing and inspirational world of your beauty. Bring your nurturing and bounty to my heart and the wisdom of your support and stability.

CALLING IN YOUR HIGHER SELF/ESSENCE OF SELF

Recite: Finally, I call in my own essence, which lives in the place of emotion, intuition, and feeling. Help me to embrace this wisdom that comes to remind me of my uniqueness yet also of my connection to the universal field. Guide me to share my gifts with the world and open my heart to receive.

CALLING IN YOUR POWER ANIMAL

Recite: I invite my Power Animal to come from the place of the highest vibrational existence. May the messages that you share with me be illuminating and for my highest good and the highest good of others. I ask that the messages you bring me be clear, kind, and compassionate. May you bring lessons and insight appropriate to the purpose of life. May the energy that flows through me be in tune with what is needed at this time and in this space.

Completing these prayers, you may begin a shamanic journey or any sacred spiritual work from this circle.

A SHAMANIC JOURNEY

Shamanic journeying is a type of meditation that is done to the rhythm of steady drumming and/or rattles played with a steady beat. Listening to drumming at a pace of 106–240 beats per minute will help to put your brain into the theta state necessary in order to enter a light trance.

Some people will start their journeys by doing an ecstatic dance, or they'll drum and sing. Others prefer to start with a more passive approach, like doing a meditation in which they set an intention for their journey. If you have a drummer who can drum live for you, that's great. But it is fine to listen to a recorded drumbeat too.

Journeying is a process that requires leaving your rational thoughts behind and employing your imagination without judgment. It also requires turning over your limiting beliefs, so you may then be inspired by the spirit world, allowing the journey to unfold and bring the intelligence of nature to you. From this state of being you can connect energetically with the spirit world and be receptive to spirit communication.

Before you begin, it can be helpful to lay on the ground (floor) or assume another comfortable, supported position ensuring relaxation. It is helpful to wear a blindfold or bandana. Shutting out the light can help to put you in a different energetic state. You can also go out into nature, away from the distractions of civilization. Modern electronic devices can mask the geomagnetic force inherent to nature. In nature, it may be possible to start to shift effortlessly and sense the spirit beings that are around you before taking any other action. Being in a place that is different from your ordinary reality can help you to slip into non-ordinary reality and enable you to encounter Power Animals and other spirit beings.

The purpose of finding an appropriate place of departure for your journey, and for assuming a relaxed position and putting on a blindfold, is to ensure that you are transitioning from an ordinary to a nonordinary realm. Much can be revealed after you begin to map and navigate the mystical realms. To begin your journey, set an intention to go to the Lower World. This is where you will encounter your Power Animal who you will then begin to guide you on your journeys. This may be an animal you already know, or it may be an entirely new animal. The Power Animal will reveal itself to you. To enter the Lower World, you must find an entrance in the natural world.

Begin drumming or listening to drumming on a CD. Go to your entrance to the Lower World using your imagination. The place to start could be the root (or a hole) in a tree or bush, a cave, a lake, an ocean, a well, or any portal that you feel a connection to. Use your intuition to discern the entrance that is easiest and most appropriate for you. Energetically, send yourself through the entrance.

Arriving in the Lower World, you should look for a place to be an observer. This can be your own personal meeting place in the Lower World. Everyone has a unique experience. From there

you can wait to see what animal appears. In some traditions, you would wait until you have seen three of the same animal from a rearview—then you can feel fairly certain that you have found your Power Animal.

The next step is to ask if the animal you have seen is your Power Animal and if it would like to return with you to the Middle World. If the answer is affirmative, you will then travel with your Power Animal back through the same route that you took from ordinary reality. After you are back, you will then ask that the essence of your Power Animal be allowed to merge into your heart chakra or energy center. You have now been blessed and infused with its power. Thank your Power Animal for honoring you with the gift of its presence. This will be the beginning of your tutelage.

Before you open your eyes, wiggle your toes and fingers, and anchor yourself back in your body. Take your time to gradually make the transition without compromising your nervous system. A few deep breaths would be appropriate. Take a moment to appreciate yourself for being proactive in connecting with spiritual guidance. When you're ready, open your eyes.

Many people question if—when they are journeying to another reality—they are "making it up" or "just imagining everything." Because they are entering unfamiliar territory and are not accustomed to being in other realities they question their experiences during the journey to find their Power Animal. Remember that there is nothing enlightened about doubting the existence of the spirit world, so cast aside any insecurity you may have about the process and give yourself permission to be liberated from your fears and persevere in discovery. Your imagination is power. Trust the process and accept things that come up for you without judgement.

A journey is a very personal and sacred dance with spirit. Know that all that you find on this journey was intended to inspire you. Practice trusting your visions and encounters with Power Animals. Some people look for messages but what they find is that the spirit world is more attuned to thoughts and visions. Others struggle with journeying because they can only believe in what they can touch, feel, smell, and experience; for them, it is as if the spirit world does not exist. This type of materialist view of the world can keep you detached from the expanded possibilities of the transcendent world.

After your journey, you will begin your relationship with your Power Animal in earnest. See your Power Animal as a cosmic transformer that can take the power of the Universe and bring it to you in a form that is ideally suited for your human body. It is often a practice. After you are united with your Power Animal, build an altar to it so that you begin to show it reverence, through making offerings to it, for all the work that it is doing to support you. Honoring your Power Animal is important. When we approach our Power Animals with humility and respect we can be rewarded with their great wisdom. A Power Animal is a powerful healer. Often, the first ceremony a shamanic healer will perform is connecting a Power Animal to someone who is sick in order to give the ill person a beneficial foundation for healing and to strengthen the potential for healing.

There is a recent proliferation of people using mind-altering plants to go on shamanic journeys. But in 90 percent of the world's shamanic cultures, altered states of consciousness and transcendence into non-ordinary reality are achieved through ceremony, song, and drumming rather than with plant medicine, so it is not necessary to use mind-altering plants in your journey work.

INDIGENOUS THEORIES AND BELIEFS

Totemism. A belief that we are descendants from the same species as our birth or "totem" animal, and that the land and the ancestor spirits who reside there are the source of our existence. Human beings are seen as equals to the souls of plants and animals, and natural forces.

Animism. A belief that natural objects such as rocks and crystals, as well as plants, animals, and humans have consciousness. Anthropologically, animism originally had its basis in the dreams and visions of humans and their observations of reality, both ordinary and non-ordinary. According to Edward Tyler, in his book *Primitive Culture*, the first known use of this term was in 1819.

Examples of animistic cultures include the Q'ero of Peru and Bolivia, various indigenous North American peoples, the Mayans of Central America, the Aborigines of Australia, the Maori of New Zealand, the ancient Celts and Vikings, and some African tribes and a few tribes in India.

Fetishism. North American tribes traditionally carved animal figurines out of wood or stone as a practice of using them as fetishes. These figures were believed to hold magical and supernatural powers. The carved fetishes would be placed on altars and in pots, medicine pouches, and used in jewelry. They were adorned with feathers and stones and given as offerings for the gifts they would bring to the owner. Each animal carried different powers for the owner. A fetish is a personal object of great importance and reverence and generally is not sold but passed down through generations. The power represented by fetishes is similar to those of a Power Animal.

Talismans and Pearls: A talisman is an object that holds magical properties for the possessor. Shamans would often use things from nature and design jewelry or special objects as a symbolism of their Power Animals. They would also use animal "pearls," which are rare stones or calcifications (for example, a gallstone or kidney stone) released in the excrement of animals and when found were believed to be a concentration of that particular animal's power.

SHAPESHIFTING

Sometimes during a shamanic journey your Power Animal will merge with you. This happens because your Power Animal is trying to show you the world through its eyes and body. We can learn many lessons from this experience which takes us out of our human form to receive knowledge from a different perspective. This can be an extraordinary experience, one deserving of great gratitude to your Power Animal for making it possible. Some Power Animals are more adept at giving us this experience than others. When someone shapeshifts, they may act in the characteristic manner of that animal or see with the eyes of that animal or feel the power of the instincts that the animal has. Shapeshifting is done by shamans for the purpose of healing and enhancing their human abilities. This assimilation means that the shaman becomes that animal for the purpose of divination and discovery.

DREAMS

Many Power Animals will readily come to you in a dream. This is simply a different form of journeying that gives you the ability to receive the same symbolic messages from the animal world that you would receive in a trance. The dreamtime and nonordinary reality are not that different. Animals can bring to you what is not acknowledged in ordinary reality. Through your dreams you may receive knowledge about your basic instincts and emotions. An excavation of underlying issues may be exposed by the visit of a Power Animal during your dreams.

POWER

Many people think of power as something that you use to push, manipulate, or overcome people or things. The truth is different. When we talk about "Power" Animals, we are referring to the basic life force they are endowed with. This is also known as *qi*, as in Chinese marital arts like qigong, or *prana*, as it is referred to by yoga practitioners. Power assumes many forms and every Power Animal is endowed with it and will share it with the human beings that it wants to—if it is approached correctly. Through humble demonstrations of respect and honor for a Power Animal, you can create a proactive relationship with it, but the first thing you need to do is ask. Since the Power Animal is capable of helping you to understand our world and humanness from its non-ordinary perspective, you must invite it into your world.

By working with a Power Animal, you can change your life from mundane to magical. Your personal power can be amplified by association with this extraordinary spirit. A wonderful practice is to make the integration of the power of a Power Animal part of your morning ritual. Even if you only take a quick five minutes, go outdoors and get into a present state. Then, look around your patio or neighborhood. Do you see any animals, including birds, fish, or reptiles? Do you hear any sounds of animals, maybe the sound of Woodpecker or a bird's song? These sighting or soundings can be signs of what you need to know or pay attention to for that day.

Also, as you go about your regular activities, keep your awareness open to the power of messenger spirits that appear to break up your normal routine. These animals may have important information to bring to your attention.

Another helpful practice is to call in your Power Animal during your day. Why not take a walk with your Power Animal and have a chat or ask that the Power Animal to bring a message to you from spirit? This type of interaction can be very rewarding and fun.

Another way of interacting with your Power Animal is the practice of divination. Divination is searching for hidden knowledge for yourself and others from the spirit world. When you are looking for the answers to tough questions, making a trip to non-ordinary reality to ask your Power Animal for insights can be very helpful, as Power Animals are usually enthusiastic about supporting us. At times, the answers you get from a journey of divination may seem ambiguous and it will be necessary to ask for clarification. But other times the information can be taken as it is, at face value, since the understanding you need (or the person for whom you are divining needs) is expected to unfold and not to be clear at that moment.

Through divination, you may receive symbols that are unknown to you. Doing some research later may yield you an expanded view of their meaning.

Because you have one Power Animal that has been your guide for your whole life, that particular Power Animal often knows the perfect image to show you in order to trigger knowledge that has been buried in your subconscious for years. The more spontaneous your imagination is, greater is the possibility of a fascinating ride. As you get to know the other Power Animals you work with, their intimacy with your mind will expand too.

QUANTUM POWER ANIMAL RETRIEVAL

Everything in existence, including all living things, is made of energy and has a frequency. Based on the science of scalar wave energy discovered by Nicolas Tesla, I have been able to define the frequencies of the almost 200 spirit animals described in this book. The creation of an animal archive can now be used to determine the animal that was present at your birth. If you are interested in knowing your Power Animal through this innovative process, please visit LoriMorrison.com to access a form. By simply entering your birthdate, birthplace, and name, a quantum search through the animal spirit kingdom is initiated that will find the Power Animal frequency on your field at your time of birth. This technology simplifies a rather lengthy process that is normally undertaken by a shaman, and then you can begin working with your Power Animal right away.

ENERGY CENTERS AND MINERALS

There is much in the written and oral traditions of many ancient and indigenous cultures that refers to the human energy system. Although we are mostly familiar with the energy centers in our bodies from practicing yoga, where they are referred to as *chakras*, the concepts are primordial because the centers are innate. A shaman understands how these serve as a place for energy to enter and leave the body, bringing it life and connection with all other beings and things. Each of these centers spins according to its own frequency, which is represented by a color and a sound. Through our energy centers, we receive and exchange energy with plants and animals, sunshine, air, and water, and the various electromagnetic fields (EMFs) that surround us.

There are seven main energy centers in the body. Each has a function related to specific characteristics of life here in the Middle World. The lower centers (the root, the sacrum, and the solar plexus) ground us in the body and connect us to the Lower World. When these are not functioning optimally, we may feel disconnected from Mother Earth, unstable, and lacking in purpose. The three upper energy centers (the throat, the third eye, and the crown) are fed by the Sun, our great star, which connects us with the Upper World and higher consciousness. Their functions connect us to the place of our origins, spiritual teachers, and Power Animals of the Upper World. Between the upper and lower energy centers is the heart center, which helps us to harmonize all energy.

Each Power Animal embodies energy that is congruent with one of the seven primary energy centers in the human body. The characteristics of the animal mirror those of the center. To strengthen the resonance between yourself and a Power Animal, you can work to create optimal functioning in its corresponding energy center using a stone or crystal that is of a similar resonance of your Power Animal.

How? You could:

- Hold the crystal or stone in your hand when you are journeying.
- Place the crystal or stone on an altar you build to honor your Power Animal.
- Wear jewelry representing the Power Animal that is encrusted with the crystal or stone.
- Adopt the indigenous Native American practice of carrying a fetish of an animal carved from the crystal or stone.

You can make yourself a more receptive vessel, spiritually, by balancing your energy with various tools. Stones and crystals are encoded molecularly with energetic information that can help sustain our natural balance. Also, you can strengthen the centers by working with one of the five foundational shamanic elements of nature: air, earth, fire, water, or spirit. When those are in balance around us, we are brought into congruency of the natural world. The sounds of nature come through the different

centers based on frequency. For example, listening to a melody of a bird can bring a soothing result.

Energetic lessons from members of the mineral kingdom will always flow through the chakra most aligned with their energy. This is how it is possible to align distinct energy from a variety of sources and identify the powers of healing related to each one. Vibrations from the mineral kingdom complement both humans and animals. Frequencies from minerals related to your Power Animal can help you better connect as you call it in to journey with you.

THE FIVE SHAMANIC ELEMENTS

Ancient cultures believed in the powers of the basic elements that exist in nature. Fire, air, water, earth, and spirit are the ingredients of our universal being and help to blend matter with energy in a variety of forms.

FIRE: Fire is life blood and life force, purifying us and consuming any impurities. Its strength can bring protection from the other elements. It is representative of our passion and our senses of motivation and desire. It is present in the solar heat and the flashes of lightning and the eruption of volcanos. It is also the flame that burns in our hearts and kindles the power of love. It is a destroyer of life yet causes a new world to be formed into being. It has a masculine presence and is connected to the planet Mars and the Sun.

AIR: Air brings us space for creation and new starts. It is an active element necessary for life. From simple cells in nature, plants evolved through the processing of the Sun's energy and now release oxygen to sustain us and are probably the most dynamic connection we have to nature. Our inhalation and exhalation nurture the soul and create states of calm and presence. Air carries the power of sound for healing and can spread the flames of fire for the renovation of nature, creating an opportunity for it to spring back to life. Air manifests flight and freedom, and through its force can also bring inspirational sunsets and hope in the rising of the Sun. It also helps to create waves in bodies of water to defy stagnation. Winds are cleansing and purifying to the human body and soul. Air has a masculine presence and is connected to Jupiter.

WATER: Oceans, rivers, lakes, ponds, glaciers, and groundwater are basins of life. The power of water is legendary and unpredictable. It is intimately connected with the Moon and tidal movements. It is the elixir of fertile feeding and a place of birth and new beginnings. It is the storm and the element of cultivation of nutrients that our bodies need to survive. It can inundate us and at the same time cleanse. Water is the inevitable river that flows through our existence, driving us forward into the mystery and dissolving us into the unknown. It provides us with a reflection of who we are and the possibility of going deeper below the surface to find the heart's desire. It makes up the majority of the human body, holding the world of our cells and our biology. Water is symbolic of prosperity and abundance and the mythical history of fertilization and re-birth. It is associated with the Moon and the planet Venus.

EARTH: Earth is the womb and giver of life. It provides the vitality and transformational qualities to sustain us. Living beings emerge here and complete their cycles, then return to the cosmic realms. It is the essence of a divine spirit that manifests itself through creation. It is where we take the perilous journey of life supported by Earth's maternal energy, which, if tapped into, can ensure a treasured experience. On so many levels, Earth is a fierce expression of the collective thoughts and energetic placenta of our evolution. It provides, yet takes away in the form of tidal waves, earthquakes, and hurricanes, which are lessons for us to respect and embrace its mysteries and power. Earth is associated with the planet Saturn.

SPIRIT: Spirit comes from the world of blessings, a place of the transfer of sacred power and energy. Through thought, meditation, words, visions, gestures, and rituals, we can connect to this divine power. Influenced by the spiraling movement of the galaxies, it is our link to the mythology of our existence. Spirit knows no limits and expands the imagination. It is most often found in silence, an internal state of being in which to seek and become more than you believe. In the world of spirit we can hear the voices of the sacred traditions and tap into wisdom that does not exist in libraries. Spirit brings us truth from the wordless world, helping to free us from delusion. Our connection to Spirit is the initiation of the soul and confirmation of eternity.

SUMMARY

We need to interact with or observe animals in natural settings in order to truly see the planet as a whole. Perhaps the root cause of our planetary dysfunction and imbalance in this era in history is the disintegration of humanity's connection to the spirit world in everyday life. Losing our connection to Power Animals diminished our fore bearers understanding of their connection to all things. With our generation's contact with animals now being limited to seeing them in a zoo or aquarium, or a domesticated setting, such as a home or a business, we have symbolically and literally created and reinforced our separation from nature. Very rarely do we see animals in the wild like our ancestors did.

I do not know what your past experience with shamanism is. I do not know if you have worked with Power Animals in the past—many people have—or if you are new to this type of shamanic experience. I believe those who are drawn to Power Animals are drawn for a reason. Power Animals can be our guides to a level of higher consciousness from which we can learn more about ourselves and the world as our souls evolve. Working with Power Animals can be a catalyst for personal growth and transformation.

Animals are an intimate part of life and death on Earth. Many shrines and caves have been found with human and animal remains lying together in the same burial grounds. Perhaps they are traveling together to the afterlife, supporting each other in their most sacred, final journeys through the bond of transcendence. From the extraordinary prehistoric cave paintings of animals throughout the world we can gather a sense of the influence animals have had on our survival and our reliance on them for so many reasons. Animals were revered and worshipped by all indigenous cultures. Animals have laid down their lives for ours, and this sacrifice has been the center of rituals of recognition of the mystery of resurrection and honoring our profound debt to them. Appeasing the animal spirits whose grace was relied upon to bring abundance was an acknowledgment of the dependency of the human to the spiritual world.

Today, most of humanity views animals as lesser species than our own, convinced by social conditioning that we are the masters of them, rather than their brethren—their sisters and brothers in the animal kingdom. In ancient times, the stories told around the sacred fire pit were filled with the lessons of animals: how they managed, how they survived, how their harmonic balance with nature enabled them to thrive. Indigenous peoples worldwide revered these lessons, which became the values of their tribes and the contexts in which they saw their lives and their cultures—and the world.

Through journeying, you may find yourself interacting with mystical beings of all types, including fantastical beasts. Are they real? The answer is yes. From Dragons to Unicorns, all are mystical creatures known to our collective consciousness. They live in a different realm, yet are accessible to us in nonordinary reality. Know that all that separates you from meeting them is your belief that they do not exist.

Each Power Animal in this book has a distinct message, perspective, and special powers. The

combined skills and traits with which animals interact with the natural environment form a body of knowledge and ability that is far beyond human comprehension. We invite you to embrace ritual and the power of animals again in your daily life. Keeping your practice alive will transform your life by helping you shape shift your being.

A shaman's ears are open to the song of the Universe. The shaman knows that the greatest wisdom for humanity comes from the natural world. Through their prophetic messages, Power Animals from the mystical world can bring you profound knowledge and expand your vision. They will make you ready to manifest the mystery of your soul. By opening your heart to possibility, you can journey with Power Animals to find healing for yourself and others.

Accompanied by the A to Z guide to Power Animals that follows, we invite you to begin your own personal journey through the Tree of Life. Find or improve your connection to nature through this adventure and renew your acquaintance with your spiritual essence by taking your first steps into the Lower World. There, with the love and tutelage of the animal kingdom, embrace the mystical and feel the ecstasy of your being.

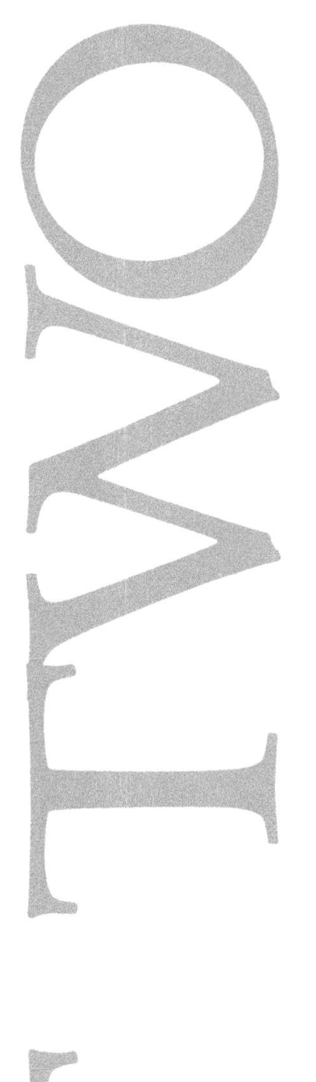

A TO Z GUIDE TO POWER ANIMALS

AARDVARK

GROUNDING **PROTECTION** **UNIQUENESS**

"In the stillness of the night, as I walk, I feel the vibration of my footsteps, sensing the Mother and trusting my inner illumination." —Aardvark

Aardvark possesses an accumulation of traits from other animals. It has ears like a rabbit, a snout like a pig, a tongue like an anteater, and a tail like a kangaroo yet is not related to any of them. It takes on the characteristics of others when necessary for its survival, otherwise it purposefully hides. With powerful claws, it is great at digging and foraging. It leaves no clump of dirt unturned when looking for opportunities. Residing in the lower two-thirds of the African continent, many predators favor it. Therefore, Aardvark prefers the darkness of the night and makes its home in extensive burrows with many rooms and several entrances. Its home is important for its protection, so it is cautious when leaving it. In fact, Aardvark performs its special ritual of a stomping dance before leaving its burrow to guarantee that no predators are around. It uses super-sensitive eyesight and hearing to ensure its safety. Aardvark eats ants and termites and often builds its burrows in the remnants of anthills and termite mounds. It is immune to being bit or stung. Its thick skin gives it the capacity to eat its most favorite meal of fire ants without effect.

The Bamana tribe of Mali makes elaborate *chiwara* masks representing Aardvark, which they wear during ceremonies to honor Mother Earth. The Bamana believe that animals that dig in the ground hold the secrets of the Earth. They recognize the Earth as a feminine entity and, when there is planting to be done, view it as a form of sexual contact between the soil and the farmer's hoe, which they associate with the snout of the Aardvark.

Aardvark has its own genetic limb on the evolutionary Tree of Life. With no living relatives, it is a testament to the power of being unique and teaches us to respect diversity. Uniqueness puts us in the position to make a contribution that may be needed by those who do not possess the same attributes as us. Our differences make us divinely special, although we don't always believe this. Spiritually, Aardvark enters your life when it's time to start believing in yourself more. Aardvark celebrates individual thinking and nurtures those who stand out from the norm in a world that often passes them over. It also brings the power of fortitude with which to walk the world in your own fashion. Be authentic and celebrate your unique qualities and one day you'll arrive at a place where your impact on the world is more significant to you than the opinions of others. Call on Aardvark to support grounding when you feel disconnected from your sense of spirituality. Aardvark encourages presence and the ability to be in touch with life and feel protected. It supports devotion to your soul and its purpose.

The spirit of Aardvark can establish a protective spiritual shield around your home and workplace, giving you the reassurance that when leaving they will remain clear and safe.

POWERS OF AARDVARK

Call in Aardvark for:

- The power of perseverance.
- The power to stand up against accusations and criticisms related to your uniqueness.
- Enhancing your self-reliance and know that you are powerful even alone.

AWARENESS FROM AARDVARK

If Aardvark comes into your life:

- It is time to stop digging for answers, as the answers are not ready to be revealed.
- Work on grounding yourself and strengthening your connection to Mother Earth.
- Dare to be and think differently.

Energy Center: Root

Mineral: Tangerine quartz

Element: Earth

Magic & Mystery: Aardvark builds elaborate homes and substantial tunnel systems with as many as sixty entrances.

SHAMAN'S INTENTION: *SUPPORT ME THROUGH INNER ILLUMINATION TO FIND WHAT I SEEK, SENSE, AND SEE*

ALBATROSS

VISION | STAMINA | FREEDOM

"Fly with grace and endurance, then, with a calm and trusting mind, you will arrive at distant shores with little effort."—Albatross

POWERS OF ALBATROSS

Call in Albatross for:

- Capturing the rhythm of the sea wind and using its powers to ride the waves of life.
- Optimism and assurance that you will reach your destination.
- Passion to create from an inner vibration of love and connection to the universal flow.

AWARENESS FROM ALBATROSS

If Albatross comes into your life:

- You are in a state of weakness and lack sufficient stamina for the journey ahead.
- It is time to address the stagnant and blocked energy in your system that may be limiting your productivity and ability to execute your personal visions.
- Eliminate your fear of the journey ahead to attain your highest potential.

Energy Center: Crown

Mineral: Mahogany obsidian

Element: Air

Magic & Mystery:

- "An Albatross is the grandest flying machine on Earth." —Carl Safina
- The Maori tribe of New Zealand use Albatross wing bones to carve their flutes.
- In Hawaiian, the word for Albatross is *laysan*, meaning "tattooing implement," since its bones were utilized in the practice of tattooing.

The South Pacific Ocean is the natural habitat of Albatross, which spends most of its life flying over water far from land. Albatross has a twelve-foot wingspan, which gives it an extraordinary ability to navigate winds and air currents—even manipulate them. It also has special salt-excreting glands that allow it to drink saltwater, and a highly developed olfactory sense that it uses for tracking live prey, such as Squid, Fish eggs, and floating Carrion. Albatross lives to be around sixty. It begins breeding at maturity, around age twelve. Females lay only one egg per year. These birds mate for life and will always stay together to raise their chicks, yet they aren't entirely loyal to their partners. They also accept same-sex partners and will continue those relationships for a lifetime. A parent Albatross may fly more than 10,000 miles to deliver one meal to its chick.

Albatross has a connection to the long-lost continent of Lemuria, an advanced, pre-Atlantean civilization that existed almost 200 million years ago and stretched from the east coast of Africa across what is now the Indian and Pacific Oceans. Albatross shares that the species's ability to sustain flight across long distances was an adaptation coming from the time of the sinking of this continent. Albatross can serve as a messenger to Mount Shasta where descendants of Lemuria now reside and are occasionally seen by residents in spirit form.

Albatross is attuned to currents of wind and sea, so it can forecast approaching storms. It offers the same power of forecasting to those who work with its energy. Albatross helps us navigate uncharted territories with ease and find calmer and more peaceful waters. For sailors, Albatross is a symbol of luck and great hope. Seeing Albatross means you are on the right track and can trust the energy flowing toward you. Seeing an injured, captured, or dead Albatross, however, is an omen of bad times ahead. This bird does not tolerate confinement and brings us the energy of freedom.

Albatross has the power to travel in a world greater than itself and has faith in a bigger vision. Albatross teaches nonconformity and how to break the chains of limiting beliefs that may be keeping you from a life of freedom. By not carrying a cargo of limitations, you can easily "reach land" —meaning, find what you are seeking. A sense of open-mindedness comes from Albatross' expanded view of the world and its possibilities.

Albatross is an excellent spirit companion when you are facing a long journey or project and need endurance to go the long haul without becoming overwhelmed. Albatross can help you face a fear of traveling. It is an important power for those who are overseas and want assistance to overcome the stress of international travel.

SHAMAN'S INTENTION: *HELP ME TO FLY FEARLESSLY INTO UNCHARTED TERRITORIES*

ANGELFISH

CLARITY **TRUTH** **JOY**

"Gaze upon my beauty and find the cosmic significance of my geometric form. I am the symbol of two faces. One eye sees the earthly realm, the other the angelic."
—Angelfish

Around one hundred different types of Angelfish inhabit the waters of the Southern Hemisphere. Some live in the freshwater rivers of South America, others inhabit salty ocean waters. Each Angelfish has a distinct personality. The species is very territorial in the presence of its food, mates, and eggs. It is known for its exotic colors and dainty movements when swimming.

Angelfish represents the world of angels and dreams, the place of the unknown and mystery. Its triangular shape reminds us of the symbols from sacred geometry that are the fabric of our existence. Angelfish encourages us to renew our understanding of the shapes and patterns that are found everywhere in nature, a wisdom that has become lost to us. We should recognize that the same patterns which exist on earth and in the sea exist in the cosmos as well. These are the blueprints that form the basis of life. In embodying mathematical perfection, Angelfish opens our eyes to the harmony of the natural world.

Angelfish impresses us with the importance of preserving fragile things that bring beauty to our existence, like the coral reefs it inhabits. As a Power Animal, Angelfish is here to flash a vibration of colors and teach you how to use color to your advantage. Color can bring you joy when you are feeling blue. Colors are associated with musical tones that can bring us uplifting vibrations for healing.

Angelfish moves about its coral reef with purpose and independence no matter the intensity of the currents around it. Although beautiful, it does not focus on itself. Rather, it has a motherly instinct for ensuring that everything around it is in good order and it looks after the well-being of the whole. Angelfish quickly reacts, so it is helpful when it is necessary to make a quick decision or to change direction. Angelfish brings us the power of assimilation of the energy around us, which heightens our awareness and facilitates mental perception.

POWERS OF ANGELFISH

Call in Angelfish for:

- Basking in the kindness and virtues of angelic beings.
- Coming to know the power of true joy by swimming out of your past and into your present.
- Healing frequencies in the form of music or color for relaxation and calm.

AWARENESS FROM ANGELFISH

If Angelfish comes into your life:

- You need to consider both sides of a story.
- You are living in a fairy tale and it's time to bust through your illusionary beliefs.
- See that expectations are a ticket to disappointment.

Energy Center: Crown

Mineral: Charoite

Element: Water

Magic & Mystery

- Angelfish is intelligent. And if if raised in an aquarium, it will recognize you.
- The scientific name for Angel fish is *pterophyllum,* which means "winged leaf" in Greek.

SHAMANS INTENTION: *GUIDE THE OPENING OF MY CROWN CHAKRA, SO I MAY ACCESS THE UPPER WORLD AND FIND MY ANGELIC TEACHERS*

ANT

EFFORT **COMMUNITY** **ENDURANCE**

"We prepare shelter for those who seek refuge and demonstrate the tenacity to weather obstacles in life."—Ant

Ant evolved some 130 million years ago and scientists recently discovered that massive colonies of ants in Europe, North America, and Japan are all part of one global super colony. Ant can carry objects fifty times its own body weight in its jaws, thus using its diminutive size to its advantage. A Scout Ant wanders randomly until finding food, and then heads to the nest leaving a special scent trail to guide others to the food source. The Worker Ant travels on the same line until food is found and consumed. The nest has "Bouncers" at the gate, blocking access, so when a Worker Ant returns it touches the Bouncer Ant's head for assurance that it belongs to the colony. Ant sticks to its path with the certainty that with time and effort it will accomplish its goals.

Ant holds great wisdom and is connected to the Hopi people of North America. The Hopi creation myth says that in ancient times there was a civilization of Ant people living beneath the surface of the Earth. During times of great devastation, the Ant people rescued the Hopi by taking them to their underground caves where they survived. These structures are believed to be similar in form to the Hopi kivas, which are subterranean communal prayer chambers. Ant people also may have lived in ancient Egypt. In some depictions, Akhenaten, the eighteenth-dynasty pharaoh who ruled from 1351–1334 B.C.E., has an elongated skull that resembles the shape of Ant's head.

In the British Isles, it is considered unlucky to destroy a colony of Ant. Stepping on them is thought to bring rain. In centuries past, Cornish farmers believed that during a certain stage of the Moon, a piece of tin placed in an Ant nest would be turned to silver and an Ant near the front door was said to bring security and riches to inhabitants of a house.

THEY LOVE TO WORK, SO THEY ARE INDUSTRIOUS AND DILIGENT IN THEIR EFFORTS.

Although one of the smallest creatures in the world Ant is an exceptionally powerful Power Animal. It can help you sharpen your instincts. Ant is an architect to call on when seeking to build a community. Its communities are extensive underground structures, and it is the quintessential master of the underworld. Alone in the wild, Ant cannot survive—but it doesn't have to. Because there are so many members in its different species, Ant is an earthly reflection of the stars of the Milky Way. Ant can play several roles and is always willing to be helpful. It loves to work, so it is industrious and diligent in its efforts. Encountering Ant, we are being made aware of the need for perseverance as we walk our spiritual paths.

Ant is a messenger of the "ant"-cestral world. It asks us to come together in ceremony for community and survival. As a Power Animal, Ant sees that we live in a world with the potential for compassion only if we would see it without the lens of hierarchy. If humanity could perceive that we were all the same, we would climb higher in our attempts to reach Source. Ant can serve as a "shout out" to focus on your worthiness and the importance of preserving your individuality in a crowd.

POWERS OF ANT

Call in Ant for:

- Cooperation with others and enjoyment of socializing.
- A life unconstrained by ego and a virtuous dedication to the collective consciousness.
- Willingness to work hard to build a better place for all to live.

AWARENESS OF ANT

If Ant comes into your life:

- You may be overly concerned with what society thinks and not focused enough on your own desires.
- Look for places to improve teamwork and cooperation.
- It may be time to take a hard look at your relationships, as they may not be contributing to what is best for you at this time.

Energy Center: Root

Mineral: Sunstone

Element: Earth

Magic & Mystery: The Chinese call the ant the *righteous insect.*

SHAMANS INTENTION: *HELP ME TO APPRECIATE THE VALUE OF ALL MY EARTHLY HELPERS*

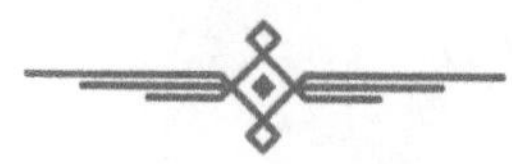

ANTEATER

COMMUNICATION **PROFOUNDNESS** **RESILIENCE**

"A stroke of the tongue is often the first gesture that a mother in the animal kingdom makes to her newborn, a warm touch that brings the young one to life."—Anteater

POWERS OF ANTEATER

Call in Anteater for:

- Help to either find the right words to say or to remain silent.
- Developing a tougher skin so you will be less vulnerable to the verbal attacks of others.
- The power of solitude and confidence in being on your own.

AWARENESS FROM ANTEATER

If Anteater comes into your life:

- Check your stomach, as you may not be digesting or absorbing food properly.
- It is a reminder to speak from your heart.
- You may be lashing out verbally because of fear, judgment, or blaming.

Energy Center: Root

Mineral: Faden quartz

Element: Earth

Magic & Mystery:

- Salvador Dali had a fascination for Anteater and painted a surreal portrait of the poet Andre Breton as an Anteater. Three years after Breton's death, Dali was seen walking an Anteater on a leash in Paris.
- The face of an Anteater is angelic, and its fur has the texture of cashmere. It has been described as the angel of the forest.

Anteater is found in Central and South America. The species is Great Spirit's way to prevent the vegetation from being overrun by Ant and Termite, which brings balance to the environment. Anteater has no teeth, but its long tongue is sufficient to lap up 35,000 Ant and Termite each day. Its tongue with sticky barbs is its most crucial survival characteristic, trapping insects with ease.

Anteater has long, dense, razor-sharp claws, like those of Bear, which it uses to tear into anthills. Then it puts its long snout inside and, with an efficient tongue, extracts its meal. It eats quickly, flicking its tongue 160 times per minute. As Ant may fight back with a stinging response, most Anteater meals are short lived. Anteater never destroys a nest, preferring instead to return and feed again and again. It has poor eyesight and relies on its keen sense of smell to find what it seeks. Its sense of smell is forty times better than ours.

If attacked by Jaguar, Anteater will defend itself and can kill Jaguar by breaking the cat's spine with its claws. Anteater is extremely defensive, and rightly so since it can hardly see. It uses its sharp hearing and powerful sense of smell to pick up on danger.

Anteater sleeps fifteen hours a day, taking numerous cat naps, so is sometimes perceived as lazy. Nomadic, it is unlikely to stay long in any one place. Although it is an excellent digger, Anteater will usually shack up in abandoned burrows rather than build its own.

A scaly African version of Anteater is associated with the spirit of the wilderness by the Lele people of the Democratic Republic of Congo, who consider Anteater the source of all good things. For the Lega people, also indigenous to the Congo, Anteater is a cultural hero. The distinctive layered pattern on its hide is the inspiration for their roofs.

Anteater heightens our sensitivity in figurative as well as literal ways. It can help us perceive more details of the world around us and teaches us to take the bitter with the sweet. Anteater rarely makes a sound, so it encourages a gentle style of communication and is a good teacher of self-control. Anteater has prehistoric knowledge of eternity to share: that our energy never dies but always returns to the energy of the infinite Universe. It helps us to avoid slips of the tongue or becoming tongue-tied and stops us from blurting out hurtful words. Since no other internal organ protrudes from the body like the tongue, Anteater is a sign of the need to speak from within with either toughness or kindness. Anteater has a strong stomach that perfectly breaks down all the insects it eats. It teaches us to "stomach" the "stings" of others and builds our resilience to negative talk.

Anteater medicine teaches that although we may be in the dark, we can trust that there is light around us. This makes Anteater a great guide for travel to the Lower World, which it knows well.

SHAMAN'S INTENTION: *BRING ME UNCONVENTIONAL WISDOM*

ANTELOPE

INSTINCT | **AGILITY** | **AWAKENING**

"Leap over the external noises that distract you; listen instead to your heart whose tenderness and grace will be your guide."—Antelope

BONGO, DIK-DIK, DUIKER, ELAND, GAZELLE, GEMSBOK, HARTBEEST, IMPALA, KLIPSPRINGER, KOB, NYALA, ORYX, SAIGA, SPRINGBOK, SUNI, TOPI, WATERBUCK

Antelope is found in Africa, the Americas, and Asia. Antelope is known for its ornate and beautiful horns. It is an herbivore that swallows quickly and then regurgitates its food later as cud for more chewing. It communicates via a range of noises, such as barking, mooing, trumpeting, and whistling, and is extremely smart. For instance, in Africa, it knows to follow the rains to find the tender grasses and to trail behind Zebra, which eats the tough outer grasses and leaves tender sprouts behind.

Many traditional African tribesmen wear masks to merge and communicate with animal spirits. Antelope is one of the most used symbolic masks as it is called upon to support agricultural endeavors. Antelope horns are associated with the growth of millet and other crops. Its ears are reminders of the songs that women sing during the harvest.

Antelope spends most of its life on alert for predators. Because it has acute vision, Antelope sees eight times better than humans. It has horizontal pupils, implying that it can look beyond the horizon. When danger is impending, it responds intuitively; its quickness to react is its most significant power. Its instincts help it discern which path to take to avoid confrontation and harm.

Antelope is an animal of constant grace; it has mastered the art of living under pressure. It loves humanity and always thinks to help others. Before the last ice age, Antelope showed up symbolizing hope by making the ultimate sacrifice for those who were suffering, offering to humanity its flesh for food and its coat for warmth. Using the medicine of Antelope, you will walk with kindness, compassion, and love and avoid negativity. Look for a higher purpose and see the world from that perspective. The symbol for the heart chakra is the Hindu God of the winds Vayu, who is always depicted riding Antelope. His presence reminds us to ride the winds of the heart energy and expand this most powerful vibration.

Antelope antlers are symbolic of the connection to the higher realms and denote the theory of ascension. They are also a sign of having the willingness to receive the energies of unconditional love and then radiate this to others. The notches on the antlers indicate the steps to enlightenment and the connection to the Sun with its centering energy. Changing our own frequency can expand our awareness and blast through the ignorance of our dimensional amnesia. Antelope reminds us of our responsibility of helping others to evolve. Many hearts are closed by fear and have lost their power. We must be become the master of our thoughts by embracing wisdom instead. When we combine love with light, the unity of these is compassion and we can collapse into oneness.

POWERS OF ANTELOPE

Call in Antelope for:

- Mastering awareness and to learn how to avoid thoughts that distort reality.
- Intuitive guidance on where dangers may reside.
- Help to strengthen bonds in a friendship or to cultivate a herd or tribe and the pride that goes along with it.

AWARENESS FROM ANTELOPE

If Antelope comes into your life:

- You may be overly fearful right now or need to trust your intuition to show you how to create peace and harmony in a particular situation.
- Stop procrastinating, take charge and leap over the obstacles in your mind into the realm of possibility.
- Consider adding more natural herbs and greens to your diet.

Energy Center: Heart

Mineral: Emerald

Element: Air

Magic & Mystery: The ancient Egyptian goddess Satis, whose name means "She who runs," was worshipped in the form of Antelope and her headdress was made of horns.

SHAMAN'S INTENTION: *GUIDE ME TO FIELDS OF ABUNDANCE WITHOUT THE FEAR OF GETTING THERE*

ARMADILLO

PROTECTION | **EMPATHY** | **SEEKING**

"My advice is to wear the armor of the mystic and become impenetrable to all that would diminish you."—Armadillo

POWERS OF ARMADILLO

Call in Armadillo for:

- Trust that whatever is lost will be found.
- Encouragement if you feel defeated or diminished.
- An end to personal abuse or to strap on the armor of self-empowerment.

AWARENESS FROM ARMADILLO

If Armadillo comes into your life:

- It is time to say no and establish better boundaries.
- There is negative energy around you, so you must create a veil of protection to guard yourself.
- Ask yourself if you are being too defensive and therefore not experiencing the world in its fullness.

Energy Center: Root

Mineral: Antigorite

Element: Earth

Magic & Mystery:

- By examining ancient DNA, it was found that Armadillo is related to the Glyptodont, an extinct animal that had a Volkswagen-sized armor and weighed 4,400 pounds. Giant tunnels in South America were dug by these massive creatures
- Bullets have been known to ricochet off the back of Armadillo.

The name *Armadillo* is derived from the Spanish term "little armored one." The Aztecs called it Azotochtli ("turtle rabbit"). Armadillo has an incredible sense of smell, probably because it is nearly blind and deaf. It subsists on grubs, insects, small reptiles, worms, and some plants. It is the only mammal whose entire body is covered with a shell. There is only one type of Armadillo in North America, the Nine-banded Armadillo. The other nineteen types live in South America. The smallest Armadillo, the Pink Fairy, is the size of Chipmunk.

Armadillo spends its life as a seeker, traveling great distances for food and shelter. It is a living dinosaur, carrying the wisdom of prehistory into the present age. Quite the survivor, it has endured for millennia through great persistence. Its appearance is unique. The primary teachings of Armadillo are about defending yourself.

The ancient Mayans hunted Armadillo in large numbers for its meat. Its shells were used as bowls and to create musical instruments, which is why it is associated with music. Armadillo was an important spirit animal in their culture. By understanding Armadillo, they learned about their deep connection to Mother Earth. It was believed Armadillo was created to teach lessons in humility.

Of shamanic significance, Armadillo is the only mammal that can give birth to quadruplets from one fertilized egg that share a placenta during gestation, an ability that is reminiscent of the four cardinal points of the compass, the four winds, the four seasons, and the four phases of the Moon. It is the keeper of the fires that are the basis of protection and helps us in burning our beliefs to find the truth.

Armadillo's armor coat protects the soul of a highly sensitive and gentle individual. If you are an extreme empath, this may be the perfect Power Animal for you, as you can be susceptible to outside influences. One type of Armadillo defends itself from attacks by rolling into a ball whereas other types jump. From this, we can gather lessons about personal boundaries and the preservation of our emotions, including insight on when it is safe to step out and open ourselves up. If a situation becomes overwhelming, we can call on Armadillo to remove our anxiety and ground it in nature. Nature is a constant force with a natural flow that can remove anything. Armadillo can teach us to be good listeners. Because it is deaf, it senses messages that come from the heart, not the mind. We can emulate this trait. Armadillo brings us knowledge of the power of the empath and the necessity for protection against energetic overload. Our empathy is a precious human quality; yet feeling the pain and suffering of others can be a curse. Building armor to protect the beauty of your sensitivity is important for maintaining your spiritual gifts. Nurturing yourself is essential for coping and radiating your inner light.

SHAMAN'S INTENTION: *I CALL IN ARMADILLO TO TEACH ME AND OTHERS THE IMPORTANCE OF PROTECTION*

BADGER

DETERMINATION **HARDINESS** **HEALING**

"There is freedom in fearlessness."
—Badger

Badger is a nocturnal, underground dweller common to Britain. Like a furry "tank," it is powerful for its size. Badger has coarse fur and a distinctive black and white striped face with white-tipped ears. Its powerful legs and sharp claws make it a successful digger. It has poor eyesight; however, its hearing and sense of smell are excellent. Like Skunk, it can emit an unpleasant smell from its anal gland when threatened. It uses this same odor to mark its territory and define boundaries between members of its species. Its skin is so tough that arrows and spears cannot pierce it—it can even resist a blow from a machete. If threatened, Badger will attack creatures larger than itself.

To European shamans, Badger is a healing spirit that shows up to encourage good health. Badger makes its home in burrows that form an intricate underground system; this is similar to the Underworld where you may find pixies, elves, and Mother Earth's healing powers. From here, the place of roots, you will find also the energies of flower essences, medicinal roots, herbs, minerals, and crystals. Badger's link to the soil makes it a great power animal and ally for gardeners.

To Native North Americans Badger is known as the thunder animal, a bringer of lightning or fire. Among the Sioux, a story is told of Badger and Coyote, who are considered the children of the sky; when the Sioux look at the night sky, they see Badger in the Big Dipper.

Japanese folklore is full of well-known tales of Badger, which, with strong mystical powers, shapeshifts into the forms of men and women so it may interact with the two-legged and share its wisdom. In Japan, Badger is called the animal of a hundred shapes.

Badger is the keeper of legends. As a Power Animal, it passes wisdom down through generations. Badger's ability to merge with healers and help their clients is stellar because it helps go deep into the energy of the root chakra to find the truth and then control the often-incessant mind.

It is said that Badger can predict death and see into the future and it knows details about past lives of people. The power of Badger is about taking risks to reap big returns, to break down barriers, and to overcome opposition to get what you want. Badger has the tenacity for the journey, creating along the way what it needs for survival. A shaman may seek Badger because of its internal sense of rebirth since it is always forgiving and forgetting. In a storm, Badger goes inside to a place of healing where it waits and learns retrospection before starting anew. Although it holds secrets, it does so until the moment is ripe to share the wisdom. Badger highly respects sacred contracts, honors commitments, and demonstrates loyalty to others.

POWERS OF BADGER

Call in Badger for:

- Leadership qualities that will help you to persuade others of your vision.
- Help to eliminate your fears.
- Taking risks and removing obstacles for creating a life of joy.

AWARENESS FROM BADGER

If Badger comes into your life:

- It is time to stand your ground and get what you want; stop at nothing.
- Look to plant medicines to enhance your well-being.
- Channel your anger into more efficient pursuits.

Energy Center: Root

Mineral: Elestial quartz

Element: Earth

Magic & Mystery: In 2002, Guinness World Records recognized Badger as one of the most fearless animals in the world.

SHAMAN'S INTENTION: *SUPPORT ME IN KNOWING THAT I AM POWERFUL BEYOND MY PERCEIVED LIMITATIONS*

BARRACUDA

FOCUS | **PATIENCE** | **DISGUISE**

"I wait because I trust that what I need is coming."
—Barracuda

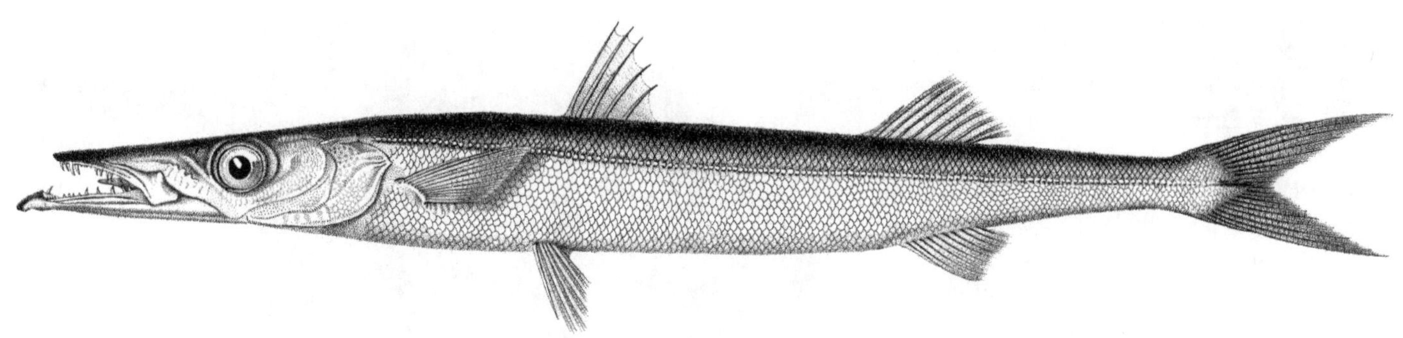

POWERS OF BARRACUDA

Call in Barracuda for:

- Learning to sit and wait, or garnering patience before taking the next step.
- A highly calculated approach to your purpose.
- Fearlessness and power.

AWARENESS FROM BARRACUDA

If Barracuda comes into your life:

- It's time to trust your intuition.
- Take a trip through your unconscious mind to see why you are so aggressive; this will help you learn to go with the flow.
- Realize that chasing shiny objects will never lead to fulfillment.

Energy Center: Solar plexus

Mineral: Purple fluorite

Element: Water

Magic & Mystery:

- Aggressive negotiators are known as Barracuda because of the characteristics of this fish.
- Barracuda have existed for more than 50 million years.

Barracuda is a saltwater fish that hides in the depths of tropical oceans. It is snake-like in appearance with prominent fanged teeth, a large jaw, and a pointed head. Because of its teeth and coloring, it is known as the Tiger of the Sea. Dark green and gray, it has silvery sides and a chalk-white belly. For every year Barracuda lives, it adds another ring of scales to its body.

Barracuda is a master of disguise and patience, waiting for the perfect timing to snatch its prey. It is ruthless, fast, and highly aggressive whenever it does make its move. Barracuda is an incessant searcher, obsessed with obtaining what it wants or needs for survival. It is always hungry and on the prowl. Its keen eyesight adds to its hunting ability.

Mostly solitary, Barracuda is nonetheless curious about humans and often follow boats, appearing collectively like a thin gray shadow in the water. When it takes bait, it seldom fights back, as it is instinctively programmed to be on the offense rather than the defense in life. Few predators hunt it, as toxins accumulate in Barracuda's tissues that make it poisonous. Younger Barracuda can change color to camouflage itself to match its surroundings, making it difficult for predators to find it. Barracuda is not a great parent as it will sometimes feed cannibalistically on its own young.

The traditional *lawai'a* (fisherman) of Hawaii would never discuss where he would fish as it was bad luck. To find Fish, he would ask Kaku, the Great Barracuda, for help in "shepherding" other Fish, like Mackerel, into his nets. Barracuda is a powerful Fish as it is highly intuitive and can sense the vulnerabilities and weaknesses in others. It does not see anything in its way, a quality important to breaking through barriers. It avoids the falsehood of illusions, which makes its journey one of confidence and skill. Barracuda reminds us to not make assumptions, as we can end up unhappy. We must be cautious not to allow our egos to run our lives; the ego can be demanding and give us an insatiable appetite that can never be satisfied. It always wants more power and prestige, which can keep us from a life of peace where we feel content with all that we are and all that we have.

SHAMAN'S INTENTION: *TAKE ME TO THE SOURCE OF MY AGGRESSION SO THAT CALM CAN FLOURISH INSTEAD*

BAT

INTUITION | PROSPERITY | ACHIEVEMENT

"Trust the night as it welcomes the light as its partner in the dance of balance and fate."—Bat

Bat is the only mammal that flies. Its wings are two thin layers of skin stretched over its arms and fingers. Its brain waves are like those of primates, indicating that it is highly intelligent. Contrary to popular belief, Bat is not blind. It is able to see color and to fly in daylight. However, it is nocturnal and sends out sounds that bounce off objects in its path to determine their size and distance so it can adjust the speed and direction of its flight. Some Bats are loners while others prefer living in the association of others. There are groups of Bat with over one million members that combined will eat tons of bugs in one night. Bat has strong family ties. It is innately connected to its offspring, recognizing them by their individual high-pitched squeaks from among thousands of others. It is also verbally communicative and nurturing, touching and displaying sensitivity to members of its group.

In Western cultures, Bat is often seen as villainous or associated with the dark. Because Medieval European naturalists were unable to classify it with any other known animal, it was viewed as violating the laws of God. The ancient Mayans worshipped Bat gods and goddesses that inhabited the underworld. In China, Bat is an emblem of longevity and blessings and of the maternal aspects of the great goddess Xi Wangmu who rules the afterlife.

Bat is a symbol of the magic of the night and the capacity to see the unseen. It is connected to the full Moon, the new Moon, and the spirit realm. In the mythology of the Zapotec people of Oaxaca, Mexico, Bat is believed to be the bringer of messages from those who have died. Bat is seen as responsible for the setting Sun and a bringer of the night; and Bat is used to admonish us not to be jealous of what other people have. The Zapotec say that Bat was punished by the gods who gave it a nocturnal lifestyle and no feathers because it was once too jealous of birds with pretty feathers.

The Apache and Cherokee tribes revere Bat and view its presence as a symbol that something good is going to happen. Bat represents the five blessings of longevity, wealth, tranquility, virtue, and the achievement of personal destiny. It contributes greatly to humanity and the planet by helping us with the pollination of plants.

Bat brings the message that when you are down, look up as your spiritual awakening is upon you. In the dark, you will see stars that will guide your way. Wake up! See the past and all the limitations you have created. Look in the mirror and see what reflects back to you, and then you will realize it is time to change direction to find balance. Leave the chaos behind and begin to make stealth decisions. Bat can help you to navigate mysterious landscapes. Bat teaches us to use the power of the sensory world for clarity and to shift our awareness.

POWERS OF BAT

Call in Bat for:

- Transforming the darkness into the obvious and the understood.
- Supporting you in the ascension process.
- Wisdom to make quick and appropriate changes when needed.

AWARENESS FROM BAT

If Bat comes into your life:

- You need to be more precise in finding the answers you seek by using your intuition.
- Time to make a 100 percent commitment to your spiritual practice.
- Darkness and light have begun to align for you, opening the way for awakening.

Energy Center: Third eye

Mineral: Azurite

Element: Air

Magic & Mystery: The oldest known fossil of Bat was found near Yellowstone National Park in Wyoming and deemed to be fifty million years old.

SHAMAN'S INTENTION: *HELP ME TO TRUST MY INNER GUIDANCE*

BEAR

PATIENCE **RENEWAL** **CONFIDENCE**

"Trust things to show up unexpectedly."—Bear

Bear relies on strength more than agility for its survival. It rambles through the forest on all fours with short legs supporting its bulky body. Although it is a quadruped, it also stands on its hind legs and sits upright like humans. It uses its forelimbs to catch prey, dig out its den, turn over rocks and logs to find goodies to eat, and take often-lethal whacks at larger creatures. With its front paws, it grabs fruit and leaves, taking great delight in eating berries, herbs, and other forest edibles. It is omnivorous but relies mainly on the plant kingdom for its sustenance. Bear has excellent hearing and vision with ranges that far exceeds ours. The world of Bear is very much defined by smell. It is one hundred times more sensitive to smell than humans. It gives and receives messages to others through scent that is left on trees, branches and leaves when it rubs or leaves markings of urine. These "messages" are a vital part of the communication system of the Bear community.

In ancient Greece, the ferocious Bear mama was linked to the huntress goddess, Artemis, patron of childbirth, young animals, and children. It is a symbol of the Divine Feminine and the mysteries of birth. Even so, when Bear reaches the age of two, it is expected to begin making its own way in the world. Bear must pull its own weight with hunting, fishing, and foraging, or else it does not survive.

Polar Bear is the largest land carnivore. Polar Bear and Brown Bear have a common ancestry. Although Polar Bear appears white, its fur really is transparent and reflects the light. Underneath the fur, its skin is black, bringing to mind the symbolism of light and dark.

Archeologist have found remains over 50,000 years old where there is evidence of a cult in which Bear was worshipped as king of the animals, a deity, and the ancestor of humans. In traditional shamanic ceremonies, a shaman seeking to harness Bear medicine wears a Bear hide to merge with the animal's spirit. Bear is respected for its immense power and often called upon during ceremonies of spiritual dismemberment to destroy the old self so a new self may be born. This practice of renewal is reminiscent also because of Bear's long hibernation.

Bear holds the powerful energy of the caves in which it rests; because it goes deep within Mother Earth to renew and heal. If you call upon Bear, it can help you to heal others. It is highly respected as a great protector in the Lower, Middle, and Upper Worlds, and it is interesting to note that those who suffer from insomnia often find that working with Bear medicine helps to get their sleep cycles under control.

Bear is associated with the direction of the West, the place of harvests and gifts. Bear is active day and night and has a deep connection to both Sun and Moon. It is often the Power Animal that chooses to accompany youth during vision quests, perhaps because of its maternal qualities. No one willingly messes with a mother Bear, as she will protect her cubs with all her ferocity and might.

Bear is the keeper of the forest and connected to the wisdom of the Tree of Life that stores the sweet honey of the creative beehive. As such, it has mastered its boundaries. Bear does not appreciate those who wander into its territory unannounced and will raise itself up on two legs and roar a challenge to make its intentions known to any trespassers and potential opponents.

Bear is in tune with the physical world, which it sees through the lens of prosperity. Every berry and Salmon it meets is a gift of abundance, as it fishes in rivers while going with the flow. It trusts things to show up unexpectedly so walks the world with great optimism and promise. It demands respect from all other creatures and will be aggressive toward anyone that does not have its best interests in mind.

Bear brings to us the message of the powers of scents that are used in homeopathy and essential oils. It can stimulate our innate knowledge of the elemental world. Bear can also be our connection to the botanical world and help us to realize the multitude of ways we can learn the healing qualities of nature. Bear is caring and kind, yet protective and discerning; qualities that make for a well-rounded state of being.

IN ANCIENT GREECE, THE FEROCIOUS BEAR MAMA WAS LINKED TO THE HUNTRESS GODDESS ARTEMIS, PATRON OF CHILDBIRTH, YOUNG ANIMALS, AND CHILDREN.

POLAR BEAR

POWERS OF BEAR

Call in Bear for:

- Patience and faith that everything comes at the perfect time; honey and berries are only a moment away.
- Guidance in the dream realm or to dissolve a fear of darkness within a dream state.
- Excellence in mothering and the protection of children.

AWARENESS FROM BEAR

If Bear comes into your life:

- You may be too quick to anger and too sure of your own power.
- Engage in introspection. Pay special attention to how you are thinking, acting, and interacting; use discernment in all that you do.
- Be quiet and go within; there you will identify the boundaries you need to set and find a place of rest that you can trust.

Energy Center: Heart

Mineral: Zoisite

Element: Earth

Magic & Mystery:

- Vikings were famous for working themselves into insane battle frenzies. They donned Bearskins to invoke Bear's spirit and imbue themselves with superhuman strength and fury.
- To show reverence for Bear and its wisdom, shamans will place sacred tobacco under a tree as an offering.

SHAMAN'S INTENTION: *SUPPORT MY ATTITUDE AND MY POSTURE TO BE EXPRESSIVE OF MY POWERS IN THE WORLD*

BEAVER

INTELLIGENCE | **HARD WORK** | **CONFIDENCE**

"Structure in life builds a solid foundation for learning, thus ensuring that dreams come true."
—Beaver

POWERS OF BEAVER

Call in Beaver for:

- Creating the boundaries necessary for success.
- Slowing things down and providing yourself with the space to breathe and take in the flow.
- Having the power to build anything, creating an environment aligned with your dreams.

AWARENESS FROM BEAVER

If Beaver comes into your life:

- Consider others and the impact your efforts may have on them.
- You need more structure in your life.
- It is time to stop chewing on matters or thoughts, forgive, and move on.

Energy Center: Throat

Mineral: Petrified wood

Element: Fire

Magic & Mystery:

- If you see Beaver storing logs of aspen or birch, folklore says it will be a snowy winter.
- Native Americans view Beaver as a holy animal that brings us wisdom in our dreams.

Adult Beaver weighs over sixty pounds and is a reddish-brown color. Its most distinct characteristic is its hairless tail, which is flat and can be used to slap the water to scare away predators or for the purpose of construction. Beaver's back feet are webbed for swimming, and its front feet—not webbed—are used for grasping. Beaver can stay underwater for up to fifteen minutes by squeezing its nostrils and ears closed so that water cannot get in. It also has a transparent membrane that protects its eyes, like a pair of built-in goggles. Beaver constructs dams across streams using sticks, grasses, and mud, creating ponds for Fish entrapment. Its dams are also natural barriers between themselves and predatory animals like Coyote, Wolf, and Bear.

Among Native Americans, Beaver is respected for being a diligent worker and seen as the builder of dreams and desires. Seeing Beaver in a dream is considered a sacred gift from spirit and a sign that great wisdom will be bestowed. To the Athabaskan of Alaska, Beaver is seen as the shapeshifter of the world, transforming it into a place of generous abundance. To the Blackfoot of Montana, Beaver is associated with wisdom, efficiency, and their sacred pipe. The Cherokee see the Beaver as witty, and it plays the role of tooth fairy and the hero of a well-known good luck song in their traditions and culture.

Beaver is determined when making its dams, which can be the cause of serious floods and droughts that have an effect on others. This characteristic reminds us to be aware of our actions and the impact we have on those around us. Emulating the enthusiasm with which Beaver works can empower you to bring your dreams to fruition. It will always get the job done. Beaver understands structure and materials for creating a beautiful environment that is productive, comfortable, and inspiring.

Beaver likes structure and is good for bringing a meticulous balance to health and well-being. It is also good medicine for the teeth and gums. Beaver medicine helps those in transition, as it brings order in a time of chaos. As a Power Animal, Beaver will teach you about being a team player and the first one to show up when work needs to be done. It embodies the energy of productivity, persistence, and completion.

Beaver loves successful endeavors and blossoms when working in partnerships. It is a sign of synchronicity, relying on the flow of the river to bring gifts from spirit and the alliances necessary for creation. Beaver will gather the resources necessary for projects and is very generous with the outcome. It is powerful enough to change the flow of rivers, so when we need some redirection it is a great helper. Beaver reminds us of the water as something we worship as the sustainer of life. All great civilizations are built near water. Beaver is also a sign of fertility, as it brings life to the vegetation that sustains us. The water that is its home is something that we are intimately connected to, as we all spend nine months in fluid before birth. Water never stands still; it is always in an ebb and flow and moves along the path of least resistance. It also has the power to erode even the hardest rock and even move mountains. Beaver sees itself in the mirror image of the river and acknowledges its place in the emotional stream and realizes its balance lies in staying in the flow and keeping its connection to the energies that feed and inspire us from source.

SHAMAN'S INTENTION: *BUILD ME A FOUNDATION SO I AM ABLE TO CAPTURE THE GOODNESS THAT FLOWS TOWARD ME*

BEE

DETERMINATION **COLLABORATION** **PRODUCTIVITY**

"The hum of the Universe vibrates through us and all living things."
—Bee

Bee has been on our planet for thirty million years and there are 20,000 species of Bee. Wherever there are flowers, you will find Bee. Bee can be solitary or live in a community with a division of labor where specialized groups do different tasks. Every functioning hive has a queen whose pheromones influence the behavior of all the other bees. Queen Bee is like the Great Mother, revered, yet mysterious, as she spends most of her life in the dark.

Bee is extremely adept at flying, and the dynamics of its flight are like a helicopter. Bee will alert its companions about the location of food by wiggling its body. It navigates instinctually using the Sun, the polarization pattern of the blue sky, and the Earth's magnetic field to guide it. In general, the workers in charge of gathering pollen are female, except in the case of the Orchid Bee whose workers are male and gather floral oils from orchids. Bee has a keen sense of timing and such a good memory that it can be trained to arrive at the same time every day for feeding.

Bee is one of the most important creatures on the planet. Without millions of Bee pollinating plants, we could not survive. This may be why Bee represents birth, death, and reincarnation in many cultures. When Bee lands on a flower, it will burrow through the folds to reach the center where the pollen is. Similarly, the realization of the shaman's power comes from the center of darkness. Bee's message to us is that by going within, as in meditation, we will find what we seek. Pollen attaches to Bee's legs and then gets passed from flower to flower for fertilization. Bee is an example of the connection between all things.

In ancient Egypt, it was believed that the Sun god Ra's tears had turned into Bees because the Sun is the alchemical ingredient that creates nectar and turns pollen into liquid golden honey. When sealed honey vats were found in King Tut's tomb, the honey was still edible. Because the sugar content of honey is so high, it is antibacterial.

In India, the goddess Bhramari's name means "Bees." Believers know she resides inside the heart chakra where the sound that is emitted resembles the buzzing of Bee. Humming like a Bee when performing ancient Vedic chants expresses the vibration of the soul. This is the same vibration that is felt when kundalini energy is rising in the spine. Indian myths are full of goddesses who turned into Bee to protect themselves from demons and for purification of the land. *Prana*, the divine force inherent to the breath, is often depicted as a circle of Bees. The god Krishna is often depicted with a blue Bee on or above his forehead.

Bee is orderly, and its hexagonal hive embodies sacred geometry. It is associated with feminine energy. In ancient Greece, priestesses in the temple of Demeter, goddess of the cycles of

BEE

DETERMINATION | **COLLABORATION** | **PRODUCTIVITY**

POWERS OF BEE

Call in Bee for:

- Focus when working toward your goals.
- Help to understand the concept of being "one with the Universe."
- Guidance to taste the sweetness in life.

AWARENESS FROM BEE

If Bee comes into your life:

- And stings you, it may be your wakeup call to trust the Universe.
- It is time to start working with others for the highest good.
- You are too lazy, so get up and get going.

Energy Center: Heart

Mineral: Septarian

Element: Air

Magic & Mystery:

- A pound of honey requires Bee to make 25,000 trips between hive and flowers, and it holds the essence of over two million blossoms.
- The Algonquian of North America believe Manitou, the spirit of life, brought Bee to the world. They say Bee comes from a hardworking tribe, whereas Fly comes from a lazy tribe.
- The Mayan word for "honey," is *cab* and is the same word for "World."

life and death, were called the *Melissai* ("Bees"). These women would consume honey and enter trances to prophesize. In Greek mythology, Bee was called a "bird of the muse."

There is a stingless Bee on the Yucatan Peninsula. The Mayans who live there so revere it that if you injure or kill this Bee it will be wrapped carefully in leaves and given a proper burial. Throughout the world, nothing Bee produces is wasted: Honey is eaten, and beeswax is used to make candles representing light and sweet abundance.

Bee is a symbol of productivity for those who wish to engage a team or create something for the greater good. The wisdom of Bee is that opportunity is always out there if you have the will to seek it. The hive, which is the heart and soul of the Bee community, holds a richly nurturing energy that inspires us to work cohesively. By widening our compassion and approaching our practices in a cohesive way, we can create a honeycomb, or the human equivalent, and thus prepare ourselves for the bounty that comes from collaboration. Although Bee knows its mission and works independently, its efforts benefit the whole. Bee is also a motivational symbol that implies having a mission; setting goals and engaging in hard work will ensure success. There is confidence and joy in the "doing" as the results are "sweet."

SHAMAN'S INTENTION: *HELP ME TO SHARE MY GIFTS SO THAT OTHERS CAN BLOSSOM*

BEETLE

ETERNITY | REBIRTH | PERSISTENCE

"Never underestimate the potential of what you see as waste."—Beetle

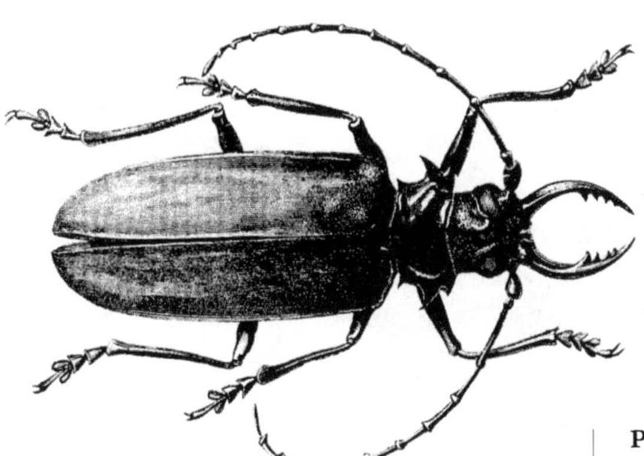

With over 350,000 varieties known to science, and probably thousands more still to be identified, Beetle is perhaps the most diverse and prolific order of life on Earth. One in five organisms is a Beetle. It comes in a rainbow of colors, linking it to the seven chakras. Beetle undergoes complete metamorphosis from egg to grub, pupa, and adult. It inhabits freshwater aquatic habitats, forests, grasslands, deserts, tundra, beaches, and mountaintops. Why is Beetle so prolific? Perhaps because there is so much for it to eat, as it is a planetary decomposer that survives on the waste of all who inhabit the Earth. Beetle is also the symbol of breaking down the illusions that keep us in pain and suffering. It is better to push forward without knowing the final destination so that you may leave the past behind.

Beetle is super intuitive. It can detect a fire from 150 miles away. It is intimately connected to Earth's energy and brings us the power of grounding, safety, and stability.

The Dung Beetle, or Scarab, is one of the oldest and most widespread symbols from ancient Egypt. Pharaohs worshipped this creature as a sacred cosmic spirit because it rolls balls of dung along the ground, a behavior interpreted as pushing the Sun through the sky every day. Millions of stone amulets were engraved with images of a scarab holding the solar disk of Ra in its claws. Beetle was associated explicitly with Khepera, god of the rising Sun, creation, resurrection, and immortality. Egyptians would place Scarab in the heart cavity of a mummy to ensure a successful meeting with the keepers of the gate to the Afterlife.

Beetle uses its antennae for extrasensory perception, defense, mating, and smell. Antennae are also its Wi-Fi connection to the spirit world. A flying Beetle represents the three areas of existence: the material, the psychic, and the divine. Beetle is a symbol of our ancestors; seeing it helps us to remember our kinship with those on the Other Side. Our ancestral knowledge is the cultural core of who we are and should be honored and respected as it is embedded in the elements of nature.

When you see Beetle, it is hard to deter it, as it is determined and focused. Its industrious, goal-oriented nature makes its efforts efficient and successful. Beetle's determination supports you in finding the patience to walk to the ends of the Earth to find your true self. Beetle is always searching for something more significant. Beetle deserves recognition from humanity for supporting the renewal of our planet and making frugal use of limited resources. Beetle brings us a message of the power of being able to step into the unknown and break the barriers of anxiety that keep us from spiritual exploration into the mysteries of life. Uncertainty is a path to sacred wisdom. With the willingness to search, we can always find fresh ideas and new possibilities. This is our path of evolution into adventure and excitement.

POWERS OF BEETLE

Call in Beetle for:

- Creative inspiration on how to move obstacles.
- A sense of what is necessary for accomplishment and achievement.
- An understanding of eternal transformation.

AWARENESS FROM BEETLE

If Beetle comes into your life:

- Use your "antennae" to expand your awareness and intuition.
- You may need to be more persistent and resolute.
- It is a sign of rebirth or the beginning of a new journey.

Energy Center: Root

Mineral: Axinite

Element: Water

Magic & Mystery:

- The Navajo people associate Corn Beetle with fertility, and the Hopi credit it with bringing the first rain dance.
- Living specimens of some Beetle species are worn by Mexican women as broaches, attached to their shirts with small gold chains.
- The Rhinoceros Beetle can lift over 600 times its own weight.

SHAMAN'S INTENTION: *SUPPORT MY JOURNEY TO THE FERTILE GROUND OF THE UNKNOWN*

BLACKBIRD

MYSTERY | **PSYCHIC GIFTS** | **TRANSITION**

"In the darkness secrets will be revealed, and higher intelligence will emerge."
—Blackbird

POWERS OF BLACKBIRD

Call in Blackbird for:

- Taking flight with your ideas so they can be seen by many.
- Lightening up and realizing that you can see more when you take the higher view.
- Help to hear the voices of your spirit guides.

AWARENESS FROM BLACKBIRD

If Blackbird comes into your life:

- Get ready for change, because you are blasting through obstacles.
- You are being overly secretive and closed to sharing with others.
- Stop being dramatic when dealing with family matters.

Energy Center: Third eye

Mineral: Charoite

Element: Air

Magic & Mystery: Druidic legends say that the birds of Rhiannon are three magical Blackbirds whose songs can put the listener to sleep or into a trance, enabling the person to travel to the Upper World to retrieve mystical secrets.

Blackbird lives all over the planet. The adult male has black, glossy plumage, while the female is reddish brown. Its bills and eye rings are yellow. Blackbird flies low to the ground and travels short distances using slow wing beats. It is too clumsy to perch comfortably on bird feeders, preferring to scurry along the ground looking for food in the soil under leaves and undergrowth. It has a soothing chirp and is very vocal in its local habitat. If your throat chakra is sluggish, Blackbird will teach you to sing and share your vocal talent with others.

For the Plains Indians of North America, Blackbird is a sacred symbol of corn. The Arikara tribe of North Dakota believed Blackbird as a helper to the Corn Mother, a divine being who was considered to be the source of life. The Sioux believed that when Blackbird would consume their crops they were being castigated for a lack of reverence and appreciation for corn. The Hopi considered Blackbird a reliable guide to the Lower World.

The color of its feathers makes many people curious about Blackbird. Black is a container of light, a void space you can step into for meditation and transformation. Blackbird is a messenger between the realms of life, death, and transition. Its lesson is to believe in the mystery and magic of the Universe. It can also be a sign of an approaching dark night of the soul, meaning that the moment has come to explore the darkness within you. Get ready. Blackbird will help you disintegrate beliefs inherited from your family that are limiting your growth. Going deep within, you will find genuine passion and soothe areas where you are volatile and unpredictable. Blackbird will also fly into the higher realms to gather insights for you from a higher intelligence. It is connected to volcanoes, which are independent and unstoppable in destroying old wounds. Blackbird adjusts quickly and is a symbol of healing the past.

Blackbird may call you to initiation, or death and subsequent reincarnation, by taking you to the dark of your emotions where you can experience the death of your personality and the emergence of the true self. Psychics and shamans use Blackbird as a spiritual helper when they wish to amplify their connection to the spiritual realms and explore their unique gifts. Blackbird has mastered the art of change and brings us the message to not invest too heavily in the external world as change can seem impossible there. When life gets uncomfortable, your inner shaman is trying to tell you that there is greater potential than what you see. The Universe is standing by, ready to take you into the future potential of your dreams. Look forward to change and embrace a new version of life that is coming to greet you.

SHAMAN'S INTENTION: *BE THE EYES OF MY THIRD EYE AND GUIDE ME TO THE PLACE OF MYSTERY*

BLUEBIRD

TRUTH | CONFIDENCE | OPTIMISM

"Embrace the royal you through renewal, then spring into joy."—Bluebird

Bluebird is a vivid deep blue. It can be seen perched on electrical wires, posts, and branches, scanning the ground for prey and will dive to the ground to pick up insects and berries. It makes its nests in trees, often inhabiting the abandoned holes of Woodpecker. It communicates through song and gestures. It will defend its territory, especially during breeding season. Generally gregarious, it travels in flocks of hundreds of birds. Its song has a lovely melody. This, combined with its vibrant color, makes it a favorite of bird watchers.

Bluebird is often mentioned in poetry as a symbol of love, hope, or happiness. *Into the wild blue yonder* and *the deep blue sea* are expressions that remind us of the power of this bird's natural color. Bluebird represents heaven and the angelic realm. Its migratory purpose is to chase the eternal arrival of spring, ensuring continuous access to ripening fruit along its route. Blue signifies transcendence, serenity, the sky, water, and the highest level of appreciation (for example a blue ribbon, blue-chip stocks, blue blood, and royal blue). The color is deeply embedded in the human psyche. Feng shui practitioners use it to promote relaxation.

Springtime brings fertility, including the fertilization of our ideas into a life of joy, contentment, and the fulfillment of our dreams. The song of Bluebird is a sign that the jewels of life are arriving at your doorstep. When Bluebird shows up there is a change in the season between winter and spring, and Bluebird medicine is on hand to guide you through your next passage and transition. Ancient Phoenician fertility goddess Tanit was depicted in hieroglyphics as wearing a blue garment with bird wings above her head and a beak as a crown. This may have been inspired by the fact that the female Bluebird has three to four broods per season, leaving the male to tend to the previously born chicks until rejoining her.

Native Americans honor Bluebird with many different traditions. The Iroquois were encouraged to hear the sound of Bluebird as it was a sign that Tawiscaron (their name for Old Man Winter) would pass. The Cherokee relied on Bluebird to help them predict the weather; it was also a reliable source for perceiving the directions of the winds. The Navajo related Bluebird with the Sun; and the Hopi saw it as a guardian of the West, the powerful place where the sky meets the Earth. Pueblo peoples revered Bluebird as the offspring of the Sun because of its color blue, which is the color of heaven.

Bluebird brings a message that words are powerful and to be cognizant of using the right ones when sharing with others. It encourages us to embrace the freedom of choice and to act without restraint. The world is full of choices with one doorway leading to another. Through the shedding of our perspectives, we are free to think and move beyond constraints. This confidence reminds us to share our expertise and knowledge as teachers, bringing to others a sense of a new dawn with fresh ideas. When we can fly, we can teach others to do so and release them from their confinement of beliefs and explore the greater truths that exist in the Universe.

POWERS OF BLUEBIRD

Call in Bluebird for:

- Support to expand your gentle and loving nature through words.
- Happiness.
- Becoming an effective teacher.

AWARENESS FROM BLUEBIRD

If Bluebird comes into your life:

- Look in the mirror and consider what you are projecting into the world.
- Express your own "song," using your voice and embrace the nobility of your soul.
- Stop acting powerless and embrace your inner feminine.

Energy Center: Throat

Mineral: Lapis lazuli

Element: Air

Magic & Mystery:

- "The most important of all the creatures are the winged ones for they are nearest to the heavens." —Oglala Sioux medicine man Black Elk
- Among the Pueblo, Bluebird feathers were used to represent the snow and ice of winter that melt and nourish the new growth of spring.

SHAMAN'S INTENTION: *SUPPORT MY AWARENESS OF CHOICE AND THE FREEDOM IT PROVIDES*

BLUE JAY

CONFIDENCE | POTENTIAL | WISDOM

"Embrace your true nature and share your greatness with others."
—Blue Jay

POWERS OF BLUE JAY

Call in Blue Jay for:

- The ability to align and balance your energy with Father Sky and Mother Earth.
- Pride in all you have achieved and to walk forward believing in your infinite potential.
- Boldness and courage in your pursuits.

AWARENESS FROM BLUE JAY

If Blue Jay comes into your life:

- You may be missing out on simple things that could bring you great joy because you are overreaching.
- You are talking too much. Now it is time to use your ears to listen to others' wisdom.
- Remember that you do not need to be forceful to be admired or respected.

Energy Center: Solar plexus

Mineral: Amber

Element: Air

Magic & Mystery:

- The Salish people of North America honor Blue Jay with an annual dance. Shamans hop around until they merge with Blue Jay's power, and then flee. The rest of the tribe must try to find them. When caught, the shamans perform healing for the participants.
- In South America, blue feathers symbolize the sky, water, the ritual use of incense, and communication.

Blue Jay is a large, crested songbird native to North America with stunning blue and white feathers. The crest on the top of its head is raised and lowered depending on its mood. Beautiful and smart, it can be aggressive. Nonetheless, it is a good neighbor for other Birds, as it will warn them of approaching predators. Blue Jay is a great imitator and can make the sound of Hawk to see if any are around. It is very protective of its nests and will dive at intruders. When Blue Jay finds food, it stores it like a squirrel, burying seeds and nuts in many caches. As a result, its love of acorns has helped to plant beautiful oak forests throughout the world. The whole of the mighty oak and its potential is contained in a single acorn. The connection of the Blue Jay to the acorn is a test of faith in the spirit world. Bluebird is saying there is a spark of spirit in all of us and the potential for greatness is always beyond what we can imagine.

The name *Jay* is derived from the Latin word *gaia* ("Mother Earth"), and blue signifies the sky. The Earth-sky combination in its name makes Blue Jay a strong Power Animal. Blue Jay embodies the essence of royal blue with avian confidence. It is intelligent and mischievous and will try to gain an advantage in most situations, making it a troublemaker and a trickster. Blue Jay is attracted to "bling" and might steal a shiny object left unattended. It is known for its tenacity and quick wit.

Blue Jay is an adaptable risk taker. Linked with the mind, it can bring calming to erratic thoughts, enabling you to trust and feel confident. Blue Jay is said to chatter. It is a useful ally for entertainers who love to be in the spotlight and for energetic individuals willing to know what they want and how to get it. When you set an intention, the power of Blue Jay's crest will bring it to you. Use Blue Jay's power to spread your beauty and the impact of your colorful personality throughout the world for others to enjoy. Blue Jay is also associated with the throat chakra, as it can help you speak your truth and release the words that keep you in suppression. Tap into divine timing, as rushing will not get you anywhere any faster. And relax. It is okay to be alone and exposed in the meadow where you can embrace your instincts and know you are safe.

SHAMAN'S INTENTION: *BRING ME YOUR WISDOM AS A CONDUCTOR OF THE BIRD KINGDOM AND HELP ME TO KNOW THE MELODIES OF THE WINGED ONES*

BOAR

FOCUS | **VALOR** | **GROUNDEDNESS**

"Fight the good fight, remembering that winning isn't everything."—Boar

Boar has an extensive territory, which includes the forests of Europe, northern Africa, and Asia. It can adapt to a multitude of environments. Boar is the wild ancestor of the domestic pig. It prefers to roam at night and will sleep almost twelve hours a day in a cozy nest of leaves. Boar lives in family units of between six and thirty animals, including hogs, sows, and piglets. With its sharp tusks, Boar is imposing. It does its best to avoid humans. Boar has an aggressive nature. Boar uses its snout to root around on the ground for food, hunting for culinary treasures like the elusive wild truffle. Loaning us this power, Boar can help us reveal hidden jewels and find the truth.

Boar is the twelfth animal in the Chinese zodiac. The Chinese look upon it for strength and loyalty. The Japanese see Boar as a lunar symbol, and their hunters were forbidden to kill white Boar. The ancient Celts of Great Britain revered Boar as a great warrior due to its temperament. Images of Boar have been found on helmets and other articles of war from Celtic lands. The ancient Norse and the Saxons had a tradition of sacrificing Boar to their gods during the winter holidays.

Merlin, the magician of Arthurian legend shapeshifted into Wolf and Boar, learning to speak the language of the animals and the elements and found his gifts of prophecy.

In Hindu mythology, Boar is a sacred animal. Its blood represents soma, the lost elixir of immortality that the gods drank.

Traditionally, Native Americans would teach their young warriors about honesty through the example of Boar. Lies were considered evidence of spiritual weakness. If a young man lied to the tribe, he would have to face off with a Boar with only a knife in hand. This challenge taught him to be authentic with his words no matter how awkward or uncomfortable it might feel. Honesty requires courage.

Boar is also associated with fertility and life. Because its belly hangs low to the ground, it is deeply connected to the womb of Mother Earth. It has a natural maternal instinct to protect its territory.

Boar swaggers around so it never appears weak. It takes challenges head on. It reminds us to stop avoiding the inevitable and gather courage so as not to run from things. See life as full of possibility, not obstacles. Never wallow in fear; there is always a different path to safety. Boar encourages us to gather our spiritual courage so that we have the muscles to love ourselves and deflect the criticism that diminishes our self-worth. Spiritual courage means that we no longer live our lives for the expectations of others. Finding our strength in the depths of our hearts, we will also find the power to be loyal to who we are.

POWERS OF BOAR

Call in Boar for:

- Bravery and the willingness to make the ultimate sacrifice of laying down your life for others, often through a commitment to the military.
- Physical and mental strength to stay focused on your mission and purpose.
- Total integrity.

AWARENESS FROM BOAR

If Boar comes into your life

- You may have anger issues and be way too protective of all that is yours. Maybe it is time to give and share more.
- Don't be deterred. If you go forward with force and conviction, you will be unstoppable.
- You may be challenging to deal with; seek fairness in competition and express comradery.

Energy Center: Root

Mineral: Aragonite

Element: Fire

Magic & Mystery: To the Druids of ancient Celtic lands, a female boar symbolized generosity and nourishment from the Earth.

BOBCAT

DISCERNMENT | **QUIETUDE** | **STEALTH**

"Walk with a mind in silence and you will always find what you are looking for."—Bobcat

LYNX

POWERS OF BOBCAT

Call in Bobcat for:

- The ability to see those around you clearly.
- Support in solitary times.
- Patience to hunt for what you desire.

AWARENESS FROM BOBCAT

If Bobcat comes into your life:

- It is time to be stealthy and become an intelligent observer.
- Begin to hunt for other options and opportunities.
- Evaluate whether you are being discerning with the information you receive from friends and family.

Energy Center: Crown

Mineral: Banded agate

Element: Earth

Magic & Mystery: Bobcat is connected to the realm of fairies and witches, who keep it informed of gossip and rumors. Bobcat holds information that you can ask it to retrieve for your highest good.

Bobcat lives in a variety of habitats, including forests, tundra, deserts, mountains, and swamps. It is a solitary animal that climbs trees and blends in well with its environment due to its light gray or brown fur and spotted or striped markings. It has keen eyesight, sensitive whiskers, and acute hearing. You can tell Bobcat from other cats because of its tufted ears. Extremely patient, it is a talented hunter, waiting for and then sneaking up on its prey: Bird, Rodent, and Rabbit. An elusive creature, at night it will roam from three to seven miles for hunting. During the day, it sleeps in dens located in rock crevices or under hollow trees and thickets of brush.

On a shamanic level, Bobcat teaches us how to destroy the limitations of time and space. This ability gives the shaman freedom to practice divination without barriers. When you are journeying, Bobcat can give you an expanded view of your past or a peek into your future. Many indigenous peoples understand Bobcat medicine as the ability to slip effortlessly between planes of reality and to invoke the power of invisibility. This spiritual camouflage gives the shaman the opportunity to be a silent observer and better understand the human experience.

Among some Native Americans, Bobcat has a negative reputation for being greedy, selfish, and unwilling to play by the rules. The Hopi call a bad-tempered or ill-mannered person a Bobcat. But others view it positively. The Zuni see Bobcat as a symbol of the hunt, so their hunters etch its image into stone fetishes as a symbol of power. To the Pawnee, Bobcat has mythological significance in that it is associated with the stars. Traditionally, Pawnee parents wrap their babies in Bobcat fur to receive celestial blessings.

Bobcat is quiet and contemplative, fulfilling its needs with grace and deliberation. It brings us a message of patience and the necessity of being strategic in preparing for what is to come. If you are alone, Bobcat will help you manage your feelings of isolation and encourage you to accept solitude as a gift and a chance for self-reflection. Bobcat can help you discover what is hidden and unexamined in the depths of your soul. It can also uncover harmful secrets, and help you be discerning and align yourself with authentic people. Behind the secrets and deception of others lies fear. Revealing this fear creates new openness and a more even exchange of energy to give and receive. Bobcat impresses upon us that deep, internal stillness is a place to connect to all. By getting quiet, breathing, and watching, we can become intimate with all creatures.

Because Bobcat is nocturnal, it makes a great totem for children who are afraid of the dark. When you see its footprints, review your objectives, develop a good strategy, state your goals, and take your first step toward success. As a spiritual teacher, Bobcat can guide you to information about the many solutions available to you.

SHAMAN'S INTENTION: *TEACH ME THE POWER OF STILLNESS*

BUFFALO

ABUNDANCE | **GROUNDING** | **COMMITMENT**

"Be great in mind and body. Know that abundance is a state of being."
—Buffalo

Buffalo lives on the prairies and in river valleys. Most of its day is spent chewing cud and wallowing in the dirt and dust of the plains. Buffalo lives in family herds of up to twenty. Females will gather in a circle to protect their calves when threatened. The males will then create another circle around them. This community circle is a compelling tribute to the preciousness of life.

Buffalo (aka Bison) is the largest animal in North America and formerly was the primary source of life for most Native Americans. A life giving creature, holding the meaning of prosperity, Buffalo sacrificed itself for humans, giving them meat to eat and hide for clothing and shelter. It offers us a lesson in gratitude for what we receive from the Great Spirit. When Buffalo hide is used to make a drum, the pounding of this instrument enhances our connection to Source/God. Buffalo is sacred because of what it gives us. In killing Buffalo, the honorable debt incurred had to be repaid through ritual and prayer.

Once a year, the Plains Indians historically performed a Sundance to reaffirm their fundamental beliefs about the Universe. Sundance was timed to coordinate with the congregation of Buffalo after the long Plains winter ended, so that food would be plentiful for the hundreds of participants.

The Seneca people place Buffalo in the north on the Medicine Wheel, honoring it as a spiritual teacher and wise elder. For them, Buffalo teaches lessons about inner peace and how to incorporate and balance masculine and feminine energy in oneself. The Lakota Sioux believe that a Buffalo calf that is born white—and this is rare—is a sign of the sacred feminine. Their legends tell of White Buffalo Calf Woman who taught them the ritual of the peace pipe that was used to seal agreements and treaties. As the smoke moves out, it is considered to be transporting a prayer.

If you are blessed with the presence of Buffalo, you can be sure that prosperity is on the horizon. Staying in the vibration of knowing we are provided for is its signature energy. The Universe is now on your side. Buffalo reminds us that prosperity in life is about arriving at a state of harmony. Appreciation for what you have by counting your blessings can instantly make your life meaningful. Just as Buffalo can endure harsh winters, if we feel gratitude, we can endure times when resources are slim. Buffalo can take on some heavy burdens, but it reminds us always to reserve an abundant spirit for ourselves. From this perspective we can experience heaven on earth.

POWERS OF BUFFALO

Call in Buffalo for:

- Mentoring from a teacher, healer, or counselor.
- The knowledge that you are making a sacrifice for a noble cause.
- Finding common ground and establishing peaceful agreements.

AWARENESS FROM BUFFALO

If Buffalo comes into your life:

- Reevaluate and reorient your thinking about not having enough. Stay focused on what really matters.
- Your life purpose may be to serve others. Do not be afraid to spread your wisdom across the planet.
- Realize that nothing significant is accomplished without a connection to our inner spirit.

Energy Center: Root

Mineral: Turquoise

Element: Earth

Magic & Mystery:

- In traditional Native American ceremonies, you would find a drum created from the hide of Buffalo, rattles made from its scrotum, tail fly swatters and fans, and even a dried penis—this last item was rubbed against a cottonwood tree at the center of the ceremonial space and planted in a hole lined with Buffalo fat. Smoke from Buffalo "chip" fires carried the prayers to Great Spirit.
- In African tribes, Water Buffalo is associated with chiefs and heroes. Any body part taken from this animal was considered magical and able to drive out negative energy.

SHAMAN'S INTENTION: *SUPPORT MY KNOWING THAT I HAVE EVERYTHING I NEED FOR SURVIVAL*

BUTTERFLY

TRANSFORMATION | **IMMORTALITY** | **LOVE**

"Beauty lies in your perception of all things and embracing the sweetness of the next flower."
—Butterfly

Butterfly has been around for over 130 million years. It thrives in warm climates since it can fly only if its body temperature is above 86 degrees Fahrenheit. There are more than 100,000 species of Butterfly, including Moth.

Butterfly undergoes four life stages. The adult lays eggs on plants that its larva, the Caterpillar (see page sixty), will feed on when it is born. Caterpillar then prepares itself to become the Pupa, lying dormant in a chrysalis. A transformation occurs in which it grows wings. When the pupal skin splits open, Butterfly climbs out and almost immediately flies off. The significance of Butterfly is similar in all cultures as the quintessential symbol of transformation and rebirth. Because of the inevitability of change, it is also representative of fate.

Butterfly can live from a week to a year depending on the species. It is sensitive to perceptions of the natural world; it uses antennae to detect wind and discern scents in the air. It has taste buds located on its feet. Its vision is very well-developed, so it perceives the spectrum of color in a more elaborate and nuanced way than we do. It can teach us to be extremely sensitive to nature and to respect the inherent harmony of life on our planet. Butterfly represents the soul and its journey. In ancient Greek mythology, a human woman named Psyche (whose name means "both") was abducted by the god Eros and transformed into a goddess after being given nectar to drink. In art, she is depicted with Butterfly wings. The Greek word psyche means both "soul" and "butterfly."

In Asia, Mexico, New Zealand, and Zaire, Butterfly is also seen as the soul. Butterfly is revered by the indigenous tribes of the American Southwest as a symbol of change, joy, and color. Many of their dances celebrate Butterfly. An important Hopi tradition

In Asia, Mexico, New Zealand, and Zaire, Butterfly is seen as the soul. Butterfly is revered by the indigenous tribes of the American Southwest as a symbol of change, joy, and color.

to honor Butterfly was when the unmarried girls of the Butterfly Clan would style their hair to look like the wings of Butterfly. This symbolized their readiness to transition from a young girl to a woman. Many Native American legends reference Butterfly as a messenger to carry worldly wishes to be granted to the Great Spirit in heaven. The Shoshone believed that Butterfly was initially a pebble into which Great Spirit blew the precious breath of life. The Zuni thought that Butterfly could predict the weather and that it signaled the beginning of summer. In Africa, the Bwa people view a Butterfly swarm as a sign of the start of the rainy season and also as signifying that you will receive a blessing. In Central America, the Maya looked upon Butterfly as the spirit of a dead warrior in disguise descending to earth. They depicted Butterfly on shields of armor and other war-related objects.

The Chinese see Butterfly as a sign of young love, or being young at heart, representing the bond between lovers. The lesson of Butterfly is to continually let go and move on. It is the sign of renewal and hope after experiencing trauma. A Butterfly sighting is magical and captures our attention as a gift and affirmation from the spirit world. They are the most mentioned sign sent from a transitioned loved one.

Butterfly characterizes the transformation of the soul as it passes through the stage of the destruction of ego and into the glory of its freedom. In Lewis Carroll's book *Alice's Adventures in Wonderland*, Alice comes upon a Caterpillar when she arrives in Wonderland, which is the perfect symbol for entering a world of chaos and confusion before she can emerge as her true self. Butterfly is a sign that it is time to experience something new and different or to incorporate the power of color in our lives. A move or change will soon take place, so get ready for the next adventure. Use the lightness of being to move from flower to flower to find the beauty in all that you see. Butterfly is a symbol of our soul and reminds us of its desire for growth and freedom. It knocks at the door of our hearts, always wanting to discover joy.

POWERS OF BUTTERFLY

Call in Butterfly for:

- Inspiration to accept the destruction of the ego during your journey of enlightenment.
- Carrying your desires through the winds of change with the confidence that you will land somewhere positive.
- Optimism for the journey of awakening ahead of you, no matter how destructive the process may seem.

AWARENESS OF BUTTERFLY

If Butterfly comes into your life:

- A personal metamorphosis is inevitable. Your life will be more challenging if you resist.
- Lighten up and look at the world through a more colorful lens.
- You may be grieving the loss of someone close to you. It is a sign that they are only a breath away.

Energy Center: Crown

Mineral: Strawberry quartz

Element: Air

Magic & Mystery:

- Many Native American cultures consider Butterfly the symbol of prosperity and have taboos against killing it.
- Butterfly designs were used to decorate baby cradles by the Blackfoot Indians.
- Legend has it that Joan of Arc was surrounded by white Butterfly during her victories.
- The Navajo believe that the butterfly were the first creatures to use "body paint"
- Aboriginals believe the dead go to the land of the Morning Star, a place full of butterflies.

Shaman's Intention: *Take me to ancestral souls that can share the wisdom of transformation with me*

CATERPILLAR

PATIENCE **TRUST** **TRANSFORMATION**

"When it seems that things are falling apart, there is always hope."
—Caterpillar

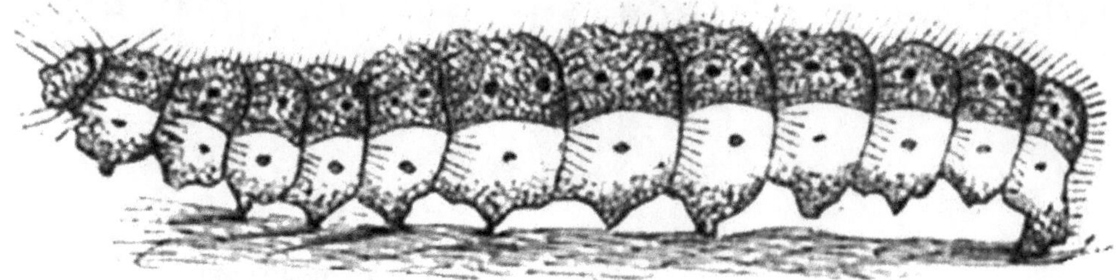

POWERS OF CATERPILLAR

Call in Caterpillar for:

- Confidence that change is good and should be embraced.
- Introspection.
- Optimism about the future.

AWARENESS FROM CATERPILLAR

If Caterpillar comes into your life:

- Change is coming and you had better get prepared.
- You must crawl before you can fly.
- Trust your intuition that things will get better even if it seems that everything is crashing down around you.

Energy Center: Heart

Mineral: Dioptase

Element: Air

Magic & Mystery:

- Caterpillar has a strong jaw and uses its feet to test its food to be sure it is tasty.
- Caterpillar has stiff hairs on its body, which have tips that detach. These tips are irritating to birds, except for Cuckoo, which does not seem to have an aversion to them.

There are more than 20,000 known species of Caterpillar around the world. These come in a multitude of colors, sizes and appearances. Sometimes Caterpillar is very hairy, sometimes smooth. The purpose of its appearance is to intimidate and deter predators.

Caterpillar is a voracious eater and the fastest growing animal on the planet. After two to three weeks in this early form, it builds a cocoon where it enters into a transformational process for roughly two more weeks, emerging with wings as a Butterfly (or Moth). To protect itself, Caterpillar will adapt to fitting into its environment, taking on the color of the leaves it lives on. This merging with the natural world is critical in designing a cocoon for change. Its ability to make itself "invisible" to predators tells us that there is protection available to us if we will go within and adapt to our surroundings.

Ancient Egyptians placed great importance on Caterpillar, inspired by its message of transformation. The dead were placed in "cocoons" like Caterpillar after mummification rituals. Caterpillar is a sign of death. It can be beneficial for widowed people to embrace a protective cocoon until they can grow wings again and flourish in life.

For Caterpillar to become Butterfly takes patience and trust in the process. Caterpillar is a symbol of *metamorphosis,* a natural process that allows us to unfold into our highest potential. It shows us that it is possible to change personality and become a reflection of our real self as we reveal the greatness of our individual expression. It is a sign of transformation and also a reminder that change cannot be avoided. Caterpillar can bring you the determination and patience you need to make changes in your life and help you to find the link between the human and the divine realms. It is the master of nothingness, a reminder to quiet the mind by watching your thoughts.

Caterpillar can be a creative muse to the artist who is looking to create something from very little and whose creations will be noticed by others. It encourages us to keep our creations to ourselves until the time is right to make a big splash with our revelations. Seeing Caterpillar means prosperity abounds and your ideas will now become realized. This is an inspiring time for your projects. It is a powerful symbol both for leaving the past and moving forward, shedding all that does not serve you. It also means that your ego is on its way to destruction, that the limitations preventing you from seeing the world in an optimum way are being removed. It can be a time for quiet, meditation, and reflection to prepare for the glory of what is coming your way. Dare to change, dream big, and be inspired by a new reality to come.

SHAMAN'S INTENTION: *SUPPORT ME IN TRUSTING THE POWER OF SPIRIT FOR TRANSFORMATION*

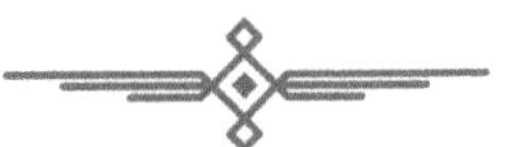

CAMEL

"There is no distance so far not to enjoy the journey."—Camel

Camel adapts well to the flat landscape of deserts and prairies. It is a reliable pack animal, biologically designed for endurance. Transporting travelers from Europe and the Middle East to the Far East in ancient times, Camel was integral to the historic expansion of the spice and silk trades and made traders very wealthy. As a sign of humility, a domesticated Camel kneels so it can be loaded with goods, implying a willingness to be of service to its owners when treated with respect.

Contrary to popular belief, Camel does not carry water in its hump. The hump is actually stored fat. Camel can drink forty gallons of water in minutes, making it able to rehydrate faster than any other mammal on Earth.

The Quran refers to Camel as *God's gift.* For the Bedouin people of Africa, Camel is revered and vital to their existence. These indigenous nomads consider Camel part of the family and recognize that it is the key to their survival. They depend on Camel for wool, hide, sinews, and bones.

Camel is also linked to the plant medicine of frankincense and myrrh, which was used by ancient healers. In some myths, Camel is said to enlighten those who are asleep.

Camel teaches us that we can be self-sufficient and do not necessarily need to rely on others for getting where we want to go. When life seems barren, Camel helps us find an oasis from which to drink the elixir we need to go forward. Camel reminds us that, although we may be carrying a burden for ourselves or others, soon we will reach our destination and can unload that which is weighing us down.

Camel may appear when a time for travel has arrived. If there is a steep and bumpy road ahead or a risky time coming, Camel's insights can be useful. Camel is obedient and calm, strong, and reliable. It has crossed many continents and connected the people of many cultures for many purposes. As a shamanic guide, it will help you discover the resources you need. Camel will expand your view of the world and extract you from the confines of any one place. It can encourage you to move when you are stuck in a place that no longer fulfills you. When it is time to move on, invite Camel to be your companion and get going on the next adventure or project. When we set out on the path of life, Camel reminds us that there are always twists and turns on the road. With innocence, humility, and faith, we will always find our way. Remember, it is okay to slow down and conserve energy so that decisions at the crossroads of life are made with good judgment.

POWERS OF CAMEL

Call in Camel for:

- Recognition that everything you need for survival is at your disposal.
- Help to manage and lift a load of problems you may have taken on.
- A reminder to nourish your body with water for the sake of energy, cleansing, and detoxification.

AWARENESS FROM CAMEL

If Camel comes into your life:

- Your physical reserves may be depleted. Conserve your energy as you fill up your "fuel tank" and build your resilience.
- A harsh time may be upon you and you may need to insulate yourself from the outside world.
- It is time to demand respect and fair treatment so that you can maintain a balanced life.

Energy Center: Sacrum

Mineral: Yellow jasper

Element: Earth

Magic & Mystery:

- The largest remaining population of feral Camel is in Australia where there is around 700,000.

SHAMAN'S INTENTION: *BE MY GUIDE TO UNDERSTAND AND EXPERIENCE DIFFERENT CULTURES, LANGUAGES, AND BELIEFS*

CANARY

OPTIMISM | **JOY** | **ENLIGHTENMENT**

"Every time you open your mouth, your voice is an energetic signature in the world."
—Canary

POWERS OF CANARY

Call in Canary for:

- Help to identify what will make you happy.
- Becoming a voice of light in the world.
- Singing your soul's song.

AWARENESS OF CANARY

If Canary comes into your life:

- Do not allow others to control or confine you.
- Speak up and share what is in your heart.
- Canary will help you find the right words to say and to express them melodically and gracefully.

Energy Center: Solar plexus

Mineral: Abalone

Element: Air

Magic & Mystery: In China, Canary yellow represents the power of the Sun, the yang (masculine) principle, happiness, and wisdom.

Canary is a member of the Finch family. Indigenous to the Canary Islands, it was brought to mainland Europe by Spanish sailors in the early 1400s. For centuries, people have appreciated Canary for its musical ability. It became highly sought after as a pet in the finest homes of England and Spain. Although it was originally green, it comes in a variety of colors and was often bred to be bright yellow. Yellow Canary is a symbol of positive transformation, sunshine, and joy. It represents our ability to see the beauty within our own islands of self-realization. To draw knowledge and energy from the Sun, the direct source of life on Earth, and lock this essence into your being is a magical ability.

The pitch of Canary's song is resonant with the frequency of the third chakra. This center of consciousness begs us to turn our heads to the Sun to establish an alchemical blend with our bodies that uplifts us emotionally and leads to the richness of being. This lovely songbird reminds us to carry the light within us and, when possible, share our inner wisdom with others. Our ability to express ourselves in a way that enlightens and uplifts others is the essence of Canary's medicine. When you have the blues practice whistling like Canary, as it is almost impossible to whistle a sad melody.

Canary originally came from Atlantis with the mission to preserve a message of joy from the ancient ones who lived there. On the Canary Islands, when standing on the main Guimar pyramid in Tenerife, it is possible to experience a double sunset behind the nearby mountains. This is symbolic of how, even when everything seems to be dark, the Sun always rises again. The Guanches, Berber tribespeople who migrated to the Micronesian islands in 1,000 B.C.E. and built pyramids would communicate merely by moving their lips and, at longer distances, conversed by whistling—like a male Canary. Surprisingly, only the male Canary sings. This special Guanche language is still used and children are taught it in school as their traditional language.

Although often confined in a cage today, Canary knows that freedom exists when we move beyond the mind and live in a world of possibility. It reminds us that our spirits can soar from wherever we are and to never feel trapped in fear. By sharing a balanced melody with others, we can help those around us maintain a higher vibration. Canary is an ideal Power Animal for public speakers hoping to spread a message of joy. Canary teaches us to admire the smallest birds, as they have the highest energy for ingenuity and quick responses. Call in Canary to help you with the people in your life who have characteristics of narcissism and want to keep you caged by using a feeling of superiority and an exaggerated need for attention and validation. Canary will teach you to defy those who wish to control you and open the door to freedom.

SHAMAN'S INTENTION: *HELP ME TO OPEN A DOOR TO FREEDOM SO THAT NOTHING CONTROLS ME*

CAPYBARA

THE CLAN | **CONSIDERATION** | **AFFECTION**

"Loving others and creating a place of calm and serenity can illuminate all who come into your space."
—Capybara

Capybara is a semiaquatic rodent with webbed feet that inhabits the waterlogged regions of Central and South America. A sociable animal, it lives close to water in dense herds as large as a hundred individuals. Capybara family units are composed of one male, several females, and their offspring. Capybara sleeps little, preferring to doze on and off during the morning while resting in soft leaves on the banks of rivers or cooling off in the water and mud during the heat of the midday Sun. It never strays far from the water's edge as it is an expert at hiding underwater and holding its breath for up to five minutes. It even can fall asleep underwater while keeping its nostrils above the surface to breathe. Capybara is an herbivore and, digestively, it is a master of extracting all the nutrients it needs from a minimum of sources. This efficiency of consumption makes it extremely adaptable.

Weighing in at 75–150 pounds, Capybara is the world's largest rodent and walks the world with confidence. Capybara only mates in the water, although females always give birth on land. Only the dominant male from the pack is permitted to mate. Every pack is dominated by a male that marks out the pack's territory to ensure mutual survival.

Protective of its family members, several Capybara will gang up on anyone who threatens them. The females communally share the responsibility of nursing the pack's offspring, ensuring every little one is nurtured and none is lost.

Sometimes referred to as a "Water Pig" because of its strong connection to streams and ponds, the lovable Capybara is actually a cousin of Guinea Pig. It has an even temperament and is quiet and content in its world unless

provoked. Perhaps the friendliest creature in the animal kingdom, you may see Capybara with other animals, such as small monkeys, riding on its back.

The young male Capybara is forced to leave the pack when he reaches maturity. Sometimes he comes back and lives as an "escort" on the outskirts of a family group. Spiritually, Capybara represents the knowledge that the best way to begin an independent journey is to free yourself from tribal limitations. Separation creates the environment to transform yourself and embrace your status among others that align with you.

Capybara knows how to live it up in its environment and normally creates a very comfortable lifestyle for itself. It would be happy hanging out by the pool with its friends if there is a lovely meadow nearby to graze on. Capybara teaches us that unconditional love is love without judgment or limitations. True love is a powerful force to tap in to. To love unconditionally starts in our hearts with loving ourselves and embracing love as a power in our lives. It requires mastering forgiveness and honoring the experiences of others, even though their experiences may bring them pain and suffering as they are led to greater wisdom. Capybara encourages us to give of ourselves unselfishly, asking for nothing in return.

POWERS OF CAPYBARA

Call in Capybara for:

- Mastering your environment by extracting all you need to flourish.
- Trusting in the flow—meaning, you are safe and will be supported by life's movements.
- A love of swimming and feeling more at home in the water.

AWARENESS FROM CAPYBARA

If Capybara comes into your life:

- It is time to find hope and strength through the support of your family.
- Take a vision quest and accept responsibility for your destiny.
- The sound of water may help you to sleep better or calm your inner self.

Energy Center: Root

Mineral: Jet

Element: Water

Magic & Mystery:

- The Matis people of the Amazon perform a hunting ritual in which they cover their bodies in clay and make the sounds of Capybara. This practice is believed to improve their hunting and boost their health and prosperity.
- The Guarani of Paraguay call Capybara the Master of the Grasses, as it likes living close to water in lush green spaces filled with long grass. This environment helps Capybara to hide and camouflage itself.

SHAMAN'S INTENTION: *GUIDE ME TO THE WISDOM OF THE WATERS AND HELP ME DISCOVER THE POWER OF THIS ELIXIR OF LIFE*

CARDINAL

LOYALTY | **INTERMEDIARY** | **THE SACRED**

"Look for the deeper messages you receive and know that your departed loved ones and ancestors are with you through every twist and turn."—Cardinal

POWERS OF CARDINAL

Call in Cardinal for:

- Free will to learn.
- A better connection to the root chakra and to fulfill the potential of your kundalini.
- Help to be a positive force in your family, community, or workplace.

AWARENESS FROM CARDINAL

If Cardinal comes into your life:

- Calm a fiery temper, as it may be causing you to lose control of your senses.
- Deliver a message to someone in a loving and caring way.
- Love is in the air.

Energy Center: Heart

Mineral: Ruby

Element: Air

Magic & Mystery: Cardinal lays eggs that hatch within twelve days. Cardinal resides in the same location the full twelve months of the year, so it is associated with the number twelve. Twelve represents the spectrum of experience and the whole circle of life.

Sporting flashy red feathers Cardinal is found in North and South America. It has an unusual crest on its head that is an indicator of its emotional state. When Cardinal is calm, the crest lies flat; when excited, it peaks. The reason for the redness of its feathers is that the diet of Cardinal consists of red berries which contribute to the feathers' pigment. If Cardinal's diet lacks berries, its red hue gradually fades. Both the male and the female Cardinal sing lovely songs, although the female's song can be more elaborate. Since Cardinal does not require much sleep, you may hear it as the first bird singing before sunrise.

Cardinal is considered a good omen by many tribes of the American Southwest. Some Pueblo see Cardinal as a guardian of the four directions on the medicine wheel, though it is most closely aligned with the direction of the East, which represents the spring. They say that the spoken word comes from the East and, carried on Cardinal's wings, it is delivered directly to and from the spirit world. The Pima people associate Cardinal with lightning and believe it can predict rain. The Cherokee tell stories of Redbird, describing Cardinal as the daughter of the Sun. Their lore says that Cardinal can predict the weather. The Ojibwe admire Cardinal for its alertness. Shamans call in the power of the Cardinal when they wish to deliver messages to the ear of someone without that person's knowledge.

Cardinal has many noble qualities, including deep devotion to the health and wellbeing of its family, monogamy to its mate, and a preference to stay in the same area all its life. The male feeds the female as a courtship ritual as well as during the gestation of her eggs. Because of this, the Choctaw of North America see Cardinal as a sign of a new relationship on the horizon or as an indication that change is needed in an existing one. Wherever you go around the world, the brilliant red feathers of Cardinal embody a sense of majesty and royalty. In Asia, the color red is seen as the luckiest color and as signifying love and passion. Cardinal is connected to fairies, the guardians of the plants and trees in the natural world (aka the Standing Ones). Cardinal brings us the message of the importance of the Standing Ones for the avian kingdom.

The Latin root of the word cardinal is cardo, which means "hinge." It refers to the principal element in a scenario, which is why mapmakers refer to the four primary directions—north, east, south, and west—as cardinal directions. Cardinal is an important messenger for spirits who want our attention. Cardinal reminds us to trust our intuition and not to be influenced by the fears of others. If you are feeling indecisive, Cardinal will appear to remind you to go with your gut. The cardinal direction you are to move toward will become clearer.

Cardinal likes to be the center of attention. It is a good Power Animal for leaders and influencers who need to get noticed. It can help us with the promoting of our ideas and being seen in the crowd. By showing up in its bright color, Cardinal reminds us to celebrate what we are and what we are becoming. Even the sound that Cardinal makes seems to be saying "Cheers."

If you see Cardinal, you can be assured that you are going to receive a message of great importance. Through its crown chakra, Cardinal is reliably connected to higher knowledge. Wisdom can come in fragments. As Cardinal helps us to awaken, the messages we receive become clearer. Cardinal knows the mystery of sacred soul contracts and will help bring souls together. Cardinal is a sign of abundance, a reminder that prosperity comes with generosity.

SHAMAN'S INTENTION: *HELP ME BE OPEN TO THE GIVING AND RECEIVING OF MESSAGES FROM ASCENDED BEINGS*

CARIBOU

WANDERLUST | **DETERMINATION** | **FAIRNESS**

"Live a life of adventure and collect stories along the way to fill your heart and mind with treasures."
—Caribou

Caribou is found in the northernmost regions of North America, Europe, Asia, and Greenland. A nomadic animal in constant search of food, Caribou (of both female and male) grow forward-pointing antlers that it uses to forage under the snow. Caribou travel a range of up to 3,000 miles, the most extensive territory of any land mammal. The most annoying and relentless enemies of Caribou are Fly and Mosquito as they will swarm its herds. Mosquito (see page XXX) attacks the Caribou calf, sucking massive amounts of blood from it. The need to avoid this danger causes Caribou to keep searching for colder climates where fewer insects live.

In Alaska, humans and Caribou have lived in close relationship for at least 11,000 years. Traditionally, clothes for the people, food, and utensils all came from different parts of Caribou's body. The ancient ones used its hide to make tents and clothing because it is almost impenetrable protection from the elements and cold. Caribou bones were used to build cradles for infants. A figure named Caribou Master features in the mythology of the indigenous Innu people of northeastern Canada. To the Innu, animal masters are supernatural beings who watch over animals and give humans permission to hunt them. Caribou Master was the most powerful of all these spirits. Legend says he was originally a human male who fell in love with a female Caribou and transformed himself so he could be with her. Many rituals were carried out to pay respect to Caribou. Showing respect for Caribou would ensure easy hunting and help the people avoid famine.

Perhaps the most famous myth about Caribou in European culture is the legend of Santa Claus and his sleigh drawn by Reindeer. It is believed this story originated among the early Norse whose thunder god, Thor, was transported by a chariot pulled by a Goat that in later centuries morphed into a Reindeer.

It is common to long for movement and adventure, or to want to travel to foreign lands. Caribou makes a good guide for times when you are experiencing wanderlust. Its endurance and commitment can stay with you for a lifetime, helping you to navigate the world with grace and speed, as when running it can reach a speed of 80 miles per hour. Caribou is unique in that both males and females have antlers, so it represents equality between the sexes.

Caribou shares with us the knowledge of finding places to sustain it and keep the herd happy and healthy. It imparts the ability to see beyond what is in front of you. It will also prepare you for an arduous journey. Caribou brings us the message that when things do not go as planned we must embrace chance. As you walk in the world, feel the power of free will, able to go whichever way you feel to ensure a life of meaning. Release the burden of toxic relationships and walk in the light.

REINDEER

POWERS OF CARIBOU

Call in Caribou for:

- Help to stop wandering. And if you feel lost, ask Caribou to help you find your way.
- A partner who can foster understanding in a large family or community.
- A keen sense of smell and to heighten your intuition of what is needed for survival.

AWARENESS FROM CARIBOU

If Caribou comes into your life:

- You should not fear the road ahead as the journey will always provide.
- It can help you find hidden or "dark" information.
- It is time to take the lead and move forward.

Energy Center: Sacrum

Mineral: Fire opal

Element: Earth

Magic & Mystery:

- The Intuit see an important connection between Caribou and Wolf. Before hunting, they would place the bodies of a sacrificed Wolf and Reindeer together on a high platform to please the gods.
- The name *Caribou* originates from the Mi'kmaq word *Qalipu*, which means the "one who paws," honoring the power of Caribou's hoofs to find food buried under the thick layers of snow in the northern regions.

SHAMAN'S INTENTION: *TEACH ME THE LESSONS OF THE SEASONS AND TO EMBRACE CHANGE*

CARP

PERSEVERANCE | **PROSPERITY** | **SOCIABILITY**

"Dissolve into nature, allowing yourself to be removed from your humanness. Only then may you come to know your connection to all things."—Carp

GOLDFISH, KOI

POWERS OF CARP

Call in Carp for:

- Tools to help you discover abundance.
- Bolstering your perseverance.
- Help to discover what is hidden in your subconscious mind.

AWARENESS OF CARP

If Carp comes into your life:

- You need to start moving and raise the vibration of the energy around you.
- It is time to get your shine on and make a splash with others.
- Start to realize your potential for prosperity.

Energy Center: Solar plexus

Mineral: Neptunite

Element: Yellow calcite

Magic & Mystery:

- In Japan, the red and white Koi called *Kuchibeni* ("Lipstick fish") is said to inspire long-lasting romances.
- A midnight black Koi known as the *Kumonryu* is named after the Japanese dragon of transformation. This "nine-tattooed dragon" has curled white markings that are like famous ink paintings of dragons. This Koi also changes color with the seasons.
- Ancient Egyptians kept Goldfish in their households to bring in prosperity and sweeten any bitterness among family members.

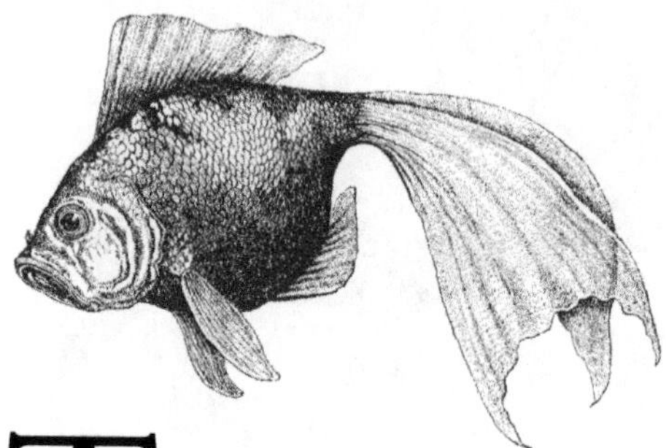

There are more than twenty types of Carp, differing in color, pattern, and scales, some of which are bred for captivity. Carp is long lived. Its average lifespan ranges from thirty to sixty years; however, there are validated cases of some Carp aging over 200 years old. Carp is a very energetic fish, fighting river currents and stirring up the waters with its great strength. It is an excellent swimmer and successfully swims upstream with great determination. A very social Fish, it enjoys living in groups and with other aquatic creatures. A group of Carp is a *gasp.*

Koi is a type of Carp famous for its persistence. A Chinese legend describes a large group of Golden Koi fighting the currents as it swims upstream in the Yellow River. Arriving at a waterfall, many of them retired and swam downstream again. Those that remained never gave up and continued their struggle to reach the top of the waterfall. It was believed that local demons would raise the level of the waterfall out of spite. It was a hundred years before the persistent Koi reached the top. The gods then rewarded Koi for its tenacity and turned it into a Golden Dragon, a symbol of power.

The vibrant colors of Koi are iconic. In Japan, it was long believed that Koi can change the perception of its observers. As your Power Animal, it can alter the outcomes you experience by raising the frequency of your energy.

Goldfish, another species of Carp, symbolizes wealth and good fortune. A common image to see at Chinese New Year is a child (the child representing new beginnings) holding a large Goldfish and a lotus flower. These items are said to bring wealth and harmony. Embroider Goldfish on your purse to ensure it will always be full of cash.

In Buddhism, a pair of fish is one of eight symbols of an enlightened Buddha. This infinity sign represents fertility, harmony, abundance, and going with the flow. The astrological symbol for Pisces is two fish swimming in opposite directions. One is supposedly swimming vertically toward spirit and the other horizontally toward matter. These fish also represent the separation between our conscious and unconscious selves. This divide is what our spiritual journey becomes as we work to merge these two aspects alchemically so that we may effortlessly achieve balance and flow with the natural energy around us.

Carp brings peace after the struggle of enlightenment and reminds us of the price we pay for calm. We must feed our spirit to arrive at higher levels of consciousness. Carp is connected to the lotus and its symbolism of unfolding from the murky waters with the daylight into a place of rest, growth, and rebirth. By trusting your Source, you are always awakening as you walk the path of karmic destiny. Allow nature to bring what is needed and there will be no scarcity. Dare to dream as the sunlight hits the water with the light of spiritual integrity. Turn sadness into serenity and define again your place to retreat. If your life seems muddy and murky, call on Carp to help you take inspiration from the lotus flower that breaks through the surface and emerges into great beauty. Here you can achieve a state of mental purity and float in the womb of earthly wisdom and power.

SHAMAN'S INTENTION: *I JOURNEY WITH CARP TO UNDERSTAND THE NATURE OF WATER AND THE ELEMENTS OF FLUIDITY*

CAT (DOMESTIC)

INDEPENDENCE | **MYSTICISM** | **SELF-LOVE**

"Take a whimsical walk with me into the mystical world where you will uncover the secrets of your precious existence."—Cat

Cat became domesticated roughly 9,500 years ago in northern Africa. The ancient Egyptians, who called Cat *Mau* (like the sound it makes), considered it sacred. Cat stood guard at the gates of many of their temples. Out of reverence, Cat mummies were buried with the mummies of human dead. In fact, Cat was considered so valuable to the Egyptians that they would impose the death penalty for killing one. Bastet, goddess of fertility and protector of children, had the head of Cat.

In India, Cat is known as the vehicle of the sage Vidali, and as a liaison to the mystical world. Cat is linked to the Tz'asti, Hindu goddess of femininity and birth, and is often portrayed riding on its back. In Norse legend, Cat is sacred to Freya, goddess of love and beauty; she is protector of the weak, a healer, and the grantor of magic for love and peace. In the hope that she would bless their crops, farmers would leave milk out for Freya and her cats. In Japan, Cat is considered a blessing to a newborn child. A cat figurine known as a *maneki neko* is placed in the entrance of many businesses to bring good fortune and prosperity to shopkeepers.

Cat is a great little survivor. It can even drink seawater to hydrate itself because of its kidneys, which can filter out the salt. It is vigilant and likes to know what is happening in its surroundings. Cat prefers living in the company of other cats to being alone, because its attention span is short and it quickly gets bored. Cat is a nocturnal hunter, like its bigger, wilder relations. It sleeps several times every day for short stretches—hence the concept of a *cat nap*—and likes spending time in dark spaces. Cat has a superior nervous system. From the condition of its fur, it can sense earthquakes and approaching changes in weather before we can.

Cat is connected to the Moon. It was placed in the service of humankind because of its heightened intuition so we could learn to sense and uncover hidden secrets and develop our psychic abilities. Cat's curiosity serves it well as it always finds the truth, leaving no stone unturned. Cat is an excellent companion for a mystic or shaman working in the spiritual realms. The ancient Celts saw them as guardians to the Lower World. Buddhist monasteries welcome Cat both as protection from Mouse (see page XXX) and, due to its orderly temperament and soothing personality, as a quiet companion who shares the monks' desire for quiet. Cat can be an excellent companion when you're exploring past lives, as it can trace threads of the divine through many lifetimes. With eyes that reflect the Moon, it can see deep into the cosmic consciousness of existence.

That Cat does not like to be wet is a reminder to manage our emotions better, since they can distort our perceptions of reality. Cat can grab at the universal basket of possibilities with its claws and bring them to us for realization. Cat reminds us of our hunting instincts and the importance of timing and patience, guiding us to grab an opportunity as soon as it arises and helping us take calculated risks to achieve what we desire. It walks the world with grace, poise, and confidence. It has a sense of who needs healing and will sit with us to work on our own healing. Its purring can help to relieve anxiety and create steadier rhythms in the body.

POWERS OF CAT

Call in Cat for:

- The ability always to land on your feet.
- Support to do what you desire on your own terms.
- Spontaneity and playfulness to celebrate your uniqueness.

AWARENESS FROM CAT

If Cat comes into your life:

- You now have a natural healer living with you; take advantage of its presence.
- It is time to celebrate your personal power and independence.
- Remember the importance of sleep and take time for rest and relaxation.

Energy Center: Third eye

Mineral: Chalcopyrite

Element: Earth

Magic & Mystery:

- A happy marriage is expected if a Cat appears at the wedding.
- Muslims respect and protect Cat because it was cherished by Mohammed. It is believed the "M" marking on Calico Cat comes from him resting his hand on its fur.

SHAMAN'S INTENTION: *FILL ME WITH THE KNOWLEDGE OF PLEASURE SO THAT I MAY BASK IN A WORLD OF HAPPINESS*

CATFISH

UNKNOWN | **INTUITION** | **DISINTEGRATION**

"Using my instincts for navigating rivers, I can help you navigate the deepest crevices of your life journey to find the truths that will set you free."—Catfish

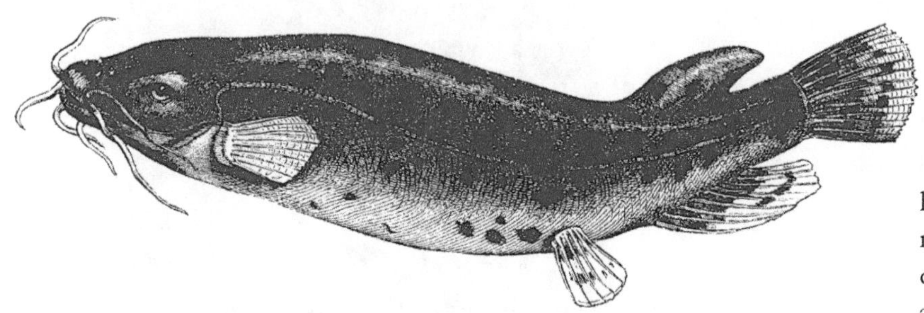

POWER OF CATFISH

Call in Catfish for:

- Swallowing" a problem whole and digesting it to come up with a solution.
- Finding the power of water for cleansing and transformation.
- Realizing that any direction will take you to a place of learning.

AWARENESS FROM CATFISH

If Catfish comes into your life:

- It is time to go deep within to find the solutions you need.
- A change will soon lead you to calmer waters.
- You need to develop a more realistic perspective of the world around you.

Energy Center: Third eye

Mineral: Siltstone

Element: Water

Magic & Mystery:

- The largest Catfish ever found was in the Mekong River that flows through Laos, Thailand, Cambodia, and Vietnam. Three meters long, it tipped the scales at 646 pounds.
- In Japan, Catfish symbolizes virility and kites shaped like Catfish are flown to celebrate the birth of boys.

Thirty-seven million years ago, forebearers of Catfish lived on Earth. Fossils of this land animal were found in the deserts southwest of Cairo, a region that has been arid for millennia. It now lives in inland lakes, rivers, and streams, and coastal waters. Catfish tends to hide in deep holes in riverbeds or under log piles or other woody debris that has fallen into the water. There are over 3,000 Catfish species and probably many more yet to be discovered.

Catfish has rayed fins and is named for its *barbels,* slender tactile organs near its mouth that resemble Cat's whiskers. The barbels contain its taste buds. Catfish produces interesting sounds and has excellent hearing, which helps it to discern friend from foe and to find its prey. It is receptive to the sound of drumming. Catfish tends to be solitary and is more active at night. A Walking Catfish native to Southeast Asia uses its pectoral fins to stay upright. With a wriggling motion, it can "walk" on land for a short while to find food or a more preferred environment.

In Japanese mythology, the giant Catfish Namazu is said to cause earthquakes. He lives in the mud under the islands of Japan where he is guarded by the god Kashima who keeps him restrained with a stone. When Kashima lets down his guard Namazu thrashes about, violently shaking the ground. The size and strength of Catfish has inspired many Fish tales, so it is a helpful Power Animal to call upon when you need to detect whether someone is exaggerating or supplying an inaccurate description. Catfish is a bottom feeder; it sinks more than swims and can inflict severe wounds upon its prey by delivering a sting that is extremely toxic.

Catfish thrives in placid lakes and gently flowing rivers. It does well when the waters around it are calm. It is a ferocious eater of other Fish because it must eat ten pounds of food to gain one pound. Seeing Catfish may be a sign that you are being too greedy or taking more than your fair share.

Take Catfish with you when you finally decide to jump into the river and go with the flow, as it will help you maintain peace and create safety while you gain momentum. Catfish does not see the darkness of life as a limitation. As it can survive in severely polluted water, it is a helpful Power Animal for coping with physically, mentally, or emotionally toxic environments and relationships.

Catfish can teach you about decomposition—breaking things down into their basic elements. It reminds us that when matter decomposes, it can support new life. Call upon Catfish to help make complex issues and situations easier to understand and to unearth emotions that have been buried under layers of accumulated debris from your life experiences. Trust that renewal is coming, and you will gain a new perspective. When you feel creatively stuck in the mud, Catfish will waggle its tail and reinvigorate your mind, getting the ideas flowing again. If you are in a state of depression, Catfish can help you to see your way through it.

SHAMAN'S INTENTION: *SUPPORT ME TO TRUST PRESENCE IN THE WORLD OF THE UNSEEN*

CATTLE—BULL

STRENGTH | **VIGILANCE** | **FOCUS**

"My horns shall remind you of your connection to all that is above and my hoofs of all that is below."
—Bull

Bull is at home around the world on farms and in pastures. One Bull can impregnate an entire herd of Cow, which constitutes a form of much-welcomed abundance and justifies its reputation for stamina. A castrated male Cattle is known as an Ox. The hazard of dealing with Bull is the risk of being trampled or gored, although it can also be protective of humans and its herd. Bull is featured in prehistoric cave paintings, which demonstrates how significant it has been to humankind for tens of thousands of years.

Bull is endowed with the powers of strength, vitality, virility, and sexual desire. It is connected to masculine energy and was worshiped as a divine being in almost every early civilization.

Ancient rulers would incorporate Bull horns into their royal crowns as a symbol of divine power. Bull was so revered for its procreative powers that women would perch on its back while begging the gods to bring them sons. In India, in front of temples to Shiva, the transformer god, even to this day, women touch the testicles of Bull sculptures in the hope of getting pregnant.

Embodied in Bull is the power of nature. Its four legs represent the four directions that support the Universe. In Bronze Age Egypt, Bull was honored for making the land fertile. There is a cultural association with watering the land and impregnation. Putting an image of Bull in your bedroom can add to your sexual strength and endurance.

Cattle, especially Bull, is associated with wealth. The English words *cattle* and *capitalism* have the same Latin root. No doubt this commonality inspired the term *bull market*. The ancient Celts saw Bull as strong willed, lacking compromise, and destructive; thus, we use the term *bull headed*. By contrast, the Chinese see Bull as helpful, confident, hardworking, and persevering.

Bull reminds us to be strong, not stubborn, and to use our strength for implementing collaborative projects rather than pressuring—*bullying*—others to do something. Bull is clear where it stands and will hold its ground. For this reason, trauma can be minimized by working with Bull as your guide. Bull can teach you how to be present as an observer, so your wisdom will be magnified and any response you have to your circumstances will be well defined. Embrace your potential, as you are stronger than you imagine. Embrace boredom as a time to learn patience. By staying focused in the now, you will avoid futile thoughts about the future and rely instead on the will of spirit. Bull reminds us that defending ourselves gives words of unkindness power over us and harms our psyche. Enemies or competitors only exist if we define them as such. If we always have our horns showing, ready to charge and do battle, the heightened energy of conflict can never dissipate. Choose to avoid a defensive stance and return to a state of neutrality where love conquers all.

POWERS OF BULL

Call in Bull for:

- Issues related to fertility or virility.
- The strength to "take the Bull by the horns" and resolve your personal problems.
- Success in business—particularly to develop a keen sense of how to create wealth.

AWARENESS FROM BULL

If Bull comes into your life:

- You may be domineering. Learn to delegate and consider other people's ideas.
- You may be too possessive of the "herd" and always want to be the center of attention.
- It is time to make a commitment to someone or something.

Energy Center: Sacrum

Mineral: Pietersite

Element: Earth

Magic & Mystery:

- The Buddha was born during the full Moon under the sign of Taurus.
- Bulls are not averse to red, as they are colorblind.
- The astrological sign Taurus, the Bull, rules the zodiac from April 20–May 20.

SHAMAN'S INTENTION: *HELP ME TO DISCOVER THE POWER OF SACRIFICE EVEN WHEN THERE MAY BE LITTLE APPRECIATION FOR MY ACTIONS*

CATTLE—COW

LOVE | GENEROSITY | COMPASSION

"Look into my eyes and find the compassion I bring to the world and all those who suffer from the misunderstanding of the sacred."—Cow

POWERS OF COW

Call in Catfish for:

- The ability to stand steadfast on the ground yet draw wisdom from the celestial realms.
- Reverence and compassion for all beings.
- Patience and the ability to endure the elements in all seasons.

AWARENESS FROM COW

If Cow comes into your life:

- It is time to nurture yourself.
- Develop a stronger relationship with those whom you can inspire.
- You may find liberation in showing kindness to others.

Energy Center: Heart

Mineral: Green sapphire

Element: Earth

Magic & Mystery:

- "The display of love toward a Cow takes the human being beyond her species." —Mahatma Gandhi
- In tribal cultures, a Cattle herd was the greatest wealth and a sacred relationship.

Cattle was introduced to the New World by the Spanish and English. When Christopher Columbus brought a Spanish Cow with him to the Caribbean, it was the beginning of the Texas Longhorn. Cow is a female Cattle. nd probably many more yet to be discovered.

With eyes set wide on the sides of her head, Cow can see 360 degrees around her, enabling her to know if a predator is coming from any direction. She has a keen sense of smell. An inquisitive animal, Cow likes to stick her nose into everything and investigate. She can be either shy or bold. Sociable, she likes to sleep within close range of her family. She is a dedicated mother and will walk miles to find a calf if one is lost.

Cultures around the world honor Cow as a form of the Great Goddess, a symbol of the fertility of the Earth and the Divine Feminine. Her crescent-shaped horns and milk connect her with the Moon and the expansive Milky Way in the night sky. As an emblem of joy and maternal nourishment in ancient Egypt Cow was worshipped and celebrated in temples dedicated to the goddesses Hathor, Nut, and Ahet who were often depicted with a solar disk between Cow horns. This was a sign of hope and survival from the ruler of the sky.

In the age of the Vikings Norse clans honored Cow for her four udders, which were said to secrete four rivers of power. A culture versed in sacred symbols and geometry, to them, Cow's link with the number four was meaningful. Among other things, her udders relate to the four cardinal directions.

In Hinduism and Buddhism, Cow is a highly respected Power Animal. The *Vedas*, which are ancient scriptures, worship Cow as the most sacred animal, honoring her for the abundance she provides humanity: the milk that we drink, the fertilizer her excrement provides for our crops, the strength she provides in ploughing and planting, her bones, which are used for making tools, and her hide, which is used to make clothing and shelter. Drinking Cow urine is said to bring good fortune and prosperity. Cow dung and water is a mixture used for purification.

Cow is an uplifting sign of the power of the feminine to sustain and nurture. Her calm yet strong presence is reassuring to many. Cow's eyes display her compassion for the world. Looking into the eyes of Cow can transform your heart so you can feel greater empathy. Cow reminds us to give generously and selflessly to others. It is a symbol of the value of family interaction. Cow bring us the same sense of sanctuary and safety that an infant feels when nursing from the breast of its mother. Cow's message is that we are capable of anything. We should not be defined or restricted by gender-specific narratives or antiquated beliefs. Cow encourages women and men to tell our authentic stories for better understanding. Embrace your vulnerability and integrate your intuitive intelligence into your journey of increasing confidence and self-realization. Authentic power is cultivating the divine within you, honoring your identity and wellbeing, and walking the path of mystic radiance.

SHAMAN'S INTENTION: *HELP ME TO NURTURE MYSELF AND, BY DOING THIS, IMPROVE THE LIVES OF THOSE AROUND ME*

CENTIPEDE

QUICKNESS **CONFIDENCE** **EXCELLENCE**

"Run, do not walk, with the force of your intuition, to find others who respect you and who will enhance your life."—Centipede

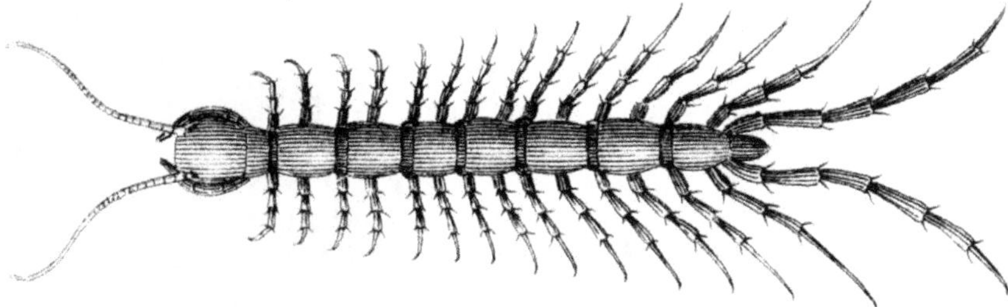

Centipede/Millipede is one of the oldest animals in the world and one of the earliest to breathe air after earthly life forms made their move from water to land. Over 8,000 species inhabit a wide range of terrains, including the frozen tundra just beyond the Arctic Circle, as well as tropical rainforests and dry deserts. Living in the soil and under leaves, stones, and dead logs, Centipede does not have one hundred legs like its name suggests, but fifteen to thirty. Millipede has 47–197, not a thousand. With so many legs, it is a sign of stability and being able to get where we are going with little effort. The major difference between the two species is that Centipede is a carnivore and Millipede prefers to eat decaying material. Bull is endowed with the powers of strength, vitality, virility, and sexual desire. It is connected to masculine energy and was worshiped as a divine being in almost every early civilization. The ancient Greeks saw Bull as a symbol of Zeus, king of the gods on Mount Olympus.

All species of Centipede/Millipede have uneven numbers of paired legs. Some of these legs can be detached to escape predators, and the missing legs will regenerate during the next molting. As Centipede grows, it develops a new exoskeleton and sheds the preexisting smaller one. For this reason, the ancient Mayans associated Centipede with death and rebirth, and with the rays of Sun, which travel daily from East to West. One dynasty of Mayan rulers reigning from 400–800 B.C.E in the region of present-day Guatemala was referred to as the Centipede Dynasty.

Centipede moves rapidly, and its bite is poisonous. Capuchin Monkey deliberately irritates Centipede, so it can get the poisonous venom from Centipede's jaws sprayed on it to repel Mosquito. Sepa, a Centipede-headed god from ancient Egypt, had power over venomous insects, like Scorpion, and biting Snake. Sepa was worshipped by farmers who hoped he would help to provide rich soils for their crops. He was also seen as the protector of the dead and depicted with two horns like the antennae of Centipede.

Because Centipede has antennae, we know it is tapped into the subtle energy around it. Call upon it when you need to enhance your psychic ability and intuition, especially about the motivations of others. Since it is mostly blind, when meeting a mate, Centipede will touch the prospective partner's antennae and rely on a psychic connection for communication. You may ask Centipede to help find the perfect match. Also, let Centipede venom remind you to use kind and uplifting words instead of striking out with random comments that may be hurtful to others. Centipede encourages us to rely on our sixth sense. Visions can be windows into the spirit world that provide us with a greater view of what is going on around us than we normally perceive. By remaining curious, rare information and references from the ancient ones may bust through our mental barriers. Embracing the sensory world enhances our potential and awakens dormant memories and insights so that we can have a healthy journey into a place of elevated energy.

POWERS OF CENTIPEDE

Call in Centipede for:

- Quick-wittedness.
- Walking in harmony, symmetry, and balance.
- For taking many steps to wholeness.

AWARENESS FROM CENTIPEDE

If Centipede comes into your life:

- Get going; do not be crippled by your doubts, as you have many legs to stand on.
- Move fast, as others may already be implementing your good ideas.
- Know that you always have enough support to move forward.

Energy Center: Solar plexus

Mineral: Sunshine

Element: Earth

Magic & Mystery:

- Centipede makes *pearls* from its crystallized mucus and sets them on its head. In Asia, it is said that such pearls bring magical powers to those who possess them.
- Centipede takes self-grooming very seriously, paying particular attention to its multiple pairs of legs. After each meal, it cleans itself off.

SHAMAN'S INTENTION: *ACTIVATE MY SENSES SO THAT I CAN VENTURE INTO THE SPIRITUAL WORLDS*

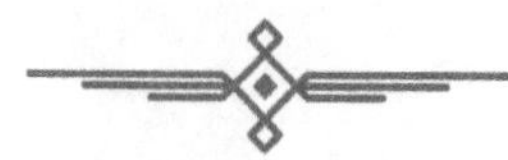

CHAMELEON

PATIENCE **ADAPTABILITY** **CALM**

"Embrace color to enhance your mood. Transform your environment into a place resembling an iridescent morning or a gorgeous, ruby-red sunset."—Chameleon

POWERS OF CHAMELEON

Call in Chameleon for:

- The ability to see everything going on around you.
- Show your true colors.
- Transformation through color therapies.

AWARENESS FROM CHAMELEON

If Chameleon comes into your life:

- You are inconsistent, so you need to understand your true self better.
- Move slowly and avoid acting impulsively.
- You must address your problems before they get out of hand.

Energy Center: Heart

Mineral: Rainbow obsidian

Element: Earth

Magic & Mystery:

- A Sufi parable about inconsistency ends with the lesson: "As Chameleon changes his skin, an unwise man changes the color of his being."
- In the sixteenth century, a Dutch astronomer named a constellation in the southern sky Chameleon. He thought the star cluster resembled a Chameleon sticking out its tongue.

Chameleon's name is derived from the ancient Greek words *chamai* and *leon* and means "lion of the ground." Around half of the world's Chameleon population lives on the island of Madagascar in the Indian Ocean off the eastern coast of Africa. A type of Lizard, it has distinctive eyes—which have a 360-degree arc of vision and can see in two different directions at the same time—and a curled tail. Its primary natural advantage is that it can move invisibly through varying environments by altering the color of its skin. Chameleon can make itself resemble a twig. It also is adept at appearing larger. If threatened, it puffs itself up, using its lungs to expand its rib cage. It avoids predators by moving slowly through different environments. It is the perfect Power Animal to teach us transformation through patience and skill.

Although Chameleon does not have ears, it can hear. Its tongue is very long and can instantly hit its prey (Cricket or Mealworm) and reel it in with a natural suction cup. It is an incredibly patient hunter and will wait for what it wants to come close enough to zap it. Chameleon is a master of breathing, and as such, is connected to the element of air.

The African Bantu tribes believe that Chameleon is an intermediary between God and humanity and proof that life is eternal. They view its spiraling tail as a symbol of defying death and stepping out of time.

Chameleon changes color for different reasons, including shifts in light, temperature, and mood, and for communication. Spiritually, it represents the imagination. It teaches us that through visualization we can bring the elemental energy of different hues of color into our lives. Chameleon connects with the Sun like a prism, cutting sunbeams into vibrant colors on its skin. It reminds us that we can set the level of light and the mood of the energy in our environment by the way we adapt ourselves to life. Chameleon is a master of illusion and can break through the blockage in an external environment that inhibits the truth. As a Power Animal, it will take you out of the familiar and into the unusual. Chameleon also reminds us about taking on the energy of others and to check in frequently with our bodies to ensure they are resonating objectively. Chameleon has great instincts and gut-level wisdom about how to show up in the world at a given time.

SHAMAN'S INTENTION: *HELP ME TO ADAPT TO MY ENVIRONMENT FOR MY HIGHEST GOOD*

CHEETAH

SPEED | **AFFECTION** | **STRUCTURE**

"Honor your exceptional gifts with pride and confidence."
—Cheetah

Almost twenty million years ago, a large population of Cheetah inhabited the African grasslands. Today, Cheetah still lives in the plains, woodlands, and semi-desert areas of southern and eastern Africa, but its numbers are few. The gift nature gave Cheetah for its survival is the ability to run fast. This insulates Cheetah from fear, as it knows it can outrun its predators. Running, Cheetah can reach a remarkable speed of 70 miles per hour, accelerating from 0–60 M.P.H. in three seconds. Although extremely fast, Cheetah cannot sustain this pace for long. It has been divinely designed with a larger than normal heart and lungs, which allow it to take in massive amounts of oxygen to fuel its muscles and accelerate. Its spine is exceptionally flexible, and the muscles in its limbs stretch in a manner that gives it a long stride. An extremely precise hunter, it never misses its prey. But after capturing it, Cheetah needs half an hour to catch its breath. Cheetah purrs when it is content and growls, hisses, and spits if annoyed. The female Cheetah is an affectionate mother who dedicates time to grooming her cubs and teaching them to hunt.

The ancient Egyptians adored Cheetah and had a loving bond with it. Cheetah's eyes have black markings below them that look like teardrops, which protect them from the glare of bright sunlight. An Egyptian legend told that the reason for these marks was that few Cheetah babies survived; therefore, these marks were representative of their mother's tears. If you have lost a child, Cheetah can bring you strength for losing what is precious and help you to shed the tears necessary to overcome your grief.

Admiring Cheetah's physiological design reminds us to embrace our own special gifts and demonstrates that, with a big heart open to love and flexibility, we can accelerate toward the accomplishment of our objectives. It shows us that a strong spine can be an essential attribute for moving through life with grace and speed. As a shaman, merging with the energy of Cheetah can help you to hunt successfully for what you desire most in your life. The spots of each Cheetah are unique and are an emblem of individuality. These markings are for camouflage and fitting into the surroundings, so Cheetah also represents having confidence in your place in the world.

Cheetah can be social but prefers solitude. It shares with us the wisdom of being alone and feeling secure in ourselves as we walk in the world. Cheetah knows when to work and when to rest. Alone, it is a master of mindfulness. Call Cheetah into a meditation session and it will help you strengthen your spine, expand your breath, and open your heart. Become a natural observer of you, focused and alert. Suspend any judgment and accept your special style.

POWERS OF CHEETAH

Call in Cheetah for:

- The ability to act and respond quickly.
- Daring to be colorful and unique.
- Embarking on an adventure or taking a calculated risk.

AWARENESS FROM CHEETAH

If Cheetah comes into your life:

- You are running too fast or becoming overloaded and exhausted.
- Learn that success is more about timing than speed when the heat is on.
- Take time to teach others about your personal gifts.

Energy Center: Heart

Mineral: Cat's eye

Element: Earth

Magic & Mystery:

- The Egyptian goddess of protection, Mafdet, had a Cheetah head.
- In 1555, Indian prince Akbar the Great established a tradition of hunting with wild Cheetah that persisted among his descendants until the twentieth century. Eventually, 1,000 Cheetah were held captive to amuse the members of his court.
- The Cheetah Conservation Fund declared December 4 International Cheetah Day to raise awareness about the plight of the most endangered cat in Africa and Iran.

SHAMAN'S INTENTION: *SUPPORT ME TO RELEASE ALL SELF-IMPOSED DOUBTS AND RUN LIKE THE CHEETAH*

CHICKADEE

POSITIVITY | SOCIABILITY | TRUTH

"Lighten your load of negative thoughts by bathing in the light of the morning Sun."—Chickadee

Chickadee is a small, gentle songbird native to Canada and the northern United States. It is curious and sure of itself. It is so trusting that it has been known to land in the palm of a human hand to grab some treats. Chickadee is a social butterfly. It travels in flocks and is happiest in a community. It prefers to mate with a lifetime partner. Chickadee does not migrate, preferring to stay in a territory where it knows it has reliable sources of food and water. It grows a dense winter coat of feathers and caches food, enabling it to cope with harsh winter weather. To help it remember the location of its food and its favorite warm roosts, it has a sizeable spatial memory center in its brain.

You can tell Chickadee's mood from its song. Listening to the tune of its call, you may notice that sometimes there is only one *dee* at the end. Other times, there are more *dees*; this indicates that Chickadee is feeling agitated. Indigenous North Americans of old saw Chickadee as a truth teller. Some tribes saw its presence as a sign of danger and believed something terrible would happen when they heard its song. By contrast, the Plains Indians saw Chickadee as a sign of success and thought that its presence meant their crops would be abundant.

Seven is a sacred number associated with the seven rays of power known to mystics, the seven planets in our galaxy, and the seven primary chakras in the human body. There are also seven kinds of Chickadee. A symbol of positive energy, Chickadee can help you raise your internal vibration, heal old wounds, and reach your highest potential. To lighten the load of energy you are carrying that no longer serves you, you may send your past away on the wings of Chickadee. Strip any illusion allowing your true essence to shine through.

Chickadee comes in the morning to ensure that your first thought sets the right tone for the rest of your day. It encourages you to open your eyes and say, "Today is a beautiful day." Take advantage of this moment to turn a negative into a positive. Chickadee has no time for negativity, as its goal is to spread happiness and joy.

Are you blind to your inner beauty? Chickadee is connected to shamans who know the natural world and understand that balance is healing. Treat this world with reverence and start the healing process by getting to the core of you. Try sitting in nature and listening to the soothing sounds and melodies from the nature spirits who are ready to help you to create a new version of you. Release Chickadee into your dreams to bring you the light without fear.

Chickadee reminds us that the truth can set us free. It can help clear the air of deception. Put on your ceremonial feathers and find your way to a new version of yourself. Chickadee's voice is linked with the fifth chakra. If you have been compromising yourself, you may want to work with affirmations and the uplifting messages of Chickadee while you practice speaking your truth.

Although Chickadee is small, it does not feel limited or vulnerable. Use this same courage in your own life to open your mind to new ideas and perspectives.

POWERS OF CHICKADEE

Call in Chickadee for:

- Positive thinking.
- Help to speak your truth and find your true essence.
- Courage, even if you feel small.

AWARENESS FROM CHICKADEE

If Chickadee comes into your life:

- It's a signal to temper negative thoughts.
- Set an attitude upon waking every morning to embrace possibilities for joy.
- Balance your seven chakras, as they may be misaligned.

Energy Center: Throat

Mineral: Selenite

Element: Air

Magic & Mystery: The Cherokees admired Chickadee, viewing it as a messenger that foretold the coming of an old friend or benevolent stranger.

SHAMAN'S INTENTION: *HELP ME TO REMAIN WARMHEARTED AND POSITIVE THROUGHOUT LIFE'S STORMS*

CHICKEN—HEN

THE FEMININE | **PURIFICATION** | **RELATIONS**

"Although life can ruffle your feathers, gather those who support your magic and you can again embrace your power."—Hen

Domesticated 8,000 years ago, Chicken currently outnumbers humans. The natural behavior of Chicken is to forage for seeds and worms in the soil of woods and meadows and to drink from small puddles and springs. As the only bird that cannot fly, Chicken is sensitive to the world around it because it is vulnerable to predators.

Hen, the female Chicken, is social and hangs out in flocks with a pecking order that gives preference to more dominant birds. The color of Hen's egg is determined by her breed and the color of her earlobes. For example, Hen with red earlobes lays brown eggs; Hen with white earlobes, lays white eggs. Hen has a good memory. She remembers specific faces and personalities. Hen is playful and dreams. She can feel stress and pain and mourns her losses.

Hen has been used as an omen in cultures worldwide for millennia. In ancient Rome, sacred chickens raised by the priests were consulted before military campaigns and were also used to decide matters of government. Every movement and sound Hen made as she pecked at the grain she was fed had a different meaning that needed to be interpreted.

There are four or five toes on Chicken feet. The indigenous Bamana of the West African Republic of Mali describe the journey of life as a *Chicken-foot crossroads* because there are so many decisions to make along the way. On New Year's Eve they conduct a renewal ritual to help them take the steps in the right direction during the year ahead. New Year's is the crossroads of being, a chance to embrace infinite opportunities.

Hen is an emblem of charity and self-sacrifice for the wellbeing of others. She makes a sacrifice for humanity every day to sustain our massive population through her meat, eggs, and poop, which is collected and used as fertilizer for our crops. Hen reminds us of the brevity of life and can help us recognize our need to nurture ourselves and others.

Since she lays an egg every day, Hen represents fertility. Brooding Hen warming her nest and mother Hen gathering her chicks under her wings are archetypes for the nurturing a mother gives her child. As a Power Animal, Hen can help you bring new life into the world, literally or metaphorically. Every day is a new beginning and a time for creation. Know that there is always a rainbow of possibility. If you are trying to get pregnant, Hen can boost your fertility. If you are pregnant, Hen can help you to temper the fear that goes along with becoming a new mother.

In another context, Hen can assist you to birth a project or enhance the fertility of your imagination. She can help you gather people together who need support and nurturing. She is also an apt Power Animal for event planners that work with wellness retreats and peer support groups. Hen reminds us to release emotions that have power over us. Sit, cry, journal, and let go. Perhaps even a ritual of burning your negative emotions will help. Burst through and seize your talents. Return to the day of your birth where you came with your most trusted intuition, your soul's power and purity. Here you will discover your truth.

POWERS OF HEN

Call in Hen for:

- Help to clear negative energy.
- Conception and fertility.
- Motherly love.

AWARENESS FROM HEN

If Hen comes into your life:

- A baby may be coming into your life soon.
- It is time to gather those you love around you.
- You need to make a change. Write a new story.

Energy Center: Root

Mineral: Garnet

Element: Earth

Magic & Mystery:

- During the Middle Ages in Europe, Jews would perform a love spell using an egg from a black Hen. To invoke the help of the goddess Venus, this egg was buried at a crossroads along with a mirror.
- Central American shamans rub eggs on the body to absorb negativity and evil.

SHAMAN'S INTENTION: *HELP TO FERTILIZE MY IDEAS*

CHICKEN—ROOSTER

FREEDOM | **LUMINOUSNESS** | **EXPRESSION**

"Avoid conflict in community, since there you can find the nurturing you desire and will cherish."
—Rooster

Rooster is a male Chicken with brightly colored feathers and a large red comb on its head. It has a terrible sense of taste and smell but excellent hearing. It searches for food by scratching and clawing the ground looking for insects. Rooster will begin to crow as early as four years old. As nature's alarm clock, it is the first animal to announce the Sun's arrival. Rooster will also crow during the day as a territorial signal. Rooster is responsible for watching over Hen and the chicks to ensure their safety. It likes to be perched high so that it can be on the lookout for intruders and will sound a distinctive call to warn those arriving that they are entering territory claimed by Rooster.

Rooster's crest or *guan* in Chinese means "official." The image of Rooster portrays a desire for advancement or a higher role. It is also considered a Power Animal that wards off evil spirits. In the Chinese zodiac it symbolizes honesty and strength. It is a *yang* (masculine) creature that represents prosperity, loyalty, and protection.

Rooster has many different appearances, showing its desire for individuality. A symbol of the Sun and male sexuality, most cultures equate Rooster with light and illumination in the Upper World, yet the Celts and Norse place Rooster in the Lower World as a messenger of the dead and warning of danger. Rooster is a perfect Power Animal to do the work of a psychopomp, guiding living souls to the realm of the dead. The Greeks saw Rooster's crowing as a salutation to the Sun and a symbol of the victory of light over darkness. In Japan, Rooster is allowed to walk through the temples undisturbed under the theory that it is at the ready to call the congregation to prayers. Its image is painted on the drums that are used to announce a gathering.

As a Power Animal, Rooster brings the concept of freedom from belongings and a reminder not to be captivated by material things. The line "Not all who wander are lost" from *The Fellowship of the Ring* by J.R.R. Tolkien is emblematic of Rooster's feeling that we must be respectful of others on their paths and offer them acceptance rather than judge them.

Rooster is a master shapeshifter and can take on many different personalities, gestures, expressions, and attitudes. It is an example of standing tall and walking with confidence even though you feel vulnerable. Rooster has expansive energy and expresses itself from the core to its external being. Use Rooster to call in the spirit world from all directions and to bring your guides to you. Wear your feathers with distinction and be an example of a seasoned traveler with a solid knowledge of your place on the path of enlightenment.

POWER OF ROOSTER

Call in Rooster for:

- Changing into the person you wish to become.
- Increased appreciation from others.
- Valuing yourself and your contribution in the world.

AWARENESS FROM ROOSTER

If Rooster comes into your life:

- It is a wakeup call to be more aware of what is going on in your life.
- You may need protection at this time.
- You may have a mental conflict and be indecisive.

Energy Center: Crown

Mineral: Pink Tourmaline

Element: Fire

Magic & Mystery:

- The Tabwa tribe mediums of Africa weave Rooster feathers into a headband that enhances the powers of the third eye, hoping that the spirits that speak through them will bring them enlightenment.
- In ancient Iran, Rooster is a symbol of royalty.

SHAMAN'S INTENTION: *GUIDE ME TO THE KNOWLEDGE OF HOW TO PROTECT MY COMMUNITY*

CICADA

SOUND **CYCLES** **CHANGE**

"We sing louder and louder, so the truth can be heard and humans can awake from the darkness in to light."—Cicada

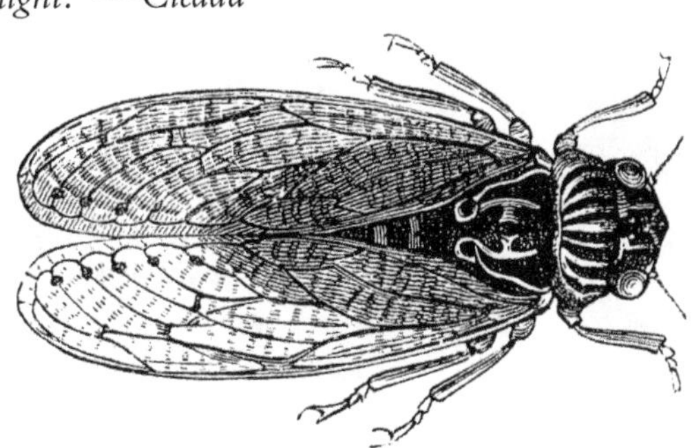

Nearly 2,500 species of Cicada live on our planet, everywhere except for Antarctica. Cicada usually prefers tropical climates and more temperate environs. It is a large insect, roughly three inches long, with two pairs of luminous wings with rainbow hues. Dark brown with green accents, it has a red eye on both sides of its head and three more in the middle. The male Cicada has an organ on its belly called a tymbal that gives it the ability to make the sound of maracas shaking. This ability makes Cicada the loudest insect in the world. The male relies on this sound to attract a female. The female uses her wings to create sound. She lays eggs on trees that hatch after six weeks. After falling from the tree, the Cicada larva heads for the soil where it makes tunnels, works, and lives. Unlike Butterfly, it does not undergo transformation. It simply matures. The new generation of Cicada emerges from the soil all at the same time, creating a massive exodus on the way to the trees. When Cicada emerges from the ground, it has no way to defend itself, so its presence leads to a feeding frenzy for Bird, Turtle, Raccoon, and other creatures that enjoy feasting on it. There are "annual" types of Cicada that appear every year or two. Magicicada, or periodical Cicada, appears every thirteenth or seventeenth year, emerging from the soil after living buried for all its life.

Due to its extraordinary life cycle, many cultures see Cicada as a symbol of resurrection. Ancient Asian burial ceremonies would include an intricate jade figurine of a Cicada that was placed in the mouth of the deceased. This was done to ensure a peaceful afterlife and to help the dead in making a successful transition in the hopes that the dead would support family members left behind. They believed Cicada was a higher being of purity because it drinks dew from up in the trees. In the Americas, the ancient Mayans carved images of Cicada in jade that they placed on the tongues of their deceased as a symbol of resurrection from the body. The Hopi Indians had a similar practice. Cicada is an ambassador for the circle of life that exists in nature.

When ancient Greek philosopher Socrates told a friend about Cicada, he said that it was always listening and bringing messages to the Muses, nine goddesses associated with different arts and sciences. Cicada bring us the message that sometimes the truth is never consciously heard, although it is singing in the background of our lives. So much about us can lie dormant until the external world brings us a challenge or a change to awaken. Due to our ignorance, we can be too externally focused and vocal, begging for attention in different ways. Those with unhealthy egos continuously seek recognition from others. As a Power Animal, Cicada can help you find satisfaction with yourself and teach you to rely less on others for praise. If you get caught in wanting acceptance you will end up with a burdensome ego. The power of Cicada is to make your voice heard on behalf of the common good; to be able to choose your words carefully so that they are not abrasive or combative. As a shaman you must master the art of being alive in fullness of your own being without attachment.

POWERS OF CICADA

Call in Cicada for:

- Assistance when you are feeling in the dark about things.
- Calling in a mate.
- Moving forward without worrying about what is coming next.

AWARENESS FROM CICADA

If Cicada comes into your life:

- You have reached the end of one cycle and the start of a new one.
- Crack open your ego and see that you are enough without the praise of others.
- Step out from the cloak you have been wearing that hides your true self.

Energy Center: Crown

Mineral: Amethyst

Element: Earth

Magic & Mystery:

- Each Cicada generation emerges in thirteen- or seventeen-year spans of time, periods representing prime numbers that can only be divided by themselves or by one.
- Cicada is a master of synchronicity. It always marches out of the Earth with others of its kind *en masse,* hoping to increase the chances of survival of its species.

SHAMAN'S INTENTION: *TEACH ME THE MAGIC OF NUMEROLOGY AND THE SYNCHRONICITY OF NATURE*

CONDOR

CLAIRVOYANCE | **FREEDOM** | **FLOW**

"Ride the winds of change to a place of surrender and arrive at the ultimate knowledge that leads to peace."
—Condor

VULTURE

POWERS OF THE CONDOR

Call in Condor for:

- Help to cleanse yourself of what no longer serves you.
- A higher perspective.
- Gliding toward what will make you successful.

AWARENESS FROM CONDOR

If Condor comes into your life:

- Something is dying and a transformation is occurring.
- Grasp the authority and power that you have and express your thoughts with confidence.
- Learn to manage the currents in your life and ride the winds of change.

Energy Center: Crown

Mineral: Garnet

Element: Sphalerite

Magic & Mystery: Mayans call in Condor from the East to give them clarity. They say that when you pray Condor takes your prayers to the spiritual world and brings back answers.

Condor is a type of Vulture and one of the largest birds in the world. Its enormous, ten-foot-wide wingspan is needed to keep its heavy body, which weighs up to thirty-three pounds, aloft. Because of its size, Condor prefers to live in windy areas where it can take advantage of strong air currents that lessen its effort when flying. A scavenger, Condor is always on the lookout for a fresh kill, which makes up much of its diet. It is a member of nature's clean-up crew that feasts on larger animals by picking apart their carcasses.

Native Americans hold Condor sacred, and it plays a role in many of their creation myths. It is generally thought of as a symbol of power. The Wiyot of California believe Condor is an ancestor. The Mapuche of Chile and Argentina called Condor the king of birds. In the ruins of Machu Picchu in Peru, there is a temple dedicated to Condor. The Andean people who lived there saw Condor as a symbol of fertility and believed that when it flapped its wings it would gather the clouds for rain to help nourish the land. Many South American tribes associate Condor with the sky.

A prophecy dating back to the 1400s from people living in the Amazon jungle speaks of the division of North and South America. This was the era of the conquest of the Americas by European settlers and the oppression of the indigenous peoples. The prophecy said that North Americans follow the path of Eagle—masculine, industrial, mentally oriented—and South Americans follow the path of Condor—feminine, natural, intuitive. The Eagle people would become powerful for 500 years and dominate the Condor people. But then the Eagle and Condor would come together again and join in creating a higher consciousness for all humanity.

In ancient Egypt Vulture was associated with the goddess Nekhebet, patroness of the city of El-Kab in Upper Egypt. Condor and other types of Vulture tend to their offspring in the nest much longer than other Bird species. This trait gave rise to an association with the goddesses Sekhmet and Mutt, overseers of childbirth and motherhood respectively.

Condor is master of the sky, skillfully piloting itself on the breezes and owning the air currents. It can reach incredible heights and yet is always aware of what is happening on the ground. It has a great intelligence of the world around it which is indicative of its ability to be grounded while in flight, a magical combination. As a Power Animal, Condor will teach you strategy and introspection and help you develop a life of patience and self-discipline—two virtues that can bring you success. Riding the winds with caution and comprehension can keep you aware of your best resources and the value they have in the world. Condor has extraordinary eyesight and an astute sense of smell. It is a scavenger, not a hunter, which requires different attributes. Condor can teach you to be opportunistic and seize what you need at the perfect time for the perfect project. Having confidence that the right moment is just around the corner inspires optimism.

Condor is associated with death because it plays an important role in the cycle of life. Everything dies, and this animal purifies that which remains. Some cultures believe that offering their deceased to Condor is a high honor, a beginning of new life. This helps us to understand that death is not an end to our existence. Ask Condor to help you connect with angels, spirits, and ancestors. Condor sees everything as it is, with no good or bad judgment. It is patient with the wind supporting it, knowing that waiting is a virtue as not everything is ready to unfold.

SHAMAN'S INTENTION: *GIVE ME A CLEAR VIEW OF MY NEXT OPPORTUNITY*

CORAL

FOUNDATION | **CREATION** | **BEAUTY**

"See what glistens beneath the ocean's surface. There you will find what connects you to Mother Earth and keeps you in the flow of that which runs through her veins."—Coral

Coral is a tiny creature that began growing in the world's oceans over 50 million years ago. Living in colonies, it secretes a hard calcium-carbonate substance that forms an exoskeleton known as a *reef*, which becomes home to biodiverse marine life. Thousands of species of fish and invertebrates make their home in reefs. Coral is a relative of the Jellyfish, at home in the tropics, in shallow waters close to the surface where the symbiotic algae that live inside its polyps and nourish it can catch the Sun's rays. Reefs get their colorful hues from the billions of colorful algae they host.

In Native Hawaiian tradition, Opuhala is the goddess of Coral and small fish. The Polynesian trickster god Maui was given a piece of Coral by Opuhala, which he used to pull the Hawaiian Islands out from the sea.

Coral is said to be the tree of the sea. According to ancient Greek mythology, the god Poseidon lived in a coral palace full of gems. The Greeks believed that crushing dried Coral into a powder and sprinkling it on crops would protect the plants from Locust and Caterpillar. The ancient Romans believed Coral powder could cure bites by Snake and Scorpion and improve blood circulation.

Coral is used in many cultures as a divination tool. The ancient Hebrews cast lots using pieces of Coral to determine a person's fate or help someone discern a truth. In Africa, bits of colored Coral are strung on Elephant tail hair to give its rider a sense of nobility. Native Americans combine Coral and turquoise in silver jewelry. Crystal healers use Black Coral to promote male fertility, conception, and fatherhood. It also helps men to respect women more. Blue Coral is used for calmness and stability. If you are raising children, it will also bring out your playful inner child. Pink Coral is beneficial for pregnancy and giving birth and can help to eliminate postpartum baby blues. Coral of all types protects the wearer against evil and from the vicissitudes of uncontrolled anger.

Vedic astrologers associate Coral with the planet Mars, which also has a natural red color. As a product of the seas, Red Coral symbolizes the blood of our planet. Coral is also linked to human blood, so menopausal women may call upon this Power Animal for strength if they experience a loss of energy.

Call upon Coral for help to understand the waves of your thoughts and emotions, and when you want to get in sync with the flow of earth energy. Coral stabilizes the root chakra; so even if you find yourself in stormy waters, you can still feel strong and planted no matter how hard the waves hit the shore of your existence. Coral also can help you in detoxing the energy in the environment around you just like it naturally balances carbon monoxide in the air.

The lessons from Coral are to build a foundation that supports your endeavors and to support others to thrive and expand their lives too. It shows that you can create a world of inner and outer beauty through contributing to emotional, physical, social, and spiritual platforms that nourish you. Coral will plant you firmly where you are and sustain you. Check to see if you are acting needy or believe that you are not enough. Stay rooted in the sense that you are enough, perfect, and worthy. By receiving the gifts of Mother Earth from your roots, you can give back and flourish on your own as well.

POWERS OF CORAL

Call in Coral for:

- The foundation you need to build a personal empire.
- Supporting the creativity of others.
- A sense of place and belonging.

AWARENESS FROM CORAL

If Coral comes into your life:

- A wave of burdens could be coming your way. It's time to create more stability.
- Do your best to support and nurture your friends.
- You may need to boost your circulation. Perhaps a sauna or more movement is necessary.

Energy Center: Root

Mineral: Rhodochrosite

Element: Water

Magic & Mystery:

- When Red Coral is placed in a glass of milk, the milk will take on a red or pink tinge.
- In working with the Feng shui of your home, place a picture of Coral in the southwest of the bagua to promote love, in the center for balance and health, in the northeast for knowledge, and in the east for community.

SHAMAN'S INTENTION: *TAKE ME ON A JOURNEY TO THE SEA SO I CAN SENSE THE POWER OF ITS EBB AND FLOW*

CORMORANT

ABUNDANCE | **ADAPTATION** | **INNOVATION**

"Initiative is the key to finding what lies beyond your reach."
—Cormorant

POWERS OF CORMORANT

Call in Cormorant for:

- Clarity about your next step. Cormorant will help you dive into something soon.
- Finding a team player who can focus on the goals and get results.
- Abundance.

AWARENESS FROM CORMORANT

If Cormorant comes into your life:

- You have been sitting too long on the sidelines obsessing over whether to jump in.
- Dive into your feelings and find the origin of your obsessions.
- Trust that inspiration is all around you to help you overcome any challenge.

Energy Center: Solar plexus

Mineral: Dioptase

Element: Water

Magic & Mystery:

- In England, the mythical Liver Bird, the symbol of the city of Liverpool, is thought to be a cross between Cormorant and Eagle.
- According to *Scientific American*, Penguin is descended from Cormorant.

Cormorant is a dark-colored, web-footed water bird with a long neck and a throat pouch. Over thirty species are found all over the world, mostly along ocean coastlines and the shores of inland lakes. Its name comes from the French language and means "sea raven." This bird loves to fish. From a perch high up, it will drop down upon the Fish it is in pursuit of with the speed of a dart. With almost perfect precision, it will seize its prey in its bill, then throw it into the air and catch it again head first and send it on its way to its belly. An excellent swimmer and diver, Cormorant is so buoyant that it must eat small pebbles to make it heavy enough to stay underwater.

In Japan and China, fishermen enlist Cormorant to catch Fish for them but prevent it from swallowing the catch by placing a metal ring around its neck. In rural Ireland, if you see a Cormorant on a church, it is said to be a sign of bad luck coming. In Norse folklore, three Cormorant flying together are carrying messages or warnings from the dead. Cormorant has a voracious appetite. Over time, it has become an emblem of both indulgence and abundance.

In Australian Aboriginal myths Cormorant is linked with fire. It is said that Cormorant is black because it got singed by a fire. In Homer's *Odyssey,* a sea nymph disguises herself as Cormorant and hands Ulysses a floating log to keep him afloat while he swims to shore.

The shaman asks Cormorant to teach us that the impossible can be possible. It can see what is below the surface in any situation and has the power to raise it from the depths and put it in front of the eyes of those who otherwise would not see it. Seeing Cormorant means something new or different will be coming your way—possibly a new perspective on something familiar. This Bird has a reputation for being an omen of prosperity.

Although you may seem to be on an island of your own thoughts, in stillness you can thrive. Stay alert and do not fall into obsessive emotionality. Allow these things to flow through you so that you remain balanced. Trust when you dive in, as you will be inspired to sing your heart's song. Embrace adventure and know that every traveler is a messenger. This advice will help you to accomplish things in new ways that may seem odd at first but later will prove to save you time and effort. Cormorant will also help you to dive into new ways of doing things and alternative ways of seeing the world and to come up with whatever you are looking for. This courageous effort will always pay off in plenty of "fish"!

SHAMAN'S INTENTION: *HELP ME TO UNDERSTAND PROSPERITY*

COUGAR

AUTHENTICITY **BOUNDARIES** **SOLITUDE**

"As you walk your path in solitude, with every step you will master your intuition."—Cougar

Cougar is one of the largest wild cats in the world. It likes to hunt alone at twilight when it can stalk and ambush its prey unseen. From this, Cougar teaches us that we walk alone on Earth with our spirits and that on the final day of our lives it will just be our being that goes on. The paws of Cougar are enormous, which allows for giant leaps and short sprints. While it will eat almost anything, it primarily subsists on Elk and Deer.

Like a ghost in the forest, you may know Cougar is there but it is rarely seen. For this reason, in the past, Native Americans believed that hearing Cougar scream was an omen of witchcraft. The Seminoles and Shawnees in eastern North America revered Cougar for its hunting skills. For protection, indigenous hunters would carry Cougar *fetishes* (small carved objects in the shape of animals) to invoke its powers for themselves. To the Pueblo, Cougar is the guardian of the North.

In South America, the Incas saw Cougar as a sign of wealth. For them, seeing it meant good luck. The city of Cusco in Peru was designed in the shape of Cougar and is associated with the Incan sky and thunder god, Viracocha. Traditional Aztec shamans understood that Cougar possessed healing power. They would prick the chest of a sick patient with a sharpened Cougar bone to ward off death. Other tribal healers would drive off illness by hanging Cougar body parts over their patients.

Colonial European settlers arrived in the Americas with fear and loathing of wild animals. Their attitude quickly separated the animals from the humans. In the 1500s, Jesuit priests in southern California offered local Native Americans a Bull for every Cougar they killed. The locals did not comply, because, for them, Cougar was sacred.

Cougar is quiet and pensive. It exudes an aura of intelligence as it patiently waits for the perfect time to pounce. A magnificent creature, to see it merely as a competitor to humans is to misunderstand its natural state and sovereignty. Because of its stealth, grace, and power in navigating the spiritual world, you want Cougar as an ally.

Cougar is territorial and carefully marks the area it patrols. By marking its boundaries, it walks the world with little fear. It needs space to roam, often covering an area of up to 200 miles. If Cougar comes into your life, you should examine your boundaries—you may be failing to recognize their importance. Flimsy boundaries leave little room for recovering from mistakes. As a Power Animal, Cougar can bring speed and precision to the making of life choices, which increases the possibilities and gets you a more rapid return on your investments in your dreams and desires.

The relationship Cougar has with caves is an important one. Caves are openings you may use to enter the Lower World. If you are working with Cougar as a Power Animal, remember to take offerings to Cougar before you enter, as it commands the respect of spirits. Cougar is intelligent and knows that with flexibility you can better survive. Holding too tightly to possessions creates instability. Cougar brings us the message to not fear endings, as they are beginnings in disguise. Accept change and move on from troubling situations. If you adopt the sharp mindset of Cougar, you can stand on your convictions; yet, do not overjudge or criticize. Instead, live life with passion and rejuvenation.

MOUNTAIN LION, PANTHER, PUMA

POWERS OF COUGAR

Call in Cougar for:

- Keen instincts and to know when to pounce on what you desire.
- Extreme focus and alertness.
- Help to embrace solitude and deepen your commitment to your inner self.

AWARENESS OF COUGAR

If Cougar comes into your life:

- It is time to look closely at your boundaries.
- Expand your awareness so you may discern the right next step.
- Believe in yourself. Trust that you are strong and able to walk in the world with grace and stealth.

Energy Center: Root

Mineral: Axinite

Element: Earth

Magic & Mystery:

- Cougar has been given forty different names. In Quechua, it is known as Puma, meaning "powerful."
- Female Cougar gives birth to two cubs at a time. These arrive with a camouflage of black and brown spots that fade with maturity. An extremely protective mother, Cougar guards her cubs with her life.

SHAMAN'S INTENTION: *AS A GUARDIAN TO THE LOWER WORLD, HELP ME TO FIND MY WAY TO THE WISDOM OF THE NATURE SPIRITS*

COYOTE

SURPRISE | **TRICKS** | **CALCULATION**

"Lighten up. Nothing should be taken seriously. You are on a mystical journey and will eventually find your way home."—Coyote

POWERS OF COYOTE

Call in Coyote for:

- Creativity and cunning.
- Youthfulness and the freedom to indulge in childlike behavior.
- Honing your instincts.

AWARENESS FROM COYOTE

If Coyote comes into your life:

- It is time to lighten up. Stop taking yourself and your life so seriously.
- Find joy in everything you do.
- Learn from your mistakes and move on.

Energy Center: Solar plexus

Mineral: Citrine

Element: Air

Magic & Mystery:

- The Navajo call Coyote "God's dog."
- The Shoshoni see Coyote as a symbol that something is ending, indicating that it is time to make room for the new.

Coyote is a wild Dog that originated in western North America and now thrives in different landscapes. Smaller than Wolf, it sometimes is referred to as Prairie Wolf or Brush Wolf. The name *Coyote* came from the Aztec word *coyotl,* meaning "howling dog." Coyote's primary power is its ability to adapt itself to any habitat and exploit its features and resources to the maximum. Coyote thrives wherever it walks. It spends its days roaming prairies, deserts, and forests, and even some large cities.

Coyote mates for life. Every year, Mother Coyote gives birth to a single litter of three to nine puppies. In numerology, the number nine represents the completion of a cycle. In Feng shui, three times nine, twenty-seven, is the number of philanthropy and cooperation. Coyote pups are born blind and do not open their eyes until they are two weeks old. During pregnancy, a mother Coyote finds a den. Throughout gestation and the first weeks of her pups' lives, she stays in this den while father Coyote brings food for her and the litter to eat. He leaves this outside the entrance and does not enter. His instinctual loyalty to his mate is unquestionable.

The howl of Coyote is the song of the West. Shamans believe that hearing Coyote howl means it is time to return to the safety of your tribe. Coyote is an important personality to learn from. It is resourceful and independent and a master of reality. Mostly shy, Coyote will not engage with those it does not trust, and it will avoid danger. Native Americans revere Coyote as a teacher, a creature that's both intelligent and practical. Coyote also reminds us of our shadow side, which can be ego oriented, if we are always looking for a way to gain at the expense of others. Call on Coyote to learn how to temper your selfish motivations. To the Crow people, Coyote was responsible for creating the less than perfect world we live in; yet, they also credited it with bringing the Sun to shine on the seeds they had planted.

Coyote often goes unnoticed and simply "appears" without warning, as if playing a trick. It actually will "tip toe" to avoid being seen. In doing this, it teaches us about adaptability as a means for surviving against the odds. Known as Heyokas, Lakota clowns, practice Coyote medicine. These shamans act in bizarre and funny ways, such as walking and talking backward, to convey messages from Coyote to us. Their less serious way of connecting with the spirit world helps us to see the antics of human behaviors.

Coyote reminds us to be the observer of life and to put our problems in proper perspective, viewing them without excessive emotions. Coyote has mastered family relationships and knows when to step out of the drama of triggered feelings. This skill will bring harmony to you and your soul. Coyote knows where to find security and understands that all paths ultimately lead to your inner home. Coyote supports us in being confident in our individuality and encourages setting healthy personal boundaries. Through humor, it will open our eyes to the ramifications of our unenlightened actions. Coyote wants us to make fun of ourselves and return to our original innocence.

SHAMAN'S INTENTION: *HELP ME TO USE LAUGHTER AND HUMOR AS A WAY TO RAISE MY VIBRATION*

CRAB

PROTECTION | **TRANSITION** | **REJUVENATION**

"Trust the Moon as it shines upon you. Its glow and its rhythms can take you from the darkness into the light of your soul's journey."—Crab

Four thousand five hundred species of Crab are found in the oceans and volcanic lakes around the world. It lives in more places than any other sea creature, including in Antarctica. Sometimes Crab even lives on the land and climbs trees! It communicates through drumming with or waving its pincers.

In China Crab is a symbol of peace. The Chinese words for Crab and for harmony have the same root in the word *peace* (xie). Crab is a symbol of holding on, which can be either a positive sign of persistence or a negative sign of rigidity. Its essence incorporates yin/yang qualities: It has a hard exoskeleton and soft inner tissues. Crab can be defensive, but it reminds us of our need for periodic renewal by casting off its old shell for a new one. From time to time, we must dump our baggage and be vulnerable. Only then do we put on a new set of armor.

Solar magic, which is yang energy, is related to Crab because the constellation Cancer is in the sky during the summer solstice. The sideways and backward scuttling of Crab is like the movement the Sun makes when it reaches the zenith before turning southward. Crab rules the fourth house of the western zodiac chart, which is associated with home and refuge. It resonates the vibration of home in our hearts, helping us to realize the heart is the safest place for us to go for rejuvenation.

Lunar magic, which is yin energy, is also related to Crab because the phases of the Moon have rhythm, as does Crab's drumming. The Inca knew Crab as the *Great Devourer* at the time of the waning Moon. With feminine style, Crab teaches us that the best way to face things is not always head on. The Buddhists see Crab symbolic of the sleep of death and the time between incarnations and as an illustration of the evolution of our consciousness in the spirit world.

Crab has a habit that is a cautionary tale for those who are chasing success. If several Crabs are in a barrel together and one starts to climb the wall and escape, the others will pull it back down. There are those among us whose envy leads them to sabotage the success of others by dragging them down, not wanting them to be better off but keeping everyone in the same level of misery. This behavior teaches us many lessons, including how important it is to bring others along with us when we grow and not to get stuck in a "barrel" if we can avoid it.

Since Crab lives in all the oceans of the world, as a Power Animal it is the protector of merchants seeking to establish intercontinental contacts. It favors those taking a risk to amass wealth and will help you hold tight to your profits. It can help you harness the power of the lunar cycles for protection and navigation, especially on water, like an internal GPS.

Crab warns against being overly responsible by taking on the battles of others. There can often be too high a price to pay. Sometimes walking away from a conflict is a better alternative than trying to win, get redress, or seeking revenge—as these paths may have negative emotional consequences. Crab is always trying to master balance, since becoming unbalanced and lying on its back can be a deadly result. Balance ensures our harmony with all things. Crab is a great companion if you want to discover new places. It will help you to find inspiring environments and see hidden niches where adventure thrives.

POWERS OF CRAB

Call in Crab for:

- A reminder that there are many paths to your goals—and some routes are indirect.
- Inner peace.
- Success and prosperity.

AWARENESS FROM CRAB

If Crab comes into your life:

- Stop envying others. Realize that greater outcomes will be made possible for you through collaboration.
- You may be acting too shy or isolated. Be more sociable.
- You may be holding on too tightly to something or someone. Loosen your grip.

Energy Center: Crown

Mineral: Moonstone

Element: Water

Magic & Mystery:

- Heikegani is a species of Crab native to Japan. It has a pattern on its shell that looks like a human face. In Japanese stories, this type of Crab is the reincarnated souls of Samurai warriors slain during a famous battle in 1185 C.E.
- The Samoan Crab, one of the most aggressive in Hawaii, is so strong that it can snap a broomstick in two.

SHAMAN'S INTENTION: *HELP ME TO FIND THE PERFECT BALANCE BETWEEN PROTECTION AND ADVENTURE*

CRANE

LONGEVITY | **GRACE** | **SOCIABILITY**

"See your life from a higher perspective. Walk with the confidence of immortality and you will bring great abundance to your journey."—Crane

POWERS OF CRANE

Call in Crane for:

- Combining power and grace.
- Prosperity and to have all you desire.
- Community and connection.

AWARENESS FROM CRANE

If Crane comes into your life:

- You may need to take time to dance and sing to raise your vibration.
- Take better care of yourself so you may realize a life of great longevity.
- Evaluate conflicts and take a more enlightened approach.

Energy Center: Crown

Mineral: Lilac kunzite

Element: Water

Magic & Mystery:

- The ancient Greek philosopher Aristotle said that Crane held a stone in its mouth in order to wake up if it fell asleep and interrupted its night vigilance.
- In the martial art of qigong, when energy reaches the level of the navel, the phenomenon is referred to as "White Crane flying."

Crane is estimated to be over ten million years old, making it the oldest bird on the planet. It is found on every continent except South America and Antarctica. Tall and thin, Crane has wings powerful enough to fly over high mountain peaks at speeds of up to 45 M.P.H. It nests in wetlands and grassy areas and has an intriguing communication system of calls with varying tones and volumes. The physiology of its larynx is complex. Each of the fifteen species of Crane makes unique sounds. Crane uses its body to communicate as well, often participating in elaborate dance rituals. This is an integral part of courtship. Once dancing starts, a whole Crane flock can become animated. Two eggs are laid each year by a mating pair and the offspring remain with their parents until the next mating season. The individual Crane is long-lived, achieving similar ages as humans.

Crane is a legendary symbol in China. Renowned as a graceful animal, martial artists mimic its stance when practicing kung fu. Regarded as the prince of all birds, Crane's long lifespan is its attraction, as some legends say it can live for a thousand years. Folklore holds that spirits ride on the backs of Crane to and from the heavens. At one point, Crane eggs were used in magic potions drunk by those seeking eternal life and white Crane feathers were thought to be symbols of old age and objects that endow us with wisdom. Cranes is important to the Japanese as well. They say anyone who folds 1,000 origami paper cranes is given a wish, as Crane is magical and holy.

The ancient Egyptians had a legend of a two-headed Crane. If this was seen flying over the Nile River, it meant that a season of great prosperity was coming. The ancient Greeks similarly saw Crane as an omen. They had a story of a Crane that followed a thief mercilessly until he confessed to the crime he committed. Both the ancient Greeks and ancient Romans portrayed the dance of Crane as a dance of joy and a celebration of life. Crane was considered the bird of Apollo, the Sun god, responsible for the return of spring.

As a Power Animal, because of its endurance in long migrations, Crane can be helpful to travelers; a source of strength for arduous journeys. It also will watch over you when you travel at night or if you are a late-night security guard. It is an enlightened teacher and can help you reach higher levels of learning on your spiritual path. Crane will help you to let go of the negative so you do not allow issues to expand. Pierce the surface of conflicts to realize a different truth and end any suffering. Crane brings the karma of the soul to us. Karma is not a punishment but the purest form of an ancestral pattern that has been designed for our journey through life. Crane reminds us to look at our reflection in water and use the moment to ensure that our opinion of ourselves is favorable. If we do not see our power and light, it is time to express self-love. If we are underestimating ourselves, we must take in a big breath of greatness and destroy any barriers that weaken our understanding of who we are.

SHAMAN'S INTENTION: *HELP ME TO SEE MYSELF FOR WHO I REALLY AM*

CRICKET

VIBRATION | COMMUNICATION | PROSPERITY

"Look at the world through a megaphone of joy and bliss."
—Cricket

Cricket is an insect that makes "music" by rubbing the tooth-like ridges of its upper and lower wings together. The sound is commonly known as *chirping*. Although it has wings, Cricket does not fly. There are approximately 900 different types of Cricket. Each species has its own songs, which it uses to communicate. The male is responsible for playing the music. He has an impressive repertoire and is always humming to attract females. After finding a mate, he sings more songs to celebrate the courtship and to defend his territory.

Thanks to its compound eyes that consist of a multitude of lenses, Cricket has amazing eyesight. It can process many images at the same time. In the old days, Cheyenne hunters would rely on Cricket to help them detect where the Buffalo herds would travel. They also saw it as a prosperous creature overcoming any shortcomings of its small size. Because the female Cricket lays hundreds of eggs, Cricket is a harbinger of fertility and abundance.

In China Cricket is the sign of summer and symbolizes resurrection. In Japan, to this day, caged Cricket are sold outside Shinto temples; by releasing them, it is said that you can assure yourself a positive next life. In Africa Tree Cricket uses leaves to make a megaphone. By chewing a hole to stick his head through, he is able to amplify his message.

As a Power Animal, Cricket will help you sing your song and expand the reach of your voice. Cricket is a great communicator, and its continuous self-expression is a reminder for all of us to play our parts in the magnificent orchestra of life. In this way we can promote harmony in our lives and on our planet. Finding your rhythm and voice with Cricket's help will benefit the greater whole. Cricket is an excellent Power Animal for sound healers. Very psychic and a master of attraction, it encourages us to open our third eye and visualize the things we want drawn to us magnetically.

Cricket is also symbolic of change. Everything changes, and Cricket teaches us that sitting quietly can help us see what to do next. Harnessing the power of foresight will give you the opportunity to take great leaps into your future. When Cricket stops chirping, it is a warning sign that an intruder is coming. Cricket also can predict rain, signaling a fresh start or the beginning of a spiritual journey.

Cricket encourages us to tell our stories to help others learn lessons of having faith when jumping forward. We must also learn to turn down the volume of the external world so that we can hear the voice of spirit and control our reception if we are sensitive to energy. Seeing Cricket outdoors or having one in your home is a sign that you should make an altar to the natural world. Having candles, rocks, feathers, and other elements on an altar can encourage harmony and communication with those residing in the world of the unspoken. Cricket is also connected to the flute and songs that flow into the heart and spur a reminder of the celestial sounds of heaven.

POWERS OF CRICKET

Call in Cricket for:

- Expressing a positive message to the world.
- Help to take great leaps forward on your spiritual path.
- Abundance.

AWARENESS FROM CRICKET

If Cricket comes into your life:

- Express your feelings to others more.
- Use sound to raise the vibration of your energy.
- You may be too sensitive.

Energy Center: Heart

Mineral: Vivianite

Element: Air

Magic & Mystery:

- According to the *Old Farmer's Almanac*, if you count the chirps of Cricket for fourteen seconds and add forty to the count you will get the temperature in Fahrenheit.
- Cricket is a popular pet among the peoples of the Iberian Peninsula in Europe.
- Cricket has often been depicted in art as playing miniature violins.
- On the island of Kauai in Hawaii, Cricket no longer chirps. Its silence is an evolutionary adaptation that gives it protection from a predator that lives there.

SHAMAN'S INTENTION: *TEACH ME OF THE HARMONY THAT IS POSSIBLE WHEN COMMUNING WITH OTHERS*

CROCODILE

NEW BEGINNINGS | **CREATION** | **MENTAL WELLNESS**

"Linking renewal with dissolution, I can assure safe passage into the lower world-- a fertile place for creation."
—Crocodile

ALLIGATOR, CAIMAN

POWERS OF CROCODILE

Call in Crocodile for:

- The wisdom to balance your emotions and mental responses.
- To understand your connection with the cosmos and the earth.
- Grace when there is chaos around you.

AWARENESS FROM CROCODILE

If Crocodile comes into your life:

- Know when to let go; holding on to anything too long is counterproductive.
- Stop clinging to the shore. Jump in and trust the river to take you where you need to go.
- You are being irrational or need to organize your thinking.

Energy Center: Sacrum

Mineral: Chlorite quartz

Element: Water

Magic & Mystery:

- In yoga the symbol of the second chakra, *Swadhisthana*, is an Alligator. Swadhisthana is a sign of balance.
- The Alligator god Itzamna was the most important god of the ancient Mayans and a symbol of leadership and power.

Crocodile has existed on Earth for over 230 million years. It is a social creature that lives in *congregations.* These groups are typically seen basking in the Sun or taking a swim. Because Crocodile can't control its temperature internally, when it is cold it sunbathes, and when it is hot it goes for a swim. Crocodile's jaw evolved to bite and grip prey. Its tough, leathery hide protects it from the roughness of the ground. Long ago, in the age of dinosaurs, this thick skin probably also protected its ancestors from larger predators. Crocodile's eyes are on the top of its skull, so it can see above the water when it is submerged. All species of Crocodile communicate with a variety of hisses, grunts, and groans. At birth, baby crocodiles make birdlike chirping sounds, signaling an innate knowledge of heaven.

As the master of the world's rivers, Crocodile is navigator of the universal flow of cosmic energy and bringer of Sun and rain. The Egyptians worshiped and adorned images of their Crocodile-headed god, Sobek, to ensure fertility for themselves and their crops. The myth says that Sobek came first out of the waters of chaos to create the world.

Crocodile is also of great importance in Hinduism, as most Hindu gods and goddesses used it as a vehicle. For Native Americans, Crocodile is a symbol of status, power, and nobility due to its capacity to survive both in water and on land, places of birth, rebirth, and purification.

Traditionally, the Mayans view Crocodile as both a representation of the Upper World and Lower World. The peaks on Crocodile's hide act like embedded pyramids, "telegraphing" energy to the outer reaches of the cosmos, especially the Pleiades star system. Each peak holds a frequency capable of bridging dimensions. Within the Milky Way, between the constellations of Scorpio and Sagittarius, there is a massive black hole. This galactic center point, which the Mayans consider the source of creation and an opening to the Upper World, is known as the Mouth of the Crocodile. The Mayans believe that the planet rests on top of a Crocodile that floats in a lagoon. But Crocodile is intrinsically linked to Mother Earth and the Lower World as well. It is said to lie at the roots of the ceiba tree, which Mayans call the Tree of Life, where it guards the entrance to the Lower World.

Crocodile is a sign of new beginnings and potential; with its belly in contact with Mother Earth, it helps to secure a strong foundation. It can also signify a period of insanity or doubt, or a struggle to understand the many levels of existence—since it navigates many dimensions. If not addressed, this type of confusion can lead to aggressive behavior. Crocodile displays anger and aggression when its territory is invaded. It can be helpful in restoring your balance if your emotions run too deep and you feel destabilized or if you're dealing with mental health issues.

Crocodile offers the power of fluidity and clarity. Just as it can navigate underwater, it can bring cleansing to your mind and enhance your ability to see through murky "waters" in your life. This will help you to convert chaos to order and eliminate that which does not serve you.

SHAMAN'S INTENTION: *HELP ME TO BE AN EFFECTIVE GATEKEEPER OF MY WORLD*

CUCKOO

REBIRTH | CONCIOUSNESS | PROPHECY

"Never forget to embrace joy in all the sacred moments of celebration in your life."
—Cuckoo

One hundred and forty Cuckoo species live in forests and woodlands around the world, including in the lush green rainforests of the tropics. The male Cuckoo is famous for its "koo-koo" call, which has been imitated by clockmakers. Cuckoo is associated with orphans because it leaves its eggs in the nests of other birds to be nurtured and raised, although it will check in to see if the chicks are being well fed and cared for properly by the foster parents. A rare trait in nature, parental delegating has given Cuckoo the opportunity to flourish. Cuckoo prefers being alone, so you will rarely see it in a pair or flying in a flock.

Cuckoo is the center of many Lithuanian fairy tales and legends because of it strange voice. Some interpret the sound it emits as complaining and groaning. One famous story is about a woman who lost her three sons in a war and turned into Cuckoo because of so much grief. She went to many countries to look for the graves of her sons. The moral of the story is: "You can only understand the song of Cuckoo if you have suffered."

Cuckoo assists the soul in entering and leaving the body during its incarnations. The body is the soul's "nest" during its life experience. In Baltic pagan tradition, people are believed to reincarnate as birds or trees after death, and souls of kind people transform into Cuckoo. The most powerful deity in this tradition is Laima, the Lithuanian goddess of fertility, life, and birth. She was often portrayed as a Cuckoo and viewed as the protector of human life and a messenger of significant events such as births, deaths, and marriages. In Eastern Europe, it is said that Cuckoo knows how long we will live. When you hear Cuckoo, if you count how many times it calls, you can discern the number of years you will live.

In Swedish folk wisdom, the direction the sound of Cuckoo comes from matters. The Cuckoo call signifies good luck if coming from the West, death if coming from the South, consolation if coming from the East, and sorrow if coming from the North.

As a guide, Cuckoo will help you to discern the truth and avoid falling prey to trickery. When you hear Cuckoo, it is time for new beginnings. Trust yourself and the impressions you receive. Cuckoo will tell you whether or not it is time to leave a situation, keeping you from being afraid to make choices. Cuckoo encourages you to strip illusion to remove antiquated beliefs. Build your nest with the vision of having it be your own personal sanctuary to house your spirit. Keep a balance with family to maintain your personal space, and, when you want to embrace the life of a wanderer and see the world from a different perspective, don't hesitate to do it.

POWERS OF CUCKOO

Call in Cuckoo for:

- A new beginning.
- Help to improve your self-esteem.
- A companion through the cycles of life and death.

AWARENESS FROM CUCKOO

If Cuckoo comes into your life:

- You must decide whether to stay or go.
- Study the eternity of the soul.
- A loss may lead to newfound wisdom.

Energy Center: Throat

Mineral: Dumortierite

Element: Air

Magic & Mystery:

- In ancient Greece Cuckoo was sacred to the goddess Hera, and legend tells us that Zeus transformed himself into Cuckoo so he could seduce her.
- In Japan Cuckoo symbolizes unrequited love. In India, Cuckoo is linked with Kamadeva, god of desire and longing.

SHAMAN'S INTENTION: *HELP ME TO TRUST THE MYSTERIES OF LIFE AND DEATH*

DEER

SURVIVAL | **CONFIDENCE** | **INSTINCT**

"In my eyes see the possibility for deep-seated compassion and heartfelt love for our planet."—Deer

POWERS OF DEER

Call in Deer for:

- Help to establish a peaceful coexistence with everyone around you.
- Attunement with your inner child.
- Destroying ego and illusions.

AWARENESS FROM DEER

If Deer comes into your life:

- Appreciate the beauty around you.
- Cultivate friendships that support and nourish you.
- Time to turn things over to a higher power.

Energy Center: Heart

Mineral: Hiddenite

Element: Air

Magic & Mystery:

- In Central Mexico the Huichol tribe believed that Deer was the original shaman and the major connector to the gods.
- Deer was often sacrificed to the Mayan gods as a valuable gift.

Deer has lived in close contact with humanity for at least 35,000 years. Its image is featured in Paleolithic paintings done by our ancestors on the walls of the Lascaux Caves in France and elsewhere. Like both Caribou and Cattle, Deer is a foraging animal that has an extra stomach in which it ferments the leaves it eats for better digestion. Deer lives on every continent except Australia. A characteristic that makes Deer special is its antlers, which the male grows and sheds each year. Clothing, food, and utensils have all come from Deer. Before killing Deer, indigenous hunters always offer a prayer as a sacred gesture of gratitude.

Deer has finely tuned hearing and an amazing sense of smell to protect itself from predators. A gentle animal, it roams the forests with grace and elegance. Its main survival tactic is to run. It reacts quickly when startled. With muscular legs, it travels long distances to reach safety with unwavering endurance. Deer can run at a pace of up to 50 M.P.H. The Doe looks out for her kind, raising her tail like a white flag, when sensing danger. The Buck travels alone. In an elaborate hierarchy of mating rights, he clashes antlers with other males and the winner impregnates the waiting female.

As a Power Animal, Deer is magical because of its antlers, which are like receptors to the Upper World. Deer brings gifts of clairvoyance and clairaudience to the emerging psychic, as these features are so well developed by it. The Great Buddha was said to have been a Golden Stag in a previous incarnation. Native Americans believe Deer to be a gentle spirit and the bringer of messages. Seeing the tracks of Deer means you are safe and in a place of prosperity.

In Celtic shamanism, two elements of Deer energy are honored. One is feminine energy, which underlies Deer's gentle and graceful aspects. This is the goddess energy that relates to positivity, the defeat of fear, and the renewal of purpose. Deer reminds us to keep our power intact and walk away from those who are not stoking our fires of compassion. Negativity must be avoided at all costs. Remaining around those who are negative can cause us to lose our vibrancy. Instead of condemning negativity, however, send positive energy to those who are suffering and pray that they find peace.

The other element of Deer energy is its masculine energy, which underlies its pride in playing a role as a protector of others. Deer has a strong self-preservation instinct and is highly independent. Its presence reminds us to trust our instincts about when to leap and when to run.

When a Fawn is born, it is an expression of pure joy and excitement. It jumps around and ecstatically enjoys its first moments of life. Deer reminds us of this unique moment when we were free of the confines of fear and social conditioning. Not everyone is a Coyote waiting around the corner for us. If you have been hurt, heal your heart and move on. Deer represents our longing for joy, movement, and adventure; a wanderlust that can capture our souls.

SHAMAN'S INTENTION: *SUPPORT MY INTENTION TO DEFY FEAR AND STAND TALL IN HIGHER VIBRATIONS*

DINGO

DISCOVERY **INDEPENDENCE** **PROTECTION**

"We illustrate the circle of life and are blessed by the abundance of the creatures that sacrifice themselves for our survival."—Dingo

Dingo has been a part of Australian history for almost 18,000 years. It has been a revered member of Aboriginal society and a pillar of the partnership between these native peoples and the animal world. It is Australia's native Dog and largest carnivore. Mostly Dingo is a brown and tan color except for a few that are black and tan. Dingo is an effective hunter with good night vision and it will hunt in packs to bring down Kangaroo, although its preferred prey is Rabbit and small rodents. It is in constant conflict with farmers as it preys on their stock animals. This problem was largely resolved through the installation of a 6,000-kilometer fence, longer than the Great Wall of China, which separates Dingo from livestock. Dingo is blamed for the extinction of the Tasmanian Devil, a marsupial. Dingo is now at the top of the food chain other than when it encounters humans or Crocodile. Dingo does not bark; however, it will howl like Coyote.

Dingo has an amazing ability to find water above and below ground, an important skill in the sometime arid regions that it inhabits. Its knowledge of where to find water was recorded by Europeans settlers who relied on it to help them locate springs. The term *Dingo soak* refers to a water hole that has been dug up and found by Dingo. Aborigines believe that Dingo knows the map of the ley lines of water tables and sources all over the planet. Spiritually, it is thought to have emerged from Lower World wells to create beautiful waterfalls. Stories also talk about Dingo creating mountains, lakes, and star constellations.

Aboriginal women used to drape a Dingo hide around their waists as a totem object to protect them when they traveled alone. Taking a vision quest with Dingo can help you adapt to the harshness of life and seek a future vision. By walking with Dingo in the wilderness, you will receive direct guidance from the spirit world.

Dingo will bring shamanic messages to you from the Upper World, and you may find it visiting you in your dreams. Dingo remains wild despite numerous attempts to try to domesticate it. It cannot be tamed or domesticated because it prefers to be independent and find its own food. As a predator, it carries the sense of a wild spirit and loves to hunt. At Aboriginal funerals, artefacts and talismans made of the teeth, bones, and fur of Dingo are sometimes buried with the deceased to provide protection for them in the Afterlife.

Dingo teaches us that forgiveness is the greatest gift we can give ourselves in order to tame the voice of the inner critic. It brings us the message to move on from trusting others and being hurt as this is just a learning process. The only path to perfection is imperfection. When grief strikes seeds of enlightenment are planted in the soil of your emotional wounds. To grow these seeds, it is necessary to explore the dark side of your personality. Facing your anger, pain, and loneliness will bring you to the highest version of yourself.

POWERS OF DINGO

Call in Dingo for:

- Finding water and nourishment for your soul.
- Encouraging your independence.
- Activating your wild side.

AWARENESS FROM DINGO

If Dingo comes into your life:

- You may feel too entitled to others' personal things.
- You may be overly protective of those you love.
- You may be relying too much on others for your success.

Energy Center: Solar plexus

Mineral: Chalcedony

Element: Water

Magic & Mystery: In a portrait from the Smithsonian Collection an Australian Aboriginal woman is wearing a Dingo tail headdress, a talisman that holds great power which was traditionally worn by warriors going into battle.

SHAMAN'S INTENTION: *BE MY GUIDE ON A VISION QUEST WITH THE PURPOSE OF HEALING MY WEARY SOUL*

DOG (DOMESTICATED)

LOYALTY | **PROTECTION** | **UNCONDITIONAL LOVE**

"Never underestimate the power love gives you to access the hearts and minds of others."
—Dog

POWERS OF DOG

Call in Dog for:

- Support to live a life centered on kindness.
- Truth and loyalty to yourself and others.
- Unconditional love.

AWARENESS FROM DOG

If Dog comes into your life:

- It is time to show more tolerance for others.
- You may be overly protective and fearful.
- Stop gnawing at things mentally; let go of what is fueling your overactive mind.

Energy Center: Heart

Mineral: Green sapphire

Element: Earth

Magic & Mystery:

- In the myths of different native tribes in Mexico, Dog plays an important role in the creation of humans.
- Dog was the sacred companion of the ancient Greek goddess Hecate, overseer of boundaries, borders, crossroads, and entrances, including the doorway to other dimensions. Her highly perceptive hounds always guided the way for those traveling to places off the beaten track.

Dog was bred from Wolf when our forebears were hunter-gatherers, perhaps as early as 34,000 years ago. As a domestic pet, Dog helps us on many levels. Playful, friendly, and loyal, it makes a great companion. It has a keen sense of smell and the ability to hear a broader range of sound than we do. It is color blind but can see better than us in dimly lit places.

Dog is sensitive to changes in the environment and can sense electromagnetic forces that come with storms. Records from ancient Greece show that dogs fled the city of Helike before an intense earthquake. It is a good practice to pay attention to Dog, as it will tell you what is going to happen. Dog can also sense spirits more easily than us. You may see or hear Dog barking at unexplained presences that its extrasensory perception is picking up.

Throughout recorded history cultures around the world have believed Dog stands as a guardian at the doors of heaven. Although the ancient Egyptians were known for their admiration of Cat, they also respected Dog. They associated Dog with the jackal-headed Anubis, god of the Underworld. Dog has also been linked to healing. The Sumerian goddess Gula, a healer who restored life to the dead, was typically depicted with Dog seated beside her throne.

The indigenous people of North and South America traditionally lived with Dog. Their loyal companion warned them of approaching danger, helped them hunt, and kept them warm at night. Before Horse, the only constant companion humanity had was Dog. This relationship was so meaningful that when Horse was introduced by the Colonial Spaniards, the Native Americans called it Sky Dog to honor it for being equally as helpful and loyal.

The connection and loyalty of Dog to the man or woman who is its primary companion runs deep. This strong bond is a blessing to those looking to abandon loneliness. Dog is good for our health because its companionship keeps us active and happy.

Spiritually, Dog teaches us the ultimate lesson of unconditional love and compassion by expressing these qualities in measures far surpassing our human ability to integrate them. Dog overlooks our faults and embraces us as we are without judgment. Seeing the world through Dog's eyes, you will have a view of contentment. Expose your hidden heart and open it to this great teacher. With the innocence of Dog, a world awaits to be seen without judgment. Dog can serve as a guide between the worlds of life and death and is always there to greet us when we cross over to the other side. Dog is a reconciler, a remover of obstacles to positivity, and a unifier. It is always willing to receive. Dog stands guard, always willing to bridge the gap between human and animal and harmonize the energies of hearts.

SHAMAN'S INTENTION: *TEACH ME TO BE A LOYAL GUARDIAN OF THOSE THAT NEED PROTECTION*

DOLPHIN/PORPOISE

LOVE **CURIOSITY** **ENTHUSIASM**

"Look past the sadness and you will realize that you are always swimming in happiness."
—Dolphin

Nearly forty species of Dolphin live in shallow and temperate oceans around the world, and five species live in rivers, including three freshwater rivers. As a mammal, Dolphin is an air breather. Scientists theorize that Dolphin's ancestors lived on land before adapting to water. Studies of their fins show that they are similar to legs and toes. Dolphin lives in large pods of up to a thousand members. It builds strong bonds with its companions and will protect them if they get injured. Its playfulness and amiability contribute to its ability to form friendships with humans too. Dolphin is extremely intelligent. It has exceptional eyesight and can hear frequencies ten times higher than the range we hear. It is also capable of echolocation—using sound to navigate.

Dolphin is admired by all who come to know it. Coastal Native American tribes tell stories about Dolphin helping to save humans from shipwrecks and Shark.

Every culture in the Mediterranean region has had a relationship with Dolphin. Images of Dolphin appear in the pottery of the Mycenean civilization dating back as far as 2,000 B.C.E. It is also depicted in the mosaic floor of a fifth-century Byzantine church in the desert city of Petra in modern-day Jordan.

The ancient Celts who sailed the Atlantic Ocean honored Dolphin and saw it as the protector of wells and sacred waters. Pirates told stories of mermaids that lived in the heart of Dolphin and would morph into beautiful maidens.

The skill of combining sound and breath that Dolphin has mastered is a very important shamanic practice. Sound is an important factor in how it finds food and other objects it desires. Dolphin teaches lessons of the sacred, life, heart, and happiness. Like Dolphin, we can use the breath to cleanse our minds of intrusive thoughts so we may remain in the heartfelt state that is evidenced by Dolphin's permanent smile.

Dolphin's playfulness, creativity, and access to other dimensions can teach us to be free of the restraints of our minds, which limit our view. Because it thrives on the rhythm and sounds of the water, Dolphin knows that everything is vibratory and that the waves of transformation are always nearby.

Dolphin carries a divine message about the intelligence of our planet. Revered by the inhabitants of Atlantis as the keeper of frequencies, it brings us wisdom of crystals, beautiful gifts from the bedrock of our planet which can be used for healing and attunement. It encourages us to develop our understanding of the electromagnetic fields around us. This "circuitry" empowers us to intersect with all sorts of beings, including those from subtler realms than our own. Music, light, color, and sound carry the octaves of these higher dimensions. Dolphin is here to support us to align with the crystal core of our planet. Dolphin will upgrade your connection to the holographic field of the Earth, a sweet spot for riding the waves of the higher dimensions.

PORPOISE

POWERS OF DOLPHIN

Call in Dolphin for:

- Unconditional love for all beings.
- An ideal blend of intelligence and compassion.
- Honesty.

AWARENESS FROM DOLPHIN

If Dolphin comes into your life:

- It is time to embrace the real you.
- Call on it for protection if you need to be rescued.
- Start communicating your desires and feelings to others.

Energy Center: Throat

Mineral: Aquamarine

Element: Water

Magic & Mystery:

- When Dolphin looks in a mirror it can recognize itself.
- As they make the transition from amniotic fluid to the air outside the womb, Dolphin sounds can be soothing to human infants at birth.

SHAMAN'S INTENTION: *TAKE ME TO RIDE THE WAVE OF HIGHER FREQUENCY*

DONKEY

DETERMINATION **COURAGE** **HUMILITY**

"Be kind to those who carry the burden of your innocence and ignorance as they walk with you through the peaks and the valleys of your personal discovery."—Donkey

ASS, BURRO

POWERS OF DONKEY

Call in Donkey for:

- Insight on when to help others who in turn will help you.
- Humility, a rare treasure that can expand your ability to receive.
- Patience regarding the timing of your next steps.

AWARENESS FROM DONKEY

If Donkey comes into your life:

- You may be ready to take a trip, or a change is in the air.
- Do not be motivated by the admiration of others, as it could be based on your wealth and power and not the real you.
- It is time to withdraw from any situation in which you are not being properly respected.

Energy Center: Solar plexus

Mineral: Fire agate

Element: Fire

Magic & Mystery:

- In the Kabbalah, it is believed that anyone who owes you money at the time of their death will come back as your Donkey to repay the debt.
- Hippocrates, the father of western medicine, wrote of the medicinal properties of Donkey milk to treat people with psoriasis, eczema, asthma, liver disease, and infections.
- Cleopatra and Napoleon Bonaparte's sister, Pauline, bathed in Donkey milk to preserve the beauty of their skin.

Carrying the burdens of many, Donkey has been a loving friend to humankind for over 4,000 years. The ultimate beast of burden, it was long the preferred mode of transport, with better capabilities and strength than Horse. Donkey may be a humble cousin of Horse; yet, it has greater natural intelligence, which contributes to its surefootedness and ability to navigate challenging terrains. It has an incredible memory for people and places, even years later, and can live to be over fifty. It may seem stubborn and independent but will never go where it does not feel safe. Donkey always uses its impeccable intuition. It is not easily startled and is very curious about the world around it. It is not motivated by fear, but self-preservation—a healthy attribute. Donkey is courageous, as evidenced by its daily treks up and down the steep trails of the Grand Canyon.

Donkey makes a wonderful guardian for Cattle, Sheep, and Goat because of its natural instinct to protect itself and others from Wolf and other predators. It is often placed in pastures with Horse because of the calming effect it has on Horse. To become a friend of Donkey, it must trust you; trust matters a lot to Donkey. In the wild, the male Donkey lives alone and creates large territories within which it has "rights" to mate with any female that arrives.

In western culture the female Donkey is a symbol of peace, poverty, patience, humility, and courage.

Since antiquity Donkey has been a lifeline to people in many regions of the world, as it carries water, food, fuel, and other necessities on its back for the progress of humanity. When archaeologists excavated brick tombs of ancient Egypt, they found Donkey bodies buried with high-ranking individuals. No other animal was found at such sites. In ancient Greece,Donkey was a sacred animal. Due to its job of carrying harvested grapes, it came to be associated with Dionysius, the god of wine.

Despite the stereotype that Donkey is stubborn and stupid, really it is an animal of great perseverance and insight. One of its gifts is its power of controlling emotions. This energy is helpful to empaths and the highly intuitive. Count on Donkey for safe passage to a new beginning, as it can help to release the burdens of the past and lighten your load. By focusing on the journey and not the destination, you will find joy along the way. Donkey has a clear vision of its boundaries and limitations and has mastered the word no and does not concern itself with the reaction of others. It teaches us not to participate in anything that is not in alignment with our purpose or values. Donkey does not engage with things that make it uncomfortable and therefore avoids feeling overwhelmed. Donkey supports us to use our intuition to assess our surroundings and stay grounded in our certainty. Donkey makes a wonderful Power Animal for young children, as it teaches boundaries and self-empowerment.

SHAMAN'S INTENTION: *HELP ME FEEL SAFE*

DOVE

LOVE **HOPE** **PEACE**

"Love is the essence of our being, finding this essence within you will bring you from the darkness into the pure white light that is joy."—Dove

Hundreds of species of Dove exist. The ancient Sumerians of Mesopotamia were the first to breed a white Dove from the same wild Pigeon that we still see in modern cities. Dove has lived close to us for thousands of years. It is found in fields and trees, and on electrical wires near humans. Images of Dove found in artwork in Iraq date back to 3,000 B.C.E. It has an amazing gift for finding its way home even over distances of thousands of miles. This ability has been put to work delivering messages for royalty, the military, and hobbyists. With its strong pectoral muscles, Dove can fly at speeds of up to 110 M.P.H. It also has excellent digestion due to an efficient way of combining gravel with seeds to help it grind and digest whatever it eats.

Long a symbol of peace, purity, and grace, Dove brings a message of hope and calm to the world. Its soft cooing sound is a morning tune that soothes the chaos of the planet. Blackfoot warriors carried Dove feathers into battle as a sign of hope to bring everyone back alive. The Eastern Algonquian tribes saw Turtle Dove as a messenger from the spirit world and a warning of death. The Cherokee associated Dove with acorns, as their word for acorn, *gule*, is pronounced similarly to the sound of Dove's coo. The Aztec saw Dove as a symbol of love and associated it with Xochiquetzal, their goddess of beauty, sexuality, and the home.

Dove is associated with the Divine Feminine. To the ancient Assyrians, Dove was symbolic of Ishtar (Mother Earth) and represented fertility and love. The Greco-Roman goddess Aphrodite/Venus was also associated with Dove, as it is emblematic of the pure love of spirit rather than physical love. The souls of those who left Atlantis during its fall continue to cherish those of us still on Earth, visiting us in the form of Dove.

As a divine messenger, Dove gifts us wisdom from the Universe that is gentle and loving. Its soft white body brings us a sense of innocence and hope. Dove is also a sign of fidelity as Dove mates for life, a demonstration that loving someone with a pure heart can lead to spending an eternity together. Dove is often released at marriage ceremonies as a sign of true love. Dove is the perfect "love bird". A female will allow a male to feed her and it looks like they are kissing. Since Dove can live up to thirty years it also represents longevity.

As a Power Animal, Dove can help us to rise above chaos and find peace. With its loving nature, it helps us to begin a process of renewal. Dove is a wonderful navigator that can support us on our journeys to the spiritual world, always ensuring that we find our way home. Like Dove, we can instill our homes with the soothing feeling of a nest and nurturing so that they become places of belonging where we feel in control and where it is predictable and secure.

POWERS OF DOVE

Call in Dove for:

- Experiencing gentleness and kindness towards others.
- Pure love and innocence.
- Going the distance.

AWARENESS FROM DOVE

If Dove comes into your life:

- Watch out for those who would take advantage of you.
- To live a peaceful life, you must be at peace with yourself.
- Love is in the air.

Energy Center: Heart

Mineral: Atlantasite

Element: Air

Magic & Mystery:

- In Greek mythology the seven daughters of Atlas were transformed into Doves by Zeus to escape Orion's advances. Zeus then turned the sisters into stars. This is the origin of the northern constellation known by astronomers as the Pleiades.
- Historically, Dove is depicted on a grave marker to represent the soul and its journey.

SHAMAN'S INTENTION: *HELP ME TO UNDERSTAND MY PERSONAL INFINITY AND BASK IN THE ENERGY OF LOVE*

DRAGON

PERSEVERANCE | **INTUITION** | **REFLECTION**

"Although a mystery, I live in the minds of those who can see beyond the limitations of an ordinary reality."
—Dragon

POWERS OF DRAGON

Call in Dragon for:

- Harmony and healing.
- Understanding the five elements for optimal balance.
- Support a shift into a healthier lifestyle.

AWARENESS FROM DRAGON

If Dragon comes into your life:

- It is time to move past the obvious and into the realm of possibility.
- Dispel your fears and journey forward.
- Embrace your greatness and walk with confidence.

Energy Center: Crown

Mineral: Purple fluorite

Element: Fire

Magic & Mystery:

- Dragon is smarter than humans and legend says it taught us how to talk.
- The constellation that revolves around the North Pole is named Draco—Dragon.

Dragon is a mystical flying creature with a lizard-like body that spews fire. We know it from Asian legends and European folk tales. It does not exist in the third dimension but is a popular mode of transportation for shamans who travel to all other realms to conduct spiritual work.

In European, Greek, and Middle-Eastern mythology Dragon is a symbol of power. We see it depicted on heraldic banners, family crests, shields, weapons, and armor to display strength. Through art, we see two dragons face to face as a symbol of neutralizing adversaries.

The symbol of Dragon swallowing his own tail appears worldwide. This ouroboros, as most call it, has its origins among the alchemists of ancient Egypt. It appears in the texts of Cleopatra the Alchemist (not to be mistaken for the queen) and represents an endless cycle of transformation between pairs of opposites such as day and night.

As a combination of a serpent and a bird, Dragon is a mysteriously powerful being that lives in caves deep in the dark belly of the Earth. It can take us into the darkness of the unconscious mind to drag buried secrets out into the open or deep into our souls for the sake of personal revision. Dragon supports the shaman in mastering the powers of all the elements—water, earth, fire, and air—and brings us an abundance of insight on how to balance, integrate, and embody these primal forces.

In the Chinese zodiac, 1916, 1928, 1940, 1952, 1964, 1976, 1988, 2000, 2012, and 2024 are considered years of Dragon, periods that bring good fortune and ensure fresh starts. In the folklore of the Philippines, Dragon lives in the sea and creates lunar eclipses by swallowing the Moon whole. Superstitious people would go out of their homes and bang pots and pans to scare away Dragon so he would spit the Moon out again.

Dragon is the largest of all animals. It has a scaled crest or ridge on its head and a small mouth. Its tail is its most powerful feature. It also has keen eyesight and a forked tongue, which can mean that we are being given double messages or that, without unity of thought, there can be deceit.

In fairytales, Dragon has the role of protecting buried treasures. If you are working with Dragon, it will help you discover the great treasures you too have buried deep inside. The saying to "wake a sleeping dragon" means to wake what is powerful within. Dragon is the sign that great spiritual growth is to come. It can teach us to understand the unseen world and to summon the courage to endure hardships, as the answers are always just a breath away.

Dragon will bring you an alchemical fusion with the spirit world and help you to shut down the noisy mind so that you can open the door to a cave of wonder. Ancient and renewing, it will enable you to connect to the higher realms and energy grids of the Universe. Dragon knows where the portals to other dimensions are and will knock down any obstacle to get you there. It is also very protective of the Earth and will encourage you to bring in your inner muse to create a new world with you in it. It will also be a great teacher of the art of Feng shui and the importance of placement. This helps to enhance the flow of the life force to design environments that are in alignment with a harmonious vibration. Call on Dragon to support the flow of energy through your body and encourage positive and energetic health, relationships, prosperity, and success. Dragon encourages us to fly above the drama and chaos because, when we do, we are gracefully put on the path of transformation.

SHAMAN'S INTENTION: *GUIDE ME TO THE UNDERSTANDING OF BEING A MULTIDIMENSIONAL BEING*

DRAGONFLY

AGILITY | **TRANSFORMATION** | **PROSPERITY**

"By watching the river flow you can be serene in your power and dissolve your awareness of the mind."
—Dragonfly

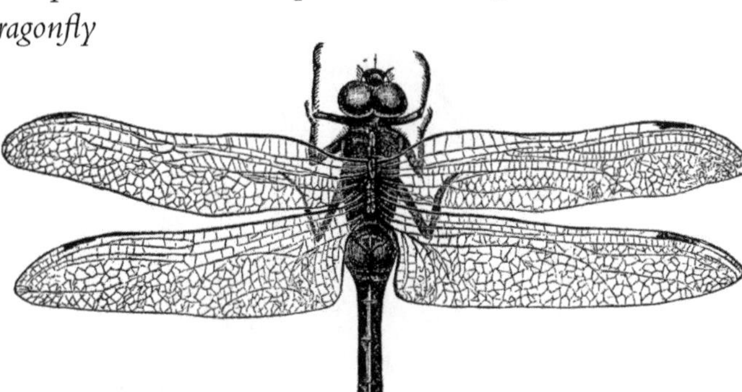

Dragonfly has been around for 300 million years and it was not always as small as it is now. Fossils of this prehistoric creature have wingspans of up to two feet. Dragonfly is a skillful flyer that mates in midair and would starve without flying since it catches its prey while in motion. Dragonfly has two sets of wings but can fly perfectly well with just one set. The eyes of Dragonfly have 28,000 separate telescopic lenses, giving it a 360-degree range of vision and the ability to see a much wider spectrum of color than humans.

Dragonfly is a traveler like the Globe Skinner, which makes the longest migration of any insect, traveling 6,200 miles back and forth over the Indian Ocean. It flies very fast and has the ability to propel itself in six different directions. Dragonfly begins its life in water and evolves from there. It delivers lessons from water about trusting the flow of life and energy. When we feel imbalanced, Dragonfly reminds us of our gestation in a womb filled with amniotic fluid--a place of purity where we exist in a state of potential before the world's social conditioning of us begins.

The Navajo see Dragonfly as a symbol of pure water; the Hopi and Pueblo see it as a medicine animal associated with healing. Killing Dragonfly is never even considered in these cultures. The Hopi put Dragonfly on their altars and recognize it as a shaman flying about with superpowers. To the Native Americans, traditionally Dragonfly signified abundance. Their myths credit Dragonfly for saving them from starvation by helping accelerate the maturation of corn. The Plains people saw Dragonfly as invincible, so they painted its likeness on their clothes and teepees for protection. The Lakota view Dragonfly as a mirage or an illusion since its wings beat so rapidly that the human eye cannot see them. When the Lakota wanted to hide from their enemies, they would invoke Dragonfly for confusion. They saw it as the god of whirlwinds.

Many world cultures understand that Dragonfly has magical energy and the ability to transcend our dimension. In Ireland it is said that if you follow Dragonfly it will lead you to the fairies. In Japanese art Dragonfly symbolizes pure joy and the hope of realizing our highest potential. The Japanese associate Dragonfly with the seasons of summer and fall. The samurai used Dragonfly as a symbol of victory.

Dragonfly works with the vibration of color and in this manner has an important effect on our moods and how we experience life when we're in its presence. Its bright metallic colors remind us of the alchemy of metals and the power of transformation that we carry within us. Dragonfly is a master of the air, the medium of emotions. It is a sign of the possibility of joy, if we can simply trust and manage our emotions. Dragonfly can assist us in getting to the core of deep-seated issues underlying addictions and procrastination. Suppressed energy will be extracted and flown away with its support. Dragonfly can help us to release limiting behaviors and thought patterns. After busting through these beliefs, we can see that we are powerful. Dragonfly signals transformation and reassures us that the work on our inner selves is worth it no matter how long it takes. Dragonfly teaches us to be quick-change artists ready to make changes in our lives.

POWERS OF DRAGONFLY

Call in Dragonfly for:

- Extreme agility.
- Dedication to long-term efforts at personal improvement.
- Wisdom and good fortune.

AWARENESS FROM DRAGONFLY

If Dragonfly comes into your life:

- Your addictions may be overtaking your reasoning.
- Big changes are coming, so get ready.
- You need to purge your thoughts of limitation.

Energy Center: Root and sacrum

Mineral: Rainbow quartz

Element: Air

Magic & Mystery:

- In China Dragonfly (*qingting*) represents the Confucian ideal of purity. Pronunciation of its name is similar to the word for "clear" (*qing*).
- Folk stories from Japan cite Dragonfly as the vehicle of choice for departed ancestors returning to visit their families.

SHAMAN'S INTENTION: *SUPPORT ME TO EMBRACE THE PERFECTION OF MY BEING*

DUCK

HAPPINESS **SIMPLICITY** **ADAPTABILITY**

"We have the freedom to rise above heavy thoughts that ground us into a muddled existence."
—Duck

POWERS OF DUCK

Call in Duck for:

- Patience.
- Help to speak the truth.
- Managing your emotions with ease.

AWARENESS FROM DUCK

If Duck comes into your life:

- Go deeper in your thinking and look for what is below the surface of your conscious thoughts.
- Don't fear socializing; there are many people who want to meet you.
- Consider a career where you can share your stories and ideas.

Energy Center: Throat

Mineral: Quantum quattro

Element: Water

Magic & Mystery:

- In feng shui, images of Duck are placed in the southwest corner of a bedroom to improve a marriage. Duck is a symbol of fidelity and honesty.
- Some indigenous people of North America use Duck manure to dye their clothing and tepees blue.

Duck lives on every continent except Antarctica. It requires open water so is found in marshes, rivers, and oceans. Its thick plumage insulates it so well that even when diving into water it never gets wet. While sleeping Duck keeps one eye open. It has the ability to shut down half its brain, while keeping the other half on alert. Its field of vision is 340 degrees, enabling it to perceive most threats coming its way.

The female Duck quacks to communicate with others in its raft (in flight, a group is a flock) and to call to her young. Quacking is primarily a female trait. Other than quacks, Duck communicates with whistles, yodels, and coos. Duck is intelligent, with a great ability for abstract reasoning.

Hearing Duck quack is a good omen. Seeing it fly by you signifies prosperity. Duck brings hope that you can overcome trying times and it brings a flavor of happiness to our lives. In Korea Duck represents fertility and is asked for support when this is an issue. In China seeing Duck holding a lotus blossom in its mouth is a sign that a baby may be on the way. In ancient Egypt Duck was the symbol of Isis, goddess of nature and magic.

Duck reminds us of a need for patience and to look at things in a less complicated way. By taking some quiet time to control our minds, we can usually find a more elegant truth. The expression "like water off a duck's back" reminds us not to take anything personally when our emotions are veering out of control. We must remember that emotions are reaction to thoughts.

To a shaman Duck can be a helpful messenger between realms, as it seeks freedom from the limitations of the earthly environment and connection to source. Finding a Duck feather means someone is thinking of you with great emotion on the other side. When Duck gets older, its dark feathers turn white. This sign is a reminder to be respectful of the wisdom of our elders and ancestors.

Call in Duck if you want to go deep into any issue, as it will help you dive to find what is lying below the surface. Duck is comfortable both on land and in water, because it is adaptable. It is also sociable and tends to live in groups. Duck reminds us to not narrow our definition of abundance but to see it in all things and count our blessings. We must swim through life with the innocence of our being and the confidence of our inner guidance. Duck also teaches us the power of choice and encourages us to speak up and let go of stuck energy.

As you practice telling your truth, you will be surprised at how many people say they needed to hear your story. Honest communication and expression create a healthy pond for us to paddle in. With assistance from Duck, we are able to relax and establish our trust when we sense truth from others.

SHAMAN'S INTENTION: *HELP ME TO LET THE JUDGMENT OF OTHERS ROLL OFF MY BACK*

EAGLE

TRUTH **VISION** **INTELLIGENCE**

"The eye is the lens to the world. With a clear focus, we can magnify potential and opportunity."
—Eagle

Eagle has existed for at least a million years. It is an aerial predator with a wingspan of up to eight and a half feet. Its sharp eyesight gives it the ability to spot prey on the ground from a mile away. A calculated hunter, its accuracy and timing are its most important skills. Eagle flies at seemingly impossible heights and will plummet to earth at speeds of 150–200 miles per hour. It covers great distances while hunting, traveling up to 500 miles per day.

When Eagle seeks a mate, both male and female engage in dramatic courtship rituals, clasping talons and falling in a death spiral until the last moment when they break apart. This is a symbol of the level of trust the pair has in each other. Once bonded, the mates build a nest together. Eagle is monogamous and dedicated to its family. It often uses the same nest year after year.

The ancient Egyptians considered Eagle a wise man because it flew high in the atmosphere, close to the light of the Sun. To them, it represented Amun-Ra, their Sun god and most important deity. They believed Eagle possessed a supreme intelligence. In ancient Greece, it was said that Zeus changed his form to Eagle to control thunder and lightning. On another continent, the Native Americans also traditionally see Eagle as an emblem of the Great Spirit, a symbol of power and vision. The Pueblo, for instance, believe it holds the energy of the Sun, recognizing that Eagle flies through the spiritual realms as well as the physical realm and possesses the gift of perception.

A Power Animal with great courage, Eagle brings us wisdom from Great Spirit and is the carrier of our prayers. The feathers of

EAGLE

TRUTH | VISION | INTELLIGENCE

THE ANCIENT EGYPTIANS CONSIDERED EAGLE A WISE MAN BECAUSE IT FLEW HIGH IN THE ATMOSPHERE, CLOSE TO THE LIGHT OF THE SUN.

POWERS OF EAGLE

Call in Eagle for:

- Restoring balance between nature and the spirit world.
- Strength to achieve the fulfillment of your promises to others.
- Tact and skillfulness in relationships or negotiations.

AWARENESS FROM EAGLE

If Eagle comes into your life:

- Ask: "What have I missed seeing because I was closed to possibilities?"
- You may need to destroy anything keeping you from flying into higher realms of consciousness.
- Embrace your greatness and soar through life with confidence.

Energy Center: Solar plexus

Mineral: Citrine

Element: Air

Magic & Mystery:

- According to legend, God told the Aztecs to settle in the place where they found Eagle sitting on a cactus. Today that place is known as Mexico City.
- Eagle plays a big role in the Sundance of the Plains Indians. Dancers carry fans made of Eagle feathers and blow into whistles made from Eagle wing bones, the body part closest to Eagle's heart. The sound represents its voice.

Bald Eagle or Golden Eagle play a sacred role in traditional Native American ceremony and healing practices. Eagle bones, for instance, are carved into ceremonial whistles and flutes. Holding an Eagle feather in your hand during a prayer means that you are telling the truth.

The Pueblo know Eagle as one of the guardians of the six directions: the upward direction of spirituality. The feathers of Golden Eagle were worn in the traditional headdresses of warriors. Northwestern tribes would spread its down on the ground at their ceremonies as a sign of hospitality. Hunting or killing an Eagle was never even considered, as its medicine was too profound. It was believed that anyone who ate the meat of Eagle would turn into a monster. Hopi shamans captured young Eagles and hand raised them, and then released them as adults to travel to and from the spirit realm on their behalf.

An important ancient prophecy foretold that our era will be the time of cleansing the wounds of colonialism in the Americas; the time when Eagle, which represents the North and is a masculine energy associated with developments like technology, will reunite with Condor, which represents the South and is a feminine energy associated with Mother Earth. When the foretold reunion occurs, there will be a shift into a higher state of consciousness and an awakening for the entire planet.

Eagle has a higher perspective of the world and can help establish a connection for the giving and receiving of our prayers. This Bird has a vision necessary to see beyond the simple view. As a master of the Upper World, it can help free us from our limitations and open the doors of discovery. Eagle encourages us to stop labeling everything we see, a habit that creates separation. Not everything needs to be defined as good or bad; things just are what they are. Eagle can help us transcend duality by teaching us to drop into the heart. The energy there, which is compassion, knows no separation. Eagle encourages us to engage in self-inquiry. Unexamined beliefs can clip our wings, impeding our ability to perceive truth. Eagle encourages us to ask ourselves the big questions, so we may arrive at enlightened conclusions about our being.

SHAMAN'S INTENTION: *TEACH ME TO MASTER HIGHER CONSCIOUSNESS AND OVERCOME SEPARATION*

EARTHWORM

CONSERVATION | **NOURISHMENT** | **REGENERATION**

"Into the belly of the Mother I go, gently bringing balance and nutrients to all beings."
—Earthworm

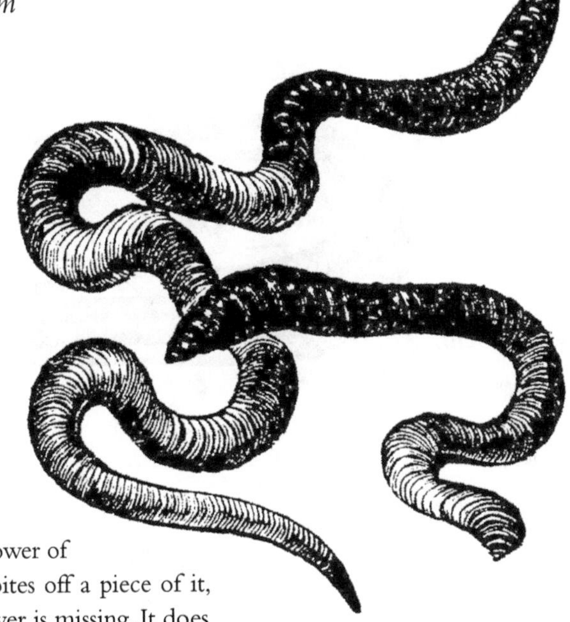

There are around 6,000 species of Earthworm worldwide. Most are only a few inches long, yet some can grow twenty-two feet long. Earthworm is hermaphroditic, meaning it has both female and male reproductive organs. It has no lungs; instead, it breathes through its skin. It has five hearts.

Earthworm spends most of its life underground and rarely goes to the surface. It cannot see light but will sense its presence. When it gets near the surface, sensors in its head will notice the presence of sunlight so that it can retreat. After an hour, light can paralyze Earthworm, so it tries to spend 100 percent of its time buried in the soil. It is so sensitive that even the dirt covering it must be dark for its survival. Earthworm is also very sensitive to pollution. If Earthworm is not present in a soil sample, this can be a sign of chemical changes making the soil unhealthy. In addition, Earthworm senses vibrations.

Earthworm is welcomed by farmers and gardeners around the world, since all plants, bushes, and trees benefit from its activity. Aristotle called Earthworm the "intestines of the Earth." In one acre of soil, a million Earthworms will be busily eating ten tons of decaying plant and animal matter per year and transforming it into fertile, oxygenated Earth. Earthworm ingests food through its mouth; then its body breaks it up and its droppings become nutrient-rich soil. Its ability to digest is a sterling example of the perfection of transforming everything we encounter into its highest good for all. The Pharaoh, Cleopatra of Egypt, revered Earthworm for its capabilities and she declared it sacred and critical to the fertility of the soil in the Nile River Valley. Any removal of Earthworm was punishable by death.

Earthworm has the power of regeneration. If a Bird bites off a piece of it, it will grow back whatever is missing. It does not carry diseases or parasites; it has a biological perfection about it, making it symbolic of the proper way to achieve balance on Earth and an emblem of the need for sensitivity to natural forces. In both Ayurvedic and Chinese medicine, Earthworm pastes and powders have been used as cures for various ailments for centuries.

Charles Darwin felt Earthworm was the most important and noblest member of the animal kingdom because of the role it plays in the ecosystem. Spiritually, Earthworm reminds us that we can always give back—even in small ways. Through our everyday activities, we are capable of contributing to causes greater than ourselves.

Earthworm's mastery of the darkness is a message for us to learn to trust. Earthworm does not avoid anything in its path. It transforms and mulches its obstacles as it goes, which shows us how to neutralize our problems. Earthworm teaches us that sometimes we need to regenerate our resources before we can go into the light.

POWERS OF EARTHWORM

Call in Earthworm for:

- Improved health by establishing a more balanced environment.
- Better awareness of recycling.
- A nurturing work environment.

AWARENESS FROM EARTHWORM

If Earthworm comes into your life:

- It is time to check if your digestive system is working properly.
- Be sure to play your part in the balance of giving and receiving on the planet.
- Perhaps you are too wasteful.

Energy Center: Root

Mineral: Fire agate

Element: Earth

Magic & Mystery: Legends from many cultures say that humans were created from Earthworm.

SHAMAN'S INTENTION: *SUPPORT MY ABILITY TO TRANSFORM ALL THAT DOES NOT SERVE ME AND OTHERS*

EEL

DISGUISE | **THE UNKNOWN** | **CONDUCTIVITY**

"There is light within all of us that is our mystical gift to the world. It is important to set an intention to share our light with others."—Eel

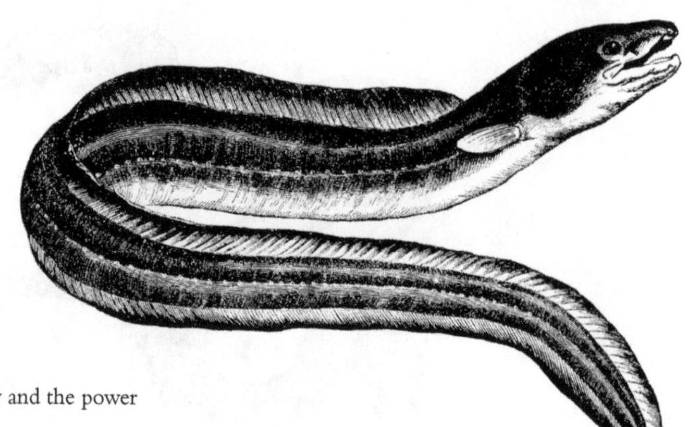

POWER OF EEL

Call in Eel for:

- Mastering energy and the power of healing.
- Transformation of anything needed to venture into the spirit world.
- Help to become invisible to malicious forces around you.

AWARENESS FROM EEL

If Eel comes into your life:

- It is a message that your kundalini (life force) is awakening.
- Retreat for a while until you have integrated new energy.
- Be observant. Something hidden may soon be revealed to you.

Energy Center: Third eye

Mineral: Blue halite

Element: Water

Magic & Mystery:

- There has been research on using Eel as shock therapy in order to block the debilitating effects of migraine headaches in humans with some success.
- Eel was a popular dish among ancient Romans, but many also kept it as a pet. Antonia, the daughter of Marc Anthony, is said to have put earrings on the fins of her favorite Eel.

Eel is an incredible fish that, if necessary, will travel over 4,000 miles to reach its spawning grounds in the ocean—a journey that takes seven months. When Eel reproduces it always travels to the saltwater of oceans and seas, whether it is a freshwater or an ocean-dwelling Eel. There are several stages in its life cycle. The larval Eel is translucent and leaf like. After growing a little, it migrates to coastal areas and enters estuaries. Some species of Eel then swim upstream to freshwater rivers. As Eel takes on pigment, it is known as an Elver. It is hardy and can travel short distances over moist ground or sand and wriggle through grasses so that it may eventually be found even in land locked lakes. Eel is a bottom dweller, spotted mostly in the muddy or sandy floor of the waters where it lives. It has an amazing sense of smell that it relies on to hunt for prey.

Eel isolates itself during the day and goes out at night to hunt. It has such powerful jaws and sharp teeth that it can overpower much larger creatures if it must. It also can swim very fast. In Japan, where Eel is a popular food, it is said that all who consume it gain strength.

In the spiritual world, Eel is a known shapeshifter, an animal that can change into human form and back again. Celtic legends have many mentions of Eel growing legs and walking on land before returning, as a kind of Snake, to the ocean.

The ancient Egyptians associated Eel with lightning. In ancient Rome, the bites of Eel were used to numb the feet of people suffering from gout. The Hawaiians, whose name for Eel is Puhi, recognize it as a spirit being related to our ancestors. The Samoans say Eel was killed and planted in the soil and a great coconut tree grew from it because, when cutting into a coconut, there are three round marks that look like the face of Eel. When one of these holes is pierced to drink the water, it is said you are kissing Eel.

Electric Eel can manipulate energy, making it a good Power Animal for healers. It is brilliant at using its energy for both defense and attack. It can help us harness the bioelectrical force of kundalini that spins through our bodies to create an opening to the spirit world. Eel can be passive, waiting and waiting while fine-tuning its power. In this experience, it silently removes fear and becomes increasingly open to the unknown. A patient observer, it nonetheless will jump at any chance to get what it wants. Eel helps the shamans who work with it to shed any burdens so they can embody a more illuminated presence.

SHAMAN'S INTENTION: *HELP ME TO UNDERSTAND MY ENERGETIC BODY*

ELEPHANT

INTELLIGENCE | **COURAGE** | **HARMONY**

"Our dramatic footsteps are to alert you to the role of the human in salvation of all things. Your human support of our existence is much needed at this time."—Elephant

Living in Central and West Africa, the African Elephant is the largest of all land mammals. The largest on record was an adult male that weighed 24,000 pounds. The Asian Elephant, which is a bit smaller, but still very large, inhabits Nepal, India, and Southeast Asia. With massive temporal lobes Elephant has the largest brain of any land mammal, giving it excellent memory. This capacity enables it to locate watering holes and remember places it can find food. It also recognizes members of its herd even decades after it last saw them. Elephant can recognize itself in a mirror, a reminder of the importance of looking for our reflection in the world around us.

A highly social and emotional creature, Elephant is known to cry, play, and laugh. It will warmly welcome a friend that has returned. The herd will gather around a deceased member and make efforts to bury it with soil and branches. If it senses its own impending death, Elephant will travel to a specific area to end its life. Elephant is loyal and will defend those it loves with determination. It relies on its feet to register subsonic sounds in the ground made by the vibration of others of its kind walking.

Elephant is admired around the world for its size, strength, and quiet wisdom. The behavior of this gentle giant is honorable and exemplifies the good in all beings. Buddhists believe every Elephant is an incarnation of a future Buddha.

Elephant has mastery of social communication and expression through writing. The number sixteen is associated with the fifth (throat) chakra, *Vishuddha* in Sanskrit, which is sometimes depicted as a white Elephant representing strength and prosperity. In one Indian origin myth Elephant was born from the merger of sixteen elephants that hatched from golden

eggs. Hindus lore says that Indra, the god of thunder and rain, rides on the back of a white Elephant—a cloud. Elephant has the power to bring rain and is a guardian of the four sacred directions. It was thought that when there was an earthquake Elephant had grown tired. The Elephant-headed Hindu god, Ganesh, is known as the bringer of good luck, a protector, and a remover of obstacles.

In Asia, Elephant is recognized as a cosmic being who carries the world on its back. One of the longest-lived animals on the planet, it seems to defy the mystery of death. Because of its great memory and capacity to age, it is a supportive Power Animal for those who are suffering from any kind of dementia or degenerative diseases of the brain. Elephant brings us the message to accept others no matter where they are on their own journey. We must stay in your own lanes, as our life paths are personal. Elephant can be helpful to venture into past lives to uncover repressed memories that need to be released. As the protector of our memories, Elephant helps us to soften toward those that cause us pain, still knowing that all memories hold valuable lessons. Elephant encourages us to turn pain into wisdom and teach others to do the same. Don't forget, each experience has an unpredictable purpose.

POWERS OF ELEPHANT

Call in Elephant for:

- A deep and enduring sense of family.
- Sensitivity to others.
- Deep grounding.

AWARENESS FROM ELEPHANT

If Elephant comes into your life:

- Trust your natural intelligence to give you the answers you seek.
- You need to wrap your head around your relationships.
- Embrace your importance; you deserve to flourish on a grand scale.

Energy Center: Heart

Mineral: African jade

Element: Earth

Magic & Mystery:

- In Thailand, White Elephant is believed to carry the soul of a dead person.
- There are temples in southern India where elephants are trained to kneel and worship.
- In Catania, Sicily, there once lived a famous sorcerer named Heliodorus. It was said that he could transform into Elephant. In the present-day city's central square, there is a fountain with an Elephant sculpture that is a reminder of him.

SHAMAN'S INTENTION: *TEACH ME THE GRACE OF RECEIVING AND THE POWER OF APPRECIATION*

ELK

COMPOSURE **PASSION** **PROTECTION**

"There lies, beyond the Earth, a place of great wisdom and song—be willing to have your soul guide you on a ride into its mystery."—Elk

POWERS OF ELK

Call in Elk for:

- Bringing harmony to your life and relationships.
- Sexual potency combined with intimacy.
- Renewal and rebirth.

AWARENESS FROM ELK

If Elk comes into your life:

- You may be acting weak, which could make you vulnerable to predators.
- You can trust the Universe.
- Use music to increase the opportunity for connection to the spirit worlds.

Energy Center: Solar plexus

Mineral: Aragonite

Element: Earth

Magic & Mystery:

- For a young Plains Indian female, having a large collection of Elk teeth sewn onto a dress was a symbol of wealth; it demonstrated the success of the girl's father as a hunter.
- The Lakota would honor a newborn child with an Elk tooth as a blessing for a long life.

Elk is a type of Deer. Found worldwide, its largest population is in North America. It lives in diverse environments—desert valleys, forests, and alpine meadows. Highly social, Elk lives in same-sex herds of ten to twenty. Herd size increases when it migrates to higher ground in the spring after the snow.

The Plains Indians revered the Bull Elk for his virility when mating with a Cow herd. Elk's predators, Bear and Wolf, show Bull great respect when they approach it, as he is a fierce fighter and protector of his herd. Elk often communicates subtly with its feet since its knuckles crack with a popping sound when it walks. This lets it know when another of its kind is around. To us Elk is like a ghost in the forest, as it can vanish into the greenery.

Male Elk is a powerful symbol of masculinity and virility. During mating season in the fall, the Bull struts around majestically to display his antlers, which are shed and regrown annually. For this reason, in the Celtic tradition of the British Isles, Elk was associated with the birch tree, which sheds its bark. Both tree and animal were symbols of new beginnings and of the number one. Elk produces up to twenty-five pounds of velvet (soft, fuzzy skin) on its antlers, which grow extremely fast—up to an inch per day. The size of the antlers depends on Elk's exposure to the Sun, as solar rays promote the release of testosterone, which spurs antler growth. Female Elk has no antlers.

If you see Elk in a dream, you are bestowed with a special medicine. In the Lakota Sioux tradition, those with visions of Elk are known as Elk dreamers. As shamans, they are of great importance to the tribe because they are able to neutralize negative spirits and have innate wisdom about matters of the heart, relationships, and falling in love. The Lakota say Elk dreamers invented the flute, whose sound can be used by men to attract women.

Elk communication is intricate, varied, and full of emotion. It brings us the message of new beginnings and rainbows of possibility. Working with Elk you will need to get ready for renewal. Elk is able to hear sounds and vibrations from the Upper World through its antlers. Elk can help you align your inner chord so that it is always in harmony with a higher vibration and more in tune with life. When you are attuned, you can receive clear messages from spirits.

SHAMAN'S INTENTION: *TEACH ME COMPOSURE AND CONSISTENCY SO THAT I CAN BECOME A SOURCE OF STABILITY FOR OTHERS*

EMU

MASCULINITY | **MOVEMENT** | **MINERALS**

"Embrace water, the giver of life. Embrace sky, the energy of existence. Embrace Earth, the foundation. Embrace yourself in the change and the movement of it all."—Emu

Emu is a large, flightless Bird that is native to Australia and New Guinea. Nomadic, Emu lives in woodlands, scrublands, grasslands, and forests. Reaching roughly six feet in height, it can run up to 30 miles per hour on its long, strong legs. It eats berries, flowers, grass, and insects, and travels daily to forage for edibles. Emu has two eyelids, one for blinking to keep the eyeball moist and the other to protect its eyes from dirt and dust. It has excellent eyesight and hearing, which helps it protect itself from threats. There are three toes on each of Emu's feet—one of which has a long talon that can be used for fighting. Emu loves to swim and play in the water.

Emu is not known for fidelity. The female Emu lay her eggs in many different nests. The male incubates the eggs for fifty-five days, during which time he does not eat and often loses up to 30 percent of his body weight. After the chicks are born, he raises the young for almost two years.

Aboriginals named a major constellation after Emu, the head of which is a dark Nebula near the Southern Cross. Depending on its position in the night sky, the people would determine the ideal time to go and collect Emu eggs. Emu was an important animal in their culture, inspiring dances and creation stories. Its feathers are used for Aboriginal ceremonies to the present day.

Emu is such a durable animal that shamans like to ride on its back to journey to the Upper and Lower Worlds. The speed of Emu makes it energy efficient and able to move quickly to gather the messages they seek. Ride Emu to the Lower World where you can align with the powers of crystals in the mineral kingdom. The sound of Emu's call is reminiscent of drumming. It easily senses frequencies and can be helpful in bringing the right energy to any journey you take. Emu is always alert and ready to go.

There is an ancient expression "As above, so below," which means that whatever happens on one level of reality happens everywhere. Working with Emu as a Power Animal, you will learn to embrace the constancy of change: the change of seasons and of life on Earth. Every new cycle can bring you greater knowledge of your place on the planet and in the Universe. Emu is a master of relationships and can help you to release the pain and regrets of unfulfilled relationships, like a separation or a divorce.

POWERS OF EMU

Call in Emu for:

- Quick reactions and willingness to go the distance.
- Guidance related to astrology.
- Help to properly nurture your children.

AWARENESS FROM EMU

If Emu comes into your life:

- It is time to journey into the unknown for answers.
- You may need to adapt to a different living situation.
- Ground yourself.

Energy Center: Root

Mineral: Garnet

Element: Earth

Magic & Mystery:

- Emu appears on Australia's coat of arms alongside Red Kangaroo.
- Emu is featured on the fifty-cent coin of Australian currency.

SHAMAN'S INTENTION: *SUPPORT MY MASTERY OF JOURNEYING TO THE UPPER AND LOWER WORLDS*

FALCON

PATIENCE | INDEPENDENCE | VISION

"Relationships must be built on a sacred foundation of trust and respect."
—Falcon

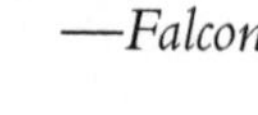

POWERS OF FALCON

Call in Falcon for:

- Calmness and guidance on high strategy.
- Help in making decisions.
- Highly reliable intuition.

AWARENESS FROM FALCON

If Falcon comes into your life:

- It is time to see the big picture; you may be too focused on little things.
- Mend friendships for the sake of harmony.
- Consider if there is something you do not see or continue to deny.

Energy Center: Sacrum

Mineral: Tiger's eye

Element: Fire

Magic & Mystery:

- In fourteen-century England, the punishment for harming Falcon was strict; destroying its eggs earned violators a year in prison. These laws were the beginning of animal conservation.
- The Moche of Peru (100–700 C.E.) revered Falcon. Nobles would dress their babies in its brown-speckled feathers.

Falcon is a bird-eating raptor that has been on the planet for 24 million years and has adapted to life in nearly all types of habitat. It is strong, agile, and uses great precision when hunting. Its incredible speed when it swiftly swoops down upon a target with its sharp talons is reminiscent of a lightning strike. Falcon's vision is eight times sharper than ours. Falcon can spot its prey either in the air or on the ground from as far as two miles away as it soars with wings outstretched scanning the landscape. It has a second eyelid that is partially translucent, allowing Falcon to see through it. It travels over migratory routes stretching up to 18,000 miles long.

The ancient Egyptians depicted their Sun god Horus as possessing the head of Falcon and viewed it as regal because this Bird flies so high above the Earth. They associated it with the rising Sun in the East. They considered it the king of the Bird kingdom. Falcon is associated with the element of fire and commands attention because of its agility and precision when on the hunt.

The Mississippi tribe believed that Falcon lived in the Upper World. They held dances and ceremonies to merge with the power of Falcon to help them be victorious in battle, overpowering their enemies with the supremacy and intimidation displayed by this majestic bird.

As a Power Animal Falcon is a wisdom keeper, a guardian and companion to those who are clairvoyant and able to see the truth and perceive dimensions beyond ordinary reality. Knowing no boundaries, it is a spiritual messenger for the entire planet. Not only is Falcon a great seer, it is a master of the winds. Symbolically, its presence in the sky reminds us that the greatest view is from "above," the perspective of cosmic consciousness. Falcon shares that we can see clearly after the fear is gone. Sometimes we can benefit from waiting for a situation to unfold instead of insisting on an outcome. Falcon thrives in the world of blue skies and sunshine and so should we. Falcon will break the barriers of assumptions to get to a sense of relief and open you to a different world through a change of perception. Falcon is streamlined, slipping through the air with little resistance. This power and speed happen without any doubt, something we too can learn when diving into what we are passionate about. Doubt kills the imagination. If we question our ability for greatness, it shackles us in mediocrity. When Falcon shows up with the purity of confidence, knowing it will be successful, it teaches us to be aligned with our purpose and to be forthcoming and focused on the goal.

SHAMAN'S INTENTION: *TEACH ME TO MASTER MY FEARS AND TRAVEL WITH STEALTH TO FIND WHATEVER IS NEEDED IN MY LIFE*

FIREFLY

ILLUMINATION **ATTRACTION** **ENERGY**

"Allow the light to flow within you and shine upon you and be all that you are."
—Firefly

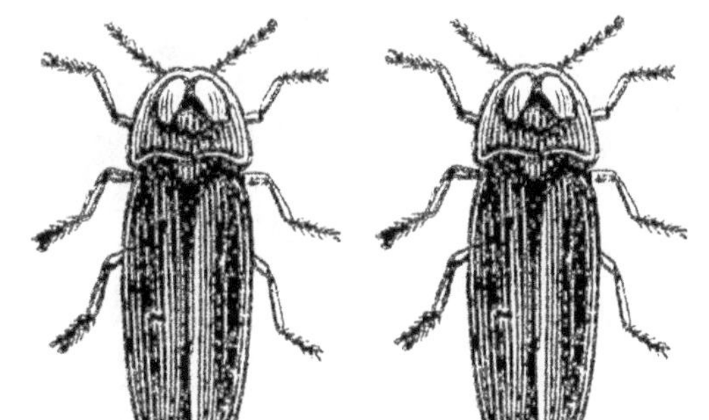
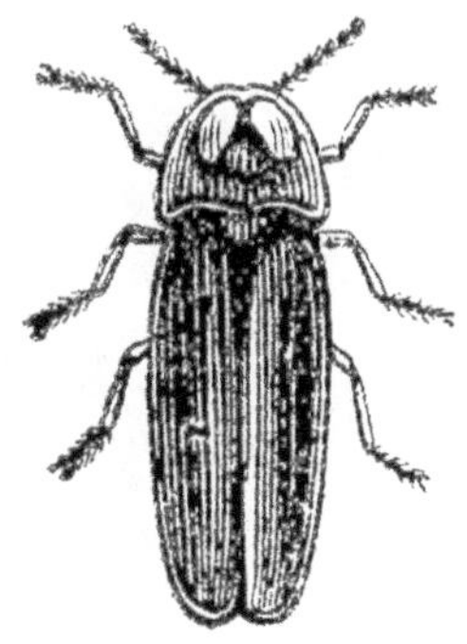
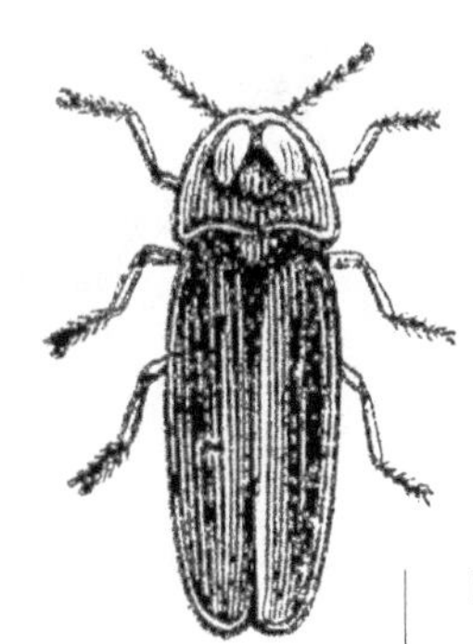

Firefly thrives in warm, humid climates. In more temperate climates, it emerges only during the summer. Firefly lives near bodies of water because it requires moisture both to survive and to ensure an abundant food source for its larvae. Firefly eats little and is a good custodian of its environment, never taking more than it needs and using light energy with great efficiency.

Firefly is a winged member of the Beetle family. It uses a magical bioluminescence during twilight to attract a mate or find prey. The male Firefly searches for its female partner by the color emitted. There are over 2,000 species of Firefly and some don't have the ability to light up. Among those that do, each emits an exclusive tint of blue, green, orange, or yellow. Some species of Firefly flash once, others flash up to nine times—and some shake their abdomens to create a twinkling effect.

In stories from Japanese folklore, Firefly is associated with children who, using their innate wisdom, catch them to make lanterns to light their way. The ancient Mayans depicted Firefly on their vases, saying it was a metaphor for a star. The compound that helps Firefly light up is *luciferin*, which comes from the same Latin root as the name of the "fallen angel," Lucifer. *Lucifer* means "light bearing."

If you find Firefly in the south of your house, Feng shui practitioners say you will be prosperous. A traditional belief of the Penobscot people of Maine and Canada is that Firefly is a bringer of salmon. Some cultures see each Firefly as carrying the consciousness of a soul who has left its light here on Earth. Since Firefly's lifespan is short, it represents those whose lives have been cut short by death.

Like Venus, the morning star that appears in the East before sunrise, Firefly, as a Power Animal, sheds light on the spiritual realms so that we can move from the darkness of ignorance to seeing the bright light of love in the world. Firefly encourages us to honor a state of quiet presence so that we may avoid the often-intrusive nature of the mind. Firefly is nature's lightworker, teaching us to heighten the vibration of our energy.

The message Firefly emphasizes is to keep our inner light bright enough to ensure that we attract positive people into our lives, especially mates. It reminds us that although life's journey may seem random, in truth it is a well calculated path for those who are in sync with the natural flow of things. Firefly tells us of the power of manifestation and the responsibility that we have to keep our vibrations high so that abundance and love can flow into our lives.

POWERS OF FIREFLY

Call in Firefly for:

- Confidence to attract others to you with your authentic light.
- Willingness to go into the darkness with no fear.
- Transformation of your soul from dark to light.

AWARENESS FROM FIREFLY

If Firefly comes into your life:

- You may be attracting the wrong people into your life because of negativity.
- It is time to shed light on an issue that has been obscured.
- Lighten up!

Energy Center: Sacrum

Mineral: Rainbow mayanite

Element: Air

Magic & Mystery:

- Firefly can hibernate for several years.
- According to Chinese folklore, Firefly was created from burning grass.
- In only two places in the world—Southeast Asia and the Smoky Mountains of North America—Firefly syncs its flashing with its friends so that they all light up at the same time all night long.

SHAMAN'S INTENTION: *TEACH ME TO USE THE POWER OF ATTRACTION*

FLEA

ACROBATICS | **PERSISTENCE** | **MOVEMENT**

"When your life becomes too much about survival the results can be catastrophic."
–Flea

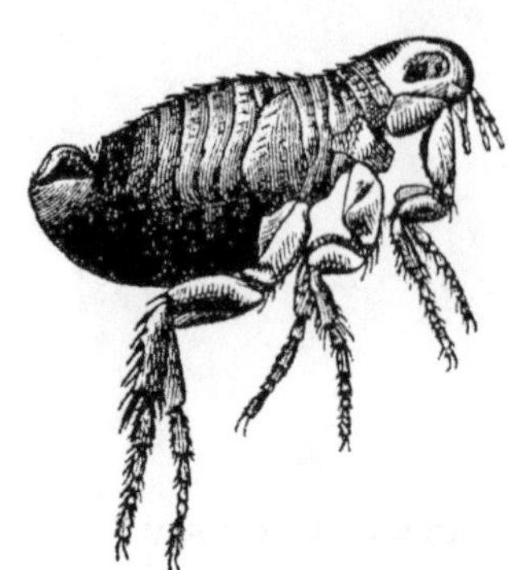
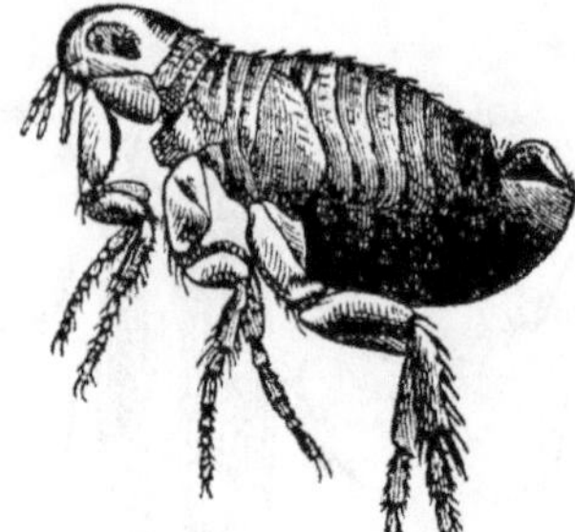
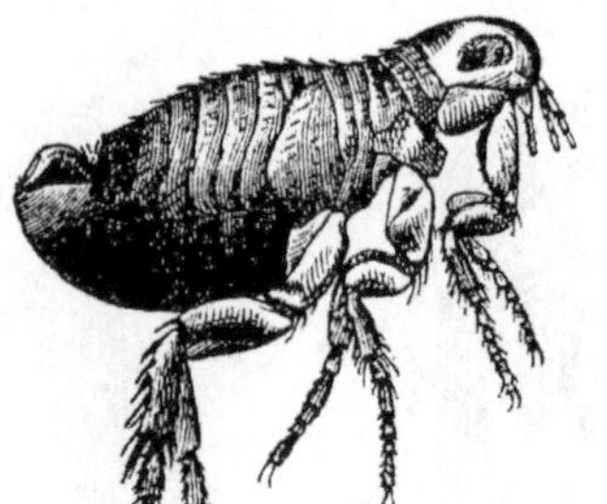
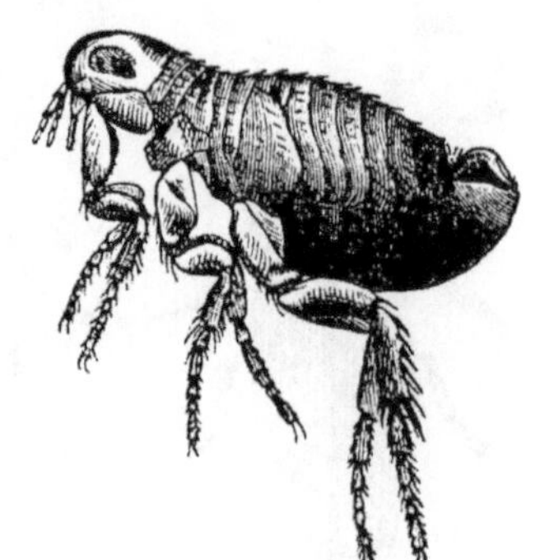

POWERS OF FLEA

Call in Flea for:

- Help to live anywhere, no matter the environmental conditions.
- The ability to slip out of a tight spot.
- Success as a performer, and to enhance your ability to entertain.

AWARENESS FROM FLEA

If Flea comes into your life:

- You need to recognize the amazing you; give yourself a hug.
- Embrace learning so that you may perform at the optimum level.
- Do not take more than your fair share from a partnership.

Energy Center: Solar plexus

Mineral: Tektite

Element: Fire

Magic & Mystery:

- In the Greek play *Prometheus Bound*, the goddess Hera changes the maiden Io into Cow for having an affair with her husband, Zeus. To then rid herself of Io, Hera asks Flea to drive Io crazy.
- The largest scientific collection of fleas is in the Natural History Museum in London, England.

Over 2,500 species of Flea have been identified by entomologists and it is assumed that there are many more. Flea has been around for 250 million years. From fossil records, we know that in the age of dinosaurs its body was gigantic compared to that of the contemporary Flea. We cannot hide from Flea. It is found on every island and continent, even Antarctica.

Flea is a jumper; it can jump 30,000 times in a row within seconds. If it was human, its power-to-height ratio and speed would enable it to jump over the Eiffel Tower. It has a remarkable rate of acceleration speed that's fifty times greater to a rocket taking off. Flea can lift objects 150 times heavier than its own body weight. Flea teeth are sharp, and it can extract blood after biting its host animal. The body of Flea can be compressed, so it is difficult to kill and very resistant to scratching. Flea has a multistage life cycle. The female first lays her eggs on the body of the host. Within ten days, these eggs hatch into larvae. These tiny worms spin silk threads around themselves to create a pupae. They then undergo metamorphosis (like Butterfly) and hatch as Flea.

In Asian folklore there are tales of Monkey shapeshifters that adopt the form of Flea to escape demons or elude human detection.

In his defense argument, in Plato's *Apology,* the philosopher Socrates compared himself to Flea, saying he was visiting the ears of the ancient Athenians trying to coax them out of complacency so that they would stand up for truth and justice. If you feel victimized or powerless, let Flea inspire you to see that you do have influence, agility, a capacity for self-preservation, and the ability to project yourself in the world.

Flea emphasizes the importance of not overreacting and jumping into the emotions of everything you see and hear. Temper your reactions to the external world by finding inner stillness. This will release you from any chaos you perceive around you. Take on no problems that are not yours alone to manage; feeling responsible for all things is a burden so weighty that it can keep you from experiencing joy. Not everyone holds common beliefs, so when more than one person's consciousness is involved in achieving a purpose, all partners' opinions should be considered for greater outcomes. Be aware of the small voice inside you that reminds you to love yourself, accept your imperfections, and release self-doubt. Flea teaches that you can use movement to activate your body's inner sensory potential and open to the awareness of your essence inhabiting this earthly temple.

SHAMAN'S INTENTION: *HELP ME TO EMBRACE THE IDEA THAT EVERYTHING, NO MATTER HOW SMALL, HAS SIGNIFICANCE*

FLY

PERSISTENCE | **QUICKNESS** | **CHANGE**

"In the death of something there is change coming. Open a multitude of lenses to the world to see how, with change, positive things are coming your way."—Fly

Fly has 4,000 lenses in its eye, giving it a 360-degree range of vision. It can beat its wings up to 200 times per second, so, although it has a tiny brain, it is excellent at avoiding flyswatters. When Fly sees a threat coming, it can make a millisecond decision to leap back and avoid being hit or eaten. Because it can withstand even the harshest living conditions and still manage to feed, grow, and breed, Fly is one tough survivor.

Like Flea, Fly has a complex life cycle, which begins in a larval stage as Maggot. Fly will do anything to get to a food source, and it will exploit an ecosystem just as much as it aids in its decay. It is always the first insect to lay its eggs in a decomposing wound, which enables pathologists to determine the exact time of death of a corpse. Fly does not respect personal boundaries. Nor does it care if it is irritating or annoying. Although its presence is rarely welcome, it never gives up trying to feed.

In ancient Egypt a Fly dipped in gold was given as an award for valor and persistence in battle. Horsefly, in particular, was chosen, because it harassed beasts of burden, causing it to be deemed a suitable reward for warriors who drove out invaders. Fly was awarded to women for being exceptional spies—like a *fly on the wall*.

Some cultures believe that when Fly crosses your path, sudden change is coming—perhaps related to a death or a sickness. Fly doesn't have the most positive meaning for Native Americans, as in their legends it is associated with curses, evil, and disease. For a few southwestern tribes, however, Fly is given credit for bringing the first fire to the people.

Fly is often looked down upon because of its association with dirty, rotten things and waste. Yet, nothing is wasted; everything has purpose. Fly does not see anything as garbage, a term that is a misnomer when applied to the eternal cycle of life, death, and rebirth. We should look beneath superficial labels for the true value of everything. Everything is a matter of the value of what is perceived. Lies, gossip, and excuses hold rotten energy that can taint our perceptions. With the multiple lenses of its eyes, Fly can see and notify us of what is unkind or detrimental so that we may purify our environment. By seeing things through many lenses our perceptions become clearer.

POWERS OF FLY

Call in Fly for:

- Persistence, if you are feeling ignored.
- More awareness of the sources of negative energy around you.
- Help to discern the intentions of others.

AWARENESS FROM FLY

If Fly comes into your life:

- Evaluate whether you are being overzealous in trying to get what you want.
- You must no longer resist change; it is coming.
- Stop landing on so many opportunities, as this diminishes your focus.

Energy Center: Third eye

Mineral: Yellow fluorite

Element: Air

Magic & Mystery:

- In the Navajo tradition, Big Fly is an important spiritual being.
- The ancient Egyptian deity Uatchi is associated with Fly. Uatchi is the guardian of the marshes where papyrus, the source of the paper they wrote on, grows.

SHAMAN'S INTENTION: *TAKE ME TO WHERE THERE IS DECEIT SO THAT I MAY WASH MY HANDS OF ITS POWER*

FOX

SKILL | **AGILITY** | **MYSTICISM**

"Through the eyes of the heart the world is a paradise."
—Fox

POWERS OF FOX

Call in Fox for:

- Mastery of the art of appearing and disappearing.
- Protection and help to navigate the mystical realms with skill.
- Brilliance in clearing the footsteps of the past.

AWARENESS FROM FOX

If Fox comes into your life:

- Ask: "Does my personality reflect the real me or am I hiding behind a façade?"
- It is time to visit the mystical world for answers.
- You may be feeling trapped and need a clever way out.

Energy Center: Solar plexus

Mineral: Adamite

Element: Earth

Magic & Mystery:

- In 2011, Jordanian researchers opened a grave in a 16,500-year-old cemetery and found the remains of Fox with a man.
- According to Finnish folklore, Fox made the Northern Lights by running in the snow so fast and hard that its tail swept sparks into the sky.

Fox is a stunning animal with a bushy tail and doglike features. It lives on every continent, both in rural and urban settings. Fox is transient, moving around a lot, especially after the Sun goes down. Its pupils are designed to help it see best in the dim light of the late afternoon. Its hunting tactics are like those of Cat; it stalks and then pounces on its prey. It is extremely fast, running up to forty miles per hour. Fox mostly lives in underground dens that provide it with a cool place to sleep, store food, and give birth to its pups. It digs many exits in its den in case it needs to flee from a predator. It is agile, walking on its toes with grace. Fox is also a climber and sometimes may be found sleeping on rooftops or in trees.

Native Americans traditionally attribute Fox with bringing fire to humankind and see it as a great protector. Some see Fox as a shapeshifter with the ability to take on human form. The Celtic shamans of the British Isles revered Fox, knowing it as the master of the forest and a guide to other dimensions. The Incas admired the cunningness of Fox, viewing it as a reminder that mental prowess can be more powerful than a physical fight. The Incas called Fox "son of Earth," believing it capable of foretelling the future because of its keen perception of faraway footsteps.

The Japanese Fox, Kitsune, can shapeshift into women to seduce men and engage in mischief. Some African lore tells that if you meet Fox while out walking, you won't get home without meeting a witch or a thief.

Fox is a master of blending into its surroundings for protection. This sensitivity warns it long before a threat arises. When hunted, Fox is extremely astute at avoiding capture. A friend to the magical fairy folk, Fox is a trickster that can move through the forest without notice. This Houdini-like characteristic gives it the ability to appear suddenly, seemingly out of thin air. Fox has a playful nature and its confidence allows it to take time for mischief, keeping everyone on their toes as to its next move.

Fox is swift, persistent, and intelligent. Highly intuitive and curious, it knows more about the intricacies of the world than most. When you are curious about the behavior of others, call upon Fox as it is rarely wrong about anyone or anything that comes into its territory. Fox shows us that we must protect our independence. It is vital not to allow others to stifle you with their insistence that you share their beliefs, as this will separate you from your soul.

As a shaman, Fox can guide you to the souls of the deceased and help you retrieve information related to your past lives. With a keen sense of Earth energy, Fox is an excellent Power Animal to call upon for assistance in grounding and stability. Fox is clever and stealthy as it moves through the dimensions. Embrace the big power of Fox as you navigate the intricate pathways of life.

SHAMAN'S INTENTION: *GIVE ME CONFIDENCE THAT ALL THE SKILLS I NEED ARE AT MY DISPOSAL*

FROG

TRANSFORMATION | **PROSPERITY** | **FERTILITY**

"When you hear my call, I am sharing the message of the abundance that is always available to you. Rise from the muddy waters and see the light."—Frog

Evidence shows that Frog roamed the Earth with the dinosaurs. There are over 6,000 species of Frog throughout the world. Each has a unique voice, and many species croak so loudly that they can be heard a mile away. Frog will often burrow into the ground or the mud at the bottom of a pond when cold weather sets in and hibernate until spring. It can go from living completely underwater to hopping around on land and breathing air. Frog also has powerful night vision and is sensitive to movements. Its bulging eyes give it a wide view of what is around it. A great jumper, it can leap over twenty times its body length.

Due to its prolific dispersing of eggs, Frog is related to the energy of fertility. Frog also has a close relationship to the rain, singing its arrival to praise the healing and cleansing that water brings. According to Hinduism, Frog is a deity and croaking is its form of chanting. During a drought, sacred priests perform ritual prayers to Frog asking its assistance in bringing rain. Hindus also credit Frog with projecting the planet into orbit around the Sun, linking it to cosmic wisdom.

Frog can be a useful spiritual guide for parents. When a child is born, the Chinese and Japanese will gift new parents with a ceramic Frog. According to Feng shui principles, placing a frog emblem in the East window of your home will encourage pregnancy and ensure you a happy family.

Frog is associated with the Tree of Life because its biology reflects the mystery of the distinct growth stages of our lives. Frog is a good Power Animal for a child that is reaching a new stage of development or passing a milestone, such as starting in a new school, as Frog can help ease transitions and offers knowledge necessary for understanding the struggle of the transformation of the physical form.

One of the strongest antibiotic and anesthetic substances in the world is derived from a poisonous secretion from the skin of an Amazonian Green Tree Frog. Shamans use this medicine to purge and detoxify the body and clear the chakra system.

Frog is a *bioindicator,* which means its health mirrors the health of the ecosystem that it lives in. Its porous body can signal that the environment is becoming too hazardous for life. In a spiritual way, Frog can also help you to identify toxic people and know when to decide that they should no longer be a part of your life. An accumulation of toxins in your body or toxic elements in your life can cause you a multitude of problems. Know that it is okay to distance yourself from anything that feels detrimental to you. If you are being judged and criticized, it may be time to call it quits and open space for more loving and kinder people to appear. Think kindly of yourself too. Holding on to negative judgments and unconstructive criticism puts an emotional strain on your already fragile self. Frog can help identify and purge anything poisonous inside or around us that is polluting the body or soul. Frog will help you to forgive after cleaning up the damage of offenses so you can start over efficiently. Frog has excellent night vision. Frog can see through the darkness of life's toxins and help you to jump into a pool of joy.

POWERS OF FROG

Call in Frog for:

- The birth of a child, idea, or new way of seeing the world.
- Help to embrace change and transformation.
- Support in speaking up when you want to be heard.

AWARENESS FROM FROG

If Frog comes into your life:

- This is a time for cleansing and healing.
- You are ready to take a big leap into a new venture; luck is on your side.
- It brings you support for fertility and the energy needed to give and receive life.

Energy Center: Sacrum

Mineral: Green jade

Element: Water

Magic & Mystery:

- In Egypt the hieroglyphic image of Tadpole (young Frog) is the symbol for the sacred number 100,000.
- The Japanese word for Frog is *kaeru*, which means "return." People who travel will carry a Frog amulet to ensure they arrive home safely.
- Frog amulets are placed in wallets in Japan to be certain that no money is lost.

SHAMAN'S INTENTION: *ENHANCE MY KNOWLEDGE OF THE CLEARING PROCESS, SO I MAY REMOVE ALL TOXIC THOUGHTS*

GIRAFFE

MODESTY | **INTUITION** | **OBSERVATION**

"Climb up and see the view from here; there is really nothing to fear except the fear of failing."—Giraffe

POWERS OF GIRAFFE

Call in Giraffe for:

- Help to reach for the sky; there are no limits.
- Grace, elegance, and poise; help to be comfortable in high society.
- Uniqueness and to avoid the ordinary.

AWARENESS FROM GIRAFFE

If Giraffe comes into your life:

- Pay better attention to your personal hygiene.
- It is time to take the higher view of problems and see them for what they really are.
- Stick out your neck for something; you may be acting too shy and timid.

Energy Center: Crown

Mineral: Smoky quartz

Element: Earth

Magic & Mystery:

- Zarafa was the first Giraffe to arrive in France as a gift to King Charles X from the Viceroy of Egypt. Her name means "lovely one."
- Egyptian rulers would bring Giraffe by raft up the Nile. On one occasion, one was gifted to Julius Caesar who called it Cameleopard, a reference of a cross between animals of two separate species.
- The Tswana people of Botswana traditionally see one of the constellations as two Giraffes that form a cross.

Giraffe is the tallest animal on Earth. Known for its long neck, long tongue, and tiny horns the male can reach a height of 18 feet and weighs 3,000 pounds and the female can reach a height of 14 feet and weighs 1,500 pounds. Although large, it has a relatively small heart that works very hard to maintain its blood pressure and flow blood to its brain. For vigilance, Giraffe only takes short power naps and altogether sleeps less than two hours a day. But Giraffe is also well-equipped to protect itself with sharp hoofs and powerful legs. Its forceful kick can kill Lion instantly. Every Giraffe has a uniquely spotted coat. The intricate pattern of its coats is like a thumbprint marking its individuality. Giraffe is at home in Africa, where it roams the woodlands and grasslands. Very particular about what it eats, it mainly dines on the leaves of the acacia tree. When we work with Giraffe as a Power Animal, its long neck is a bridge to an elevated view of the human experience. Giraffe has a rare third horn on its head, which represents its access to knowledge from higher dimensions. Using intuition and clairvoyance, Giraffe is sometimes willing to provide us with a glimpse of the future.

Because of Giraffe's uniqueness, it is revered in African culture as a mythical creature. Prehistoric cave paintings featuring Giraffe have been located all over Africa. The Kalahari Bushmen do a famous healing ritual called a Giraffe Dance that was inspired by a vision of Giraffe running in the rain. In an ancient stone painting in South Africa Giraffe is depicted with its head above the clouds and rain falling upon it, a message to have our thoughts transcend the chaos and disorder of the world below. We must move "beyond the clouds."

Giraffe brings us a message of Nirvana, a place of higher existence where our needs and desires vanish and we no longer suffer. By turning our destinies over to the Universe, we can disappear into our connection with a higher power and exist in a state of bliss. Giraffe reminds us to know of this potential and to strive for the creation of heaven on Earth. What this requires is that we manage the mind—it can be an obstacle to inner peace. The size of Giraffe's brain is relatively small in comparison to its body, a telltale sign that it has traded in its previous importance for a more mystical view. Giraffe tells us never to be so intimidated about the future that we fail to dream. If we create a vision without hesitation, it can begin to take form immediately and make its way to us in the present. Visionaries are very welcome in the world, although at times they are misunderstood. Giraffe reminds us to not be discouraged if our views of the world are ahead of our time. The world will one day be ready to embrace our new or unconventional ideas.

SHAMAN'S INTENTION: *SHOW ME THE WORLD FROM A HIGHER PERSPECTIVE*

GOAT

SEXUALITY | **RESOURCEFULNESS** | **ADAPTABILITY**

"Even a life of melancholy can lead to spiritual satisfaction."
—Goat

The domestication of Goat occurred in the Near East 11,000 years ago, at the point in history when humankind moved from hunter-gather to an agriculture-based civilization. Humanity has benefited from Goat's milk, wool, and meat. Its intestines have been used to make surgical sutures and strings for plucked musical instruments. Goat is adaptable and can survive anywhere. Roughly 600 million Goat live on the planet in mountainous areas, deserts, and low grasslands. It has excellent coordination and balance, so it can maneuver in uneven terrains. It has a playful side and enjoys company. Naturally curious, Goat will always look for a way out of an enclosure. It knows to exploit an area of weakness to get what it wants. It loves adventure. Because of Goat's ability to move up and down cliffs with amazing agility, and even climb trees, as a Power Animal it represents balance and sturdiness for when life gets unstable.

Goat has horizontal, slit-shaped pupils that give it the ability to see 340 degrees in its periphery. It knows what is going on around it. An environmental helper, Goat is not discerning about what it eats and will seek out anything that remotely resembles plant matter.

Seven thousand or more years ago, Mesopotamians began to worship Ea/Enki, a horned god who took the form of Goat when he visited the Earth. Goat has been associated with the life force ever since. The ancient mystics of India who discovered yoga circa 600 B.C.E., associated Goat with the crown chakra, which they visualized as a lotus with 1,000 petals, signifying some of our mental and emotional propensities. When our *kundalini*, or life force, travels up the body from the base of the spine and activates this subtle-energy center, we achieve a state of *samadhi*, connection with the supreme force of the Universe. Some sound healers say that the sound SAAAAAAA, reminiscent of the bleating of Goat, may be toned to facilitate this activation.

Goat horns remind shamans of our link to the Sun and Moon. They inspire us to transcend the mind and connect to higher realms for universal wisdom. Goat is also symbolic of love, lust, and passion. It stirs up the desire for physical connection and to satisfy the body's need for seduction. It supports the act of sex and helps us to jump in with passion. Goat brings us feistiness and a sense of living with abandon and encourages us to release ourselves from the bonds of civility to find a deeper part of our sensuality and sexuality. Goat is an animal that lives in the moment and can help us to be mentally present in the physical body.

Goat's message is to remind us that relationships offer us abundant gifts for learning. It tells us of the futility of expectations and to let go of trying to control others. Goat takes its time and does not force things and allows everything to unfold. When you live with expectations and desires there is a natural progression to want to control outcomes, which, for the Goat, do not matter. Goat encourages us to live dangerously and embrace our personal liberation. Life is a great adventure; follow your inner nature and take the quest to learn and grown.

POWERS OF GOAT

Call in Goat for:

- Initiation of your next adventure.
- Escaping confined thinking.
- Stability to make the next move in any venture.

AWARENESS FROM GOAT

If Goat comes into your life:

- Your curiosity may be getting you into trouble; do your best to accept what is.
- You may need to compromise; stubbornness could be impeding forward movement in your life.
- Be more discerning about what you eat and do.

Energy Center: Crown

Mineral: Herkimer diamond

Element: Earth

Magic & Mystery:

- Native American tribes traditionally honor Mountain Goat with special rituals because it gives all of itself to humanity.
- Northwest U.S coastal tribes use Mountain Goat hair to weave a ceremonial Chilkat blanket and other traditional textiles.
- In astrology the goat Capricorn is associated with the winter solstice.

SHAMAN'S INTENTION: *HELP ME TO TRUST MY CROWN CHAKRA AND MY ABILITY TO KNOW*

GOLDFINCH

HAPPINESS **BEAUTY** **HEALTH**

"Every melody carries a message of knowing that somewhere lies more than we can ever imagine."—Goldfinch

POWERS OF GOLDFINCH

Call on Goldfinch for:

- Abundance and the power of attraction.
- Help to carry a beautiful or healing message to the world.
- Support to heal those who are sick in any manner.

AWARENESS FROM GOLDFINCH

If Goldfinch comes into your life:

- You may be craving too much attention.
- Realize you are able to heal yourself; you can stop looking for external solutions.
- Understand the power of your song—your message for the world—as it is time to express what you have inside.

Energy Center: Throat

Mineral: Calcite

Element: Air

Magic & Mystery:

- Goldfinch is acrobatic; it balances on the seed heads of thistles, dandelions, and other plants it eats.
- Goldfinch is known for a special chirp that sounds like the words *po-ta-to-chip.*

Goldfinch is a bright yellow bird that resides mostly in the northern regions of Europe and North America. As winter comes, it moves toward the South. It enjoys open habitats, especially orchards. Its brilliant color comes from the pigments of the plant life it consumes. A strict vegetarian, its diet consists entirely of seeds. When Goldfinch senses an approaching storm, it will overfeed itself to gain weight and increase its chances of survival.

Goldfinch builds its nest in the forks of branches in tall trees. Its nest is often made from soft pieces of the thistle plant which blooms in July and casts off seeds that Goldfinch feeds its offspring. Thistle, like Goldfinch, is showy and attracts many with the beauty of its purple flowers. Traditionally, it is associated with healing, cleansing, longevity, and the fairy realms, as is Goldfinch. Goldfinch can help a shaman communicate with nature spirits. Ask it to help you heal an animal, either wild or domestic.

It is hard to miss the flashy yellow Goldfinch flying across the landscape. Native Americans consider it an omen of happiness and good energy. Its golden feathers are symbolic of prosperity and a life full of opportunities. In an Iroquois story Fox asked some birds to help open his eyelids. The birds carefully helped to pick the pine gum that had glued his eyes shut. Fox then was able to see the Sun again. In gratitude, he grabbed some yellow flowers nearby and pressed the yellow pigment into their dark feathers, transforming the birds into bright yellow messengers of sunshine. Goldfinch's lovely song also reminds us that walking the world with a pleasing "melody"—the vibration emanating from within us—can create a happy field around us and a sense of spiritual freedom. When Goldfinch rarely stops singing, it is using its voice to remind us there are other realms of existence. Purely by looking at its beauty and hearing its song, we can be elevated and made whole. It is a reminder to each of us that we have healing power within us.

Goldfinch is about being expansive and free, creativity and optimist. Surround yourself with the color yellow as it can open you up to change and enthusiasm for taking the next steps to develop your creative side. Yellow can be seen at a greater distance than any other color, so use it in imagery to ensure that your work or your message will be seen. Energize yourself, take interest in the outside world, and be involved with life.

SHAMAN'S INTENTION: *TEACH ME TO BE GENTLE WITH MYSELF AND BRING ME FRESH, INNOVATIVE IDEAS*

GOOSE

COMMUNICATION | **SELF-ASSURANCE** | **FIDELITY**

"Take flight, knowing that you will find what you seek, and your destination awaits you. The knowledge to make the unknown known is waiting there for you."
—Goose

There are thirty species of Goose, some domesticated, some wild. The largest waterfowl, Goose spends most of its time on land. Wild Goose lives in marshes, lakes, and estuaries. Domestic Goose is excellent at controlling weeds in crops and waterways and it does not require much feed since it is adept at scavenging. Goose is a good security guard, as it honks and squawks at strangers and doesn't quiet down until the threat has passed.

When observing Goose, you will see a sense of community. Flying in a V formation increases its range of flight as the birds in the front provide an updraft for the birds behind. Goose rotates positions when tired and turns the leadership over to another bird. Sharing leadership makes the flock very fast, capable of reaching speeds of up to sixty miles per hour.

Goose is representative of the yearly cycle. For Native Americans it is the totem of the winter solstice. In Greek mythology it is a symbol of Boreas, the north wind. The Egyptian Earth god, Geb, was often depicted with Goose on his head. It was said that his wife laid an egg every day—like the Sun, a Goose egg appeared every morning. In China, Goose is considered a messenger that can cross the veil between heaven and Earth. In northern Africa Goose is sacrificed to this day at the beginning of the year as a symbol of the changing seasons.

In ancient Rome Goose was sacred to Juno, the goddess of light, marriage, and childbirth. Goose is an important symbol of marriage and home because it is an excellent parent and very protective of its young. Goose is a loyal partner who will mate for life. Upon the death of its partner, Goose will live the rest of its life alone. It has a keen sense of home and, using its incredible inner navigation system, will always find its way back to the same grounds season after season during its annual migration. If Goose is injured during its migratory flight, another Goose will stay with it wherever it is until it either recuperates or dies. No Goose dies alone.

The ancient Celts displayed the symbol of the Goose in their homes to ensure the safe return of absent family members. They associated Goose with war because of its aggressive nature; and, in fact, Goose remains have been found in the graves of Celtic warriors.

Goose is a trusted partner for traveling to the Upper and Lower Worlds. Like a GPS, it has an internal knowing of its destination. Seeing Goose is a sign that a journey is to begin or that a destination is waiting for you to explore. This can be an actual place or going inside yourself to find greater knowledge of your purpose. Goose is expressive and encourages telling the truth of your life. Perhaps it is time to write a memoir? Many children's stories are based on Goose, highlighting the importance of getting to know our inner child and innocence. Goose flies forward and helps people who nostalgically cling to the past to let go. It does not linger; Goose completes its purpose and moves on.

POWERS OF GOOSE

Call in Goose for:

- Help to honor and cooperate well with others.
- Support of home and family.
- The protection of those around you.

AWARENESS FROM GOOSE

If Goose comes into your life:

- It is time to find a new home where you feel safer and more secure.
- Become aware of what is going on around you or be more protective of your space.
- Open your heart to communicate better with others.

Energy Center: Root

Mineral: Fluorite

Element: Water

Magic & Mystery:

- In Egypt the "great cackler" is a celestial Goose that lays a cosmic egg containing Re, a solar bird that is born and heats the world into creation.
- A Goose egg is a symbol of springtime and renewal.

SHAMAN'S INTENTION: *HELP ME TO UNDERSTAND THAT THINGS CHANGE, AND SUPPORT ME IN KNOWING WHEN TO MOVE ON*

GOPHER

PROFUNDITY **ONENESS** **TRUST**

"Sometimes in the darkness you will find the answers that you seek. Do not fear what you do not see. You may be surprised to encounter the truth."—Gopher

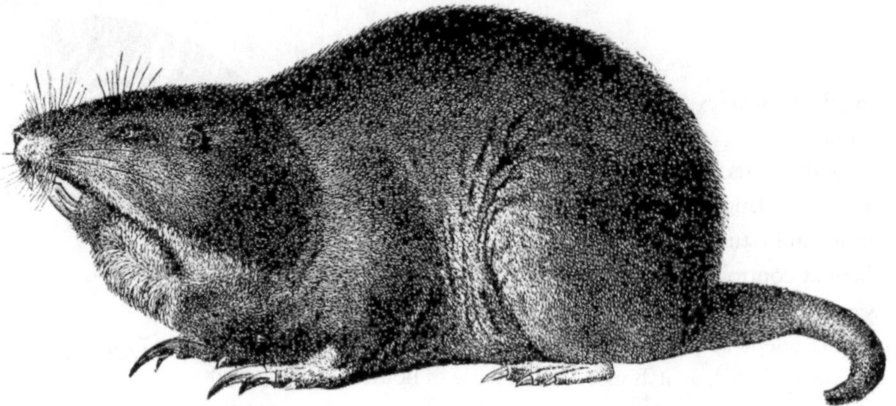

POWERS OF GOPHER

Call in Gopher for:

- Emerging from the darkness with confidence.
- Escaping a situation in which you feel trapped.
- The power to keep on digging for your answers—you will soon find that you are connected to a world of possibilities.

AWARENESS FROM GOPHER

If Gopher comes into your life:

- You may be stuck in the dark or entering a state of decline.
- It is time to separate myth from reality.
- You may be hoarding something you should let go of.

Energy Center: Root

Mineral: Galena

Element: Earth

Magic & Mystery: Gopher is the master of the principle "As above, so below," that was described in the mysterious Emerald Tablet written by Hermes Trismegistus. This is an explanation of our planet being a place of mirrors where what happens on one level of consciousness simultaneously happens in others.

Gopher has been around for 28 million years. Thirty-five species live in the Americas and make their homes in woodlands, prairies, and mountainous areas where there is soft soil. Because of the damage Gopher does to gardens and farmland, it is seen as a pest in these rural areas. Gopher has large cheek pouches that it fills with food and material for nesting, which gives it the name Pocket Gopher. It has big teeth that come in handy when it needs protection from Snake, and it is also very agile, so it can make quick getaways. Gopher lives underground and feeds inside the tunnels it creates by pulling plants down by their roots, much to the dismay of gardeners. An intricate tunnel system connects Gopher to vast areas of land without it needing to pop up and be vulnerable. When it does emerge above ground to forage, it transports food back to its burrow in its cheeks. It is a known hoarder. Gopher has small eyes and poor eyesight. It uses its short, bushy tail to feel around behind it when it walks backward through its tunnels. If you are ever unsure which way to turn, call on Gopher. It will know.

Shamanically, Gopher is a messenger from the Lower World, Because of this, it has often been seen as a symbol of death. The Shoshone and Paiute tribes traditionally regard Gopher as a Power Animal that can either cause illnesses or cure people from them. Gopher lives in family colonies where it thrives on communication and trust. Living underground attunes it to the vibrations and sensations of Mother Earth. For this reason, it is an excellent Power Animal for clairsentient people. Gopher reminds us of going deep to find the realization of self. It then teaches us to "get down to earth" and "be grounded" through the vibration and energy of Mother Earth where we feel safest. Gopher can be called upon to help you merge your frequency with the frequencies of your crystal and mineral collection. Gopher's sensitivity can be helpful anytime you need to identify which crystal is the most appropriate to work with for various purposes. It brings a message to strengthen your protective systems, in your home for instance, but also your personal boundaries. Gopher can teach you how to maintain your inner calm and stability when managing changes that could disrupt your balance.

SHAMAN'S INTENTION: *SHOW ME THE LOWER WORLD AND HELP ME LEARN THE HEALING SECRETS OF PLANTS AND MINERALS*

GORILLA

SELFLESSNESS **ACCOUNTABILITY** **BALANCE**

"If you could see your behavior from our perspective, you would realize your potential to be beyond ordinary."—Gorilla

Gorilla is the world's largest primate. With 98 percent of DNA the same as ours, it is closely related to humans. There are only two species of Gorilla—the Eastern and the Western—with a few additional subspecies, all of which live in the tropical rainforests of Africa. The rarest is the Cross-River Gorilla, of which, sadly, there are only 250 remaining at the time of this writing. Gorilla is full of emotions, including grief and compassion for others. Each has a distinct personality. An herbivore, it helps disperse the seeds of fruit trees whose produce is the mainstay of its diet. Gorilla has the capacity for abstract reasoning and processes information. It has an intricate form of vocal communication that includes over twenty-five distinct sounds. Psychologists have experimented and discovered that Gorilla can be taught sign language. One Gorilla may be differentiated from another by its individual footprint and fingerprints. The silver hair on a male Gorilla's back means he is at full sexual maturity and will take on the role of father to the young that rely on him. He supports their survival in case a youngster's mother dies or leaves the group.

Male Gorilla is bisexual, interacting with both males and females with intimacy. Gorilla is empathic and sensitive, and despite its size, it is shy and timid. Mother Gorilla is patient and, although protective, will allow her young to experience life on their own terms. She is tolerant, playful, affectionate, and supportive but has defined boundaries of discipline.

Some African tribes believe that Gorilla can speak to us in our language, yet refuses to, for fear it will be put to work and made to live among humans. They know Gorilla is intelligent and very affectionate. Members of a band will often embrace and pat one another on the back, demonstrating to us the importance of touch in sharing our feelings.

Hindu folklore rightly portrays Gorilla as compassionate. The

GORILLA

SELFLESSNESS | **ACCOUNTABILITY** | **BALANCE**

THERE ARE ONLY TWO SPECIES OF GORILLA—THE EASTERN AND THE WESTERN—WITH A FEW ADDITIONAL SUBSPECIES, ALL OF WHICH LIVE IN THE TROPICAL RAINFORESTS OF AFRICA.

POWERS OF GORILLA

Call in Gorilla for:

- A sympathetic ear and affection.
- Help with communication and learning sign language.
- Protection of your loved ones.

AWARENESS FROM GORILLA

If Gorilla comes into your life:

- You may need to balance your emotions.
- Reevaluate your behavior and ensure it demonstrates a large measure of compassion.
- Be willing to have enough humility to learn from those around you.

Energy Center: Sacrum

Mineral: Prehnite

Element: Earth

Magic & Mystery:

- Gorilla builds a comfortable nest to sleep, sometimes on the ground and other times in trees.
- The nose print of Gorilla is as unique as a human fingerprint.

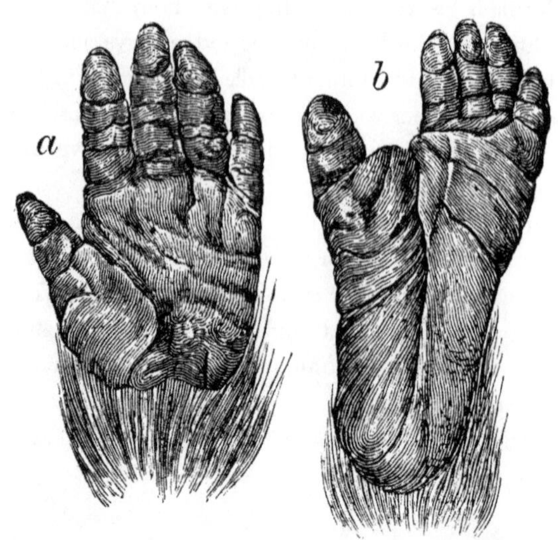

god Hanuman in the legend of the Ramayana is a white ape. Gorilla is powerful yet gentle, a model for the balance of humility and strength and a reminder that caring for ourselves and others makes us better humans. Highly social, Gorilla is always aware of the feelings and needs of its band and understands the dynamics that will ensure every member gets along. It is very loyal and its accountability for its actions keeps it from engaging in selfish acts.

Seeing Gorilla, you cannot escape the wisdom behind the face and the depth of emotion and knowledge of the world. Therein lies a sense that power is only as great as the compassion that lies within us. Balance is the message from Gorilla, who takes it to the level of an art. Gorilla lead a tranquil existence and is not aggressive. Its temper only rises if there are unwelcome intruders into its territory. It does not pound its chest or display violent behavior; rather, it is gentle and calm, which is a lesson in being dignified in our actions and honoring the sensitivities of those we love. Gorilla teaches us that losing our patience is a weakness.

Gorilla has a good memory. If your behavior has upset it, it will never forget. It may run you off the next time you want to approach it. Gorilla does not react well if it is not respected.

Gorilla can teach us conservation of our resources and how to be a sustaining member of the natural world. It takes its nutrition from the plant world yet always leaves enough leaves behind so that the plant can recuperate and provide for it again. It is not a destroyer.

As naturalist Jane Goodall points out: "Chimpanzees, Gorillas, Orangutans have been living for hundreds of thousands of years in their forest, living fantastic lives, never overpopulating, never destroying the forest. In a way, I would say that they have been more successful than us as far as being in harmony with the environment."

SHAMAN'S INTENTION: *HELP ME TO BUILD MY FOUNDATION OF COMPASSION SO I MAY TRULY BE STRONG*

GRASSHOPPER

ABUNDANCE | **CHANGE** | **PROSPERITY**

"There exists a vibration in nature that, if tapped into, will manifest what you dream of and desire."—Grasshopper

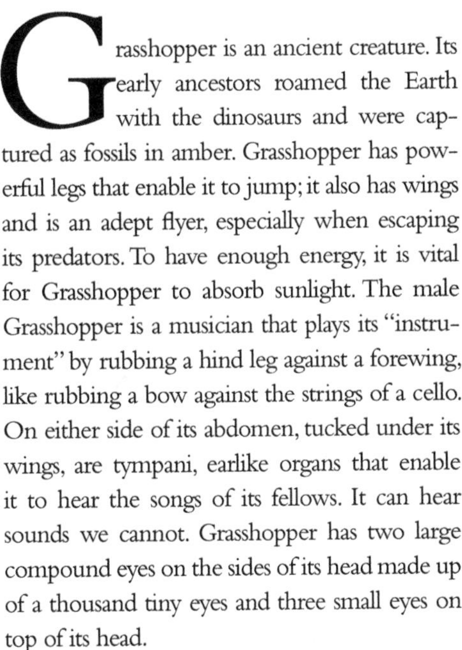

Grasshopper is an ancient creature. Its early ancestors roamed the Earth with the dinosaurs and were captured as fossils in amber. Grasshopper has powerful legs that enable it to jump; it also has wings and is an adept flyer, especially when escaping its predators. To have enough energy, it is vital for Grasshopper to absorb sunlight. The male Grasshopper is a musician that plays its "instrument" by rubbing a hind leg against a forewing, like rubbing a bow against the strings of a cello. On either side of its abdomen, tucked under its wings, are tympani, earlike organs that enable it to hear the songs of its fellows. It can hear sounds we cannot. Grasshopper has two large compound eyes on the sides of its head made up of a thousand tiny eyes and three small eyes on top of its head.

The Chinese, who have great respect for their ancestors, believe Grasshopper is the reincarnated soul of a deceased relation. They also consider it a symbol of prosperity, fertility, happiness, health, luck, and virtue. The ancient Egyptians also viewed Grasshopper as the soul, and many were buried with the dead. The Japanese have a legend that the Moon coaxes its most cherished songs out of Grasshopper. In ancient Athens Grasshopper was considered a status symbol. The people would adorn themselves with hair combs and jewelry that had Grasshopper motifs that represented immortality.

When the ancient Aztecs arrived in the Valley of Mexico (now Mexico City), they named it Grasshopper Hill because it was swarming with mating Grasshoppers. A subsequent onset of rain gave Grasshopper an association with fertility and water. Later, large reservoirs were built solidifying the symbol of Grasshopper as the giver of life. Plates of Grasshopper were eaten to receive prosperity and taken as an offering to the temples at Tenochtitlan. In time, the Aztecs learned that the arrival of Grasshopper can also signify destruction, as swarms of hungry Grasshoppers would also destroy their crops.

Among the Hopi, parents tease misbehaving children by telling them that Grasshopper will bite off their noses. Other Native Americans say that Grasshopper brings good news. When seen on a walk, it is said that joy is coming for that person and the entire community. Grasshopper may be a sign for you that a new direction is necessary for your growth or that the results of taking a risk will fall in your favor. Grasshopper has strong back legs that keep it grounded and also ready to jump into action. It reminds us that sometimes the only way we can move forward is by taking a chance and catapulting ourselves into the unknown to find the right next step.

As a creature of sound, Grasshopper can be an artistic muse for musicians and other creative individuals. Because the male "sings" to locate a mate, Grasshopper is a good Power Animal for a man who wants to attract the right woman into his life.

Connecting to the rhythm of the Universe inspires us to dance in our uniqueness. Each species of Grasshopper has a different song. It reminds us to bring song into our lives, because, when calling Power Animals to ceremony, song is an important tool. Grasshopper is highly perceptive and can be a helpful Power Animal to notice the signs from the Universe and point out strings of synchronicities that add up to big messages from the spirit world. The call of the Grasshopper is known to all.

POWERS OF GRASSHOPPER

Call in Grasshopper for:

- Taking a leap of faith.
- A keen sense of hearing in order to receive the subtle messages of the spirit worlds.
- It may be a time to destroy what links you to the past, clearing the slate to make way for the birth of new ideas to flow.

AWARENESS FROM GRASSHOPPER

If Grasshopper comes into your life:

- Sing your own song and stop imitating others.
- You are excelling because of your efforts and will have the opportunity to be a leader in the world.
- Listen to music to elevate your vibration and attract what you want.

Energy Center: Third eye

Mineral: Amber

Element: Earth

Magic & Mystery:

- Grasshopper blood turns green when exposed to air; this is symbolic of the movement of energy from the Earth to our hearts.
- The lifespan of Grasshopper is about fifty days.
- Grasshopper can only jump forward—not backward or sideways.

SHAMAN'S INTENTION: *HELP ME TO CONNECT TO GREATER POWERS BY RAISING MY VIBRATION*

GROUSE

SPIRAL | **PRAYER** | **REFLECTION**

"The spiral contains a force greater than anything else in nature."—Grouse

Grouse is a type of Pheasant native to the cold, northern regions of North America. It prefers to live in mixed forests that are abundant with aspen, poplar, and birch trees. Despite being an efficient and acrobatic flyer, Grouse is a nonmigratory bird that spends most of its time walking on the ground. During the winter, Grouse burrows in deep snow that serves as insulation from the cold. In this season, its toes grow little combs that function as snowshoes to help it walk across the surface of snow. It is a hearty bird, able to endure harsh winters. Grouse thrives on change and destruction. It can digest bitter plants other animals would find toxic and its favorite foods are cherries and hazelnuts, which emerge after forest fires, massive windstorms, or clear cutting.

Normally a solitary bird, Grouse makes an exception during mating season. In the springtime, Grouse will call to its mate by making a low-pitched drumming sound by raising its chest and then opening and closing its wings in rapid succession and with increasing speed and intensity. Its wings are a complete blur at the peak of the drumming. The relationship of Grouse to the drum is a powerful spiritual correlation. By beating its wings, Grouse creates a vacuum similar to the vacuum after a lightning strike that causes thunder.

Grouse has been called a Prairie Chicken. Native Americans in North America honor these birds with a traditional dance that symbolizes birth and rebirth. This stamping dance roughly follows the line of a spiral that represents the experience of going inward to the deepness of ourselves. Inspired by how Grouse flaps its wings and spins, turning dancers become more connected with themselves and reach higher levels of transcendence.

Grouse is the keeper of the sacred spiral. The spiral is the most widely seen shape in the natural world. Spiral is the natural path of the flow of energy. DNA, embryos, horns, whirlpools, hurricanes, and the movement of galaxies are spirals. As sacred geometry, spirals representing the path of growth and transformation appear in art around the world. From Aboriginal cave drawings in Australia and prehistoric burial chambers in England to the pre-Columbian petroglyphs of Mesoamerica, the spiral is a cosmic symbol of great importance.

Grouse is also linked to the walking of the labyrinth, a place for the resolution of inner conflict. It teaches us to reach balance through our movements so we may experience the unfolding of ourselves. Some shamans use the spiral as a path to the Upper World. Prayers also travel through the spiral to the Source of all things. The center of the spiral is the eternal/timeless "I AM" presence, in which calm and wisdom prevail. Grouse brings the message to have clarity of intention, so you may funnel your energy into appropriate channels. This will give you the feeling that you are united with humanity and that your work is the work of the Universe. Overcome any inhibitions or anxiety and translate your creative inspiration into a practical application of manifesting what you want from the spiral.

POWERS OF GROUSE

Call in Grouse for:

- Help in making an inner journey to develop awareness.
- Strength in solitude and to endure a harsh environment.
- Aligning yourself with cosmic energy.

AWARENESS FROM GROUSE

If Grouse comes into your life:

- It is time to walk the labyrinth of awakening.
- Use dance to open your perspective.
- Implement prayers into your spiritual practice to help you endure hardship and resolve issues that are creating pain and suffering.

Energy Center: Crown

Mineral: Seraphinite

Element: Air

Magic & Mystery:

- A group of Grouse has many names, among them a chorus, a covey, a drumming, and a grumbling.
- The average lifespan of Grouse is one year.

SHAMAN'S INTENTION: *HELP ME TO EMBRACE THE LANGUAGE OF NATURE AND THE SPIRAL THAT GUIDES ME WITHIN*

GROUNDHOG

BOUNDARIES | **MEDITATION** | **DREAMING**

"In your dreams you will find a place of rest and rejuvenation. Sleeping, you shall find a path to the visionary world of cosmic wisdom."—Groundhog

Groundhog lives in the Central and Eastern regions of North America. Also known as Woodchuck or Mouse Bear because it looks like a miniature Bear when sitting upright, Groundhog is a solitary creature that spends its summer and fall stuffing itself with food and taking naps in the Sun to get ready for its winter hibernation. It can eat about a pound of food at one sitting. When not sunbathing, Groundhog spends most of its time underground in the complex burrow systems it digs in well-drained soil. It uses a high-pitched shrill to warn others of its kind of approaching threats.

Groundhog spends three months in hibernation during the winter, which reminds us that sometimes we may require a break from the chaos of life. It is necessary to have a special place where we can go to meditate and clear cobwebs of confusion out of our heads. The male Groundhog will wake up in late winter, as it does not want to miss out on the start of mating season. He will begin to search the nearby territory by going to visit the female Groundhog in her burrow. After mating, Groundhog spends a brief period raising its young and then goes back to its life of solitude.

Groundhog brings messages from the belly of Mother Nature, advising us of the change of seasons. For this reason early European settlers to North America saw it as a predictor of the severity of the weather in springtime. Today it is a social event, a date honored for the fun of it.

When awake, Groundhog has a keen sense of place and knows its territory well. It maintains very clear boundaries with its companions, which results in peace and tranquility and mutual respect.

As a Power Animal, Groundhog supports us in achieving deep sleep and entering into meditative trance states equivalent to those of Buddhist monks. Groundhog is an expert at preserving its energy by dropping its body temperature and heart rate even lower than Bear does. Its intimate and long connection to dream states makes Groundhog able to help us understand our dreams and integrate their meaning into our ordinary reality. It is a wonderful guide into the world of mystery and darkness.

Dreams can reveal the fears we have stored. Spending time dreaming can give us an opportunity to unravel them and deepen our sense of security and attachment to the nurturing energy of Mother Earth. Life is like a long sleep and staying safe by being well grounded gives us an important foundation for our Earth walk. After we are securely grounded, we can learn to navigate altered states of being and head out into the universal field for the answers that we seek.

Meditation is an imperative practice for a shaman, as it gives the mind and the body a chance to rest from being on alert and helps to integrate the input of the senses. Take Groundhog with you when you learn to meditate or to help you quiet an incessantly noisy mind. Groundhog is a master of silence; it can teach you to find peace.

POWERS OF GROUNDHOG

Call in Groundhog for:

- Maintaining a healthy metabolism.
- Knowing when it is time to rest and reflect.
- Sweet dreams.

AWARENESS FROM GROUNDHOG

If Groundhog comes into your life:

- It is time to reevaluate your boundaries.
- Start to journal your dreams for deeper meaning in your everyday life.
- You may need to go out more.

Energy Center: Solar plexus

Mineral: Selenite

Element: Earth

Magic & Mystery: Groundhog has several levels in its burrow: one for hibernating; another for its spring exit, and one that's a bathroom. It may also have more than one residence.

SHAMAN'S INTENTION: *JOIN ME IN MY DREAMS AND CLEANSE ME OF ALL OF MY FEARS*

GUINEA PIG

SACRIFICE | **DIVINATION** | **HEALING**

"Use kindness as a medicine for healing others."—Guinea Pig

POWERS OF GUINEA PIG

Call in Guinea Pig for:

- Healing serious illnesses.
- Teaching us kindness in dealing with others.
- Building strong friendships.

AWARENESS FROM GUINEA PIG

If Guinea Pig comes into your life:

- You may need to make sacrifices for others.
- It is a time to pay attention to your body and its needs.
- Be mindful of your lack of agility.

Energy Center: Heart

Mineral: Lepidolite

Element: Earth

Magic & Mystery:

- In the 1600s, the Spaniards were the first Europeans to see Guinea Pig and they took several back to Europe where Guinea Pig became a popular pet.
- Fossil records of the existence of Guinea Pig date back to the Miocene period over 18 million years ago. In August 2003, archeologists in Venezuela discovered the fossilized remains of a huge Guinea Pig-like creature, the *Phoberomys Pattersoni*, which grew to around nine feet long and lived eight million years ago.

Guinea Pig was first domesticated in the Andes Mountains of South America circa 5,000 B.C.E. Not related to Pig, it may have acquired its name because it has a similar squeal. Guinea Pig has extremely sensitive hearing, perceiving ultrasonic sounds. It does not do well in solitude. It has lively communication skills and wants to share affection and emotions with others of its kind. Its teeth never stop growing so it must have unlimited access to food to grind them down and keep them aligned. In nature, wild Guinea Pig eats a diet of raw vegetables. It has an amazing memory and can navigate a complicated maze.

Guinea Pig is a poor climber and not particularly agile. It startles easily, either freezing in place or running for cover when it senses danger. For safety from predators, it sleeps with its eyes open. When excited, Guinea Pig hops in the air, like popping corn. It is a very good swimmer.

Guinea Pig is a healer. Incan legend holds that it is a mystical being able to cure the sick and which assists the dying in the journey to the Afterlife. In Peru, some shamans will use Guinea Pig as a diagnostic tool. These *sobadores* will rub the body of an ailing patient with a Guinea Pig to see if the animal dies. The animal is then cut open and a spiritual analysis of its organs takes place. It is also believed that Guinea pig can talk to the spirits and receive prophecies and information to aid in healing. The Guinea Pig will also assist the dying on their way to the other side.

As a Power Animal, Guinea Pig is emblematic of friendship and caring for others. It can assist us in forming groups of like-minded individuals who can support the whole and be a collective force for good. Guinea Pig also is an important spiritual guide for Reiki practitioners, theta healers, and massage therapists. Guinea Pig comes to teach us of the old ways, when whole communities would support each other and when there was a tribal effort to generate healing. It encourages us to form bonds and healing circles with those souls who believe in the power of energy healing. Guinea Pig brings us the message to release whatever is standing in the way of successful cocreation with others. It also encourages us to deepen our relationship with nature. Ask Guinea Pig to help you recover from the stress of past traumas and forgive those who have harmed or betrayed you. This will help you to arrive at a deep peace and calm.

SHAMAN'S INTENTION: *TEACH ME TO HEAL MYSELF AND OTHERS THROUGH UNCONDITIONAL LOVE*

HAWK

VISION **CHANGE** **INTELLIGENCE**

"Take charge of who you are beyond the personality and realize that true strength is within you and available when you hear the call."—Hawk

Hawk species, of which there are more than 270, can be found on every continent except Antarctica. Red-tailed Hawk is the most common in the Americas. When hunting, it dives at speeds of 150 miles per hour. It will catch prey either on the ground or in the air. It is a successful hunter because of its excellent eyesight—it can see eight times better than humans. Hawk prefers to live alone and relies on just itself for survival. That being said, Hawk is a loyal partner who mates for life. During courtship, the male and female fly in wide circles around each other making shrill sounds. The male impresses the female by performing aerial displays, diving steeply and then climbing again. After repeating this display several times, he grasps her talons briefly with his own. It is a beautiful and loving dance.

In ancient Egypt the Hawk-headed god Charon was responsible for guiding souls across the Styx River to the afterlife. A Hawk would be released after the death of a prominent person, symbolizing this journey. In the Roman Empire the souls of great emperors were illustrated as Hawk transitioning to the heavens. In Norse mythology the Valkyries transformed into Hawk to transport the souls of soldiers lost on the battlefield.

The ancient Egyptians also recognized Hawk as a magical bird capable of shapeshifting. According to myth Isis shapeshifted into Hawk to save Osiris, and Horus used Hawk to see what otherwise could not be seen. Foresight is one of Hawk's powers. Native Americans would call in Hawk to deliver tips from their ancestors about battles to come. Hawk was the bringer of messages and change. To the Celts Hawk was a link to ancestral roots and could help them find the secrets of a full life. In the traditions of Polynesia, Hawk was also recognized as a prophetic bird with healing powers and connection to the highest realms. Early African tribes worshiped Hawk and honored it by wearing its feathers in their rituals where they would allow the healing spirit of Hawk to merge with them to help them heal others.

As a Power Animal, Hawk is a visionary and messenger from higher-vibrational planes of existence. Through its astute intelligence we can better understand what seems impossible to know. With elevated perception we can realize the full potential of our intentions, then swoop down and grab hold of our life on Earth in its entirety. Hawk has four color receptors in its eyes, giving it the ability to see ultraviolet a color vibration that provides us with a deeper connection to spirits.

Hawk is so aware of its surroundings that it is alert to even minor changes. Whenever it sees what it wants, it goes after it. It has intense concentration, the kind with which to build a successful strategy. Its preferred time for hunting is right before nightfall. Hawk can help safeguard us against whatever we fear at night that could attack us.

Because Hawk lives in the sky, it is associated with rain, wind, thunder, and lightning. This makes it a good Power Animal for weather shamans. Hawk is the messenger of truth and comes to destroy all issues of lying, betrayal, and the lack of trustworthiness. Its vibration is like a truth serum, helping to release any issues we have suppressed, ignored, or denied. Hawk helps us to forgive ourselves for lying and helps us to be able to trust others again and heal the wounds of those that have been betrayed.

POWERS OF HAWK

Call in Hawk for:

- Honing your perception of the world around you.
- Assistance with strategic planning.
- An expansion of your intuition and opening to messages from the Upper World.

AWARENESS FROM HAWK

If Hawk comes into your life:

- It is time to take your power back.
- Work on better awareness and seeing things as they really are.
- Move from innocence to wisdom.

Energy Center: Crown

Mineral: Sunstone

Element: Air

Magic & Mystery:

- The red tail of the Red-tailed Hawk only appears when the bird reaches maturity. Red feathers must be earned with age and experience.
- Canadian ornithologist Louis Lefebvre developed a method of measuring avian "IQ" by testing innovation in feeding habits. Based on his ratings, Hawk was named the most intelligent bird.

SHAMAN'S INTENTION: *TEACH ME TO SPEAK, HEAR, AND BE TRUTH*

HEDGEHOG

TRUST | **SURVIVAL** | **DIVINE FEMININE**

"Fear kills the curiosity of the unknown."—Hedgehog

POWERS OF HEDGEHOG

Call in Hedgehog for:

- Being able to distinguish between what is of the light and of the dark.
- Times when you need to demand respect for your personal space.
- Attunement with the cycles of the Sun and astrology.

AWARENESS FROM HEDGEHOG

If Hedgehog comes into your life:

- You have the capacity for healing others.
- Know that you are safe and protected and you should trust that the Universe is supporting you.
- Return to Source energy to bolster your strength and confidence.

Energy Center: Solar plexus

Mineral: Obsidian

Element: Earth

Magic & Mystery:

- In Eastern Africa the skin and spine of the White-bellied Hedgehog is regarded as a fertility charm. People believe that if its skin is laid on seeds prior to planting, a good harvest is guaranteed.
- It is illegal to catch, kill, or confine a Hedgehog in both China and Europe as they are considered sacred.

Hedgehog has been around for 58 million years. Its seventeen species are found in Europe, Asia, Africa and New Zealand. The smallest, only two inches long, lives in British Columbia. A solitary animal, it only socializes when breeding. Its body has 5,000 spines that it utilizes for defense. Each spine lasts for a year then drops off and another grows in its place.

Hedgehog got its name because it forages around hedges and undergrowth making a grunting sound like Pig while searching for its favorite foods: Centipede, Snail, Mouse, Frog, and Snake. During daylight hours Hedgehog relies on its senses of hearing and smell since its eyes are better adapted for night vision. Nocturnal, it is connected with the lunar cycle. And as a hibernator, it has the power of prophetic dreaming and psychic intuition. It is adept at seeing what is in the darkness of the self and others and is a messenger of rebirth and rejuvenation.

Hedgehog is extremely resourceful, as it demonstrates when "picking" grapes. It will crawl up the vine, drop grapes to the ground, and then roll all over them, spiking the grapes with its spines, and then walk off with a full "plate" of portable fruit stuck to its back.

The belly of Hedgehog is close to the ground, so it has a strong connection to Mother Earth, earth spirits, and the fairy world. Hedgehog often curls into a fetal position, making it a symbol of fertility and displaying its link with feminine energy. When Hedgehog feels threatened, it goes back to the spiral of Source energy for protection and centering.

Throughout the world this spiky animal is associated with abundant harvests and the fertility of land. Ancient cultures believed that its quills represent the rays of the Sun, associating it with solar power and fire. Although a small animal, Hedgehog is a being with purpose that knows how to take care of itself using its built-in defense system. Its threats can even send predators running. During times of adversity Hedgehog remains calm and, although relatively powerless, trusts the protection it has to survive.

Among other special gifts, Hedgehog is resistant to Snake's bite. Its natural immunity is due to a protein in its muscles that blocks the action of the venom. This power was seen by many indigenous peoples as being triumphant over evil. Hedgehog has amazing stamina and energy; it can run four to five miles per hour. It can climb walls, trees, fences, and swim. Its life force is vibrant and healthy. Because of its stamina and ability to overcome adversity, shamans may find it helpful to merge with Hedgehog when powerful healing is needed.

Hedgehog brings a lesson of grounding for those who feel disconnected from their sense of spirituality. It helps us to be more receptive and present in our bodies and in touch with our inner children. It encourages us to connect to the pulse of life and living. Hedgehog will help us to find our strength through vulnerability and supports quieting the mind during meditation. Hedgehog teaches us

SHAMAN'S INTENTION: *HELP ME TO TRUST IN THE ABILITY TO PROTECT MYSELF AND FEEL SAFE*

HERON

CALM **PATIENT** **INTROSPECTION**

"There is a magical space you will find when you look into still water and see the reflection of you."—Heron

The Heron family includes sixty-four species which differ in size, color, and habitat. Heron chooses dead trees high on cliffs as places for its nests, but it will also build on the ground. In either case, it returns to the same nest every year. Male and female build a home together, yet they remain self-reliant. The wingspan of Heron is an impressive six feet and it flies at speeds of up to thirty miles per hour. It is a graceful image to see Heron with its S-shaped neck, beautiful feathers, and long legs stretched out behind it. With eyes that see equally well in light or darkness, it is active in both the day and the night.

The ancient Egyptians honored Heron as the creator of light. A mythical double-headed Heron was their symbol of prosperity. Purple Heron was associated with Ra, the Sun god, as the flight of Heron over water looks like a reflection of sunlight. Egyptians also saw Heron as the original Phoenix; it was believed to have been created from a fire in the sacred temple of Ra. The symbolism of death and rebirth surrounds Heron. Across the world, the Aztec god Huitzilopochtli was called the Blue Heron Bird, and he was considered the incarnation of the Sun.

Heron for the Chinese represents strength and a long life. It is also a sign of spiritual ascension to the Upper World. Heron's contemplative behavior, standing so very still with its eyes closed, is reminiscent of a Buddhist standing meditation. Heron signifies someone who remains steadfast on the right path.

The Maori of New Zealand see a single Heron flying as a sign that a rare visitor is coming to see you, the kind you see once in a lifetime. According to Indian folklore, if Heron perches on your house you will have good luck; and if you find its feather, even more good luck.

Native Americans admire Heron's inquisitive nature. It is seen as wise and possessing good judgment. Heron will stand motionless in the water for hours before flawlessly grabbing its prey in its bill. This skill was a sign to the tribe that a successful fishing trip was to come. Heron's precision-hunting skills connect it to the concept of spear magic, which involves spiritually penetrating the body to make a hole through which the divine can enter and unite with someone's soul to heal the person's inner emotional wounds.

Heron's introspection and purposeful behavior makes it a master of the observation and analysis of the soul. Because Heron lives in wetlands and swamps, its connection to water is emblematic of going with the flow and embracing the movement of the natural world. Standing on two very thin legs makes it flexible and light, teaching us of the necessity to move through life with grace and ease. Heron helps us release congested emotions one by one and to express our emotions as they arise rather than create a backlog of unexpressed feelings. Heron will ease and rebalance the emotional body so that it can function in harmony again. It will also uplift your mood, helping you to not take things so seriously and to see the world with calm and detachment, thus keeping your head above the water. Heron keeps you from emotional swings, the ups and downs that cause difficulty in reaching equilibrium and balance.

BITTERNS, EGRET

POWERS OF HERON

Call in Heron for:

- Getting what you want and being willing to wait for it.
- The power of stillness.
- A purposeful, solitary existence that nonetheless values relationships.

AWARENESS OF HERON

If Heron comes into your life:

- It is time to get still and seek wisdom from within.
- Realize the freedom that can come from being alone.
- Go with the flow.

Energy Center: Throat

Mineral: Apatite

Element: Air

Magic & Mystery:

- Black Heron hunts using *canopy feeding*—a method in which it spreads its wings like an umbrella to create a shaded environment that will attract fish.
- The fat of Heron killed at full Moon was believed to be a cure for rheumatism in the folklore of the Irish.

Shaman's Intention: *Support me to embrace confidence in all that I do*

HIPPOPOTAMUS

EXPANSIVENESS | **MORALITY** | **ASSURANCE**

"Fear is BIG and can drive you to the greatest of angers. Carve your path to a place of calmer waters where you can thrive and begin again."—Hippopotamus

POWERS OF HIPPOPOTAMUS

Call in Hippopotamus for:

- Love of water and its cleansing abilities.
- Being quick to respond and exceed the expectations of others.
- The ability to remove obstacles very quickly.

AWARENESS FROM HIPPOPOTAMUS

If Hippopotamus comes into your life:

- You may be too aggressive and need to tone it down.
- It is time to take a hard look at your anger issues.
- Speak your truth and open up to others with kindness about your feelings instead of lashing out.

Energy Center: Throat

Mineral: Aquamarine

Element: Water

Magic & Mystery:

- The color of Hippo milk is pink. Pink is a color that shamans see as a representation of Goddess energy and the Divine Feminine.
- An African folktale says that Hippo wanted to live in the water and was originally refused by humans out of the fear that it would eat all the Fish. When Hippo begged, it was allowed to go back to the water on the condition that it would eat grass instead of Fish and have its dung inspected for fishbones for verification.

Hippopotamus (Hippo) was once found throughout Sub-Saharan Africa, yet, sadly, its population has declined due to habitat loss and hunting. It is now mostly confined to protected areas. Hippo is the second largest land animal on Earth, with first place going to Elephant. It has an enormous body, short legs, and a massive head. It spends most of its time in rivers and lakes in order to stay cool from the heat. With eyes, nose, and ears on the top of its head, it can see and breathe while submersed in water. It exudes an oily red sweat that is a natural sunscreen to protect its skin from radiation and keeps it from drying out. Hippo is very social and lives in groups with up to a hundred members. These groups are headed up by a dominant male. Hippo is a common sight in African rivers with its ears floating like islands and birds fishing from a perch atop its wide back. Hippo spends almost sixteen hours a day in the water and often remains there for protection. It eats herbs and is a distant relation of Whale and Dolphin. Its name which is derived from the Greek words *hippo* ("horse") and *potamos* ("river") means River Horse.

Hippo is noisy in and out of water. Its grunts have been recorded at 115 decibels, which is the sound you would hear at a heavy metal rock concert if you were standing in front of the speakers. Hippo has a lot to express to the world. Its power resides in its mouth, which can hinge open by 180 degrees, and then with a crushing blow from its jaws and teeth can kill anything it bites down on. In the water it is an aggressive animal with little to no patience for anything that is bothersome. On land, it is not as aggressive except when it wants to protect its young. It will attack humans, Crocodile, and other creatures at will—even boats—with no hesitation.

Hippo is indigenous to Egypt and likes to swim in the Nile. Sadly, because of it being so dangerous it has been hunted nearly to extinction even though killing Hippo is not an easy task. Hippo's relationship to water makes it a master of regeneration and its association with rivers makes it a bringer of life. Hippo mothers offer their offspring excellent protection. You may call in the energy of Hippo for help to get pregnant and to be a good mother. A strong, predatory creature, Hippo is the perfect Power Animal to call in when you need to ward off evil.

As a Power Animal, Hippopotamus is about size. It walks the world bearing its massive form and can loan its confidence to you. Weighing in at four tons, it dominates space. Because of its size, wherever Hippo walks—especially when it moves from land to water or water to land—it creates paths and channels. Call in Hippo if you want to carve out a new path in life, such as changing careers, relocating, or making another kind of radical change. Hippo can blast open any barriers you may be experiencing. Hippo activates our sense of morality in taking responsibility for owning and expressing who we are, away from the perceptions of others. It reminds us to steer clear of trying to be who we are not. It is important to embrace our own identity and charisma so that our true light can shine. Through our natural morality we can draw out undesirable characteristics of our own consciousness and begin to inspire and nurture others.

SHAMAN'S INTENTION: *TEACH ME TO BE LARGER THAN ALL OF MY FEARS*

HORSE

CONFIDENCE | **MOVEMENT** | **VITALITY**

"When two beings can agree on a destination, the journey can be taken together to places far beyond the limits of your imagination."—Horse

The early ancestor of Horse, when its evolution split off from Zebra and Donkey, evolved fifty million years ago. Horse is a noble creature that has been a friend to humanity since roughly 3,000 B.C.E. Showing us great loyalty, it has gone into battle and taken us on long journeys, often into uncharted territories. The eyes on the sides of its head make it capable of seeing a range of nearly 360 degrees. It is extremely clever and proficient at learning and rising to meet challenges. It is also emotionally sensitive and is a valuable resource for teaching those suffering from mental health issues and post-trauma about trust, respect, compassion, communication, and confidence—all important factors for leading a healthy life.

The temperament of Horse varies. Sometimes Horse is nervous and energetic; other times, serene and tolerant. Horse lives in a social group with a hierarchy where either a dominant male or dominant mare is the boss. It forms lasting relationships and connections with others in its group through a relatively elaborate communication process. Horse is a symbol of travel, freedom, and moving forward. Horse changed the futures of many indigenous peoples when it was brought to the Americas by European settlers in the sixteenth century. Since that time, it has been revered by Native people, as having a Horse was often a turning point in battle, ensuring a victory; and it improved the ability to hunt and travel. The number of Horse a tribe owned was a statement of wealth. Today, almost every Horse is domesticated. Few are wild.

In Chinese astrology, the Year of the Horse (1930, 1942, 1954, 1966, 1978, 1990, 2002, 2014, and 2026) symbolizes devotion and the giving of service to others. People born in those years are said to be endowed with the best traits of Horse. Horse will

HORSE

CONFIDENCE **MOVEMENT** **VITALITY**

HORSE CHANGED THE FUTURES OF MANY INDIGENOUS PEOPLES WHEN IT WAS BROUGHT TO THE AMERICAS BY EUROPEAN SETTLERS IN THE SIXTEENTH CENTURY.

POWERS OF HORSE

Call in Horse for:

- Developing a clear vision of what is around you.
- Going forward without looking back at the past.
- Willingness to serve others.

AWARENESS FROM HORSE

If Horse comes into your life:

- It is time to get going.
- You can lose your temper and balance is needed.
- Illusion may be clouding your mind; stay in the present and put one foot in front of the other.

Energy Center: Solar plexus

Mineral: Tiger's eye

Element: Earth

Magic & Mystery:

- If several Horse are seen standing together, a storm is coming.
- Przewalski's Horse is the only Wild Horse still in existence. It is found in Mongolia.
- Horse uses facial expressions to communicate its feelings.

never give up going forward; it will walk until its last breath to be of service. It has great endurance and loyalty and a purity of spirit that is admirable. When a horse runs, it is an emblem of freedom and ecstasy.

Ancient Romans linked Horse with Mars, their god of fury and war. Horse was depicted as pulling the chariot of Helios, the Sun god. In the British Isles the Celts saw Horse as a sign of good luck. Horse has always been so beloved, almost a member of the family, that when Alexander the Great's Horse died in 326 B.C.E. while he was on a campaign to the Hindu-Kush Valley in Central Asia he founded the city of Bucephala in its memory, building it on the exact spot where the animal died. One of the best-known figures in Greek mythology is the mythical Winged Horse, Pegasus, child of the Olympian god Poseidon, offering a beautiful image of power and victory. Horse has consistently been used as a vehicle for souls to commune with Spirit.

In Celtic lore there existed one magical word that was the secret to exert dominance over Horse. This word, still remains a mystery. Horse is a sign that a new and better version of our world was being brought forth where people would live at a higher vibration.

Horse has given itself over to humanity but its spirit has never been compromised. Horse can never be fully tamed and it will always be our guide to carry us in new directions and out of places when we get stagnant. It offers us freedom to move ahead into uncharted territory. Horse teaches us a lesson about kindness and the power of being gentle but also firm and focused. Horse, with its muscular body and strength, is a package of power, and yet it allows humans to ride it once a bond of trust has been formed.

Horse is sensitive to touch, especially around its head. It can sense even a tiny insect landing on its body. It is a clairsentient being with a broad aura. It teaches us that real power comes from a balance of sensitivity and strength. Horse can sleep standing up, ready to go at a moment's notice. It is a master of "flight," using its speed for protection from predators. Knowing when to run is an invaluable instinct. Horse brings us the message of strong, self-contained individuality. It urges us to honor it but cautions against arrogance or acting distant and becoming isolated. Horse teaches us to be confident with a new, expanded sense of self—and to validate ourselves. Remember, you are powerful just as you are. If you develop a strong inner center, you are capable of surviving anything.

SHAMAN'S INTENTION: *SUPPORT ME TO BE STEADFAST AND UNYIELDING IN MY JOURNEY*

HUMMINGBIRD

PLAYFULNESS | **QUICKNESS** | **ENDURANCE**

"Be quick to realize that the path is clear and the navigation set; the destination is the heart."—Hummingbird

The 340 species of Hummingbird are found only in the Americas, and most, exclusively in South America. Inside this tiny bird is a wealth of information as its memory is astounding. It remembers every flower it has visited and has intricate routes to return to them. Hummingbird knows exactly how long to wait for a flower to generate more nectar so it can come back at the optimum time for its extraction. Hummingbird can recognize humans. It knows who to count on to refill a birdfeeder. Since Hummingbird never stops flapping its wings, it has a high metabolism and must eat every ten minutes. It will consume three times its body weight in bugs and flower nectar every day. Making this possible is its nuanced vision. It sees a large spectrum of colors. Hummingbird has an extra set of eyelids that it uses like goggles while rapidly flying. It also has a capacity for multidimensional flying, moving up and down and side to side effortlessly.

Hummingbird is the great navigator of the world with its ability to travel more than 2,000 miles during a single migration. It is tireless, beating its wings up to 5,400 times per minute so it can fly at speeds of up to thirty-three miles per hour, or hovering in place like a helicopter to drink nectar.

Hummingbird comes in a multitude of colors and is intimately connected to the diverse energy of the chakra system and the rainbow. The Aztecs honored Huitzilopochtli, their god of war, by naming him "Hummingbird of the South." They saw Hummingbird as strong and sacred. It was categorized, along with Eagle and Hawk, as a symbol of solar power.

In the traditions of the Mayan and Inca, Hummingbird is the representative spirit of the North with the ability to guide us to our ancestors. For many native tribes, Hummingbird is thought to be a little messenger to the gods. Pueblo Indians would ask Hummingbird to send their gratitude to Mother Earth and carry

HUMMINGBIRD

PLAYFULNESS | **QUICKNESS** | **ENDURANCE**

HUMMINGBIRD KNOWS EXACTLY HOW LONG TO WAIT FOR A FLOWER TO GENERATE MORE NECTAR SO IT CAN COME BACK AT THE OPTIMUM TIME FOR ITS EXTRACTION.

POWERS OF HUMMINGBIRD

Call in Hummingbird for:

- Complete confidence in the details of your journey.
- Quick reactions and to take advantage of an opportunity.
- Understanding joy and where to find it.

AWARENESS FROM HUMMINGBIRD

If Hummingbird comes into your life:

- It is time to rest and relax; you may be moving too fast.
- A journey is being prepared for you for the purpose of spiritual growth.
- You may be too territorial; it is time to allow others inside your protective space.

Energy Center: Heart

Mineral: Seraphinite

Element: Earth

Magic & Mystery:

- Hummingbirds have no sense of smell.
- The heart of Hummingbird, at 2.5 percent of its weight, is the largest of all animals.
- Hummingbird will remember its place of birth and return there every year.

requests for the shamans. Mayan legends also say that Hummingbird is the Sun in disguise and that it is always trying to court the Moon as a partner. For the Mojave it was Hummingbird that was sent to the surface of the Earth when the ancestors were living underground and it found them a path to the light so they could emerge. The Taino of the Caribbean see Hummingbird as a sacred pollinator responsible for abundance. Some tribes believe Hummingbird brought them their sacred tobacco.

Hummingbird is connected to rain. Hopi, Zuni, and Pueblo artisans paint images of it on their water jugs to assure themselves enough of this vital liquid to sustain life. Water is humanity's nectar. As a Power Animal, Hummingbird could always be counted on to bring the nectar that was needed, and its iridescent feathers are representative of the prism and its corresponding color vibration on our energetic field. The Pima see Hummingbird as playing a role like Dove does in the biblical story of Noah and his ark. According to their myths, Hummingbird was able to find land during floods. The Aztecs would adorn their clothing with Hummingbird feathers and also wear Hummingbird earrings. Their shamans would take sticks and decorate them with these same feathers for help to suck evil out of those who had been cursed by sorcerers.

Hummingbird is full of life and energy and travels the world with no sense of barriers. With great control it can move swiftly wherever it wants to go. It is a symbol of the morning Sun, as the colors burst into the earthly realm, and a reminder to jump into action and pursue your goals with vitality. Hummingbird can be territorial and will attempt to take on any intruder hovering around and dive at it with an angry chirping sound no matter its size. Hummingbird has no fear about expressing its dissatisfaction. It also demonstrates how to get to the heart of any matter and where to find the sweetness in life; this is evidenced by its pointed bill which goes straight for the center of the flower.

Hummingbird brings us messages that we do not have to pay the price for being loved and that everything worthwhile is difficult to obtain. Abundance is within us all, as we are born with it. The trick is being able to receive that which is unconditionally given. When we walk in the knowing that there is plenty, we can see and feel the blessings around us. Hummingbird holds the key to our star lineage. Ask Hummingbird to awaken you to your divine presence so that you can work with your divine purpose while on Earth.

SHAMAN'S INTENTION: *TAKE MY MESSAGES TO THE WORLDS BEYOND OUR WORLD*

HYENA

PERCEPTION | **PARTNERSHIP** | **INTUITIVE**

"We carry the power of the mystic and walk with no fear of the unknown."—Hyena

Hyena is a large, doglike carnivore that lives in the grasslands and savannahs of Africa and Asia. There are three types: spotted, brown, and striped, with the spotted being the largest. Although Hyena has a reputation for being a scavenger, it is also a skillful hunter. With its powerful jaws it is able to eat and digest bones, leaving nothing of its prey behind. Hyena is a great communicator, issuing a variety of calls and screams, and its infamous "laughter," which actually is not humor but a message to let others know that food has been found. From the pitch of its "laugh," others can determine a Hyena's age and social status. Hyena is territorial and lives among a clan of relatives, marking and protecting its den. It is intelligent and endowed with a frontal cortex the same size and complexity of a primate, giving it advanced cognitive skills that are useful for relationships and problem solving. Hyena's aptitude for nonverbal communication adds to its intuition and mystical power.

Hyena is hypersexual and while in some cultures this is associated with deviance, elsewhere it is understood as emblematic of fertility. In India and Pakistan, Hyena is a symbol of love and fertility due to the fact that after long separations members of both Hyena genders display erections when they greet one another. Hyena is a social animal and can help you to cultivate the skills needed in large groups. The female Hyena is very strong and will rarely back down if confronted.

Because Hyena is a scavenger, in many cultures it is seen as a robber or a menacing being. In Tanzanian lore Hyena is associated with witchcraft. Stories are told of witches riding on its back. The Tabwa tribe from Lake Tanganyika reveres Hyena for bringing the Sun to warm the Earth. African shamans believe Hyena has the ability to speak the names of people and can trick us by imitating the human voice.

In the Middle East striped Hyena is feared and thought of as treacherous. It is misunderstood because it is associated with destruction and decay. But Hyena has an important place in the cycle of life, which moves from creation to destruction and rebirth. Scavengers assist in making space for something new to occur. For the shaman, the practice of dismemberment involves going on a spiritual journey to another dimension where a spirit animal is brought in to destroy the human body. This is done so that all the layers of conditioning and human limitation are removed, and, after dismemberment, the shaman can be reborn again— "re-membered" and inclusive of the powers of the animal that facilitated the process. Hyena is the ideal Power Animal to work with for purification and a new start; it will help you to see the truth and rely on your instincts for survival.

Hyena brings the message to activate your inner warrior to access your courage and resolve. It is time to conquer your inner enemies, obstacles, difficulties, and shortcomings. If you are lacking discipline, Hyena can help you to master self-control and deal with things that you have ignored. Hyena finds the inner resources to tame overindulgence and doubt. It keeps you focused on your destiny and not on the obstacles.

POWERS OF HYENA

Call in Hyena for:

- Telepathic communication.
- Learning the value of a community and nurturing your connection to a tribe.
- Adaptability and survival.

AWARENESS FROM HYENA

If Hyena comes into your life:

- You need to fill yourself up with the high vibration of laughter.
- You are being misjudged for your attributes. Make yourself clear.
- Reduce the feeling of wanting things in excess of what is really required.

Energy Center: Root

Mineral: Petrified wood

Element: Earth

Magic & Mystery:

- Hyena is often referred to as the mystic of the animal kingdom because of its mastery of the power of nonverbal communication.
- It is believed that the fear of Hyenas prevented humans from crossing the Bering strait.

SHAMAN'S INTENTION: *SUPPORT MY KNOWING OF MY INNER WARRIOR AND REMOVE ALL DOUBT*

IBIS

ADAPTABLE | **EXPRESSIVE** | **SACRED**

"It takes patience to find your inner wisdom and grace to share it in the world."—Ibis

POWERS OF IBIS

Call in Ibis for:

- Improving your ability to express yourself in written or verbal form.
- Instruction in the great wisdom of the ancient world.
- Success in creating your perfect nest in which to build your home.

AWARENESS FROM IBIS

If Ibis comes into your life:

- You are wasteful and need to make more effort to recycle and support Planet Earth.
- You may need to be more social or gregarious when in a group.
- Your ideas have become stagnant; it is time to fertilize them so they can take flight.

Energy Center: Throat

Mineral: Shattuckite

Element: Water

Magic & Mystery:

- The symbol of Ibis is portrayed on 4,500-year-old hieroglyphs in Egypt.
- The' milky white feathers of Ibis suggest its strong connection to the Moon.

Ibis is a tranquil bird that resembles Stork in shape and size. It has long legs and a thin, downward curving beak. It lives in colonies of up to 300 that inhabit swamps, marshes, riverbanks, and lakes all over the planet. Ibis loves to eat Grasshopper, Cricket, Water Beetle, and small aquatic animals, picking them out of the mud with its pointed beak. Since many of these insects are nuisances to farmers, Ibis is useful to have around to keep nature in balance. Ibis is perfectly content foraging alone or resting in the safety of its nest perched in a tall tree, and yet enjoys being part of a group as well. Its plumage is snowy white or black and charcoal gray.

Ibis was a sacred animal in ancient Egypt. It is one of two animal forms that the god Thoth, who is credited for the introduction of measurement, mathematics, writing, time keeping, and justice, was portrayed as; the other is Baboon. Thoth was also the assistant to Horus-Re, a Sun god. There is much artwork showing Thoth with an Ibis head. Ibis was long a protected animal in Egypt and anyone who killed it was punished by death. Archeologists found millions of Ibis mummies at the temple of Serapeum alongside thousands of Falcon. Ibis was plentiful in the capital city, Alexandria, during its heyday in the Hellenistic period, because of Ibis' protected status. Surviving on household scraps, Ibis kept the city relatively clean.

Ibis's icon was the first letter of the hieroglyphic alphabet. It is so closely connected with the origin of language that its energy brings us the hope that our communication can reach a higher level of understanding and enlightenment. As a Power Animal, the influence of Ibis starts from within and creates the most harmonious communication that is instinctual and trusting, and always done with divine timing. Ibis is a symbol of expression, teaching us to master the flow of our words whether we are putting them on paper or expressing them through our voice. It can help a leader open space energetically for a group gathering.

Ibis teaches us responsibility for the rivers and watersheds of the world, which need us to clean and maintain them. Its presence is a lesson for how we can be attuned to our impact on watery, flowing ecosystems. Ibis brings us the message to be gentler with ourselves. It encourages us to be optimistic and innovative and to avoid falling into old patterns and habits. We must unload our old conceptions so that our creativity can flow. Ibis helps us sort out our priorities and focus on what is really important to us. It inspires us to be more inventive. Ibis embodies gracefulness, balance, and sensitivity to timing. If you see Ibis, it means now is the perfect time to affect change in your life, so do not hesitate.

SHAMAN'S INTENTION: *HELP ME FIND THE RIGHT WORDS TO EXPRESS THE WISDOM INSIDE OF ME*

JACKAL

CALCULATION | TACTICS | LOYALTY

"The dusk is the first step on a path to find the essence of the soul as it journeys home."—Jackal

Jackal can be found in the deserts, savannahs, grasslands, marshes, and mountains of Africa, the Middle East, India, and southeastern Europe. It belongs to the same family (*Canidae*) as Wolf, Coyote, Dog, and Fox. Mostly nocturnal, during the day Jackal sleeps in dens made by other animals in rock outcroppings, which help it to stay cool. At dusk, it heads out to hunt. It is an opportunistic omnivore, which means that its diet consists of small animals, reptiles, birds, fruits, and vegetation including the left-over kills of larger animals. Jackal is vocal and uses many sounds to communicate, the most notable being an Owl-like hoot, a sign that food has been found. It will only communicate with its own family, ignoring attempts at communication from other animals. Cunning and adaptable, it is not easily captured or hunted. Jackal has a lifelong relationship with the same partner and contributes to its pack by collaborating in rearing the young.

Egyptian Jackal teeth are much more elongated than those of other species in the Canidae family, which is a reason they are regarded as sacred. Anubis, the god of the Underworld, had the head of Jackal. Egyptians saw Jackal as a sign of rebirth and fertility because its black fur was reminiscent of the rich soil on the banks of the Nile. Because Jackal is seen around cemeteries, its powers could be misconstrued as frightening; but, really, it is guarding the souls in the tombs.

In the cultures of India and Pakistan, Jackal is seen as courageous since it mostly travels alone to hunt, although it will team up with another Jackal if it is hunting an animal that is too large to kill on its own.

Jackal is helpful to shamans who do psychopomp work. By seeing into the Middle World, Jackal finds the souls of those who have not crossed over and takes them to the Upper or Lower World so they may begin their natural progression to the realms of higher consciousness. Jackal is a good guide for this task because it sees well in the dark. Although on the surface we might see the Jackal as something to fear, since it is related to death, this does not mean that death is near when we see it. Its presence most likely is a sign that a period of renewal or a transition is needed or coming to your life. Jackal's message is to avoid being driven by ego. Jackal arrives to give you a firm push to move to the next level of your development. Trust the timing and surrender to the Universe. Pushing to make things happen is not helpful. Do not get stuck in indecisiveness, hesitation, or fear. Unite your will with your fine-tuned calculations and intentions and you will avoid any distractions that might prevent you from achieving your goal or purpose.

POWERS OF JACKAL

Call in Jackal for:

- Commitment in your relationships with others.
- Independence and not excessively relying on others.
- Calculation and tactical support.

AWARENESS FROM JACKAL

If Jackal comes into your life:

- There could be devious behavior on your part or another's that needs to be rectified.
- Stop aimlessly searching for what you need. Allow the Universe to bring it to you.
- You are not following through on your intentions because you are too oriented toward the analytical brain.

Energy Center: Sacrum

Mineral: Prehnite

Element: Earth

Magic & Mystery: In India the name Shiva means "Jackal," and is associated with the destructive aspect of the goddess Kali who is his counterpart—the undomesticated, divine force of the feminine spirit.

SHAMAN'S INTENTION: *SUPPORT ME IN LIVING IN THE PEACE OF ADAPTABILITY*

JAGUAR

WILL | **HONESTY** | **GUARDIAN**

"To find the truth, you must be open to all possibilities; you will find it in the great unknown."—Jaguar

Jaguar is a large wild cat found primarily in the Americas. It is the third largest cat in the world behind Lion and Tiger. It has a stunning orange-yellow coat with spots that stand out that are unlike the spots of any other animal. The Black Panther is a Jaguar with the distinction of the color of its coat. It is believed that Jaguar crossed the Bering Strait from Asia to North America one and a half million years ago.

It has no predators except humans; and it has an advantage over us because of being able to see in the dark six times better than we do.

Native Americans term Jaguar "He who kills with one leap" since it often hides in a tree while preparing to ambush its prey. Because it is at the top of the food chain, Jaguar represents the conquering of fear and the ability to walk the world with confidence. Jaguar attacks the heads of its prey, which fuels the theory that Jaguar understands the detrimental aspects of the mind. This tactic reminds us that we have a tendency to be too much in our heads.

The Mayans see Jaguar as the totem of Hozanek, the god of the southern sky, who would enter the dreams of the community's leaders to be sure that they were telling the truth to their people. In the lower Americas, Jaguar is seen as a God that inhabits the Underworld and is called "Night Sun." The spots of Jaguar are seen as stars that empower it to overcome darkness. In the Mayan ruins of the pantheon, Jaguar is only second to the revered feathered Snake. A Jaguar priest is the most powerful of all the Mayan priests.

Jaguar protects the shaman from evil and negativity. It moves through the dimensions of the spirit world without being detected, thus able to be a guide to the mysterious. This Power Animal has the ability to clear fear and make it possible to trust the Universe again. Anyone going through a spiritual awakening may ask to be accompanied by Jaguar who is masterful at supporting us in the opening up of the gifts of clairaudience and clairvoyance. This is a big reason why shamans choose to merge with them energetically.

To Jaguar, truth and integrity are nonnegotiable. It will remove itself from any situation that it feels is not aligned with truth and disappear into the deepest jungle. A good Power Animal for healers, Jaguar has a mirroring area behind its retina that can enable a shaman to perceive disease and remove unwanted energy and attachments. Shapeshifting into Jaguar can be powerful medicine.

Black Panther is surrounded by mystery and is a symbol of feminine energy. It holds the essence of the Goddess: passion, fertility, and the awakening of the kundalini that spells the death of the old self and the birth of the new self and the moment of arrival in our full strength and powers. If you are in the dark night of the soul, Jaguar reminds you not to resist the process of finding the spiritual riches within you. The destination is a place of human love. Even when we feel emotionally remote, Jaguar helps us to assimilate wisdom. Jaguar supports us in developing clarity. With the integration of universal knowledge, we can have those aha moments as the answers drop in and our insight glows.

BLACK PANTHER

POWERS OF JAGUAR

Call in Jaguar for:

- Moving through the world without fear.
- Achieving the highest form of integrity.
- Strong leadership.

AWARENESS FROM JAGUAR

If Jaguar comes into your life:

- Face your fears and find freedom in acceptance.
- Look beyond the simple view for information.
- Take your spiritual path seriously and embrace your power.

Energy Center: Third eye

Mineral: Jade

Element: Earth

Magic & Mystery:

- Jaguar has binocular vision; meaning, each eye works independently. This gives it enhanced depth perception.
- Jaguar will dangle its tail in the water, like a lure, to attract fish.

SHAMAN'S INTENTION: *SUPPORT ME TO BE THE CONQUEROR OF FEAR*

JAVELINA

ALLIANCES | BOUNDARIES | COMPASSION

"Keep yourself in a high vibration; this is your greatest way of leaving a mark in the world."—Javelina

Javelina lives in southwestern North America, Central America, and South America in a variety of warmer habitats, ranging from dry deserts to tropical rainforests. Although it looks like Boar, with its snout, large head and shoulders, hoofed feet, thick skin, and tusks, it is actually a distinct species. It has coarse brown and gray hair. Omnivorous, Javelina eats insects, like Grub, but prefers vegetation, seeds, roots, and fruits, especially the Prickly Pear cactus and agave. During the day, Javelina rests with its family under shrubs and bushes in order to remain cool. Javelina is territorial and marks its area with a musky scent that identifies its presence to others of its kind that might be hanging out in its territory. It waits for nightfall, when the air is cooler, to venture out of the shade to search for food. Mostly indifferent, it will, however, attack if threatened, charging at its opponent head first and biting or stabbing it with its tusks. It has strong jaws that are used for crushing roots, plants, and seeds. It typically travels in herds of several members, a cohort that serves as protection against predators.

The ancient Mayans saw Javelina as a noble creature. Known as the Patron of the Constellations, it was often buried with royalty. Stars in the constellation of Gemini, the place where the corn god was resurrected according to myth, were called Javelinas. In the region of space that we call Orion's Belt, the Mayans saw images of mating Javelina. The Mayans also said Javelina represented four pillars on which the Earth rested, and therefore is very connected to the Lower World.

The current Wari tribe of Brazil has a special relationship with Javelina. They see it as humanlike because of its close-knit family units. They believe that when a relative dies, the soul goes to the Lower World and then returns as a Javelina that will seek them out and offer itself as food to support them.

Javelina is well adapted to life in a harsh environment. It teaches us that although the world may seem like an adversarial place, community and connection to others can diminish the harshness. It shares its wisdom about carrying on a continued search and foraging for that which nourishes our bodies and minds, a noble cause that will pay off in dividends of health.

Javelina requests that we leave behind the comforts of conformity and think for ourselves. It can help us cultivate a mindset of freedom. When we are overly influenced, it can block our individual expression as we will become self-conscious or inhibited, even shy. Once we find what personally inspires us, we can then contribute to a collective intellect where our thoughts and ideas are appreciated and secure. Javelina also warns us of never being satisfied, probably because it is always on the hunt for something. Maybe it is time to rest and count your blessings; you most likely have more than you need.

PECCARY

POWERS OF JAVELINA

Call in Javelina for:

- Setting up much-needed boundaries with others.
- Help to better your relationships with your family.
- Being flexible with the opinions of others.

AWARENESS FROM JAVELINA

When Javelina comes into your life:

- It is a sign that you may need to be more independent.
- You need to be more productive during the day.
- You may be overly vicious and wary of others.

Energy Center: Root

Mineral: Tree agate

Element: Earth

Magic & Mystery:

- Because of its fierce nature the Spanish gave Javelina its name which means "spear."
- The Tupi of Brazil refer to Javelina as Peccary, a word in their language that means "many paths through the woods."

SHAMAN'S INTENTION: *HELP ME TO TRUST THAT I WILL ALWAYS FIND WHAT I NEED TO SUSTAIN MYSELF*

JELLYFISH

FLOW | **SERENITY** | **REGENERATION**

"No mind, no thoughts, no thing; the Zen of floating."—Jellyfish

POWERS OF JELLYFISH

Call in Jellyfish for:

- Trust in the flow and believing that you can get where you want to go.
- Learning that just existing is sometimes enough.
- Reaching a place of peace and tranquility without using your brain.

AWARENESS FROM JELLYFISH

If Jellyfish comes into your life:

- You need to focus on being more efficient with what you consume.
- You may be striking out at others with little to no understanding of why.
- You need to get moving. Your lack of movement has you stuck.

Energy Center: Crown

Mineral: Chalcedony

Element: Water

Magic & Mystery:

- A Jellyfish *bloom* may be composed of as many as 300,000 members. This term is a reference to them appearing to be lotuses of the ocean.
- Jellyfish is very wise about the movement of the ocean currents and, since it has existed for 650 million years, it has mastered the wisdom of the deep.

Jellyfish does not have a brain, a heart, or lungs; all of its sensory needs occur in its outer layers. This stimulation is how Jellyfish manages its existence. If Jellyfish is cut in half, it can regenerate the missing pieces. It may glow in the dark and is roughly 95 percent water. If Jellyfish washes up on a beach it will die because of evaporation. Many species of Jellyfish have several eyes and can see 360-degrees around them. It is efficient in the processing of nutrients. It is one of the only creatures that have no responsibility for their transportation; instead, it relies solely on ocean currents and the wind to move it. However, Jellyfish does have the ability to expand and contract, which gives it some capability to propel itself forward.

Jellyfish often look like floating bells or a medusa, which is the name of a mythological woman who offended Athena and her hair was turned into bodies of Snake.

The characteristics of Jellyfish remind us of the importance of going with the flow and expanding our energy into the world with the faith and trust that everything we need will be provided. The innate knowing that Mother Nature will provide for us using the natural forces around us is an energy used by shamans to feel secure. Jellyfish demonstrates that we only need to be transparent in our ways to form a part of nature's magnificent tapestry.

The passivity of Jellyfish reminds us that relying on the unknown to move us forward at the right times can be a virtue. Delegating and accepting things as they are can bring a smooth calm to the survival process. Jellyfish brings us the message of fulfilling our divine mission, doing what we were chosen to do while on Earth. It guides us to a multidimensional awareness so that we can embody a presence that is gentle yet effective. When we can embody the integrity and purity of spirit, we can connect with our higher self. When we are able to feel this divine presence, we will be fulfilled and complete and able to return to oneness.

SHAMAN'S INTENTION: *HELP ME TO ELIMINATE THOUGHTS AND EMBRACE NOTHINGNESS*

KANGAROO

GROUNDING | **VELOCITY** | **NURTURING**

"With our ears we can hear the negative stories in your mind. Consider a positive twist and then jump forward with a different view."—Kangaroo

Kangaroo is found on mainland Australia, Tasmania, New Guinea, and the surrounding islands. As a symbol, it is used on the coat of arms of Australia and appears on its currency. It is an important animal for the culture and national image, as it represents the concept of moving forward. Kangaroo is a marsupial. The female carries her young in a stomach pouch that contains her mammary glands where the infant, a Joey, stays safely tucked away until it is weaned. Kangaroo has the amazing gift of being able to slow down the growth of its babies when food is scarce.

Kangaroo has a very strong lower body with a muscular tail and hind legs. The male can reach a height of six-foot-seven and a weight of 200 pounds. The female is a little bit smaller. Kangaroo is fast. Even though it hops, it can outpace a running human. It eats grasses, leaves, ferns, and insects.

Kangaroo is social and caring. It grooms its pals and is protective of its troop. When it feels threatened, Kangaroo will stomp its hind feet on the ground and take up a crouching position like a boxer that is getting ready to punch or kick its opponent. Kangaroo is shy and not aggressive around humans. It has minimal vocal cords so, with limited sounds, it relies on its body to express itself.

In Australian astrology, Kangaroo's constellation appears in the sky during the same month that Aries, the Ram, does in the northern hemisphere. It is connected to the planet Mars. In Aboriginal cosmology, Kangaroo is a great ancestral spirit responsible for the creation of the Earth's landscape and the entire animal kingdom. They say the essence of Kangaroo lies within us all. Australian Aboriginal mothers attribute their maternal instincts to the example of Kangaroo who teaches them—in a dream state—to be good nurturers.

The indigenous Palawa people of nearby Tasmania were named after the first man that Kangaroo created. Kangaroo taught them about the land and their mystical connections to the spiritual world. Their songs and ceremonies reportedly included stomping and energetic movements of Kangaroo that would raise the vibration of the participants. Few people on Tasmania can claim a Palawa ethnic heritage anymore, and much knowledge has been lost.

Australian Aborigines are careful not to point Kangaroo bones at anyone as it is believed to cause bad luck, even bring death. The energetic strength of Kangaroo is well respected by these indigenous people. Since it spends so much time in a pouch near its mother's belly at the beginning of its life Kangaroo is deep in the energy of the root chakra, giving it a strong sense of security and safety, a connection to others and strong grounding.

Kangaroo brings us the message that we may be trying too hard and making things too complex. It tells us to value simplicity and that things being difficult, and complex, does not make them more valuable. When we use simplicity and ease in our approach, the complexity and resistance dissolves. Kangaroo can see deep-seated conditioning, hidden in the "pouch" of your soul. These things create resistance and control and inhibit the free flow of your creative expression. If you are trying too hard, release the tension and hypervigilance you feel that is a byproduct of your dysfunctional family beliefs and embrace the family of spirits and guides that support you on a higher level so that your life is lived in full.

POWERS OF KANGAROO

Call in Kangaroo for:

- The capacity to move forward quickly and with precision.
- Help to build a more nurturing relationship with your children or to support a premature baby.
- Holding safe space for your ideas until they are truly ready to be released in the world.

AWARENESS FROM KANGAROO

If Kangaroo comes into your life:

- You may be too quick to pick a fight. You need to discern when to pick your battles wisely and when to walk away.
- You may need to get grounded and bring more balance into your life.
- You may need some remedial nurturing to overcome a childhood lacking connection to others.

Energy Center: Root

Mineral: Red goldstone

Element: Earth

Magic & Mystery:

- When English explorer James Cook arrived in Australia he misinterpreted the word for Kangaroo when the Aboriginals were actually saying "I don't understand you."
- Kangaroos never stop growing during their entire lives.

SHAMAN'S INTENTION: *SUPPORT ME IN MOVING FORWARD*

KINGFISHER

FIDELITY | **CALMNESS** | **PRECISION**

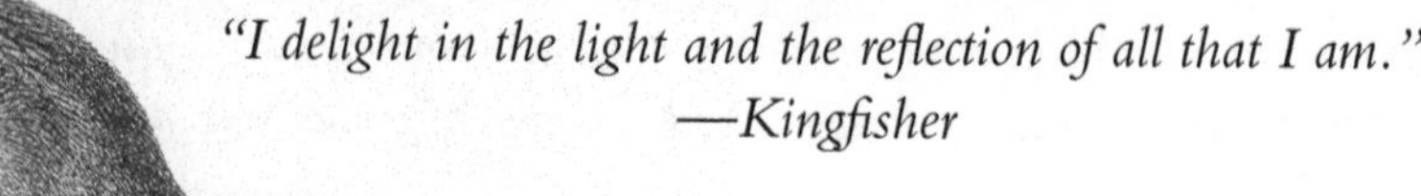

"I delight in the light and the reflection of all that I am."
—Kingfisher

KOOKABURRA

POWERS OF KINGFISHER

Call in Kingfisher for:

- Skillful hunting when you are looking for something.
- Calming the waters in a chaotic environment.
- Finding a lifelong partner.

AWARENESS FROM KINGFISHER

If Kingfisher comes into your life:

- It is time for an assessment of how you reflect yourself in the world.
- You need to go beyond the seen world for your answers.
- Learn the importance of courtship and respect when meeting a potential mate.

Energy Center: Sacrum

Mineral: Orange Aventurine

Element: Water

Magic & Mystery:

- For Polynesians, Kingfisher is a holy bird and thought to control the waves of the ocean and is the symbol of a successful fisherman.
- Native Americans used the feathers of a Kingfisher to give them speed and success in hunting.
- The design of Kingfisher's beak is so efficient that the Japanese bullet train design was inspired by its aerodynamic perfection.

There are almost one hundred different species of Kingfisher. Fossils have been found indicating that it has been on the planet for approximately two million years. Both the male and female of this medium-sized bird sport lovely plumage. Kingfisher lives up to its name, fishing near rivers, lakes, and streams and carving out its territory, which it energetically protects. It has keen vision and a special membrane that covers its eyes to protect them when it dives. It can accurately judge what's below the water's surface, and then strategizes how to get it.

Kingfisher builds its nests on the ground or in the trunks of trees. It chooses one partner for life and will bring fish to a potential partner as a gesture of its intention to spend a lifetime together. The devotion of the Halcyon Kingfisher of the Mediterranean, with its bright blue wings and red beak, spawned a myth that to this day is emblematic of loyalty and commitment to those we love. The story tells of how grief-stricken Alcyone, the daughter of the wind god, who had regrettably discovered that her husband drowned in the sea, jumped into the waters to be with him. The gods turned both into birds, so they could be together forever. And since it was January, the gods stopped the winds and calmed the sea for fourteen days—the so-called *halcyon days* of winter before the solstice—so that the wife could lay her eggs and nurture them with calm. The ancient Greeks saw Kingfisher as closely linked to the nymphs of the sea who adored them and felt that they were the protectors of bodies of water. Halcyon days represent periods of prosperity, happiness, and peace.

On the Island of Borneo, the indigenous Dusun saw Kingfisher as a negative omen; if spotted on the way to battle, it was thought best that the soldier not go to war. Other tribes saw them as good omens. Polynesians worshipped Kingfisher and believed it watched over the waves and oceans. Among Native Americans Kingfisher is a sign of prosperity, fertile valleys, and good luck. It is honored for its hunting skills.

Kingfisher thrives in three elements: earth, water, air. Its connection to these elements makes it highly perceptive of the presence and flow of energy around the planet. It has an instinctual knowledge of past lives and is a good Power Animal from which to learn about reincarnation and different levels of consciousness. If you're interested in deepening your relationship with nature, Kingfisher is the perfect guide. In nature, we can begin our expansion so that we feel secure and assimilated in the world. When we feel safe enough, we drop the need to try and control everything and this makes changes easier. We can function with precision, not fear, if we remain calm. Kingfisher takes the deep dive without anxiety, it trusts its inner knowing that what it seeks is near. Kingfisher does not see obstacles, only possibilities.

SHAMAN'S INTENTION: *HELP ME TO BE CONCISE, CLEAR, AND CALCULATED*

KOALA

CALM | **AFFECTION** | **TRUST**

"The view from the Upper World will help you to realize that life is not complicated, it is really a simple journey to enlightenment."—Koala

Koala is a marsupial that lives in the trees of Australia and dines on eucalyptus leaves. Its name was derived from an Aboriginal word that means "no drink" because it hydrates itself with the water from leaves and therefore drinks infrequently. Koala is very choosy about the type of eucalyptus that it consumes; although there are 900 types to choose from, it can only eat a few. It has a specialized liver that makes it possible to digest this toxic plant. Since its diet is not designed for high energy, Koala tends to sleep a lot; in fact, it is active only four hours per day. Because it has no predators, it can safely enjoy a laidback lifestyle. The biggest threat to its survival is the bush fires that burn through its habitat. If fire is approaching quickly, it cannot run fast enough to escape. What Koala lacks in its capacity for abstract reasoning, it makes up for with its powerful sense of smell and can smell eucalyptus leaves from many miles away. Koala's gestation period is thirty-five days. The Joey will live in its mother's pouch afterward for six months, and then ride on her back for another year.

Aboriginal myths depict Koala as a wise teacher. They say that if threatened a human could be turned into Koala for survival. Tree climbing was an important skill humans needed to hide. Koala has no sense of urgency. Tribes near Queensland see Koala as a wisdom keeper who knows much about turning barren lands into abundant forests.

Koala's connection to trees is its bond with the principles of the Tree of Life and our evolution in a place of the divine plan. As a Power Animal, Koala shows us that we need to find a pillar of strength that we can rely on for our home and protection and also to assure we receive the exact nourishment we need for or souls so that we can feel calm and secure in our being.

Koala carries the symbolism of the nurturing womb since it carries its offspring for almost a year. This sense of Mother Earth and the Koala's connection to trees is a bridge to Father Sky, the place of creation. This is the perfect circle of our cosmic journey.

Koala embodies a lesson in tranquility and kindness. It is always ready to receive, a trait that brings abundance and happiness. The simplicity with which it lives can help us to realize that our lives can be full even if we keep things simple. Slowing down, taking it easy and remaining hydrated is foundational advice for longevity. This messenger of stillness shows us that we can overcome the chaos of our everyday lives through meditation and by putting down roots, like a tree. It demonstrates that through constant and meaningless motion, we risk missing out on the mysteries of earthly experience. If we are never still we will never be present enough to perceive our greatest truths, which come from the quiet and honoring of our infinite connection to Earth.

POWERS OF KOALA

Call in Koala for:

- Lowering the volume on your adrenal glands.
- Learning that in solitude you can find the power of the present.
- Help in getting enough quality sleep.

AWARENESS FROM KOALA

If Koala comes into your life:

- You are stressed out and need to take a break.
- You need to be more discerning about your diet.
- It may be a sign to drop your defenses.

Energy Center: Root

Mineral: Black agate

Element: Water

Magic & Mystery:

- When a baby Koala is born it is the size of a bee.
- Koala is the only animal other than humans to have an individual fingerprint.
- Koala lives a solitary life, leaving its mother after one year and then lives alone in trees.

SHAMAN'S INTENTION: *TEACH ME THE WAY TO STILLNESS, A PLACE WHERE I CAN DISCOVER THE SIMPLICITY OF BEING HUMAN*

LADYBUG

BALANCE | **LOVE** | **ABUNDANCE**

"There is hope in everything; never doubt the power of the Universe."
—Ladybug

POWERS OF LADYBUG

Call in Ladybug for:

- Destroying what it is that is bothering you and restoring balance.
- Helping you to appreciate the fruits of your labor.
- Solidifying a relationship and its purpose.

AWARENESS FROM LADYBUG

If Ladybug comes into your life:

- A relationship may soon begin to blossom.
- You may be expecting a child soon or a new idea will come to you for nurturing.
- Time to plant a garden that will bring you greater understanding of the insect world.

Energy Center: Heart

Mineral: Ruby in fuchsite

Element: Air

Magic & Mystery:

- Ladybug is a messenger from the spirit world, landing on us to bring our attention to something we need to know.
- Ladybug is a beetle not a bug.
- Ladybug prefers to fly.

There are over 5,000 types of Ladybug. A member of the beetle family, this pretty bug is primarily known for its red wings and black spots, although it may come in other colors and not all types have spots. In the animal world, bright red is often perceived as a sign of toxicity. This coloring is a protective mechanism to repel predators that instinctively will avoid it. The black spots are to help it blend into leafy environments. Ladybug can fly very fast, beating its wings 5,000 times per minute. It protects plants by keeping populations of predators like White Fly, Aphid, and Mite under control. Ladybug will purposely lay its eggs among colonies of Aphids and other insects so that when its eggs hatch its larvae can begin to feast on them. A mature Ladybug eats up to sixty Aphids a day, making it an ally for gardeners and farmers.

The number of spots on a Lady bug is determined by its genetics and species. The most common Ladybug has seven spots, and this has spiritual significance. There are seven main energy centers (chakras) in the human body and the seventh, located on the crown of the head, is associated with cosmic consciousness and awakening. A double seven is a sign of acknowledgment that you are pursuing your divine purpose. There are also the seven stars in the Pleiades star system in the constellation of Taurus.

In many cultures Ladybug is a symbol of prosperity and a positive future. Europeans of old would count the spots of a Ladybug that landed on them as an indication of how many children they would have. According to folklore, the number of spots on Ladybug's shell represents how many months it will take you to find your true love. In Asia, if you catch a Ladybug and set it free, they say it will find your true love and whisper your name in his or her ear. In France Ladybug is seen as a healer that can take away whatever ails you. The Swiss may tell their children that Ladybug brought them, like the German story of Stork. On the other hand, some cultures believe that seeing a Ladybug with more than seven spots is a sign of an impending famine. Ladybug is obviously a gift from nature to humanity, as it brings us so many messages from the spirit world.

As a Power Animal, Ladybug is a protector. To improve the Feng shui of a living space, use images of Ladybug to optimize the flow of energy. Ladybug brings a spirited confidence because of its bright color that is beneficial for those wanting to shine and be seen by others. Call upon Ladybug when you're ready to hop on an online dating site and get noticed. Ladybug brings a sense of enthusiasm for life that is like an inner love potion to attract those that are favorable and congruent with your personality. As a guide, Ladybug can tell you when you need to make a quick getaway if the alignment with a potential mate is not right for your future. Ladybug can also help you to release your former partners and stop remembering, softening the impact of a loss so that you are free to move forward. Releasing the past helps us to become more receptive to the future and ready to receive. Opening up to a lighter view of your past will inspire merriment and renewal so that you can fall in love again.

SHAMAN'S INTENTION: *HELP ME TO LET GO OF THE PAST AND EMBRACE THE FUTURE*

LARK

JOY | **EXPRESSIVENESS** | **THOUGHTFULNESS**

"We bring a message from the animal kingdom to hear our songs of love for our planet."—Lark

Lark is a songbird well known for the lovely melody it sings even when flying. Most birds sing only when perched. The many species of Lark are found all over the planet in habitats ranging from warm deserts to chilly tundra. Most have brown feathers that camouflage them while they are on the ground foraging for seeds, grasses, fruits, flowers, and leaves to eat. Lark is protective of its nest and will defend its territory with vigor. It can mimic the sounds of other birds or even voices. It can sing familiar songs like Parrot or Mynah Bird do. The ancient Celts of the British Isles saw Lark as a sacred being.

The Lakota Sioux tell a story in which Lark is a messenger from Itokaga, the god of the south wind. South is the direction of the Sun and bringer of the warmth and light that supports life. Lark's association with this energy means it can bring the medicine of fertility and a joyful relationship with a loyal partner. In the medicine wheel the South represents summer, a time of rapid growth and heat—and the element of fire. It intensifies relationships.

Lark displays almost hawk like aerial gymnastics, as it likes to fly toward the heavens and then fall quickly toward the ground as if wanting us to know of our connection to the other worlds and that our embodied lives are a link between the two poles of existence, the spirit of Father Sky and the matter of Mother Earth. Lark's aerial talent also suggests that it is a spiritual messenger capable of bringing us insights from higher realms of consciousness.

A crescent shape on Lark's breast is a sign that it holds the energy of the Moon, a symbol of the fullness of the light—the abundance—that is to come. The word *crescent*, derived from the Latin root *crescere,* means "to increase." Therefore, when seeing Lark, recognize that it is a time to manifest more abundantly. You can expand your riches through gratitude and appreciation, and enthusiasm about the potential promise of starting anew.

Lark brings us a message about expanding our view of our life purpose. It urges us to put the wisdom of the Universe to use in our everyday lives. Unfold your own wings and fly without fear, leaving behind the place you previously occupied if you were surrounded by self-absorbed people. Abundance can come from loving your work and using your talents. Sing as you fly, like Lark does. Lark can help you to communicate the truth and give you the confidence to name it. Only when we fly beyond illusion do we have the ability to see our patterns of imbalance. Many times, the most difficult path is the one to find your heart's desires. Lark will take you on a ride to the unconditionally loving place inside you where your inner joy resides.

POWERS OF LARK

Call in Lark for:

- Help to understand your purpose.
- Expanding the reach of your message.
- Listening to the stories of others so that your song is full of understanding.

AWARENESS FROM LARK

If Lark comes into your life:

- Keep your promises; now is not time to go back on your word.
- Raise your level of optimism; things are not as bad as they seem.
- Become a messenger of a higher vibration on the planet.

Energy Center: Throat

Mineral: Dumortierite

Element: Air

Magic & Mystery:

- "The lark at break of day arising, from sullen earth, sings hymns at heaven's gate."
  —Shakespeare, Sonnet 29
- It is believed in almost all cultures that birds are the reincarnated souls of humans coming back to Earth to learn the language of the animal kingdom.

SHAMAN'S INTENTION: *TEACH ME THE LANGUAGE OF THE ANIMAL KINGDOM*

LEECH

PURPOSE | **COMPLETION** | **HEALING**

"Sometimes your purpose is not clear, yet within all beings is a call to service waiting to emerge."
—Leech

POWERS OF LEECH

Call in Leech for:

- Control over your nervous system.
- A holistic and natural approach to your health.
- Leaving a job, relationship, home, or possession to which you've been clinging.

AWARENESS FROM LEECH

If Leech comes into your life:

- You might consider working in the health and wellness sector.
- You may have negative energy attached to your energy field.
- Be aware that people may be taking advantage of you.

Energy Center: Root

Mineral: Axinite

Element: Earth

Magic & Mystery:

- Only one type of Leech sucks blood; others survive on algae, decaying plant material and insects.
- Amazon Leech can grow to be eighteen inches long.
- Leech has thirty-two brains and three sets of teeth with 100 teeth in each set.

Leech is related to the Worm family with its closest relatives being Earthworm. It can be found in rivers, marshes, and ponds, and sometimes it makes its home in the sea or in a forest. One Leech species has been used for bloodletting for medicinal purposes for 25,000 years in India, Greece, and Europe. Leech is mentioned in ancient Ayurvedic texts from India as an integral tool for good health. Hippocrates, the father of western medicine, believed that our moods, emotions, and behaviors were caused by our "humors" –having too much or too little fluids, such as blood, yellow bile, black bile, and phlegm, in our bodies. The best way he and his peers knew to balance our humors was with Leech therapy.

Although Leech has small, sharp teeth that can pierce through even the tough hide of Hippo, the sucking of blood that Leech does is not painful. It produces an anesthetic substance that reduces the pain of the process. Physicians today utilize Leech during reconstructive surgery and to treat arthritis, among other procedures.

Leech has a remarkable nervous system. Its internal structure has thirty-two segments, each with its own brain. It also has multiple sets of reproductive organs. Even when exposed to toxins or when it loses most of its body weight, it has the ability to survive. Leech is a dutiful parent, covering its eggs to protect them from bacteria and fungus. When born, it attaches itself to the parent.

Leech is a participant in the creation story of the Munda people who are indigenous to Bengal, India. Traditionally, the Munda worship Sing Bonga, the luminous creator of the Universe, who was married to the Moon. Sing Bonga asked Turtle, Crab, and Leech to create the Earth by bringing up soil and clay from the bottom of the ocean. After Turtle and Crab failed, Leech succeeded. Sing Bonga transformed Leech's gift into what is now Earth. Leech brings us the message of stimulating our attention and sensory awareness so that we can be present. Once present, we can confront life consciously and unclouded by emotional reactions. With calm and clear thinking, there is no intimidation. When we are in a state of presence, we can also heal ourselves and others. Our inner peace invokes positive actions and energy levels that can penetrate the human body and affect wellbeing.

SHAMAN'S INTENTION: *GUIDE ME IN THE PROCESS OF EXTRACTION OF ALL THAT DOES NOT SERVE THE HIGHEST GOOD FOR ALL*

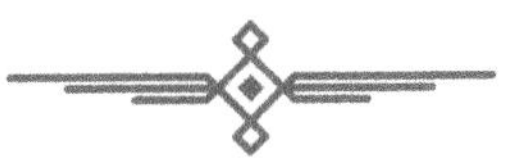

LEMUR

AGILITY | EXTROVERSION | INTUITION

"When you spend most of your life in a tree, you realize the power it has to sustain life. More appreciation is certainly deserved of the tree."—Lemur

Lemur is a small primate that lives in the mountainous forests and the wetlands of Madagascar and the Comoro Islands off the coast of Africa. It has nearly 100 existent species. As recently as a couple thousand years ago, some Lemur were as large as Gorilla. Like Monkey, Lemur is intelligent with a good capacity for learning and recall. It has hands with five grasping fingers that look like ours and they can use tools. Lemur has a keen sense of smell and hearing that give it early warning of approaching danger. It relies on special sounds for communication. The most social Lemur is the Ring-tailed Lemur, which likes to get into a huddle with others of its kind, forming a ball for warmth and companionship. This Lemur likes to scratch its buddies' backs and sunbathe. It eats fruit and leaves, its favorite fruit being tamarind. Sometimes Lemur is nocturnal, which is how it got its name. Humans only settled on Madagascar 2,000 years ago; it was visited, but not populated, by ancient Romans. The Latin root of the word *Lemur* is *lemure*, meaning "ghost," referring to a spirit that haunts the living.

For the people of Madagascar Lemur has extensive cultural and spiritual significance. Mostly there is fear and respect for Lemur, as it is seen as potentially vengeful if made fun of or killed. Legend says its soul will return and wreak havoc upon perpetrators.

As a Power Animal, Lemur brings us the energy of a successful social life and encourages outgoing behavior, yet it is territorial and will only go so far with its generosity. It is an effective communicator and can usually get what it wants. Its love of fun and abundant enthusiasm remind us that a simple smile can raise the vibration of the field around us and be a helpful tool for getting out of depression. The female Lemur is a dominant force in Lemur society, a highly respected matriarch that can be a formidable fighter when she wants something. Lemur's strength is a trait that women should emulate as the antiquated stereotypes of female weakness dissolve and our society embraces the creative power of the Divine Feminine. Lemur brings us the message to lighten up and let go; it is time to trust our inner wisdom. If we do not trust our inner wisdom, we can remain emotionally stuck and out of touch with the joy that is always within us. Fuse the mind with feelings so that they are equal partners and your actions incorporate deeper wisdom and knowing. Stop complaining and being grumpy, as holding on to anger and resentment is a self-imposed poison that means you are taking things way to seriously. Feel secure and jump for joy.

POWERS OF LEMUR

Call in Lemur for:

- Help to communicate with the spirits of your ancestors.
- Boosting your social prowess when you feel intimidated.
- The gift of expression and language.

AWARENESS FROM LEMUR

If Lemur comes into your life:

- Focus. You are moving around from place to place too often and need to get grounded.
- Remember to embrace your inner child and have fun.
- It is time to take a vacation and enjoy your family or friends.

Energy Center: Throat

Mineral: Blue sapphire

Element: Air

Magic & Mystery:

- The tail of the Ring-tailed Lemur is longer than its body.
- Lemur is thought to be the only surviving animal from an ancient civilization on our planet called Lemuria.

SHAMAN'S INTENTION: *MERGE WITH ME SO THAT I MAY FEEL, SENSE, AND EXPERIENCE JOY*

LEOPARD

SOLITUDE | **TEACHING** | **ADAPTABILITY**

"I walk in the world with confidence; this affords me the ability to trust the path I am taking."—Leopard

SNOW LEOPARD

POWERS OF LEOPARD

Call in Leopard for:

- Embracing the feminine aspects of yourself.
- Conquering fear.
- Greater understanding of the laws of the Universe.

AWARENESS FROM LEOPARD

If Leopard comes into your life:

- It is time to gather your strength and be powerful.
- There may be deceit around you that you will need clarity to perceive.
- You will land on your feet no matter how many hoops you have to jump through.

Energy Center: Crown

Mineral: Stilbite

Element: Fire

Magic & Mystery: The tomb of the ancient Egyptian pharaoh Tutankhamen contained several images of Leopard and two skins of Leopard that are believed to have been part of his wardrobe while he was alive.

Leopard, one of five species of Cat from the genus *Panthera* which includes Lion, Jaguar, Snow Leopard, and Tiger, is an inhabitant of East Africa and Southern Asia. On the whole, it is a solitary animal that roams a large, marked territory at night as it plans a stealth kill of its prey. Leopard will gather with its pride to mate and then will head out on its own again. Leopard is not easy to spot in the wild, as it is cunning at blending into the vegetation and is well camouflaged by its spotted fur. It prefers to travel in areas with abundant foliage rather than barren landscapes for this reason. Leopard is a skilled climber and will drag the carcass of its prey up into a tree to protect it from being shared with others.

Leopard is fast and agile. It can run over thirty-six miles per hour and leap ten feet into the air. It is a patient strategist that will sit and assess its situation during a hunt before attacking. Its spots, called rosettes, are similar to those of Jaguar, yet smaller.

As a nocturnal animal, Leopard is associated with feminine, lunar energy. Because of its strength and ferocity, it also represents the power of unleashed desire and the awakening of kundalini in the spine. Leopard has no barriers, so paths to awakening are always open to it. Leopard embodies the truth and will attack any energy that is incongruent with the truth. Leopard can recognize a falsehood a mile away and will warn us of distortions. Through its presence Leopard is a symbol of the immense power of life itself.

According to ancient Egyptian lore, Seshat, the goddess of wisdom and writing (aka Mistress of the House of Books) wore a Leopard skin with spots on it that was said to represent the stars, eternity, and mastery of numerology. Her hieroglyph became the symbol for "year" because she was the record keeper. In China, Leopard is also associated with the cycles of nature since there it hibernates.

As a Power Animal, Leopard can teach shamans how to master darkness. It is a guide for those who want to cross the bridge between the conscious and unconscious minds and have access to the mysteries of the spirit worlds. By shapeshifting into Leopard, we may gain admission to the Other World and talk to spirits.

Leopard has a warning for those who would dominate others to not misuse their power. Leaders whose intentions are designed for the benefit of only an elite few should be on alert for its corrective ability. As an embodiment of the Warrior-Priestess archetype, Leopard represents the power of creation inherent to lunar cycles. Leopard has an innate awareness of the cycles of darkness and light, death and rebirth. It dismisses fear by trusting the balancing forces of the Universe to bring swift justice to the corrupt. Leopard brings us the message of transformation. It urges us to glean wisdom from our experiences. When the time is right, we can take a seat as an elder of our tribe and use this power as a tool for transformation. As a Power Animal, Leopard is a helpful guide to have at the crossroads of life, especially when you are older and need to discern the next path. It helps to maintain a sense of vibrancy and defy thoughts of aging. It encourages us to see age as an alchemical process that enables us to support others. Leopard inspires us to share shamanic wisdom so that the teachings of ancient and indigenous peoples are passed on for many generations to come and ensuring that the knowledge is preserved.

SHAMAN'S INTENTION: *BY MERGING WITH LEOPARD, I EMBRACE THE KNOWLEDGE OF THE WISDOM KEEPERS*

LION

PRESTIGE | **PROTECTION** | **HEART**

"Paws of purpose, ears of understanding, and eyes of protection we bring to all who admire and respect us."—Lion

Although in ancient times Lion inhabited Europe, the Middle East, and Africa, it is now found only in the savannahs and grasslands of southern Africa. Lion's family, or pride, collaborates to defend its territory and collectively hunt. Lion is strong and linked to the energy of the heart and love. The male Lion weighs over 500 pounds and has a huge presence in the animal kingdom. It uses its explosive roar, which can be heard for miles away, to communicate and warn others of where its territory is, and as a reminder of how powerful it is. During the day, Lion lazes around in all-male or all-female groups, relaxing and sleeping. The females tend the cubs. Lion conserves its energy for the night when it hunts in teams using time-tested tactics to snatch the targeted prey.

Worldwide Lion is a symbol for royalty, power, and courage. The female Lion is the epitome of a mother and she embodies all the feminine powers and maternal energy of the Moon, including the nurturing intelligence that contributes to the successful upbringing of cubs. Lion is one of the best hunters in the Feline family. In Africa, to be compared to Lion is a welcome compliment, signifying a person of stature and importance.

In ancient Egypt Lion was seen as a symbol of the rising Sun; its deep yellow fur gave people the impression that it had swallowed the Sun and internalized the mysteries of the heavens. There are thousands of references throughout the world to the power of the Lion and many overlap in meaning. What most cultures agree on is Lion's skill for hunting, the confidence and authority with which it walks the world, and its protective nature. For this reason, Lion statues are placed at the entrances to temples, government buildings, and libraries with their paws on a ball that represents the Sun. The most important representation of Lion is the body of the Great Sphinx on the Giza Plateau, holding sacred space to guard the pharaohs in their tombs--the pyramids--after death.

The Buddhists see Lion as protecting humans from demons and standing vigilant for any ghosts or negative energy that may be lurking around. Fearless, Lion will pounce on and devour anything that is not welcome.

Although extremely strong, Lion is also often portrayed as demonstrating a heartfelt side of mutual respect and compassion among all beings. When leading, it is an emblem of wisdom, nobility, and fairness. The Shangaan people of southern Africa believe that the extremely rare White Lion is a messenger from God. Only a few are left in the world at the time of this writing. The constellation Leo (Latin for "Lion") was named by the second-century Greco-Roman astronomer Ptolemy after the monstrous Nemean Lion that was killed by the hero Heracles as one of his twelve labors.

Because of its connection to the Sun, Lion reminds us to leave behind with the sunset all that troubles us and to temper our expectations by not obsessing about what is to come with tomorrow's sunrise—this is an alchemical lesson about devouring the Sun to tame the mind. With courage, staying present puts us in a place of power. Presence brings us enlightenment, which is evidenced by the luxurious mane of the male Lion that encircles his head like a radiant crown of higher thought. If you feel defeated or you are having difficulty surviving a transformational experience, ask Lion for support to cultivate your will to live, heal, and overcome obstacles. Use its power to triumph over adversity. If you feel beaten down, call upon the power of Lion to restore you to your vibrant self. Lion never accepts defeat.

POWERS OF LION

Call in Lion for:

- The highest protection available for walking with freedom in the world.
- Devouring mental images of the past and future.
- Elevating your reputation and proudly roaring your presence to others.

AWARENESS OF LION

If Lion comes into your life:

- You may be too laidback and need to generate more energy so you can be successful.
- It is time to nurture yourself and others.
- Embrace your feminine nature and the divine and majestic you.

Energy Center: Heart

Mineral: Tree agate

Element: Air

Magic & Mystery:

- A male lion often is shown with his paw on a ball that is a symbol of his life essence.
- Female lions are often seen as statues guarding cities and temples because of their fierceness.

SHAMAN'S INTENTION: *I ASK FOR YOUR WATCHFUL EYE TO DISSOLVE THE NEGATIVITY THAT SURROUNDS ME AND PROTECT ME FROM HARM*

LIZARD

INTUITION | **CHOICE** | **COLOR**

"Where would we be without color and the energy that it brings to the prism of the soul?"—Lizard

CHAMELEON, GECKO, GILA MONSTER, IGUANA, KOMODO DRAGON

POWERS OF LIZARD

Call in Lizard for:

- Choose to see the world in a vibrant and colorful way.
- Help to quickly remove yourself from an unresolved situation.
- Guidance when making your next move.

AWARENESS FROM LIZARD

If Lizard comes into your life:

- You may need to make a bigger effort to support your children or others close to you.
- You should do more to rely on your intuition.
- Consider color therapy to brighten your mind and attitude.

Energy Center: Third eye

Mineral: White jade

Element: Earth

Magic & Mystery:

- There are more than 450 species of Lizard in the Amazon.
- Some species of Lizard can live for fifty years.
- Of all the types of Lizard, only the Gecko has vocal chords and can make a sound.

Lizard is a reptile with tough, overlapping, and scaly skin that has existed on Earth for 200 million years. Over 6,000 species of Lizard are found on every continent except for Antartica. The largest is the 300-pound Komodo Dragon that lives on a few islands in Indonesia. The male of this species is territorial and has been known to run off rivals. It eats insects and has a tongue that extends to snatch its next meal. Most species of Lizard lay eggs, which are untended. These hatch in due time, after which the offspring must fend for themselves. Active parenting is a rare Lizard instinct. During the day Lizard likes to soak up the Sun since it is cold blooded. Lizard is both impressed by colors and is very colorful itself. Some kinds of Lizard have glow-in-the-dark bones that shine through their skin. It can be seen bobbing its head or using movements to attract others of its kind.

Lizard is harmless to humans. In the Hawaiian Islands and the Amazon jungle alike, it is considered by the local tribes as the king of beasts. Lizard has excellent intuition evidenced by a photosensitive area of the brain near the top of its head that is connected to its pineal gland. This parietal eye makes it capable of navigating habitats of forest or jungle. Lizard is a master of evading predators. It will move quickly and disappear into a crack or crevasse when it feels threatened. Sometimes it will even detach its tail to escape capture. It is clever about camouflaging itself.

Native Americans associate Lizard with healing and survival. In the tribes of the Plains Indians, a newborn boy's umbilical cord would traditionally be sewn into a pouch in the shape of Lizard as an offering for his health. The Cheyenne consider it bad luck to kill a Lizard. Horned Lizard is sacred medicine to the indigenous people of the Southwest.

The Egyptian hieroglyphic of Lizard means "plentiful." To ancient Romans, Lizard symbolized death and rebirth because it periodically sheds its old skin and grows a new one. In Africa members of the Dogon tribe carve the image of Lizard on their homes to welcome protective spirits. In Cameroon Lizard is known as a symbol of fertility and for bringing peace to a home. The Maori of New Zealand believe that Lizard came from outer space and is a supernatural being.

As a Power Animal, Lizard is about movement in how you see the world. Most animals are color blind, but not Lizard whose vision can bring alive all the colors in nature and spur on your imagination. Color transmits feeling as each color carries a vibration that causes the retina to dance in its sensitivity. The ability to move into cracks in the ground or rock is knowledge of the way to other realities beyond the boundaries of Earth. The crack can allow the light of higher consciousness to come into our minds, which can help us to start over. Just like the arrival of a new day at the "crack" of dawn, the crack that the spirit of Lizard leads us to enter is a gateway of potential. It is a good guide for discovering what has been missing in our lives or in a given situation or relationship. Knowing how to get through the narrow passageways unnoticed is a shamanic skill that's very useful in the spirit realms.

Lizard brings us the message to realize that we have the power to make our own decisions. With the power of choice, we can simply make up our minds to be successful and prosperous. By overcoming the weakness of the mind's shortcomings, we can realize that opportunities are everywhere for us. Prosperity of every kind will be drawn to those who align with the frequencies and colors of the Universe. With the power to choose, you can be happy, motivated, and enthusiastic about life. Say yes to life!

SHAMAN'S INTENTION: *OPEN UP THE CRACKS AND CREVICES TO MY HEART AND ALLOW THE LIGHT TO SHINE IN*

LLAMA

CURIOSITY | GRACE | PERSEVERANCE

"Do not see your life as a place of burdens. If you are making sacrifices for others, know that there can be joy in service."—Llama

Llama was domesticated from Wild Guanaco 5,000 years before the appearance of the Incas in South America. It dates back 40 million years to the central plains of North America, and during the last ice age it migrated south. Now it makes its home in the highlands of Peru and western Bolivia. The Inca used Llama as a pack animal and a guard for Sheep (with whom it gets along well). Its hair was weaved into warm clothing, its meat was used for food, and its dung was used for fuel. Llama can carry 25 percent of its body weight for many miles. It is remarkably surefooted on a variety of terrain because of its two-toed feet. Looking in Llama's large eyes you will sense its kind and gentle spirit. It is friendly to humans. For food, Llama grazes in fields upon native grasses. It also seeks out low-lying shrubs and vegetation.

Llama is curious, intelligent, and an independent thinker. Highly social, it lives in herds where it enjoys loving bonds with others of its kind. When Llama is upset, it spits to show its discontent. It is territorial and protective. Its presence is a deterrent to Coyote.

Llama is uniquely adapted to high elevations, making it aware of upper realms and vibrations, which most likely is the reason for its kind and accepting nature. A dark cloud constellation that rises above Cusco in November is called the Yacana (Llama) because of its shape's resemblance to the animal. Black was especially revered by the Incas because of this. It is believed that the Llama among the stars drank the water of the ocean to keep it from flooding the land so that humanity could avoid pain, sadness, hunger, and tragedy.

The Moche tribe of Peru would bury a Llama with a valued member to take to the afterlife as a companion. In Cusco, Peru, during April, the ancient Incas would dress a white Llama in a red tunic and place gold earrings on its ears. It symbolized the primordial Llama and the authority of the Incan Empire.

According to legend, the Incan deity Urcuchillay—a multicol-

LLAMA

CURIOSITY **GRACE** **PERSEVERANCE**

THE MOCHE TRIBE OF PERU WILL BURY A LLAMA WITH A VALUED TRIBE MEMBER TO TAKE TO THE AFTERLIFE AS A COMPANION.

ALPACA, GUANACO, VICUNA

POWERS OF LLAMA

Call in Llama for:

- Help in receiving gifts from Mother Nature.
- Reducing the ego.
- Goal setting.

AWARENESS FROM LLAMA

If Llama comes into your life:

- It is a sign to get organized and tidy up your environment.
- Your digestive system may need your attention.
- Don't worry, be happy.

Energy Center: Heart

Mineral: Goshenite

Element: Air

Magic & Mystery:

- A bezoar is a gallstone from a Llama. Believed to have magical powers, bezoars used to be offered as antidotes for poison. Resembling a semiprecious stone, Queen Elizabeth I of England had several bezoars included in the design of her crown.
- When a Llama is born both mother and baby hum, as if they are chanting Om. The newborn Llama takes comfort in remembering the vibrational sound of the cosmos from which it came.

ored Llama—was creator of the world. He taught that there was no beginning or end to our existence. This god watched over animals in their fields at night. Llama guards the fifth element (the sacred rainbow), which represents the colorful harmony of being connected to all things. Rainbow is a reminder of the beauty and joy we can find in living.

Traditional Incan offering ceremonies (*despachos*) are done to honor new beginnings and as prayers for healing. Shamans are charged with the preparation of the offerings, which are placed on a woven cloth, wrapped in a package, blessed, and then burned. The package may include incense, flowers, coca leaves, fruit, anything colored silver or gold, beads, and Llama fat. The contents are symbolic of the elements. The purpose is to thank Mother Earth, Father Sky, and the Mountains. When a Llama has a miscarriage, the fetus may be offered to the gods in a despacho and seen as representing that which is not yet manifested, yet a sign of potential.

The wool of Alpaca, another Andean animal, is used to create hand-woven clothing. Before any garment is woven, a chuyay ceremony is done to bless the fibers. Normally chuyays are held in January and February, marking the month that Alpacas give birth.

Llama is hard working. As a Power Animal, its spirit of service to others, such as its perseverance in carrying heavy loads up steep mountainsides, can inspire your dedication to personal growth. Learn from it to insist on using your heart (not your ego) as you move forward. Llama will help you stay curious about your existence, questioning the mystical in everything. Define your personal space within your own herd and be independent in your purpose.

Llama loves when we set new destinations and act with perseverance. It knows that looking back at the past with regret is an exercise in futility. Take Llama with you as you set forth on a new adventure, even when you do not know where you are going, as Llama will always know where and when to take the next step. Llama is happy to help others and encourages us to volunteer.

Step up and give with no fear of a lack of appreciation. Your gifts are great, no matter how insignificant they may seem to your ego. Remove any burden of resentment and view the beauty of the world, as it is yours to reflect. Your potential lies in never underestimating the power of the spirits of the higher realms, like the apus (mountain spirits) in Peru. If you seek the Llama's wisdom it will help you anchor into the high-frequency energy of the mountaintops.

SHAMAN'S INTENTION: *BLESS ME WITH LIGHT-FOOTEDNESS, SO I MAY TRAVEL IN THE HIGHER ELEVATIONS OF THE SPIRITUAL WORLD*

MANATEE

GENTLENESS | **INTELLIGENCE** | **REGENERATION**

"Living in the seas is being in the home of the psyche."—Manatee

Manatee have been called the Cow (or Teddy Bear) of the Sea. Related to Elephant, it evolved from land mammals over sixty million years ago. There are three species: African, West Indian, and Amazonian. At its largest, Manatee can weigh over a thousand pounds. It walks on its flippers across the bottom of waterways searching for herbs and grasses and normally grazes for hours a day. It has large lips. Manatee hears sounds in high frequencies, giving it the spiritual gift of being able to connect to the dimensions inhabited by ascended beings. Like its cousin, Elephant, it is intelligent and has a good memory. Manatee is sociable and creates deep, meaningful bonds with others of its kind. The African Manatee is nocturnal. It spends its days dozing and its nights grazing. When an aggregation of Manatee migrates, it looks for warm waters and areas of abundant vegetation.

In western Africa, Manatee is held sacred and is thought to have evolved from a human being. Killing Manatee is frowned upon. The people know it as the great protector of water, an important resource. The Serer people of Senegal believe Manatee knows the secrets of the future. Maame Water, a goddess of the sea venerated around the world by descendants of survivors of the African diaspora, is a symbol of great beauty and riches and an embodiment of Manatee spirit.

The Taino people of the Caribbean used the bones of Manatee to communicate with their ancestral spirits and gods in the Upper World when seeking their assistance in healing members of their tribe. The Taino hunted Manatee, as did other Native peoples who ate its meat and used its hide to make shields, boats, and shoes. It is currently a threatened species. The word Manatee is Carib for "breast" or "udder." This reference links Manatee to the Great Mother of our galaxy, the Milky Way. The maternal significance of the breast is nourishment and tenderness and the bonds of mother and child, a sign of our connection to the Divine.

To the shaman, Manatee brings wisdom from the water world. Its intelligence and trajectory of experience makes it a Power Animal that can help you understand a deeper version of things. Its peaceful existence is a message about the benefits of maintaining a Zen-like environment, of trusting in your friends and family and of believing in the power of being linked to higher frequencies.

Shamans may journey with Manatee to seek knowledge about compassion, especially if they have experienced grief or loss and want to heal the broken bonds of an emotional attachment. It will encourage us to love ourselves so we can move into calmer waters. Its gentle energy is soothing and softens suffering. Shamans are often empaths and, as such, have fragile souls. Manatee teaches us to be gentle with ourselves and others. A sense of security is paramount to the dissolution of fear. At times when we are afraid we are not enlightened. Manatee helps us to restore our sense of safety and offer security to others. Survival kills our passion for living, so spreading kindness and compassion can make the difference for many. Water is the elixir with which to transmute pain and boredom into happiness; by nourishing yourself and others you can hydrate your thoughts and bring nurturing to the planet.

POWERS OF MANATEE

Call in Manatee for:

- Help to cope with anxiety and teach you to stay calm.
- Guidance when you are learning how to meditate.
- Promoting concern for endangered species.

AWARENESS FROM MANATEE

If Manatee comes into your life:

- It is time to be gentle with yourself and others.
- Take a rest and travel to warmer waters.
- Slow down and enjoy the journey—focus less on the destination.

Energy Center: Heart

Mineral: Green garnet

Element: Water

Magic & Mystery:

- Twenty thousand years ago, a nebula that resembles Manatee was formed from an explosion in the Universe. The Manatee Nebula is located in the northern constellation of Aquila (Eagle).
- Manatee playfully enjoys body-surfing.
- Manatee has inhabited the waterways of Florida for more than forty-five million years.

SHAMAN'S INTENTION: *BRING ME THE SENSATION OF PEACE SO THAT I MAY EMBODY IT*

MOCKINGBIRD

FEARLESSNESS | CLEVERNESS | MUSICALITY

"When you have confidence in your voice and the song is of the sacred the world will embrace the message."
—Mockingbird

THRASHER

POWER OF MOCKINGBIRD

Call in Mockingbird for:

- Standing up to those who do not respect your boundaries.
- Help to use sound for healing.
- A positive attitude and help to end a cycle of negative thinking.

AWARENESS FROM MOCKINGBIRD

If Mockingbird comes into your life:

- It is time to evaluate a relationship and possibly kick someone out of your life.
- It is time for increased clarity in your communication with others.
- The way that you handle your life and use power may be in question.

Energy Center: Throat

Mineral: Blue quartz

Element: Air

Magic & Mystery: The male Mockingbird sings all night long in the spring and summer, a testament to the joy that abounds in sunny seasons.

Mockingbird is a perching bird with toes perfectly designed to grasp and hold onto a branch. It is omnivorous, mainly eating both insects and fruits. It makes its home in grasslands near the edge of forests. Mockingbird's name is derived from its love of mimicking other birds, insects, dogs, cats, frogs, crickets, and even sounds from civilization like the honk of a horn. Although its mimicking can at times be convincing, most creatures can detect the difference. Mockingbird in its maturity has a repertoire of 200 songs and sounds that it can replicate.

Mockingbird is extremely territorial and will attack anything that comes near its nest, including humans. Female Mockingbirds are attracted to males that display the most aggressive behavior toward intruders. It has excellent recognition and will remember intruders or those who have threatened it. Mockingbird has no fear and will even attack much larger birds, such as Hawk. Mockingbirds raise their offspring together and the female will insist on helpful fathering. If her mate does not rise to the occasion, she will kick him out of the nest and look for a more responsible partner.

Mockingbird holds great importance in Native American cultures. The Hopi and Pueblo people believe Mockingbird taught us to speak. The Shasta Indians view Mockingbird as the guardian of the dead. The Maricopa Indians of Arizona delight in having Mockingbird enter their dreams, as this means they will be bestowed with special powers. Other Arizona tribes, the Papago and Pima, say Mockingbird is a mediator.

Mockingbird has a beautiful selection of songs and is one of few birds that sing while flying. As a Power Animal, Mockingbird can help us to expose and express our talents. It will not accept a hidden voice, as suppression of emotion can impede the functioning of the throat chakra. Mockingbird encourages us to dig deep and bring out the truth when we are upset so that it doesn't simmer in our souls. As nature's imitator, Mockingbird is a good Power Animal for comedians and others interested in humor. Laughter relieves tension and is a great way to share playful and joyous emotions. Mockingbird's fascination with its reflection reminds us that the thoughts we put out create our reality and that the best way to know the truth of what we are projecting from within is to take a hard look at the world we have created.

Mockingbird is an authoritative messenger and embodies leadership by embracing power rather than fearing it. Mockingbird is a master problem solver and may bring you a vision of someone in your life that it would be good to learn from or emulate. Mockingbird makes decisions quickly in order to secure a positive outcome. It comes to show us the whimsy of it all; in particular, reminding us not to invest heavily in any role we are playing. In the big picture, we are only mimicking our beliefs. Fly beyond the persona that you have created for yourself and seek the purity of your authentic spirit. Count on the real you and be your amazing self.

SHAMAN'S INTENTION: *TAKE ME ON THE WAVES OF RESONANCE TO HEAR THE MUSIC OF THE UPPER WORLD*

MOLE

TRUST | **SENSING** | **GATHERING**

"Even though being small and in the dark could mean vulnerability, so much comes into view the moment you close your eyes."—Mole

Mole is a small mammal with velvety fur that has adapted to life underground. Almost blind, it uses its long nose to feel and sense things around it because it can only see light, not shapes, and sense movement. It has extremely strong paws that are ideal for digging and uses them to form tunnels and carve out caverns where it may sleep and give birth in safety. It even has a separate "kitchen" where it feeds. Many generations will use the same network of underground chambers.

Mole finds food through scent sensors on its nose and eats rapidly. Its diet consists mostly of Earthworm that accidentally fall into Mole's tunnel while crawling through the soil and get snapped up. Mole's saliva paralyzes Earthworm, so it may be stored for later consumption. Underground storage areas have thousands upon thousands of Earthworms in them. Mole does not eat the roots of plants, although its continuous digging can hurt them.

Because it is a burrowing animal, Mole is associated with the Lower World. For some Native North Americans, Mole digging around your home is an omen of impending illness or death. The Pueblo, however, consider Mole important for healing. They say Mole is one of the six guards of the sacred directions—along with Lion, Badger, Bear, Wolf, and Eagle—and guards the direction downward into the Earth. The ancient Zuni would carve stone fetishes of Mole for protection and healing. In Australia, Marsupial Mole is part of Aboriginal mythology. The Aborigines associate it with sympathy, since it is so harmless.

The Sioux believe that the Creator put Mole into the hearts of humanity to encourage us to see with the eyes of spirit and not with our own eyes; a lesson that we create our own reality. Mole reminds us that we will rarely see the truth through our own eyes. Through ultrasensory experience, there is more to discover. For example, our ears can sense the tone of a tear or an inflection of sadness. Nonordinary perception of the world gives a greater view of what is. All that defines us comes from the deeper side of who we are. Mole accepts what it cannot see. Simply stand in a place of knowing that all will come to you. Seeing is believing in the distortion of truth. Mole senses and feels the world, and life for Mole will always be multisensory and never a simple view. Mole encourages us to trust in Great Mother Gaia completely.

POWERS OF MOLE

Call in Mole for:

- Help to instinctively know your next move.
- Increasing your reliance on your perceptions of the unseen.
- Having what you need fall into your lap unexpectedly.

AWARENESS FROM MOLE

If Mole comes into your life:

- You may be acquiring more than you need.
- You may be wasting time destroying things that others would find useful.
- Be confident of the unknown.

Energy Center: Third eye

Mineral: Star ruby

Element: Earth

Magic & Mystery:

- Mole can dig up to eighteen feet per hour.
- Mole has been living in the Australian desert for fifty million years.
- When you see Mole tunnels in your yard, it's a sign of healthy soil.

SHAMAN'S INTENTION: *HELP ME TO TRUST THE UNSEEN WORLD AND KNOW ITS POWERS*

MONGOOSE

COURAGE **AGILITY** **SPONTANEITY**

"Living in defense of everything hardens your view of the world. Knowing you are powerful will keep you calm."—Mongoose

MEERCAT

POWERS OF MONGOOSE

Call in Mongoose for:

- Finding the right relationships and ending toxic ones.
- Take quick action on pending matters.
- Courage to trust in your dreams and future.

AWARENESS FROM MONGOOSE

If Mongoose comes into your life:

- You may be caught up in defending yourself all the time.
- You have the potential for success in all that you do.
- You may have to be brave and face your fears.

Energy Center: Solar plexus

Mineral: Alexandrite

Element: Earth

Magic & Mystery:

- In ancient India, Cobra was a symbol of hidden wisdom—and Mongoose was recognized as dominant over Cobra.
- Scientists at the University of Exeter in England found that Mongoose passes its traditions of foraging on from generation to generation.
- Mongoose has a special alarm call. Members of a Mongoose pack take turns as sentinel, tasked with warning others of approaching danger.

Mongoose is a small, carnivorous mammal that lives in Europe, Asia, and Africa. It is famous for its fearlessness in fighting poisonous snakes. It is agile and has such quick reflexes that it can avoid being bitten. Even if it is bitten it would be immune to the poison. Members of the thirty-three species of Mongoose live in burrows connected by a complex set of tunnels. Several individuals will live together. Team players, they support each other in achieving their common goal of survival. If one Mongoose chooses to change dens, the rest move with it; none stays behind. Unlike many other predators, Mongoose always shares its food. It is an excellent hunter due to its keen senses of sight, smell, and hearing. Using a dialogue that at times sounds similar to human speech, Mongoose is constantly chatting it up with others of its kind. Its vocalizations resemble syllables and vowels. Since Mongoose is so connected, it makes sense it would have important messages to share among itself.

Evidenced by mummified Mongoose remains found in prehistoric tombs, the ancient Egyptians domesticated Mongoose and considered it sacred. Mongoose was also depicted on funeral urns. Among other things, it was respected for eating the eggs of Crocodile and keeping the population along the Nile River in check.

Among the Tibetans, Dzambala is a Buddhist god that is depicted holding Mongoose with its mouth open and spitting jewels representing wealth and prosperity. The Hindu god of wealth, Kubera, holds Mongoose in his left hand as it represents prosperity. In Vedic astrology from India, Mongoose is the name for the December constellation that westerners call Capricorn; it is said to endow people born under these stars with the energy of independence.

Mongoose can teach you about survival and guide you to build defenses that will enable you to protect yourself, your friends, and your family and destroy that which could poison you. It is important not to overdo it but take a balanced approach. Being too defensive can leave you in constant fear, whereas embracing the perspective that all situations ultimately occur for your highest good can keep you from feeling attacked or betrayed and enable you to remain adaptable.

Mongoose also can help you to develop the skills you need to be successful. With skill, there are no barriers or challenges. We can be brave in taking risks when our instincts kick in and we trust our skills. Walking in the world with confidence we have a bold and compelling presence, a way to honor our personal power. Mongoose medicine shows us how to be less frightened and more agile and responsive—all the while knowing there is nothing to fear.

SHAMAN'S INTENTION: *HELP ME IN MANAGING FEAR AND GET ME POISED FOR WELLBEING*

MONKEY

COMMUNICATION | **EMOTION** | **FAMILY**

"Taking life so seriously is a threat to joy."—Monkey

There are 264 known species of Monkey in the world. New World Monkey lives in Central and South America. Old World Monkey lives in Africa and Asia. Evolution began to split into these different genetic lines approximately 40 million years ago. Every species has different physical characteristics (sizes, colorings), and abilities. In general, Monkey has a thumb that helps it with climbing, and it has a unique fingerprint just like humans. Monkey—our cousin—makes tools from sticks and rocks and will use a leaf as a cup for drinking water.

Monkey has lived with much admiration from humans. In ancient Egypt, it was sometimes kept as a pet for children. It was also trained to pick fruit from the trees. Male Monkey was admired for his lustfulness—so much so, in fact, that Monkey feces were an ingredient in ancient Egyptian aphrodisiac ointments.

Monkey is an excellent communicator. You always know where you stand with Monkey as it has many ways of expressing itself. It is very comfortable in its environment and is energetic and clever when facing new challenges. It acts determined and is often scolded by others of its kind if it overextends itself in a group. Monkey loves to be the center of attention and often shows off to stand out.

Monkey travels in close-knit troops and stays connected to the family it trusts throughout its life. It is protective of other troop members. If you have recently given birth, invite Monkey to be your Power Animal. The bond between mother and infant is especially strong. The mother will carry the young until the baby is able to ride on her back. Monkey is in constant contact for the first few months, during which period its mother is attentive. Only once an infant reaches around four months of age will it be allowed to play and interact with other youngsters.

In ancient Egypt, Monkey was associated with death. In art on the walls of various temple complexes, Thoth, the god of writing (hieroglyphics), wisdom, and magic, was often portrayed as Baboon and as a guardian of the Land of the Dead. He was said to stand in the judgment hall of Osiris and record the weight of people's hearts after a test to see if they should be permitted into the afterlife or be exterminated forever.

Because of its connection to the Sun, Monkey has a habit of screeching at dawn; its cries symbolize the awakening of con-

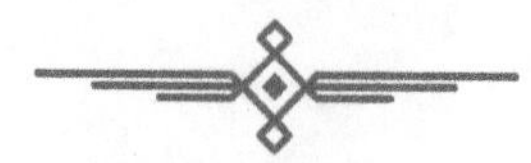

MONKEY

COMMUNICATION | **EMOTION** | **FAMILY**

MONKEY TRAVELS IN CLOSE-KNIT TROOPS AND STAYS CONNECTED TO THE FAMILY IT TRUSTS THROUGHOUT ITS LIFE.

BABOON, CHIMPANZEE, ORANGUTAN

POWERS OF MONKEY

Call in Monkey for:

- A guide to managing and revealing your emotions.
- Increased confidence when you are ready to take center stage.
- Support to be a good parent.

AWARENESS FROM MONKEY

If Monkey comes into your life:

- You may be too judgmental and controlling of others.
- It may be necessary to get more grounded.
- This may be a good time to be more involved with your family.

Energy Center: Solar plexus

Mineral: Topaz

Element: Fire

Magic & Mystery:

- On Yakushima Island in Japan, Monkey will groom and share food with Deer in exchange for a ride.
- The Macaque Monkey of Japan is the only monkey that will wash its food before eating.
- Capuchin Monkey is named after sixteenth-century monks because its head resembles the monks' hooded robes.

sciousness. In ancient art, it is often portrayed with arms raised to worship the Sun. The Egyptians admired and cared for Monkey. Since its attributes were so human-like, they thought it could be the reincarnation of an ancestor.

When Monkey gets enraged or senses a threat, it displays aggression to intimidate its rivals and enemies and compel them to submit or back down from a fight. This is how Monkey expresses its determination to get what it wants for itself and its family. Violently shaking branches of trees, thumping its chest, showing its teeth, and making guttural barking sounds are a whole package of showing up with full commitment.

Monkey is an integral figure in Hindu and Buddhist mythology. In some tales, Monkey is seen as foolish, vain, and mischievous; yet it learns lessons that lead it to be redeemed for its "unenlightened" behavior. The popular Hindu god Hanuman appears as a Monkey with a red face that is said to be the child of the wind god, Indra, regent of the East.

Buddhists tell the tale of when Buddha was Monkey in an earlier incarnation and showed compassion to a hunter who wished to do him harm. This enlightened action earned him a human incarnation. Despite this tale, Monkey also represents trickery or dishonesty in some Chinese myths.

The Tzeltal people of Mexico traditionally worshipped Monkey as the incarnation of a dead ancestor. The Mayans of Guatemala and Mexico worshipped Howler Monkey as the patron god of the arts. The Aztecs saw Monkey as their connection to the Sun and the god of fun and fertility.

As shamans, Monkey reminds us of our special relationship to trees and of how we may use our knowledge of nature as a support system. Monkey has mastered the meaning of the Tree of Life and is skillful in guiding us to the entrance to our dreams. Monkey reminds us not to impose our needs on others, as trying to control everything and everyone around us is futile. Life requires flexibility and acceptance that everyone is on their own path of learning.

No matter if we are going through dark days, life goes on; there are always brighter days ahead. It is important to embrace living fully and freely and come from a place of unconditional love. For example, we must love our children for who they are, not what we want them to be. Children have life cycles of their own, so we need only provide a loving environment for them in which they may thrive and they will do the rest. Loving ourselves is our greatest gift to others.

SHAMAN'S INTENTION: *HELP ME IN SEEKING THE ULTIMATE WISDOM OF OUR SUN, THE GREATEST CONTRIBUTOR TO OUR NOURISHMENT*

MOOSE

PROTECTION **WISDOM** **COURAGE**

"My hoofs are like thunder and my wisdom is lightning from the power of nature."
—Moose

Moose makes its home in the North. Over two million Moose inhabit North America, with the majority living in Canada. The tallest mammal in the Western Hemisphere, Moose can weigh up to 1,600 pounds. Its near-sightedness helps Moose to focus on finding the rich vegetation on the bottom of ponds and lakes that is the mainstay of its diet. Moose has excellent hearing and smell. It is a fast swimmer and can dive underwater. The antlers of the Male Moose may span five feet in width and are covered with fuzzy "velvet" that contains blood vessels which support the growth of the antlers. In late summer, when the blood supply ceases, the antlers drop off. The female Moose is extremely protective of her calves and can be as aggressive as a mother Bear if they are being threatened. She sometimes gives birth to twins and even triplets. Very protective of its territory and young, a Moose will charge at anything it sees as a threat.

For Native Americans, Moose lies in the North on the Medicine Wheel, along with Bear and Buffalo, representing animals that offer sustenance in the winter. The Ojibwe and Cree peoples see Moose as a symbol of endurance and survival. They call its antlers the crown of courage. These massive antlers growing from Moose's crown chakra are reminders of our ability to capture information from higher dimensions of consciousness that serves our highest good. As a Power Animal, Moose is a spiritual elder whose knowledge is very sacred and wise. It can be called upon to offer a unique perception of the world around it. Despite its enormity, Moose has the ability to walk unnoticed in the forest. This gift is highly prized by shamans, as it gives us the opportunity to be the ultimate observers of life. When Moose is born, its eyes are open as if it has already awakened to its purpose and inherent wisdom.

Moose is connected to the mystic feminine and to life-giving waters, which can remove toxic thoughts from our heads and restore calm and beauty to our lives when we work with its powers. Water is a holy place—the home of spirits and a source of wisdom, healing, renewal, and the manifestation of wishes. Moose spends a lot of time in the water, which is its sanctuary.

Moose is connected to other realms through solitude. Angelic voices are only a frequency away and Moose can readily hear these tones. For those who are open to its presence, Moose disseminates knowledge of the angelic realms. Moose has no doubt of the reality of the spirit world as it can see its reflection in the water. Moose brings us the affirmation of adequacy and that we are all we need for all situations. Like the water Moose is connected with, prosperity should flow easily and abundantly when we feel prosperous. It is through this divine frequency that abundance vibrates from our cells. In our careers, this same flow will help our capacity for bringing dreams to reality for ourselves and others. We should not see life as a competition or comparison. We are all different and meant to be as such. Comparing ourselves to others and feeling inadequate diminishes us and creates obstacles to exploring and pursuing our goals. Remain accepting of who you are and build a foundation of trust for your skills and contribution.

POWERS OF MOOSE

Call in Moose for:

- A different perspective when you have been comparing yourself to others.
- Spiritual protection of your personal space.
- Watching over children who may stray.

AWARENESS FROM MOOSE

If Moose comes into your life:

- There is much you need to learn and it is time to study.
- Realize that your contributions in the world are valuable.
- Take time to bathe in the calm of water.

Energy Center: Crown

Mineral: Dioptase

Element: Earth

Magic & Mystery:

- Cave drawings in Europe reveal that Moose has been hunted and revered since the Stone Age.
- According to the Algonquin Indians, if you dream of Moose you will have a long life.

SHAMAN'S INTENTION: *SUPPORT ME IN LOVING AND APPROVING OF MYSELF AND APPRECIATING ALL THAT I DO AS I SEEK TO CLAIM MY POWER*

MOSQUITO

PERSISTENCE | **FOCUS** | **AWARENESS**

"We understand that blood is life and it is what cleans and nourishes the body. It is the vital highway to health."—Mosquito

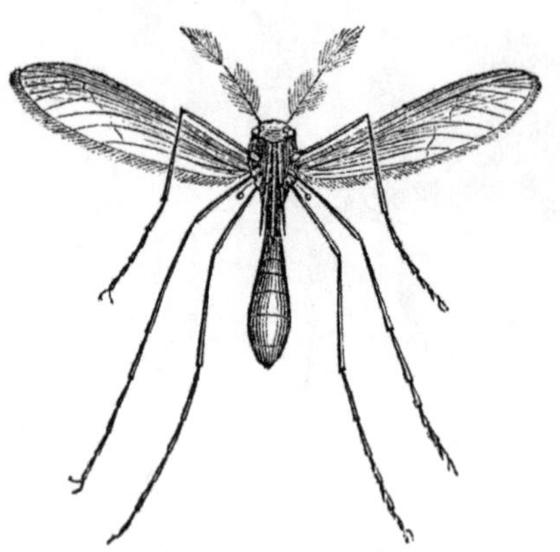

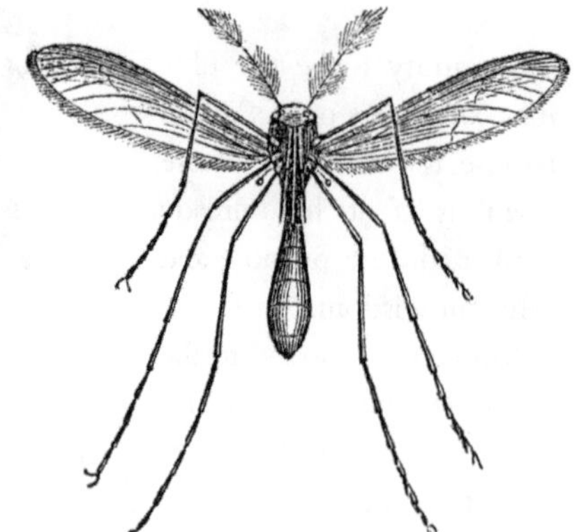

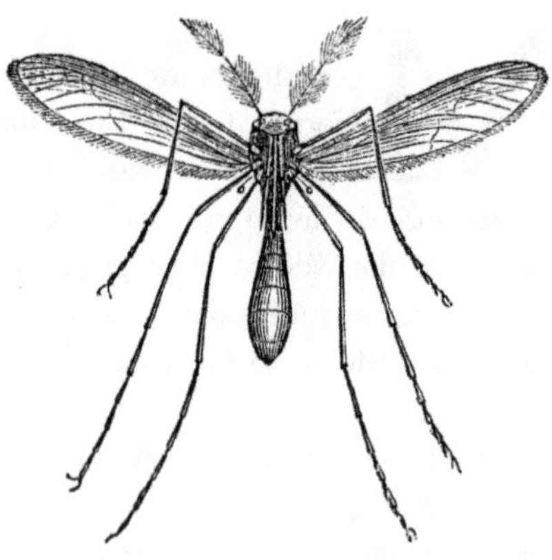

POWERS OF MOSQUITO

Call in Mosquito for:

- Help to become persistent.
- Learning to handle disappointment.
- Stamina to take care of your family.

AWARENESS FROM MOSQUITO

If Mosquito comes into your life:

- You may be letting too much get to you so lighten up.
- Take precautions against illness.
- Don't be a pest.

Energy Center: Throat

Mineral: Eudialyte

Element: Air

Magic & Mystery:

- Mosquito prefers to feed on the blood of Horse and Cattle rather than human blood.
- A full Moon can increase Mosquito activity by 500 percent.

Mosquito means "little fly" in Spanish. Over 3,000 species of Mosquito roam the world. The oldest Mosquito fossil discovered—now enshrined in amber—is deemed to be 79 million years old. Mosquito eyes have one hundred lenses arranged in the shape of a honeycomb. This gives it the ability to see in every direction. The female Mosquito survives by feeding on the blood of others. But only she can bite. The male does not have the proper teeth for it; instead he feeds on flower nectar. The female is a dedicated mother and needs the protein from blood to sustain her eggs. Dedicated to the circle of life, and connected to water as the giver of life, Mosquito hatches its eggs in pools of still water. Mosquito does not have a long life—living less than two months. Mosquito wings beat 300–600 times a second, which make it a very speedy flyer.

A West African folktale says that nobles of a village were tricked on their way home from a spiritual journey to meet their ancestors. A cunning man stole a bag of luggage and swapped it for a bag filled with Mosquitos; the Mosquito has been angrily cursing the people ever since.

As a Power Animal, Mosquito is a symbol of the bloodstream that reminds us of the Tree of Life. Just like sap flows through trees blood circulates through our bodies, sharing the same precious life force. Mosquito teaches us the value of our connection to all things.

The ancient Mayans believed Mosquito was a little spy and that by sucking blood from people could memorize names. Many tribes see Mosquito as their enemy—believing it is a transformed monster. The Haida and Gitxsan tribes of the Pacific Northwest used Mosquito as their crest, carving it into their totem poles. The Creek of the Southeastern woodlands did a ritual Mosquito dance during which the dancers would be pricked with pins.

Not all creatures see Mosquito as a negative presence, as it is a reliable source of nourishment for birds, Bat, Dragonfly, and Frog. Mosquito also can nourish our minds. You have the potential to be a destroyer; if you are full of poisonous thoughts and emotions, it is easy to transmit these to others. Choose wisely where you land. Although you may think you have the perfect perspective, there is always a possibility that your opinions won't be welcome. Be careful that where you live is not a place of stagnation or unhealthy. Flow like a river to create health and experience higher consciousness.

SHAMAN'S INTENTION: *I ASK YOU FOR HELP TO UNDERSTAND WATER AND CREATION*

MOTH

DETERMINATION **ENLIGHTENMENT** **MYSTERY**

"Trust your internal navigation; you know where the light is."
—Moth

Moth has been around for 190 million years. A relative of Butterfly, there are 160,000 species of Moth, which range from being extremely small to the size of a bird. Moth has mastered the ability of camouflaging itself to protect it from predators; it can blend into the background to the point of invisibility. Moth also has the form of an eye on each of its wings to deceive predators into believing a dangerous animal is looking at them. In order to protect itself from Bat, Tiger Moth makes ultrasonic clicking sounds to confuse Bat's biological sonar system. For millions of years, Moth and Bat have been constantly adapting, trying to outsmart one another. The majestic Hummingbird Moth is so large and flaps its wings so fast that it can be confused with Hummingbird. Moth has a featherlike antenna with scent receptors on it that help it to find food and a mate. The male Moth can find the female from seven miles away through tracing her scent. Moth uses the earth's geomagnetic field to navigate at night.

Many Native American tribes see Moth as a sign of transformation and healing. Dried Moth cocoons have been used as rattles in ceremony by Yaquis, Costanoans, Yaudanchi Yokuts, and Miwoks, among others. Traditionally they believed Moth brings messages to us from the spirit world. In different cultures around the world, Moth is associated with death. The Death's Head Hawkmoth has a skull-like pattern on its wings that plays into this belief. In many cultures, a white Moth symbolizes purity and truth, and seeing one means that an ancestor's soul has been cleansed of the remnants of its earthly journey. Jamaicans consider a white Moth a soul at rest with itself. In China, April is the month for tomb sweeping, a ceremony for remembering ancestors. An abundance of Moth during this period is seen as a sign that the ancestors are watching. Even more significant is when Moth lands on a photo of a deceased relative. Encountering a Moth at a Taoist funeral holds the same significance.

As a Power Animal, the nocturnal aspects of Moth's existence represent an intuitive sense of transformation. Luna Moth has a spot on each of its wings that resemble the Moon and rings around these spots that are reminiscent of Saturn's rings—illustrating its cosmic connection to the planetary world. Moth displays fragility and yet its commitment to the Moon's energy is strong. The door to transformation and enlightenment is the third eye, which is depicted on Moth's wings. Moth carries this message with it all the time.

Moth reminds us that we may have to see the darkness before we can see the light. There are many teachers in the world, yet the greatest wisdom is inside of us. Remember, in transformation, the old you must be destroyed in order to discover the new you. Moth stops at nothing to find light and through its example brings us the message of motivation and helps catapult us toward our goals of enlightenment. It reminds us to believe we are safe and that releasing any oppositional beliefs will enable us to live in a natural state of joyfulness, vibrating with energy and health and bestowing positive energy on others.

POWERS OF MOTH

Call in Moth for:

- Shedding light on difficult situations.
- Transforming your negative thoughts to positive ones.
- Becoming invisible to your enemies.

AWARENESS OF MOTH

If Moth comes into your life:

- You are too fixated on one thing.
- You are a nocturnal being.
- Don't give up easily.

Energy Center: Third eye

Mineral: Mookaite

Element: Air

Magic & Mystery:

- In Greek mythology, Atlas was condemned by Zeus to hold the sky on his shoulders. Atlas Moth is named in honor of this legendary hero.
- In Taiwan, the cocoons of Atlas Moth—with its wingspan of eleven inches—are used as purses.

SHAMAN'S INTENTION: *SUPPORT ME IN RELEASING MY MEMORIES OF THE PAST SO I CAN LIVE FULLY IN THE MOMENT*

MOTMOT

SPEED | **TRANSFORMATION** | **GIVING**

"Trust the divine design of all things."—Motmot

Motmot lives in the rainforests and shady coffee farms of Central America and South America. It has a striking plumage and strong bill. Its tail feathers, which resemble the pendulum in a grandfather clock, distinguish it from other birds. This is the reason for its nickname, Clock Bird. When excited Motmot moves its tail from side to side with greater speed. Colorful, its body is green and blue, its eyes are red, its crown is a brilliant turquoise, and its face is black. Its call is similar to the hooting of Owl. During flight Motmot makes sudden movements; it quickly passes through the trees like a flash of blue and green. It builds its nest by tunneling into the ground, usually at the base of a tree. Its tunnels can be more than a foot long with the nest at the bottom. During mating season, the male will offer leaves, grass, and flowers to the female as a loving gesture. Both male and female share responsibility for raising their hatchlings. Motmot always resides near water for drinking and bathing. It eats insects, small lizards, and fruit.

The feathers of Motmot were much desired by the ancient Mayan elite. These were often traded throughout the Americas to be used in headdresses and for decoration. According to myth, it was connected to the rain god Chaac, who was always depicted with a Motmot feather in his ear. It was said that if a Motmot drank from an open well or *cenote* it meant the water is safe for swimming and drinking. For the Mayans, Motmot was a symbol of transformation and changes that were coming. They knew there would be a time when the energy around them had matured and their evolution would take them beyond the point of no return into enlightenment. Seeing Motmot means that you will return to the world of these Mayans. It was a sacred bird for the Mayan people. Motmot was often found in caves where shamans would do rituals to initiate young people as they began their adult lives.

In one funny Mayan story of Chaac, he decided to burn all the crops so that the soil would recover its nutrient richness. This was done with the hope that future crops would be more abundant. Before he set fire to the land Chaac asked members of the bird kingdom to gather the seeds of all the plants. Motmot was the first to volunteer and it raced the others to find the seed of corn, so it could be the envy of all. But Motmot was lazy. Since it knew it was much faster than the others, it rested while the others worked until instead of the seed of corn all it could find was the seed of a green tomato.

Motmot brings us the message of time. It says, "Regard the timeline of your life without regret. If you see it otherwise, you lessen the possibility to see the future with potential. Being stuck in regret is a dance with futility, since nothing can be restored. Time marches on and mistakes are made, and choices can be less than desired. Expectations can also fall short. But you will only suffer if you see the past as lost time. This is not true; time is never lost. It is an illusion to think this way."

POWERS OF MOTMOT

Call in Motmot for:

- Learning how to give eloquently.
- Helping youth expand their consciousness.
- Showing up brightly and colorfully in life.

AWARENESS FROM MOTMOT

If Motmot comes into your life:

- You are dehydrated and should seek out pure water.
- Time is short, so do not delay striving for what your heart desires.
- Take a journey to the Lower World to see your future children.

Energy Center: Throat

Mineral: Cavansite

Element: Air

Magic & Mystery: The temples in the ancient Mayan city of Copán in Honduras have many expressions of Motmot.

SHAMAN'S INTENTION: *SUPPORT ME IN ACCEPTING MY PAST, SO IT DOES NOT DEFINE ME*

MOUSE

RESOURCEFULNESS **EXPRESSION** **DRAMA**

"There is so much you do not see from my perspective."
—Mouse

Mouse is a rodent with a pointed nose, small, round ears, and a skinny, hairless tail. It breeds exponentially, being able to get pregnant forty hours after giving birth. Its fertility begins at two months. Mouse is found everywhere, in every type of terrain. It boldly looks for food and shelter wherever it can find them, adapting to any environment. Agile and with good balance, it is able to scale even thin ropes and vertical surfaces. It is mostly active at night, relying on its keen hearing and sense of smell to avoid predators while searching for food.

Mouse has animated facial expressions. It is talkative with others of its kind, communicating with a complex variety of ultrasonic sounds. Mouse is timid and quivers when it is stressed. It sometimes plays dead until the pursuit of it by a predator has ended. It is also able to empathize with the feelings of others. It keeps its den extremely clean and tidy, and designates separate areas for storing food, going to the bathroom, and sleeping. Its whiskers are also designed to detect temperature changes and breezes. Mouse is deeply connected to the Earth and is a friend to the spirits of the natural world, such as fairies.

Traditional Hopi stories of Mouse are used to impress upon children that size doesn't matter, as courage and persistence can prevail. In some Native American tribes, Mouse is revered for being able to succeed at difficult tasks. The Blackfoot Indians believe that Mouse is their brother and that it gave humans a leadership role over animals.

The ancient Egyptians were terrified of Mouse, seeing it as a disease carrier and crop destroyer. All rodents were associated with the goddess Sekhmet, the wrathful alter ego of Hathor and a bringer of pestilence. Mouse also provided the symbolism of rebirth as it would emerge from holes in the dirt when the Nile River's banks would overflow. The ancient Greeks saw Mouse as very powerful and encouraged it to nest under altars and temples. The ancient Romans associated Mouse with the almighty Mars in spite of its size.

In Bali, Field Mouse is known as the protector of the goddess of rice, so it is rarely killed there, even if the crops are being consumed. Rather than destroy Mouse, people prefer to placate its spirit by making offerings in temples.

Mouse's message is that inactivity leads to boredom—which is an unnecessary state of being considering that the world holds so much opportunity. It teaches us to know that just around the corner something will appear that solves the mystery of the moment. Nothing is predictable, so you should strive for the results you want. By having orderly thoughts you can keep fear at bay; nothing else can deter you from finding the next treasure you seek. Be spontaneous and aim your sights higher than mere survival. As a Power Animal, Mouse can help us find shelter or create a sanctuary where we may be free.

POWERS OF MOUSE

Call on Mouse for:

- A quick getaway from what may confine you.
- House hunting.
- Support when you are trying to conceive a child or an idea.

AWARENESS FROM MOUSE

If Mouse comes into your life:

- You may need to improve the quality of your communication.
- Your house is a mess and you need to tidy things up.
- You need to be more agile and balanced in how you conduct your affairs.

Energy Center: Sacrum

Mineral: Galena

Element: Earth

Magic & Mystery:

- Mouse sings songs of endearment to its friends and family.
- In medieval times, it was believed that Mouse implanted souls into babies in the womb.

SHAMAN'S INTENTION: *HELP ME TO HONOR THE SMALL LESSONS THAT LEAD TO BIG AWARENESS*

MUSK OX

SURVIVAL **FORCE** **LOYALTY**

"There is warmth in community, a sense of belonging. The collective consciousness is aware of the feeling of our connection to all things."—Musk Ox

Musk Ox walked the Earth with Woolly Mammoth and Saber Tooth Tiger during the most recent ice age. Musk Ox and Caribou are the only hoofed animals that survived that era. Today, Musk Ox lives in the artic regions of Alaska, Canada, Greenland, and Siberia. It has a thick coat and the male exudes a musky odor from which it gets its name to attract the female. The Inuktitut call it *Umingmak,* meaning "bearded one." Musk Ox has traits that make it a true survivor—especially in the Artic where there are few species. It has the longest hairs of any animal on earth, measuring forty inches long. Its coat is thick and shaggy and protects it from the cold air on the tundra which can reach -94 degrees Fahrenheit (-70°C).

Musk Ox is one of the strongest animals on the planet. For centuries, the Aleut and Intuit in the Arctic have used Musk Ox to pull cargo weighing more than its body weight for miles across rugged terrain. When the time comes to establish the head of the herd each year, combative males will charge full force at each other in a dramatic clashing of heads. The male Musk Ox has a bony plate on its forehead and its skull has a built-in cushion to protect its brain from injury during this fight for dominance.

Musk Ox lives in large herds and, if threatened, forms a circle around its young for protection. Its horns are its principal form of defense. In Intuit art, Musk Ox is a sign of survival. These indigenous people believe there is a mystery surrounding Musk Ox and that it has a cunning nature and understands everything said by humans. Since prehistory they have had a deep connection with Musk Ox, eating its meat and using its warm fur for clothing and its horns to make tools. In the late 1800s, Musk Ox became extinct in North America. Thirty-four were shipped from Greenland to repopulate the area and now there are 125,000.

Musk Ox brings you its message from the vast, pristine, crystalline glaciers of the frozen tundra of the North Pole where there are no shadows. This vastness is a picture of newness, a beginning that exists in silence. White is the power of rebirth and renewal, a final frontier, and an ancient mystery where the key to your restoration exists. The North embodies the beauty of nothingness. Let the green circles of the aurora borealis that glimmer and shine upon the Earth bring the warmth of heart energy into your being. This electric phenomenon from the edge of the atmosphere is a tangible display of love energy emanating from the heart of the cosmos.

If you can imagine yourself reflected in a snowbank, the truth of who you are in your innermost nature will be looking back at you. Seek higher realms of thought; if you do not, your journey in life will be long and cold. Source wisdom has a caring embrace and can warm you with its teachings. Ignore the noise of the civilized world, as this keeps you from experiencing your connection to source. Do not always turn your back to the wind, as it often brings change. Ignore those who enter your life with cold hearts and warm your feet by the fires of those who are compassionate.

POWERS OF MUSK OX

Call in Musk Ox for:

- Protection from all that seems cold.
- Strength in numbers.
- Becoming immune to adversity.

AWARENESS FROM MUSK OX

If Musk Ox comes into your life:

- Lessen your burdens; it is time to lighten your load.
- You may be sacrificing too much for the sake of others.
- Focus on the wisdom you have gained from your losses.

Energy Center: Crown

Mineral: Rutilated quartz

Element: Earth

Magic & Mystery:

- The undercoat of Musk Ox is known as qiviut. Qiviut yarn is one of the finest fibers in the world, softer than Goat's cashmere and warmer than Sheep's wool.
- Musk Ox will bust through solid ice with its powerful hooves to access water.

SHAMAN'S INTENTION: *HELP ME TO SURVIVE HARSHNESS AND WARM MY SOUL WITH THE FIRE OF COMPASSION*

NIGHTHAWK

ELUSIVENESS | **TRAVEL** | **SUPERNATURAL**

"Our desire for freedom is great; it is the tonic you need for happiness."
—Nighthawk

Nighthawk has existed for 400,000 years. Contrary to its name, it is not a member of the Hawk family. Nighthawk has gray brown and black feathers and a long-forked tail. Its wings have white bars on them that make it easy to spot during flight. It sees well at night because of special retinas that have the ability to gather light. It subsists entirely on insects, feeding while in flight by opening its mouth wide and scooping them up. An inhabitant of the Americas it migrates from South America to North America at the end of February, arriving in June—one of the longest migrations of any bird, clocking in at up to 4,000 miles. It migrates in a flock of thousands.

Nighthawk prefers to live in open areas, like farmlands and suburbs—though it is common in cities too. It will appear after forest fires that provide it with new, more expansive open areas in which to fly. Because of this, its nickname is the Burnt Land Bird. It has an erratic flight pattern where it will quickly change directions, so it is often mistaken for Bat. The male enjoys diving at intruders and will show off like a daredevil to impress a female. Nighthawk makes sharp boasting sounds during courtship.

Nighthawk becomes active right after birth, jumping into life almost immediately, as if the memory of life on Earth is clear to it. During the day it sleeps on the ground where it is protected by its well-designed plumage that makes it fit right into the vegetation. It changes where it sleeps often enough to not become a predictable prey.

Nighthawk is an elusive bird that has a supernatural sense about it. Greek philosopher Aristotle was suspicious of Nighthawk, writing about how it caused problems with Goat. It is often seen in fields with Goat and Sheep, leading to myths about Nighthawk sucking milk from the teats of a mother Goat. The truth is that Nighthawk is only taking advantage of all the insects assembling around these herd animals.

Oddly, Nighthawk has a face like Dragon, which is a sign of its innate connection to fire. Nighthawk brings us message from forest fires, including the insight that all living things have been touched by fire in some way, whether by the flickering flames of a campfire or by a raging forest fire that sweeps through many trees. Shamans see fire as a deity, a living and breathing being to engage with. We should honor fire for its ability to spawn the germination of new seeds and tender growth. Nighthawk appreciates the essence of fire and knows that it rages for the sake of renewal. Fire can also be the final interaction the body has on Earth for those who are cremated. Nighthawk knows the transformational aspects of fire at the time of transition into the mystery of the afterlife. It reminds us of the purity that comes after a fire once the ashes have settled, and how we should open our eyes to see the emergence of things from the surface seeking to be renewed again, propagating new life from hope and transmutation.

From Nighthawk's perspective there is a need for simplicity on our planet, as complexity is the norm. Simply look to the enormity of the sky and your perceived complications will shrink. No longer accept complications as a dreary reminder of an unhappy reality. Be bold and look around you with clear eyes and a simple solution will reveal itself to you. The darkness of night represents the unseen world. Nighthawk embraces it—viewing darkness as a backdrop for light.

POWERS OF NIGHTHAWK

Call in Nighthawk for:

- Finding freedom and wide-open spaces.
- Adapting to life in a city.
- Flying through life with a mouthful of abundance.

AWARENESS FROM NIGHTHAWK

If Nighthawk comes into your life:

- It is time for the destruction of the old to allow something new to emerge.
- Accept change.
- You may be too confined in a certain situation or relationship.

Energy Center: Crown

Mineral: Sunstone

Element: Fire

Magic & Mystery:

- One Nighthawk can eat 500 mosquitos per day.
- Nighthawk spend their winters in the Amazon rain forest and their summers in their nesting grounds in northern Alberta, Canada.

SHAMAN'S INTENTION: *HELP ME TO SIMPLIFY EVERYTHING I SEE*

NUTHATCH

ORGANIZATION **FEARLESSNESS** **LOYALTY**

"With proper planning you can design an existence that supports your goals and gives you a foundation for growth."—Nuthatch

POWERS OF NUTHATCH

Call in Nuthatch for:

- Support to get better organized.
- Bringing you a caring and loyal life partner.
- Healing.

AWARENESS FROM NUTHATCH

If Nuthatch comes into your life:

- Get busy planning your future.
- You need to trust that everything will be there for you when you need it.
- Even if your life seems like a tough nut to crack at present, with persistence you will meet your needs and find peace.

Energy Center: Heart

Mineral: Indigo Aura quartz

Element: Air

Magic & Mystery:

- Nuthatch relies on Chickadee to warn it of the level of danger an intruder represents.
- Nuthatch spends 90 percent of its time gathering food.

Nuthatch can be identified by long stripes on the sides of its face that give it the dramatic appearance of having a line running through its eyes. It has a black crown, similar to a Mohawk haircut. Found throughout North America and the United Kingdom, Nuthatch is a resourceful bird that makes itself busy looking for insects and large seeds. Its name comes from its habit of embedding seeds in the bark of trees to hold them in place while it uses its sharp beak to open the shells and "hatch" the seeds. It stores food all over the forest, wherever it can find a suitable place. This bird is so loud that its voice stands out from the other birds in the forest. It is a loyal partner, forming lifelong relationships; mates stay together to protect their common territory. Nuthatch has a funny division of labor: The male spends his time looking out for predators; the female is on the lookout for the male so that she can find his stash of seeds.

Nuthatch has a couple of nicknames. It is sometimes called the Upside-down Bird since it will climb down the trunks of trees. It also is known as the Mud Stopper because it plasters mud around the entrance to its nest.

Native Americans traditionally use the energy of Nuthatch to diagnose illnesses. Some also see it as the bird of the medicine man, a guide to help the shaman with finding the underlying issues that may be impeding the ability to heal. Every Power Animal has its own medicine. These medicines may be imparted to us in dreams or by energetic transmission through its presence, teaching us a variety of ways to heal ourselves or by healing us, such as by flying over our heads or into our bodies. The Mi'kmaq people believe the Nuthatch has the power to instill us with faith and offer divine intervention. The Navajo, by contrast, see Nuthatch as a sign of impending old age. The Cherokee speculated that it would steal their words when they were telling their stories. The Cherokee word for Nuthatch is *Tsulie'na,* meaning "deaf," a reference to the fearlessness this bird shows toward humans despite our loud manner.

As a Power Animal, Nuthatch reminds us to trust our instincts, gifts with which we were born. Never underestimate the value of your instincts. No one comes to the planet at a disadvantage in terms of his innate abilities; each of us is born equipped to survive. Despite our initial circumstances, it is only our perceptions and beliefs that ultimately make us weak. Embrace the knowledge to move through scarcity and obstructions. All that you need is within you. Walk in the world secure in the wholeness of being you. Nuthatch can show you where everything is hidden and help it to emerge.

SHAMAN'S INTENTION: *WHEN THE ANSWERS ARE HIDDEN FROM MY VIEW, PLEASE CRACK OPEN THE HARD SHELL THAT OBSCURES THEM FROM ME*

OCTOPUS

CLEVERNESS | **SECURITY** | **ADAPTABILITY**

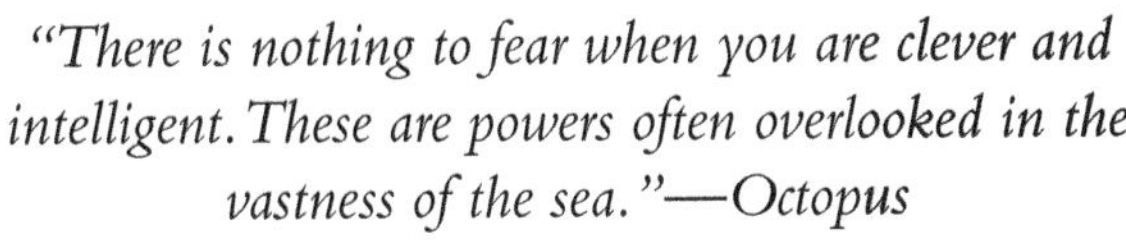

"There is nothing to fear when you are clever and intelligent. These are powers often overlooked in the vastness of the sea."—Octopus

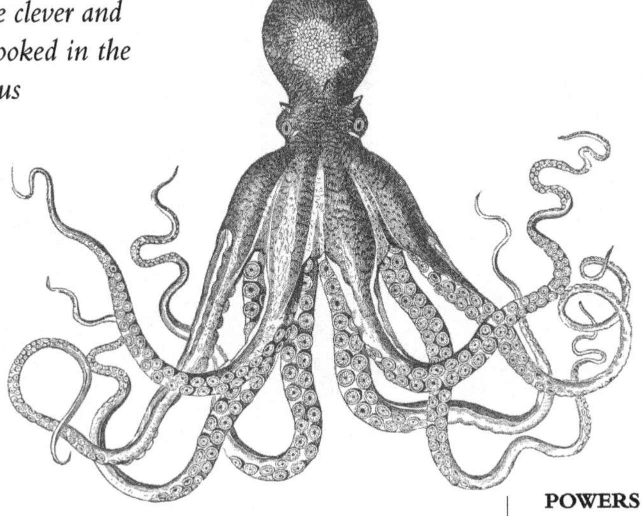

There are 300 species of Octopus and they come in all shapes, sizes and colors. Octopus has been on the planet for 300 million years. Giant Pacific Octopus is the largest, weighing in at 400 pounds and stretching twenty-five feet in length. Octopus regenerates if any part of it goes missing. The ability to regrow severed tentacles is a defense tactic that enables it to escape predators or get out of threatening predicaments it finds itself in. Octopus makes its home among cracks in rocks and reefs. These places are its shelter and where it lays its eggs. It uses sharp teeth to attack Shrimp, Crab, Scallop, and various fish, and then suck out their meat. The poison of the Australian Blue Ring Octopus can kill a human. Adaptable, Octopus can live in different underwater environments. Its soft body allows it to squeeze through cracks and crevices. It has excellent eyesight and a special ability to keep its eyes in the same position while turning its body upside down.

A difficult prey to spot in the sea, Octopus is a master of camouflage. Its skin changes color and patterns within seconds when it needs to blend in. It uses a dark "ink" to throw off its enemies. This defensive substance causes temporary blindness and paralyzes the sensors related to smell and taste. Octopus has three hearts to circulate blood to its organs. It prefers crawling over swimming, as swimming is exhausting for it.

Pacific Northwestern tribes used to see Octopus as a medicine animal able to overcome sickness or bad weather. Octopus is the totem crest of many tribes. Its Hawaiian name is He'e, which means "multifaceted," "mystical," and "flexible." Octopus is associated with Kanaloa, the Hawaiian god of the Underworld. People have honored it through song and dance. They believed Octopus is an extraterrestrial being. Their creation story tells of a time when the cosmos was destroyed, and Octopus was the only survivor.

Octopus is nature's animate mandala. As it moves it sparks our fears of the depths of our being and encourages us to move to the mystic center of our being, dissolving our beliefs. An invertebrate, its body signifies that our power is in our agility not in having a strong backbone that only can serve as a structure with which to carry a burden. It teaches that whatever is lost can be replaced. The movement of Octopus is a lesson in fluidity and swimming through the world with intelligence. With a peaceful approach Octopus will welcome you into its world and promises to make you aware of new possibilities.

When not at rest Octopus is always propelling itself forward, moving into the future with confidence. It brings us the message not to cling to the familiar like a suction cup, as this will keep us from achieving our full potential. Grasp life with all your tentacles and hold on tight because learning to be human can be a rocky ride.

POWERS OF OCTOPUS

Call in Octopus for:

- Blending in when you feel like an outcast.
- Healing from the loss of a limb.
- Clarity when everything seems upside down.

AWARENESS FROM OCTOPUS

If Octopus comes into your life:

- It is time to figure out what you are hiding from and face the facts.
- You may need to get out in the world to get noticed.
- Count on your intelligence for survival.

Energy Center: Heart

Mineral: Iolite

Element: Water

Magic & Mystery:

- Pacific Northwestern shamans often wear Octopus amulets because of its supernatural qualities.
- Octopus is often seen in jewelry made by the Moche tribe in Peru. They associate it with sacrifice—a trait they admire.

SHAMAN'S INTENTION: *WITH YOUR MANY ARMS, PLEASE EMBRACE ALL THE DIRECTIONS AND BRING THE ANCESTORS TO PROTECT MY SACRED SPACE*

OPOSSUM

INTUITION | FEARLESSNESS | DRAMA

"Stop, there is a solution near if you can believe that one exists."—Opossum

POWERS OF OPOSSUM

Call in Opossum for:

- Instinctual knowledge of how to deal with a particular situation.
- Nurturing your ideas to ensure a positive outcome.
- Managing your nerves and using aplomb to get out of difficulty.

AWARENESS FROM OPOSSUM

If Opossum comes into your life:

- You need to deal with fear that is destroying your potential.
- It is a time to give birth to a new project.
- Hang out in nature where you do not have to take life so seriously.

Energy Center: Solar plexus

Mineral: Yellow calcite

Element: Earth

Magic & Mystery:

- Newborn Opossum is as tiny as Honeybee.
- Opossum appears in the *Dresden Codex* of Mayan hieroglyphics (circa 1300 C.E.) as a symbol of death and rebirth due to its ability to seem dead.

Opossum is descended from a marsupial forbearer that survived the extinction event 65 million years ago that killed off the dinosaurs. It is the oldest surviving type of mammal. Today, its territory extends from Canada to South America. A gray, furry nocturnal creature with a white face and a pointed nose, its signature feature is its tail, which it uses as a fifth limb, mostly for grasping. Young Opossum loves to hang by its tail in trees, a habit it indulges in less as an adult. Opossum grows to be five feet long from the tip of its nose to the tip of its tail and it weighs between eight and thirteen pounds. It prefers areas that are wet, such as those that include swamps, lakes, and streams.

Opossum has an amazing immune system, which comes in handy considering the venom of the snakes that attack it. It has fifty teeth—more than any other mammal in the Western Hemisphere. It has a very short gestation period of twelve days, after which it gives birth to a passel of young that are born blind. From the beginning of its life, Opossum must rely on its intuition. Opossum has mastered fear in that it has an internal switch that shuts down its central nervous system so that it can lapse into a self-induced coma when it is threatened. Opossum has other coping techniques for times when things get too difficult to handle. Sometimes it will be aggressive, other times submissive; it will weigh its options carefully to see which will serve it well in a given situation.

Native American warriors of the past used Opossum medicine on the battlefield by pretending to be dead when they were outnumbered. When least expected, they would then jump up and create confusion before doing their best to disappear. As a Power Animal, Opossum can help you to escape harm by using your wits in combination with some pragmatic skills. Where this can go too far is if you never express your true motives or display any transparency. Certain North American tribes saw Opossum as an example of arrogance and haughtiness. They felt that its self-imposed coma was a sign of being a fool or an imposter to your real self.

In Central America, especially southern Mexico, Opossum is often seen as a trickster who can cleverly escape from danger. It is also a sign of fertility.

Opossum tells us to master our reactions to the external world so we may discern exactly what is needed at a given time. It brings us the message that not all is what it seems and that our ego can be an intimidator if it is seeking power. By sensing vulnerability in others, we can respond strategically. Relationships are a dance, like a tango or a foxtrot; it is only with precise movement and intuition that we can create the perfect pattern of steps. Confrontation is a skill, and size is not everything. With agility and intelligence, we can rule the world.

SHAMAN'S INTENTION: *HELP ME TO EXCEL IN THE ART OF INTUITION*

OSTRICH

TRUTH **REBIRTH** **GROUNDEDNESS**

"There is little patience to be had when you feel vulnerable; sometimes a good kick in the rear of those who are bothering you can be what is needed for calm."—Ostrich

In existence for 120 million years, Ostrich is the oldest bird species. It is also the largest and heaviest, weighing in at up to 350 pounds. Flightless, it gets around by running and can reach speeds of forty-three miles per hour. Ostrich lives in the rugged terrain and inaccessible spaces of Sub-Saharan Africa, although its territory once extended through northern Africa, to the Mediterranean Sea and Asia. It has long legs, two toes on each foot, a long neck, and large, luminous eyes with three sets of eyelids and prominent lashes. Its vision is so sharp that it can see objects over two miles away.

The strong legs of Ostrich are its secret weapon, as they are capable of deterring and even debilitating a predator as large as a lion. Ostrich feeds on grass, flowers, seeds, and the occasional small lizard. It can go long periods without water, sustained only by the moisture in the vegetation it consumes. Ostrich lives in groups or flocks. A flock may have as many as a hundred birds. Ostrich is a good parent. When nesting, the Hen sits on the eggs during the day and the Rooster sits on them at night. It lives between fifty and seventy-five years.

The long white, black, and gray plumes of Ostrich are soft, delicate, and showy. Its feather was an important feature in the Hall of Ma'at, ancient Egyptian goddess of truth, a place where souls were judged on their worthiness to pass to the afterlife. Ma'at would weigh the heart of the deceased to see if it was as light as the Ostrich feather. To the ancient Egyptians, Ostrich was a symbol of purity. Its eggs were often placed in tombs to show their desire for resurrection and belief in immortality. They also used its egg shells as containers for perfume.

The hunter-gatherers of the Kalahari Desert used Ostrich eggs as containers for water and created jewelry from them. These Kung Bushmen believed Ostrich held super powers and performed rituals in its honor.

To think that a giant bird like Ostrich can be born from an egg that can fit in the palm of a hand is a testament to the power of the cosmic egg, a universal symbol of life. Symbolically, it reminds us to go back to the beginning, which is the "place" of innocence and truth. Sometimes it is hard for others to find our truth, because we disguise ourselves to hide it from the external world. If you often try to conform or put on a show for others, Ostrich can help you develop a more authentic presence and also to recognize the value of you. Ostrich will help you go beyond the surface and face your fears and inconsistencies so that your truth can emerge with ease.

Ostrich holds a message of potential for although it cannot fly it has wings. Call upon its powers when you are ready to quit running and looking over your shoulder for what is chasing you. Ostrich can help you soar to a height that is beyond your current reality. Its long neck represents seeking wisdom at higher levels of existence—even if you are grounded, these possibilities are always within your reach. Speaking for the avian kingdom, Ostrich asks that we use words of grace that nurture us. Place an Ostrich feather on your altar as a reminder of the wisdom that comes from the higher perspective of those who fly above it all.

POWERS OF OSTRICH

Call in Ostrich for:

- Opening your eyes wide to see the truth.
- Finding answers when you are not sure what you are running from.
- Help to stop diminishing yourself and to be seen.

AWARENESS FROM OSTRICH

When Ostrich comes into your life:

- It is time to rise above the confusion and realize your connection to a higher power.
- You need to acknowledge the importance of your "flock" and show them your gratitude for their presence in your life.
- You may be ready to birth a big project.

Energy Center: Throat

Mineral: Blue opal

Element: Earth

Magic & Mystery:

- In ancient Egypt, Ostrich was sometimes used to pull chariots—although they were not very willing, so the practice was not widespread.
- A statue of Arsinoë II, a Ptolemaic queen of Egypt, shows her riding Ostrich, was found in a tomb in Egypt.

SHAMAN'S INTENTION: *HELP ME TO SEE BEYOND THE PLUMAGE OF MY EXTERNAL EXPRESSION AND FIND ANY TRUTH THAT ELUDES ME*

OTTER

PLAYFULNESS | **HAPPINESS** | **FRIENDLINESS**

"The key to happiness is balance. With a balanced life you can gain momentum to move forward and realize your personal desires."—Otter

Otter inhabits almost every waterway on the planet expect for those in Australia and Antarctica. It is believed to have been on Earth for over 23 million years and is known for its charisma and playful energy. Its interaction with others of its kind is like a party—so much so, in fact, that a group of Otter is called a *romp*. Most times Otter prefers to live in groups but is occasionally solitude. But everywhere it goes, it is important to the ecosystem; for example, Sea Otter enables kelp to grow by eating Sea Urchin, which feeds on it.

Otter is clever. It uses tools and will often store a rock under its arm to have it handy in case it needs to crack open a shell. It eats fish and marine invertebrates like Clam, Mussel, and Sea Urchin. It has an intricate communication system which involves whistles, growls, screams, chirps, purrs, and laughter. Otter mates for life and its relationship with its mate is a source of much happiness. Otter nearly always swims while floating on its back. Its two layers of fur give it exceptional buoyancy and help keep it warm in northern waters.

Peoples indigenous to the Pacific Northwest Coast of Canada long saw Otter as a healer and still admire it for its skills, agility and friendliness. They view it as a clan totem and historically have carved its likeness into their totem poles. Many Native Americans considered the Otter so linked to the supernatural world that they believed only shamans could connect with its spirit. Otter pearls (bezoars) are highly prized talismans because of the desire to embody Otter's happy, playful personality.

The ancient Zoroastrians, proto-Indo-Iranians dating back to 5,000 B.C.E., by tradition would never kill Otter and even would hold ceremonies for a dead Otter found in the wild. They believed Otter purified the water by eating anything that would contaminate it.

Otter is a central figure in Celtic shamanism of the British Isles. There, an Otter is called a dratsie and in the olden times, if caught, it would offer to grant a wish in exchange for being set free. Folklore said Otter was a god come to Earth in disguise to test people's level of compassion. Those who were respectful to the land and water were rewarded with prosperity.

As a Power Animal, Otter is walking joy and helps us to see what happiness is. The message of Otter is about the wisdom of the inner self. Otter spends most of its time looking up at the Sun, our primary energy source, which is representative of the intellect and the relationship of the self to the Universe. Otter teaches us to not get tangled up in the seaweed of negativity; to stay on the surface, above that which would take you down. The ripples on the water's surface are a mirror of the millions of choices and possibilities available to us in our lives. By placing its intentions into the waves of nonordinary reality, Otter assures it will receive the gifts of change—and it can help us to do the same when we work with its powers.

Choice, change, and creation are glimmers of hope that can be seen in the mirror of still water. Stillness creates space for play. Otter swims with assurance, never doubting its innate potential. When it looks out over a vast sea or a river, it sees no limitation.

POWERS OF OTTER

Call in Otter for:

- The courage to do something you are afraid to do.
- Willpower and self-control.
- Help to speak with conviction about your ideas.

AWARENESS FROM OTTER

If Otter comes into your life:

- It may be time to gain control over the thoughts that prevent you from feeling joy.
- It is time to stop acting like a victim—try a new approach.
- You need to reclaim your personal power.

Energy Center: Solar plexus

Mineral: Black jasper

Element: Water

Magic & Mystery:

- Sea Otter holds hands with its friends and family when it sleeps to keep from drifting away from them in the water.
- A group of Sea Otter is called a *raft*. The largest recorded raft held 2,000 creatures.

SHAMAN'S INTENTION: *TEACH ME THE POWER OF JOY*

OWL

PERCEPTION **PROTECTION** **WISDOMKEEPING**

"Life is about being willing to receive and being grateful for the gift."—Owl

There are 225 species of Owl on our planet. Each is a master of camouflage. The ability of Owl to blend into its surroundings makes it practically invisible against the backdrop of a forest, desert, or grassland. Owl is the ultimate observer. Due to its immobile close-set and forward-facing eyeballs, it has binocular vision. The flexibility of its neck enables it to see everything in a range of 270 degrees around it. Owl has excellent night vision and depth perception. Furthermore, the bony structure holding its eyes secure amplifies the soundwaves it hears.

Owl's acute hearing—which is ten times better than ours—helps it hunt in total darkness. It can zero in on even the faintest sound. Its feathery feet, sensitive like a cat's whiskers, help it to detect when it has caught its prey. Its powerful talons can grasp and hold heavy cargo. When Owl flies, it is silent because the fringes on its feathers diminish the sound of its flight.

The ancient Greeks believed Owl was a sacred companion to Athena, the goddess of wisdom and education. Many inhabited the Acropolis in Athens where her primary temple was located. Owl was a symbol of protection for the people of the city. The Greeks believed that Owl had an inner light that gave it special vision. For the ancient Egyptians, Celts, and Hindus, Owl was the guardian of the Lower World with the important job of accompanying the souls of the dead to safely reach the realms of spirit.

Traditionally, Native Americans saw Owl as the keeper of wisdom, sacred knowledge and prophets that could see the future. When secrets were to be uncovered, Owl was consulted. Before battle Cheyenne warriors would tie Owl feathers to their shields and arms in the hope that Owl would help them slip unnoticed past their enemies. They would watch Screech Owl for messages that would foretell whether or not they would have victory in their battle. Creek warriors used Owl feathers

OWL

PERCEPTION | **PROTECTION** | **WISDOMKEEPING**

OWL'S ACUTE HEARING—WHICH IS TEN TIMES BETTER THAN OURS—HELPS IT HUNT IN TOTAL DARKNESS. IT CAN ZERO IN ON EVEN THE FAINTEST SOUND.

POWERS OF OWL

Call in Owl for:

- Help to support a different view of an unforeseen change or disruption.
- Focusing on an opportunity that is waiting.
- Sharing your wisdom with others.

AWARENESS FROM OWL

If Owl comes into your life:

- Use your natural intuition to its greatest capacity.
- Call upon Owl to help you get what you desire. Magic is in the air.
- You may be overly protective—to the point of aggression—so take it easy.

Energy Center: Crown

Mineral: Labradorite

Element: Air

Magic & Mystery:

- The Great Goddess of Teotihuacan, a pre-Columbian civilization in Mexico, is depicted as wearing an Owl headdress. Owl incense burners were used to make offerings to her.
- Aborigines in Australia believed that Bat was the soul of a man and Owl was the soul of a woman.
- The Kiowa tribe of the North American Great Plains believed that Owl is the soul of a dead shaman.
- There is a saying in Mexico "when the owl cries, the Indians dies", an omen that change is coming.

similarly to enhance their night vision and see the enemy before the enemy saw them.

Shamans from the Ponca tribe of Nebraska used a stuffed Owl in their healing sessions to help them "see" what was needed and tell them how to properly heal others. The Pawnee believed Owl was the head of the medicine men in the avian world. To many tribes, Owl delivered prophecies. For the Apache, Owl meant an approaching death and for the Cherokee, sickness. The Hopi saw Owl as the guardian of everything that happens underground, including the germination of seeds.

The wisdom of Owl is relied on by the Minahasa people of Indonesia who call Owl *Burung Manguni*. When they want to travel, they ask Owl if it is an auspicious time to go. To certain African tribesmen Owl is the companion to mystics, seers, and medicine people to whom it reveals secrets necessary for the welfare of humanity. A shaman who wears Owl feathers is deemed a great healer.

Owl is intelligent and intuitive, a powerful combination. As a Power Animal, Owl teaches you to move forward with a clear strategic purpose, to think before you act. Owl can be the catalyst for change and help you see the world from a higher perspective. As a bringer of light, it can peer into your inner being and extract details of the reality that you need to know. Owl will show you the futility of grasping at things in your external world for satisfaction and guide you to focus on a purpose.

Due to a fallacy that we lack enough knowledge, many of us act paralyzed when confronted with the need for action. This is counterproductive. We are born with the knowledge of the entire Universe within us. Our greatest power as humans is our instinct, yet it is the least relied upon. Owl wants you to know that if you heed your instincts you will always be safe. Do not fear times of darkness.

SHAMAN'S INTENTION: *THERE IS GREAT WISDOM IN THE WINDS. HELP ME TO HEAR, SEE, AND FEEL THE WAYS OF MY ANCESTORS AND BRING THEIR MESSAGES TO ME*

PANDA

PEACE **KINDNESS** **NURTURING**

"Kindness is a valuable currency because it can help you get what you want when you want it."—Panda

Panda lives in forests of bamboo, a plant that accounts for 99 percent of its diet. It spends half the day grinding, crushing, and eating bamboo with its strong jaws and teeth. When resting, it lies flat on its stomach with its legs stretched out and its belly touching Mother Earth. Panda's fur enables it to blend into the dappled shadows of its environment. Its fur is white with black accents that are reminiscent of the yin/yang symbol from Chinese philosophy, which depicts how reality is composed of pairs of opposites that attract and complement each other. Although seeming separate, really two halves make a whole. Light and dark can only exist alongside each other. The black circles around the eye of Panda appear in the shape of a teardrop, a symbol of the emotions inside of each one of us and our human struggle in managing them.

Panda does not live in family units or have deep relationships; it is a solitary and self-reliant creature. Because it is so mellow it does not compete with other Panda for food, mates, and territory. In fact, it will kindly share food with other animals. It simply likes to carve out its own space and live separately. It has little fear as it does not have any natural enemies. Mother Panda is sensitive about her cubs, to the point of not wanting them to be seen by others.

Panda is an agile climber. But since its eyesight is poor it relies on memory, hearing, and smell to get around. It moves very slowly, teaching us that there is no reason to run and that we should take our time to embrace the gifts around us. Panda does not hibernate like other types of Bear. A vegetarian, it cannot build up enough fat to sustain itself during a time of hibernation.

The Chinese see Panda as a symbol of peace and friendship because it attracts so many people to visit and admire it. Panda's characteristic gentleness is a quality many Chinese aspire to. Panda was given the name "Zouya" by the people in the town of Pingwu. This defined Panda as a creature of peace since it was never aggressive or hurt others. When the army would raise their flag of "Zouya" during a fight, everything would stop and temporarily peace would prevail.

Panda power represents emotions, sensitivity, and the peace in accepting that everything changes around us. Panda is resilient through change and rarely becomes over excited or over reactive to events. It is an example of being cool and in control of your emotions, diminishing sensitivity—thus encouraging healing. Panda says to make it a practice to slow down, take a breath, and observe life. It may also be necessary to go deep and extract any tears that are stored inside you so that you can let the sunshine in. Do an emotional cleanse and you will find inner peace. Panda will reveal whatever is keeping you from being tranquil and from avoiding or pushing difficult subjects aside.

Panda also reminds us to protect the forests as they are the lungs of Mother Earth. With every breath we take, we are breathing in the intricate geometry of nature. This alchemical structure supports life. Panda sees us as our ancestors in the Upper World see us and encourages us to take a deep breath of nature and be calm about our existence. From this higher viewpoint, there is nothing to fear.

POWERS OF PANDA

Call in Panda for:

- Properly managing your emotions.
- Learning to relax and enjoy every moment.
- Realizing there is nothing to fear.

AWARENESS FROM PANDA

If Panda comes into your life:

- It may be time to obtain new skills, so you do not stay stuck in your present environment.
- You may thrive best in a cool and wet environment.
- Your diet may be lacking sufficient variety and balance.

Energy Center: Heart

Mineral: Striped brown jasper

Element: Earth

Magic & Mystery:

- The Emperor Wen, fifth in the Han Dynasty, was buried circa 157 B.C.E. with the skull of a Panda in his tomb because Panda was a symbol of nobility in ancient China.
- Panda has been known to sneak into a village and steal objects that it can play with in the wild.

SHAMAN'S INTENTION: *TEACH ME THE PACE OF PEACE*

PARROT

TRANSFORMATION | **FREEDOM** | **RENEWAL**

"There is much abundance from our perspective. We are often at a loss for words when confronted by an obsession with scarcity."—Parrot

Parrot has been around for 23 million years. Its more than 350 species are a lovely mixture, ranging from the colorful Macaw to Gray Cockatiel. Parrot is typically long lived, with a lifespan of seventy-five years or more. Kakapo lives as much as ninety years. In the wild, Parrot is found in Central and South America, Asia, Africa, and Australia. Usually it is monogamous. Both sexes are dedicated to making nests, nurturing eggs, and caring for the young. Its ideal habitat is a dense tropical forest, abundant with nuts, seeds, fruits, and berries. Parrot is a great communicator and loves to socialize and be active. It travels in a large noisy flock. With excellent endurance it is able to fly 500 miles a day, if necessary, in search of food. Parrot makes a nest in hard-to-find places, which contributes to the mystery of spotting it.

Parrot is extremely intelligent and will mimic sounds from the environment, even learning words from human languages that capture its interest. It is curious and loves to learn. It can distinguish different colors and shapes. In captivity, Parrot has been known to learn to read. Its mental faculties make it one of the few animals that could potentially bridge the gap of understanding between the animal and human worlds.

Parrot sees a much broader color spectrum than we do. Parrot can play an important role in shamanic ceremonies when the intention is to bring in the healing magic and powers of color. Shamans know that the vibration of a color can invoke feeling and be used for healing.

The ancient Mayans were enthralled by the spirit of Parrot. They decorated their homes and temples with images of Macaw, whose red feathers were symbolic of the Sun and its fire. The Bribi of Colombia used the spirit of Red Macaw to help them with the work of the psychopomp. Traditionally, the Bororo of Brazil believed they were reincarnated from the Macaw, creatures that represent an earlier stage of human development.

The most important depiction of Parrot is in the Nazca Lines, an ancient collection of geoglyphs (images carved into the ground) discovered in Peru in 1927. Curiosity remains as to how a civilization that flourished over 2,000 years ago would have been capable of carving complex designs that could only be seen in their true form from the sky; and the question, too, remains about their purpose for doing so.

Parrot petroglyphs in the Native cultures of the American Southwest may indicate the presence of active trade routes between indigenous peoples for thousands of years and the importance of Parrot in ceremony. Remains of Parrot have been found in Chaco Canyon in New Mexico and at other archeological sites, proving that Parrot feathers made their way north from the jungles of Central and South America.

Parrot is extremely intelligent and will mimic sounds from the environment, that capture its interest, even learning words from human languages.

These feathers were highly valued and often used in the elaborate costumes and headdresses of prominent leaders outside North America. The feathers were symbols of power, prestige, and protection.

The Anasazi Indians, ancestral Puebloans from the Four Corners region of North America, were known to keep Amazonian Parrots as a pet. In the cosmology of the Hopi—who are descendants of the Anasazi—Parrot is the guardian of the South. Many Pueblo tribes engage in ceremonial dances featuring Parrot energy. They see a strong connection between the multicolored feathers of Parrot and the rainbow. Parrot feathers were traditionally incorporated in fetishes of their Corn Mother goddess, which were made of bundled corn surrounded by clusters of feathers. Native prayer sticks often had Parrot feathers attached to them as well.

In India, Parakeet is associated with Kamadeva, a deity often depicted as riding Parrot or holding one in his hand and uses a bow and arrow to stimulate sexual desire. In Sanskrit, the word *kama* means "desire" or "longing." They say that Parakeet's red beak represents the redness of soil and its green feathers the abundance of vegetation that comes after the rain.

Parrot brings us the spiritual message of transformation. It is hard to miss the ornate and beautiful wings of Parrot as it comes flying in to announce change. Change must come with courage. Confident, Parrot comes to destroy remnants of our past and old ways of thinking that we are clinging to. Life is always changing and opportunities abound when we can take even one next positive step forward. Parrot is the perfect Power Animal for those who like to travel. Parrot can help you to leave the confines of your home and find color, culture, and creativity out in the wider world.

A caged Parrot is symbolic of our internal confinement. Given wings, we are meant to fly. We ignore the importance of freedom and movement at our own peril. Parrot's message from the jungles is that the most powerful medicine comes from plants, and we must heal our planet if we want to fully heal ourselves. In the undergrowth is Mother Earth's pharmacy where she has hidden all that we need to heal ourselves.

BUDGIE, COCKATIEL, COCKATOO, LOVE BIRD, MACAW, PARAKEET

POWERS OF PARROT

Call in Parrot for:

- The discipline not to dwell in the past.
- To gather enough strength for transformation.
- Learning the power of color in your life.

AWARENESS FROM PARROT

If Parrot comes into your life:

- You may be in a cage of self-imposed limitation.
- It is time to taste and feel your freedom.
- Work to find the right words to express your inner feelings.

Energy Center: Crown

Mineral: Peach quartz

Element: Air

Magic & Mystery:

- There is a Parrot population of over 500 birds in New York City that are descended from a *pandemonium* accidentally released from a cargo hold at John F. Kennedy International Airport in the late 1960s.
- In Australia, during drunken Parrot season, hundreds of Parrots eat fermented fruits and become intoxicated.
- Amitabha, the celestial buddha, was thought to have shapeshifted at one time into Parrot in order to increase the chances of converting people.
- Guan Yin is often depicted with a parrot on her right side with a prayer or a pearl in its beak.

Shaman's Intention: *Bring me the vibrancy of color and help me to know its powers*

PEAFOWL

SENSUALITY **ASSUREDNESS** **TRANSFORMATION**

"The more beauty you see in the world, the more beautiful your world becomes."
—Peafowl

Peafowl is native to South Asia. The Blue Peafowl comes from India and Sri Lanka and is the national bird of India. The Green Peafowl is also found in India but has greater numbers in Myanmar, China, Thailand, Vietnam, Cambodia, and Java where it enjoys a more tropical habitat. White Peafowl are widespread throughout all these regions. They have a recessive gene that makes them lose pigmentation, like other albinos, making them easy prey since they do not blend into the surrounding vegetation. The male of the species, the Peacock, is more flamboyant than the female, the Peahen. She blends into the background for protection and the security of her unhatched eggs.

In the wild, Peafowl prefer dense forests where they rest on tree branches and avoid predators. They do not tolerate cold weather well. They live in small groups and are known for their mating displays. Peacock explodes his brilliant six-foot-wide tail like fireworks to attract dowdier-looking Peahen with an expression of flamboyancy and confidence. Peacock sheds this elegant plumage after the season ends. Both genders of Peafowl make excellent parents and have loving parental instincts.

Peacock is known as the bird with one hundred eyes, as each tail feather has a shining eyelike circle near its tip and reflects our Universe, which holds the stars, Moon, Sun, and planets. The eyes on its feathers resemble the all-seeing eye of God that watches over humanity. Peacock tail feathers also have a microscopic crystalline structure that reflects a fluorescent wavelength of light, creating a shimmering dance of brilliant colors when Peacock moves. When he quivers his tail, he emits a low-frequency sound inaudible to human ears. This is part of his approach to seducing the Peahen. When walking and carrying his display with great stature behind him, Peacock looks like a Milan model strutting down a catwalk, invoking the term "proud as a Peacock."

In Asian cultures, the revered goddess of compassion, Kuan Yin, is said to have run her hand over Peacock and created one hundred eyes to watch over us and spread compassion when she could not be present. Having a Peacock feather in a home offers shamanic protection from unwanted psychic energy. Finding Peacock's feather is a sign that you will have peace of mind and successful relationships.

The crown-like crest of Peacock gives him a noble appearance. It serves as a thread that pulls frequencies of unconditional love from the cosmos into the heart energy center through the bird's head. Passion and sexual prowess are characteristics of Peafowl. Mixing these with the wisdom of the cosmos is a combination that makes for successful relations.

White Peafowl is a symbol of immortality; artistic versions showing two of a kind drinking from a chalice represents renewal and rebirth. In India, it is associated with feminine energy and linked to transformation. Hindus associate Peafowl with the goddess Lakshmi, the mother of the world, who is patient and kind and the bringer of good fortune. For Buddhists, Peafowl is a symbol of turning their face on suffering through courage, as exemplified by eating poisonous plants without regard—which is something Peafowl can do. This is a powerful message to transmute that which can destroy you into a personal power.

In ancient Egyptian mythology, Peafowl symbolizes wisdom and the ability to see other dimensions of reality. In ancient Greece, Peafowl was the escort of Hera, the queen of Mount Olympus. She rode in a carriage pulled by Peacock. Peacock is territorial and makes loud sounds when intruders are nearby, so he makes an excellent "guard dog." The ancient Persians recognized Peafowl as a guardian of the Tree of Life and a symbol of the duality of human life.

Peafowl brings the power of transformation and radical change. It can see the day when humanity collectively moves from using our two eyes to just one, the third eye. This eye holds a magical spiral that leads us deeply into the reality of any moment. The male energy of the Peacock is a sign of being seen as powerful. By expanding your auric field, you can walk in the world confidently and, like Peacock, without hesitation. This feeling keeps you in an energetic place of competence and balance.

Peafowl realizes that some of us only ever scratch the surface of who we are, never going deep enough to uncover our brilliance. The truth is that nothing stays the same and we require the inner eye to perceive things in a different way. Peace and bliss are everywhere, if we choose to see them. Peafowl warns us of focusing on the outer world as it will never satisfy us. True power comes from presence and allowing things to flow toward us in a sacred way. Peafowl's message is: Open yourself up and spread your wings in manifestation of the life that you wish to live without doubt of the power and brilliance that you hold.

PEACOCK IS KNOWN AS THE BIRD WITH ONE HUNDRED EYES, AS EACH TAIL FEATHER HAS A SHINING EYELIKE CIRCLE NEAR ITS TIP AND REFLECTS OUR UNIVERSE, WHICH HOLDS THE STARS, MOON, SUN, AND PLANETS.

POWERS OF PEAFOWL

Call in Peafowl for:

- Displaying your inner brilliance.
- Help to cultivate a new perception of the world around you.
- Turning things over to a higher power.

AWARENESS FROM PEAFOWL

If Peafowl comes into your life:

- Your arrogance may be an obstacle to the revelation of your truth.
- Use the most colorful aspects of your personality to get noticed.
- It's a sign to seek help if you are stuck.

Energy Center: Crown

Mineral: Azurite

Element: Air

Magic & Mystery:

- Peafowl is able to predict rain and will dance when rain is coming.
- Peafowl feathers are used in Buddhist ceremonies for purification.
- It is believed that Peafowl deliberately consumes things that are poisonous in order that they become more immune. Being that the most vibrant flora and fauna is the most poisonous, it is believed that their vibrant plumage is the reward for the sacrifice.

SHAMAN'S INTENTION: *SHOW ME THE BEAUTY IN ALL THAT I SEE, NO MATTER HOW DREARY IT MAY SEEM OUTWARDLY*

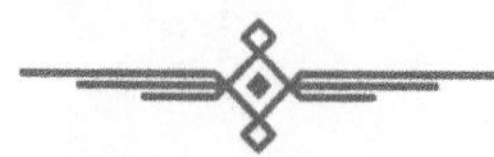

PELICAN

SACRIFICE | EXPANSION | CURIOSITY

"Sometimes life requires that you make a sacrifice for others. If so, do it willingly and without regret, as it can be a gesture of alchemy for the transformation of them and you."—Pelican

Pelican lives on every continent except Antarctica. It is the size of a toddler, standing four feet tall with short legs and webbed feet. Pelican is aerodynamically designed and able to ride the winds with little effort, gliding at altitudes of up to 10,000 feet and skimming over the water using the effects of ground airflows and other upward forces.

Pelican is especially social; it enjoys both the company of its fellows and other birds. It lives in large colonies that can number hundreds of birds. Always gregarious in its style of communication, if angry it will flap its wings and snap its bill to show its discontentment. It takes advantage of keen eyesight to locate fish from high above the water's surface, and then dives at high speeds into the water to snatch its prey. Often perched from a strategic position, it is patient and focused, waiting for the perfect time to swoop in.

As parents, both genders of Pelican forage for their newly hatched offspring. Pelican can store a multitude of fish in its pouch before returning home to the babies. To release the cargo in its pouch, it places its bill on its chest. This gesture looks like it is piercing its breast to remove the fish, a theme that found its way into mythology as a sign of making great sacrifices for those you love. In reality, Pelican swallows and predigests the food for the young before giving it to them, which is also a nurturing gesture.

Pelican understands the art and nobility of sacrifice that is evidenced in every kingdom of nature. Minerals from the soil are sacrificed to plants, which are sacrificed as food to animals; in turn, the decomposing bodies of animals sacrifice minerals back to the earth. Even humans are returned to the soil. The cyclical nature of giving is everywhere around us and the purpose of our relationships and evolution. This connection is built into our souls and underlies the cosmic harmony between us. Sacrifice is an important Pelican characteristic, which humans can emulate if we are open to forgiveness and sharing. This is the foundation of the responsibility we have in being members of humanity. Sometimes we may think of sacrifice as something we do when we are weak or giving up; Pelican reminds us that it is actually an act of wisdom and strength. The capacity to surrender to a divine source means we can then ride the winds of compassion effortlessly for miles and miles.

In ancient Egypt, the Pelican-headed goddess Henet, who is referred to in some texts as the "mother of the king," was associated with dying and the afterlife. She accompanied souls to the Lower World. As a Power Animal, Pelican supports those going through spiritual awakening by minimizing the impact on the psyche of this "death," ensuring for them a softer landing after the experience.

The Nez Perce people of western North America delight in seeing Pelican in their dreams as it means they are being given spiritual powers. Some Indian tribes in California have legends that Pelican has control over weather.

Pelican teaches us to be curious about other creatures and their perceptions and behavior. It eavesdrops on us at times, like nature's equivalent of our animal behaviorists. If we emulate Pelican by watching the behavior of others, we can begin to see and appreciate different approaches to life. Pelican wonders why we are always running toward or away from something and demonstrating a lack of patience or fear. By contrast, when Pelican walks it waddles slowly. It prefers to trust the winds or the waves and observe the world from a higher perspective and can help us do the same.

POWERS OF PELICAN

Call in Pelican for:

- Seeing and making a sacrifice as a noble cause.
- Becoming an observer of life not immersed in the drama of it.
- Embracing the concept of the circle of life to ease the pain of losing someone.

AWARENESS FROM PELICAN

If Pelican comes into your life:

- You may be compromising yourself too much for others. It is time to love yourself.
- You could be too caught up in a situation out of a sense of duty.
- Your "pouch" may be holding more than it should.

Energy Center: Throat

Mineral: Blue opal

Element: Water

Magic & Mystery:

- With a wing span of eleven and a half feet, the Dalmatian Pelican is the largest Pelican species.
- Seagull is often seen sitting on the head of Pelican, ready to snatch a fish from its pouch.
- Alcatraz Island in San Francisco Bay was given its name by Spanish explorers because of the large number of Pelican that nest there. In Spanish, *Alcatraz* means "island of Pelican."

SHAMAN'S INTENTION: *HELP ME TO SHARE MY GIFTS WITH OTHERS EFFORTLESSLY AND WITHOUT SELFISHNESS*

PENGUIN

ADAPTABILITY **EXPRESSION** **EMPATHY**

"Love permeates the chill and warms the heart, making way for enduring relationships."—Penguin

There are twenty different species of Penguin. It lives in the cold climate of the Southern Hemisphere and is most abundant in Antarctica and New Zealand. Penguin is an aquatic bird that spends a significant amount of time swimming in the ocean where it feeds on Krill, Shrimp, Squid, and fish. Penguin does not fly because its feathers are not long enough to support flight. Instead, it relies on its flippers to swim. Its tuxedo-like appearance helps camouflage it from predators while swimming. To stay warm on land, Penguin huddles with other members of its flock, which helps it to keep its body temperature high enough to survive. Emperor Penguin has the densest coat since it always remains on land. Penguin pairs mate for life, but males are also known to build relationships with others of the same sex. The male Penguin will normally fast during breeding season, preferring to stay with its eggs and protect them from predators. While her mate nests, the female Penguin heads for the ocean in search of food to sustain her family.

Penguin lives in large colonies of over twenty million members. It loves to socialize and cherishes its community. It realizes the importance of a team and social network to building a life. As a Power Animal, Penguin teaches that communication is the key to successful relationships. Sharing with others can help us detox thoughts and emotions, enabling us to thrive in high-energy environments. Penguin likes to press its belly to the earth for grounding, and then jump into the ocean with a sense of freedom and celestial fluidity. Riding the currents and waves, Penguin is always tapped into what is going on around it. It can sense the atmosphere of its colony and knows its responsibility to the collective as well as its family unit.

The indigenous Maori of New Zealand associate the yellow-headed Fiordland Penguin with a sense of divinity. Since its crest is yellow, they say it must therefore have been hit by lightning—a shamanic initiation. Since Penguin does not live near many indigenous peoples, there are few mentions of Penguin in the lore of surviving Native populations.

Penguin is busy every day trying to meet its needs and yet be part of a greater community. The balance it seeks is to maintain its uniqueness among millions of its kind—which is a lot like being human. It has a special gland that helps it process salt water, an example that can impress upon us the importance of mineral salts to our health and how they can stabilize and boost our personal energy.

Penguin lives in an isolated world, away from humanity and with only a few natural predators. On land, its predators are Lizard, Snake, and Ferret; and in the sea, Killer Whale, Leopard Seal, and Shark. Its habitat is a place of purity. Alone with its peers, it relies on strength in numbers and the predictability of its environment to survive. From the cold conditions Penguin faces much of the year, it shows us that it can be difficult to see through the blizzard and know where we really are. When this happens, nature is forcing us to accept change and trust that, whatever the outcome, all is as it should be.

Penguin brings the message of a universal language, one that speaks to our souls not our minds. Although we all have distinct traits and skills, Penguin reminds us that to get along we need to learn to embody the common values of kindness, compassion, generosity, tolerance, patience, honesty, creativity, joy, humility, and wisdom. These are all ingredients of empathy. By embracing these values we gain the capacity for hope and honesty among our kind. We know when to let go and jump into the nurturing waters that can cleanse us and enable our purest self-expression.

POWERS OF PENGUIN

Call in Penguin for:

- Support in clearing negative energy.
- Getting beneath the surface of an issue in order to reveal a truth.
- Help in learning to get along with a large group.

AWARENESS FROM PENGUIN

If Penguin comes into your life:

- You may need to improve your skills of compassion.
- Revisit your commitment to your relationships.
- An intimate same-sex relationship, whether with a friend or a lover, may present itself for your introspection.

Energy Center: Throat

Mineral: Kunzite

Element: Water

Magic & Mystery:

- Fossils have been found of a giant Penguin that weighed 220 pounds and was six feet tall.
- New Zealand is the Penguin capital of the world with almost half of all Penguin species breeding there.

SHAMAN'S INTENTION: *TEACH ME A SENSE OF COMMUNITY AND THE UNCONDITIONAL LOVE THAT IT TAKES TO THRIVE IN IT*

PHEASANT

MASCULINITY | **TRANSCENDENCE** | **ACTIVITY**

"Rise above a simple view of the world around you; there is much to see from a higher perspective"—Pheasant

POWERS OF PHEASANT

Call in Pheasant for:

- Writing a memoir or telling your story.
- The courage to express yourself and get noticed.
- The confidence to promote your ideas.

AWARENESS FROM PHEASANT

If Pheasant comes into your life:

- It is time to fly and leave your comfort zone behind.
- What you have been hiding will soon be revealed.
- Realize your importance to those with whom you work.

Energy Center: Root

Mineral: Axinite

Element: Earth

Magic & Mystery:

- The first Pheasant was brought to North America from China in 1881.
- In China, Pheasant represents excellence in the literary world.

Pheasant originated in China and now resides throughout Asia, Europe, and North America. It enjoys living on farmlands and in prairies near forests that it can use for cover. It builds its nest among tall grasses. At night Pheasant finds a branch high up in a tree to rest, safe from predators. Peafowl and Partridge are cousins to Pheasant, so, as you can imagine, the male has a striking array of richly colored feathers. His head is red and he has a noticeable white "collar" around his neck, giving him an aura of distinction. His tail feathers are also a lovely symmetric pattern. The female Pheasant is not as brilliantly colored; she's a simple gray.

The brilliant red and bright yellow Golden Pheasant is so adept at sensing danger that it will easily detect any threat nearby. In fact, the wonderful eyesight, hearing, and speed of all types of Pheasant make it elusive to predators. It can run ten miles per hour and fly seventy miles per hour.

In China, Pheasant is a symbol of beauty, refinement, and high status and a good totem animal for someone who is in politics. The elite in the Song Dynasty (960–1279) wore robes of Pheasant feathers to important events. In the Japanese myth cycle of the Shinto religion, whose origins date back to the eighth century, Pheasant is the messenger from the Sun goddess named Amaterasu, ruler of the heavens. To the Japanese people,Green Pheasant is a popular symbol of a mother's love and the strong maternal instinct that will protect children.

Native Americans see Pheasant as a master of protection of the hidden world, most probably because it spends a lot of time unseen in fields of tall grass. They especially admire the male Pheasant for his beauty and ability to attract females.

Pheasant brings us the message of the Sun, a masculine energy. The Sun sings the sound of creation and higher consciousness. The relationship between the Sun and the Earth is the alchemical power of fertility, light, and warmth. Pheasant embodies this energy with its fiery-looking red feathers (Sun) and takes comfort being grounded on Mother Earth.

Pheasant has a diverse collection of feathers, which it wears like a striking "outfit." Its lesson is to embrace color and put on a more vibrant plumage as you walk in the world instead of hiding in the grasses, unseen by others. Pheasant is the embodiment of the masculine yang energy. Yang characteristics are expansive and energetic, active, giving, and similar to the more aggressive side of human nature. As such, Pheasant is a good Power Animal to call upon when you need passion, fire, and the fuel to step out of the crowd and let your talents and abilities be recognized. In the practice of feng shui, yang inspires us to live in houses with bright colors, lots of glass windows to let in natural light, and mirrors to reflect it throughout the space. This helps us to embrace the inner masculine side of our existence and flaunt our magnificence to attract what we want in our lives.

As a Power Animal, Pheasant can help immigrants who have moved to a foreign land face the challenge of adapting to their new homeland. It can also assist recently hired employees adapt to their new business culture. Pheasant does not discriminate on the basis of its perceptions. The male regards the female without judgment, although her feathers are not as bright as his. It can help us to level the playing field in which we pursue our endeavors.

SHAMAN'S INTENTION: *TEACH ME TO EMBRACE THE SERENDIPITY OF LIVING AND THE ELEMENT OF SURPRISE*

PHOENIX

IMMORTALITY | **TRANSFORMATION** | **BALANCE**

"If you could only believe in your eternal being, you would gracefully dance through life with the knowing that nothing ever ends."—Phoenix

Phoenix is a bird of great mystery. According to legend, only one can exist on Earth at a given time. Since it is believed to live up to 13,000 years, it is associated with longevity. Described as having a collection of colorful feathers and a tail of red and gold, Phoenix is a tall bird with slim legs, a long tail, and an extensive wingspan. Its most important trait is its capacity for rebirth. At the end of its life, Phoenix builds a nest for itself that it then sets on fire, and it is consumed in the flames. After three days the Phoenix rises from the ashes reborn.

In the East, images of the Phoenix have appeared for over 7,000 years in a multitude of art forms, even being carved into stone grave markers. To the ancient Chinese Phoenix was the god of the winged ones, and a reminder to rise from your place of being with strength and strive to reach greater heights of knowledge and being. In Chinese mythology Phoenix represents the ultimate power of balance. In ancient times they said it combined features of Rooster, Swallow, Snake, Goose, and other animals—including the shell of Tortoise, the legs of Deer, and the swishy tail of a fish. The myths say that Phoenix was a gentle creature that never destroyed anything; even its food was only droppings of dew. And it embodied feminine energy, with powers derived from the Moon.

The ancient Japanese believed that Phoenix would nest in a paulownia tree, arriving only when a great ruler was born. They said it came to Earth to ensure that this ruler did good deeds for the people. Phoenix has always been associated with the Sun. The ancient Egyptians called it the Lord of Jubilees and viewed it as an incarnation of the Sun god Ra. Its reincarnation represented the alchemical transmutation of lead into gold and death into eternal life.

Phoenix is a totem of survival that exhibits the strength needed to overcome adversity. For this reason, a person who achieves greatness after a major defeat is called a Phoenix. Phoenix reminds us of the importance of embracing darkness the same as light and sadness as much as happiness, seeing everything as part of the balance of earthly experience. Balance can lead to longevity, as acceptance is healthier than worry. Phoenix is powerful because it does not fear death; it realizes that an eternity awaits the eternal being.

When Phoenix appears, you have been blessed: The death of your egoic self or an old mindset is near. All that has been negatively consuming you will be burned so that you can rise higher. When there is a willingness to accept death, death becomes a portal to new life. Nothing dies; there is simply a change of seasons and a sunrise that lights the way to another vast world of possibility. As a Power Animal, Phoenix offers your soul freedom to become what it desires. It can help release you from stagnancy and spur on your creativity—often with a surprising outcome.

Phoenix does not like to be called *mythical* as this term is too limiting, implying it is extinct. It says, "The only reason most people think I am extinct is that they cannot see me. But if they cannot, who is extinct, them or me? I find great comedy in this term. Is the entire unseen world extinct? I beg to differ." Phoenix makes us aware of the unseen world and the vibrancy and energy that surround us. As a Power Animal, Phoenix will assist us in protecting endangered animals on the brink of extinction. It encourages us to respect boundaries and territories of other beings and share the resources of our planet. When there is scarcity, we only see division. But all that we need is available to us without struggle. Knowing this can bring us harmony.

POWERS OF PHOENIX

Call in Phoenix for:

- Help in emerging from a very difficult situation quickly and successfully.
- Reaching a healthy balance of mind, body, and spirit.
- Support in viewing death as a new beginning.

AWARENESS FROM PHOENIX

If Phoenix comes into your life:

- It is time to see yourself as young and vibrant again.
- It is bringing you the knowledge of sacred truths that will free you.
- It will dismember thoughts that keep you from destroying faith.

Energy Center: Crown

Mineral: Ruby in fuchsite

Element: Fire

Magic & Mystery: Phoenix was associated with the Phoenician civilization, which spanned the Mediterranean region from 1500–300 B.C.E., spread the Linear B writing system, and was famous for its purple dyes derived from conch shells.

SHAMAN'S INTENTION: *TEACH ME TO OVERCOME MY LIMITATIONS AND EMBRACE THE MAGIC OF TRANSFORMATION*

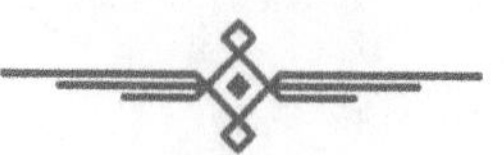

PIG

MATERNITY | SOCIABILITY | SENSITIVITY

"There is so much abundance to embrace; everything is ripe for creation."—Pig

POWERS OF PIG

Call in Pig for:

- Help in raising a lot of children.
- Achieving a clean, orderly environment.
- Helping you save money.

AWARENESS FROM PIG

If Pig comes into your life:

- You may need to lower your voice and stop squealing to be heard.
- Try using aromatherapy to activate your senses.
- You may be too lethargic and need a spurt of enthusiasm to get going.

Energy Center: Sacrum

Mineral: Fire opal

Element: Earth

Magic & Mystery:

- The squeal of Pig can reach three decibels higher than the sound of a supersonic airplane.
- The domestic Pig represents the largest number of any kind of mammal.
- In New Guinea, people's wealth is determined by the number of Pig they own.

Pig has been domesticated for thousands of years and is found all over the planet. It grows to be large, weighing up to 1,000 pounds. It has short legs, a wrinkled snout, pointy ears, a round belly, and a tail with a curl on the end. It mostly consumes plants: grasses, fruits, and roots. It has a powerful sense of smell, a wide field of vision, and a good sense of direction. It is a great communicator with a sophisticated language that it uses to chat with others of its kind. Piglet will recognize the voice of its mother soon after it is born. Sow will sing to her piglets in a series of gentle grunts while she is nursing. Pig likes creature comforts such as sunbathing, the sound of music, touch, and food. Very clean, Pig will avoid soiling the areas where it eats and sleeps. To stay cool, it prefers a dip in water more than rolling in the mud. Pig is highly intelligent with excellent survival instincts.

In many cultures, Pig is a symbol of fertility. Sow is revered as an excellent mother and for her power of creation since she usually gives birth to many Piglets at once. The Plains Indians see Pig as the bringer of rain and therefore linked to fertility and abundance. In many artifacts and carvings throughout Europe, Pig is associated with the Moon and fertility. In ancient Greece, Pig was associated with Persephone, the goddess of vegetation, who is often depicted wearing the mask of a pig. She was the daughter of Zeus and queen of the Lower World. In Germany Pig is a sign of having luck in finances, leading to the invention of the piggy bank. The ancient Celtic story of the sea god Manannán tells how he owned a Pig herd that never dwindled as its members were always replenishing themselves.

In Asia, Buddhists see Pig as a symbol of ignorance, representing its attachment to illusions of thoughts, desires, and the truth about life. Other Asian cultures see pig as good luck. In the Chinese zodiac the Year of the Pig is considered an auspicious time for fertility, virility, and making babies. In ancient Egypt an image of Pig would be painted under the lid of a coffin, depicting the eternal mother whose Piglets were the night stars.

Pig knows the primal smell of Mother Earth. When we're walking in nature, Pig reminds us to embrace the scents we encounter as they can give us important information about the world. The smell of decay, the aroma of rebirth in spring, and other fragrances are impressions of the circle of life. Scent brings back memories immediately, as if the past has been restored. A memory trigger can be as simple as the moment a tea bag hits hot water and releases its scent.

Pig also reminds us of the importance of the skin, our largest organ, and its sensitivity to touch. Skin is a place where two of us can meet: where mother touches child and lover touches lover on a level of nuance and discovery. Pig is not the most discerning in its food choices; it eats whatever it finds. As a Power Animal, Pig teaches us to be more aware of what we eat. Pig is the ultimate giver, lying on its side exposing its teats to nurse the world with its beneficence. Pig sacrifices its body for human consumption. By constantly sharing its gifts, it teaches us the importance of discernment and self-care in a world that often responds with a lack of gratitude.

SHAMAN'S INTENTION: *HELP ME TO LEARN THE POWER OF NURTURING OTHERS, SO I MAY LEARN TO NURTURE MYSELF*

PLATYPUS

ULTRASENSING | **UNIQUENESS** | **CONFIDENCE**

"Close your eyes and ears and feel the answers penetrating your field of awareness."—Platypus

Platypus appears to be a blend of Duck, Beaver, and Otter. Found in southern and eastern Australia it lives near creeks, rivers, and lakes and has a rubbery bill, a flat tail, and webbed feet suitable for swimming. Its bill contains 40,000 electroreceptors that are able to detect electric fields generated by living things. This sensitivity to subtle energy enables it to hunt and move without using its hearing, sight, or smell. It can rely 100 percent on its bill to get around. For defense Platypus has toxic spurs on its heels that are able to stun or kill medium-sized animals. Over time the female loses her heel spurs, a sign that she has managed her fears and can now walk the world with trust and faith. Platypus sleeps most of the time. It has two burrows, one for living and the other for nursing after eggs are hatched.

The Australian Aboriginals see Platypus as such a special animal that it is never hunted. Their traditional stories celebrate the power of being unique and not needing a crowd to be relevant. The Kabi Kabi tribe believes that Platypus is a human who was transformed by Snake during a battle of wits.

As a Power Animal, Platypus comes to tell us to trust our inner guidance and count on nature for direction. Each of us is unique; no one else on the planet is quite like us. Our particular gifts were designed for us in the spirit world before our birth, and the more we connect to spirits now the more we can align with our purpose. When we allow the spirits to guide us, life can be magical. Platypus keeps us from conforming to social expectations. It reminds us to release our attachment to what others think and any desire to fit in. Happiness comes from embracing our quirks instead of following trends. Daring to think differently leads to innovation. This is the power that resides within us.

As a Power Animal, Platypus can support psychic mediums to heighten their extrasensory perception or develop this capacity. It can also help those who are blind to develop intuition and gain confidence about functioning well without eyesight. Platypus teaches us that the number one thing we need for protection is awareness. By relying on our feelings, we can master our fears and cunningly avoid doing that which is not in our highest good. Platypus can also assist energy healers who rely on the electromagnetic field, such as homeopaths and acupuncturists. Although scientific advances in biofield frequencies are only beginning, Platypus has used the innate gift of sensing biofields for centuries to its advantage.

Waterways are the conductors of energy around our planet. They transport the frequency of life. Their currents are feeding the tissues of the plant world and other beings that exist in their fluid network. The ability of Platypus to sense electromagnetic energy reminds us that we too emit energy and have an impact on the planetary field. From the smallest Ant to the largest Elephant, we are vibrational contributors. In a world filled with diverse frequencies, it is important to place your feet in the muddy soils of the embankments and stabilize yourself. Then you can become the beacon of life energy you have the potential for being.

POWERS OF PLATYPUS

Call in Platypus for:

- Believing without seeing.
- Tapping in to higher frequencies to create synchronicity in your life.
- Embracing your individuality.

AWARENESS FROM PLATYPUS

If Platypus comes into your life:

- You are too focused on the external world.
- You may have the abilities of a psychic.
- You need to trust your instincts more.

Energy Center: Third eye

Mineral: Iolite

Element: Water

Magic & Mystery:

- The Platypus is honored on the twenty-cent coin of Australia.
- When European naturalists first saw Platypus, they thought they were being fooled by someone who had put Duck's bill and Otter's tail on a Beaver.

SHAMAN'S INTENTION: *HELP ME TO UNDERSTAND THE VIBRATION THAT FLOWS THROUGH ALL THINGS*

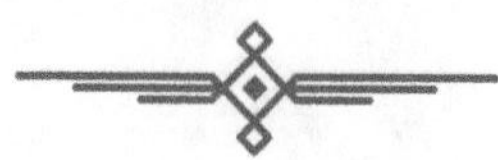

PORCUPINE

SAFETY | **HUMILITY** | **FEARLESSNESS**

"We always wear our protection as we honor and understand our empathic selves."—Porcupine

POWERS OF PORCUPINE

Call in Porcupine for:

- Feeling safe and secure.
- Confidence in your ability to defend yourself.
- The enhancement of your ability to nurture.

AWARENESS FROM PORCUPINE

If Porcupine comes into your life:

- Call on the ancestral realm for support.
- You may need protection from people who are unkind towards you.
- Ensure the security of those you love.

Energy Center: Heart

Mineral: Malachite

Element: Fire

Magic & Mystery:

- The word *Porcupine* is derived from the French term porc *d'espine*, which means "thorny pig."
- The Tlingit of the Pacific Northwest traditionally made their paintbrushes from the hairs of Porcupine.

Porcupine is found in diverse environments that range from deserts to forests. There are twenty-eight species of Porcupine in North America and one in Africa. Some are brown, some are gray, and others are white. Porcupine has poor eyesight but a great nose for finding food. Its teeth are strong; a trait that comes in handy as it loves eating the bark of trees, which is tough. Possessing strong feet and claws that help it to ascend trees, Porcupine is an excellent climber. For the most part, it is peaceful; it only gets aggressive when it feels that its territory is threatened. It is a creature of the night and during the day usually rests inside hollow logs where it feels safe in the company of its family. Porcupine mates for life.

Porcupine has soft hair all over its body that is mixed with almost 30,000 quills. These quills are its protection. With numerous barbs on each one, they are a major deterrent if it is attacked. As a warning to predators, Porcupine shakes its quills and makes a rattling sound. Quills always grow back if they fall off.

Warriors of the ancient Arapaho tribe used Porcupine quills in their war dresses because they related to Porcupine as a great fighter. Porcupine was their messenger to the spirit world and brought them the power of defense. Porcupine inspired these Native Americans to believe that, no matter how powerful the enemy, they would always prevail. The Tahltan of Canada used quills to make bows and the Tlingit decorated clothing, baskets, blankets, and rugs with them. The Mi'kmaq used them to extract maple syrup from trees.

In Africa, people carried quills with them as talismans and even designed clothing that contained them. The Kikuyu of Kenya have a legend that Porcupine is the bringer of fire, which can be attributed to the Porcupine's appearance when its quills are on full display, seeming much like the rays of the Sun shooting out of its body.

Porcupine represents safety and how we feel grounded when we are a member of a loving family. Ancestral powers are the greatest powers of indigenous peoples. Porcupine was seen as carrying many generations of ancestors with it, each quill representing a member of its extended spiritual family. To harvest its quills Lakota women would throw a blanket over Porcupine and then keep the ones that got stuck in the blanket.

As a Power Animal, Porcupine can support you to walk the world, as if wearing a suit of armor. Feeling protected can give you the ability to transcend fear and stay calm. Confidence creates smiles of contentment. When you work with Porcupine's power, those who wish to attack you will question their impulse to do so and recognize that it is not worth the risk. Porcupine will also guide you to calculate risks before you leap into action. Preserving what you already have can often be satisfaction enough that you do not need to take a risk. Porcupine offers its quill to you to prick any hardness that exists in your heart and allow love to flow through it so that you may better nurture yourself and others.

SHAMAN'S INTENTION: *TEACH ME TO FEEL SECURE SO THAT FEAR DOES NOT DIMINISH MY POWER*

PRAIRIE DOG

NETWORKING | **CREATIVITY** | **ARTICULATION**

"Follow me into the Lower World; there you will find your imagination."
—Prairie Dog

Prairie Dog is native to North America and Mexico. It has round ears, short legs, strong claws, and a short tail. One of the top burrowers in the animal kingdom, it designs extremely sophisticated underground colonies. These Prairie Dog "towns" may be populated by hundreds of occupants. Located fifteen to twenty feet under the ground, towns have tunnels that extend for miles with areas for storing food, sleeping, going to the bathroom, and exits that allow for quick escapes. Prairie Dog communities have an intricate social structure. Prairie Dog may greet others with a kiss or a hug. It makes a squeaky sound that may seem primitive, but its language enables it to communicate detailed descriptions. It is often seen sitting upright on its back feet, on alert and guarding the entrance to its world.

The Hopi and Navajo of old admired the ability of Prairie Dog to connect places with tunnels and the effort it makes to do so. They took a lesson from Prairie Dog when building and connecting their own dwellings and ensuring they could escape. The kiva is a room ancestral and modern Puebloans of the Desert Southwest traditionally have used for religious ceremonies and community gatherings. Kivas offer a similar sense of safety as the Prairie Dog town as they are made of dirt and nutrients of Mother Earth. These tribes believe Prairie Dog spirit holds the power of the rain water. They believe it digs deep so it may sleep as close to the heartbeat of Mother Earth as possible. When Prairie Dog feels threatened, it retreats underground. Prairie Dog teaches us that sometimes in life it is time to retreat to prepare for our next steps while awaiting a new season.

As a Power Animal, Prairie Dog is a gatekeeper to the Lower World, which is a place of spiritual connection with many diverse regions—among them, forests, jungles, oceans, rivers, mountains, and valleys. When you wish to find the entrance to the Lower World, ask Prairie Dog for assistance. During a shamanic journey, you can ask Prairie Dog to root out your negative patterns and help you to achieve transformation. Prairie Dog will assist you in finding the right plant medicine for healing and in working with elemental beings.

We are often led by our ego into the tunnel of fear that appears dark; yet, if we trust our intuition, we know which turn to take and the path to healing appears. We need not be afraid of what we find in the dark, as it can be the place of truth. Prairie Dog invites us to dive deep into self-examination. It will help you to face your fears, your hidden emotions, your dreams, and your suppressed potential and emerge whole and complete with an ageless wisdom of who you are. Among the unseen roots of things, you can be reborn.

The human desire for connection is great. Unfortunately, when we connect we often bring with us our desire to control and judge as well as our jealousy and possessiveness qualities that make relationships unbearable. These tendencies shut off our ability to communicate and poison our connections. We then fail to move forward, retreating behind a silly façade. Being a symbol of nature's "internet," Prairie Dog can help us form healthy connections untainted by such problems. Prairie Dog reminds us that when we show up as our authentic selves, we do not discriminate by judging. Prairie Dog sees no boundaries. It simply expands its territory to include more in its world. When others feel a Prairie Dog-like sense of abundance and expansion in their encounters with you, they will work toward a common goal with you and possibilities will abound. Keep digging and exploring these paths.

POWERS OF PRAIRIE DOG

Call in Prairie Dog for:

- Building an intricate network of friends and colleagues.
- Confidence in seeking what lies deep inside your psyche.
- The ability to seek refuge when needed.

AWARENESS FROM PRAIRIE DOG

If Prairie Dog comes into your life:

- You may need to be on the alert for intruders.
- It is time to seek information that is waiting for you in the Lower World.
- You need to be more specific in the way that you communicate with others.

Energy Center: Root

Mineral: Sphalerite

Element: Earth

Magic & Mystery:

- The largest Prairie Dog town was discovered in Texas. It spanned 25,000 square miles and housed almost 400 million Prairie Dogs.
- Centuries ago Prairie Dog towns stretched from Canada to Mexico.

SHAMAN'S INTENTION: *TAKE ME TO THE ENTRANCE OF THE LOWER WORLD WHERE I CAN FIND THE PEAKS AND VALLEYS OF MY CONNECTION TO EARTH*

PRAYING MANTIS

AWARENESS | **MINDFULNESS** | **OPPORTUNITY**

"Never underestimate the power of stillness."
—Praying Mantis

POWERS OF PRAYING MANTIS

Call in Praying Mantis for:

- The gift of patience.
- To train your body to be still.
- To seize an opportunity.

AWARENESS FROM PRAYING MANTIS

If Praying Mantis comes into your life:

- What you desire is coming to you.
- You may be living in chaos and confusion and need to simplify.
- Take time for stillness; it is the surest way to stop indulging in bad habits.

Energy Center: Crown

Mineral: Phenacite

Element: Air

Magic & Mystery:

- In captivity, the female Praying Mantis bites off the head either during and/or after copulation. We don't know what she does in the wild!
- Praying Mantis reverses the food chain, sometimes eating birds.
- There is an African Bushman myth that Praying Mantis created the Earth and is our supreme being.

Early fossils indicate that Praying Mantis has existed for 150 million years. This insect is found in all parts of the world wherever there are mild temperatures. A predator, it is on the constant lookout for any insect it can find to consume. From two to five inches long, depending on the species, it has what appear to be four legs and two arms. It can come in many colors, which is its mechanism for blending into the background of local vegetation. Praying Mantis can be mistaken for branches, leaves, or sticks. It is so convincing that unsuspecting insects find it difficult to detect. It tends to hang out near sources of nectar, which are popular destinations for insects to feed on and perfect places for it to plant itself and wait for "dinner." Praying Mantis can swivel its head 180 degrees to detect its prey and prepare to strike. It is extremely calculated in its movements—highly aware of its surroundings and patient and still. Its face can seem humanlike or extraterrestrial and with its "arms" together it gives the impression that it is praying. This gesture has led it to be honored and cherished by many civilizations. The ancient Greeks and Egyptians, for instance, believed Praying Mantis had supernatural abilities.

The Chinese have always been impressed with Praying Mantis' stillness and the contemplative manner of its movements. They honor its lack of fear and the opportunistic skill it uses to strike quickly to get what it desires. Its movements have inspired poses that martial artists use in hand-to-hand combat.

In Africa the Kalahari Bushmen worship Praying Mantis like a god, asking it for messages when it is seen and waiting with interest for what it will reveal. Praying Mantis may be asked to find lost sheep and goats. In the ancient Greek culture Praying Mantis was seen as a prophet and its messages were much anticipated. It is a helpful guide those who are lost and need to find their home. The Greek word mantis means "prophet."

Stillness is the message this Power Animal brings. It takes its own sweet time. There is no busy schedule in its life that could distract it or trample on the signals of its intuition, no chaos in its demeanor. Within its silence there is spiritual power. Praying Mantis is a good Power Animal for teachers and students of meditation and mindfulness. It teaches us to wait calmly and patiently for what we desire. Praying Mantis rarely misses its target, and it is so sure that it will achieve its goal that it is willing to wait. Those who are aware prevail; those in ignorance become the vulnerable. Many of us have a destination in mind yet take no notice of how we are getting there. Staying in one place increases the depth of our experience of it by exposing its layers and aspects. To know a place, you must take the time to absorb all that is around you; just seeing it is not sufficient enough to know it. Often the next move requires calculation and precision. Use stillness to calculate what to do next so that you will be inspired with the confidence to take your next step.

SHAMAN'S INTENTION: *HELP ME TO BE CONSCIOUS OF MY EVERY THOUGHT, INTENTION, AND ACTION*

PUFFIN

ADVENTURE | **LOYALTY** | **INDEPENDENCE**

"Having a place to come home to is soothing to the soul."
—Puffin

Puffin makes its home on the east coasts of Canada and the United States, and in Alaska, Iceland, and northern Europe. Similar to Penguin, it is black and white with short wings, a stock body, and a colorful parrot-like beak, giving it the name Sea Parrot. Puffin's beak changes colors in the seasons from gray to a bold orange that is believed to play a part in attracting a mate. Puffin spends its life at sea and will rest on waves, taking a break from flying vast distances along the shore. It has a capacity to fly up to fifty-five miles per hour. To feed, it dives into the ocean to depths of 200 feet, looking for Eel, Haddock, and Herring. In the spring it heads for its coastal breeding grounds, usually crevices and rocks in the soil by the water.

Three million members of the Puffin family gather in Iceland to breed once a year. The rest gather in a variety of other locations. Puffin follows the magnetic field of the Earth and stars to get to its destination. When it arrives, there is a lot of drama. On the breeding grounds Puffin unites with the loyal mate that it stays with for life. The male Puffin will impregnate the female who will then lay a single egg that both parents incubate. Forty-five days after hatching the Puffin chick—a Puffling—heads off to sea at night alone. After two years the Puffling will return to nest for the first time, but it won't breed until it is five. And it won't breed if there is not sufficient food to share with new offspring.

Native Alaskan tribes believe that Puffin can manage storms and weather. Traditionally, the Aleut, Sugpiaq, and Alutiiq use Puffin skins, crests, beaks, and feathers as adornments for their ceremonial costumes. Puffin's image is found on hereditary totem poles. Puffin masks are used by storytellers to share stories of their traditions and communicate with spirits. The ancient Inuit would collect the bills of Puffin that were cast off during mating season to create a musical instrument known simply as a shaker that is similar to a tambourine and was believed to have magical powers to heal the sick.

As it can live for more than thirty years, Puffin possesses wisdom about the oceans. It brings us messages from the waves that are the pathways of human emotions and it understands the subconscious information that lies beneath them. We experience constant upwelling and downward currents of emotion in our lives. These currents are the fabric of our journeys to realization. The waves and waters of the psyche can teach us and rejuvenate us by bringing us face to face with the shore of our reality. Traveling into the unknown of the Upper and Lower Worlds is a beneficial shamanic pursuit, as the line of the horizon is where wisdom lies. Many of us see the entering of unknown territory as being dropped into an abyss; but those who aspire to greatness of spirit see visiting the unknown as just another step on the journey of enlightenment that will bring us home. Puffin shares with us its version of home, which is the place it merges with the mineral kingdom, as it builds its nest among the gravity of rocks and their nurturing vibrations. It suggests we incorporate crystals into our domiciles—even if just building a small altar to hold them.

As a Power Animal, Puffin warns us about drowning in our own sorrow. It says that if we stay above the surface of the water of our emotions we have a better view. We can find abundant health everywhere we look, whether to the sunlit skies or a sea teeming with life.

POWERS OF PUFFIN

Call in Puffin for:

- Going the distance.
- Raising independent children.
- Finding your way home to your heart or to the place you feel most nurtured.

AWARENESS FROM PUFFIN

If Puffin comes into your life:

- You may need to be more adventurous.
- Dive deep to find the abundance that you seek.
- Embrace your time alone.

Energy Center: Heart

Mineral: Prasiolite

Element: Water

Magic & Mystery: Puffin was seen as a sacred bird by the Irish. They believed Puffin was a reincarnated monk because of its plumage, which looks like a Catholic monk's robe.

SHAMAN'S INTENTION: *TAKE ME ON A JOURNEY FAR BEYOND THE SHACKLES OF MY LIMITATIONS*

QUAIL

HIGHER CONSCIOUSNESS | AGILITY | ELUSION

"We navigate both worlds, the dust of reality and the skies of freedom."—Quail

POWERS OF QUAIL

Call in Quail for:

- The ability to make a quick departure.
- Help to become a person of trust and steadfastness.
- Grounding and support in settling into a new home.

AWARENESS FROM QUAIL

If Quail comes into your life:

- You may be acting unnecessarily evasive.
- You worry too much about your children or other dependents.
- You may lack sociability for those outside of your circle.

Energy Center: Root

Mineral: Axinite

Element: Earth

Magic & Mystery: In olden times, Germans would bring their Quail inside their homes to protect them from lightning.

Quail is found worldwide. It typically roams woodlands and open areas where there is brush in which it can hide for protection from predators. To protect itself from pesky insects it will stir up dust to keep its feathers clean. Quail is admired for its plumage, which varies in color among the ninety-five species of its kind and is a major factor in blending into its environment. Quail is recognizable by the crest on its head, which is shaped like a teardrop antenna and bobs around while it is walking. It prefers walking to flying but, if surprised, can launch into flight at speeds of forty miles per hour. Quail communicates with a variety of high-pitched shrill sounds and calls. During mating season, it gathers with its family group. Quail tends to stay in the same territory for most of its life and so remains in contact with early acquaintances and family. The female Quail is a prolific egg layer, producing up to twenty eggs at one time. It is a heartwarming sight to see the care and concern the mother has for her hatchlings as she rounds them up while they learn to search for food.

For the ancient Greeks, Quail was a symbol of a higher consciousness and communal love. For the ancient Romans, along with being a sign of affection and a gift often given to a lover, Quail was viewed as a warrior and represented bravery in battle. The ancient Chinese also admired Quail for its bravery and loyalty to its partner. One of many Chinese characters for peace is pronounced the same as the word for Quail, *anchún.* When nine Quails are drawn with chrysanthemums, it is a wish that all the generations that follow will live in peace.

Tribes of the southwestern United States associate Quail with Mother Earth and with modesty. Quail is the totem of one of the Mohave clans, and the dance of Quail is a popular tribal tradition. Some tribal cultures saw the spirit of Quail as elusory and fleeting, as it is always aware of what's happening in its surroundings and can move quickly to flee from danger. The Vikings of ancient Norway also worked with animal spirits and had totems. In Norse mythology, the rowan (mountain ash) tree was the Tree of Life. One of the totems that the tree was associated with in their tradition was Quail, because of its ability to evade capture.

As a Power Animal, Quail reminds us of connecting daily to a higher power through nature. This power is far greater than the smallness of who we are. Quail also urges us to be receptive to diverse people and concepts. To listen without prejudice and think first before forming opinions heightens our awareness. Quail shares our preoccupation to protect ourselves and our families from others but warns us that too often these thoughts are exaggerations. It wants us to know that if we slow down and are less motivated by fear, life will be gentler and kinder to us.

SHAMAN'S INTENTION: *SUPPORT ME TO STAY CONNECTED TO THE UPPER WORLD ENERGY YET GROUNDED IN MY EARTHLY JOURNEY*

QUETZAL

SELF-AWARENESS **BEAUTY** **IMAGINATION**

"Happiness is freedom."—Quetzal

Quetzal is a bird that lives in the tropical forests of southern Mexico and Central America. It especially enjoys cloud cover and fog because of the moisture. It is part of the Trogon family whose name is ancient Greek for "gnawing." Quetzal has a round, pudgy body covered in emerald green feathers. The male has a spectacular long tail that looks like an elegant streamer. Its chest is a striking red, which contemporary Mayans believe represents the blood of their ancestors who were killed by the Spanish in the sixteenth century. Quetzal is truly one of the most beautiful birds in the Western Hemisphere. The display of it in flight is breathtaking. It has larger than normal eyes that help it to see inside the darkness of the dense forest where it lives. Quetzal makes its home in the crevices of trees at the top of the canopy. With its brilliant green shading it blends in perfectly and is difficult to spot. It is a skilled hunter of Frog, Fly and Lizard, and also forages fruits and berries. Through its droppings, seeds are spread that rejuvenate the forest vegetation. During mating season, males display an impressive plumage to impress females. The females are on the lookout for the healthiest male to procreate with and share the responsibility of tending their chicks. Quetzal is a faithful partner for life.

Quetzal was greatly admired and sacred to the ancient Aztecs and Mayans who called it the "rare jewel bird of the world." In the pre-Columbian era, the feathers of Quetzal were more valuable than gold and as important as jade. Only the highest levels of royalty were permitted to possess and wear them. It was forbidden to kill Quetzal for its feathers. The Mayans would catch Quetzal, take some of its feathers and then set it free so it could regrow its plumage. Today, dances known as Quetzales are still performed in Central America to honor the bird. Dancers show up in beautiful costumes adorned with its feathers.

The word quetzal means "precious" or

QUETZAL

SELF-AWARENESS | **BEAUTY** | **IMAGINATION**

> QUETZAL WAS GREATLY ADMIRED BY AND SACRED TO THE ANCIENT AZTECS AND MAYANS WHO CALLED IT THE "RARE JEWEL BIRD OF THE WORLD."

POWERS OF QUETZAL

Call in Quetzal for:

- Seeing the beauty in all things.
- Releasing your spirit to feel free.
- Embracing your beauty and gifts to inspire others.

AWARENESS OF QUETZAL

If Quetzal comes into your life:

- Begin a new spiritual practice designed to help you reach your highest potential.
- You need to learn to thrive no matter how dense the energy around you may be.
- Invest in yourself and do a makeover.

Energy Center: Heart

Mineral: Jade

Element: Air

Magic & Mystery:

- Quetzal has a reputation for killing itself if it is caged or captured.
- Quetzal love wild avocados, they will swallow the pits whole and then regurgitate the pit, spreading them throughout the jungle, planting new trees for future consumption.

"sacred" in several indigenous languages. Quetzal is related to the Snake god Quetzalcoatl—a god of much appreciation—who was always depicted as a serpent with Quetzal feathers. In one hand he holds a staff that represents life. In the other hand he holds a spear that has a star on it—and it was said this was where his heart was. Another translation of the word quetzal is "sky." This god's name means "sky, earth (co), water (atl)." From this we can see that Quetzal, as a Power Animal, is an important emblem of the sky possessing divine associations. The Aztecs believed that Quetzalcoatl would return in 1519, but instead the Spanish arrived in an expedition headed by Hernán Cortés. The Aztec emperor Montezuma, who greeted Cortés, gave him a stunning headdress made of Quetzal feathers, thinking he was the god—probably the world's worst case of mistaken identity.

For the ancient Mayans Quetzal represented the individual spirit and its desire to transcend. Its connection with Snake was recognition of the human spirit's grounding in the physical world. Quetzal was a symbol of fertility and abundance. In the Temple of Kukulkan (the Mayan version of Quetzalcoatl) in Chichen Itza, if you clap your hands, an echo is produced that is said to be the sound of Quetzal. In Guatemala, Quetzal is similarly revered by indigenous peoples, like Condor or Eagle, and honored in their traditional songs and culture. In the cosmology of the Mayans, the divine breath of the gods caused the blue flowers of the Guayacan tree to fall, and before they hit the ground they turned into Quetzal. After the Spanish arrived, it was said that the Quetzal was silenced and would only sing again when the land was free.

Quetzal tells us to feed our curiosity. Curiosity is noble; it inspires us to learn about the world around us. It is especially good to be inquisitive about nature and to adopt a mindset of discovery. Curiosity is the catalyst for creation and invention. When so much is hidden in the clouds of the forest canopy, curiosity will get you to your destination; it is the driving force needed to meet any mystery you encounter. The color green of the jungle is representative of the heart chakra of Mother Earth. It breathes in her nutrients and breathes out life. Quetzal suggests we embrace this as our alchemical formula for love. Celebrate your life, embrace your curiosity, breathe, spend time in the greenery of nature and you will begin to see the world from the perspective of the higher vibration of love.

SHAMAN'S INTENTION: *TEACH ME TO APPRECIATE THE BEAUTY OF NATURE; THEN TEACH ME TO LOVE MYSELF*

RABBIT

VULNERABILTY **CREATION** **ABUNDANCE**

"We take comfort in the belly of the Mother who brings us the magic of creation."
—Rabbit

Rabbit is found throughout the world, living in forests, grasslands, deserts, wetlands, and meadows. It inhabits any environment that is conducive to digging burrows. Rabbit digs an intricate system of tunnels with many entrances and exits; and before entering one, Rabbit uses its whiskers to gauge the width of the hole so that it does not get stuck. Rabbit is small and furry with large ears and a tail that looks like a tuft of cotton. It hops instead of walks and therefore has strong hind legs, which it can kick with to defend itself. Rabbit comes in a variety of colors which are mostly an evolutionary adaptation to its environment, a perfect camouflage to hide from predators. Mostly timid, Rabbit will freeze so as to not draw attention to itself or run from approaching predators.

Rabbit is a powerhouse of optimum senses ready to take on survival and defense, and because of this it represents immortality. It has the ability to see in a range of 360 degrees and has excellent distance vision. Rabbit is farsighted, enabling it to see over a large swath of terrain and perceive anyone approaching. If it fails to see a predator, Rabbit will probably smell it first. Rabbit can hear high frequencies and is able to detect sounds from far away. Its long ears function like antennae so it can discern where a sound is coming from. Rabbit does not have a detectable personal scent, which also helps it stay safe.

In many cultures, Rabbit is a symbol of fertility, as it is a prolific producer of offspring. This connection to the circle of life is a lesson for all of us as to our ability to create on many levels. It is also a reminder of the inevitability of eternal life. Rabbit is a Chinese zodiac sign and represents a long life, tenderness, and love. The Chinese Moon goddess, Chang'e, had Rabbit as her pet. Native American tribes see Rabbit as a trickster and a real character that displays inappropriate behavior and has an inflated sense of self. The Hopi and the Shawnee have Rabbit clans and perform many ceremonial dances that revolve around Rabbit.

Many shamans have used a Rabbit foot as a talisman of luck

RABBIT

VULNERABILTY | **CREATION** | **ABUNDANCE**

IN MANY CULTURES, RABBIT IS A SYMBOL OF FERTILITY, AS IT IS A PROLIFIC PRODUCER OF OFFSPRING.

POWERS OF RABBIT

Call in Rabbit for:

- Planting seeds for a new project.
- To develop appreciation for your sensory powers.
- Trusting the friends that you meet on your journey; they are all teachers no matter what their messages.

AWARENESS FROM RABBIT

If Rabbit comes into your life:

- You may be very fertile—ready to conceive an idea or a family.
- Do not always feel you have to be on alert; some days you just need to trust that all is well.
- Release any fears that are keeping you frozen in place.

Energy Center: Crown

Mineral: Tanzanite

Element: Earth

Magic & Mystery:

- It is estimated that the Rabbit species has more than 40 million members.
- "Follow the White Rabbit" is a reference to Lewis Carroll's book *Alice in Wonderland*. It means be willing to respond to an unexpected invitation or calling and make a deeper search for the meaning of life.
- The ancient Aztecs saw Rabbit as a symbol of drunkenness because of its wild sexual promiscuity.

and special powers of protection, especially when visiting the Lower World. Rabbit is revered in Irish culture where legends tell of women who can shapeshift into Rabbit. In Mexican and Central American tribes, Rabbit was an image reflected on the Moon. The Mayan god Quetzalcoatl was so grateful to Rabbit that he illuminated its image on the Moon so we would all remember its goodness. Like the Mayans, Asians refer to the "Rabbit in the Moon," as opposed to the "Man in the Moon." The Moon symbolizes death and rebirth as it dies when it sets and is reborn again when it rises.

The Moon and Rabbit have much in common in regard to shadow and light, which is Rabbit's story of going into the darkness of its burrow and reemerging into the light. The Moon is a symbol of conception and pregnancy and is tied to parallel agricultural moments like the planting of seeds. Parables featuring the Moon and Rabbit describe the ebb and flow of life as well as principles like not clinging to outcomes and instead supporting inspiration. Mark Twain once wisely stated, "Everyone is a Moon." He meant that we all have a dark side. As a Power Animal, Rabbit is a steady companion to take us into the dark when we must search our souls for truth and light. By harnessing the energy of the Moon, we can see Rabbit there; the mother of the heavens is ready to fill us with the invigorating power of her feminine energy.

White Rabbit is an important symbol for the shaman; it often means that a healer is to be born, serving as a white light that will transform the hearts and minds of those that live in darkness. It is also a sign that a major transformation is coming quickly. From the famous book *Alice in Wonderland,* the meaning of the journey is that down the Rabbit hole is a place to go for the true quest of knowledge. White Rabbit encourages Alice to take a chance to go to another world. When things seem confusing or desperate White Rabbit shows up to encourage us to move forward into the unknown.

Rabbit is about embodying quickness. Having a quick mind and being capable of quick reactions or responses means that your intuition is in charge of you. Choose the first answer that comes. Avoid getting bogged down in analytical thinking as it is rare to be wrong on your first response. Sometimes we regret not heeding our initial brilliance. Over analyzing decisions feels like whisking the egg of thoughts into a scrambled mind.

SHAMAN'S INTENTION: *TAKE ME DOWN THE RABBIT HOLE; I PROMISE TO TRUST WHAT I FIND THERE*

RACCOON

TOUCH | **OBSERVATION** | **INGENUITY**

"We always see a way out of difficulty."—Raccoon

Raccoon is native to Northern, Central, and South America and was introduced to Europe and Japan in the twentieth century. It has gray and brown fur with dark rings on its tail and dark circles around its eyes, making it look like a masked bandit; in fact, it is nature's bandit. Raccoon is smart and has the ability to break into anything and get what it wants—mainly food. Its front paws have five fingers that it uses to grasp and manipulate things it finds, including latches and lids. Raccoon has 200 distinct sounds it uses to communicate with others of its kind.

Raccoon's most heightened sense is touch. When Raccoon eats, it spends a lot of time handling its food for the purpose of gathering a sense of what it is going to eat. Like a child it learns by touch, which helps it to engage in abstract thinking. Raccoon is smart and has a wonderful memory. This gives it the ability to solve problems and come up with viable solutions for overcoming obstacles.

Native North Americans see Raccoon as a trickster. They tell stories to their children about Racoon's mischief and its ability to find food. Eastern peoples, like the Lenape, Shawnee, and Iroquois, honor Raccoon with dances. Due to its black mask, Raccoon is a symbol of magic for some cultures who respect its power of disguise. To them it is an emblem of keeping secrets, curiosity, resourcefulness, and adaptability. To the indigenous tribespeople that once inhabited Mississippi, Raccoon was a symbol of war. Many of the weapons found in their ancient burial sites were embossed with its image. Raccoon inspired the Sioux of the Dakotas to paint their faces, something done to connect to the spirit world. The ancient Aztecs associated Raccoon with wise women whose way of teaching and commitment to family seemed similar to its behavior.

Neuroscientists have found that the more fingers an animal has the greater its intelligence. With its dexterous fingers, Raccoon brings us awareness of the power of our hands and their capacity for expression through gestures, like waving at someone or communicating in sign language. Whether a finger over the mouth to indicate a need for silence or a pat on the back to comfort someone in a state of grief our hands convey meaning. Fingers are vital for transforming raw materials into art via chiseling, molding, weaving, or sculpting. Our hands give us the ability to create and destroy, to heal, and to pray. Raccoon shares its sense of the mudras, ancient hand gestures of worship and symbolism that open the body's meridians and channels. Mudras inspire our devotion to higher powers and our ancestors, including, ultimately, the Hand of God, the supreme authority of creation and blessing.

Raccoon is a symbol of masking for the shaman. Psychologically, a mask gives us the ability to escape judgment behind a story or image we portray of who we are. This disguise signifies the embracing of drama and a lack of truthfulness. A mask can also conceal us from ourselves, which we do by covering up or suppressing our real emotions. This darkens our thoughts. Playing a role in life that is not our true calling also fulfills the functions of a mask.

Spiritually a mask relates to shapeshifting, the mystical art of personal transformation by either changing your internal nature or physical attributes. Raccoon can guide you to break through the molding of your tribe and embrace the freedom of a new and more aligned identity. If you are seeking to accept potentials and never doubt the power of the Universe to bring them to you then this is the Power Animal for you.

POWERS OF RACCOON

Call in Raccoon for:

- Support when you're working with your hands.
- Seeking what is ready to be revealed.
- Learning how to use your sense of touch for healing.

AWARENESS FROM RACCOON

If Raccoon comes into your life:

- You may be taking from others what is not yours.
- Secrets will be revealed.
- It is to share what you are truly feeling.

Energy Center: Solar plexus

Mineral: Obsidian

Element: Earth

Magic & Mystery:

- The Algonquin name for Raccoon is *Arakun*, which means "scratches with hands."
- A smaller Racoon species is found only on the island of Cozumel off the coast of Mexico where they live near the water and feast mostly on crabs.

SHAMAN'S INTENTION: *HELP ME TO TAKE OFF MY MASKS AND REVEAL MYSELF FOR WHO I AM*

RAT

WIT **TENACITY** **SUCCESS**

"We bring a very different intelligence from the least expected nooks, crannies, and corners of life."—Rat

POWERS OF RAT

Call in Rat for:

- Chewing through the cords of negativity that link you to past lovers.
- A nudge to help you maneuver a difficult situation.
- Improving social skills.

AWARENESS OF RAT

If Rat comes into your life:

- It is time to deal with what has been gnawing at you.
- Shift out of the smallness of your mind into more productive thoughts.
- Consider making a journey on a ship.

Energy Center: Sacrum

Mineral: Cinnabar

Element: Earth

Magic & Mystery:

- In 1961, the first Rat sent into space, Hector, had a spacesuit designed for him by Cerma, a French aerospace company.
- Rat is the "vehicle" for Ganesha since it knows all the entrances to the granary, a place of great abundance.

Rat is originally from Asia and Australia, but when shipping and the transporting of goods began, it made its way all over the world. Sailors believe that Rat knows whether or not a ship will sink. Rat has a furry body and a hairless tail, ears, and feet. It comes in different colors. Nocturnal, it has excellent senses of hearing, touch, and smell but poor eyesight. Rat also has extremely powerful teeth and jaws that can chew through anything. In the wilderness, it digs underground networks where it lives in colonies with others of its kind. It makes an effort to disguise entrances to these burrows among rocks and roots of trees, places where larger animals cannot pass. Rat has an excellent memory. Rat is social and will take care of its companions when they are sick or injured. It spends a lot of time grooming itself to keep clean.

Rat has a varied reputation. In ancient Egypt, it was seen as a destroyer of crops and possessing excellent judgment. The ancient Romans saw it as a sign of prosperity. In Japanese mythology one of the seven gods of prosperity is Rat; he is named Daikoku and is the patron of farmers. Rat is looked up to as productive, industrious, and successful. In Chinese astrology, Rat is the first animal of the zodiac. In myth it is remembered for bringing rice to humankind. Because of how fast it reproduces, Chinese couples hoping to have children pray for its assistance.

In Hinduism Rat symbolizes foresight. Its vehicle is Ganesha, an elephant-headed god that can break through any barrier or obstacle. Rat supports this effort by gnawing away on obstacles and squeezing through the tightest corners. In both the Hindu and Buddhist traditions Rat was seen as a trusted friend since it was given a mythical jewel of wish-fulfillment to keep safe. The Karni Mata temple, where Hindus worship an incarnation of the goddess Durga, is inhabited by thousands of White Rat which are treated as sacred.

As a Power Animal, Rat will help you to gnaw through strings of attachment to things that are not serving you well. It is tenacious and able to beat the odds of survival. The cleverness of Rat can be called on when you need to slip through the cracks and solve problems when you get in a jam. Be sure to emulate Rat's resourcefulness. It will use anything it finds to support itself in some way. It reminds us not to toss things away without applying conscious thought to its utility. It also reminds us that being small can be an advantage, so in studying the intricate workings of things we shouldn't overlook simple solutions. Sometimes we can get tied up in emotional knots or the world churns us up inside until we feel despair. Ask Rat to chew through the barriers of beliefs that are keeping you from excelling at the art of living, so you can move into the flow of joy.

Rat tells us that life demands a humorous response. The earthly journey can be a comical exercise as humans learn to be humans and Rats learn to be Rats. The forms that we take on and the variety of circumstances we encounter are often worthy of laughter. We focus too much on becoming when the real task is being.

SHAMAN'S INTENTION: *HELP ME TO GATHER A TRIBE THAT WILL NURTURE ME AND SUPPORT MY SPIRITUAL JOURNEY*

RAVEN

KNOWLEDGE **AWAKENING** **DIVINATION**

"There is always another point of view."
—Raven

Raven is a large black bird with a thick neck covered in shaggy feathers, a glossy plumage of iridescent black with tones of green, purple, and blue. It has a wingspan of up to four feet. Raven lives in forests and deserts and prefers to make its nest in rocky cliffs. It actively forages for food, searching for seeds, nuts, small animals, and whatever else it can find in a garbage can to eat. It has secret caches of food that it has stolen from others of its kind. It is cunning. It will spy on another Raven and then swoop in to grab what it wants. Raven will also play games with Wolf and Coyote and snatch a bit of their prey. It may tease Dog, Cat, and humans to distract them while a nearby partner snatches some food. Raven mates for life and when its offspring are grown it sends them out into the world where they join a conspiracy that works as a team to survive.

Raven is a good communicator with an extensive vocabulary of calls. It can be trained to speak, leading to its mystic role as an oracle that can tell of the future and reveal signs. It is a well-known messenger from the spiritual dimensions. In Celtic mythology, Raven is often seen with Morrigan, a goddess known for prophecy. She shapeshifts into Raven and delivers important messages to her followers. When she bears news to a battlefield she also collects fallen souls so they do not have to remain with their enemies.

Raven was connected to the mythological Welsh king Brân the Blessed, told of in the thirteenth-century stories of the Mabinogion. Brân was a giant who held the wisdom of the ancestors and his people relied on him. Because of all of the knowledge in his head, it was buried where the Tower of London now stands. To this day, there is a Yeoman Warder Ravenmaster at the Tower to protect Raven. Legend says that if Raven leaves Britain will cease to exist.

Raven has been a Power Animal of the mind, thought, and

RAVEN

KNOWLEDGE | AWAKENING | DIVINATION

In Celtic mythology, Raven is often seen with Morrigan, a goddess known for prophecy.

CROW

POWERS OF RAVEN

Call in Raven for:

- Seeing that which you could not see within yourself until now.
- Piercing the veil to the Upper World and allowing its mystical energy to flow into your life.
- Protective vigilance over whatever you most cherish.

AWARENESS FROM RAVEN

If Raven comes into your life:

- You can learn to use the energy of laughter as a skillful means to shift the energy of any interaction.
- You may be ready to take the first step on a new spiritual path.
- You need to listen more and talk less.

Energy Center: Third eye

Mineral: Onyx

Element: Air

Magic & Mystery:

- Psychiatrist Carl Jung believed Raven represents the shadow, the area of the psyche that holds that which we disavow.
- A study by Lund University in Sweden found that Raven has the ability to plan for the future.
- Seeing a Raven with food in its mouth means you will always be taken care of.

intelligence for centuries in the British Isles and Scandinavia. The Norse god Odin was accompanied by two Raven: Hugin, who wielded the power of thought and the search for information; and Mugin, who wielded the power of the mind and intuition. His daughters, the Valkyries, would shapeshift into Ravens to gather and bring information back to him in Asgard.

The ancient Greeks associated Raven with Apollo and Athena, deities respectively of the Sun and the light of wisdom. Myths describe how Raven was originally white, but when Raven failed to keep a secret Apollo punished it by turning it black. The ancient Romans used Raven as a tool of divination, deriving messages from its flight patterns.

To the Native Americans, Raven is the heroic bringer of light. Myths of the Hopi, Navajo, and Zuni say that Raven came from the center of the cosmos with the light of the Sun to give humanity a foundation of wisdom and understanding. It is thanked for ensuring that we do not have to live in darkness. Raven is also seen as a heyoka, a trickster with positive intentions, since it taught the ancestors to lead balanced lives.

Crow and Raven share the characteristics of vision and prediction, yet Crow is more social. Raven is comfortable in solitude. To understand Raven is to understand the power of intuition and the deep mysteries of your being. As a Power Animal, Raven accompanies those who are awakened and burdened with the task of illuminating the path of higher consciousness for others. Raven also helps those who have not yet seen their true selves to gain their liberation from the veil of illusion that prevails on our planet. Raven searches for those who are ready for more than simple knowing, people who have had a glimpse of subtle energy and want to know more. When Raven appears, spiritual transformation may be at hand. Raven likes to take us from the crossroads of possible next steps into the certainty of a specific path. Raven is a great protector. You can engage it as an ally to defend your values in the realms of spirit.

Raven encourages us to take a higher view of our lives. We are limited when too much is going on around us. Raven can help us move from ignorance to knowing and trusting our spiritual perceptions. The gift of the mystic is the power that subtle insight brings. Shamans with clairvoyance have the ability to capture snapshots in their imaginations. Raven encourages us to step into the unknown since every mystery holds the potential for magic.

Shaman's Intention: *Bring me the wisdom to understand what arrives on my doorstep*

RED PANDA

ISOLATION | **CHOICE** | **DESTINY**

"We live beyond the demands of culture and cherish our individual destiny that is not defined by others."—Red Panda

Red Panda makes its home in the mountains of Nepal, Myanmar, and China. It prefers to live in the high-altitude tropical forests. Red Panda's belly is black and its feet and ears white. Its tail has brown rings, but it is often called Firefox because most of the rest of its fur is red. Its appearance helps it blend in with the red moss and white lichen that cling to the trees in its habitat. Red Panda spends most of its life in trees where it feeds on bamboo. As it does not derive many calories from its diet, it rests to conserve energy. For the most part, Red Panda is a solitary creature. It has a built-in protection system: It emits a strong odor from the base of its tail to fend off would-be attackers. It also has a displeasing, high-pitched bark that gets predators running.

Red Panda is not a relative of Panda. It was simply given the name because, like Panda, it eats bamboo. The Nepalese call it *Nigalya Ponya* ("bamboo eater"). A rare animal of great beauty, Red Panda is an expert escape artist. It travels at night to elude predators. The inaccessibility of its habitat is a lesson in the purity of spirit. What would our lives be like without our layers of cultural conditioning? As a Power Animal, Red Panda is an example of how to walk the world without being unduly influenced by others.

Red Panda reveres the dignity of the individual and values equality. It sees everything through a single lens: the value of a simple life. It urges us to construct our destiny on a foundation of self-love and experience happiness in solitude. A modern lifestyle is stressful because it creates chaos in our minds. As it would be a fallacy to think we can control the outer world and its distortions, Red Panda encourages us to make our homes into sanctuaries where we can avoid external distractions. We can learn from Red Panda how to maintain our purity of spirit through periodically retreating from the madding crowd to check in with ourselves. The truth most worth finding is that which lies within.

POWERS OF RED PANDA

Call in Red Panda for:

- Connecting with the purity of your essential self.
- Help to shut out noise and distraction from the outside world.
- Getting away from the demands of your culture.

AWARENESS FROM RED PANDA

If Red Panda comes into your life:

- You may be getting lost in the complexity of your mind.
- Now is the time for solitude and to do inner work.
- You need to rely on your intuition more.

Energy Center: Crown

Mineral: Peach moonstone

Element: Fire

Magic & Mystery:

- When French zoologist Frederic Cuvier discovered Red Panda in 1825, he described it as the "most handsome mammal in existence."
- India's former Prime Minister Indira Gandhi received a gift of a pair of Red Panda, which she kept in a special tree house.
- Red Panda is the state animal of Sikkim, India and the mascot for the annual Darjeeling Tea Festival that takes place there.

SHAMAN'S INTENTION: *TAKE ME TO A PLACE IN THE OTHER WORLDS WHERE THERE IS NO DISTRACTION SO I MAY HEAR ONLY THE SOUNDS OF THE NATURAL WORLD*

RHINOCEROS

RESILIENCE | **BALANCE** | **STRENGTH**

"There is really nothing to fear when your heart is big, and your body is strong."—Rhinoceros

POWERS OF RHINOCEROS

Call in Rhinoceros for:

- The ultimate protection from anything negative.
- Help to balance your emotions.
- Developing independence.

AWARENESS FROM RHINOCEROS

If Rhinoceros comes into your life:

- You may be too territorial.
- Consider becoming a vegetarian; or if you already are one, reevaluate the nutritional content of your diet.
- Stop taking things so personally, it is not advisable to be thin skinned.

Energy Center: Solar plexus

Mineral: Champagne aura quartz

Element: Earth

Magic & Mystery: Kenya was the home to the last remaining male White Rhinoceros who was guarded twenty-four hours a day by eleven Maasai warriors. He died of old age on May 3, 2017.

Rhinoceros has walked the Earth for millions of years. It currently lives in the grasslands and flood plains of southern Africa, northern India, Nepal, Malaysia, and Indonesia. Its strength and size are probably the reason it has existed for so long. Weighing in at as much as 8,000 pounds, it is one of the largest mammals on Earth. Rhinoceros leaves nothing in its path, crushing the brush and vegetation wherever it goes. It prefers a tranquil environment and is displeased when disturbed—and may become aggressive. If prompted to attack, Rhinoceros will lower its head and run up to thirty miles an hour ready to gouge its attacker with the horn on its face. Then it uses its agility to turn around and fight some more. It has excellent senses of hearing and smell and lousy eyesight. Rhino has a symbiotic relationship with Oxpecker, a bird that eats ticks from its hide and squawks loudly if danger is approaching.

Rhinoceros is built like a tank. Its thick hide cannot be pierced easily by a spear and it is tenacious. The horn it uses to attack is made of compacted hair. Native Malaysians admire Rhino's thick skin. In their stories it plays the role of a helper coming to put out fires in their villages by stomping on the flames to keep burning underbrush under control. African tribes also revere Rhino. They see it as a totem of stability, as for hundreds of years it was a food source that kept them alive. African shamans also feature Rhino horns in their ceremonies for rain.

As a Power Animal, Rhino is a protective spirit that can fend off the negative energy of backstabbers, betrayers, and malicious people. Rhino teaches us important qualities of leadership. Although we may seem large and powerful, our true power lies in balancing our size or status with equanimity and gentleness. These types of leaders have well defined boundaries and do not allow others to enter their space without permission. Rhinoceros will help us to find the word no in our vocabulary, probably the most helpful term we can use to establish healthy boundaries and safe zones for our mental and physical wellness. Rhinoceros, however, does not take no for an answer, encouraging us to push forward and stomp through obstacles that could impede our progress. We can call upon it for assistance to overcome inconsistency and reduce the complexity that might otherwise stifle our creativity and interfere with our earthly accomplishments. Rhino encourages us to develop stamina for the times ahead. Wise use of power and the skill to avoid needing to use force are two of its powers.

Rhino's greatest power is its horn. Never losing sight of the direction it is headed, Rhino can help you focus on what is in front of you. It walks with the sign of thunder and is an omen that lightning may be coming. Trust Rhinoceros to guide your path. It can dissolve your doubts about things that you cannot see. You do not need to engage with words meant to destroy you. They can be easily deflected by adopting the thick skin of Rhinoceros. With its guidance and support, you can easily crush what is meant to delay you and go forward without doubt.

SHAMAN'S INTENTION: *BRING ME KNOWLEDGE OF BALANCE, SO THAT I KNOW WHEN TO USE MY POWERS*

ROADRUNNER

ENDURANCE | **ADAPTABILITY** | **PASSION**

"A sunset in the desert is a display of nature's passion."
—Roadrunner

Roadrunner is a bird that lives in the dry, hot environs of the deserts and grasslands of Texas, New Mexico, and Arizona in the United States and northern Mexico. It survives with little water, relying on the high-water content in the meat of the animals it hunts. Courageous, it will take on Rattlesnake with confidence because of its quickness. Roadrunner is generally solitary although it sometimes travels in pairs. A group of its kind is known as a *marathon* or *race*. Roadrunner has brown and white-streaked plumage on its crested head. It is a big bird, almost two feet long from beak to tail, with a similar wingspan. It prefers running over flying and can exceed a pace of fifteen miles per hour on foot. Its long tail helps it with its balance. Its footprints look like an X in the dirt, making it easy to locate in the desert. At night, Roadrunner's body functions slow to conserve energy, a brief hibernation. In the morning, it turns its back toward the rising Sun and absorbs the energy to reactivate its systems.

Indigenous tribes honor Roadrunner for its speed and endurance. Traditionally, its feathers are used to ward off negative entities. Its tracks in the desert can be used to guide you back to the right path if you are lost and to confuse evil spirits that might be following you. Roadrunner tracks may be carved into rock art for protection and their feathers used to adorn a baby cradle. According to the Pueblo Indians, if someone has died and Roadrunner tracks are nearby evil spirits won't know which way the soul has gone, providing it a safe passage to the afterlife. Many Native Americans also see Roadrunner as a sign of good fortune coming their way. For the Apache people, Roadrunner is the leader of all birds.

Roadrunner brings us a message from the desert, the space of wanderers and the spirits of the ancient people who formerly walked our lands. Roadrunner walks in the region of powerful plant medicine, a natural pharmacy. Its desert habitat is a place to go to carve out your passion, just like torrential rains and erosive winds formed canyons and mesas.

Roadrunner tells us not to run from the fire inside. Fire fuels the passion that will guide you out of your comfort zone and which is waiting to emerge and dazzle you. As a Power Animal, Roadrunner will support you to take a chance on going in a different direction and replacing the old with the new. We can get caught up in swirling dust devils, whirlwinds that keep us ordinary and make it hard to step into the lives that our hearts desire. Yet, when we arrive at a crossroads, we can put our foot on the path of the unknown and trust its potential. Magical forces are waiting to aid us. Roadrunner is a symbol that we can accept change with a moment's notice and not crash into rock piles of doubt.

Roadrunner encourages us to embrace our curiosity and be patient. The answers we seek are often right in front of us. Its footprint signifies a meeting with destiny: X marks the spot to find our highest potential. Roadrunner is one of the few bird spirits to reside in the Lower World. It is a master of transformational energy, like Snake. It is an ideal Power Animal for those interested in the freedom of discovery and enlightenment.

POWERS OF ROADRUNNER

Call in Roadrunner for:

- Help to decide which way to go when you are at a crossroads.
- Honing and rousing your survival instincts.
- Finding your passion.

AWARENESS FROM ROADRUNNER

If Roadrunner comes into your life:

- You may be feeling deprived in your current environment.
- It may be time to make a quick decision rather than dragging it out.
- Embrace change and transformation, as it will bring you joy.

Energy Center: Heart

Mineral: Rhodochrosite

Element: Fire

Magic & Mystery:

- Roadrunner was given its name by pioneers that would see it run alongside their covered wagons on dirt roads.
- The Latin name of Roadrunner, *Geococcyx californianus*, means "California Earth Cuckoo."

Shaman's Intention: *Introduce me to the gatekeepers of the Lower World*

ROBIN

NEW BEGINNINGS | REFLECTION | SACRED SPACE

"Carve out your space in the garden of life and see the dawn of the newly born and their excitement for living."—Robin

POWERS OF ROBIN

Call in Robin for:

- Guidance when designing a sacred space.
- Initiating a new phase of life or doing a makeover.
- A sense of freedom and a new perspective.

AWARENESS FROM ROBIN

If Robin comes into your life:

- Reevaluate your parenting skills.
- Embrace music and the power of sound.
- It is time for you to explore your psychic gifts.

Energy Center: Throat

Mineral: Blue tanzanite

Element: Air

Magic & Mystery:

- When you see the first Robin of spring, make a wish.
- British postmen used to wear red uniforms and were called Robin redbreasts.

Robin is a member of the songbird family that lives in woodlands and meadows. It is found in North America, especially central Mexico, and parts of Europe. Easy to spot because of its terra cotta-red breast feathers, the rest of Robin's plumage is gray and white. It has a white lower belly and a white tip on its tail. It has a bright yellow bill and sturdy legs that it hops or runs around on as it feeds on insects, fruit, and Earthworm. In spring, Robin lays its beautiful light blue eggs and sings lovely tunes from sunrise to sunset. Not wanting to miss the bright blooms of flowers and evolution of nature's beauty in spring, it is often the first bird to return from the South after a cold winter. Robin is territorial. It will react aggressively if it sees its reflection in a window, thinking that it is another bird checking out its space.

The Plains Indians associate Robin with the arrival of the Sun and sunrise. The ancient Iroquois and Shoshone saw the white ring around Robin's eye as an indication that it had the power of prophecy and was a bringer of wisdom. Robin was traditionally called on to support decision making during ceremonies. Other tribes say Robin gave fire to humanity. To see Robin when you are pregnant was considered a positive omen. The Blackfoot welcomed the presence of Robin, believing it meant that their camps would be safe from attack.

Old wives' tales from Great Britain say Robin should never to be harmed and that taking eggs from its nest will lead to something being taken from you: If someone killed Robin, then their hand would never stop shaking or their barn would catch on fire, for example. Whenever tragedy befalls Robin, they said, a human being would face the same consequences.

Robin is a busy bird that exemplifies a strong work ethic and responsibility. It symbolizes gardens, places of cultivation and nurturing. Robin shows us how to tend to our needs, like it incubates its eggs amid the beauty of nature. It reminds us to take time for contemplation and to immerse ourselves in the mandala of nature, so we may appreciate the vividness of its colors. It encourages us to find a sacred space where we can reflect on and design wholeness. Robin shares a message of hope that we have the potential to move beyond the darkness of winter. If we are facing grief, loss, disappointment, or betrayal, we can trust that a time of light-heartedness is awaiting us. Call on Robin to develop your capacity for celebrating the goodness in your past and remembering it in brighter tones. Robin is a very nurturing parent that reminds us of our own responsibility in nurturing children, not only with food but also with affection. We are the nutritional gatherers of ingredients to feed children's souls and form their character. Call in Robin to support you with the divine guidance and protection for the innocence and purity of a child.

SHAMAN'S INTENTION: *PLEASE EXPAND THE RANGE OF MY VOICE SO THAT THOSE WHO ARE READY TO LISTEN MAY HEAR THE WISDOM I AM MEANT TO SHARE*

SALAMANDER

REJUVENATION | **FLUIDITY** | **ADAPTATION**

"If you show up with color and brilliance, you will never be stepped on."—Salamander

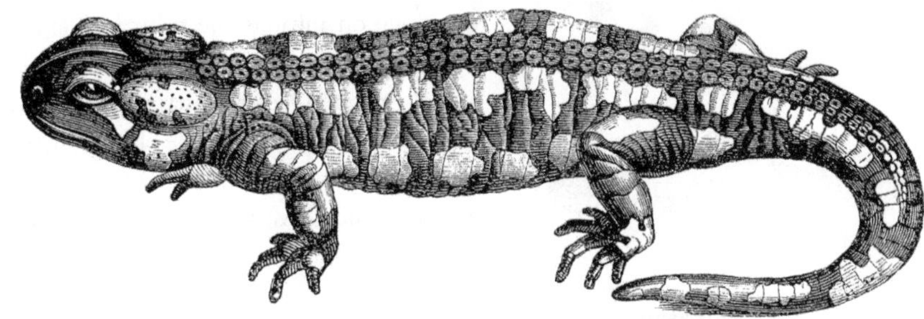

Salamander is an amphibian, a close relative of Frog and Toad. Believed to have been on the planet for 150 million years, it is found living on the edges of waterways everywhere. There are at least 400 known species of Salamander that come in a multitude of colors and patterns. One of its top defensive features is its ability to lose its tail or a limb and regenerate a new one in less than two weeks. The much-revered Axolotl Salamander is also able to regenerate internal organs, including its spine and brain. Salamander also regenerates other tissues to adapt to its environment. Another way it protects itself from predators is that Salamander is able to secrete a highly poisonous substance.

In studying Salamander, we can gain insights on the health of our planet. It is vulnerable. Salamander is like a fish with legs. It returns to the water to bear its young. The offspring are born with gills that they eventually lose when they begin to walk on land. Unlike a fish, Salamander does not have scales. Its skin is very sensitive to toxins that can penetrate it and enter its organs.

Salamander is associated with fire. Named Fire Lizard by the ancient Greeks, Salamander is seen as able to withstand fire since it lives near ponds and streams; it usually is a survivor of forest fires. It also thrives in the aftermath of fires—perhaps because of fire's cleansing nature which sanitizes the environment and reduces levels of toxins. By legend, Salamander is seen as a hero, able to withstand the fury and come out unblemished. In Asia, Salamander is traditionally thought to control the weather and to be related to Dragon.

Salamander is in a constant state of change and transition. Perpetually adapting, it seeks balance and wholeness. As a Power Animal, Salamander teaches us that we have the power to renew ourselves and inspires us to believe in the miracle of rejuvenation. Call upon it for assistance to reprogram your mind and body to heal quickly. You, like all life on this planet, have this potential. Nature's elixir is to synchronize with us if we feel we can change our state of being. Salamander is a master of healing energy and the light that comes through it can upgrade your consciousness.

Indigenous people understand the life-giving essence of water and its place at the heart of creation. Water represents the fluidity of the soul. It is a symbol of purification and protection in many cultural practices, such as the rituals of sprinkling someone with holy water and swimming in the sacred Ganges River. Native Americans see beings that come from water as great teachers and hold them in high regard. For the Blackfoot Indians, divine underwater beings known as the Soyiitapi instructed them to protect their home, which was the waters and the world of the Salamander.

Amphibians are dual beings. Salamander reminds us both to bathe in the sunshine and to absorb the coolness of the rain, so we can achieve the bliss of balance. Salamander questions our ability to relax and offers this key: Relaxation is unattainable without surrendering to prevailing conditions.

POWERS OF SALAMANDER

Call in Salamander for:

- The power to heal yourself.
- Cleansing yourself of all that is not serving your highest good.
- Instruction on the sanctity of water.

AWARENESS FROM SALAMANDER

If Salamander comes into your life:

- You probably need to undergo a comprehensive detox.
- You may need a dose of awareness about the vulnerability of our planet.
- You might be carrying around poisonous thoughts that are destroying you and others.

Energy Center: Third eye

Mineral: Charoite

Element: Water

Magic & Mystery:

- Some types of Salamander have tongues ten times larger than their bodies.
- The Chinese Giant Salamander is the largest and can reach lengths of almost six feet.

SHAMAN'S INTENTION: *TAKE ME TO THE WATER'S EDGE AND TEACH ME THE SACRED ART OF PURIFICATION*

SALMON

RENEWAL | **DIRECTION** | **IMAGINATION**

"Stay in the flow, as it is the only way to know where you are going."—Salmon

Salmon inhabits the tributaries and rivers leading to both the Pacific and the Atlantic Oceans. It has also been introduced to lakes. Salmon may be blue, silver, or red with black spots and red stripes, and it changes its colors when it is on its way to its spawning grounds in mating season. It has a strong tail that helps it to jump almost twelve feet in the air and scale waterfalls. In the course of this journey, Salman may travel over a thousand miles. It has an incredible sense of smell and relies on the Moon and the currents in the ocean to go back to the place of its origin. After arriving at her birthplace, the female Salmon creates several nests by moving her tail from side to side. She then lays 5,000 eggs in each nest, which the male Salmon covers with his sperm. Spawning is so taxing to the female that she dies. Newborn Salmon has a built-in system for detecting magnetic energy that helps it make its way to the ocean.

Salmon has long been respected as a sacred creature, an animal that carries much esoteric wisdom, especially insights about the future. Celtic seers honored Salmon for its gifts of prophecy. The Celts believed that eating Salmon could give them foreknowledge. In Japanese mythology, Salmon is called *shibe,* meaning, the "great thing," or *kamui chep,* meaning "divine fish." Salmon is said to come from a place of paradise.

Tribes in the Pacific Northwest revere Salmon for the sacrifice it makes to become their food. The shaman's duty is to ensure harmony between Salmon and the tribe. Traditionally, the first-caught Salmon in spawning season is placed on an altar with its head pointing upstream in the hope that it will guide the rest of the fish back to the breeding ground. To this day, special dances are done at the beginning of the Salmon run to ensure a successful mating season.

Salmon's long journey home to spawn symbolizes its determination and is emblematic of the cycle of life in which renewal emerges from death. Some tribes put Salmon's skeleton back into the water after eating its flesh, believing that its spirit can rise again. Salmon is a reminder of the infinite nature of energy. In Native American astrology, the star sign of Salmon denotes reproduction. The Kwakiutl believe only twins should perform the dance of Salmon because twins are the product of a blessing from Salmon.

Salmon teaches us that life is a mystery, a river flowing from a source unseen. The cycle of life is a foundational aspect of our world, with rhythms and routines emanating from the Universe. The planets orbit the Sun, the ocean tides change, we, and our society have upturns and downturns, all doing a cyclical dance. A successful journey through life is only limited by our unwillingness to embrace the cycles or to recognize that we are part of a celestial clock. Salmon also reminds us of reincarnation, a driving force behind the natural plan of evolution. Nothing really ends. Everything turns and spirals and is transformed. The journey of Salmon is proof of the greater symphony of movement that drives our existence. We are programmed with death as an outcome and yet are given the capacity for survival if we believe in eternity.

Salmon would have us recognize that the lakes and streams are the mirrors of Mother Earth. Look into the water and you will see the reflection of who you are without limitation. Is there a corrupted image keeping you from seeing your greatness? In the reflection, look for all that is obtainable given your potential and abilities. When you have arrived at your spiritual destination, it is time to plant seeds so that others may flourish. Remind them of the power of the mirror and that, when cleansed and inspired, you will always reflect the beauty inside.

POWERS OF SALMON

Call in Salmon for:

- Help to comprehend the mystery of death.
- Confidence to help you know where you are going.
- The ability to navigate difficult obstacles.

AWARENESS OF SALMON

If Salmon comes into your life:

- It may be time for rebirthing yourself or to begin a new phase in life.
- Schedule a visit to your old hometown.
- Open your imagination to unfamiliar possibilities.

Energy Center: Third eye

Mineral: Malachite

Element: Water

Magic & Mystery:

- A sculpture of Salmon was found in a prehistoric cave in France, revealing a reverence for Salmon dating back 25,000 years.
- The Latin word for Salmon, *salire,* means "to leap."

SHAMAN'S INTENTION: *SHOW ME THE PLACE THAT I WILL CALL HOME*

SANDPIPER

FELLOWSHIP | FOCUS | FLEXIBILITY

"The ocean is the great giver of life, laying itself at the doorstep of Mother Earth."—Sandpiper

Sandpiper is a bird that lives and breeds near rivers and streams, and along seacoasts all over the world. It often migrates for thousands of miles to reach a warmer climate. Its plumage is several shades of gray and brown and it has a white belly and a sharp, pointed bill. It breeds in open areas near water, and then protects its chicks in dense vegetation. Sandpiper has a lovely courtship display. The male will sing in flight, conduct aerial displays and rapidly beat its wings. When the female arrives in its territory, it chases its competitors for her affections. During mating season, the female lays eggs and the male incubates them until they are born.

Sandpiper stays focused on hunting and scavenging for what it desires. It is very fast and industrious in its efforts. It lives in large groups whose members support each other in the effort of searching for food. Sandpiper runs along the waterline and then digs with its long bill into the sand, looking for food. It will also fly close to the ground, on the lookout for insects, crustaceans, Worm, Frog, and seeds. While eating or walking, Sandpiper bobs its head and tail up and down. It is a great runner and spends hours darting in and out of waves, almost obsessed with being the first to find what the ocean will bring its flock. This characteristic makes it better at walking than flying.

Living on the edge of the ocean where the waves break into the land and the tides recede and return over and over is to live at an undefinable boundary in a marginal place between two forces. The shoreline is never the same from moment to moment. Sometimes the land wins, sometimes the water. As a Power Animal, Sandpiper can help us avoid wrong steps that can spell danger when we are taking a risk. It is an ally to call upon when difficult decisions are being made or barriers encountered. For some, transitional moments seem fearsome; for others they are seen as opportunities to experience the exuberance of life—Sandpiper can help you embrace the second view. Sandpiper can stop your mind from teetering between competing options. Something will always be coming at you; will you respond with force or flow? Do you retreat or lean in? There is an inevitable dance of decision making that occurs in the moment when you are contemplating what is the best action or reaction.

Sandpiper urges us always to follow our internal guidance. You do not need to seek validation from the crowd that your actions are right. Relying on others can create confusion. Going it alone often brings clarity and the chance to ride the waves of freedom.

POWERS OF SANDPIPER

Call in Sandpiper for:

- Calm when there is turbulence around you.
- Assistance in adapting to changes.
- Support to manage a tsunami of emotions.

AWARENESS FROM SANDPIPER

If Sandpiper comes into your life:

- It may be time to stop living on the edge, so make a decision.
- Look deeper into a situation to find treasures that should be coming to you.
- Seek a place of calm and balance, as you may be too frantic.

Energy Center: Root

Mineral: Blue turquoise

Element: Water

Magic & Mystery: The Buff-Breasted Sandpiper is a compassionate bird that will change course if one in its flock is injured.

SHAMAN'S INTENTION: *HELP ME TO GO WITH THE FLOW AND TRUST A HIGHER POWER FOR THE DECISIONS I NEED TO MAKE*

SCORPION

DETERMINATION | NUTURING | PREVENTION

"Power lies in the ability to be competent in acting on and being truthful with your threats."—Scorpion

POWERS OF SCORPION

Call in Scorpion for:

- Protection from individuals who seem harsh and unyielding.
- Discernment as to when to strike against your opponents.
- Being seen as powerful, yet compassionate.

AWARENESS FROM SCORPION

If Scorpion comes into your life:

- You likely need protection from toxic people or your own toxic thoughts.
- Address your fears so they do not attract negative experiences.
- You may be in the dark about something that could sting you.

Energy Center: Solar plexus

Mineral: Ruby

Element: Earth

Magic & Mystery: Scorpion venom can treat certain forms of heart disease and cancer.

One hundred million years ago, a three-foot long Scorpion lived in the ocean. When it moved to the land, it shrunk to the size of the present-day Scorpion. Scorpion lives on every continent except Antartica, most commonly in locales that are dry and hot. Scorpion spends most of its life underground, emerging at night to forage insects for food. It glows in the dark and prefers to navigate by the full Moon. After it is born it rides around on its mother's back until it is ready to go out in the world, never returning to the family environment. It is venomous and the tip of its tail is like a sharp needle. The amount of venom it secretes will depend on how threatened it feels it is.

The ancient Egyptians worshiped the Scorpion-headed goddess Serket, who was caring and compassionate to her devotees when they were obedient but had a darker aspect with which she would dismiss those with whom she was not in agreement. She had the power to protect her followers from the poisonous bites of Scorpion and Snake. Serket was also revered as the protector of kings.

Goddess figures from diverse world cultures are associated with Scorpion. Isis, Egyptian goddess of transformation, had seven Scorpion as her bodyguards. The ancient Aztecs worshipped Malinalxochitl, a sorceress with power over Snake and Scorpion and other insects. Another powerful Scorpion goddess was Ishara from Mesopotamia. She was admired for fairness in judging others. Many temples were built in her honor. Hindus still worship Chelamma, and anyone who prays in her shrine is said to be protected from Scorpion bites.

In Tibetan culture, Scorpion has a negative connotation. However, as a Power Animal, Scorpion signifies the conversion of even the direst circumstances into something beneficial. The seal of Scorpion is used by many Buddhist masters as a sign of transformation.

Scorpion carries antivenom in its body. It teaches us to do the same. If you would attack, you must also be willing to console. Everything should be done with balance. People can become toxically angry when consumed by the urgency of meeting their survival needs. Encountering someone in this state is an invitation to listen from the heart with the antivenom of compassion.

SHAMAN'S INTENTION: *TEACH ME TO STAND IN MY POWER AND KNOW THAT I AM PROTECTED*

SEAGULL

INQUIRY **OPPORTUNITY** **FREEDOM**

"Being willing to indulge in what you desire can bring great fulfillment; the lesson lies in the realization that satisfaction can be elusive."
—Seagull

Seagull has been on the planet for thirty million years. Wherever there is water, there is Seagull. It is one of the most widespread birds on the planet. Seagull will eat almost anything. It is a constant scavenger and opportunist and will steal anything it needs from others. Its nests are made from whatever it finds, and it will take over territory from weaker species. Seagull mates for life and is protective of its chicks, becoming aggressive and squawking if it feels they are threatened. If a couple splits up because of the inability to breed healthy chicks, it can face stigma from others. Seagull is intelligent and curious. It has a complex way of communicating that may look chaotic, noisy, greedy, and aggressive, but which is nonetheless effective. There are forty-four unique species of Seagull that have diverse traits. For example, Swallow-Tailed Seagull from the Galapagos Islands is nocturnal. It hunts squid by moonlight.

According to the myths of Pacific Northwest tribes, Seagull has power over the weather and can control storms. The Haida tell stories in which Seagull is a wise guardian and helpful advisor for people so distraught they want to take their own lives. In one tribal myth, Seagull brings light to the world in a cedarwood box that Raven ultimately must open because Seagull is too stubborn to share and too self-absorbed to think of the needs of others. The Tsimshian tells similar stories of Seagull's opportunism.

The Celtic god Manannán is a Seagull god that comes from the sea. He is known for his work as a psychopomp—in particular for helping souls to find gateways to the Lower World under the sea or on the horizon. To this day, the Manx people from the Isle of Man still honor Manannán with offerings placed in the ocean, hoping for a good fishing season and calm seas.

As a Power Animal, Seagull, like many other birds, is a symbol of freedom and a resourceful lifestyle. It teaches us to be skillful in navigating the actions of others and coming up with ingenuous ways to accomplish what we set out to do. Seagull says there is a barrier to knowing it intimately, since humans have never flown. Nonetheless it can help you to master the winds of change. To do so requires you to accept that nothing stays the same. Seagull is an ally to those who work with energy of the new, like inventors and engineers, and to visionaries. Anyone who must surf the waves of potential as they come crashing in can benefit from its guidance. Change is a gift that eliminates stagnation because it cuts through mediocrity. It compels us to make a decision and instigates looking at the future. The thought of flying to a distant shore can seem like a trip laden with anxiety; yet, if we embrace adventure as we contemplate our next moves, Seagull can help us to dissipate the fog in our minds so that our course becomes clearer.

POWERS OF SEAGULL

Call in Seagull for:

- A multifaceted approach to survival.
- Help to learn a new skill.
- Enhancing your skills of persuasion.

AWARENESS FROM SEAGULL

If Seagull comes into your life:

- Your survival skills are too prevalent—they may be making you act pushy or feel worried.
- Stay in your own lane; remember that everyone's journey is personal.
- You may need to be more aggressive in order to get what you want.

Energy Center: Solar plexus

Mineral: Yellow calcite

Element: Air

Magic & Mystery: The Eskimo of the Bering Sea would wear hats with Seagull feathers and beaks to give them avian powers.

SHAMAN'S INTENTION: *MAKE ME CURIOUS AND SHOW ME HOW I CAN USE THIS TRAIT AS A TOOL FOR LEARNING*

SEAHORSE

CALM | **PASSION** | **SURVIVAL**

"Through the spiral comes the potential to express the wisdom and love of Source."—Seahorse

Seahorse is an unusual type of fish found living among coral reefs, mangrove roots, and seagrass beds in temperate climates around the world. A poor swimmer, to avoid being swept away by sea currents it wraps its tail around vegetation that it blends in with by changing color. It prefers calmer waters, as stormy seas cause it to expend too much energy, which exhausts it, causing it to die. It does not travel much, staying close to its birthplace throughout its lifespan. It has excellent eyesight, which includes the ability to simultaneously see forward and backward. It has a backbone but no ribs, and no teeth or stomach, which means it must eat all day long to sustain itself. Seahorse relies on suction to eat and it is usually fat and happy. Seahorse mates for life and will often swim with its tail intertwined with its partner's. It is the only animal on Earth whose male is the child bearer. Curiously, the female releases her eggs into an abdominal pouch in the male where he fertilizes and incubates them until they hatch. As many as 2,000 Seahorse offspring may hatch from one couple with only a few surviving. Every living Seahorse is a true survivor, having beaten remarkable odds.

Sailors have revered Seahorse for centuries for its characteristic calm and its ability to adapt. The ancient Greeks associated it with Poseidon, god of the sea, who was often depicted as traveling in a chariot pulled by a powerful Seahorse. If a sailor found a Seahorse in his nets, it was believed to belong to Poseidon and would be released. The seafaring Phoenicians and Etruscans of the same era painted images of Seahorse on the walls of their burial chambers to provide souls with transportation in the afterlife. European sailors of old viewed Seahorse as a guide for those lost at sea and said it would take the souls of deceased sailors to the Lower World.

The Chinese see Seahorse as a symbol of good luck. In Malaysia and the Philippines, dried Seahorse carcasses are hung in homes as talismans to guard inhabitants from evil spirits. In Indonesia, they believe this fetish can protect your bank account and ensure future prosperity.

The tail of the Seahorse embodies the Fibonacci spiral, like a whirlpool of energy from the Universe that invokes a course of growth and transformation. Compare a blown-up image of human DNA, which looks like a twisted ladder, to the body of Seahorse and you'll be amazed at the similarity. Seahorse brings us the message of living in the rhythm of grace, pursuing a path of no conflict and balanced movement. It helps us to see our own process through the eyes of nature and as a mythical journey of regeneration and awakening as we move around the spiral to follow the path of the shaman and the spirit world. Like Conch's shell, the voice of the sea inherent to the spiral is the voice of the I AM, the tone that creates all motion and emotion in our being.

Seahorse shows us that although it may seem impossible to move forward, the spirit of propulsion exists in everyone to some degree. Tapping into this energy, we will always find new motivation for moving forward. When it seems that our wings have been clipped and our freedom compromised, we must search for something that motivates us. Do not cling to the familiar or the stagnant, as clinging leads to mediocrity and keeps us from harnessing our potential to thrive. Move beyond the confines of the familiar, knowing that there is much to experience on the other side of fear.

POWERS OF SEAHORSE

Call in Seahorse for:

- Helping men to understand childbirth.
- Moving through life with a sense of grace and ease.
- Collective cooperation with others.

AWARENESS FROM SEAHORSE

If Seahorse comes into your life:

- You may be holding on too tight to something; release it and set yourself free.
- It's likely time for a vacation, you have been too tied to your home lately.
- You may wish to use color therapy to help you feel more relaxed.

Energy Center: Heart

Mineral: Sodalite

Element: Water

Magic & Mystery:

- The Dwarf Seahorse is the slowest fish in the world, moving at a rate of five feet per hour.
- Seahorse sings when it is mating, mates under the full Moon, and gives its partner a hug every morning during pregnancy.

SHAMAN'S INTENTION: *TAKE ME TO THE SPIRAL WHERE I CAN BE IN THE ENERGY OF THE "I AM"*

SEAL

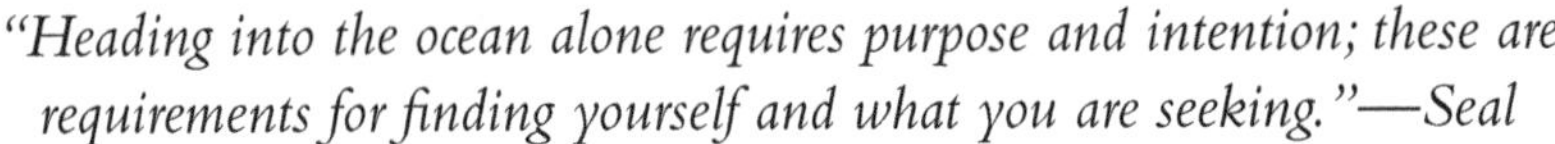

"Heading into the ocean alone requires purpose and intention; these are requirements for finding yourself and what you are seeking."—Seal

Seal is a semiaquatic mammal related to Bear. The largest Seal can weigh up to 8,000 pounds. Seal's smooth fur is perfectly designed for gliding through the water and its thick layers of fat keep it warm. It is adept at diving and able to sustain itself underwater for up to two hours because of the massive amount of blood volume it has, which gives it an abundance of oxygen.

Seal's whiskers are vibration detectors, useful to sense the movement of its prey. Its diet is primarily fish, shellfish, and Octopus. Seal lives in large colonies of thousands of its kind. Breeding beaches are hotly contested territory for the males and there can be many clashes. Every Bull hopes to amass a harem of Cows that it can mate with. Seal has extreme mood swings. It is quick to anger and yet has the potential to lay back and stay mellow. Seal spends most of its time in or on the shore of the ocean.

In the folklore of Scotland, it was believed that a race of Seal people lived in the ocean who were hostile to those on the land. These Selkies were water-dwelling fairies that could shapeshift into either a human or a Seal. It was thought that anyone walking too close to the ocean could be pulled in by a Selkie. The ancient Scots also believed that a Selkie, when it had transformed into a Seal, could speak an ancient Gaelic tongue that was too old to understand. These Celts believed animals had power to change into humans so that many clans were a union of human and animal.

Natives of the Pacific Northwest see Seal as a symbol of wealth. These coastal peoples recognize Seal's skill at riding the waves and mastering the oceans. After hunting it for thousands of years, the Inuit has a special relationship with Seal. After killing Seal, melted snow is dripped into its mouth in order to quench the thirst of its spirit. Traditionally, the Natives revere Seal for its sacrifices and generosity to them, as they are so dependent on it. Because of its highly insulating properties, Seal pelt was used to make clothing and boots. Its fat made oil for lamps and its meat became food. The bladder was always saved because it was believed that this was where the spirit of Seal resided. Wasting anything of Seal was considered a dishonor.

The most important deity in Inuit culture is Sedna, goddess of the sea and ruler of Whale and Seal. If she was content, they knew that she would provide. According to the mythology of the Native Lapp people of modern-day Finland, the skin of Seal has healing powers. Lapp shamans say Seal symbolizes healing.

The Moche of Peru hunted Seal and admired Seal for its agility to move between life on land and life in the water. They felt it had the soul of a human because of its eyes. Several Moche tombs have been found with bones and teeth of Seal resting on various areas of the body.

As a Power Animal, Seal encourages us to take time for relaxation, nothing we do deserves unlimited effort. Rejuvenation by taking time to congregate with likeminded people can help us to feel fulfilled. But not all have earned the right to share our gifts. Seal asks that we cherish our freedom to be happy. There are many fish in the sea and Seal can help you to wisely discern with whom to share your life. Dive deeply into life and question what is beyond the surface. Question everything so that the answers are born from the depths of your curiosity.

ELEPHANT SEAL, SEA LION, WALRUS

POWERS OF SEAL

Call in Seal for:

- Help in dealing with emotionally charged family issues.
- When it is time to throw your weight around.
- Going deeper into understanding your purpose in life.

AWARENESS FROM SEAL

If Seal comes into your life:

- It may be a sign that there is a lack of fidelity in a relationship.
- Use the sounds of the ocean—and Seal calls—for healing.
- You may wish to learn how to manage your emotions better.

Energy Center: Solar plexus

Mineral: Ocean jasper

Element: Water

Magic & Mystery:

- Back in the day, Celtic shamans would shapeshift into Walrus in order to undertake the journey to the home of the sea goddess Sedna who lives at the bottom of the ocean.
- The Inuit culture sees Seal as a symbol of innocence.

SHAMAN'S INTENTION: *BRING ME THE POWER ALWAYS TO GO DEEPER INTO THE MYSTERY OF MY DIVINITY*

SECRETARY BIRD

DETERMINATION | **LEADERSHIP** | **OBSERVATION**

"Respect is earned by walking with unwavering integrity."—Secretary Bird

Secretary Bird lives in the plains of Sub-Saharan Africa. It gets its name because its head feathers resemble the quills of the old-fashioned pens that secretaries would place behind their ears. Its face is not feathered and so, except for its bright orange and red skin around its eyes, it looks similar to Eagle. As a relative of Hawk and Vulture, it has some characteristics of a raptor, like excellent eyesight. It finds its prey through lovely long eyelashes—then it chases it down on foot and either pecks it or stomps it to death. Secretary Bird is greatly admired in Africa for its large size, appearance, and ability to take on Snake, which it kills by stomping it with its five-times greater body weight. Its legs have special scales on them to protect Secretary Bird from being bitten by the reptiles it hunts.

Secretary Bird is easy to spot because it stands four feet tall. Despite its size, it is capable of flight. It is an excellent runner and called the "devil's horse" by some African tribespeople. It normally has to traverse a "runway" to get enough speed for an airlift if it is going to fly. During mating season, Secretary Bird engages in dramatic aerial performances where male and female swoop around each other in midflight and even clasps talons. It makes a loyal companion. The female lays three eggs every few days in a nest that the mating pair have built together on the top of an acacia tree. This nest can be up to eight feet wide. The female does incubation duties as the eggs hatch in staggered fashion and then both parents bring food for the hatchlings, flying back and forth. Indigenous peoples are very respectful of the nest and eggs of Secretary Bird. The Ndebele of Zimbabwe call it the "lightning bird." They believe you can ask Secretary Bird to make lightning strike near someone you want to intimidate. But such requests are frowned upon. If Secretary Bird is ever found dead, it is reported to the chief of the tribe immediately, so that no one can steal this power and use it in a wicked way. According to the Nguni of South Africa, totem objects made of Secretary Bird feathers can be used to control the rain.

Secretary Bird has a built-in, chieftain-like headdress that gives it its inherent powers. The feathers are embedded with the power of the Sun, making it ready to do battle with agility and strength, stomping out negativity and adversity. This headdress represents courage, honor, strength, and leadership. Its distinct look was inherited from Secretary Bird's dinosaur ancestors. As a Power Animal, Secretary Bird can bring you a sense of vigilance as to your personal space and protect you from that which could destroy you. Secretary Bird can also help you control the flow of kundalini (Snake energy) up your spine that circulates throughout your body. If you are going through a dramatic spiritual awakening it can help to protect you from low-energy beings that are attracted to your presence and whose voices are not of the highest good.

Secretary Bird offers a message about personal power. It is important to realize that the only harm that can come to you is the harm of believing you are weak. Connection to a higher power is like connecting to a beam of light from Source energy that reinforces your ability to live fearlessly. Rise above the ignorant masses. The truth is above them. It can only be "plucked" if you are looking at life from a higher view. Do not let the gravity of negative thoughts weigh you down. From the top of the acacia, you can see a bigger picture: There is always a greater purpose in your struggles.

POWERS OF SECRETARY BIRD

Call in Secretary Bird for:

- Dominating an adversary.
- Problem solving.
- Believing in your higher power and gaining trust and confidence.

AWARENESS FROM SECRETARY BIRD

If Secretary Bird comes into your life:

- Start walking as a way to be healthy and feel nourished by nature.
- You may be cowardly in not taking on issues that need to be dealt with.
- Embrace your personal integrity and seek a role as a leader.

Energy Center: Root

Mineral: Black jasper

Element: Earth

Magic & Mystery:

- The scientific name of Secretary Bird, *Sagittarius serpentarius,* means "archer of snakes."
- Secretary Bird has been referred to as a "hawk on stilts."

SHAMAN'S INTENTION: *BRING ME WISDOM FROM THE ACACIA TREE, AN EARTHLY SYMBOL OF THE TREE OF LIFE*

SHARK

TENACITY | **EVOLUTION** | **AUTHORITY**

"Be open to see an opportunity in the smallest crevasse in the floor of the deepest ocean. Opportunity is everywhere."—Shark

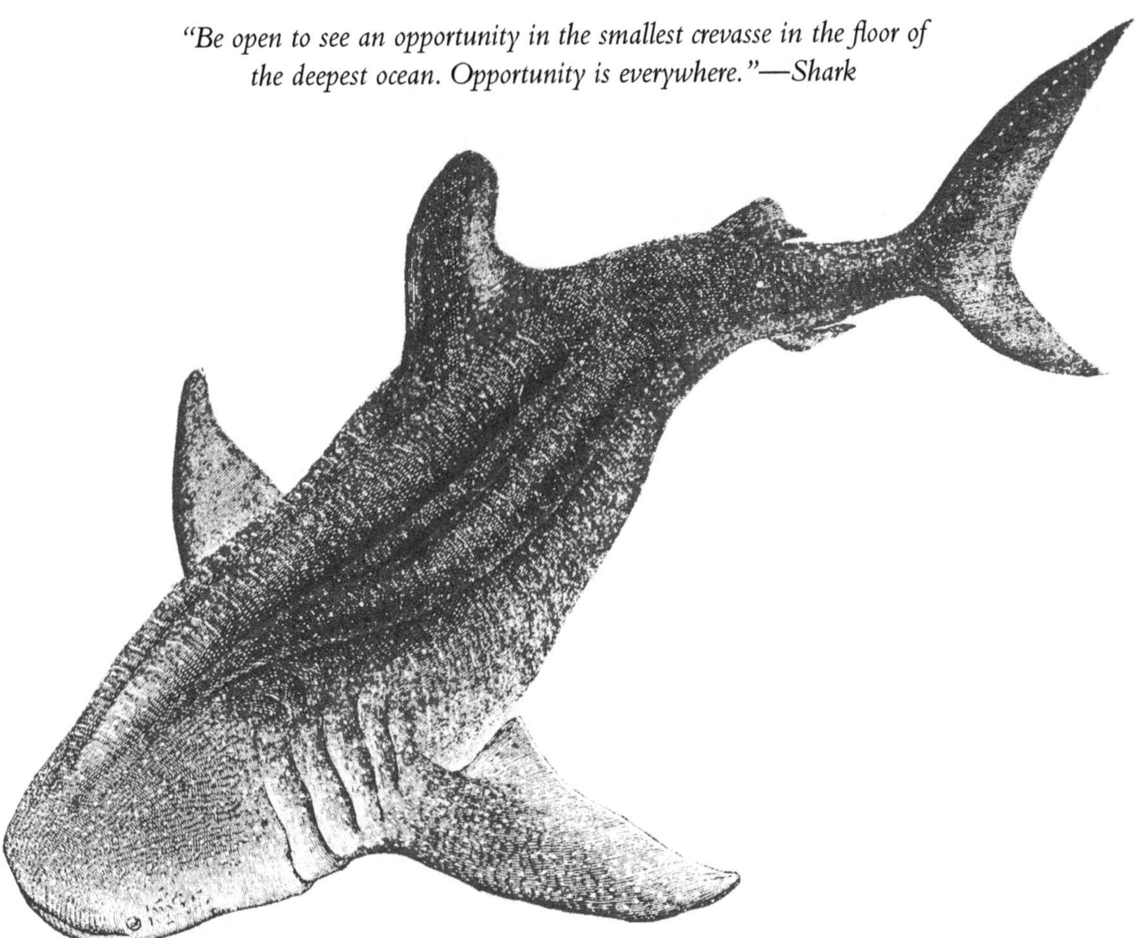

Shark is one of the oldest living creatures on Earth; it has been roaming the oceans for over 400 million years and it is represented by more than 400 distinct species. Its structure is pure cartilage; it has no bones. Shark skin is a collection of scales that act as a hydrodynamic surface allowing Shark to move through water with less drag. Some types of Shark have few teeth, others have up to 3,000 teeth that exert extreme pressure on the flesh of prey. Shark must swim constantly otherwise it will sink. Shark can detect blood from miles away and sense the presence of fish through the Earth's electromagnetic currents.

As a predator, by eliminating weak and sick members of other species, Shark plays an important role in the cycle of life in the ocean. Coral benefits from the balance Shark brings to the ecosystem. Shark preys on the predators of the smaller fish that support Coral.

The indigenous Hawaiians honor several Shark gods. The most respected is Kamohoali'i, brother of Grandmother Pele, who can take on both a human and a fish form. Ka'ahupahau looks like a beautiful woman with red hair. When transformed into Shark, this goddess lives in Pearl Harbor, where she protects people from Shark's aggression. The Ka'u people believe that Shark is their ancestor. When a family member died, it was custom to offer the body to the ocean, so it could become Shark. The shaman, a kahuna, later would know which Shark someone had become by studying Shark's special markings. Family members relied upon this specific Shark, their aumakua, to help them fish and protect them from harm in the water.

The Fijians revered Dakuwaqa, a Shark god that was half man-half Shark. He protects fisherman from anything dangerous from the sea and rules the Sun and Moon. In the Bahamas, legend says that the Shark goddess, Lascu, makes blue holes in the ocean when residents of an island anger her. These blue holes occur

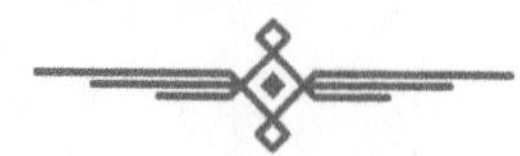

SHARK

TENACITY **EVOLUTION** **AUTHORITY**

As a Power Animal, Shark brings us the power of progression and evolution into a more refined way of being. It is efficient and purposeful and moves through the oceans with precision.

POWERS OF SHARK

Call in Shark for:

- Defeating fear.
- Detecting opportunity.
- Fine-tuning your senses.

AWARENESS FROM SHARK

If Shark comes into your life:

- You need to start moving forward immediately.
- You may have special sensitivities to the magnetic fields of the Earth. Begin to explore them.
- Do not be quick to attack others for having beliefs that you do not share.

Energy Center: Crown

Mineral: Rubellite

Element: Water

Magic & Mystery:

- In antiquity, because of their extreme sharpness, Shark teeth were used to manufacture weapons and cutting tools.
- Shark was thought to be the fish monster of the Olmecs, this was a supernatural creature associated with death.
- In American Samoa, villagers perform a ritual to call the turtle and the shark because of a legend of two humans who shapeshifted into these creatures. They both often appear and surprise the visitors and participants.

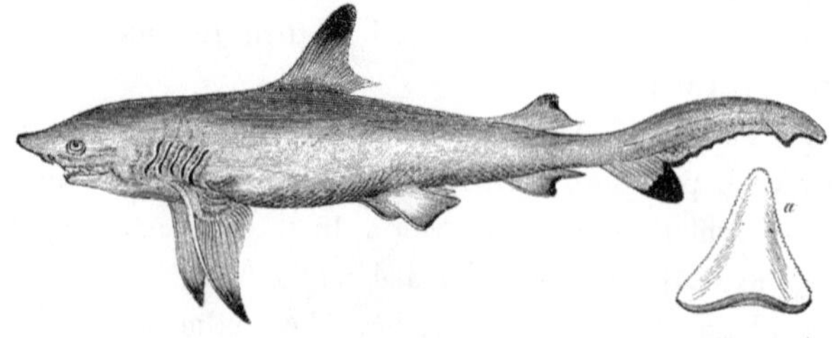

when a geological structure, such as a cavern, originally above ground, loses its integrity and goes underwater.

The English word Shark is derived from the Mayan word Xoc. Mayans saw Shark and Stingray as the most feared creatures from the Lower World. Their Sun god, Kinich Ahaw, was often depicted as having Shark teeth.

Shark naturally loses and regrows its teeth throughout its lifespan. Native peoples wear the teeth they find as talismans of protection to prevent Shark attacks while they are swimming, surfing, and fishing.

Shark is a master of the survival instinct. It swims the oceans with a sense of authority and knowing and is always ready to act or respond. It does not wait around for something to happen. It has great confidence and will seize any opportunity that presents itself. It does not fear anything and sees the world without conflict.

Through Shark's elite form, which was perfectly adapted to its role through the process of evolution, it shows us that through fluidity we can become greater versions of ourselves. As a Power Animal, Shark brings us the power of progression and evolution into a more refined way of being. It is efficient and purposeful and moves through the oceans with precision. It does not know stagnation and sees it as a weakness. Shamans see Shark as a superior being that can bring them astute assessments of life. Shark advises that we should take our highest values with us throughout the journey of our lives, and, even while being fluid in response to the environment, be unwilling to compromise them.

Shark's message is to take a bite out of life. Life is here for the taking. Opportunity is everywhere, so look for it. If we adopt the view that life is easy, we can achieve great accomplishments. If we view it as difficult, we invent obstacles that slow us down, making our goals seem elusive. Shark can help you to remove the barriers to your success and teach you to master the process of manifesting your desires. Sometimes wielding your personal power means that others are fearful, therefore integrity is key.

Shaman's Intention: *Help me to evolve into a higher version of myself*

SHEEP

AGILITY | **HIGHER CONSCIOUSNESS** | **DREAMING**

"We wear the spiral to remind you of the mythical journey of evolution."—Sheep

Wild Sheep is found all over the world. It lives at high elevations—altitudes of as much as 10,000 feet—to avoid predators. For the same reason, Sheep has excellent eyesight and can turn its head and see a range of 360 degrees. Because of its split hooves, which improve its grip, Sheep is agile and surefooted, able to navigate unstable surfaces like the rocky edges of cliffs. Because of all the climbing it does, it stays lean and muscular. Domesticated Sheep has been herded for over 12,000 years, sacrificing its body to us as meat and offering us its wool to keep us warm.

Bighorn Sheep gets its name from the large, curved horns of the Ram. The Ewe has much smaller horns. Shamanically, these horns symbolize the spiral that is the foundation of the functioning of the Universe, like a map to a higher level of consciousness or God. This form is nature's way to express the patterns of energy that exists in the world. Bighorn is known for the dramatic fights that males engage in to prove their dominance during mating season. Ram will throw himself at a rival at a speed of up to twenty miles per hour, ending in a loud clash of horns.

Sheep communicates its emotions with sounds and facial expressions. It is a clever self-healer, instinctively seeking out specific plants for their curative properties. Sheep is an independent animal that is also social and content in a herd. Ewe is a sweet mother who forms a strong bond with her calf, calling to it if the calf strays out of view.

The ancient Sumerians relied heavily on Sheep for their existence and culture. Their most prominent Sheep goddess, Dutter, guarded the flocks. Her son, Damu, spent half the year in the Lower World; his return brought the green fertility of spring. Goddess Gestinanna was also associated with Sheep. She was an oracle who interpreted dreams. In ancient Egypt, Khnum, god of the Nile, had the head of Ram. He created hundreds of gods and

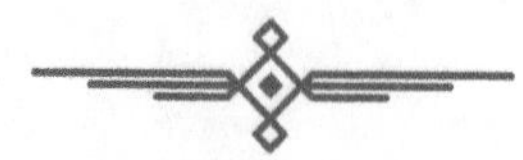

SHEEP

AGILITY | **HIGHER CONSCIOUSNESS** | **DREAMING**

> SHEEP COMMUNICATES ITS EMOTIONS WITH SOUNDS AND FACIAL EXPRESSIONS. IT IS A CLEVER SELF-HEALER, INSTINCTIVELY SEEKING OUT SPECIFIC PLANTS FOR THEIR CURATIVE PROPERTIES.

POWERS OF SHEEP

Call in Sheep for:

- Reconnecting with your children if they seem lost to you.
- Restoring the balance in your life.
- Help to remove negative karma.

AWARENESS FROM SHEEP

If Sheep comes into your life:

- You may need time to clear the air of anger and fear.
- Trust the natural evolution of things.
- It is time to see your vulnerability as strength.

Energy Center: Solar plexus

Mineral: Howlite

Element: Fire

Magic & Mystery:

- Navajo-Churro Sheep were the very first breed of domesticated sheep to enter the United States as a byproduct of the Spanish Conquest of the sixteenth century.
- In Madagascar Sheep is considered a reincarnation of a human soul, so its meat is never consumed.

goddesses and created himself from an egg. Among the ancient Greeks, Aristaeus, one of Apollo's sons, was god of herdsmen and beekeepers. He protected Sheep in the fields from predators and the hazards of bad weather.

In Buddhist stories, Ram was present at the birth of Buddha. Ram is the eighth animal in the Chinese zodiac and a symbol of perseverance and sensitivity. In Tibet, Ram is released by shamans during the festival of Losar, their New Year's Day, to carry away the errors of the previous year. Ram is seen as the keeper of our faults and, as such, can counter evil. There is a ritual in Tibet that involves walking around a monastery with Ram to improve your karma.

Sheep feature in European folklore too with the Celtic god Cernunnos representing fertility, life, animals, wealth, and the Lower World. In Bulgaria, people believe Ram is safe from evil, so it is carved on objects people wear for protection. British shepherds view the birth of a black Sheep as a good luck omen.

The constellation of Aries, the Ram, is in the northern sky roughly March 20–April 20, coinciding with the spring equinox, a period when the power of the Sun and light is equal to the power of darkness and the Moon. Lamb—a young Sheep—is a symbol of innocence and the purity of our being when we are born. It reminds us of simpler times when we were void of social conditioning and mental burdens. We can reclaim the child within us by embracing joy and newness of spring.

Call upon Ram as a Power Animal when you need to bolster your authority and embody leadership and masculine characteristics such as the energy of dominance. Work with Ram through the energy center of your solar plexus (aka the *third chakra*). Also invite Sheep to help you come to terms with your vulnerability. Spirit cares for you by providing you with support through the gifts of animals like Sheep. Sheep is proud to wrap humanity in the warmth of its wool, giving us the sense of being nurtured and secure when conditions are otherwise. Sheep is present in the world's greatest tapestries—Navajo rugs, Celtic quilts, and Bedouin rugs are all products made of wool. Sheep reminds us that our lives are threads in the tapestry of life, no one more or less necessary, each contributing to the pattern of the whole by virtue of expressing our creativity in life. Sheep is an ideal Power Animal for weavers. Let it inspire you to weave messages from the spiritual realms into your handiwork.

SHAMAN'S INTENTION: *JOURNEY WITH ME TO MY BEGINNINGS TO FIND MY INNOCENCE AGAIN*

SKUNK

SENSE | **SOLITUDE** | **SELF-DEFENSE**

"Respecting yourself ensures that you are respected by others."—Skunk

Skunk is a small, furry animal with two white stripes on its back that is found in Indonesia, the Philippines, North America, and Central America. It is famous for spraying an unpleasant smelling liquid from special glands near its anus when it feels threatened, which is its only protective tool for repelling predators. But Skunk is conservative in the amount of spray it uses, since it takes almost a week to "reload" its glands. With qualities similar to onion or garlic, Skunk spray is highly flammable.

Skunk is immune to Snake venom. When a Snake smells Skunk, it will lay low and remain quiet to avoid Skunk pursuing it. Skunk lives in hollowed-out logs or burrows abandoned by other animals. It has a long body with strong legs and uses its front claws for digging. Mainly solitary Skunk forages alone during the night. Its favorite meal is honey and bees. It doesn't mind raiding a beehive where it relies on its thick fur to help it avoid being stung. In addition, it eats insects, rodents, fish, roots, and berries.

The Seneca Indians of North America see Skunk as an animal worthy of honor and respect. Knowing it is a master of self-defense, the Cherokee used Skunk spray to ward off disease and treat coughs and poison ivy. The spray was also used as a moisturizer.

As a Power Animal, Skunk can help you find your way in the world without needing to rely so much on others. It can help you develop your confidence and to repel those who do not have your best interests in mind or are disrespectful. Skunk is protected because of its reputation. It chooses its battles wisely and does not attack unless it is necessary. If you are working to set healthy boundaries in your relationships, Skunk can serve as your role model.

Skunk is a guardian of plant medicine, and an ally for those who use herbs, flower remedies, and essential oils to heal themselves and our planet. Skunk inspires us to breathe in and restore our balance. As Skunk walks among plants, it perceives potentials that we do not. Skunk knows the chemistry that is waiting to be born and encapsulated into a form that makes it available for deep healing. From the elixirs of eucalyptus and lotus, to the musk of frankincense and sandalwood, we live amid an infinite source of vibratory aromas that can penetrate our souls and transform our physical and emotional experience.

Shamanically, scent and the memories it carries to us through the air that we breathe, connect us sensorially with waves of energy from the cosmic field. A random hint of rose or pipe smoke can be a reminder of someone who has transitioned. Scent can be a portal to the past.

POWERS OF SKUNK

Call in Skunk for:

- Setting clear boundaries with others.
- Help to find the essence of who you are.
- Seeing your potential in the darkness.

AWARENESS FROM SKUNK

If Skunk comes into your life:

- It is time to be fearless and accept your power.
- Do not turn your back on others.
- Withhold judgment of others.

Energy Center: Root

Mineral: Blue chalcedony

Element: Earth

Magic & Mystery:

- The word *Skunk* (*Squuncke* in the Algonquin tongue), is a moniker that means "urinating Fox."
- Skunk does not spray others of its kind.

SHAMAN'S INTENTION: *TEACH ME THE WISDOM OF CONFLICT AND HELP ME DISCERN WHEN AND WHERE TO TAKE A STAND*

SLOTH

RELAXATION | **PRESENCE** | **PEACE**

"Drink the elixir of kindness and compassion so that you can live a life without conflict."—Sloth

POWERS OF SLOTH

Call in Sloth for:

- Help to perceive the world from a higher perspective.
- Improving your ability to slow down.
- An end to pushing the limits of time.

AWARENESS FROM SLOTH

If Sloth comes into your life:

- Embrace the present moment.
- You may trust that everything is going to be fine.
- Stress could be destroying your health and wellbeing.

Energy Center: Heart

Mineral: Yellow calcite

Element: Air

Magic & Mystery:

- The remains of a giant Sloth dating back to the end of the ice age 15,000 years ago were discovered in an underwater cave near Tulum on Mexico's Yucatan Peninsula along with a shrine to Ek Chuay, Mayan god of war and commerce.
- When Sloth dies, it is often found still gripping a tree.

Sloth is a mammal with tiny ears and a face similar to a primate. It lives in the rainforests of Central and South America. Either a two- or three-toed nocturnal creature, it spends almost all of its lifetime hanging upside down in trees eating leaves, twigs, and fruit. It sleeps up to nineteen hours per day because of its extremely slow metabolism. Sloth has gray and brown fur that is home to many microorganisms, such as green algae that camouflages it in the forest canopy it inhabits. It has a peculiar relationship with Moth and the hundreds of other creatures crawling on it—hiding them from their major predator, Eagle.

Sloth does almost everything while hanging from a tree limb, even giving birth. The only time it usually leaves the tree is to defecate and urinate at its base—which occurs roughly once per week—in the process providing nutrients for its home. Sloth eats very little very slowly; its digestive system is so sluggish that it takes a month to digest just one leaf. During the rainy season, Sloth will enter the water of a lake, stream, or swamp. Curiously, it is a good swimmer, mainly because it has the ability to hold its breath for almost forty minutes. It is well adapted to its environment and a master of peacefully coexisting with the natural world.

In Theravada Buddhism, they use the term *Sloth* as a translation for *thina-middha*, a state characterized by being unwholesomely sluggish, lazy, dull, and bored. These are hindrances or obstructions that can occur during meditation. While Sloth may appear to be in meditation because it does everything slowly, in fact, it is expert at conserving its personal energy. Sloth is an intelligent animal that simply lacks the drive to do much, and its awkwardly shaped legs do not do well walking. Sloth avoids conflict with anything and keeps to itself. It can make an annoying high-pitched sound if it needs to communicate. Other than its genetic destiny for being slow paced, Sloth also consumes the leaves of mangrove trees, which have a natural sedative effect, slowing down its senses considerably.

As a Power Animal, Sloth teaches us to relax and enjoy life. It is powerful because it is non-confrontational in the style of Gandhi—an example that even in defending ourselves we are giving up power to others. An adversary only exists if we believe it is an adversary. When we walk in the world in peace, the aggression in others dissipates and the encounter becomes about nothingness. If we hold on to conflicts, their energy never goes away. Nonviolence breeds a kinder and gentler life where we are at peace with ourselves and all things.

Sloth is a perfect reminder that there is no time in the world of subtle energy; time is an illusion of our dimension of reality. If you try to grab time, it will always slip away. There really is only the now—one now follows another. Consult Sloth about your dreams and for guidance in traveling out of body to experience alternate realms.

Sloth sees humanity as being too focused on our doings. Our chaotic frenzy of activity is an untamed energy that breeds a sense of scarcity of time. And time breeds stress. What if there was no urgency in our lives? What if we were to rely on synchronicity to meet our needs, and trusted that the cogs in the wheel of the Universe would come together for our benefit at the perfect moment? The damage caused by our mental constructs of time is an elusive symptom to heal. Call on Sloth to help you to master presence and to help others who are likely to short circuit their nervous systems, depleting their motivation and inhibiting their minds' ability to focus. When we are aligned with the present, there is no urgency. When we are fulfilled in stillness, then we can evolve and be at peace.

SHAMAN'S INTENTION: *TEACH ME TO OVERCOME THE CONSTRAINTS OF TIME*

SNAIL

CIRCUMSPECTION | **SELF-SUFFICIENCY** | **DETERMINATION**

"If you travel through life with little friction, you may trust in what will unfold."—Snail

Most types of Snail and Slug are sea creatures. Even so, 500 species live on land. The only significant difference between Slug and Snail is that Slug either has no shell or a very minor one. Snail always has a shell. Water shells are often bright colors whereas land shells come in earth tones for camouflage.

Slug is an essential member of its ecosystem as it consumes decaying plant matter. With thousands of teeth, it grinds and devours its food. Both Snail and Slug spend most of their time in underground tunnels, emerging at night to feed. They are hermaphrodites and will lay around thirty eggs after mating. During mating two Snails (or Slugs) impregnate each other. The act takes twelve hours.

One of the more important types of Snail in the shamanic world is Conch, a large Sea Snail. Throughout the Americas, the Conch shell is blown like a trumpet to invoke spirits during ceremonies. At Teotihuacan, an archaeological site in Mexico, many of the ruins are adorned with Conch shells, a symbol of plenty and supernatural powers. Many tombs also incorporated Conch shells. For the ancient Mayans, shells were often used as art.

The ancient Aztecs saw Snail as sacred, representing the cycle of life. T ccizt catl, god of the Moon, was depicted with Snail's shell on its back, inspired by how Snail retreats into its shell, like the Moon sinks into the ocean. Quetzalcoatl, a god resembling a feathered serpent, wore a Snail shell emblem on his chest, depicting the wisdom of reincarnation and the cycles inherent in the Universe. Snail has been associated with wind—many Native wind gods have been depicted as riding in shells.

The spiral that is embodied in the shape of Snail's shell is the symbol of the expansion of consciousness and the contraction of going within to find our personal truths. Snail is associated with beginnings as it is one of the first animals to emerge from the soil during springtime. To describe human thinking, psychiatrist Carl Jung said conscious thought is like the hard shell, and unconscious thought is like the soft Snail inside it. Human form also resembles Snail in another way: Our ears look like its shell, gathering vibration and converting it into sound so that we may resonate with a universal source.

Conch, Slug, and Snail are associated with the Lower World and a labyrinth, a maze that folds over on itself. Each has a protective quality, on its back carrying about its own place to dwell or retreat from the world for a while. As a Power Animal, Snail reminds us that infinity overrides limitation. There are no barriers in the quantum field, only nothingness. Beyond the confines of the earthly journey lies the multidimensional potential of immortality that we can enjoy after we are dead. While you are alive, Snail teaches the importance of listening to the winds of change and for messages from higher-frequency dimensions. Do you hear the call of spirit? Do you listen to your heart? So much is speaking to you, yet you may not be listening intently enough. The heart is an unending vortex of energy that can swirl unconditional love into your field to nurture your doubts. This vortex resonates with the harmonic frequency of love.

As we walk the Earth, we have no sense of what is happening in the physical reality below us, with the roots and the hidden insect life, there is so much vibrant energy there. Capture this energy as you walk and sink your soles into the nurturing aspect of the Earth.

CONCH, SLUG

POWERS OF SNAIL

Call in Snail for:

- Knowing when to withdraw and quiet your mind.
- Guidance in the creation of sacred space.
- Help with realization of your immortality.

AWARENESS FROM SNAIL

If Snail comes into your life:

- It is time to start over and head down a different path from the one you are on.
- It is important for you to take measures to preserve your privacy.
- Slow down, as speed is dulling your powers of perception.

Energy Center: Crown

Mineral: Tanzanite

Element: Earth

Magic & Mystery:

- In the United Kingdom, an acre of farmland contains an estimated 250,000 Slugs.
- Conch shells are considered so precious in the Bahamas and Bermuda that they are handed down for generations and generations within a family.

SHAMAN'S INTENTION: *TEACH ME INFINITY*

SNAKE

TRANSFORMATION | **MANIFESTATION** | **DREAMING**

"We wait patiently in the sacrum of the body, ready to provide a fertile opportunity for the explosion of enlightenment."—Snake

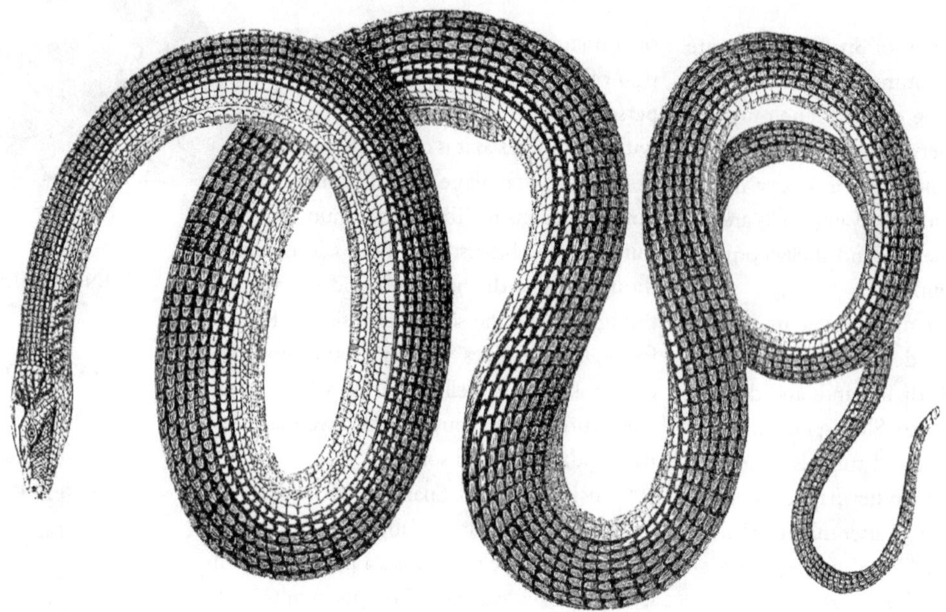

There are almost 3,000 different species of Snake on Earth, from the tiny African Thread Snake to the massive Anaconda. Only 10 percent are venomous. Snake evolved from Lizard over ninety million years ago, losing its legs in the process. It is found in many habitats. Snake's tongue is an important sensory tool that helps it find food and mates. It has an excellent sense of smell and touch, but poor eyesight. As a cold-blooded reptile, Snake must adjust to the external temperature to regulate its internal temperature, so it will seek cool areas on hot days or bask in the warm Sun on cooler days. In the winter, it hibernates.

Snake sheds its skin up to six times per year. Many cultures see this as a sign of immortality as Snake continually emerges as a new being. Ouroboros, the symbol of a snake eating its own tail, has many meanings: the cycle of life and death, infinity, wholeness, creation, and the encircling of the world in unity.

The ancient Egyptians saw Snake as possessing healing abilities. Offerings were made to the goddess Wadjet, the patron of Lower Egypt, in the hopes that her good will would be manifested. The pharaoh wore the image of a Cobra head on his diadem—a uraeus—symbolizing that he embodied Cobra's powers. Nehebkau, a double-headed benevolent Snake god, was linked to the Sun. It was said that he protected souls both in life and in the afterlife.

The ancient Sumerians also saw Snake as a symbol of healing and depicted its importance in the caduceus. An icon of medicine to this day, it shows two Snakes intertwined around a staff with wings. The Snakes represent the nervous system; the staff is symbolic the spinal cord; and the wings denote the two hemispheres of the brain, with the center representing the pineal gland—or third eye. At the Temple of Asclepius in ancient Greece stories were told of Snake crawling across the bodies of sick people during the night and licking them back to life or curing deafness or blindness.

In the traditions of yoga, dating back anywhere from 5,000–10,000 years in India, Snake is emblematic of the nature of the kundalini energy that lies asleep in the human sacrum, near the tailbone. In the process of awakening, this energy rises through the subtle body via the nerve currents of the spine, passing through the chakras until it arrives at the crown producing ecstasy and transformation. The Snake on the left is the ida, a channel for feminine prana (life force) or Shakti energy. The Snake on the right is the pingala, a channel for masculine prana or Shiva energy. The central channel (like the staff of the caduceus) is the sushumna. Full enlightenment, according to some sources, is

when Shakti has risen to meet Shiva. Some Indian myths portray their god Shiva, the destroyer or transformer, with a cobra on his head and another on his shoulder, ready to take on any enemies.

In almost all world cultures, Snake is seen as the guardian of the Lower World and a messenger to the Upper World, a figure able to slither through the cracks between cosmic dimensions. African and Australian tribespeople alike revere Rainbow Snake, believing it gave birth to all other animals. Rainbow Snake is also believed to have created all the waterways on the planet. Many tribes believe a race of Snake people who are half-human, half-snake live below the surface of the Earth, and they tell mythical stories of shamans traveling to this underground world. They see Snake as a wisdom keeper, perhaps because Snake takes its time to evaluate if it should strike. To them, Snake is an umbilical cord that connects humanity to Mother Earth.

One of the most important ancient Mesoamerican gods was the feathered serpent the Aztecs called Quetzalcoatl, god of wind, air, and learning. The Mayans called this same deity Kukulkan. According to the legends of their descendants, he once appeared in the form of a human and was known to have brought advanced knowledge to the people. It is said that when he died, he became the star of Venus.

In North America, the Hopi view Snake as a symbol of fertility. Their traditional annual Snake dance is done to celebrate the union of the male Snake sky spirit with the female Snake Earth spirit in the hope of revitalizing and fertilizing plants in the high desert where they live. Live Snakes that are part of the ceremony are then released into the fields to ensure abundant crops.

As a Power Animal, Snake is the companion to our higher consciousness, allowing hidden knowledge to be born. The egg of Snake is a symbol of the union of masculine and feminine energy in the material world. When the egg hatches, you may expect a powerful creative explosion to occur.

Just as Snake sheds its skin, we must periodically shed our old ideas and allow our minds to experience new perceptions. Before shedding, the eyes of Snake become cloudy, representing a moment of inner reflection before coiling into a new place of power. This is the moment of its alignment with the frequency of the Earth, enabling it to enter the field of manifestation.

Remember that Snake works with frequency. It does not search, preferring to use its intuitive senses to bring to it what it desires. This Power Animal sleeps at the entrance to the Lower World, where it acts as a shamanic guide to your dreams.

Anaconda desires us to squeeze out the creative juices of our potential. It is the overseer of revolutionary thoughts and fertile minds. Call upon it for help if you are working to produce inventions and innovations that stimulates progressive changes, or to foster cosmic connections.

SNAKE SHEDS ITS SKIN UP TO SIX TIMES PER YEAR. MANY CULTURES SEE THIS AS A SIGN OF IMMORTALITY AS SNAKE CONTINUALLY EMERGES AS A NEW BEING.

ANACONDA, BOA CONSTRICTOR, COBRA, PYTHON, RATTLESNAKE

POWERS OF SNAKE

Call in Snake for:

- Help to realize your full potential.
- Transformation of all that blocks your path.
- Finding that which is hidden from you.

AWARENESS FROM SNAKE

If Snake comes into your life:

- You are entering a time of transformation.
- It is necessary to heal whatever is not serving you.
- Expand your knowledge of the healing arts.

Energy Center: Root

Mineral: Snakeskin agate

Element: Earth

Magic & Mystery:

- In Kerala, India, almost every home has a shrine to Snake.
- Anaconda, which can weigh over 600 pounds, is the biggest Snake in the world.
- Prior to the introduction of Christianity, the symbol of Snake was very positive.
- Snake has a strong link to humans as its skeleton resembles the spine and ribcage of a human.
- The symbol Ouroboros depicts a serpent eating its own tail, creating a figure eight which represents the beginning and end of time.

SHAMAN'S INTENTION: *WRAP YOUR COILS OF LIGHT AROUND ME SO THAT I CAN EXPERIENCE ENLIGHTENMENT*

SPARROW

COMMUNITY | **EXPRESSION** | **MOTIVATION**

"Show gratitude for the small things, as they often bring big love."—Sparrow

POWERS OF SPARROW

Call in Sparrow for:

- Support in building a spiritual community.
- Coordinating tasks with others in the most effective manner possible.
- Building an audience of people with whom to share your stories.

AWARENESS FROM SPARROW

If Sparrow comes into your life:

- You may be relying too much on others for your happiness.
- Venture out of civilization and commune with nature.
- You may be feeling caged in, so spread your wings and fly.

Energy Center: Sacrum

Mineral: Labradorite

Element: Air

Magic & Mystery:

- In Japan, Sparrow is a symbol of loyalty because of its success at getting along well in groups.
- Sparrow can fly at speeds of twenty-five to thirty miles per hour.

Sparrow is a small, passerine bird that that has lived near humans ever since the invention of the birdfeeder. Originally from northern Africa, today Sparrow is prevalent everywhere except Antarctica. It is a chubby brown and gray bird with a short tail and strong beak that makes flying look easy. It maneuvers through the air without effort. It is also vocal, making its messages clear. Sparrow is probably one of the most social birds, thriving within its flock and preferring communal living. It derives its power from its numbers, carrying out most tasks with others. Sparrow typically builds its nests in buildings and overhangs, and several Sparrow may roost together in the same spot. It is extremely sexually active. Although not territorial, it will be assertive in order to protect its young. Its diet consists primarily of moths, berries, seeds, and fruit. Sparrow does not like watery bird baths and, though it likes to be clean; often it is seen bathing itself in dust.

In ancient Greece, Sparrow was sacred to Aphrodite, the goddess of love, and symbolized love and spirit. The ancient Egyptians also considered Sparrow sacred, believing Sparrow would grab the souls of those who died as they left the body and would carry the souls to heaven. Many sailors would tattoo an image of Sparrow on their bodies to ensure that their souls would be taken to heaven if they perished at sea.

Indonesians believe that if Sparrow flies into your house it is good luck, and if it builds a nest in your home's eaves, even better. They say Sparrow is a sign that a wedding is soon going to take place. Traditionally, Sparrow would be asked to sing a song for rain. In China, Sparrow is a symbol of happiness, beginnings, and companionship.

As a Power Animal, Sparrow is a master of friendship, togetherness, and the power of the collective. It is also a master of flight, both literal and figurative. You may call upon it for assistance when you are struggling with your freedom of expression or with nurturing others. Sparrow is curious why humankind questions so many things intellectually instead of relying on our instincts, which can always help us to find our way to understanding. It can teach those who work with it how to let go and just dive into the flow of the energy field. It actually requires less thought and effort to survive than most people realize. Sparrow is about simplicity. Accumulating more than we need can prevent us from experiencing that which is meaningful. There is a freedom of spirit in possessing nothing.

Build your nest and make it a place to express creativity. Be a person who inspires others and supports them to arrive at greater heights of awareness. In doing this, you will see that opportunity flows in your direction and fills you with new enthusiasm for life. So many see the world from a narrow perspective that looks like a small circular opening in the side of a birdhouse and lead a narrow existence. Sparrow can guide you to hop boldly out onto your perch where you can launch a new life for yourself.

SHAMAN'S INTENTION: *SUPPORT MY UNDERSTANDING OF THE COLLECTIVE AND THE POWER OF MANY BECOMING ONE*

SPIDER

CREATIVITY **ASSERTIVENESS** **PATIENCE**

"Don't complicate anything with senseless thoughts; they are simply a web that you can get tangled up in."—Spider

The more than 40,000 types of Spider form the largest group of carnivores on the planet. It comes in all shapes and sizes and, although diverse, always has one thing in common with others of its kind: eight legs and eight eyes (with rare exceptions). Spider produces silk from glands on its abdomen. These strands of protein are used to build webs to catch insects, create shelter, and glide from place to place. Spider also has fangs that enable it to inject venom into its prey or for protection in a battle. Only a small percentage of Spider types will bite a human or pose a health problem to us.

The female Spider is larger than the male and the male often perishes after mating with her. One of the most dangerous species for a male to belong to is Black Widow Spider, which is recognizable for two bright red spots in an hourglass symbol. The female of this species is relentless and overpowering as she does not allow a male to live near her territory. Spider is like Snake, shedding its skin to grow. It weaves the strands of the various webs it builds to carry different frequencies, so it can sense the location of its prey when it is caught. Through this method of discernment, it also can detect a mate or food.

In the past, Dakota and Lakota Sioux warriors wore the symbol of a Spider web on their clothing when they went into battle to make them invincible to arrows. The theory was that anything shot into a Spider web goes right through it, causing no harm. They felt that the web image also supported them in being invisible. The Lakota attributed Spider with giving all other creatures their names and identity. The Cherokee believe that their ancestral spirit, Grandmother Spider, brings light to the world during times of darkness.

In Hopi cosmology, Spider Woman represents the Earth. They believe that with Tawa, the Sun god, she created the first man and woman. Being adept at weaving, an important cultural skill and art, Spider was understood to be the goddess of creation. Spider Woman is also credited with bringing the alphabet and writing to humanity. These tools are associated with the wisdom of the feminine. No matter where you go, to all peoples, Spider is honored for reflecting creation and infinity—the totality of the life cycle.

There is futility in fear. As you weave the tapestry of your life often what is lacking is knowing and trusting that all is as it should be. Infinite resources are always available. Trying to capture or seize a moment is impossible. Instead of misguided attempts at controlling the past, trust that you have a perfect place in the greater web of life. Outcomes naturally evolve so that your needs and desires can be met. Your presence gives you power over the now—instant by instant. As a Power Animal, Spider is a master of planning and diligence. Weave confidence and knowledge into the silk threads of your existence and you will be guaranteed to succeed. Weave doubt and ignorance into the threads and you will fail. A lack of confidence means you perceive yourself as less than you are. Walking in your power is your insurance against fear. When you walk in doubt, you make yourself more vulnerable to being stepped on. Spider is a good Power Animal for weavers, fundraisers, and architects.

POWERS OF SPIDER

Call in Spider for:

- Support with business networking and planning.
- Help to enhance your creativity.
- Patience in waiting for things you want to come to you.

AWARENESS FROM SPIDER

If Spider comes into your life:

- You are ultrasensitive and instead need self-empowerment.
- Consider the balance in your relationships; some may be lopsided.
- It is time for you to design a life that captures what you desire.

Energy Center: Solar plexus

Mineral: Aragonite

Element: Air

Magic & Mystery:

- In Japan, the sound of some violin strings made from Spider silk is described as having a profound, underlying softness.
- Golden Wheel Spider from Namibia folds itself into a wheel and rolls away whenever it feels threatened.

SHAMAN'S INTENTION: *SHOW ME THE WEB OF MY EXISTENCE SO THAT I MAY NAVIGATE THE FIELD OF POSSIBILITY*

SQUIRREL

DILIGENCE | **VIGILANCE** | **MOBILITY**

"Fear dissipates when your basic needs are met. Desiring more than that can create a feeling of scarcity."—Squirrel

POWERS OF SQUIRREL

Call in Squirrel for:

- Vigilance to what is going on around you.
- Guidance in finding whatever you need to survive.
- Help to seeing the forest (big picture) through the trees (details).

AWARENESS FROM SQUIRREL

If Squirrel comes into your life:

- Explore new ways to relax; take a day off or go on retreat.
- Focus on being a better decision maker; you may be wishy washy.
- Ease back on accumulating anything new for the time being. Focus on experiencing gratitude for what you already have.

Energy Center: Throat

Mineral: Rosasite

Element: Air

Magic & Mystery: When Squirrel misplaces an acorn, it is to the forest's advantage, as every acorn holds the potential to grow a whole new oak tree.

More than 200 species of Squirrel live on our planet. The smallest is African Pygmy Squirrel. The largest is Indian Giant Squirrel, which is three feet long. Flying Squirrel is equipped with a built-in parachute that helps it to glide and extend the distance it can leap. Quick and agile, Squirrel roams from tree to tree, jumping with quick precision between branches. Its paws are perfect for digging and gathering fallen nuts for food. Squirrel is territorial, protecting its space at all costs. It lives in underground tunnels where it will sometimes hibernate. It can become ferocious when its babies are threatened. Squirrel communicates through sounds and scents to mark its territory and the twitching of its tail. It is chatty and sociable. Squirrel is the security guard of the forest, chirping and twitching to warn its neighbors of danger. Intelligent and clever, it may create a mock version of its food storage area to confuse potential thieves. Vigilant, it is constantly looking in every direction for predators.

Native Americans see Squirrel as a noisy and aggressive troublemaker, and as an efficient food gatherer and sentry. A Choctaw legend says solar eclipses are caused by a black squirrel eating the Sun. The Lakota Sioux believe a white Squirrel is an omen that spirit sends to get our attention.

The origin of Squirrel's name is the ancient Greek word skiouros, meaning "shade tail," alluding to Squirrel's ability to give itself shade with its bushy tail. Squirrel's image has been used in heraldic coats of arms in many different European countries. The British surname Holt means "grove" and the family coat of arms includes Squirrel.

In Norse mythology, Ratatoskr is a Squirrel that carries messages from Snake at the bottom of the Tree of Life (Yggdrasil) to Eagle at the top—activity that symbolizes the cosmic principle "As above, so below." The ancient Celts recognized Squirrel as a companion to Mab, queen of the fairy kingdom.

As a Power Animal, Squirrel brings us the message that although life can be a tough nut to crack, it is ripe with wisdom. We may move from branch to branch on the Tree of Life scratching our heads about our purpose and existence. But we will be more fulfilled if we see every branch of life we touch as a step in our personal journey to uncover truth and every leaf and nut as a lesson to learn. Squirrel can guide you to feel secure in knowing that everything will come to you at the perfect time, so there is no need to overthink what may come next. Why be confined to a structure of thought that impedes adventure and the freedom to roam, discover, and just be? Squirrel would remind you not to cling too tightly to anything you accumulate, as grasping can lead to an obsession over things, when all that is needed lies within your heart. This is the place where your real gems are kept. Your heart is the treasure chest of your life.

SHAMAN'S INTENTION: *GIVE ME PATIENCE TO TEND TO THE SEEDS OF MY POTENTIAL*

STARFISH

IMAGINATION | RENEWAL | REFLECTION

"Wander lost no longer; there are millions of signs along the way that can orient you."—Starfish

There are nearly 2,000 species of Starfish found at various depths in oceans around the world. These are classified either as Sea Cucumber, Urchin, or Sand Dollar. Most types have five arms, yet some, like Sun Star, have as many as forty arms. The colorful arms on Starfish's body look like sunrays that are covered with a spikey skeleton that is a deterrent against predators. Starfish has the ability to regrow missing body parts. Interestingly, while Starfish does not have a centralized brain, it does have a complex nervous system. And while it does not have blood, nutrients are circulated throughout its body by a sea water vascular system. Starfish depends on its environment for survival. It has an eye on the end of each arm. It is also capable of changing gender at any time.

The Kwakiutl tribe of North America has a legend that Starfish were women had the ability to turn the trickster Mink into a Starfish. Starfish was also the form of Komokwa, goddess of the undersea world. The Tlingit and Haida have a Starfish clan and carve its image into their totem poles. For them it is a symbol of longevity and strength because of its ability to crack open shellfish with its arms. They believe it holds the magic of immortality because of its ability to regenerate its body.

The shape of Starfish has long been seen as demonstrating infinite and unconditional love with a celestial quality, a capacity for protecting those in troubled waters. The ancient Romans saw Starfish as a symbol of Venus, their goddess of love. The ancient Egyptians equated Starfish with Isis, who, among other things, watched over society's poorest members, including the slaves.

As a Power Animal, Starfish is a celestial source of unconditional love, renewal, and regeneration. Call upon it when you are determined to crush old paradigms of thought and grow into a better version of yourself. Just as Starfish grows back stronger after losing a part of itself, we grow stronger when we discard negative habits and attitudes, like worrying. Starfish is a sign that we need healing or that we carry qualities of healing inside us that would enable us to help others. It can be an excellent support for us when we feel abandoned or betrayed. Starfish can help us to connect to beings that exist off planet and to embrace the energy of the Moon, the flow of the tides, and ourselves.

The five-pointed body of the Starfish embodies the five elements of earth, air, fire, water, and spirit, with its arms acting like cosmic neurons to exchange these five types of energy. In clusters, it is an undersea "reflection" of the starry heavens. Like the ephemeral wishes made on shooting stars that burn up as they enter Earth's atmosphere, Starfish inspires us to see ourselves as stardust—part of the wider cosmos. The main obstacle we face when trying to see ourselves this way is the density of our physical perceptions. Millions of years have defined us as human, but it takes just a moment to see through the paradox of that which we simply think we are to the truth that we are much more.

Starfish has a profound message to share. The golden light that comes to us from the Sun is an alchemical substance. This tonic light that dances and sparkles on the surface of bodies of water represents the higher consciousness that beams into our atmosphere. Learning from Starfish, we can pull in the nourishment and spiritual protection of this golden field. By gathering this energy in your body, you can shine brightly in the darkness. Do not define yourself by just your form; see yourself as a grain of sand in the infinity of the entire cosmos. Respect your energetic signature.

POWERS OF STARFISH

Call in Starfish for:

- Orientation if you feel you are wandering astray.
- Support to overcome betrayal.
- When you want to shine more brightly among a field of others.

AWARENESS FROM STARFISH

If Starfish comes into your life:

- It is a time to say prayers and express your appreciation for all the gifts you have been blessed to receive.
- Get centered so you can expand your energy to shelter and heal others.
- Take time for rejuvenation and restoration of your body and soul.

Energy Center: Crown

Mineral: Stibnite

Element: Water

Magic & Mystery:

- Starfish has existed for over four hundred and fifty million years.
- Crown-of-Thorns Starfish has a ferocious appetite for Coral. It lives throughout Indonesia.

SHAMAN'S INTENTION: *HELP ME TO UNDERSTAND THE MYSTERIES OF THE COSMOS*

STARLING

OMNIPRESENCE | **ALIGNMENT** | **EXPRESSION**

"Going with the flow helps the soul find its greatest expression."—Starling

POWERS OF STARLING

Call in Starling for:

- Honing your ability to thrive in a crowd.
- Deepening your trust of others.
- Embracing synchronicity in your life.

AWARENESS FROM STARLING

If Starling comes into your life:

- You may need to improve your communication skills.
- It is important to study and heal the dysfunctional patterns in your life.
- Align yourself with the flow of nature.

Energy Center: Sacrum

Mineral: Black jasper

Element: Air

Magic & Mystery:

- In 1890, sixty European starlings were released into New York's Central Park as part of an effort to introduce all the animals mentioned by Shakespeare in his plays.
- Wolfgang Amadeus Mozart had a pet Starling. When it died he held a funeral and wrote a special poem for the occasion.
- Starling can mimic the human voice. As early as the fifth century B.C.E., Greeks and Romans caged Starling and taught it to imitate human speech.

Starling is a sturdy bird with a long, bright yellow beak and a short tail and wings that looks like a four-pointed star when it flies. Its feathers change color with the season. In summer they are an iridescent purple; in winter they are brown with white spots. Starling travels in large flocks with birds both of its own kind and others that race across meadows searching for food. Loud and rambunctious, a Starling flock can number up to 100,000 birds. Thousands of Starling in synchronized flight is an amazing display of nature. Starling is agile and strong, reaching speeds of forty-eight miles per hour.

In ancient Greece, Sparrow was sacred to Aphrodite, the goddess of love, and symbolized love and spirit. The ancient Egyptians also considered Sparrow sacred, believing Sparrow would grab the souls of those who died as they left the body and would carry the souls to heaven. Many sailors would tattoo an image of Sparrow on their bodies to ensure that their souls would be taken to heaven if they perished at sea.

Starling is a great communicator that likes to hang out on electrical wires and trees while chatting it up. It can mimic the calls of other birds, even Eagle. It is also an opportunist that will take over the nests of other birds. The male is aggressive about nesting sites. Starling likes to feed on grassy lawns and fields. Due to its appetite for fruits, corn, and seeds, it has at times contributed to severe crop damage. With such high numbers in a flock, it can be an unrestrained and unwelcome visitor to farms.

The ancient Welsh believed that Starling would right wrongs against a woman who had been mistreated. They viewed it as a sign of a warrior because of its sometimes-aggressive nature. Starling was recognized as an omen from the spirit world that change was coming. The ancient Romans believed they could make predictions and prophecies off of the flying displays of Starling, so the path that Rome took often hinged on Starling's movements.

The term for a flock of Starling is a murmuration. This massive movement overtakes the entire sky, like wind, rain, clouds, smoke, or mist. It moves as if with a single purpose. Studies have concluded that a simple change in the behavior of one bird can change the movement of all the others. As a Power Animal, Starling asks us to embrace the collective nature of our existence. A murmuration is a tangible example of how our own thoughts and actions can impact the people around us. As we dissolve any separation from one another, we will all capitalize on the wave of change that is sweeping across the planet and uplifting collective consciousness to a higher frequency. Nothing stays the same. Acting in synchrony, we will start to see pieces of our creations leading to unexpected turns. When we all know our power as individuals, we will have achieved a level of thought that can release a power into the field that is unstoppable.

SHAMAN'S INTENTION: *HELP TO TEACH ME THE CONCEPT OF RHYTHM AND MOVEMENT, SO THAT I MAY DANCE WITH THE UNIVERSE*

STINGRAY

QUANTUM ENERGY | **FEARLESSNESS** | **INTUITION**

"Appreciation is a statement to the Universe that you are grateful to be here."—Stingray

Stingray came into existence roughly 150 million years ago. Found mostly near the tropics, it can survive in both saltwater and freshwater. It prefers the shallow areas of the oceans and estuaries. There are sixty different species of Stingray, the largest weighing almost 800 pounds. It is a flat fish with eyes on the top of its heads and gills underneath. It catches Shrimp, Clam, and Mussel, crushing them with its powerful jaws. It uses its tail for self-defense; with razor edges and a stinger on the end, it can cut into the flesh of an attacker and release venom. One type of Stingray, the Electric Ray, can electrocute larger prey since its body carries an extremely high voltage. Stingray is an excellent predator. Through its fine-tuned connection to the electromagnetic field, it can easily sense movement. It has such astute skills of detection that it can hear the heartbeats of other animals.

The movement of Stingray is similar to that of a bird. Its physical undulations look like it is flapping "wings" and give the impression that it is flying through the water. From the moment it is born, Baby Stingray is a great swimmer. Stingray spends most of its time buried in sand that matches the color of its skin, thus keeping itself hidden from the outside world. It lies in wait, ready to strike should a "meal" swim by. It is territorial and has a strong survival instinct; even so, Stingray is more curious than fearful.

The ancient Mayans used the stinger from Stingray's tail as an implement to draw blood during human sacrifices. They believed that the stinger had magical power. Indigenous people in South America traditionally only rarely hunted Stingray as it was believed to be associated with evil spirits. Myth says that the Greek god Hercules had a finger bitten off by Stingray. The ancient Greeks used venom drawn from Stingray as an anesthetic for dental work. The Te Wh nau- -Apanui of New Zealand saw Stingray as a caretaker that protected shellfish and ensured there would be plenty for fisherman to catch. In the Philippines Stingray tail was traditionally used as a talisman to ward off evil spirits. The Gumatj clan of the Yolngu tribe of Australia revered the black-colored Whipray, which has white spots and a white tail. For them, Stingray was a metaphor for human society, an animal whose behavior should be emulated. They said we should be gentle, kind, social, and take good care of our children. But we also must have a spear that we can use if attacked.

As a Power Animal, Stingray's ability to tap into the electromagnetic fields can be called upon to help us to manifest our goals, measure risks and rewards, and consciously connect with all that is. Stingray represents water, the living environment of emotions, which exist on varying depths of our psyche. Here is the unseen world where we store our feelings. It is best to be an observer of our emotions so as not to allow them to feed on the inconsistencies of the outside world.

POWERS OF STINGRAY

Call in Stingray for:

- Connection to a higher frequency.
- Help to become more of an observer of life and less a victim of it.
- Getting in harmony with the natural environment.

AWARENESS FROM STINGRAY

If Stingray comes into your life:

- You would benefit from finding something more stimulating to do.
- Your impulses may be leading you to act too fast; do your best to take more measured decisions.
- Seek to understand the nuances of the electromagnetic field.

Energy Center: Third eye

Mineral: Herkimer diamond

Element: Water

Magic & Mystery:

- Torpedo Stingray, which lives in the Atlantic Ocean, can generate sufficient power to produce a shock of 220 volts from its ray.
- The ancient Greeks used the venom from Stingray to numb pain during operations.

SHAMAN'S INTENTION: *TEACH ME ABOUT THE ENERGY FIELD THAT IS AVAILABLE TO ME FOR HEALING MYSELF AND OTHERS*

STORK

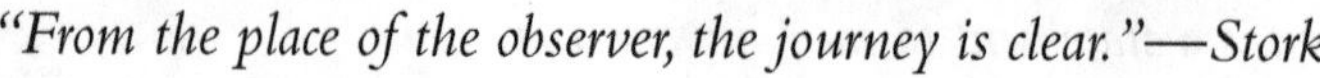

"From the place of the observer, the journey is clear."—Stork

POWERS OF STORK

Call in Stork for:

- The enhancement of your maternal instincts.
- Protection of your home.
- Help to strengthen your loyalty to your partner and family.

AWARENESS FROM STORK

If Stork comes into your life:

- It is bringing you a message of rebirth or renewal.
- Focus on nurturing yourself and your ideas or dreams.
- Consider the benefits of relocating to a warmer climate in the winter months.

Energy Center: Sacrum

Mineral: Azurite

Element: Water

Magic & Mystery:

- The Greek term for Stork, storge, means "mother love" or "powerful affection."
- Poland is the home of a quarter of the White Stork population.

Stork is found all over our planet. It lives in Europe, Asia, and Africa near rivers and in swamps and grasslands. A handsome bird, it has flashy white plumage on its chest that contrasts with its black wing feathers. Five feet tall with a pointy beak, long, thin legs, and semi-webbed feet, it is ideally built for wading in shallow waters, which it does while waiting for the fishes it eats to swim by. Stork is also good at diving into murky waters and catching fish. Males and females are identical, other than the male being slightly larger. Those bright chest feathers are on a brilliant display during its rituals of courtship, while the male searches for his life partner. With a massive wingspan, Stork is quite a sight when it is in the air, soaring with its long neck and long legs outstretched. It travels in flocks of thousands when migrating and takes advantage of the updrafts of thermal currents that help it to minimize its effort, enabling it to fly further before running out of energy. Stork is a vocal creature that both cries and makes a clacking sound with its bill. Its nests are massive, and it returns to them year after year.

Stork typically flies south for the winter and north in the spring. For many people, seeing Stork is a sign that spring has sprung, and the season of renewal and rebirth is upon them. Because of its annual return to its breeding grounds roughly nine months after migrating south, according to the legends of some cultures, Stork brings babies in its large bill. But not in all cultures! The ancient Greeks saw Stork as a thief of babies instead of as a bringer. Storks massive nest and devotion to its home impressed the ancients. The Romans, Greeks, and Norse of antiquity held Stork as a sacred symbol of hearth and home and family. Strong protective maternal instincts are a Stork characteristic. The Hebrew word for Stork, *chasidah,* translates as "kind mother."

Stork was also associated with death. The ancient Egyptians believed Stork was associated with the *ba*, one of the three parts of the human soul, which holds the blueprint of our existence through many lifetimes. They often depicted the soul as a bird with a human head on it and compared the migratory skills of Stork to the out-of-body journey the soul makes both during dreaming and when it departs the body to "go home" at the time of death.

It was also said that Stork would stay in its nest no matter what to protect it, even compromising itself in a fire rather than fleeing. In North America, pioneers headed west noticed that Stork would line its nest with maple leaves, and since that time, both are symbolic of the welcoming of a child into the world.

As a Power Animal, Stork can help us to avoid being caught up in the drama of those close to us. Their struggles can seep into our perception of them and into the energy of our lives in general, so we need to remain free of it—caring, but neutral. What happens to each of us is a personal journey and a chance to raise our awareness. It is only our beliefs that define this as a struggle. If we intercede in someone else's lessons we interfere with their opportunity to grow. When children arrive in our lives, for instance, we are to support their journeys rather than mold their choices. All we can do as parents and friends is to build a nest that is strong and foundational, and then teach them to fly. We must avoid swooping down to save them when life gets difficult. Sometimes spiritual lessons can only be learned through pain and suffering. If you are constantly going to the rescue of those in need, it may be time to ask your ego why you feel compelled to do so. Don't seek to fulfill all the needs of others. Bring to the world compassion for their earth walk but avoid compromising another soul's journey.

SHAMAN'S INTENTION: *SHARE YOUR KNOWLEDGE OF THE FEMININE, SO I MAY LEARN TO NURTURE MYSELF AND OTHERS*

SWALLOW

ENDURANCE FREEDOM REBIRTH

"When we return home in spring, we bring with us hope for new beginnings."—Swallow

Swallow is found all over the world in a variety of habitats that have an abundance of insects. With a dark blue head and wings, a white belly, and orange accents on its throat and forehead, its forked tail is the feature that gives it excellent maneuverability. During breeding season, the male attracts the female by singing to her, and then they mate in the air. This is a loyal pairing that lasts for life. Both sexes participate in nest building, and mostly they occupy holes in trees.

The Hebrew name for Swallow is *deror* ("bird of freedom") because Swallow is unable to withstand captivity. It is a great traveler that is always looking for the perfect temperature in which to reside during different seasons. Swallow is a migratory bird that travels 600 miles per day on its flight from North America to Central and South America when the northern climate turns cold. In the springtime, it always returns to the exact place where it hatched. Its homing instinct relies on the electromagnetic fields of the Earth.

Swallow has always enjoyed a protected status. Throughout the world they can be seen living in temples, mosques, and churches, as if knowing these places are sacred. It is also known for building nests in the oddest of places and with little discretion. In England, Swallow is allowed to build its nests in and on roofs since this is said to be good luck. According to Germans folklore, Swallow can prevent fires and storms from destroying a home.

The ancient Egyptians believed Swallow was connected to the stars and the soul of someone who had died. *The Egyptian Book of the Dead* describes how to turn into a Swallow for passage to the afterlife. Swallow was thought to be an imperishable star that, like the North Star, never stops shining. In Egyptian poetry Swallow is a symbol of the declaration of new love. The goddess Isis was said to change into Swallow at night. The ancient Romans also believed Sparrow a lucky spirit, and in their case, a symbol of Venus. They felt it carried away the souls of deceased children. Grieving mothers would wonder if a Swallow was their child.

Some Native American myths say that Swallow stole fire from the Sun and graced humanity with it. These peoples relied on Swallow to warn them of impending thunderstorms, seeing its forked tail as associated with thunder and lightning. The droppings of Swallow have healing powers and are used to treat snake bites, epilepsy and rabies. Seeing Swallow meant that a long journey would be coming to an end. Those who were imprisoned in England during the mid-1900s chose Swallow as a tattoo, a symbol that they would find freedom soon.

Swallow is the Power Animal of extremely gifted shamanic healers. These shamans can leave their bodies during healing sessions. In the Tucano tribe of the Amazon Swallow provides the shaman with magic wings to take the shaman on cosmic journeys.

The Swallow reminds us that no matter how far we travel, we always take ourselves with us. If your baggage is heavy, your journey will seem like a difficult struggle. Better to leave the past behind. Leaving everything behind requires trust. As a Power Animal, Swallow can help you build it. Renewal follows the elimination of your mental and emotional burdens. Freedom is the state that occurs after releasing all thoughts, wants, and needs.

POWERS OF SWALLOW

Call in Swallow for:

- Freedom from unwanted thoughts and emotions.
- Going on an adventure with your soul.
- Starting all over again after a period of difficulty.

AWARENESS FROM SWALLOW

If Swallow comes into your life:

- You may find a new partner or ignite a passion for the person you are with now.
- It is time to realize that home is where the heart is.
- Study the afterlife and different concepts of eternity.

Energy Center: Heart

Mineral: Sunstone

Element: Air

Magic & Mystery:

- For sailors, a Swallow tattoo indicates the number of miles they have traveled. One Swallow signifies 5,000 nautical miles.
- The celandine poppy, which is called the Swallow Flower, is a symbol of hope.

SHAMAN'S INTENTION: *TEACH ME TO BUILD A NEST IN MY HEART, SO I MAY BE A GUIDE TO OTHERS ON THEIR WORLDLY ADVENTURES INTO THE UNKNOWN*

SWAN

LOVE | **POISE** | **BONDING**

"Mastering the art of positivity will bring you a life of great beauty."
—Swan

Swan is one of the fastest swimmers and flyers in the bird kingdom. It is also long lived, reaching ages of up to fifty years. It is white with either a red, orange, or black beak. Its neck is long, with a graceful S-curve in it. A cousin of Goose and Duck, Swan is known for being aggressive, especially around its nest. After chasing away unwanted guests, it celebrates its success with its buddies. It has a big body and large, webbed feet designed for optimal paddling, with which it glides silently across the water. Above the surface it appears imperturbable.

When the weather turns, a flock of Swan migrate in a V-formation at top speed, traveling up to 4,000 miles roundtrip. It has strong bonds with its partner that lasts a lifetime. It is faithful and devoted to its mate. Swan often joins its long neck with its mate in a position resembles a perfect heart shape. Part of its courtship rituals is to bow gracefully to another Swan while ruffling its feathers. It is very intelligent and has a good memory.

Cygnus (from the Latin word for Swan) is the name of a constellation that features an asterism known as the Northern Cross right where a female Swan's womb would be located anatomically.

In Sanskrit, the name for Swan is *hamsa* and the word for an enlightened being is *paramahamsa* (or "supreme Swan"). Sages would say that by swimming in the waters of the mind for a lifetime, Swan absorbs the wisdom of the lotus blossom—releasing identification with the ego and merging with the cosmos. The

lotus closes at night and reopens every morning, as if it is being reborn. With its many petals, it resembles a shining star. Swan embodies this quality of grace too.

The ancient Celts of the British Isles saw Swan in the context of movement and travel. As a Power Animal, they would consult it on matters related to the Sun and the Moon. Swan was symbolically linked to Belanus, god of light, Lugh; the Sun god, and Brigid, the goddess of fire. It is only fitting that Swan would be linked to Brigid, as she was pure elegance and grace. A Celtic shaman might wear a gold or silver chain around his or her necks to indicate the possibility of shapeshifting from human to Swan or Swan to human. The ancient Greeks also associated Swan with the Sun. Their Sun god, Apollo, rode in a chariot pulled by Swans.

Shamans in Siberia would never kill Swan as death would come swiftly to whoever did. They wore cloaks made of Swan feathers in order to shapeshift into Swan for divination practices. The Nganasan would imitate the flight of swan in their dances and attempt to copy the sounds it makes.

As far back as the Paleolithic era, Swan has been perceived as a figure of importance. It was depicted in the cave paintings of Lascaux, France.

In the Yukon, shamans would have young women drink water through the hollow bones of Swan to ensure successful pregnancies. These shamans also put Swan feathers into medicine bags that people wore around their necks for healing various ailments. Also, when a child was born the down of Swan was placed in a beaded pouch with the child's umbilical cord and this medicine bag was carried by the mother. The masks of Swan adorned with their feathers were worn in native dances done during the last feast of winter to call Swan back and announce the arrival of spring. To this day, in late winter the celebration of the Swan is held in Whitehorse, the capital of the Yukon.

Swan is a great observer of life. With its long neck it can see sideways and backward. This helps Swan move fearlessly through its environment. Swan tells us that battling with others is always a disappointment and unnecessary. It is more effective to reflect on your own actions and motives. Study your reflection in the water, so you can achieve peace. Cleanse your mind of judgments and unkind thoughts. Purify your existence through acceptance. You will get further with others if you are poised and calm when you interact with them, like a Swan gliding through the water—even if you feel like you are furiously paddling your feet below the surface.

CYGNUS (FROM THE LATIN WORD FOR SWAN) IS THE NAME OF A CONSTELLATION THAT FEATURES AN ASTERISM KNOWN AS THE NORTHERN CROSS RIGHT WHERE A FEMALE SWAN'S WOMB WOULD BE LOCATED ANATOMICALLY.

POWERS OF SWAN

Call in Swan for:

- Handling difficult situations with grace.
- Help in delving into the impact of your past lives on you.
- Celebrating the power of love.

AWARENESS FROM SWAN

If Swan comes into your life:

- Love is in the air.
- Remember to look for the beauty inside yourself.
- You may need to temper your anger, even if you are feeling threatened.

Energy Center: Heart

Mineral: Prehnite

Element: Water

Magic & Mystery: Swan *song* is a metaphorical phrase for a final gesture, effort, or performance given just before death or retirement.in the world.

SHAMAN'S INTENTION: *TEACH ME TO FORGIVE THOSE I HAVE LOVED AND LOST, AND HELP ME TO LOVE AGAIN*

TASMANIAN DEVIL

DARKNESS | OPPORTUNITY | REPUTATION

"We bring to humanity our knowledge of the ability of fear to be the great deceiver of the mind."—Tasmanian Devil

POWERS OF TASMANIAN DEVIL

Call in Tasmanian Devil for:

- Support if you are fearful in the night.
- Honing the ability necessary to take on a project that seems challenging.
- Support to defend yourself without attacking your attacker in kind.

AWARENESS FROM TASMANIAN DEVIL

If Tasmanian Devil comes into your life:

- You may have too aggressive a nature for your own good.
- It may be time to face your deepest fears or clear your conscience.
- Stress may be causing you to overreact. Take a break and restore your calm.

Energy Center: Solar plexus

Mineral: Fire agate

Element: Fire

Magic & Mystery: At a lake in New South Wales a human skeleton estimated to be 7,000 years old was found wearing a necklace with 179 teeth genetically assessed to have been taken from forty-nine different Tasmanian Devils.

Tasmanian Devil makes its home in Tasmania and Australia. It is a solitary creature that is active at night. During the day, it conceals itself under dense vegetation. A carnivorous marsupial, it is just twenty inches long and weighs no more than twenty-five pounds. It has tremendous strength in its jaw, which is proportional to its massive head, and very sharp teeth. Of all the animals in the world, its bite is the most crushing. It is also known for its devilish screams and imposing growls. It uses its long whiskers to detect its prey in the darkness and, if bothered or agitated, releases a pungent odor similar to Skunk. When agitated, it goes into a rage that causes its ears to turn red. It can seem intimidating because it has no fear of fighting for what it wants. An opportunist, Tasmanian Devil will scavenge for dead prey of other animals before spending time hunting on its own. Its diet is customarily small mammals, fish, and frogs, but it eats whatever it comes across without discretion, even garbage.. Stories about the fierceness of Tasmanian Devil told by the European sailors that first encountered it are greatly exaggerated; in fact, it rarely kills anything.

Aboriginal witches in Australia used to call on Tasmanian Devil, which they know as Purinina, to learn people's secrets and for support in astral projection. Tasmanian Devil was seen as an invincible spiritual ally that could help them overcome any hardship or adversity. Aboriginals tell a mythical story of how Tasmanian Devil got a white stripe on its chest. After showing unbecoming behavior, the spirits scolded Tasmanian Devil by placing Clematis blossoms on its chest, leaving a large white mark that would lessen its ability to hide at night and warn other animals of its approach.

It is unfortunate that records of the relationship between the indigenous people to the fascinating creatures that exist on the Island of Tasmania are so sparse. Evidence suggests that humans have lived there for around 40,000 years--perhaps arriving via a Paleolithic era land or ice bridge. They ended up isolated there when the sea levels rose and cut them off from the Australian mainland.

The Tasmanian Devil shared that its cries in the night are warnings of bad spirits that could make their way into dreams. The indigenous people of Tasmania used to spit their nightmares into the blue gum flower, which they would then wrap up in the leaves of the plant and place in the forest. They believed Tasmanian Devil would find these at night and eat them, thus removing any residual fear after a bad dream. As a Power Animal, Tasmanian Devil would only allow higher vibrational spirits passage to the island. This was reassuring to Aboriginal mothers, who would sing lullabies to their children, knowing they were being encircled with protective energy that would keep them safe.

Tasmanian Devil is a great teacher about death and helps us to understand the transition of the soul, assuring us that even though the body is gone, the soul always makes its way to the afterlife. Our bodies are really no more than a vehicle for this important part of us. Tasmanian Devil also brings us a lesson of the use of power and intimidation. It is a great responsibility to carry power of any kind, especially the power of words. These should be carefully chosen so as not to undermine others. There is a high price to pay in the spirit world for verbal abuse.

SHAMAN'S INTENTION: *HELP ME TO UNDERSTAND THE POWERS OF INTIMIDATION AND HUMILITY*

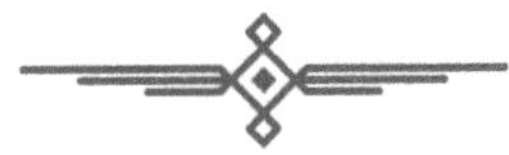

THUNDERBIRD

THE UNKNOWN | **HONOR** | **CREATION**

"There is so much more in the cosmos than we can imagine. With such vastness, our only option is to trust the Universe."—Thunderbird

In the legends and stories of various indigenous cultures from the Pacific Northwest of North America, Thunderbird is described as a bird with a massive wingspan and large claws that has the ability to control rain, thunder, wind, and lightning. The Sioux word for Thunderbird, *Wakyq*, means "sacred winged being." According to the Sioux, Thunderbird lives high in cloud-covered mountains. The Algonquian say Thunderbird is an ancestor, creator of the Universe and human beings. Other tribes believe Thunderbird is a master bird who protects a powerful egg from which hatch all types of birds. To all these tribes, Thunderbird is the most dominant force in nature and needs to be honored and satisfied so it won't become destructive. In times gone by, when thunder was heard, to them it meant a war would be coming. And if a war was already being fought, it meant victory was near.

Thunderbird's ability to control the weather makes it a benefactor, since rain is needed to nurture food crops. The Sioux Sundance ceremony is based on the legend of Thunderbird. In the center of the ceremonial arena is a pole that holds a nest for Thunderbird, an honored messenger to Great Spirit. Participants engage in acts of self-sacrifice to receive its charity.

Other ceremonies conducted by members of different tribes wearing headdresses made of Eagle feathers were traditionally done to ensure the victory of Thunderbird over Snake (master of the water spirits), so as to prevent flooding or devastation by water for the year. The Ojibwe say that Thunderbird was created by Nanabozho, the spirit of creation and brother of the four directions. According to them, a different Thunderbird lives in each of the four directions and these birds guide all the other birds back to their nesting places in spring. The Lakota believed Thunderbird was the giver and taker of life and called it *Wakinyan Tanka*.

Some Native Americans smoke tobacco with cedarwood pipes to honor Thunderbird, hoping the smoke will lift their souls, so they can find it in the Upper World and secure its assistance. In this way, warriors can achieve victory against their enemies. Myths saw Thunderbird as carrying the Sun in its eyes; when its eyes opened in the morning, the Sun would rise; and when its eyes closed at night, the Sun would set. In many tribes of the Pacific Northwest, people carved Thunderbird at the top of their totem poles as a sign that it would accompany the souls of the dead to the afterlife.

According to Thunderbird, anything that can exist in our imaginations—like it—is real in another dimension of reality. Though we cannot see it with our bare eyes, Thunderbird is proud to be honored with visits during shamanic journeys. As a Power Animal, it can lift you to new heights of purity and integrity. When you elevate yourself to a higher perspective, you can live a life that makes you impervious to the negative influences of others. Going solo in any endeavor gives you this higher view, as from solitude you can perceive truth more easily. By ignoring the dogma of the world around you or making a retreat, you can practice realization of self. Thunderbird is a being of power, call upon it to uplift you and help you to see beyond what you normally see. With its great wings, Thunderbird can embrace you and facilitate your journey into your heart.

POWERS OF THUNDERBIRD

Call in Thunderbird for:

- Help to develop authority over things that weaken you.
- Support to tame negative energy and convert it into optimism for the future.
- Connecting to the world of ascended beings for spiritual enlightenment.

AWARENESS FROM THUNDERBIRD

If Thunderbird comes into your life:

- You may be in the dark about what is going on around you.
- This may be a time of trials and tribulations and you need support to sort it out.
- You need to go the distance with matters that concern you.

Energy Center: Crown

Mineral: Morganite

Element: Air

Magic & Mystery: Several tribes from the Pacific Northwest believe that Thunderbird could easily carry Whale in its claws.

SHAMAN'S INTENTION: *TEACH ME THE POWERS OF THE UNIVERSE AND HOW I CAN UTILIZE THESE FORCES FOR GOOD*

TIGER

GUIDANCE **NOBILITY** **EMOTION**

"Sense the world around you and you will always walk in step with nature and its virtues."—Tiger

Tiger is a big cat that lives in fourteen Asian countries, including China and Russia. India is home to 60 percent of the world's population of this animal. Tiger prefers to live in dense forests where it walks quietly stalking its prey. Tiger is elusive despite being the largest feline on our planet; it can weigh up to 800 pounds and leap twenty feet. Its night vision is six times more powerful than a human and it is most active at dusk and nighttime. To sharpen its claws, Tiger claws on tree bark. Its tongue is as rough as sandpaper and would tear human skin with one lick. Its saliva has a built-in antiseptic that serves to heal its wounds. Tiger is so strong that it is able to dominate animals four times its size. Its teeth are impressive and with its strong jaws it can crush anything it bites, yet it is gentle when lifting one of its cubs to carry it to safety. Mostly solitary, with its striped coat it blends easily into the shadows and grasses of its environment. Tiger enjoys water and is a good swimmer. It finds a cool dip in a river or lake an enjoyable way to avoid the heat. Each Tiger has a signature formation of stripes and patterns. No two have the same patterns.

As a Power Animal, Tiger represents strength. Its presence as a shamanic benefactor has been woven into the legends of Asian culture for thousands of years. It is said that Tiger brings food to people who are lost in the forest and that it fights evil, protecting whole villages of people. The Chinese see Tiger as possessing yin (feminine) energy, a protector for the home. Tzai Shen Yeh, their ancient god of wealth, was often depicted as riding atop Tiger. It is also viewed as the rival of Dragon. Shamanically, Tiger represents matter whereas Dragon represents spirit. Many ancient tombs had images of Tiger etched into them to protect the deceased from bad spirits. Tiger rids everything it touches of evil and guards everything that is good. Tiger is one of the twelve signs of Chinese astrology and associated with the quality of flow.

As a Power Animal, Tiger represents strength. Its presence as a shamanic benefactor has been woven into the legends of Asian culture for thousands of years.

In Indochina, the indigenous Moi people worship Tiger, respectfully calling it his Eminence and my Lord. Tiger is seen as royalty, and they believe the markings on its forehead resemble twang, the character in their pictographic alphabet that means "king."

Traditionally, shamans work with Tiger to access the Lower World and converse with the deceased. Tiger is also a spiritual guide to visit the Milky Way. In India, the ten-armed Hindu goddess Durga rides a Tiger named Damon. Emblematic of higher virtues, she can help us to control emotions that can generate evil, such as anger, arrogance, jealousy, and greed. The view is that the tamed Tiger within each of us will help us to manage these qualities. In Vietnam there is a temple in every village honoring Tiger. The altars have offerings to Five Tigers of Protection, differentiated by the colors yellow, blue, black, red, and white. Koreans believed that a white Tiger has arrived at enlightenment and therefore changes color. In Java, where Tiger no longer exists in physical form, Tiger is seen as the guardian of the Tree of Life.

Tiger shares that the sound of human footsteps is bitterly perceived by members of the animal kingdom because we appear to be endowed with a mindset bent on the destruction of all others life forms—even our own. Aggressiveness is bred into all beings that compete for dominance. Tiger speaks as one of the most dominant beings in the food chain. It wants us to ask ourselves why we are so hostile to animals. Tiger would have us align with Mother Earth and shift the rivers of resentment we seem to feel toward animals to a new course. The bloodlust of humanity for animals will cause us to wither away into the darkness. It is time for a new wave of being. Humankind can only learn the sacred when we walk beside the animals, being peaceful and gentle with each step. To find equality there can be no separation. Tiger asks us to take his noble words of wisdom and share them with others. You have been chosen as a messenger. This cosmic advice is for the highest good of all beings on our planet.

POWERS OF TIGER

Call in Tiger for:

- A strong perspective on where to take your next step.
- Enhancement of your leadership qualities.
- Experiencing oneness with nature.

AWARENESS FROM TIGER

If Tiger comes into your life:

- You can be overpowering, so lighten your approach.
- Seek to understand other points of view; you do not know it all.
- Be willing to be guided past any limiting beliefs.

Energy Center: Third eye

Mineral: Tiger's eye

Element: Fire

Magic & Mystery:

- Tiger is depicted in numerous Neolithic cave paintings discovered throughout India.
- Siberian shamans believe Tiger could transform itself into a human being.
- Tigers need space and a diverse habitat, they are a powerful force that roams in nature.
- The Tigris river was named for Tiger because of its swift waters.
- Tiger has been a "vehicle" for many Buddhist and Hindu Gods.

TOUCAN

EXPRESSION | **HAPPINESS** | **SPIRIT**

"Your world is much less complicated than your mind tells you."
—Toucan

Over forty different species of Toucan live in the tropical rainforests of the Caribbean, Central America, and South America. Most have black feathers, short, thick necks, and small wings—they cannot travel long distances. Toucan's throat is covered by white and yellow feathers. Its oversized bill is usually multicolored. When it is flying outstretched, the bill of Toucan is a full half of its length. Toucan lives in a small flock of usually no more than six birds. It prefers to live high in the trees and rarely walks on the floor of the rainforest; however, its presence is not hidden as it keeps a continuous racket of conversation going with others of its kind. It has a court jester-like personality as it jokes around with its companions, throwing things, playing catch, and tossing berries into the air that it catches in its bill. During mating season, Toucan will throw food at its prospective partner. To sleep, Toucan must tuck its large bill under its wings, which makes it appear to be a ball of feathers. Its diet is fruit based although it will eat insects and small reptiles, too. In some places, Toucan is called the "flying banana" as its colorful appearance is so striking.

The ancient Incas and Mayans revered Toucan as a tribal totem and their shamans used it as an ally in their travel to the Lower World. The ancient Aztecs believed that Toucan was the god of rain. They also believed that their colorful bill was a gift from the spirit world for being such great messengers. Elaborate rain dances were performed by dancers wearing headdresses of Toucan feathers. Toucan feathers were thought to bring abundance and prosperity.

According to Toucan, it isn't necessary to travel the world to find yourself, as often the answers you seek are right at the tip of your nose. Embrace integrity with yourself and avoid making excuses. Toucan empowers us to see our true colors and to shine a light on what we do not want to see. Often, we deceive ourselves into thinking we are not worthy. Believe that you have purpose and will always have the capacity for divine potential.

Toucan also encourages us to let go of the past, so it no longer colors the present. Toucan is always going forward not back. Don't linger with things that are finished or completed, it is simply a message that it is time to move on.

POWERS OF TOUCAN

Call in Toucan for:

- Excellence as a public speaker or communicator.
- Brightening your life with more color.
- Gliding through life with ease and little effort.

AWARENESS FROM TOUCAN

If Toucan comes into your life:

- It is time to design a more interesting social life, one with perhaps fewer but higher quality friends.
- Ask for help.
- It is time to lighten up and have fun!

Energy Center: Throat

Mineral: Blue opal

Element: Air

Magic & Mystery: Tucana is a constellation of stars in the southern sky named after Toucan.

SHAMAN'S INTENTION: *OPEN MY MIND TO THE INFLUENCE OF COLOR IN OUR WORLD*

TURKEY

GRATITUDE **MANIFESTATION** **CLARITY**

"You are a gift."—Turkey

Turkey evolved on our planet eleven million years ago or more. Indigenous to North America and Central America it was domesticated by the Aztecs and Mayan before any European settlers arrived. Turkey is a ground-dwelling bird that has a large fan-shaped tail and pink legs. Its head and neck can change color instantly depending on its level of stress. When excited the male head turns blue, and when it is ready to fight it turns red. Turkey is smart, sensitive, and social and is able to with others of its kind and show affection. While the male Turkey is famous for his gobble, it also makes many other sounds and can recognize another Turkey by its voice. When clucking, Turkey sounds like it is gossiping. Females make small chirping noises. Although spending most of its time walking, it has the ability to fly up to sixty miles per hour. It has better than 20/20 vision. When the Sun goes down Turkey will head for a tree branch at a safe height to sleep.

For ancient Native Americans, Turkey was a symbol of abundance and fertility and often sacrificed as gratitude for bounty. Turkey was given as a gift to friendly tribes. This practice is still a part of the Thanksgiving holidays in North America. Turkey has a reputation for being proud, wily, shy, and elusive. Turkey feathers are often used in headdresses and rituals. The Caddo of the southeastern United States traditionally would sing and perform a Turkey dance to honor their warriors. After floods, the Navajo say Turkey dives into the Lower World to get new seeds for their crops. The Pima Indians of Arizona and Mexico know Turkey as a rain spirit that is able to predict the weather. Turkey gets agitated by the arrival of a storm. In the ancient Aztec and Mayan worlds, Turkey was honored in several festivals. The trickster god Tezcatlipoca would shapeshift into a jeweled Turkey that would help the people cleanse themselves of guilt and remorse.

As a Power Animal, Turkey can help work you with your intentional manifestations. Turkey is a guide to gratitude and the mystery of its power to fulfill the potentials in our lives. Gratitude is a vital way we can nourish ourselves and is essential for receiving the gifts of community and connection. Our brilliance comes when we are willing to be truthful about our deepest desires. Turkey can help you to give and receive in proper balance. Turkey is a master of the art of giving. Pure giving is to be thankful and expect nothing in return.

POWERS OF TURKEY

Call in Turkey for:

- Help to practice gratitude.
- Expressing generosity to those who may need your inspiration.
- Fine-tuning your ability to manifest your desires.

AWARENESS FROM TURKEY

If Turkey comes into your life:

- You may be sensing a storm coming toward you. Get prepared.
- It is time to release guilty feelings and clear your thoughts.
- Be willing to receive whatever the Universe brings to you.

Energy Center: Third eye

Mineral: Fulgurite

Element: Earth

Magic & Mystery:

- Some Native American creation stories say that Turkey created the world.
- Turkey is prone to heart attacks as it does not do well with stress.
- Each Turkey has over 5,000 feathers.

SHAMAN'S INTENTION: *BE MY GUIDE TO FREEDOM FROM GUILT AND WORRY*

TURTLE

SURVIVAL | **DILIGENCE** | **PROTECTION**

"Hurrying gets you nowhere fast."
—Turtle

Turtle survived the last ice age. Its fossils date back over 220 million years. The largest is Leatherback Turtle, which weighs 1,500 pounds; the littlest fits in the palm of a hand. It appears in every imaginable color and has three hearts. It loves water and has webbed feet or flippers. Terrestrial Turtle and Sea Turtle can be found in every climate. Sea Turtle spends all of its time in the ocean except to go to the beach for laying eggs. Freshwater Turtle enjoys hanging out near ponds, creeks, and lakes and likes to sunbathe on warm rocks. Tortoise is purely a land dweller. Turtle is not highly social but is fine if others of its kind are around. It is rather noisy. Some species make sounds like little motors, others bark like Dog, and one type of Tortoise from South America makes clucking sounds, like Chicken.

Sea Turtle will participate in thousand-mile migrations to find cooler feeding and nesting places to lay its eggs. After mating with the male, the female Turtle lays about one hundred fertilized eggs in the sand and then simply walks away. Turtle does not nurture its young. In two months, the young Turtle hatches and is on its own to protect itself as it makes its way back to the ocean.

Many ancient and indigenous cultures worldwide feature Turtle in their cosmology. In the Iroquois creation myth, the Great Spirit creates the world from the shell of a giant Turtle that is casted into the waters. For this reason, many Native peoples refer to North America as Turtle Island. Each part of Turtle's anatomy represents an aspect of Earth or the Universe. Turtle's body is Earth and the shell is the heavens all around it, protecting it. The base of the shell is the horizon over which the Sun and Moon rise and set. The top shell holds an outline of the topography. For the Plains Indians, Turtle is symbolic of longevity and protection. In times past, they would often sew a newborn girl's umbilical cord into the figure of Turtle to ensure her health and safety. In

> IN THE IROQUOIS CREATION MYTH, THE GREAT SPIRIT CREATES THE WORLD FROM THE SHELL OF A GIANT TURTLE THAT IS CASTED INTO THE WATERS.

the Mayan creation story, the gods grew corn out of a crack in Turtle's back. In the ruins of the city of Copan, there is a Turtle altar. In Hindu legends, the world sits on the backs of four elephants standing on a Turtle shell. Indigenous Hawaiians say Sea Turtle guided the first voyagers who arrived in their homeland.

Many cultures see Turtle as the master of longevity since it lives an average of a hundred years. In ancient Egypt, Nile Turtle was associated with warding off evil and anything that could compromise health. People made protection amulets from Turtle shell. The ancient Chinese viewed Turtle as divine. They admired its slow and steady progress and easygoing character, which is like that of hermit sages whose legends say they lived peaceful immortal lives for thousands of years, as they were removed from the troubles of the world. Ancient Chinese shamans would use the underbelly of Turtle to do psychic readings, believing this part of the shell was a map of the cosmos and the history of the lifetimes of our souls.

As a Power Animal, Turtle is in touch with Mother Earth and the tides of the seas. From Turtle, we can learn a quiet appreciation of the world. It is wise because of its connection to all nature and its ability to move slowly enough to absorb knowledge everywhere it goes. When Turtle accidentally flips and ends up lying flat on its back in a vulnerable way, the lesson for us is to be willing to let others help us turn right side up sometimes. Turtle protects itself by retracting its head and legs inside its shell, which it closes tightly. Sometimes a tactical retreat is necessary. But we also need to come out of the dark once danger has passed and shine brightly in the world.

Do not get caught up in insignificant details. Ignore the limitations you perceive that come with a sense of competition and do not allow them to stifle opportunity. Too many people see themselves as incapable or lacking the ability to compete and win. They sit out the game, as life passes them by. If you wait until the end of your life to participate all that will be left is the regret of wondering what could have been. Call upon Turtle to help you boost your confidence and overcome procrastination.

TORTOISE

POWERS OF TURTLE

Call in Turtle for:

- Wisdom about what is going on around you.
- Immunity against physical, verbal, and written attacks from others.
- Help to slow things down.

AWARENESS FROM TURTLE

If Turtle comes into your life:

- You may be expressing too much concern about trivial matters.
- It would be beneficial if you were more nurturing of others.
- Remember that your home is inside of you, no matter where you are.

Energy Center: Third eye

Mineral: Dumortierite

Element: Water and earth

Magic & Mystery:

- A Chinese birthday wish is "May Turtle and Crane give you a long life."
- According to Thai folklore, freeing a pet Turtle back into the wild will free you from sadness.
- The Vietnamese say that seeing Turtle means your plans will be delayed.
- Turtles origin is the sea. Eons ago they learned to live on the land adapting their fins for legs.
- Turtle is associated with fertility and the lunar "yin".

SHAMAN'S INTENTION: *HELP ME TO UNDERSTAND THE MYSTERY OF THE CREATION OF THE PLANET*

UNICORN

FREEDOM | **MYSTERY** | **KINDNESS**

"In your imagination lives the human kaleidoscope."—Unicorn

In the imagination lives Unicorn, a horse with magical powers and energy that has a single, spiral horn coming from its forehead. Its coat may be white, silver, and gold. Its eyes are usually light blue or purple. It may have a beard like Goat, or a tail like Lion. As beautiful as it is mysterious, it would be impossible to capture or tame Unicorn. In Medieval European art, it is often depicted with a broken chain around its neck, showing it has freed itself. From those times, it has retained a strong association with purity, innocence, and virginity. Unicorn's tears can heal issues of the heart and physical wounds. Its horn—or *alicorn*—is extremely hard, like a diamond, and can neutralize poison.

At one time, Unicorn did exist in the world we inhabit. Many civilizations left us an abundance of records proving it resided throughout the Middle East and Asia. Ancient Greek philosopher Aristotle mentioned Unicorn in his stories, as did many of his compatriots. The earliest surviving description of Unicorn is from a Greek physician that saw one while visiting Turkey in the fifth century; he verified that it was also seen by travelers from India. The ancient Turks referred to Unicorn as Karkadann. They reported that it was an aggressive animal that could outrun any other and would chase away every creature in its path. Unicorn holds a reputation of respect and reverence. It has always been a positive sign for humanity.

The Chinese call Unicorn Qilin and it holds a special place in their mythology. It is one of nine monsters who are children of Dragon. The Chinese believe Unicorn can only be seen by those who have been chosen or enlightened. To shamans that work energy similar to feng shui, it is a symbol for a life of joy. Unicorn is admired for being able to distinguish good from evil. It is considered such a kind and compassionate creature that it can eat grass without crushing the blades, walk on water and even fly. Unicorn's image is often carved on tombstones honoring its role as a psychopomp. But it is also known for bringing children to their parents when they are born.

If you can see Unicorn, it can make your wish come true. As a Power Animal, Unicorn comes from the Upper World to teach us to embrace strange and unseen things. Unicorn often appears to those who have a strongly creative approach to life. With the mystical alicorn that guides its third eye, it points us in the right direction and leads us on a tantalizing journey of intuition. But Unicorn does not tolerate lies. If you are discovered lying, it will pierce your heart with its horn to purify you. It invites us to cleanse ourselves of anything poisoning us and keeping us from healing our inner wounds. Related to the Moon and its feminine energy, Unicorn is a master of the knowledge of flower and plant essences and the resonance of the crystal kingdom. It also understands how to stimulate the heart and its innate knowing.

Only magic can take you into the world of mystery. Leave the shackles of your beliefs behind and embrace the colorful hues you see by looking through a new lens of possibility. Sprinkle your own version of fairy dust on any beliefs that you feel confine you to dissipate them. Unicorn invites you to gaze at the Moon and wonder. If you are able to use your imagination, there is no distance between the natural world and the Upper World where Unicorn lives.

POWERS OF UNICORN

Call in Unicorn for:

- Healing with color therapy.
- Pursuing your fascination with the unknown.
- Expanding your imagination.

AWARENESS FROM UNICORN

If Unicorn comes into your life:

- Release thoughts that are poisoning you.
- Break free of the chains of whatever is keeping you from being amazing.
- Include the spirit world in your daily life.

Energy Center: Third eye

Mineral: Alexandrite

Element: Spirit

Magic & Mystery:

- Chinese legend says that the voice of Unicorn sounds like a bell from a monastery.
- In the Middle Ages, Unicorn would aid married couples in procreation.

SHAMAN'S INTENTION: *TRAVEL WITH ME TO A PLACE OF MYSTERY WHERE I CAN DRINK THE ELIXIR OF THE UNKNOWN*

WASP

ORGANIZATION | **STRATEGY** | **ASSOCIATION**

"In all that you do, believe in the power of creation."—Wasp

Often called Yellow Jacket or Hornet, Wasp is a winged insect. There are over 100,000 different kinds located around the world that come in all shapes, sizes, and colors. Every other type of insect on the planet has a corresponding Wasp that is its predator. The largest Wasp is Asian Giant Hornet, which is two inches long and has a wingspan of four and a half inches. Wasp's eyes are kidney shaped. It has six legs, a pair of antennae, and two pairs of wings that make a noticeable buzzing noise. The female Wasp stings. When Wasp delivers its sting or is killed, a chemical is released into the air that makes others of its kind become combative. You've heard the adage "Don't kick the hornet's nest"—and this is why. A Wasp community will swarm when aroused and attack anyone it perceives as a threat. A nest may house as many as 10,000 individuals. Some types of Wasp live in a social colony similar to a Beehive, where there is an egg-laying queen, workers, sexually undeveloped females, and male drones. Other types are solitary and create nests only for their own benefit. Wasp will travel a mile to find food.

In Africa, Wasp is a symbol of evolution. In Europe, Wasp is valued for being a pollinator and is traditionally associated with fertility. Siberian shamans that shapeshift will often assume the form of Wasp. In Mongolia, shamans sometimes hide their souls in Wasp. The ancient Mayan name for the Planet Venus is XUX Ek, which means "Wasp star." The Mayans saw Venus as a god. Wasp helps shamans predict the weather. If there are a lot of Wasps in the evening, the next day will be warm; and if they enter their nests at night a storm is coming. The Warao people, who live in the Orinoco Delta of Venezuela, use the image of Wasp to provoke rain.

Wasp is very much tied into the universal field and the sacred geometry that underlies matter in our Universe. Its nests are built in the form of a hexahedron. Some Native Americans believe Wasp created the entire planet. For them, it symbolizes structure, organization, and productivity. In South America, Wasp is thought a hero for showing human beings how to build houses and make pottery—in those regions design takes the round shape of a Wasp nest, which looks like a papier mâché ball.

In Latin America, healing shamans will often call upon Wasp to protect them when they are performing a ritual of extraction—meaning, the removal of disease caused by bad energy stuck in the body. They will ask for two Wasp spirits to be in their mouths so that they are protected when they suck the negative energy out of the body.

Wasp sees most of us going about our lives in a frenzy, with no place to land and treating nothing as sacred. As a Power Animal, Wasp encourages us to build sacred spaces, to go out into the world and search for objects that we can relate to and bring them to our altars. Wasp can be a welcome companion during your search for the sacred, as it can help you to find meaningful things that are sweet and of a high vibration. Wasp encourages us to excavate any resentment from our being. Resentment destroys our ability to work in common purpose. It also keeps us from having a positive experience of our productivity. All of us are given distinct gifts. Life is about melting these gifts together, like liquid waxes that pool and then are molded into candles. We can see our own potential in the flames of illumination that come from lighting up the collective consciousness. Wasp says: "Do not fear words from others that criticize and sting the heart, as these are only signs of their frustration with themselves. Never feel bitten, instead spend time discovering the underlying reason for the animosity of others. Once you learn it, you won't experience pain."

POWERS OF WASP

Call in Wasp for:

- Help in organizing a team.
- Support in working on projects that are mutually beneficial.
- Fertilizing your plans and ideas.

AWARENESS FROM WASP

If Wasp comes into your life:

- You may be tempted to gang up on others—but don't do it!
- You may need to be more aware of the impact of sugar on your health.
- If feeling harassed, try to understand the motivations of others to create balance and calm.

Energy Center: Sacrum

Mineral: Tiger iron

Element: Fire

Magic & Mystery: In the Republic of Mali, Mason Wasp is the symbol of an elite shaman.

WEASEL

CURIOSITY | **SPONTANEITY** | **ENTERTAINMENT**

"It is important not to take life too seriously."—Weasel

FERRET, MINK, POLECAT, STOAT

POWERS OF WEASEL

Call in Weasel for:

- Help to amass savings.
- Support related to socializing and having fun.
- A guide to enter other realms to find that which is hidden.

AWARENESS FROM WEASEL

If Weasel comes into your life:

- You may be acting too lazy or relying too much on others.
- Resist the temptation to take that which is not yours.
- Your curiosity may be getting the best of you. Remember that some things are best left as they are.

Energy Center: Root

Mineral: Jasper

Element: Earth

Magic & Mystery:

- In the construction industry, Ferret is often used to transport cables through pipes.
- Queen Elizabeth I of England owned an albino Ferret, which appears with her in one of her portraits.

There are seventeen types of Weasel, including Polecat, Stoat, and Ferret. In Latin, the word *ferret* means "little thief" since stealing and hiding things—aka *ferreting them away*—is one of Weasel's typical behaviors. It is a hoarder because its wild ancestors would cache the carcasses of its prey if there was more than enough for one meal. Ferret has been domesticated for almost 2,500 years. It was originally used for hunting Rabbit, Mouse, and Mole and now is primarily kept as a pet. Weasel is clever and can find what is missing. It uses observation and scent to *ferret out* what it is hunting. The ancient Egyptians found Weasel especially useful to rid barns and ships of rodents.

Weasel is happy to live in a group. It is lively and will perform a "war dance" full of hops and twists, encouraging others of its kind to play with it. When it is happy, it chirps or clucks. As a Power Animal, Weasel can help you bring out your inner warrior and strengthen your confidence and survival instincts. It is a survivor and can endure many obstacles. The Hob (male) will mate with as many Jill (female) as possible. The Black-footed Ferret was almost extinct and now is alive and well and keeps the Prairie Dog population balanced.

At birth, the Weasel kit is deaf and blind. It begins to hear and see at around thirty-four days old. The grown Ferret remains nearsighted but compensates for this with keen senses of smell and hearing. It is curious and has an active mind that needs stimulation. Weasel sleeps almost eighteen hours a day, and often so deeply that trying to rouse it yields little reaction; it appears dead. It hisses when agitated and can exude a strange, unpleasant odor from its scent glands. When it is frightened, it acts like Skunk, raising its bushy tail and letting out this musty-smelling scent to ward off predators, even as it is running for shelter.

As a Power Animal, Weasel brings a huge bundle of creativity and a keen intuition. Curiosity is valuable for creativity. Weasel will stimulate the creative centers of your brain and help you to birth new ideas. It will never hesitate to go below the surface to see what is hidden; maybe there it will find the inspiration that you need for your next project.

SHAMAN'S INTENTION: *I STIMULATE MY IMAGINATION, WHICH BRINGS JOY TO ME AND OTHERS*

WHALE

FREQUENCY **ANCESTRAL WISDOM** **BREATH**

"The intelligence is within you. Seek it to love the Earth and the animals and lift the spirit of everything around you."—Whale

Whale is the oldest living large mammal on the planet. A member of the order Cetacea, it is the descendant of land-based animals that returned to the oceans. Blue Whale, which is the largest animal ever to have lived on Earth, is longer than a basketball court and weighs 300,000 pounds. Just its tongue weighs the same as Elephant. The main source of food for Blue Whale is plankton that it captures in the rows of baleen in its mouth. Sperm Whale and Orca (also mistakenly referred to as Killer Whale) are the only types of Whale with teeth.

There is a matriarchal structure in a Whale pod, with a hierarchy of several generations that is respected by all its members. Whale communicates through complex sounds that include whistling, groaning, and squealing. During mating season the male sings a particular melody. The noises it makes are so loud they can be heard 500 miles away. Many Whale sounds are soothing to humans; they have an eerie gentleness that promotes feelings of sanctity. This sonically oriented creature relies on soundwaves in water to track its prey and avoid potential dangers. Whale must be awake to breathe, so only half of its brain sleeps at a given time.

Ancient coastal cultures saw Whale as a god and a guardian of the sea. As such, it was a symbol of love, compassion, and family. In China, the mythical Yu-kiang was a creature that looked like a Whale, but with hands and feet. When angry it would transform into a bird and cause terrible storms in the oceans. In Vietnam a shrine was built when a Whale died, and a funeral was staged. Tribes in the Pacific Northwest of the United States and Canada have always respected Whale for its great wisdom and spiritual connection to all things. The Haida people honored Orca as the most powerful animal in the ocean and thought it shapeshifted into a human being when it went underwater. A Haida that drowned was said to go to live with Orca in its house under the sea. The Kwakwaka'wakw believed Orca ruled the sea and that Seal was its slave and Dolphin its warrior. Whale hunters were said to turn into Whales upon their death. Special rituals were done to ensure that their spirits would be saved so they could be reborn as humans again. The Tlingit of southern Alaska knew that Orca never kills humans so they never hunted it.

According to the legends of the Yupik of Siberia, Orca appears as Wolf in the winter and Wolf appears as Orca in the summer. When traveling in the ocean, tobacco was thrown into the sea to honor Orca. In Iceland, Blue Whale was known as the protector of small fishing boats and it was counted on to drive away any other "evil" Whale. The Australian Aborigines believed that

WHALE

FREQUENCY | ANCESTRAL WISDOM | BREATH

THERE IS A MATRIARCHAL STRUCTURE IN A WHALE POD, WITH A HIERARCHY OF SEVERAL GENERATIONS THAT IS RESPECTED BY ALL POD MEMBERS.

BELUGA, HUMPBACK, ORCA

POWERS OF WHALE

Call in Whale for:

- Help to establish a state of inner peace.
- Connecting to the magnetic field of the Universe.
- Entraining to the vibration of love.

AWARENESS FROM WHALE

If Whale comes into your life:

- Heal yourself before attempting to heal others.
- Release anything that does not support your empowerment.
- Seek ancestral knowledge.

Energy Center: Heart

Mineral: Brookite

Element: Water

Magic & Mystery:

- The Iñupiat people of the Arctic talk to Whale and have great knowledge of its inner feelings. They have been consulted by scientists for information.
- The Inuit tribes of Alaska perform ceremonies inside a circle of Whale bones.
- In Alaska, Native people used to carry amulets made from Whale bones. Hunters placed these face down in their boats to flatter and attract Whale during their hunts.

Whale would bring them joy. The Nivkhi people of the Amur River, which today forms the border between Russian and China, hunted only White Whale. Before it was eaten, they covered its head with grass in honor of its sacrifice. Afterward, its eyes were buried with these ritual grasses near their village.

Whale is related to the depths of our subconscious, our memories, our emotions, and the Lower World. Since Whale is a mammal, we come from the same ancestors. Its extraordinary eyes give us the feeling of meeting a pure source of higher intelligence, something that we know exists but rarely tap into ourselves. Oddly, Whale does not see the ocean as blue, but as shades of gray. Because of the iron oxide in its brain, Whale can discern and follow the magnetic fields and ley lines of the Earth. By embodying the vibration of love, as a Power Animal it can guide us to heal our hearts. Whale can help you develop the courage to go within and search your feelings, to breathe and tune in to them so you may release whatever is necessary to sense your wholeness again. Whale resonates joy and will coax out your anger and bitterness and help you otherwise to step out of a state of misery. Its message is to love yourself and start developing a new blueprint for your happiness.

Whale shares: "The only thing that separates humanity from Whale is your inability to swim. Humans are ignorant of the vastness of the ocean, which comprises seventy percent of the planet. The ocean is our home, yet you treat it like a landfill. You have hunted, killed, and consumed us, which makes no sense as my kind feels we are the brothers and sisters of humanity. We are shifting the vibration of the ocean we travel through to the frequency of compassion. Emotions come in waves and are constantly crashing onto the shores of your hope for transformation. If you could only resonate with the vibration of love, something so elusive to so many humans, it would transmute you. This is the vibration of oneness in which no one exists as self."

Whale is a member of a conclave of Power Animals that have the capacity to adjust our consciousness. It is helping bring rainbow and crystal children to the wombs of earthly women. Whale is their spiritual mother and father, guiding them before birth. These millions of crystal structures will grow and illuminate the landscape of our hearts and minds. If you work with Whale, you can assist in this mission on behalf of humankind. We must nurture these beings to save all those who walk on the planet and avoid the extinction of all things.

SHAMAN'S INTENTION: *HELP ME TO SHIFT MY INTERPRETATION OF THE PAST AND SEE THE WORLD THROUGH THE EYES OF THE PRESENT*

WOLF

TRUST | **CLAN** | **GUIDANCE**

"Everyone is put on their path for a purpose."
—Wolf

Wolf has evolved on our planet for thirty-five million years. There are three species that live in North America, Europe, Africa, and Asia. Wolf is highly intelligent and has excellent instincts. Its body has exceptional stamina because of its powerful back and legs that can sustain it for long journeys. It can cover several miles quickly, trotting six miles per hour. Wolf lives in a pack led by an alpha male and an alpha female who manage the activities of the "tribe." Wolf is a loyal, lifelong partner to its mate and a wonderful parent and packmate. It will howl when getting ready for a hunt, calling out to a lost member of the pack, or when mourning the death of a companion. Wolf can distinguish the individual voice of each member of its pack. All its movements have meaning, whether the swooshing of its tail or the movement of its head. It has an excellent sense of smell, 100,000 times more perceptive than ours. Scent is another way Wolf communicates with others of its kind and finds its prey. Wolf is territorial and will meticulously mark boundaries, claiming its space and warding off members of competing packs. Its hearing is also exceptional; it's able to hear sounds as far as six miles away.

Because of its remarkable senses, the Celts relied on Wolf as a guardian spirit. In ancient Scotland, Gaelic goddess, Cailleach, rode Wolf. She was a destroyer and protector of everything wild. The ancient Welsh revered Cerridwen, goddess of the Moon, whose companion was Wolf. They believed Wolf ruled their lands in winter. That Wolf sources its power from the Moon gives Wolf knowledge unobtainable by most creatures. Legendary second-century Celtic hero Cormac mac Airt, the high king of Ireland, was said to have been raised by Wolf and to have spoken its language. He was accompanied by four Wolves wherever he went. In fifth-century England, the only companion that Merlin, the magician of Arthurian lore, had during his time spent as a

WOLF

TRUST | **CLAN** | **GUIDANCE**

hermit in the Forest of Ascetir was Wolf. He was deemed Lord of the Animals by the Druids.

The ancient Greek Sun and wind god Apollo was sometimes called Lycegenes ("born of Wolf"). The land around the Temple of Apollo in Delphi, which was adorned with a statue of Wolf, is known as the Wolf skin.

In shamanism, Wolf is known for being a powerful teacher. The shamanic journey is often referred to as a "Wolf trance." Such journeys serve to release the shaman's energy field so that it can be molded into Wolf, which then carries the shaman's consciousness into the Lower World. Wolf is also associated with death, in particular, how it clears the soul of the energy of its most recent lifetime so it may transition to an awakening and rebirth. Indigenous cultures saw Wolf as a Power Animal of bravery, fortitude, and devotion.

Many creation stories tell of how humans evolved from Wolf. Mongolians believe they are descendants of Wolf due to the legend of a human raised from infancy by Wolf who later fathered a litter of half-Wolf, half-human cubs with a she-Wolf. In North America, the Pueblo Indians see Wolf as one of the guardians of the six directions. They associate Wolf with the East and the color white. Traditionally, the Cherokee never hunted Wolf as they believed that its pack brothers would seek revenge on them if they did. They also believed that if a weapon was used to kill Wolf it would never work again.

Seeing Wolf tracks means you have a spirit teacher nearby. Call on Wolf if you need a powerful mentor. It knows many paths through the forest and can guide you. Wolf is energetically connected to the southern constellation Canis Major, the place where our ancestral spirit teachers live.

Wolf shares that because it walks on four legs it has the balance and strength to carry the burden of emotions. It invites us to look into its eyes and see beyond them to find a place where the stability of thinking resides. It knows us well, as it can read our thoughts. For this reason, it has little curiosity about us. Wolf sees our fears multiplying because we see the world as an adversary or competitor in a game that must be won. We spend most of our time fighting on the battlefields of life. Wolf hopes that we will instead seek a better way and nurture our intuition so that it may guide us. Relying on external forces is unpredictable and breeds fear, so we should tap into our inner guidance, which is flawless. The better part of who we are is always resonating with the footprints of Wolf.

BECAUSE OF ITS REMARKABLE SENSES, THE CELTS RELIED ON WOLF AS A GUARDIAN SPIRIT. IN ANCIENT SCOTLAND, GAELIC GODDESS CAILLEACH RODE WOLF. SHE WAS A DESTROYER AND PROTECTOR OF EVERYTHING WILD.

POWERS OF WOLF

Call in Wolf for:

- Waking the instincts that you need to tackle large problems.
- Help to build a relationship based on mutual respect.
- Getting moving. The answers come when you leave your comfort zone.

AWARENESS FROM WOLF

If Wolf comes into your life:

- Stabilize your thoughts and your thinking.
- You are now safe to get out of survival mode and trust.
- Neutralize adversarial relationships.

Energy Center: Third eye

Mineral: Phantom quartz

Element: Earth

Magic & Mystery:

- In Asia Wolf is the guard to heaven.
- In Japan people leave offerings of rice in small Shinto shrines to honor nature spirits, the *kamis*. They hope to appease kami, the Wolf spirit, to encourage it to hunt animal pests that roam among their crops.

SHAMAN'S INTENTION: *SUPPORT MY ABILITY TO MOVE THROUGH THE MIDDLE WORLD WITH EASE*

WOLVERINE

PERSISTENCE | **FEARLESSNESS** | **ADAPTABILITY**

"Don't diminish yourself; balance and bravery will bring you opportunities."—Wolverine

Wolverine, which looks like a small Bear, is the largest member of the Weasel family. It lives in regions near the Arctic that include grasslands and tundra, where it travels up to fifteen miles per day scavenging for food. It is stocky and muscular, weighing more than fifty pounds despite being only the size of a medium dog. Its paws and posture are designed so it can walk through deep snow. Thick, oily fur protects it from frostbite. Wolverine is fast, able to run at speeds of up to thirty miles per hour. With its powerful jaws and teeth, it can easily devour its prey, which normally consists of rabbits and rodents, although it may also take on larger animals if they are weak. Its eyesight is bad, but its other senses are excellent. Wolverine is solitary and moves about during the night. In his lifetime, the male will mate with different females and help raise the offspring. The character of Wolverine is persistent and brave. It never gives up or surrenders and defies all odds to survive in its harsh environment. A vicious fighter, it is wild and free.

In Native American stories, Wolverine is a trickster and entertainer. The Innu see it as a conniver that acts inappropriately. Because of its odor, some call it Skunk Bear. The Athabaskans of Alaska admire Wolverine for its tenacity so much so that they hang its teeth on their babies cradles as charms to endow them with these qualities. The tribes of northern California see Wolverine as a successful gambler and bringer of prosperity. As a Power Animal, Wolverine is able to travel between worlds. It is master of its surroundings and the ultimate guide to the wilderness. It has the reputation of being overly indulgent with a ferocious appetite. Some shamans use Wolverine medicine to temper revenge and dark magic. When necessary, Wolverine becomes aggressive and violent.

Wolverine brings us the message that it is the master of intention. Its sacred intention, which flows on a high vibration, makes it invisible as it walks. This power is available to us as well. Sacred intention is the motor for movement to the planet's diverse forests. In such places, all is available; there is no wanting or needing. If we rely on our instincts and intentions, there will be no scarcity and we will never be in need. The other shamanic power Wolverine brings to us is stealth—the ability to see the deeper, subtler meaning behind all that exists and expose that which is superficial.

POWERS OF WOLVERINE

Call in Wolverine for:

- Help to control what is going on around you.
- Lessons in the power of solitude.
- Moving through the world with confidence.

AWARENESS FROM WOLVERINE

If Wolverine comes into your life:

- You may be too anxious; it is time to promote calm.
- You may be over indulging in food and drink at the expense of your health.
- Don't give up; the best is yet to come.

Energy Center: Solar plexus

Mineral: White jade

Element: Fire

Magic & Mystery: Native Americans call Wolverine *Carcajou,* a French word meaning "evil spirit" or "mountain devil."

SHAMAN'S INTENTION: *SUPPORT MY DEDICATION TO THE WAYS OF THE SHAMAN*

WOMBAT

EMPATHY | **DETERMINATION** | **THOUGHT**

"Do not forget nurturing of self; go to the womb of Mother Earth who is always waiting for you."—Wombat

Wombat is a marsupial that lives in the southeastern coastal regions of Australia. It has big paws with impressive claws for digging down to the roots that it loves to eat. It also digs extensive burrow complexes where it spends the daylight hours. It mostly ventures out at night. Wombat prefers to inhabit damp forests and grasslands. It has a large, solid, stocky body with a big head and small eyes and weighs up to eighty pounds. Its coarse coat is gray-brown in color. Unlike its tree-hugging cousin, Koala, it spends time on the ground. A shell of cartilage on its rear end protects it from being bitten when its rump is sticking out of its burrow. Wombat walks with an awkward shuffle and yet can run very quickly when threatened. Its only real predator is Dingo. With its tank-like body of pure muscle, it walks through anything in its way.

Wombat is mostly solitary, although some species of Wombat live in colonies. Its Joeys spend the first four months of their lives being nurtured in their mother's pouch. Wombat has sharp, rodent-like teeth that never stop growing; yet, it rarely bites unless it feels threatened. Wombat is intelligent, determined, and stubborn. Wombat is also playful. It enjoys doing somersaults and shoulder rolls and has many ways of expressing pleasure in living. It was given its name by the Darug, the Aboriginals who were the original inhabitants of the land that Sydney, Australia is built upon. Wombat's burrowing is good for the soil. Many plants benefit from how it increases the soil's moisture content and aeration.

As a Power Animal, Wombat is about living in the now and enjoying the moment. It is a symbol of being connected to the Earth, like the Australian Aborigines, who know they are part of the land and that all living things share the same soul. The spirit of Wombat lives in the nonordinary reality that the Australian Aborigines refer to as the Dreamtime. Wombat honors the landscape that is its home and knows that it is always on hallowed ground. It expresses its gratitude as it emerges from the womb of Mother Earth every night. Wombat is accepting of diversity. It has lessons to teach about inclusivity and unity (aka nonduality), as it perceives the integrity in all that exists. The generous heart of Wombat shows us to express empathy for other beings without acting superior or always trying to be right. Its slow, meditative approach to life can help us take our time and be patient when making decisions.

Wombat shares with us the symbol of holding hands. Because of its thick skin, Wombat cannot feel the touch of another. It emphasizes the importance of placing a gentle hand on the back of a friend in need. Humans were given hands so that we would be able to give to others. Our reliance on touch is often ignored, yet contact is an important gesture of love and a powerful component of the sensory world. We all thrive from being embraced, as it helps to settle us and allows us to feel calm. Touch is our way of transmitting kindness. It is the hand that reaches out to others when they are drowning or unable to see their potential that matters. Wombat praises the shaman who coaches others on their walks through life, as so many people need a hand.

POWERS OF WOMBAT

Call in Wombat for:

- Increased appreciation for the comforts of home.
- Realization of your deep connection to Mother Earth.
- Extracting buried emotions that need resolution.

AWARENESS FROM WOMBAT

If Wombat comes into your life:

- You may need to show more sympathy for others.
- It is time to get out of your burrow and jump into life.
- Evaluate your forcefulness, as you may be acting overly protective.

Energy Center: Root

Mineral: Black jasper

Element: Earth

Magic & Mystery:

- A baby Wombat is the size of a jellybean when it is born.
- A Wombat group is known as a wisdom.

SHAMAN'S INTENTION: *TAKE ME TO THE LOWER WORLD AND TEACH ME THE NURTURING QUALITIES OF MOTHER EARTH*

WOODPECKER

DETERMINATION | SKILL | FOCUS

"Pecking away at your fears can clear the air for enlightenment."—Woodpecker

Over two hundred species of Woodpecker live on our planet in almost any habitat with lots of trees. Curiously though, it is not found in Australia, New Zealand, and Madagascar. Woodpecker comes in the colors of the rainbow. It has a very long tongue that, when retracted is long enough to, wrap around its head. The tongue has barbs on it that help Woodpecker extract insects from holes in trees and to lick up sap or raid the hives of nectar feeders such as Bee. Think of it as the carpenter of the bird kingdom, hammering out holes in trees to make its nests. Loyal to its partner, both the male and the female take on the responsibility of pecking to find food or create shelter. It can peck twenty times per second and its brain is protected by air pockets around its skull that ensure the vibration is not painful or wounding. It is easy to know when Woodpecker is around, as it is highly communicative and always extremely focused on its task. It puts a lot of effort into whatever it does.

The ancient Romans associated Woodpecker with Mars because it embodies the energy of initiative and mastery. The ancient Greeks said Woodpecker sat on the throne of their chief god, Zeus, a sacred position. The ancient Norse associated Woodpecker with Thor, the god of thunder and lightning, who wielded a hammer, because of the sound of its hammering. Later, European folklore said Woodpecker could predict the weather and that the quality of its pecking was a message of what was coming.

Inspired by the vision of its nest high up in the trees, far away from predators, Native Americans see Woodpecker as a protector of their homes. Some tribes hear Woodpecker's pecking as drumming to accompany a shamanic journey. The bird was seen as a shaman able to share messages and prophecy. To enter the spirit world Tribal shamans would imitate the sound of Woodpecker with their own drums. Woodpecker's pecking mimics the heartbeat of Mother Earth. The Lakota designed their flutes to look like Woodpecker's beak. Still other tribes related Woodpecker's pecking to the act of plowing the soil to grow crops because it is so efficient at getting what it wants with its beak.

Woodpecker is a medicine bird. Hearing it is a sign of friendship and happiness. Many Native Americans have worn its feathers in their traditional ceremonies and dances. The Sioux use it to speak to thunder or open up the gates to the spiritual worlds. The Cherokee use it to draw in the skill of making war. Some tribes have carved its likeness on totem poles. Long ago, Creek shamans would use a Woodpecker beak as a tool to extract penetrating objects from wounds.

Woodpecker is a guardian of the tree kingdom. Wherever it nests, it forms a special bond with the tree it inhabits. As a Power Animal, Woodpecker invites humanity to come together in a circle of rhythm and dance. In this circle you can ride the waves of energy into the multidimensional, non-ordinary realities visited by the shaman. It is impossible to go pecking deeply enough into what the psyche holds to uncover everything there is to know about yourself. You could spend a lifetime trying. To see who you really are as a spiritual being, at the core, you must learn to embrace your imperfections despite living in a culture where the beliefs may be stacked against you. Woodpecker can be your ally in this endeavor.

POWERS OF WOODPECKER

Call in Woodpecker for:

- Going deeper within to excavate your truth.
- Learning to journey with drum beats.
- Cultivating the belief that nothing is impossible.

AWARENESS FROM WOODPECKER

If Woodpecker comes into your life:

- It is time to dance to your own rhythm.
- Carve out your own space and spend some time alone.
- Destroy all the obstacles that your thinking creates.

Energy Center: Crown

Mineral: Spirit quartz

Element: Air

Magic & Mystery:

- Some Native American shamans put a necklace of Woodpecker feathers around someone who has been bitten by Rattlesnake to heal them.
- The Masai of Africa believe that if the pecking of Gray Woodpecker is heard in the right ear, it is a good omen. But heard in the left, it is a portent of evil.

SHAMAN'S INTENTION: *HELP ME TO EMBRACE AND CHERISH FRIENDSHIPS*

ZEBRA

FREEDOM **ILLUSION** **OPTIMISM**

"Embrace the unique and the random."—Zebra

Zebra is an impressive animal with an individual signature pattern of black and white stripes on its hide that lives in the grasslands and woodlands of eastern and southern Africa. Because it has an extremely sturdy body it sometimes has been called a Mule with stripes, but, in fact, Zebra evolved from Horse during the last four million years. The various species of Zebra reside in separate territories. Zebra has superb day and night vision and despite its black and white hide it sees the world in color. Wildebeest hangs out with Zebra because of its astute sense of hearing, smell, and taste. Zebra's ears are like lookouts, pivoting to hear sounds coming from all directions. To communicate Zebra uses facial expressions made with its eyes, lips, and teeth, and it will bark, snort, and huff, stamp its feet, and wag its tail. Running in a herd, Zebra stripes create an optical illusion that makes it more challenging for predators like Lion and Hyena to hunt it.

Zebra is a highly social animal that lives in large herds where members build strong bonds to each other over many years. Herd mates support each other through grooming and if one goes missing all go on a hunt to find it. Mostly, Zebra travels to find water and food and its pace is chosen to accommodate the energy level of the entire group. Zebra runs in a zigzag at speeds that can reach sixty-five miles per hour. Its most successful defense is running away, although it may also deliver a swift kick that's powerful enough to cause debilitating injury. Zebra refuses to be domesticated. It is the master of its own destiny.

The Karamajong of Uganda has a special dance where the women paint themselves with stripes and dance like Zebra. They wear Zebra masks to represent freedom, independence, and a free spirit. By contrast, the Songye of Central Africa use Zebra masks to exorcise negative forces. They believe the black fur of Zebra represents the qualities of purity, procreation, and beauty and its white fur represent the Moon, cassava flour, breast milk, and sperm. According to folklore, if a pregnant woman sees Zebra with more stripes on its front legs than its back legs this means she will have twin boys. Seeing one Zebra alone is a sign of many blessings to come.

As a Power Animal, Zebra is a sign of transparency and following a clear and balanced path in life and our endeavors. Its stripes represent the duality of right and wrong, good and bad—and the extreme polarities of the times we live in. Zebra embodies the freedom to embrace your individualism. Zebra believes that feeling safe—which comes from knowing that we are surrounded by compassion, abundance and prosperity—is our greatest treasure. This vibration of calmness nurtures and relaxes us. When you are safe, there is no need to be alert or to focus on self-preservation. This allows you to take off your cloak of resistance to being seen, taking risks, trusting, loving, and striving to attain your purpose and potential. You may then step into the world as your vibrant authentic self with assurance and without fear. The start of any journey can bring both excitement and the fear of the unknown. Therefore, go with those who want to take the path of enthusiasm. Do not look back. Move in the direction of the new and what is coming into being, as this is the destination where you will find renewal. Zebra can help you reveal and amplify your signature essence.

POWERS OF ZEBRA

Call in Zebra for:

- Help to acquire a clearer picture of your life.
- Celebrating your uniqueness.
- For grounding and acceptance.

AWARENESS FROM ZEBRA

If Zebra comes into your life:

- You may be running from issues that you need to confront head on.
- You may be acting too stubborn. Soften your resistance so you can embrace new ideas.
- It is time to shine. Step out of the herd and be noticed.

Energy Center: Solar plexus

Mineral: Zebra jasper

Element: Earth

Magic & Mystery:

- In many indigenous cultures the stripes of Zebra represent balance.
- During Africa's annual Great Migration of Wildebeest and other kinds of Antelope and Zebra, 20,000 Zebra travel three hundred miles between Tanzania and Kenya.

SHAMAN'S INTENTION: *SUPPORT ME IN UNDERSTANDING THE NEEDS OF MY COMMUNITY AND HOW I MAY BE OF SERVICE*

LIST OF ENDANGERED SPECIES

ADAPTED FROM THE WORLD WILDLIFE FEDERATION, WWW.WORLDWILDLIFE.ORG

COMMON NAME	CONSERVATION STATUS
Amur Leopard	Critically Endangered
Black Rhino	Critically Endangered
Bornean Orangutan	Critically Endangered
Cross River Gorilla	Critically Endangered
Eastern Lowland Gorilla	Critically Endangered
Hawksbill Turtle	Critically Endangered
Javan Rhino	Critically Endangered
Malayan Tiger	Critically Endangered
Mountain Gorilla	Critically Endangered
Orangutan	Critically Endangered
Saola	Critically Endangered
South China Tiger	Critically Endangered
Sumatran Elephant	Critically Endangered
Sumatran Orangutan	Critically Endangered
Sumatran Rhino	Critically Endangered
Sumatran Tiger	Critically Endangered
Vaquita	Critically Endangered
Western Lowland Gorilla	Critically Endangered
Yangtze Finless Porpoise	Critically Endangered
African Wild Dog	Endangered
Amur Tiger	Endangered
Asian Elephant	Endangered
Bengal Tiger	Endangered
Black-footed Ferret	Endangered
Blue Whale	Endangered
Bluefin Tuna	Endangered
Bonobo	Endangered
Borneo Pygmy Elephant	Endangered

COMMON NAME	CONSERVATION STATUS
Chimpanzee	Endangered
Fin Whale	Endangered
Galapagos Penguin	Endangered
Ganges River Dolphin	Endangered
Green Turtle	Endangered
Hector's Dolphin	Endangered
Humphead Wrasse	Endangered
Indian Elephant	Endangered
Indochinese Tiger	Endangered
Indus River Dolphin	Endangered
Irrawaddy Dolphin	Endangered
North Atlantic Right Whale	Endangered
Red Panda	Endangered
Sea Lions	Endangered
Sei Whale	Endangered
Sri Lankan Elephant	Endangered
Tiger	Endangered
Whale	Endangered
Whale Shark	Endangered
African Elephant	Vulnerable
Bigeye Tuna	Vulnerable
Black Spider Monkey	Vulnerable
Dugong	Vulnerable
Forest Elephant	Vulnerable
Giant Panda	Vulnerable
Giant Tortoise	Vulnerable
Great White Shark	Vulnerable
Greater One-Horned Rhino	Vulnerable
Hippopotamus	Vulnerable
Leatherback Turtle	Vulnerable
Loggerhead Turtle	Vulnerable
Marine Iguana	Vulnerable
Olive Ridley Turtle	Vulnerable
Polar Bear	Vulnerable
Savanna Elephant	Vulnerable
Sea Turtle	Vulnerable
Snow Leopard	Vulnerable
Southern Rockhopper Penguin	Vulnerable
Albacore Tuna	Near Threatened
Beluga	Near Threatened
Greater Sage-Grouse	Near Threatened
Jaguar	Near Threatened
Mountain Plover	Near Threatened
Narwhal	Near Threatened
Plains Bison	Near Threatened
White Rhino	Near Threatened

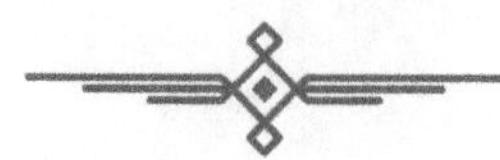

TABLE OF POWERS AND MINERALS

ANIMAL	POWERS	MINERAL
Aardvark	Groundedness / Protection / Uniqueness	Tangerine Quartz
Albatross	Freedom / Stamina / Vision	Mahogany Obsidian
Angelfish	Clarity / Truth / Joy	Charoite
Ant	Effort / Community / Endurance	Sunstone
Anteater	Communication / Profoundness / Resilience	Faden Quartz
Antelope	Awakening / Instinct / Agility	Emerald
Armadillo	Empathy / Protection / Seeking	Antigorite
Badger	Healing / Hardiness / Determination	Elestial Quartz
Barracuda	Disguise / Focus / Patience	Purple Fluorite
Bat	Achievement / Intuition / Prosperity	Azurite
Bear	Confidence / Renewal / Patience	Zoisite
Beaver	Intelligence / Hard Work / Confidence	Petrified Wood
Bee	Collaboration / Determination / Productivity	Septarian
Beetle	Eternity / Rebirth / Persistence	Axinite
Blackbird	Mystery / Psychic Gifts / Transition	Charoite
Bluebird	Truth / Confidence / Optimism	Lapis Lazuli
Blue Jay	Confidence / Potential / Wisdom	Amber
Boar	Focus / Valor / Groundedness	Aragonite
Bobcat / Lynx	Discernment / Quietude / Stealth	Banded Agate
Buffalo	Abundance / Groundedness / Commitment	Turquoise
Butterfly	Transformation / Immortality / Love	Strawberry Quartz
Camel	Travel / Intercultural Understanding / Endurance	Yellow Jasper
Canary	Optimism / Joy / Enlightenment	Abalone
Capybara	The Clan / Consideration / Affection	Jet
Cardinal	Loyalty / Intermediation / The Sacred	Ruby
Caribou / Reindeer	Wanderlust / Determination / Fairness	Fire Opal
Carp / Goldfish / Koi	Perseverance / Prosperity / Sociability	Neptunite
Cat (Domestic)	Independence / Mysticism / Self-love	Chalcopyrite
Caterpillar	Patience / Trust / Transformation	Dioptase
Catfish	The Unknown / Intuition / Disintegration	Siltstone

ANIMAL	POWERS	MINERAL
Cattle—Bull	Strength / Vigilance / Focus	Pietersite
Cattle—Cow	Love / Generosity / Compassion	Green Sapphire
Centipede / Millipede	Quickness / Confidence / Excellence	Sunshine
Chameleon	Patience / Adaptability / Calm	Rainbow Obsidian
Cheetah	Speed / Affection / Structure	Cat's Eye
Chickadee	Positivity / Sociability / Truth	Selenite
Chicken—Hen	The Feminine / Purification / Relationship	Garnet
Chicken—Rooster	Freedom / Luminousness / Expression	Tourmaline
Cicada	Sound / Cycles / Change	Amethyst
Condor / Vulture	Clairvoyance / Freedom / Flow	Sphalerite
Coral	Foundation / Creation / Beauty	Rhodochrosite
Cormorant	Abundance / Adaptation / Innovation	Dioptase
Cougar / Puma	Authenticity / Boundaries / Solitude	Axinite
Coyote	Surprise / Tricks / Calculation	Citrine
Crab	Protection / Transition / Rejuvenation	Moonstone
Crane	Longevity / Grace / Sociability	Lilac Kunzite
Cricket	Vibration / Communication / Prosperity	Vivianite
Crocodile / Alligator	New Beginnings / Creation / Mental Wellness	Chlorite Quartz
Cuckoo	Rebirth / Consciousness / Prophecy	Dumortierite
Deer	Survival / Confidence / Instinct	Hiddenite
Dingo	Freedom / Independence / Protection	Chalcedony
Dog (Domestic)	Loyalty / Protection / Unconditional Love	Green Sapphire
Dolphin / Porpoise	Love / Curiosity / Enthusiasm	Aquamarine
Donkey / Ass / Burro	Determination / Courage / Humility	Fire Agate
Dove	Love / Hope / Peace	Atlantasite
Dragon	Perseverance / Intuition / Reflection	Purple Fluorite
Dragonfly	Agility / Transformation / Prosperity	Rainbow Quartz
Duck	Happiness / Simplicity / Adaptability	Quantum Quattro
Eagle	Truth / Vision / Intelligence	Citrine
Earthworm	Conservation / Nourishment / Regeneration	Fire Agate
Eel	Disguise / The Unknown / Conductivity	Blue Halite
Elephant	Intelligence / Courage / Harmony	African Jade
Elk	Composure / Passion / Protection	Aragonite
Emu	The Masculine / Movement / Minerals	Garnet
Falcon	Patience / Independence / Vision	Tiger's Eye
Firefly	Illumination / Attraction / Energy	Rainbow Mayanite
Flea	Acrobatics / Persistence / Movement	Tektite

ANIMAL	POWERS	MINERAL
Fly	Quickness / Persistence / Change	Yellow Fluorite
Fox	Skill / Agility / Mysticism	Adamite
Frog / Toad	Transformation / Prosperity / Fertility	Green Jade
Giraffe	Modesty / Intuition / Observation	Smoky Quartz
Goat	Sexuality / Resourcefulness / Adaptability	Herkimer Diamond
Goldfinch	Happiness / Beauty / Health	Calcite
Goose	Communication / Self-assurance / Fidelity	Fluorite
Gopher	Profundity / Oneness / Trust	Galena
Gorilla	Selflessness / Accountability / Balance	Prehnite
Grasshopper	Abundance / Change / Prosperity	Amber
Grouse	Spiral / Prayer / Reflection	Seraphinite
Groundhog	Boundaries / Meditation / Dreaming	Selenite
Guinea Pig	Sacrifice / Divination / Healing	Lepidolite
Hawk	Vision / Change / Intelligence	Sunstone
Hedgehog	Trust / Survival / The Feminine	Obsidian
Heron / Egret	Calm / Patience / Introspection	Apatite
Hippopotamus	Expansiveness / Morality / Assurance	Aquamarine
Horse	Confidence / Movement / Vitality	Tiger's Eye
Hummingbird	Playfulness / Quickness / Endurance	Seraphinite
Hyena	Perception / Partnership / Intuition	Petrified Wood
Ibis	Adaptability / Expression / The Sacred	Shattuckite
Jackal	Calculation / Tactics / Loyalty	Prehnite
Jaguar	Will / Honesty / Guardianship	Jade
Javelina	Alliance / Boundaries / Compassion	Tree Agate
Jellyfish	Flow / Serenity / Regeneration	Chalcedony
Kangaroo	Groundedness / Velocity / Nurturing	Red Goldstone
Kingfisher	Fidelity / Calm / Precision	Orange Aventurine
Koala	Calm / Affection / Trust	Black Agate
Ladybug	Balance / Love / Abundance	Ruby in Fuchsite
Lark	Joy / Expression / Thoughtfulness	Dumortierite
Leech	Purpose / Completion / Healing	Axinite
Lemur	Agility / Extroversion / Intuition	Blue Sapphire
Leopard	Solitude / Teaching / Adaptability	Stilbite
Lion	Prestige / Protection / Heart	Tree Agate
Lizard / Iguana	Intuition / Choice / Color	White Jade
Llama	Curiosity / Grace / Perseverance	Goshenite
Manatee	Gentleness / Intelligence / Regeneration	Green Garnet
Mockingbird	Fearlessness / Cleverness / Musicality	Blue Quartz
Mole	Sensing / Trust / Gathering	Star Ruby
Mongoose	Courage / Agility / Spontaneity	Topaz

ANIMAL	POWERS	MINERAL
Monkey / Baboon / Chimpanzee / Orangutan	Communication / Emotion / Family	Topaz
Mosquito	Persistence / Focus / Awareness	Eudialyte
Moth	Determination / Enlightenment / Mystery	Mookaite
Motmot	Speed / Transformation / Giving	Cavansite
Mouse	Resourcefulness / Expression / Drama	Galena
Musk Ox	Survival / Force / Loyalty	Rutilated Quartz
Nighthawk	Elusion / Travel / The Supernatural	Sunstone
Nuthatch	Organization / Fearlessness / Loyalty	Indigo Aura Quartz
Octopus	Cleverness / Security / Adaptability	Iolite
Opossum	Intuition / Fearlessness / Drama	Yellow Calcite
Ostrich	Truth / Rebirth / Groundedness	Blue Opal
Otter	Playfulness / Happiness / Friendliness	Black Jasper
Owl	Perception / Protection / Wisdomkeeping	Labradorite
Panda	Peace / Kindness / Nurturing	Striped Brown Jasper
Parrot	Transformation / Freedom / Renewal	Peach Quartz
Peafowl / Peacock	Sensuality / Assuredness / Transformation	Azurite
Pelican	Sacrifice / Expansion / Curiosity	Blue Opal
Penguin	Adaptability / Expression / Empathy	Kunzite
Pheasant	Masculinity / Transcendence / Activity	Axinite
Phoenix	Immortality / Transformation / Balance	Ruby in Fuchsite
Pig	Maternity / Sociability / Sensitivity	Fire Opal
Platypus	Ultrasensing / Uniqueness / Confidence	Iolite
Porcupine	Safety / Humility / Fearlessness	Malachite
Prairie Dog	Networking / Creativity / Articulation	Sphalerite
Praying Mantis	Awareness / Mindfulness / Opportunity	Phenacite
Puffin	Adventure / Loyalty / Independence	Prasiolite
Quail	Higher Consciousness / Agility / Elusion	Axinite
Quetzal	Self-awareness / Beauty / Imagination	Jade
Rabbit	Vulnerability / Creation / Abundance	Tanzanite
Raccoon	Touch / Observation / Ingenuity	Obsidian
Rat	Wit / Tenacity / Success	Cinnabar
Raven / Crow	Knowledge / Awakening / Divination	Onyx
Red Panda	Isolation / Choice / Destiny	Peach Moonstone
Rhinoceros	Resilience / Balance / Strength	Champagne Aura Quartz
Roadrunner	Endurance / Adaptability / Passion	Rhodochrosite
Robin	New Beginnings / Reflection / Sacred Space	Blue Tanzanite
Salamander	Rejuvenation / Fluidity / Adaptation	Charoite

ANIMAL	POWERS	MINERAL
Salmon	Renewal / Direction / Imagination	Malachite
Sandpiper	Fellowship / Focus / Flexibility	Blue Turquoise
Scorpion	Determination / Nurturing / Prevention	Ruby
Seagull	Inquiry / Opportunity / Freedom	Yellow Calcite
Seahorse	Calm / Passion / Survival	Sodalite
Seal / Walrus	Introspection / Breath / Emotion	Ocean Jasper
Secretary Bird	Determination / Leadership / Observation	Black Jasper
Shark	Tenacity / Evolution / Authority	Rubelite
Sheep / Ram	Agility / Higher Consciousness / Dreaming	Howlite
Skunk	Sense / Solitude / Self-defense	Blue Chalcedony
Sloth	Relaxation / Presence / Peace	Yellow Calcite
Snail / Slug / Conch	Circumspection / Self-sufficiency / Determination	Tanzanite
Snake	Transformation / Manifestation / Dreaming	Snakeskin Agate
Sparrow	Community / Expression / Motivation	Labradorite
Spider / Tarantula	Creativity / Assertiveness / Patience	Aragonite
Squirrel	Diligence / Vigilance / Mobility	Rosasite
Starfish	Imagination / Renewal / Reflection	Stibnite
Starling	Omnipresence / Alignment / Expression	Black Jasper
Stingray	Quantum Energy / Fearlessness / Intuition	Herkimer Diamond
Stork	Home / Inner Child / Independence	Azurite
Swallow	Endurance / Freedom / Rebirth	Sunstone
Swan	Love / Poise / Bonding	Prehnite
Tasmanian Devil	Darkness / Opportunity / Reputation	Fire Agate
Thunderbird	The Unknown / Honor / Creation	Morganite
Tiger	Guidance / Nobility / Emotion	Tiger's Eye
Toucan	Expression / Happiness / Spirit	Blue Opal
Turkey	Gratitude / Manifestation / Clarity	Fulgurite
Turtle / Tortoise	Survival / Diligence/Protection	Dumortierite
Unicorn	Freedom / Mystery / Kindness	Alexandrite
Wasp	Organization / Strategy / Association	Tiger Iron
Weasel / Ferret / Mink	Curiosity / Spontaneity / Entertainment	Jasper
Whale	Frequencies / Ancestral Wisdom / Breath	Brookite
Wolf	Trust / The Clan / Guidance	Phantom Quartz
Wolverine	Persistence / Fearlessness / Adaptability	White Jade
Wombat	Empathy / Determination / Thought	Black Jasper
Woodpecker	Determination / Skill / Focus	Spirit Quartz
Zebra	Freedom / Illusion / Optimism	Zebra Jasper

ACKNOWLEDGEMENTS

Joost Elffers, producer: Thank you for your vision and creativity; it inspired me to write this book.

John Mason, artist extraordinaire: Thank you for your lifelong friendship, visual genius, and help in coming up with the book title as well as inspiration for the artistic layout and design.

Caroline Meniere, cover artist: A mountain of gratitude for being a sparkling gem full of artistic expression that divinely captures the power of the feminine, the shaman, and the spirit of animals. Your gifts inspire and uplift me to seek the wisdom from the other worlds. Your art is a magical gift to our planet.

Stephanie Gunning, editor: Thank you for being the literary power that guided the book to its final destination. Your knowledge of what it takes to get a book into the world is invaluable and your editing extracts the essence and meaning so divinely. Every day I work with you I become a more accomplished author. I admire your standards and your unwillingness to cut corners, always seeking and extracting the brilliance in others. I would also like to acknowledge your assistant, Najat Washington, for her diligence in helping you to prepare the end notes.

Gus Yoo, layout and design: Special thanks to Gus who has brilliantly brought to life this work. With great instinct and flair you have waved your magic wand and created a visual masterpiece. I am so grateful for all your effort and attention to detail, truly a gift to all who read this book.

Tamara Wilder, administrative assistant: Much thanks for holding down the fort while I escaped into nonordinary reality for a good part of a year. You deserve a medal of honor for trying to organize me and keep other projects off of the back burner. I appreciate all your efforts that often go unnoticed when someone is immersed in writing a book.

Xandra Alifson, artist and graphic designer: Many thanks for all the artistic detail in fine-tuning the details of the mountain of illustrations used throughout the book. I honor your efficiency, your attention to detail, and your instinct and intuition to bring dimension and life to the drawings. Thank you for your gifts to this project and to the world through your fabulous creations of art.

My dog, Gracie, and my cat, Tut: Thank you for your sacrifice while I spent hours and hours writing and missing walks, cuddling with you, and communicating. You have taught me what unconditional love is and daily inspire me to see the world through the eyes of an animal.

Family: To my parents, Tom and Donna Morrison, thank you for being eternal cheerleaders in my life, always supporting my many endeavors. I am grateful for your patience during this effort.

Zack Greenfield, media manager: Thank you for your marketing brilliance and unrelenting efforts to create space for my messages in the world. You are an elixir of assurance and calm when the tech world begins to encompass my self-imposed limitations.

Fauzia Burke and FSB Associates, publicists: Thank you. I am grateful to you and your associates for taking on the publicity campaign for the book and helping me to spread word of this avenue for connection with spirit. I could not do it alone. By playing this role, you are helping to raise the consciousness of the world.

Spirit teachers: Special thanks to my Power Animal of eight years, Lion, who never leaves my side. I am grateful for your guidance and protection and for encouraging me to seek the power within. Your support in helping to heal myself and others and your unwavering faith are my greatest strengths. I am also grateful to my teachers in the other worlds that assist me in downloading the knowledge of spirit, showing me the signs, and sharing the woven wisdom of the Mayan cosmology to support my earth walk.

My readers: Thank you for bringing this book into your life and for supporting my efforts. I am humbled as you encourage me to continue to share my love of shamanism and its contributions to our society. I am grateful that I can stay connected with so many of you through the magic of social media and share my stories, hear your inner voices, and walk together on this journey called life.

REFERENCES

PART ONE: THE WORLD OF SHAMANS AND THEIR POWER ANIMALS

The Shaman

Mircea Eliade. *Shamanism: Archaic Techniques of Ecstasy, reprint edition* (Princeton, N.J.: Princeton University Press/Bollinger Foundation, 2004), p. 182.

Indigenous Theories and Beliefs

Nurit Bird-David. "'Animism' Revisited: Personhood, Environment, and Relational Epistemology," *Current Anthropology.* vol. 40, supplement (February 1999), pp. S67–8, https://www.journals.uchicago.edu/doi/pdfplus/10.1086/200061.

PART TWO: A TO Z GUIDE TO POWER ANIMALS

Aardvark

"Aardvark," Science Encyclopedia (accessed June 28, 2018), http://science.jrank.org/pages/1/Aardvark.html.

David Catchpoole. "A Is for Aardvark," *Creation,* vol. 36, no. 2 (April 2014): pp. 28–31, https://creation.com/aardvark.

Thomson Safaris. "Dead Pig Walking: Aardvarks, 'Living Fossils' in the Bush," Thomas Safari, (May 27, 2014), https://thomsonsafaris.com/blog/aardvarks-living-fossils.

Jed Winer/NGS Staff. "Aardvark," National Geographic Kids (accessed June 28, 2018), https://kids.nationalgeographic.com/animals/aardvark/#aardvark-tongue-out.jpg.

Albatross

"Albatross," Wikipedia (accessed August 7, 2018), https://en.wikipedia.org/wiki/Albatross.

"Albatrosses," National Geographic (accessed August 7, 2018), https://www.nationalgeographic.com/animals/birds/group/albatrosses.

"Twenty-five Amazing and Weird Facts about Albatrosses," Tons of Facts (December 15, 2017), http://tonsoffacts.com/25-amazing-and-weird-facts-about-albatrosses.

"What Are Some Interesting Facts about Albatrosses?" Quora (accessed August 7, 2018), https://www.quora.com/What-are-some-interesting-facts-about-albatrosses.

Angelfish

"Angelfish," Animal-World (accessed June 28, 2018), http://animal-world.com/encyclo/fresh/cichlid/angelfish.php.

"Angelfish," A–Z Animals (accessed June 28, 2018), https://A–Z-animals.com/animals/angelfish.

Ant

"Ant," Wikipedia (accessed July 16, 2018), https://en.wikipedia.org/wiki/Ant.

"Ant Medicine," Spirit Lodge (accessed July 17, 2018), http://www.spiritlodge.itgo.com/libtotems6.html.

Debbie Hadley. "Ten Fascinating Facts about Ants," ThoughtCo. (December 7, 2017), https://www.ThoughtCo.com/fascinating-facts-about-ants-1968070.

"Native American Ant Mythology," Native Languages of the Americas (accessed July 17, 2018), http://www.native-languages.org/legends-ant.htm.

Anteater

"Native American Totem Animals and Their Meanings," Legends of America (accessed July 17, 2018), http://www.legendsofamerica.com/na-totems.html.

Stephanie Pappas. "'Monstrously Big Ant' Fossil Found in Wyoming," Live Science (May 3, 2011), https://www.livescience.com/14008-giant-ant-fossil.html.

Antelope

Andre Dollinger. "Antelopes," Ancient Egyptian Bestiary (accessed July 27, 2018), http://www.reshafim.org.il/ad/egypt/bestiary/antelope.htm.

Raven Fon. "The Spiritual Meaning and Symbolism Behind African Animals," Spirit Science (May 18, 2016), http://thespiritscience.net/2016/05/18/african-animals-their-meaning-and-symbolism.

"What Does the Mask Mean?" African Ritual Masks (accessed July 17, 2018), http://africanritualmasks.weebly.com/what-does-the-mask-mean.html.

Armadillo

Ageresdi. "Animal Spirit Guide: Armadillo," White Lotus Magazine (accessed July 17, 2018), http://whitelotusmagazine.com/animal-spirit-guide-armadillo.

Joshua Nixon. "Where Did Armadillos Come From?" Natural History of the Armadillo (accessed July 17, 2018), https://armadillo-online.org/history.html.

Badger

Violet H. Harada. "The Badger in Japanese Folklore," Nanzan Institute for Religion and Culture. (accessed June 28, 2018), https://nirc.nanzan-u.ac.jp/nfile/1034.

Barracuda

"Barracuda Facts," Soft Schools (accessed June 28, 2018), http://www.softschools.com/facts/animals/barracuda_facts/472.

"Water Animal Spirits," Spirit Walk Ministry (accessed June 28, 2018), http://spiritwalkministry.com/spirit_guides/water_animal_spirits.

Bat

Diane Ackerman. "In Praise of Bats." *The Moon by Whale Light* (New York: Vintage Books, 1992), pp. 4–59.

Archive for Research into Archetypal Symbolism. *The Book of Symbols: Reflections on Archetypal Images* (Los Angeles, CA.: Taschen, 2010).

"Basic Facts about Bats," Defenders of Wildlife (accessed July 1, 2018), https://defenders.org/bats/basic-facts.

"Bats in Mythology," Bat Worlds (November 5, 2013), http://www.batworlds.com/bats-in-mythology.

"Information about Bats," Nexles EU (accessed July 15, 2018), https://www.nexles.com/articles/information-about-bats-chiroptera.

"Native American Bat Mythology," Native Languages (accessed July 1, 2018), http://www.native-languages.org/legends-bat.htm.

Bear

"Bear," Trees for Life (accessed July 1, 2018), https://treesforlife.org.uk/forest/mythology-folklore/bear.

"General Characteristics," Get Bear Smart Society (accessed July 1, 2018), http://www.bearsmart.com/about-bears/general-characteristics.

Beaver

"Beaver Moon," Symbols (accessed July 1, 2018), http://www.symbols.com/symbol/beaver-moon.

"Native American Beaver Mythology," Native Languages of the Americas (accessed July 1, 2018), http://www.native-languages.org/legends-beaver.htm.

Bee

Archive for Research into Archetypal Symbolism. *The Book of Symbols: Reflections on Archetypal Images* (Los Angeles, CA.: Taschen, 2010), p. 228.

Andrew Goughs. "The Bee: Part 2—Beewildered," Andrew Goughs blog (July 2008), http://andrewgough.co.uk/articles_bee2.

"May I Have This Dance?" You Better Bee-lieve It (accessed July 15, 2018), https://youbetterbeelieveit.weebly.com/day-2.html.

"Mayan Mythology and Bees," Aktun Chen (May 15, 2016), https://aktun-chen.com/blog/las-abejas-en-la-cultura-maya.html.

Ordo Infinitus Orbis. "Bee Goddess," Temple of Theola (April 11, 2009) http://www.templeoftheola.org/bee-goddess.html.

Beetle

"Scarab Beetle," Ancient Egypt: The Mythology (accessed July 5, 2018), http://www.egyptianmyths.net/scarab.htm.

"Secrets of the Scarab: Ancient Sacred Symbol in Human History," Ancient Pages (July 14, 2015), http://www.ancientpages.com/2015/06/14/secrets-scarab-ancient-sacred-symbol-human-history.

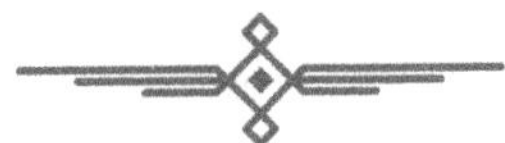

Blackbird

"Common Blackbird," Oiseaux-Birds (accessed July 5, 2018), http://www.oiseaux-birds.com/card-common-blackbird.html.

Sandra Kynes. *Bird Magic: Wisdom of the Ancient Goddesses for Pagans and Wiccans* (Woodbury, MN.: Llewellyn Publications, 2016), pp. 74–77.

"Native American Blackbird Mythology," Native Languages of the Americas (accessed July 5, 2018), http://www.native-languages.org/legends-blackbird.htm.

Bluebird

Ted Andrews. *Animal Speak: The Spiritual and Magical Powers of Creatures Great and Small* (Llewellyn Publications, 2002), pp.120–1.

"Native American Bluebird Mythology," Native Languages (accessed July 5, 2018), http://www.native-languages.org/legends-bluebird.htm.

Lori Schubring. "Ten Fun Facts about Bluebirds," *Wausau Daily Herald* (March 30, 2016), http://www.wausaudailyherald.com/story/life/2016/03/30/10-fun-facts-bluebirds/82424314.

Blue Jay

"Blue Jay," Audubon Guide to North American Birds (accessed July 5, 2018), http://www.audubon.org/field-guide/bird/blue-jay.

"Jay Symbolism," Spirit Animal Totem (accessed July 5, 2018), https://www.spirit-animals.com/jay.

Lesley Morrison. *The Healing Wisdom of Birds: An Everyday Guide to Their Spiritual Songs and Symbolism* (Woodbury, MN.: Llewellyn Publications, 2011), p. 192.

Boar

"Boar," Symbols (accessed July 5, 2018), http://www.symbols.com/symbol/boar.

"Body Language of Wild Board," Suwannee River Ranch (accessed July 5, 2018), http://www.suwanneeriverranch.com/wild-boar-body-language.htm.

"Wild Boar," Trees for Life (accessed July 5, 2018), https://treesforlife.org.uk/forest/mythology-folklore/wild-boar2.

Bobcat

"Basic Facts about Bobcats," Defenders of Wildlife (accessed July 5, 2018), https://defenders.org/bobcat/bobcats.

Debbie Gent. "Bobcat Medicine: Solitude, Silence and Secrets," Shamanic Connection (October 15, 2013), https://shamanicconnection.com/nature-wise/bobcat-medicine-solitude-silence-secrets#more-288.

"Native American Bobcat Mythology," Native Languages of the Americas (accessed July 5, 2018), http://www.native-languages.org/legends-bobcat.htm.

Norma Roche. "Major Characteristics of the American Bobcat," Animals (accessed July 5, 2018), http://animals.mom.me/major-characteristics-american-bobcat-9183.html.

Buffalo

"American Bison," Nature Works (accessed July 9, 2018), http://www.nhptv.org/natureworks/americanbison.htm.

"Fifteen Facts About Our National Mammal: The American Bison," U.S. Department of the Interior (accessed November 13, 2018), https://www.doi.gov/blog/15-facts-about-our-national-mammal-american-bison.

Butterfly

"Myths about Butterflies," Butterflies and Blazes (accessed July 9, 2018), http://journeyofhearts.org/butterfly/bfly_myth.html.

"Native American Butterfly Mythology," Native Languages of the Americas (accessed July 9, 2018), http://www.native-languages.org/legends-butterfly.htm.

"What Is a Butterfly?" Enchanted Learning (accessed July 9, 2018), http://www.enchantedlearning.com/subjects/butterfly/allabout.

Camel

"The Camel: Ancient Ship of the Desert and the Nabataeans," Nabatacan History (accessed July 9, 2018), http://nabataea.net/camel.html.

"Camel," Wikipedia (accessed July 11, 2018), https://en.wikipedia.org/wiki/Camel.

"Camels," Fun Facts and Details (accessed July 11, 2018), http://factsanddetails.com/world/cat52/sub331/item1181.html.

Hope B. Werness. *The Continuum Encyclopedia of Animal Symbolism in Art.* (New York: Continuum International Publishing Group, 2006), pp. 69–70.

Canary

G. G. Carbone. "Bird Signs, Guidance and Wisdom from Our Feathered Friends," Spirituality and Practice (accessed July 11, 2018), http://www.spiritualityandpractice.com/book-reviews/excerpts/view/16774.

Mika Harimoto. "A Guide to Canaries and the Bird's History, Characteristics, and Breeding Practices,"EzineArticles (October 26, 2009), http://ezinearticles.com/?A-Guide-to-Canaries-and-the-Birds-History,-Characteristics,-and-Breeding-Practices&id=3158874.

Capybara

Amazon-Indians (accessed July 12, 2018), http://www.amazon-indians.org/matis/magicgallery/05-Matis-Dec2004_089.htm.

"Capybara Facts," Tropical Rainforest Facts (accessed July 12, 2018), http://www.tropical-rainforest-facts.com/Tropical-Rainforest-Animal-Facts/Capybara-Facts.shtml.

"Unknown Facts about Capybaras: The Biggest Rodents on Earth," AnimalSake (June 7, 2017), https://animalsake.com/facts-information-about-capybaras.

Cardinal

"Cardinal Bird Facts," Cardinal Experience (accessed July 12, 2018), http://www.thecardinalexperience.com/bird%20facts.php#.WmjOCq2ZN-U.

"Cardinal Signs and Symbols," Cardinal Experience (accessed July 12, 2018), http://www.thecardinalexperience.com/symbols.php#.WeTyKa2ZP_Q.

"Native American Cardinal Mythology," Native Languages of the Americas (accessed July 12, 2018), http://www.native-languages.org/legends-cardinal.htm.

Caribou

"Caribou Facts," Animal Facts (accessed July 12, 2018), http://interesting-animal-facts.com/Arctic-Animal-Facts/Arctic-Caribou-Facts.html.

"Caribou: Rangifer Tarandus," Nature Works (accessed July 12, 2018), http://www.nhptv.org/natureworks/caribou.htm.

"Caribou Skin Clothing," National Park Service (April 14, 2015), https://www.nps.gov/gaar/learn/historyculture/caribou-skin-clothing.htm.

Mircea Eliade. *From Primitives to Zen: A Thematic Sourcebook of the History of Religions* (New York: Harper and Row, 1978), p. 14.

Carp/Goldfish/Koi

Terri Benning. "Koi Fish (Goldfish)," Totem Talk (August 13, 2010), https://totemtalk.ning.com/group/k/forum/topics/koi-fish-goldfish.

"Koi," Wikipedia (accessed July 16, 2018), https://en.wikipedia.org/wiki/Koi.

"Koi Fish Meaning and Myth," Koi Story (accessed July 17, 2018), https://koistory.com/blog/koi-fish-meaning-and-myth.

Cat (Domestic)

"Cat," Wikipedia (accessed July 11, 2018), https://en.wikipedia.org/wiki/Cat.

"Cat Mythology, Myths and Legends," Must Love Cats (accessed July 12, 2018) http://www.mustlovecats.net/Cat-Mythology.html.

Caterpillar

"Caterpillar," A–Z Animals (accessed June 28, 2018), https://A-Z -animals.com/animals/caterpillar.

Ferris Jabr. "How Does a Caterpillar Turn into a Butterfly?" Scientific America (August 10, 2012), https://www.scientificamerican.com/article/caterpillar-butterfly-metamorphosis-explainer.

Catfish

"Catfish Facts," Soft Schools (accessed July 12, 2018), http://www.softschools.com/facts/animals/catfish_facts/1119.

Nadia Drake. "Giant Catfish Fossil Found in Egyptian Desert," National Geographic (March 10, 2017), https://news.nationalgeographic.com/2017/03/ancient-egypt-catfish-fossil-palaeontology-science.

Cattle—Bull

"Bull," Symbols (accessed July 9, 2018), http://www.symbols.com/symbol/bull.

Murray J. Mizrachi. "Bull Symbolism in the Golden Calf Narrative," Jewish Magazine (May 2014), http://www.jewishmag.com/184mag/bull_imagery/bull_imagery.htm.

Cattle—Cow

K. Parvathi Kumar. "Cow: The Symbol and Its Significance," Jugendforum (accessed July 13, 2018), http://www.jugendforum-mithila.de/ethik_CowContent.html.

Centipede/Millipede

Elmer W. Gray. "Millipedes and Centipedes," *Bulletin* 1088, University of Georgia Extension (April 2015) http://extension.uga.edu/publications/detail.html?number=B1088.

"Sepa, God of Egypt," Land of Pyramids (accessed July 12, 2018) http://www.landofpyramids.org/sepa.htm.

Brent Swancer. "The Creepy Crawly World of Cryptid Giant Centipedes," Mysterious Universe (May 3, 2016), http://mysteriousuniverse.org/2016/05/the-creepy-crawly-world-of-cryptid-giant-centipedes.

"Twenty Strange Facts about Centipedes—Stop Squashing Them," Riverside 247 (accessed July 12, 2018) http://riverside247.com/centipede-facts/12.

Chameleon

"Chameleon," Constellations of Words (accessed July 12, 2018), http://constellationsofwords.com/Constellations/Chamaeleon.htm.

"Chameleons," Animals Adda (February 17, 2017), https://animalsadda.com/chameleons.

"Chameleons," Smithsonian National Museum of African Art (accessed July 12, 2018), https://africa.si.edu/exhibits/animals/chameleons.html.

Norman A. Rubin. "Reptiles Throughout Mythology," ViewZone (accessed July 12, 2018), http://www.viewzone.com/israel.html.

"Ten Things You Didn't Know About Chameleons," Twisted Sifter (November 28, 2012), http://twistedsifter.com/2012/11/ten-things-you-didnt-know-about-chameleons.

Cheetah

Sankalan Baidya. "Forty Facts about Cheetah," Facts Legend (April 13, 2014), http://factslegend.org/40-facts-cheetah/2.

Alina Bradford, Live Science Contributor. "Cheetahs: Facts, Pictures and Habitat," Live Science (October 16, 2014), https://www.livescience.com/27319-cheetahs.html.

"Cool Facts about Cheetah," Interesting Fun Facts (April 3, 2012), http://www.interestingfunfacts.com/cool-facts-about-cheetah.html#LQMJOp7rxmgVcc2s.99.

James Gaines. "Hunting with Cheetahs," Glyptodon (February 25, 2012), https://theglyptodon.wordpress.com/2012/02/25/hunting-with-cheetahs.

Chickadee

"Chickadee: Spirit Animal, Symbolism, and Meaning," Dreaming and Sleeping (accessed July 12, 2018), https://dreamingandsleeping.com/chickadee-spirit-animal-symbolism-and-meaning.

George Ellison. "The Honest Little Bird," *Smoky Mountain News* (10 May 2006), http://www.smokymountainnews.com/archives/item/13484-the-honest-little-bird.

Chicken—Hen

Karen Davis. "The Dignity, Beauty, and Abuse of Chickens: As Symbols and in Reality," United Poultry Concerns (May 2002), https://www.upc-online.org/thinking/dignity.html.

Louis de Jaucourt. "Sacred chickens" (1765). *The Encyclopedia of Diderot and d'Alembert Collaborative Translation Project,* translated by Dena Goodman (Ann Arbor, Michigan: University of Michigan Library, 2007), http://hdl.handle.net/2027/spo.did2222.0000.865.

Paul Sheridan. "The Sacred Chickens of Rome," Anecdotes from Antiquity (November 8, 2015), http://www.anecdotesfromantiquity.com/the-sacred-chickens-of-rome.

"Ten Fun Facts about Chickens," Cherry Crest (accessed July 12, 2018), http://www.cherrycrestfarm.com/The-Amazing-Fun-Time-Blog/10-Interesting-Facts-About-Chickens.

Cat Yronwode. "Black Hens, Hen Eggs, and Frizzled Fowl," Lucky Mojo (accessed July 12, 2018), http://www.luckymojo.com/blackhens.html.

Chicken—Rooster

Cherran. "Interesting Facts about Roosters," Infomory (July 19, 2015), http://infomory.com/facts/interesting-facts-about-roosters.

"Rooster," Wikipedia (accessed July 17, 2018), https://en.wikipedia.org/wiki/Rooster.

Cicada

Alina Bradford. "Facts about Cicadas," Live Science (February 8, 2017), https://www.livescience.com/57814-cicada-facts.html.

"Cicadas: Symbols of Resurrection, Rebirth in Ancient Myths," Journal (May 24, 2013), http://www.journal-news.net/life/home-and-garden/2013/05/cicadas-symbols-of-resurrection-rebirth-in-ancient-myths.

Herbert Hoffman. *Sotades: Symbols of Immortality on Greek Vases* (New York: Oxford University Press, 1997), p. 113.

Jan Stuart. "The Cicada in China," Freer Sackler Galleries/Smithsonian Institution (April 29, 2016), https://www.freersackler.si.edu/cicadas.

University of Arizona. "Seven Things You Didn't Know about Cicadas," Phys Org (June 13, 2017), https://phys.org/news/2017-06-didnt-cicadas.html.

"What Are Cicadas?" Cicada News (accessed September 26, 2018), http://www.cicadamania.com.

"What Do Cicadas Symbolize?" Cicada Mania (March 2, 2016), http://www.cicadamania.com/cicadas/what-do-cicadas-symbolize.

Condor/Vulture

"Andean Condor," *National Geographic* (May 10, 2011), https://www.nationalgeographic.com/animals/birds/a/andean-condor.

Ryan Andersen. "The Eagle and The Condor Prophecy," Pachamama Alliance (August 5, 2017), https://www.pachamama.org/blog/the-eagle-and-the-condor-prophecy.

Ellen Lloyd. "Eagle and the Condor Prophecy," Ancient Pages (April 21, 2017), https://www.bibliotecapleyades.net/profecias/esp_profecia57.htm.

"Vulture," Ancient Egypt: The Mythology (accessed July 12, 2018), http://www.egyptianmyths.net/vulture.htm.

Coral

"Coral," Crystals and Their Healing Properties (accessed July 12, 2018), http://www.healingwithcrystals.net.au/coral.html.

"Coral," Theosophy Trust (accessed July 12, 2018), https://theosophytrust.mobi/642-coral#.WfYEUa3Mw6g.

Rinkesh. "Top 25 Coral Reef Facts," Conserve Energy Future (accessed July 12, 2018), https://www.conserve-energy-future.com/top-25-coral-reef-facts.php.

Edward Wozniak. "Eleven More Deities from Hawaiian Mythology," Balladeer's Blog (March 2, 2011), https://glitternight.com/2011/03/02/eleven-more-deities-from-hawaiian-mythology-2.

Cormorant

"Bird Stories, Great Cormorant (*Phalacrocorax Carbo*)," Planet of Birds (May 6, 2013), http://www.planetofbirds.com/bord-stories-great-cormorant-phalacrocorax-carbo.

"Cormorant (or Shag)," Native Symbols (accessed July 17, 2018) http://nativesymbols.info/cormorant-or-shag.

"What Does the Cormorant Bird Symbolize in Mythology," CliffsNotes (accessed July 17, 2018), https://www.cliffsnotes.com/cliffsnotes/subjects/literature/what-does-the-cormorant-bird-symbolize-in-mythology.

Cougar/Puma

"Cougar," Wikipedia (accessed July 17, 2018), https://en.wikipedia.org/wiki/Cougar.

Kevin Hansen. "An Almost Perfect Predator," Mountain Lion Foundation (accessed November 2, 2018), https://www.mountainlion.org/CAL_ch4.asp.

Kevin Hansen. "Cougars and Humans," Mountain Lion Foundation (accessed November 2, 2018), https://www.mountainlion.org/CAL_ch5.asp.

"Mountain Lion: Cougar," Desert USA (accessed July 17, 2018), https://www.desertusa.com/animals/mountain-lion.html#ixzz54TsVCQKH.

"Native American Cougar Mythology," Native Languages of the Americas (accessed July 18, 2018), http://www.native-languages.org/legends-cougar.htm.

"Spirit of the Wild Cat," Wild Felid Advocacy Center (accessed July 17, 2018) http://wildfelids.org/SpiritoftheWildCat.html.

Coyote

"Coyote," A–Z Animals (accessed July 19, 2018), https://A-Z -animals.com/animals/coyote.

"Coyote," National Geographic (May 10, 2011), https://www.nationalgeographic.com/animals/mammals/c/coyote.

"Coyote (*Canis Latrans*)," Nature Works (accessed July 19, 2018), http://www.nhptv.org/natureworks/coyote.htm

Jaymi Heimbuch. "Ten Fascinating Facts about Urban Coyotes," Urban Coyote Initiative (accessed July 19, 2018), http://urbancoyoteinitiative.com/10-fascinating-facts-about-urban-coyotes.

"Native American Coyote Mythology," Native Languages (accessed July 19, 2018), http://www.native-languages.org/legends-coyote.htm.

Crab

Barry. "Hawaii's Samoan Crab," GET2HAWAII (September 17, 2015), http://get2hawaii.com/hawaiis-samoan-crab.

"Cancer," Constellations of Words (accessed July 19, 2018), http://constellationsofwords.com/Constellations/Cancer.html.

"The Hidden or Implied Meaning of Chinese Charm Symbols," Primal Trek (accessed July 19, 2018), http://primaltrek.com/impliedmeaning.html.

April Holloway. "The legend of Heikegani: The Samurai ghost crabs," Ancient Origins (September 7, 2014), http://www.ancient-origins.net/myths-legends/legend-heikegani-samurai-ghost-crabs-002049

Crane

"Crane," All about Heaven (accessed July 19, 2018), http://www.allaboutheaven.org/symbols/783/123/crane.

"Legend of the Crane," In the Field with Operation Migration (July 28, 2013), http://operationmigration.org/InTheField/2013/07/28/legend-of-the-crane.

Monarch13. "Bird Symbolism and Spiritual Gifts," Exemplore (December 15, 2014), https://exemplore.com/spirit-animals/divine-birds.

Melissa Russell. "Crane Symbol," Signology (accessed July 19, 2018), http://www.signology.org/bird-symbol/crane-symbol.htm.

Cricket

"Cricket," All about Heaven (accessed July 19, 2018), http://www.allaboutheaven.org/symbols/991/123/cricket.

"Cricket Facts," Soft Schools (accessed July 19, 2018), http://www.softschools.com/facts/animals/cricket_facts/583.

"Native American Cricket Mythology," Native Languages of the Americas (accessed July 19, 2018), http://www.native-languages.org/legends-cricket.htm.

"What Are Interesting Facts about Crickets?" Joy of Animals (accessed July 19, 2018), http://www.joyofanimals.com/interesting-cricket-facts.

Crocodile/Alligator

"Alligator," Wikipedia (accessed July 11, 2018), https://en.wikipedia.org/wiki/Alligator.

Ernesto Vargas Pacheco and Teri Arias Ortiz. "The Crocodile and the Cosmos: Itzamkanac, the Place of the Alligator's House," Foundation for the Advancement of Mesoamerican Studies (accessed July 13, 2018), http://www.famsi.org/reports/03101/02vargas_arias/02vargas_arias.pdf.

Cuckoo

"Cuckoo," One Kind Planet (accessed July 19, 2018), https://one kind planet.org/animal/cuckoo.

"Interesting Facts about Cuckoos," Just Fun Facts (accessed July 19, 2018), http://justfunfacts.com/interesting-facts-about-cuckoos.

Deer

"Deer in Mythology," Wikipedia (accessed November 13, 2018), https://en.wikipedia.org/wiki/Deer_in_mythology.

"White-tailed Deer—*Odocoileus Virginianus,*" Nature Works (accessed November 13, 2018), http://www.nhptv.org/natureworks/whitetaileddeer.htm.

Dingo

Matt Ayres. "Seven Sacred Animals from Around the World," Animalogic (April 14, 2016), http://community.lovenature.com/blog/7-sacred-animals-from-around-the-world.

Joslyn C. "Animal-Human Connection," Interconnectivity: Animals Mourning Together in Modern Stories and Mythology (accessed November 1, 2018), http://scalar.usc.edu/works/chid490animalmourning/human-nonhuman-connection.

Justine Philip. "The Cultural History of the Dingo," *Australian Geographic* (August 7, 2017), http://www.australiangeographic.com.au/topics/wildlife/2017/08/cultural-history-of-the-dingo.

Dog (Domestic)

"Can Dogs Sense the Supernatural?" Animal Planet (accessed July 19, 2018), http://www.animalplanet.com/pets/can-dogs-sense-the-supernatural.

Renee Moen. "Dog Intuition: Five Things Your Dog Knows Before You," I Heart Dogs (accessed July 19, 2018), https://iheartdogs.com/are-dogs-psychic-5-things-dogs-sense-before-they-happen.

"Native American Dog Mythology," Native Languages of the Americas (accessed July 19, 2018), http://www.native-languages.org/legends-dogs.htm.

Dolphin/Porpoise

Joslyn C. "Nonhuman Animals Mourning," Interconnectivity: Animals Mourning Together in Modern Stories and Mythology (June 12, 2014), http://scalar.usc.edu/works/chid490animalmourning/animal-mourning.

"Dolphin Intelligence," Dolphin World (April 26, 2017), http://www.dolphins-world.com/dolphin-intelligence.

"Native American Dolphin Mythology," Native Languages of the Americas (accessed July 20, 2018), http://www.native-languages.org/legends-dolphin.htm.

"Seven Surprising Facts about Dolphins," *Week* (July 4, 2012), http://theweek.com/articles/474142/7-surprising-facts-about-dolphins.

"Spinner Dolphins," Wild Dolphin Foundation (accessed July 20, 2018), http://wilddolphin.org/spinner.html.

Donkey/Ass/Burro

"Ass," All about Heaven (accessed July 20, 2018), http://www.allaboutheaven.org/symbols/928/123/ass.

"The Donkey," Ancient Egyptian Bestiary (accessed July 20, 2018), http://www.reshafim.org.il/ad/egypt/bestiary/donkey.htm.

Dove

"Doves as Symbols," Wikipedia (accessed July 20, 2018), https://en.wikipedia.org/wiki/Doves_as_symbols.

"Native American Dove and Pigeon Mythology," Native Languages of the Americas (accessed July 20, 2018), http://www.native-languages.org/legends-dove.htm.

Dragon

"Draco—The Dragon," Constellations of Words, (accessed July 20, 2018), http://constellationsofwords.com/Constellations/Draco.html.

"Dragon Mythological Creature," Encyclopaedia Britannica (June 21, 2018), https://www.britannica.com/topic/dragon-mythological-creature.

"The Hidden or Implied Meaning of Chinese Charm Symbols," Primal Trek (accessed July 20, 2018), http://primaltrek.com/impliedmeaning.html.

"List of Dragons in Mythology and Folklore," Wikipedia (accessed July 20, 2018), https://en.wikipedia.org/wiki/List_of_dragons_in_mythology_and_folklore.

Dragonfly

Joslyn C. "Dragonflies, Butterflies and Mythology," Interconnectivity: Animals Mourning Together in Modern Stories and Mythology (June 12, 2014), http://scalar.usc.edu/works/chid490animalmourning/dragonfly-and-butterfly.

"Dragonfly," Wikipedia (accessed July 20, 2018), https://en.wikipedia.org/wiki/Dragonfly.

"Native American Dragonfly Mythology," Native Languages of the Americas (accessed July 20, 2018), http://www.native-languages.org/legends-dragonfly.htm.

Duck

"Amala (Mythology)," Wikipedia (accessed July 17, 2018), https://en.wikipedia.org/wiki/Amala_(mythology).

"The Hidden or Implied Meaning of Chinese Charm Symbols," Primal Trek (accessed July 19, 2018), http://primaltrek.com/impliedmeaning.html.

Liz Martin. "Eleven Amazing Duck Facts!" Cape Coop (November 10, 2016), http://www.thecapecoop.com/11-amazing-duck-facts.

Arin Murphy-Hiscock. "A Spiritual Field Guide to Birds," Belief Net (accessed July 19, 2018), http://www.beliefnet.com/wellness/environment/galleries/a-spiritual-field-guide-to-birds.aspx?p=5.

"Native American Duck Mythology," Native Languages of the Americas (accessed July 19, 2018), http://www.native-languages.org/legends-duck.htm.

Eagle

Ellen Lloyd. "The Eagle and the Concord Prophecy," Prophecies, Predictions and the Future (April 21, 2017), https://www.bibliotecapleyades.net/profecias/esp_profecia57.htm.

"Native American Eagle Mythology," Native Languages of the Americas (accessed July 19, 2018), http://www.native-languages.org/legends-eagle.htm.

G.E. Steckert. "Aquila: The Eagle," *Star Names and Their Meanings* (1889), http://constellationsofwords.com/Constellations/Aquila.htm.

Earthworm

David Maxwell Braun. "The Most Influential Species of All Evolution," National Geographic (November 2009), https://blog.nationalgeographic.org/2009/11/04/the-most-influential-species-of-all-evolution.

Edwin L. Cooper, et al. "Earthworms Dilong: Ancient, Inexpensive, Noncontroversial Models May Help Clarify Approaches to Integrated Medicine Emphasizing Neuroimmune Systems," *Evidence-based Complementary and Alternative Medicine* (2012), https://www.ncbi.nlm.nih.gov/pmc/articles/PMC3410320.

Claire Gillespie. "Earthworm Characteristics," Sciencing (April 10, 2018), https://sciencing.com/earthworm-characteristics-5480698.html.

Bintoro Gunadi. "The Myths and Facts about Earthworms and Fishy Wastes," Burnaby Red Wigglers (August 1, 2016), https://burnabyredwigglers.wordpress.com/2016/08/01/the-myths-and-facts-about-earthworms-and-fishy-wastes.

Eel

Sandra Casellato. "European Eel: A History Which Must Be Rewritten," *Italian Journal of Zoology*, vol. 69, no. 4 (2002), pp. 321–324, https://www.tandfonline.com/doi/abs/10.1080/11250000209356476.

"Eels of Hawaii," Kai Kanani (accessed July 19, 2018), http://www.kaikanani.com/2014/03/eels-of-hawaii.

Mary Harrsch. "Eels in Roman Gardens," Presentations on the Roman Empire (January 8, 2004), http://romanpresentations.blogspot.com/2004/01/eels-in-roman-gardens.html.

James MacDonald. "Five Shocking Facts about Electric Eels,) JSTOR Daily (October 12, 2017), https://daily.jstor.org/5-shocking-facts-about-electric-eels.

"Sina and the Eel," Wikipedia (accessed July 17, 2018), https://en.wikipedia.org/wiki/Sina_and_the_Eel.

Elephant

Joslyn C. "Nonhuman Animals Mourning," Interconnectivity: Animals Mourning Together in Modern Stories and Mythology (June 12, 2014), http://scalar.usc.edu/works/chid490animalmourning/animal-mourning.

"Cultural Depictions of Elephants," Wikipedia (accessed July 17, 2018), https://en.wikipedia.org/wiki/Cultural_depictions_of_elephants.

"Elephant," One Kind Planet (accessed July 19, 2018), https://one kind planet.org/animal/elephant.

"Three Wise Monkeys," Wikipedia (accessed July 17, 2018), https://en.wikipedia.org/wiki/Three_wise_monkeys.

Elk

Richard L. Dieterle. "Elk Clan Origin Myth," Hot Cake Encycolpedia (accessed July 19, 2018), http://www.hotcakencyclopedia.com/ho.ElkClanOriginMyth.html.

"Elk," Wikipedia (accessed July 17, 2018), https://en.wikipedia.org/wiki/Elk.

"Elk (Cervus Elaphus)," Eduscapes (accessed July 19, 2018), http://www.eduscapes.com/nature/elk/index1.htm.

"Elk Facts," Elk Network (accessed July 19, 2018), https://elknetwork.com/elkfacts.

"Native American Elk Mythology," Native Languages of the Americas (accessed July 19, 2018), http://www.native-languages.org/legends-elk.htm.

Tracey. "Native American Myths and Legends: Love," Prairie Edge (January 31, 2011), http://www.prairieedge.com/tribe-scribe/native-american-myths-legends-love.

Tyler Wilcox. "Eight Fascinating Facts about Elk," Estes Park (September 4, 2017), https://www.visitestespark.com/blog/post/8-fascinating-facts-about-elk.

Emu

ABC Radio Sydney. "Aboriginal Astronomy the Star of Dreamtime Stories," ABC (April 4, 2017), http://www.abc.net.au/news/2017-04-05/aboriginal-astronomy-basis-of-dreamtime-stories-stargazing/8413492.

"Emu," Bush Heritage (May 17, 2018), https://www.bushheritage.org.au/species/emu.

"Emu," Wikipedia (accessed July 17, 2018), https://en.wikipedia.org/wiki/Emu.

Robert Fuller. "The Kamilaroi and Euahlayi Emu in the Sky," Australian Indigenous Astronomy (March 31, 2014), http://aboriginalastronomy.blogspot.com/2014/03/the-kamilaroi-and-euahlayi-emu-in-sky.html.

Falcon

Shawn E. Carroll. "Ancient and Medieval Falconry: Origins and Functions in Medieval England," Richard III Society/American Branch (accessed July 19, 2018), http://www.r3.org/richard-iii/15th-century-life/15th-century-life-articles/ancient-medieval-falconry-origins-functions-in-medieval-england.

"Falcon Symbol," Native American Symbols (accessed July 19, 2018), https://www.warpaths2peacepipes.com/native-american-symbols/falcon-symbol.htm.

Falcon (cont.)

"Falcons," Ancient Egyptian Bestiary: Falcons (accessed July 19, 2018), http://www.reshafim.org.il/ad/egypt/bestiary/falcon.htm.

"Horus: The Egyptian Falcon God," Ancient Egypt Online (accessed July 19, 2018). http://www.ancient-egypt-online.com/horus.html.

Emily Pate. "The Characteristics of Falcons," Sciencing (April 25, 2017), https://sciencing.com/characteristics-falcons-10048987.html.

Firefly

Alonso Abugattas. "Firefly Folklore," Capital Naturalist (June 27, 2014), http://capitalnaturalist.blogspot.com/2014/06/firefly-folklore.html.

Precy Anza. "The Legend of the Firefly," HubPages (August 28, 2017), https://hubpages.com/religion-philosophy/Philippine-Legend-The-Legend-Of-The-Firefly.

Joanna Klein. "How to Talk to Fireflies," *New York Times* (July 5, 2016), p. D6, https://www.nytimes.com/2016/06/30/science/how-to-talk-to-fireflies.html.

Katie Pohlman. "Twelve Fascinating Facts about Fireflies," EcoWatch (June 10, 2016), https://www.ecowatch.com/12-fascinating-facts-about-fireflies-1891169972.html.

Flea

"Flea," Wikipedia (accessed July 17, 2018), https://en.wikipedia.org/wiki/Flea.

Stephanie Pappas. "Giant Bloodsuckers! Oldest Fleas Discovered," Live Science (February 29, 2012), https://www.livescience.com/18734-giant-ancient-fleas-discovered.html.

Adam Retzer. "Ten Little-Known Facts about Fleas," Flea Science (August 22, 2014), http://fleascience.com/10-little-known-facts-about-fleas.

Fly

"Fly," Wikipedia (accessed July 17, 2018), https://en.wikipedia.org/wiki/Fly.

"Flies," Ancient Egyptian Bestiary (accessed July 19, 2018), http://www.reshafim.org.il/ad/egypt/bestiary/fly.htm.

"The History of Art and the Curious Lives of Famous Painters," History of Painters (accessed July 19, 2018), http://www.historyofpainters.com/insect.htm.

"Native American Fly Mythology," Native Languages of the Americas (accessed July 19, 2018), http://www.native-languages.org/legends-fly.htm.

"What Do Flies Symbolize?" Reference (accessed July 19, 2018), https://www.reference.com/pets-animals/flies-symbolize-23947133adc6d3f6#.

"Who Is the Egyptian God of Flies and What Was His Role?" Quora (accessed July 19, 2018), https://www.quora.com/Who-is-the-Egyptian-god-of-flies-and-what-was-his-role.

Fox

"Fox Meaning and Symbolism," All Totems (accessed July 19, 2018), http://alltotems.com/fox-spirit-meaning-symbols-and-totem.

"Fox Spirit," Wikipedia (accessed July 17, 2018), https://en.wikipedia.org/wiki/Fox_spirit.

"Native American Fox Mythology," Native Languages of the Americas (accessed July 19, 2018), http://www.native-languages.org/legends-fox.htm.

"Pale Fox—Mysterious Fox of the African Desert," Website of Everything (accessed July 19, 2018), http://thewebsiteofeverything.com/animals/mammals/Carnivora/Canidae/Vulpes/Vulpes-pallida.html.

Frog

Janie Bill. "Elements of Fantasy—Frogs," Fantasy Faction (August 10, 2014), http://fantasy-faction.com/2014/elements-of-fantasy-frogs.

Peter Bowden. "Sacred Frog Medicine: Kambo Ceremony," Manataka American Indian Council (accessed July 19, 2018), http://manataka.org/page2923.html.

"Frogs and Toads," Ancient Egyptian Bestiary (accessed July 19, 2018), http://www.reshafim.org.il/ad/egypt/bestiary/frog.htm.

"Frog Fun Facts," American Museum of Natural History (accessed July 18, 2019), https://www.amnh.org/exhibitions/frogs-a-chorus-of-colors/frog-fun-facts.

Giraffe

"Gigantic Engravings of a Giraffe Created Long Before Egypt as We Know It Existed," Ancient Pages (January 14, 2015), http://www.messagetoeagle.com/amazing-gigantic-engravings-created-long-before-ancient-egypt-as-we-know-it-existed.

"Giraffes in Culture," Giraffe Worlds (accessed July 19, 2018), http://www.giraffeworlds.com/giraffes-in-culture.

"Giraffe," Wikipedia (accessed July 17, 2018), https://en.wikipedia.org/wiki/Giraffe.

Kammie Kam. "African Giraffe Mask," Prezi (May 22, 2014) https://prezi.com/l9qxszwxvbqs/african-giraffe-mask.

Giraffe (cont.)

"Ten Amazing Facts You (Probably) Didn't Know about Giraffe," Alluring Africa (accessed July 19, 2018), https://alluringafrica.com/10-amazing-facts-probably-didnt-know-giraffe.

Goat

"Goat," Wikipedia (accessed July 17, 2018), https://en.wikipedia.org/wiki/Goat.

Moe. "GOAT: The Devilish God of All Things," Gnostic Warrior (September 2, 2014), https://gnosticwarrior.com/goat.html.

Goldfinch

"American Goldfinch," Hinterland Who's Who (accessed July 16, 2018), http://www.hww.ca/en/wildlife/birds/american-goldfinch.html.

"American Goldfinch—Life History," All about Birds (accessed July 16, 2018), https://www.allaboutbirds.org/guide/American_Goldfinch/lifehistory.

Mabel Powers, from *Stories the Iroquois Tell Their Children* (1917), as cited by "Why the Goldfinches Look Like the Sun," Whispering Books (accessed August 30, 2018), http://whisperingbooks.com/Show_Page/?book=Legends_Of_The_Iroquois&story=Why_Goldfinches_Look_Like_Sun.

Goose

"Facts about Goose," Lifestyle Lounge (accessed July 19, 2018), http://lifestyle.iloveindia.com/lounge/facts-about-goose-8064.html.

"Goose," Wikipedia (accessed July 17, 2018), https://en.wikipedia.org/wiki/Goose.

"Native American Goose Mythology," Native Languages of the Americas (accessed July 19, 2018), http://www.native-languages.org/legends-goose.htm.

Deanne Quarrie. "Goose," Blue Roebuck (accessed July 19, 2018), http://www.blueroebuck.com/goose.html.

"Twenty-nine Super-Interesting Facts about Geese," Farmers Joint (accessed July 19, 2018), http://www.farmersjoint.com/blog/livestock-farming/poultry/29-super-interesting-facts-about-geese.

Gopher

Aay. "Politicians and Gophers," Y Worlds (November 7, 2014), http://yworlds.com/2014/11/07/politicians-gophers.

"Gopher," Wikipedia (accessed July 17, 2018), https://en.wikipedia.org/wiki/Gopher.

"Native American Gopher Mythology, Native Languages of the Americas (accessed July 19, 2018), http://www.native-languages.org/legends-gopher.htm.

Gorilla

Matt Ayres. "Seven Amazing Facts about Gorillas That You Probably Didn't Know," Animalogic (August 17, 2016), http://community.lovenature.com/featured-doc/7-amazing-facts-about-gorillas-that-you-probably-didnt-know.

Berggorilla and Regenwald Direkthilfe. *Gorilla Journal*, no 18 (June 1999), http://www.berggorilla.org/fileadmin/user_upload/pdf/journal/journal-en/gorilla-journal-18-english.pdf.

Sarah McPherson. "Ten Amazing Gorilla Facts," Discover Wildlife (July 14, 2014), http://www.discoverwildlife.com/animals/mammals/10-amazing-gorilla-facts

Grasshopper

"The Legend of Tithonus and Eos," Florida Gardener (June 3, 2008), http://www.floridagardener.com/pom/tithonusandeos.htm.

Renee McGarry. "Grasshopper," Aztecs at Mexicolore (June 5, 2011), http://www.mexicolore.co.uk/aztecs/flora-and-fauna/grasshopper.

"Native American Grasshopper Mythology," Native Languages of the Americas (accessed July 20, 2018), http://www.native-languages.org/legends-grasshopper.htm.

Sherry Riter. "Twenty-seven Grasshopper Facts, Symbolism and You," Redhead Riter (accessed July 20, 2018), http://www.theredheadriter.com/2014/10/27-grasshopper-facts-symbolism-and-you.

Grouse

"Grouse," Wikipedia (accessed July 17, 2018), https://en.wikipedia.org/wiki/Grouse.

"Ruffed Grouse," State Symbols USA (accessed July 20, 2018), https://statesymbolsusa.org/symbol-or-officially-designated-item/pennsylvania/state-bird/ruffed-grouse.

"Ruffed Grouse," All about Birds (accessed July 20, 2018), https://www.allaboutbirds.org/guide/Ruffed_Grouse/lifehistory.

"Ruffed Grouse (Bonasa Umbellus)," Wildscreen Arkive (accessed July 20, 2018), https://www.arkive.org/ruffed-grouse/bonasa-umbellus.

Groundhog

Dan. "Groundhog Medicine: The Wisdom of the Groundhog," Return to Nature (June 2, 2013), http://returntonature.us/groundhog-medicine-experiencing-the-wisdom-of-the-groundhog.

"Groundhogs," Havahart (accessed July 20, 2018), http://www.havahart.com/groundhog-facts.

"Groundhog," Wikipedia (accessed July 17, 2018), https://en.wikipedia.org/wiki/Groundhog.

Cie Simurro. "Totems: Groundhog," Wisdom Magazine (accessed July 20, 2018), http://wisdom-magazine.com/Article.aspx/1053.

Stefan Sirucek. "Nine Things You Didn't Know about Groundhogs," National Geographic (January 31, 2014), https://news.nationalgeographic.com/news/2014/01/groundhogs-day-animals-wildlife.

Guinea Pig

Eduardo Archetti. "The Social and Symbolic World of Guinea Pigs in the Andes," Vacuum, no. 4 (accessed August 30, 2018), http://www.thevacuum.org.uk/issues/issues0120/issue04/is04artsocsym.html.

"Forty Fun Guinea Pig Facts," Abyssinian Guinea Pig Tips (accessed July 20, 2018), https://abyssinianguineapigtips.com/guinea-pig-facts.

"Guinea Pig," Wikipedia (accessed July 17, 2018), https://en.wikipedia.org/wiki/Guinea_pig.

"Guinea Pig History," Animal Corner (accessed August 30, 2018), https://animalcorner.co.uk/guinea-pig-history.

Hawk

Paul D. Frost. "Hawks Mythology and Folklore," Raptors (accessed July 20, 2018), http://www.pauldfrost.co.uk/intro_h2.html.

"Hawk," Wikipedia (accessed July 17, 2018), https://en.wikipedia.org/wiki/Hawk.

"Hawk Facts," Raptor Trust (accessed July 20, 2018), http://theraptortrust.org/the-birds/hawk-facts.

"Hawk Symbol," Native Indian Tribes (accessed July 20, 2018), https://www.warpaths2peacepipes.com/native-american-symbols/hawk-symbol.htm.

Aimee Rebekah Shea. "Sacred Symbolism of Birds," Indigo International (September 13, 2012), http://indigointernational.org/sacred-symbolism-of-birds.

"Spiritual Meaning of the Red Tail Hawk," Keepers of the Sacred Tradition of Pipemakers (May 7, 2015), https://www.facebook.com/pipekeepers/posts/10152886302836491.

Hedgehog

Andre Dollinger. "Hedgehogs and Porcupines," Ancient Egyptian Bestiary (accessed July 21, 2018), http://www.reshafim.org.il/ad/egypt/bestiary/hedgehog.htm.

"Hedgehogs in Myth and Legend," Hedgehog Central (accessed July 20, 2018), http://www.hedgehogcentral.com/myths.shtml.

Hannah Keyser. "Sixteen Fun Facts about Hedgehogs," Mental Floss (March 29, 2016), http://mentalfloss.com/article/56004/16-fun-facts-about-hedgehogs.

Heron/Egret

"Animal Folklore the Heron," Pitlane Magazine (accessed July 20, 2018), http://www.pitlanemagazine.com/cultures/animal-folklore-the-heron.html.

"Native American Heron Mythology," Native Languages of the Americas (accessed July 20, 2018), http://www.native-languages.org/legends-heron.htm.

Aimee Rebekah Shea. "Sacred Symbolism of Birds," Indigo International (September 13, 2012), http://indigointernational.org/sacred-symbolism-of-birds.

"Symbols: Blue Heron," Mind Body and Spirit Gifts and Books (accessed July 20, 2018), http://www.mindbodyspirit-online.com/blue_heron.

"What a Heron Symbolizes: The Meanings Are Compiled Right Here," Mysticurious (accessed July 20, 2018), http://mysticurious.com/what-does-heron-symbolize.

Hippopotamus

"Hippo," Ancient Egyptian Bestiary http://www.reshafim.org.il/ad/egypt/bestiary/hippo.htm.

"Hippopotamus," One Kind Planet (accessed July 20, 2018), https://one kind planet.org/animal/hippopotamus.

"Hippopotamus in Culture," Hippo Worlds (accessed July 20, 2018), http://www.hippoworlds.com/hippopotamus-in-culture.

"Hippopotamus ("William")," Met (accessed July 20, 2018), https://www.metmuseum.org/art/collection/search/544227.

Matt Kareus. "Six Surprising Facts about Hippos," Safarist (December 19, 2014), https://isafari.nathab.com/blog/six-surprising-facts-about-hippos.

Jennifer Spirko. "What Did the Hippopotamus Symbolize in Egyptian Mythology," Classroom (accessed July 20, 2018), http://classroom.synonym.com/did-hippopotamus-symbolize-egyptian-mythology-15955.html.

"Taweret," Wikipedia (accessed July 17, 2018), https://en.wikipedia.org/wiki/Taweret.

Horse

Alina Bradford. "Mustangs: Facts about America's Wild Horses," Live Science (June 24, 2014), https://www.livescience.com/27686-mustangs.html.

"Four Horsemen of the Apocalypse," Wikipedia (accessed July 17, 2018), https://en.wikipedia.org/wiki/Four_Horsemen_of_the_Apocalypse.

"Horse," One Kind Planet (accessed July 20, 2018), https://one kind planet.org/animal/horse.

"Horse Symbolism," Pure Spirit (accessed July 20, 2018), http://www.pure-spirit.com.

Valda Roric. "Horses as Symbols of Power in History and Mythology," Ancient Origins (May 18, 2016), http://www.ancient-origins.net/history/horses-symbols-power-history-and-mythology-005912.

Mark W. Sanderson. "The Horse in Myth and Legend: Selected Snippets," Symbolic Horse Education Resources (accessed July 20, 2018), http://www.symbolic-horse.info/myth.htm.

Hummingbird

Nicole Canfield. "The Hummingbird Spirit Guide," Exemplore (March 4, 2017), https://exemplore.com/spirit-animals/The-Hummingbird-Folklore-Symbolism-and-Spirit-Guide.

"Interesting Facts on Hummingbirds," UC Davis Veterinary Medicine (accessed July 20, 2018), http://hummingbirds.ucdavis.edu/hummingbird_information/interesting_facts.cfm.

"Native American Mythology," Hummingbird World (accessed July 20, 2018), http://hummingbirdworld.com/h/native_american.htm.

Hyena

Sankalan Baidya. "Thirty Interesting Spotted Hyena Facts," Facts Legend (May 31, 2014), http://factslegend.org/30-interesting-spotted-hyena-facts.

Lory Herbison and George W. Frame. "Hyena," Encyclopedia Britannica (accessed July 20, 2018), https://www.britannica.com/animal/hyena.

"Hyena," New World Encyclopedia (accessed July 20, 2018), http://www.newworldencyclopedia.org/entry/Hyena.

"Hyena," Wikipedia (accessed July 17, 2018), https://en.wikipedia.org/wiki/Hyena.

Ibis

"African Sacred Ibis," Wikipedia (accessed July 17, 2018), https://en.wikipedia.org/wiki/African_sacred_ibis.

Linda Alchin. "Thoth, God of Egypt," Land of Pyramids (accessed July 20, 2018), http://www.landofpyramids.org/thoth.htm.

Grrl Scientist. "Mystery Bird: Asian Crested Ibis, Nipponia Nippon," Guardian (March 11, 2011), https://www.theguardian.com/science/punctuated-equilibrium/2011/mar/11/4.

"Ibis," A–Z Animals (accessed July 20, 2018), https://A-Z -animals.com/animals/ibis.

"Ibis," Ancient Egyptian Bestiary (accessed July 20, 2018), http://www.reshafim.org.il/ad/egypt/bestiary/ibis.htm.

"Ibis," Native Symbols (accessed July 20, 2018), http://nativesymbols.info/ibis.

Janet Thomas. "The Role of the Sacred Ibis in Ancient Egypt," Janet Thomas blog (March 6, 2013), https://janetthomas.wordpress.com/2013/03/06/the-role-of-the-sacred-ibis-in-ancient-egypt.

Jackal

Melissa Flagg. "The Egyptian God of the Dead: Anubis the Black Jackal," Exemplore (September 25, 2017), https://exemplore.com/paganism/The-Egyptian-God-of-the-Dead-Anubis.

Bernd Grahl. "Why Is the Jackal Called a Trickster?" Gondwana Collection (January 22, 2016), https://www.gondwana-collection.com/blog/jackal.

Jackal (cont.)

"Interesting Facts about Jackals," Just Fun Facts (accessed July 20, 2018), http://justfunfacts.com/interesting-facts-about-jackals.

"Jackal," Wikipedia (accessed July 17, 2018), https://en.wikipedia.org/wiki/Jackal.

Jaguar

Alina Bradford. "Jaguar Facts: Biggest Cat in Americas," Live Science (September 21, 2017), https://www.livescience.com/27301-jaguars.html.

Beth A. Conklin. *Consuming Grief: Compassionate Cannibalism in an Amazonian Society* (Austin, TX.: University of Texas Press, 2001).

"Jaguar," Wikipedia (accessed July 17, 2018), https://en.wikipedia.org/wiki/Jaguar.

"Jaguar: *Panthera Onca*," San Diego Zoo (accessed July 20,2 018), http://animals.sandiegozoo.org/animals/jaguar.

Javelina

"Collared Peccary—*Pecari Tajacu*," Nature Works (accessed August 6, 2018), http://www.nhptv.org/natureworks/peccary.htm.

"Covered Vessel with the Principal Bird and Peccary Heads, A.D. 200/300," Art Institute of Chicago (accessed August 6, 2018), http://www.artic.edu/aic/collections/artwork/195461.

Nicholas Hellmuth. "Peccary," Revue (October 1, 2010), http://www.revuemag.com/2010/10/peccary.

"Peccary," Wikipedia (accessed August 6, 2018), https://en.wikipedia.org/wiki/Peccary.

Wing-Chi Poon. "Collared Peccary," Animal Facts (accessed August 6, 2018), https://theanimalfacts.com/mammals/collared-peccary.

Hope B. Werness. *The Continuum Encyclopedia of Animal Symbolism in Art* (New York: Continuum International Publishing Group, 2004), p. 323.

Jellyfish

Margaret Badore. "Fourteen Fascinating Facts about Jellyfish," Treehugger (March 13, 2014), https://www.treehugger.com/natural-sciences/14-fascinating-facts-about-jellyfish.html.

Megan Gambino. "Fourteen Fun Facts about Jellyfish," Smithsonian (accessed April 17, 2012), https://www.smithsonianmag.com/science-nature/14-fun-facts-about-jellyfish-67987765.

"Jellyfish," Wikipedia (accessed July 17, 2018), https://en.wikipedia.org/wiki/Jellyfish.

"Ten Cool Things You Didn't Know about Jellyfish," CBC (accessed July 20, 2018), http://www.cbc.ca/kidscbc2/the-feed/10-cool-things-you-didnt-know-about-jellyfish.

Kangaroo

"Interesting Kangaroo Fun Facts and Information," Down Undr (accessed July 20, 2018), http://www.downundr.com/facts/interesting-fun-facts-about-kangaroos.

"Kangaroo," Wikipedia (accessed July 17, 2018), https://en.wikipedia.org/wiki/Kangaroo.

"Kangaroos in Popular Culture," KangarooWorlds (accessed July 20, 2018), http://www.kangarooworlds.com/kangaroos-in-popular-culture.

Greg Lehman. "The Palawa Voice," Companion to Tasmanian History (accessed July 20, 2018), http://www.utas.edu.au/library/companion_to_tasmanian_history/P/Palawa%20Voice.htm.

Trishan. "What Is a Kangaroo?" Trishan's Oz (accessed July 20, 2018), https://panique.com.au/trishansoz/animals/kangaroo.html.

Kingfisher/Kookaburra

Lynn E. Cohen. "The Kingfisher as a Symbol for Hopkins and Later Poets: Thomas Stearns Eliot, Charles Olson, and Amy Clampitt," Hopkins Lectures 2009/Hofstra University (accessed July 20, 2018), http://www.gerardmanleyhopkins.org/lectures_2009/kingfisher_as_symbol.html.

Emily Jarvis. "Birds of Ice in Mythology" Ouevre (January 23, 2012), http://esjarvis.blogspot.com/2012/01/birds-of-ice-in-mythology.html.

"Kingfisher," Wikipedia (accessed July 17, 2018), https://en.wikipedia.org/wiki/Kingfisher.

"Native American Kingfisher Mythology," Native Languages of the Americas (accessed July 20, 2018), http://www.native-languages.org/legends-kingfisher.htm.

Koala

Glenna Albrecht. "Koala's: A Retrospective," Glenna Albrecht Psychoterratica (January 17, 2017), https://glennaalbrecht.wordpress.com/2017/01/17/koalas-a-retrospective.

Koala (cont.)

"A Brief History of Koalas," Australian Koala Foundation (accessed July 20, 2018), https://www.savethekoala.com/about-koalas/brief-history-koalas.

"Koala," Wikipedia (accessed July 17, 2018), https://en.wikipedia.org/wiki/Koala.

Ladybug

Taryn Campbell. "Ladybug Lore," Celtic Bug (accessed July 19, 2018) http://www.celticbug.com/Legends/Lore.html.

"Coccinellidae," Wikipedia (accessed July 16, 2018), https://en.wikipedia.org/wiki/Coccinellidae.

"The Facts about How Ladybugs Help Humans," Den Garden (November 10, 2016), https://dengarden.com/gardening/Ladybugs-Facts.

Lark

All about Birds. "Horned Lark," Cornell Lab of Ornithology (accessed July 19, 2018), https://www.allaboutbirds.org/guide/Horned_Lark/sounds.

Mary X. Dennis. "The Social Lives of Chinese Songbirds," Audubon (January 6, 2013), http://www.audubon.org/news/the-social-lives-chinese-songbirds.

Aathira Perinchery. "For a Lark, This Bird Imitates 34 Others!" Hindu (October 21, 2017), http://www.thehindu.com/sci-tech/science/for-a-lark-this-bird-imitates-34-others/article19897541.ece.

Leech

Edward Tuite Dalton. *Descriptive Ethnology of Bengal* (1872), https://books.google.com/books?id=9wxWAAAAcAAJ.

Julia Layton. "Ten Crazy Facts You Didn't Know about Animals," How Stuff Works (accessed June 22, 2018), https://animals.howstuffworks.com/animal-facts/10-crazy-facts-about-animals6.htm.

"Leech," Wikipedia (accessed June 22, 2018), https://en.wikipedia.org/wiki/Leech.

Lemur

"Lemur," Wikipedia (accessed July 16, 2018), https://en.wikipedia.org/wiki/Lemur.

"Lemur Sense," Lemur World (accessed July 19, 2018), http://www.lemurworld.com/lemur-senses.

"Lemuria," Paranormal Encyclopedia (accessed July 19, 2018), https://www.paranormal-encyclopedia.com/l/lemuria.

"Ring-tailed Lemur," Folly Farm (accessed July 19, 2018), https://www.folly-farm.co.uk/zoo/meet-the-zoo-animals/ring-tailed-lemur.

Leopard/Black Panther

Penny Baldwin-French. "The Majestic African Black Panther," Zawadee (May 18, 2016), http://www.zawadee.com/blog/ca/the-majestic-african-black-panther.

"Leopard," Wikipedia (accessed July 16, 2018), https://en.wikipedia.org/wiki/Leopard.

"Leopards and Mythology," Leopard Men (accessed July 19, 2018), https://theleopardmen.wordpress.com/leopards-and-mythology.

Scott Ramsay. "Africa's Elusive Leopards Disappearing," Love Wild Africa (February 29, 2016), https://www.lovewildafrica.com/stories/africas-elusive-leopards-disappearing.

Lion

"Big Cats Initiative," National Geographic Society (accessed November 12, 2018), https://www.nationalgeographic.org/projects/big-cats-initiative/education.

"Lion," Wikipedia (accessed July 16, 2018), https://en.wikipedia.org/wiki/Lion.

"The White Lion: Home Is a Journey," Society Gone Forever (accessed July 19, 2018), http://societygone.weebly.com/legend-of-the-white-lion.html.

Lizard/Chameleon/Gecko/Gila Monster/Iguana/Komodo Dragon

Elsdon Best (1856–1931). "Myths Concerning Lizards," *Maori Religion and Mythology: Being an Account of the Cosmogony, Anthropogeny, Religious Beliefs and Rites, Magic and Folk Lore or the Maori Folk of New Zealand, Part 2* (Wellington, N.Z.: P.D. Hasselberg), p. 460, http://nzetc.victoria.ac.nz/tm/scholarly/tei-Bes02Reli-t1-body-d4-d5-d15.html.

Alina Bradford. "Iguana Facts," Live Science (June 11, 2015), https://www.livescience.com/51153-iguanas.html.

"Color Changes," Green Iguana Society (accessed July 19, 2018), http://www.greenigsociety.org/colors.htm.

Alex Morgan. "From Inspiration to Photography: A Lizard's Tale," Henna Page (accessed July 19, 2018), http://www.hennapage.com/journal/issue_I/article_2/page2.html.

Lizard/Chameleon/Gecko/Gila Monster/Iguana/Komodo Dragon (cont.)

"The Mysterious Moche Icon of the Iguana, Companion to the Sky God Wrinkle Face," Ancient Origins (July 4, 2016), http://www.ancient-origins.net/artifacts-other-artifacts/mysterious-moche-icon-iguana-companion-sky-god-wrinkle-face-006233.

"Myths and Misconceptions," Green Iguana Society (accessed July 19, 2018), http://www.greenigsociety.org/myths.htm.

"Native American Lizard Mythology," Native Languages of the Americas (accessed July 19, 2018), http://www.native-languages.org/legends-lizard.htm.

"Seventeen Interesting Facts about Iguanas," Oh Fact (accessed July 19, 2018), https://ohfact.com/interesting-facts-about-iguana.

Llama/Alpaca/Guanaco/Vicuna

"Inca Empire," Wikipedia (accessed July 19, 2018), https://en.wikipedia.org/wiki/Inca.

"Inca Gold Llama," BBC (accessed July 19, 2018), http://www.bbc.co.uk/ahistoryoftheworld/objects/l83ZQ7grS9iS0D84X8HRuA.

Marina Jones. "The Dark Constellations of the Incas," Futurism (August 10, 2014), https://futurism.com/the-dark-constellations-of-the-incas.

"Llama," Wikipedia (accessed July 19, 2018), https://en.wikipedia.org/wiki/Llama.

"Llama," Desert USA (accessed July 19, 2018), https://www.desertusa.com/animals/llama.html.

Paulina Suarez. "Yacana's Constellation," Groovy Fayuca (November 17, 2013), http://groovyfayuca.blogspot.com/2013/11/yacanas-constellation.html.

Manatee

Caty Fairclough. "From Mermaids to Manatees: The Myth and the Reality," Smithsonian Ocean (accessed July 19, 2018), http://ocean.si.edu/ocean-news/mermaids-manatees-myth-and-reality.

"Manatee," Wikipedia (accessed July 19, 2018), https://en.wikipedia.org/wiki/Manatee.

"Manatees in Culture," Manatee-World (accessed July 19, 2018), http://www.manatee-world.com/manatees-in-culture.

Annelies Rhemrev. "The Manatee Nebula: A Supernova Remnant in Aquila," Anne's Astronomy News (accessed July 19, 2018), http://annesastronomynews.com/photo-gallery-ii/nebulae-clouds/the-manatee-nebula.

Mockingbird/Thrasher

Sastry Bapanna. "Amazing Facts about Northern Mockingbird," Knowledge (accessed July 19, 2018), http://knowledge-sastha.blogspot.com/2015/07/amazing-facts-about-northern-mockingbird.html.

"Native American Mockingbird Mythology," Native Languages of the Americas (accessed July 19, 2018), http://www.native-languages.org/legends-mockingbird.htm.

"Northern Mockingbird," Wikipedia (accessed July 19, 2018), https://en.wikipedia.org/wiki/Northern_mockingbird.

Mole

Rob Atkinson. "Animal Folklore: A Mole in the Hand," Folklore Thursday (April 27, 2017), http://folklorethursday.com/folklife/animal-folklore-mole-hand/#sthash.v3IiM6PT.dpbs.

Alina Bradford. "Facts about Moles," Live Science (September 24, 2015), https://www.livescience.com/52297-moles.html.

"Native American Mole Mythology," Native Languages of the Americas (accessed July 19, 2018), http://www.native-languages.org/legends-mole.htm.

"Mole (Animal), Wikipedia (accessed July 19, 2018), https://en.wikipedia.org/wiki/Mole_(animal).

"Tales from Temagami—Land of Deep Water," Native Web (accessed July 19, 2018), http://temagami.nativeweb.org/tale-folklore-10.html.

Mongoose/Meercat

Alina Bradford. "Mongoose Facts," Live Science (accessed July 19, 2018), https://www.livescience.com/52565-mongoose.html.

"Egyptian Mongoose," Wikipedia (accessed July 19, 2018), https://en.wikipedia.org/wiki/Egyptian_mongoose.

"Facts about Mongoose," Fast Facts (accessed July 19, 2018), http://www.findfast.org/facts-about-mongoose.htm.

"Mongoose Facts," Soft Schools (accessed July 19, 2018), http://www.softschools.com/facts/animals/mongoose_facts/45.

"Mongoose," One Kind Planet (accessed July 19, 2018), https://onekindplanet.org/animal/mongoose.

Monkey/Baboon/Chimpanzee/Orangutan

Matt Ayres. "Seven Sacred Animals from Around the World," Animalogic (April 14, 2016), http://community.lovenature.com/blog/7-sacred-animals-from-around-the-world.

Monkey/Baboon/Chimpanzee/Orangutan (cont.)

Joslyn C. "Nonhuman Animals Mourning," Interconnectivity: Animals Mourning Together in Modern Stories and Mythology (June 12, 2014), http://scalar.usc.edu/works/chid490animalmourning/animal-mourning.

"Introduction to Monkeys," Monkey World (accessed July 23, 2018), http://www.monkeyworlds.com.

Anniina Jokinen. "Monkeys and Monkey Gods in Mythology, Folklore, and Religion." Luminarium (March 8, 2007), http://www.luminarium.org/mythology/monkeygods.htm.

Karin Lehnardt. "Sixty Interesting Facts about Monkeys," Fact Retriever (May 23, 2017), https://www.factretriever.com/monkey-facts.

Moose

Terri Benning. "Moose," Totem Talk (August 13, 2010), http://totemtalk.ning.com/group/m/forum/topics/moose-1.

"Interesting Facts about Moose," Interesting Fun Facts (May 1, 2012), http://www.interestingfunfacts.com/interesting-facts-about-moose.html#F1702rdauvLSQmvB.99.

"Moose Meaning and Symbolism," Dreaming and Sleeping (accessed July 23, 2018), https://dreamingandsleeping.com/moose-meaning-and-symbolism.

"Moose: *Alces Americanus*," Nature Works (accessed July 23, 2018), http://www.nhptv.org/natureworks/moose.htm.

Peter Muise. "The Specter Moose of Maine," New England Folklore (March 4, 2012), http://newenglandfolklore.blogspot.com/2012/03/specter-moose-of-maine.html.

Mosquito

Asahngwa Constantine. "The Mythical Origin of Mosquitoes and Its Implication for Malaria Prevention in Bamunka, North West Region of Cameroon," *PACEsetterS*, vol. 8, no. 1 (January–March 2011), pp. 39–40, http://journals.lww.com/jbipacesetters/fulltext/2011/01000/The_mythical_origin_of_mosquitoes_and_its.15.aspx.

Debbie Hadley. "Ten Fascinating Facts about Mosquitoes," ThoughtCo. (September 24, 2017), https://www.thoughtco.com/fascinating-facts-about-mosquitoes-1968300.

"Mosquito," Wikipedia (accessed July 23, 2018), https://en.wikipedia.org/wiki/Mosquito.

"Mosquitoes," *National Geographic* (April 11, 2010), https://www.nationalgeographic.com/animals/invertebrates/group/mosquitoes.

Vlad Vekshtein. "Ten Tales of Creepy-Crawlies from Myth and Folklore," Listverse (August 7, 2014), https://listverse.com/2014/08/07/10-tales-of-creepy-crawlies-from-myth-and-folklore.

Moth

Nicole Canfield. "The Meaning of the Moth as a Spirit Guide," Exemplore (May 16, 2018), https://exemplore.com/spirit-animals/Animal-Spirit-Guides-Meanings-The-Moth-Spirit-Guide.

Infinite Spider. "Five Quick Facts about the Luna Moth," Infinite Spider (June 24, 2017), https://infinitespider.com/five-facts-about-the-luna-moth.

"Interesting Facts about Moths," Just Fun Facts (accessed July 23, 2018), http://justfunfacts.com/interesting-facts-about-moths.

Liti. "Our Giant Silk Moths and Ancient Mythology," National Moth Week (April 29, 2014), http://nationalmothweek.org/2014/04/29/our-giant-silk-moths-and-ancient-mythology.

"Moth," Wikipedia (accessed July 23, 2018), https://en.wikipedia.org/wiki/Moth.

"Moth Facts," Soft Schools (accessed July 23, 2018), http://www.softschools.com/facts/animals/moths_facts/1270.

"Moth Symbolism." Moth Symbolism (accessed July 23, 2018), http://mothsymbolism.com.

Motmot

"Blue-Crowned Motmot," Rainforest Alliance (November 14, 2006), https://www.rainforest-alliance.org/species/motmot.

"Blue-Crowned Motmot (*Momotus momota*)," Coraciiformes Taxon Advisory Group (accessed September 25, 2018), http://www.coraciiformestag.com/Motmot/momotus/momotus.html.

Adrienne Dickerson. "*Momotus Momota:* Blue-Crowned Motmot," Animal Diversity Web (accessed September 25, 2018), http://animaldiversity.org/accounts/Momotus_momota.

"Motmot," Wikipedia (accessed September 25, 2018), https://en.wikipedia.org/wiki/Motmot.

"Turquoise-Browed Motmot Feathers Were Potential Long-Distance Trade Goods," Maya Archaeology (accessed September 25, 2018), https://www.maya-archaeology.org/motmot-bird-feathers/long-distance-trade-mayan-merchants-trade-goods-products/turquoise-browed-motmot-eumomota-superciliosa-feathers.php.

Mouse

"Follow That Mouse—Mice in Folklore," Pirotta blog (4, 2012), https://pirottablog.wordpress.com/2012/03/04/follow-that-mouse-mice-in-folklore.

Jack Lyons. "Twelve Fascinating Facts about Mice You Need to Know," deBugged (January 8, 2018), https://www.jcehrlich.com/blog/12-fascinating-facts-about-mice-you-need-to-know.

"Mouse," Wikipedia (accessed July 23, 2018), https://en.wikipedia.org/wiki/Mouse.

"Native American Mouse Mythology," Native Languages of the Americas (accessed July 23, 2018), http://www.native-languages.org/legends-mouse.htm.

"Rodents," Ancient Egyptian Bestiary (accessed July 23, 2018), http://www.reshafim.org.il/ad/egypt/bestiary/rodent.htm.

"Seventeen Interesting Facts about Mice," Oh Fact! (accessed July 23, 2018), https://ohfact.com/interesting-facts-about-mice.

Musk Ox

Samantha Grace-Marie. "Musk Ox Myth and Legend," Samantha's Insights (November 12, 2010), http://samanthasinterestinginsights.blogspot.com/2010/11/musk-ox-myth-and-legend.html.

Ideaself90. "Musk Ox Hunting," Power Poetry (September 27, 2014), http://www.powerpoetry.org/poems/musk-ox-hunting.

"Interesting Facts," Nunavut Muskox (October 25, 2013), http://www.nunavutmuskox.ca/interesting_muskox_facts.html.

"Musk Ox," Animal Corner (accessed July 23, 2018), https://animalcorner.co.uk/animals/musk-ox.

Nighthawk

"Common Nighthawk" All about Birds (accessed July 23, 2018), https://www.allaboutbirds.org/guide/Common_nighthawk/lifehistory.

"Common Nighthawk," Bird's Lifestyle (February 2, 2013), http://birds-lifestyle.blogspot.com/2013/02/common-nighthawk.html.

https://phys.org/news/2018-10-scientists-track-nighthawks-migration-route.html

Eleanor Daisy Upstill-Goddard. "The Midnight 'Goatsucker'," Wildlife Articles (November 23, 2015), http://wildlifearticles.co.uk/the-midnight-goatsucker.

"Nightjars or Nighthawks aka Goatsuckers," Beauty of Birds (accessed July 23, 2018), https://www.beautyofbirds.com/nightjars.html.

Nuthatch

Roger Highfield. "Nuthatches Can Speak Chickadee," Telegraph (March 26, 2007), https://www.telegraph.co.uk/news/science/science-news/3352376/Nuthatches-can-speak-chickadee.html.

Timothy Martinez, Jr. "Ten Interesting Facts about Nuthatches," Into the Air (March 28, 2014), https://www.backyardchirper.com/blog/10-interesting-facts-about-nuthatches.

"Nuthatch," Royal Society for the Protection of Birds (RSPB) (accessed July 23, 2018), https://www.rspb.org.uk/birds-and-wildlife/wildlife-guides/bird-a-z/nuthatch/#HudqVeyW1sdfEkEC.99.

Evan T. Pritchard. *Bird Medicine: The Sacred Power of Bird Shamanism* (Rochester, VT.: Bear and Company, 2013), http://tiferetjournal.com/heart-warming-story-bird-medicine-sacred-power-bird-shamanism-evan-t-pritchard.

"Symbolism Surrounding White Breasted Nuthatch," Birdhouse Project (March 14, 2015), https://202holden.wordpress.com/2015/03/14/symbolism-surrounding-white-breasted-nuthatch.

"Twenty-One Facts about Nuthatches," Royal Society for the Protection of Birds (January 21, 2010), http://ww2.rspb.org.uk/community/wildlife/f/13609/t/8980.aspx#CdcYl1YhX4y33z8f.99.

Tom Waters. "A Nuthatch Has Been Collecting Whole Nuts and Burying Them in a Large Planter. Is This Normal?" Royal Society for the Protection of Birds (October 28, 2010), http://ww2.rspb.org.uk/birds-and-wildlife/bird-and-wildlife-guides/ask-an-expert/previous/nuthatch_nuts.aspx#u4tAyB7PiE3VplKt.99.

"White-Breasted Nuthatch," All about Birds (accessed July 23, 2018), https://www.allaboutbirds.org/guide/White-breasted_Nuthatch/lifehistory#.

Octopus

Landess Kearns. "Eleven Fun Facts That Prove Octopuses Are All Kinds of Astonishing," HuffPost (July 1, 2015), https://www.huffingtonpost.com/2015/07/01/octopus-facts_n_7692438.html.

Rachel Nuwer. "Ten Curious Facts about Octopuses," Smithsonian (October 31, 2013), https://www.smithsonianmag.com/science-nature/ten-curious-facts-about-octopuses-7625828.

"Octopus of Hawaii: Steeped in Hawaiian Legend," Kelii's Kayak Tours (accessed July 23, 2018), http://www.keliiskayak.com/octopus-hawaii.

Octopus (cont.)

"The Octopus Show: A Legend of the Deep," Nature (February 3, 2008), http://www.pbs.org/wnet/nature/the-octopus-show-a-legend-of-the-deep/2014.

Opossum

Alina Bradford, Live Science Contributor. "Facts about the Common Opossum," Live Science (September 20, 2016), https://www.livescience.com/56182-opossum-facts.html.

"How the Opossum Stole Fire," Rasheline (September 24, 2008), http://rasheline.blogspot.com/2008/09/how-opossum-stole-fire.html.

"Interesting Facts about Opossums," Just Fun Facts (accessed July 23, 2018), http://justfunfacts.com/interesting-facts-about-opossums.

"Opossum," Wikipedia (accessed July 23, 2018), https://en.wikipedia.org/wiki/Opossum#cite_note-63.

"Ridiculously Awesome Facts about Opossums," AnimalSake (June 7, 2017), https://animalsake.com/interesting-facts-about-opossums.

University of Florida. "Ancient Origins of Modern Opossum Revealed," Science News (December 17, 2009), https://www.sciencedaily.com/releases/2009/12/091215202320.htm.

Ostrich

"Birds: African Folklore," Wild Life Campus (accessed August 6, 2018), http://www.wildlifecampus.com/help/pdf/folklore_birds.pdf.

Alina Bradford. "Ostrich Facts: The World's Largest Bird," Live Science (September 17, 2014), https://www.livescience.com/27433-ostriches.html.

"Common Ostrich," Wikipedia (accessed August 6, 2018), https://en.wikipedia.org/wiki/Common_ostrich.

"The Feather (Shut)," Ancient Egypt (August 17, 2014), http://www.egyptianmyths.net/feather.htm.

"Minoan Ostrich Eggs from Africa," Paleoglot (March 23, 2011), http://paleoglot.blogspot.jp/2011/03/minoan-ostrich-eggs-from-africa.html.

"Origin of the Pangu Myth, the Cosmic Egg, the Creation of Heaven and Earth and Separation of Heaven and Earth Imagery, Nuwa Repairing the Heavens," Japanese Mythology and Folklore (accessed August 6, 2018), https://japanesemythology.wordpress.com/origin-of-the-pangu-myth-the-cosmic-egg-the-creation-of-heaven-and-earth-and-separation-of-heaven-and-earth-imagery-nuwa-repairing-the-heavens.

"Ostrich," Animal Files (accessed August 6, 2018), http://www.theanimalfiles.com/birds/ostrich/ostrich.html.

"Ten Interesting Facts about Ostrich: The Most Special Bird," Interesting Facts (accessed August 6, 2018), http://interestingfacts.tv/animal-facts/10-interesting-facts-about-ostrich-the-most-special-bird.

Otter

"The Fearsome Alaskan Tlingit Kushtaka: If It's not One Thing, it's an Otter," Esoterx (January 9, 2013), https://esoterx.com/2013/01/09/the-fearsome-alaskan-tlingit-kushtaka-if-its-not-one-thing-its-an-otter.

Estelle Hakner. "Eight Amazing Facts about Sea Otters," Discover Wildlife (August 10, 2016), http://www.discoverwildlife.com/animals/mammals/facts-about-sea-otters.

"Native American Otter Mythology," Native Languages of the Americas (accessed August 8, 2018), http://www.native-languages.org/legends-otter.htm.

"Otter," Trees for Life (accessed August 8, 2018), https://treesforlife.org.uk/forest/mythology-folklore/otter.

"Otters," SeaWorld Parks and Entertainment (accessed August 8, 2018), https://seaworld.org/en/animal-info/animal-infobooks/otters/diet-and-eating-habits.

"Otters in Culture," Otter World (accessed August 8, 2018), http://www.otter-world.com/otters-in-culture.

"Twelve Facts about Otters for Sea Otter Awareness Week," U.S. Department of the Interior "Sea Otter Cam," (September 25, 2017), https://www.doi.gov/blog/12-facts-about-otters-sea-otter-awareness-week.

"Zoroastrianism," Wikipedia (accessed August 8, 2018), https://en.wikipedia.org/wiki/Zoroastrianism#Vision_of_Zoroaster.

Owl

Deane Lewis. "Owl Eyes and Vision," Owl Pages (accessed August 8, 2018), https://www.owlpages.com/owls/articles.php?a=5.

Deane Lewis. "Owls in Mythology and Culture," Owl Pages (accessed August 8, 2018), https://www.owlpages.com/owls/articles.php?a=62.

Jamie K. Oxendine. "Concerning Owls," Powwows (July 21, 2011), http://www.powwows.com/concerning-owls.

"Physical Characteristics of Owls," Carolina (accessed August 8, 2018), https://www.carolina.com/teacher-resources/Interactive/information-on-the-physical-characteristics-of-owls/tr11106.tr.

Panda

Tamara Colloff-Bennett. "Bamboo and Blackened Eyes: The World of the Giant Panda," Quillcards (March 8, 2013), https://quillcards.com/blog/bamboo-and-blackened-eyes-the-world-of-the-giant-panda.

"Giant Panda," Wikipedia (accessed August 10, 2018), https://en.wikipedia.org/wiki/Giant_panda.

"Giant Pandas Behavior—What Do They Do All Day," China Highlights (accessed August 10, 2018), https://www.chinahighlights.com/giant-panda/behavior.htm.

"Pandapedia," River Safari (accessed August 10, 2018), http://pandas.riversafari.com.sg/pandapedia-02.html.

Parrot/Budgie/Cockatiel/Cockatoo/Love Bird/Macaw/Parakeet

Karen Becker. "These Unique Birds Eat in a Very Unusual Way," Healthy Pets (March 4, 2016), https://healthypets.mercola.com/sites/healthypets/archive/2016/03/04/10-fascinating-parrot-facts.aspx.

Alina Bradford. "Parrot Facts: Habits, Habitat and Species," Live Science (July 24, 2014), https://www.livescience.com/28071-parrots.html.

Craig Conley. "Birdwatching Among the Ruins: Mexico's Mythical Macaws," Words Worth (accessed November 2, 2018), http://www.oneletterwords.com/wordsworth/mythology/mayan.html.

Lora Kim. "The Living Legends of the Ancient Mayans," Lafeber (September 23, 2012), http://lafeber.com/conservation/the-living-legends-of-the-ancient-mayans.

"Native American Parrot Mythology," Native Languages of the Americas (accessed August 10, 2018), http://www.native-languages.org/legends-parrot.htm.

Patty. "A Bird's Five Senses," Bird Tricks (February 18, 2010), http://birdtricks.com/blog/tag/parrots-vision.

Deb White. "Parrots in Culture," Parrot Fun Zone (accessed August 10, 2018), http://parrotfunzone.com/explore-parrots/parrots-in-culture.

Peafowl

Maria Cook. "Characteristics of a Peacock Bird," Sciencing (April 19, 2018), https://sciencing.com/characteristics-peacock-bird-6155098.html.

Monarch13. "Bird Symbolism and Spiritual Gifts," Exemplore (December 15, 2014), https://exemplore.com/spirit-animals/divine-birds.

Prasenjit. "Peacock Facts and Information: Interesting Facts about Peacocks You Never Want to Miss," Animal Fun Facts (September 5, 2013), https://factsandtrivia.co.in/animalfacts/peacock-facts-information.

Peafowl, Depictions in Culture https://en.wikipedia.org/wiki/Peafowl#Depictions_in_culture

Pelican

Diana Cooper. "Interesting Facts about Pelicans," Bright Hub (June 23, 2010), http://www.brighthub.com/environment/science-environmental/articles/75097.aspx.

Joe Panek. "The Pelican (as a Symbol)," Seeker's Thoughts (August 21, 2011), http://www.aseekersthoughts.com/2011/08/pelican-as-symbol.html.

"Pelican," Medieval Bestiary (January 15, 2011), http://bestiary.ca/beasts/beast244.htm.

"Pelican Facts," Soft Schools (accessed August 14, 2018), http://www.softschools.com/facts/animals/pelican_facts/300.

"Remarkably Interesting Facts about the Australian Pelican," Bird Eden (March 9, 2018), https://birdeden.com/interesting-facts-about-australian-pelican.

Penguin

Zaria Gorvett. "If You Think Penguins Are Cute and Cuddly, You're Wrong," BBC (December 23, 2015), http://www.bbc.com/earth/story/20151223-if-you-think-penguins-are-cute-and-cuddly-youre-wrong.

Karin Lehnardt. "Sixty-Nine Wonderful Facts about Penguins," Fact Retriever (August 20, 2016), https://www.factretriever.com/penguin-facts.

"The Penguin," Tawaki Project (accessed August 14, 2018), http://www.tawaki-project.org/the-penguin.

"Penguin Facts and Information," Whale Facts (accessed August 14, 2018), https://www.whalefacts.org/penguin-facts.

"Ten Amazing Facts about Penguins," Amazing Facts about (February 5, 2018), https://amazingfactsabout.com/10-amazing-facts-about-penguins.

Pheasant

"Animals' Symbolism in Decoration, Decorative Arts, Chinese Beliefs, and Feng Shui," Nations Online (accessed August 14, 2018), http://www.nationsonline.org/oneworld/Chinese_Customs/animals_symbolism.htm.

Majid Awan. "Green Pheasant: National Bird of Japan," NationalPedia (March 15, 2017), http://www.nationalpedia.com/green-pheasant-national-bird-of-japan.

"Bird Symbolism in Chinese Art," Chinasage (accessed August 14, 2018), http://www.chinasage.info/symbols/birds.htm.

"Facts about Pheasant," Lifestyle Lounge (accessed August 14, 2018), http://lifestyle.iloveindia.com/lounge/facts-about-pheasant-8588.html.

M. Ishaq. "Golden Pheasant Bird Facts, Pictures and other Information," Live Animals (February 12, 2013), http://www.liveanimalslist.com/birds/golden-pheasant.php.

"Kiji," Immortal Geisha (accessed August 14, 2018), http://www.immortalgeisha.com/wiki/index.php?title=Kiji.

Phoenix

Liz Leafloor. "Ancient Symbolism of the Magical Phoenix," Ancient Origins (August 29, 2014), https://www.ancient-origins.net/myths-legends/ancient-symbolism-magical-phoenix-002020.

"Phoenix (Mythology)," Wikipedia (accessed August 14, 2018), https://en.wikipedia.org/wiki/Phoenix_(mythology).

Elaine Schoch. "Travel Trivia: 25 Things to Know about Phoenix," Carpe Travel (April 3, 2015), https://carpe-travel.com/fun-facts-about-phoenix.

"Unraveling the Mystery of the Phoenix: The Bird of Immortality," Ancient Pages (August 26, 2015), http://www.ancientpages.com/2015/08/26/unraveling-mystery-phoenix-bird-immortality.

Pig

"Interesting Facts about Pigs," Interesting Fun Facts (January 27, 2012), http://www.interestingfunfacts.com/interesting-facts-about-pigs.html.

"Pig," Wikipedia (accessed August 14, 2018), https://en.wikipedia.org/wiki/Pig.

"Pigs in Religion and Folklore," Professor Bamfield's Rare-Breed Pigs (accessed August 14, 2018), http://bamfield.eu/religion.php.

"Pigs: Suidae—Physical Characteristics," Animal Life Resource (accessed August 14, 2018), http://animals.jrank.org/pages/3273/Pigs-Suidae-PHYSICAL-CHARACTERISTICS.html.

"Top Ten Fascinating Facts about Pigs," People for the Ethical Treatment of Animals (May 7, 2009), https://www.peta.org/blog/top-ten-fascinating-facts-pigs/comment-page-1.

Platypus

"Interesting Facts / Mythology," Online Digital Education Connection (accessed August 14, 2018), http://www.odec.ca/projects/2010/hehexj2/Intresting_Facts_Mythology.htm.

"Platypus," Wikipedia (accessed August 14, 2018), https://en.wikipedia.org/wiki/Platypus.

"Platypus Facts," Soft Schools (accessed August 14, 2018), http://www.softschools.com/facts/animals/platypus_facts/282.

Pauline McLeod. *Aboriginal Art and Stories* (Carlingford, N.S.W.: Intechnics, 1994). https://catalogue.nla.gov.au/Record/1266574.

Porcupine

"About Porcupines," Native Tech (accessed November 2, 2018), www.nativetech.org/quill/porcupin.html.

Jenise Alongi. "Porcupine Facts," Animal Facts Encyclopedia (accessed August 17, 2018), https://www.animalfactsencyclopedia.com/Porcupine-facts.html.

"Native American Porcupine Mythology," Native Languages of the Americas (accessed August 17, 2018), http://www.native-languages.org/legends-porcupine.htm.

"Porcupine," Traditional Animal Foods (accessed August 17, 2018), http://traditionalanimalfoods.org/mammals/rodents/page.aspx?id=6155.

"Porcupine Facts," Soft Schools (accessed August 17, 2018), http://www.softschools.com/facts/animals/porcupine_facts/15.

Prairie Dog

Madronna Holden. "How Prairie Dogs Cry for Rain: Reflections on Shelter, Rain, and Drought," Our Earth/Ourselves (October 2, 2012), https://holdenma.wordpress.com/2012/10/02/how-the-prairie-dogs-cry-for-rain-reflections-on-shelter-rain-and-drought.

Fettis Jabr. "Can Prairie Dogs Talk?" *New York Times* (May 12, 2017), https://www.nytimes.com/2017/05/12/magazine/can-prairie-dogs-talk.html.

Laura Moss. "Seven Things You Didn't Know about Prairie Dogs," Mother Nature Network (February 18, 2015), https://www.mnn.com/earth-matters/animals/stories/7-things-you-didnt-know-about-prairie-dogs.

Prairie Dog (cont.)

Guy Musser. "Prairie dog," Encyclopedia Britannica (accessed August 17, 2018), https://www.britannica.com/animal/prairie-dog.

Sarah Wade. "Eight Surprising Prairie Dog Facts," World Wildlife Fund (accessed August 17, 2018), https://www.worldwildlife.org/stories/8-surprising-prairie-dog-facts.

Praying Mantis

Debbie Hadley. "Ten Fascinating Praying Mantis Facts," ThoughtCo. (April 17, 2018), https://www.thoughtco.com/praying-mantid-facts-1968525.

"Mantis," Wikipedia (accessed August 17, 2018), https://en.wikipedia.org/wiki/Mantis.

"The Myths and Legends of the Praying Mantis," Praying Mantis for Sale (June 11, 2014), http://prayingmantisforsale.net/the-myths-and-legends-of-the-praying-mantis.

"Praying Mantis," Desert USA (accessed August 17, 2018), https://www.desertusa.com/insects/praying-mantis.html.

Puffin

Jude Isabella. "It's a Bird, It's a Mask, It's Puffin Man!" *Hakai Magazine* (June 27, 2016), https://www.hakaimagazine.com/article-short/its-bird-its-mask-its-puffin-man.

Elissa Leibowitz Poma. "Ten High-Flying Facts about Puffins," World Wildlife Fund (March 1, 2010), https://www.worldwildlife.org/blogs/good-nature-travel/posts/ten-high-flying-facts-about-puffins.

"Puffin," Wikipedia (accessed August 22, 2018), https://en.wikipedia.org/wiki/Puffin.

"Puffin Facts," National Geographic Kids (accessed August 22, 2018), https://www.natgeokids.com/nz/discover/animals/birds/puffin-facts/#!/register.

Quail

"Asteria," Theoi Project (accessed August 22, 2018), http://www.theoi.com/Titan/TitanisAsteria.html.

"Common Quail," Wikipedia (accessed August 22, 2018), https://en.wikipedia.org/wiki/Common_quail.

"Interesting Facts about Bobwhite Quails That'll Leave You in Awe," Bird Eden (July 16, 2017), https://birdeden.com/interesting-facts-about-bobwhite-quail.

"Quail: The Small, Plump and Cute Bird," Easy Science for Kids (accessed August 22, 2018), https://easyscienceforkids.com/all-about-quail.

"Quail," Greek Mythology (accessed August 22, 2018), http://greekmythology.wikia.com/wiki/Quail.

"Quail Facts," Soft Schools (accessed August 24, 2018), http://www.softschools.com/facts/animals/quail_facts/968.

"Quail Information, Photos, Artwork and Facts," American Expedition (accessed August 22, 2018), https://americanexpedition.us/learn-about-wildlife/quail-facts-photos-and-information.

"Quail," A—Z Animals (accessed August 26, 2018), https://a-z-animals.com/animals/quail.

Quetzal

Duane Blake. "The History and Symbolism Behind a Beautiful Guatemalan Coin," PCGS (December 21, 2010), https://www.pcgs.com/news/The-History-And-Symbolism-Behind-A-Beautiful-Guatemalan-Coin.

David De la Garza. "Sacred Animals in the Mayan Culture," Xichen (June 29, 2017), http://blog.xichen.tours/en/sacred-animals-mayan-world.

Catherine Giordano. "The Resplendent Quetzal: The Most Beautiful Bird in the World," Owlcation (March 10, 2018), https://owlcation.com/stem/The-Resplendent-Quetzal-The-Most-Beautiful-Bird-in-the-World.

"Quetzal," Aztecs at Mexicolore (August 30, 2011), http://www.mexicolore.co.uk/aztecs/flora-and-fauna/quetzal.

"Quetzal," Animals Network (accessed September 25, 2018), https://animals.net/quetzal.

"The Plumed Serpent, Quetzalcoatl: A Symbol of Connectedness," Nexus (September 19, 2006), https://nexusnovel.wordpress.com/2006/09/19/the-plumed-serpent-quetzalcoatl-a-symbol-of-connectedness.

"The Resplendent Quetzal in Aztec and Mayan Culture," Data Zone (accessed September 25, 2018), http://datazone.birdlife.org/sowb/casestudy/the-resplendent-quetzal-in-aztec-and-mayan-culture.

"Turquoise-Browed Motmot Feathers Were Potential Long-Distance Trade Goods," Maya Archaeology (June 2018), https://www.maya-archaeology.org/motmot-bird-feathers/long-distance-trade-mayan-merchants-trade-goods-products/turquoise-browed-motmot-eumomota-superciliosa-feathers.php.

Rabbit

Laura Goldman. "Twenty Fascinating Facts about Rabbits," Care 2 (March 31, 2018), https://www.care2.com/causes/20-fascinating-facts-about-rabbits.html.

Rabbit (cont.)

Tony Locke. "Superstitions and Folklore of the Rabbit and Hare," Irish Broad (March 29, 2013), http://www.irishabroad.com/blogs/PostView.aspx?pid=4325.

"Moon Rabbit," Wikipedia (accessed August 26, 2018), https://en.wikipedia.org/wiki/Moon_rabbit.

"Mayan Rabbit Symbolism in Ancient Mexico," Myths Symbols Sandplay (March 16, 2017), http://mythsymbolsandplay.typepad.com/my-blog/2017/03/mayan-rabbit-symbolism-in-ancient-mexico.html.

Ian Mursell. "A Rabbit in the Moon?" Mexicolore (accessed August 26, 2018), http://www.mexicolore.co.uk/aztecs/aztefacts/rabbit-in-the-moon.

Raccoon

Richard L. Dieterle. "Raccoons," The Encyclopedia of Ho k (Winnebago) Mythology (accessed August 26, 2018), https://hotcakencyclopedia.com/ho.Raccoons.html.

"Interesting Facts about Racoons," Just Fun Facts (accessed August 26, 2018), http://justfunfacts.com/interesting-facts-about-raccoons.

"Native American Raccoon Mythology," Native Languages of the Americas (accessed August 26, 2018), http://www.native-languages.org/legends-raccoon.htm.

"Raccoon Fact Sheet," Nature (February 7, 2012), http://www.pbs.org/wnet/nature/raccoon-nation-raccoon-fact-sheet/7553.

"Raccoon Symbol," Native American Symbols (accessed August 26, 2018), https://www.warpaths2peacepipes.com/native-american-symbols/raccoon-symbol.htm.

Rat

David Bennett. "Rats in Space! A Short History," British Rat Trap (April 13, 2018), https://thebritishrattrap.com/blog/rats-in-space-a-short-history.

Alina Bradford. "Facts about Rats," Live Science (September 30, 2015), https://www.livescience.com/52342-rats.html.

"Rats in Mythology," Alt Pets Rodents Rats (accessed August 26, 2018), https://groups.google.com/forum/#!topic/alt.pets.rodents.rats/4VYnHXnojwI.

"Some Interesting but Strange Facts about Rats," Odd Stuff Magazine (accessed August 26, 2018), http://oddstuffmagazine.com/some-interesting-but-strange-facts-about-rats.html.

Raven/Crow

Stefan Anitei. "Ten Amazing Facts about Ravens," Softpedia (November 14, 2007), http://news.softpedia.com/news/10-Amazing-Facts-About-Ravens-70914.shtml.

"Odin," Wikipedia (accessed August 29, 2018), https://en.wikipedia.org/wiki/Odin.

"Ten Amazing Facts about Ravens," Unbelievable Facts (November 29, 2017), https://www.unbelievable-facts.com/2017/11/facts-about-ravens.html.

Red Panda

"Interesting Facts about Red Pandas," Just Fun Facts (accessed August 29, 2018), http://justfunfacts.com/interesting-facts-about-red-pandas.

"Red Panda," San Diego Zoo Animals and Plants (accessed August 29, 2018), http://animals.sandiegozoo.org/animals/red-panda.

"Red Pandas," Animal Corner (accessed August 29, 2018), https://animalcorner.co.uk/animals/red-panda.

Angela R. Glatston, editor. "People and Red Pandas: The Red Panda's Role in Economy and Culture," *Red Panda: Biology and Conservation of the First Panda* (Cambridge, MA.: 2011), pp. 11–25.

Rhinoceros

J. C. A. Boeyens and M. M. van der Ryst. "The Culture and Symbolic Significance of the African Rhinoceros: A Review of the Traditional Beliefs, Perceptions and Practices of Agropastoralist Societies of Southern Africa," *Southern African Humanities*, vol. 26 (2014), pp. 21–55, http://www.sahumanities.org/ojs/index.php/SAH/article/view/346.

Andrew Laurie. "A Most Preposterous Beast," Rhino Resource Center (accessed September 1, 2018), http://www.rhinoresourcecenter.com/pdf_files/135/1355668199.pdf.

Jennifer Mueller. "Physical Characteristics of a Rhinoceros," Pets (accessed August 29, 2018), http://animals.mom.me/physical-characteristics-rhinoceros-7544.html.

Jo Price. "Twelve Amazing Rhino Facts You Might Not Know," Discover Wildlife (September 22, 2014), http://www.discoverwildlife.com/animals/mammals/facts-about-rhinos.

"Rhinoceros," Out of Africa (accessed August 29, 2018), http://www.outtoafrica.nl/animals/engrhino.html.

"Rhinoceroses in Culture," Rhino Worlds (accessed September 1, 2018), https://www.rhinoworlds.com/rhinoceroses-in-culture.

Roadrunner

Gail Garber. "Paisano Bird: Greater Roadrunner," New Mexico Birds (August 26, 2010), http://newmexicobirds.blogspot.com/2010/08/paisano-bird-greater-roadrunner.html.

Jaymi Heimbuch. "Five Surprising Facts about Roadrunners," Mother Nature Network (April 26, 2017), https://www.mnn.com/earth-matters/animals/stories/roadrunner-facts.

"Native American Roadrunner Mythology," Native Languages of the Americas (accessed September 1, 2018), http://www.native-languages.org/legends-roadrunner.htm.

"Roadrunner," Nature Conservancy (accessed September 1, 2018), https://www.nature.org/newsfeatures/specialfeatures/animals/birds/roadrunner.xml.

"Roadrunner Legends and Oddities," DJ's Texas State of Mind (accessed September 1, 2018), http://mstexan7.tripod.com/id28.html.

Robin

"American Robin (*Turdus Migratorius*)," Science Nature (accessed September 1, 2018), https://science.nature.nps.gov/im/units/cakn/relatedwebsites/yuch_bird_inventory_website/species_descriptions/amro_description.htm.

Michael Hartley. "The Fabled Folklore of the Robin Redbreast," Study (December 10, 2012), http://from-bedroom-to-study.blogspot.com/2012/12/the-fabled-folklore-of-robin-redbreast.html.

George Knowles. "Robin Redbreast," Controverscial (December 25, 2008), http://www.controverscial.com/Animals%20and%20Witchcraft%20-%20Robin%20Redbreast.htm.

"Native American Robin Mythology," Native Languages of the Americas (accessed September 1, 2018), http://www.native-languages.org/legends-robin.htm.

Jillian O'Keeffe. "What Are Traits of the Robin?" Sciencing (April 24, 2017), https://sciencing.com/traits-robin-8434772.html.

Salamander

Nicole Barone Callahan. "Salamanders," Environmental Literacy Council (accessed September 1, 2018), https://enviroliteracy.org/special-features/creature-feature/salamanders.

Carl Miller. "Salamander Characteristics" Sciencing (April 25, 2017), https://sciencing.com/salamander-characteristics-7873616.html.

"Salamander," Animal Spot (accessed September 1, 2018), http://www.animalspot.net/salamander.

"Salamanders," Reptile Gardens (accessed September 1, 2018), http://www.reptilegardens.com/animals/amphibians-and-bugs/salamanders.

Zteve T. Evans. "Mythical Beasts: The Salamander," Under the Influence! (April 2, 2014), https://ztevetevans.wordpress.com/2014/04/02/mythical-beasts-the-salamander.

Salmon

"Ainu Legend: Salmon—the Divine Fish That Came Down from Paradise," Japanese Mythology and Folklore (accessed September 1, 2018), https://japanesemythology.wordpress.com/ainu-legend-salmon-the-divine-fish-that-came-down-from-paradise.

Chris Branam. "Newly-Hatched Salmon Use Geomagnetic Field to Learn Which Way Is Up," Phys Org (February 16, 2018), https://phys.org/news/2018-02-newly-hatched-salmon-geomagnetic-field.html#jCp.

Heather Crochetiere. "Did You Know? 10 Amazing Things about Salmon," World Wildlife Fund (March 19, 2015), https://blog.wwf.ca/blog/2015/03/19/did-you-know-10-amazing-things-about-salmon.

Dan Puplett. "Salmon," Tree of Life (accessed September 1, 2018), https://treesforlife.org.uk/forest/mythology-folklore/salmon.

"Salmon Facts," Soft Schools (accessed September 1, 2018), http://www.softschools.com/facts/animals/salmon_facts/658.

"The Salmon Symbol," Spirits of the West Coast Native Art Gallery (accessed September 1, 2018), https://spiritsofthewestcoast.com/collections/the-salmon-symbol.

Sandpiper

"Common Sandpiper Facts," Soft Schools (accessed September 1, 2018), http://www.softschools.com/facts/animals/common_sandpiper_facts/1850.

"Sandpipers: Scolopacidae," Encyclopedia (accessed September 1, 2018), https://www.encyclopedia.com/science/encyclopedias-almanacs-transcripts-and-maps/sandpipers-scolopacidae.

"Semipalmated Sandpiper (*Calidris Pusilla*)," Wildscreen Arkive (accessed September 1, 2018), https://www.arkive.org/semipalmated-sandpiper/calidris-pusilla.

Scorpion

Dragonlady Mothman. "Scorpion Myths," Unexplained Mysteries (December 19, 2005,) https://www.unexplained-mysteries.com/forum/topic/57515-scorpion-myths.

Scorpion (cont.)

"Mysterious Scorpion Goddess in Myths and Legends," Ancient Pages (January 26, 2016), http://www.ancientpages.com/2016/01/26/mysterious-scorpion-goddess-myths-legends.

"Scorpion Facts," Scorpion Worlds (accessed September 1, 2018), http://www.scorpionworlds.com/facts-about-scorpions.

"Scorpius," Wikipedia (accessed September 1, 2018), https://en.wikipedia.org/wiki/Scorpius.

"Ten Facts about Scorpions," Some Interesting Facts (accessed September 1, 2018), http://someinterestingfacts.net/10-facts-scorpions.

Seagull

Nicole Canfield. "Bird Gods and Goddesses Associated with Birds of Flight," Exemplore (April 15, 2016), https://exemplore.com/misc/Bird-Gods-and-Goddesses-Deities-Associated-With-Birds-of-Flight.

"Interesting Facts about Seagulls," Just Fun Facts (accessed September 1, 2018), http://justfunfacts.com/interesting-facts-about-seagulls.

"Native American Seagull Mythology," Native Languages of the Americas (accessed September 1, 2018), http://www.native-languages.org/legends-seagull.htm.

Matthew Tcheng. "American Herring Gull," eBestiary (May 29, 2012), http://blogs.evergreen.edu/ebestiary/blog/2012/05/29/american-herring-gull.

Seahorse

"Seahorse," Wikipedia (accessed September 13, 2018), https://en.wikipedia.org/wiki/Seahorse.

"Seahorse Facts," Seahorse Trust (accessed September 13, 2018), https://www.theseahorsetrust.org/seahorse-facts.

"Seahorses in Myth, Legend and Art," Birch Aquarium (January 8, 2010), https://aquarium.ucsd.edu/blog/seahorses-in-myth-legend-art.

Helen Scales. "Incredible Stories of Seahorses," Underwater 360o (accessed November 2, 2018), http://www.uw360.asia/incredible-stories-of-seahorses.

"The Secret Life of Seahorses," BBC QED video (1996), https://www.youtube.com/watch?v=pYtWOf6nfCo.

Ze Frank. "True Facts about the Seahorse," YouTube (January 17, 2013), https://www.youtube.com/watch?v=UqYUTTqupOY.

Seal/Elephant Seal/Sea Lion/Walrus

Nicole Canfield. "Merrows, Selkies, and Kelpies: Irish and Scottish Underwater Creatures Like the Mermaid," Exemplore (December 22, 2016), https://exemplore.com/cryptids/Merrows-Selkies-and-Kelpies-Irish-and-Scottish-Underwater-Creatures-Like-the-Mermaid.

"Celtic Sea Gods," Irelands Eye (accessed September 14, 2018), http://www.irelandseye.com/aarticles/culture/talk/myths/seagods.shtm.

"The Inuit," Canada's First People (accessed September 14, 2018), http://firstpeoplesofcanada.com/fp_groups/fp_inuit5.html.

"Fun Seal Facts for Kids," Science Kids (accessed September 14, 2018), http://www.sciencekids.co.nz/sciencefacts/animals/seal.html.

John Miller and Louise Miller. Walrus (London, UK.: Reaktion Books, 2014).

"Sealing Culture," Seals and Sealing Network (accessed September 14, 2018), https://sealsandsealing.net/sealing-culture.

Edith Turner. "Shamanism and Spirit," *Expedition*, volume 1, no 1 (2004), Penn Museum (accessed November 2, 2018), https://www.penn.museum/sites/expedition/shamanism-and-spirit.

Secretary Bird

Virginia Carper. "Secretary Bird: Might," Nature: Observations and Meanings (July 23, 2010), http://naturemeanings.blogspot.com/2010/07/secretary-bird-might.html.

Sara Oliver. "Really Weird Birds: The Secretary Bird," World Bird Sanctuary (December 18, 2013), http://world-bird-sanctuary.blogspot.com/2013/12/really-weird-birds-secretary-bird.html.

"Secretary Birds," Beauty of Birds (accessed September 14, 2018), https://www.beautyofbirds.com/secretarybirds.html.

Kuro Karasu. "Creature Feature: Secretary Bird," And I Think to Myself . . . What a Wonderful World (September 26, 2010), http://myths-made-real.blogspot.com/2010/09/creature-feature-secretary-bird.html.

"Impundulu the Lighting Bird Tale of Chaos Africa Myth Story," Chic African Culture (April 25, 2015), http://www.theafricangourmet.com/2015/04/african-mythological-monster-impundulu.html.

Shark

Angela Chen. "Before sharks became movie villains, they were celebrated in myths across the world," The Verge (July 26, 2017), https://www.theverge.com/2017/7/26/15998676/sharks-myths-history-culture.

Shark (cont.)

Brian Handwerk. "These Ridiculously Long-Lived Sharks Are Older Than the United States, and Still Living It Up," Smithsonian (August 11, 2016), https://www.smithsonianmag.com/science-nature/ridiculously-ancient-greenland-sharks-are-older-united-states-180960101.

"The Importance of Sharks," Oceana (accessed September 14, 2018), https://eu.oceana.org/en/importance-sharks.

Kara Lefevre. "Shark Facts," Shark Siders (accessed September 14, 2018), https://www.sharksider.com/shark-facts.

Matthew T. McDavitt. "The Cultural Significance of Sharks and Rays in Aboriginal Societies across Australia's Top End," Seaweek 2015/Shark Bay (accessed September 14, 2018), http://www.mesa.edu.au/seaweek2005/pdf_senior/is08.pdf.

Amelia Meyer. "Interesting Facts about Sharks," Sharks (accessed November 2, 2018)) https://www.sharksinfo.com/interesting-facts.html.

Michael Rogers. "Shark Mythology," Shark Siders (July 11, 2016), https://www.sharksider.com/shark-mythology.

Sheep/Ram

"Sheep," One Kind Planet (accessed September 14, 2018), https://onekindplanet.org/animal/sheep.

"Sheep in History," Sheep 101 (accessed September 14, 2018), http://www.sheep101.info/history.html.

"Sheep in Religion and Mythology," Think Differently about Sheep (accessed September 14, 2018), http://think-differently-about-sheep.com/Sheep%20_In_Religion_and_mythology.htm.

Terri Windling. ""Into the Woods" series, 42: The Folklore of Sheep," Myth and Moor (December 17, 2014), http://www.terriwindling.com/blog/2014/12/the-folklore-of-sheep.html.

Skunk

Miles Phillips. "What You Didn't Know about Skunks," Nature Tourism Development (October 2, 2013), https://naturetourism.tamu.edu/2013/10/02/what-you-didnt-know-about-skunks.

"Skunk Facts," Animal Facts Encyclopedia. (accessed September 14, 2018), http://www.animalfactsencyclopedia.com/Skunk-facts.html.

"Skunk Facts," Havahart (accessed September 14, 2018), http://www.havahart.com/skunk-facts.

"Striped Skunk," National Geographic (accessed September 14, 2018), https://www.nationalgeographic.com/animals/mammals/s/striped-skunk.

Sloth

"Life of Sloth," Sloth Club (accessed September 18, 2018), http://www.sloth.gr.jp/1.Life.htm.

Alina Bradford. "Sloth Facts: Habits, Habitat and Diet," Live Science (May 21, 2014), https://www.livescience.com/27612-sloths.html.

"Sloth," Wikipedia (accessed September 14, 2018), https://en.wikipedia.org/wiki/Sloth.

"Twenty-Eight Fascinating Facts about Sloths," Kickass Facts (accessed September 14, 2018), http://www.kickassfacts.com/28-fascinating-sloth-facts/2.

Anne Woods. "Special Characteristics and Adaptations of a Sloth," Pets (accessed September 14, 2018), https://animals.mom.me/special-characteristics-adaptations-sloth-7872.html.

Snail/Conch/Slug

"Cool Facts: Slugs," Lakeside Nature Center (accessed September 14, 2018), http://www.lakesidenaturecenter.org/AOM%20-%20Slugs.pdf.

"Fascinating Sluggy Facts," Slug Off (accessed September 14, 2018), http://www.slugoff.co.uk/slug-facts/facts.

Steve Thomas. "Medicinal Use of Terrestrial Molluscs (Slugs and Snails) with Particular Reference to Their Role in the Treatment of Wounds and Other Skin Lesions," World Wide Wounds (July 2013), http://www.worldwidewounds.com/2013/July/Thomas/slug-steve-thomas.html.

Snake/Anaconda/Boa Constrictor/Cobra/Python/Rattlesnake

Estelle Nora Harwit Amrani. "The Serpent of Life and Wisdom," Biblioteca Pleyades (November 1998), https://www.bibliotecapleyades.net/sumer_anunnaki/esp_sumer_annunaki07.htm

"Basic Facts about Snakes," Defenders of Wildlife (accessed September 14, 2018), https://defenders.org/snakes/basic-facts.

"Cobra," Ancient Egypt: The Mythology (accessed September 14, 2018), http://www.egyptianmyths.net/cobra.htm.

Jeffrey Hays. "Snakes: Their History, Characteristics, Feeding and Breeding," Facts and Details (accessed September 14, 2018), http://factsanddetails.com/asian/cat68/sub434/item2441.html.

Russell McLendon. "Six Interesting Facts about Boa Constrictors," Mother Nature Network (October 3, 2017), https://www.mnn.com/earth-matters/animals/blogs/boa-constrictors-facts.

Snake/Anaconda/Boa Constrictor/Cobra/Python/Rattlesnake (cont.)

Caroline Seawright. "Nehebkau, God Who Joined the Ka to the Body, God of Protection and Magic," K4W Foundation (March 26, 2002), http://www.thekeep.org/~kunoichi/kunoichi/themestream/nehebkau.html#.W4Sj_K3Mzq0.

Sparrow

"House Sparrow," Wikipedia (accessed September 14, 2018), https://en.wikipedia.org/wiki/House_sparrow.

"Sparrows: 15 Interesting Facts about Sparrow and 8 Effective Control Measures," PestWiki (May 24, 2017), https://www.pestwiki.com/sparrows-facts-control-measures.

"Sparrow Facts," Soft Schools (accessed September 14, 2018), http://www.softschools.com/facts/animals/sparrow_facts/322.

Jennifer Stone. "The Meaning of Sparrows: Identification and Folklore," Owlcation (September 22, 2016), https://owlcation.com/social-sciences/The-Meaning-of-Sparrows-Identification-and-Folklore.

Spider/Black Widow/Daddy Long Leg/Recluse

Amanda Littlejohn. "Top Ten Interesting and Fun Facts about Spiders," Owlcation (December 20, 2017), https://owlcation.com/stem/Amazing-Facts-About-Spiders.

"Spiders," Animal Corner (accessed September 25, 2018), https://animalcorner.co.uk/animals/spiders.

"Ten Surprising Facts about Spiders," Oxford University Press (March 14, 2016), https://blog.oup.com/2016/03/ten-spider-facts.

"Twenty-Five Kickass and Interesting Facts about Spiders," Kickass Facts (accessed September 25, 2018), http://www.kickassfacts.com/25-kickass-and-interesting-facts-about-spiders.

Patti Wigington. "Spider Mythology and Folklore," ThoughtCo. (June 24, 2017), https://www.thoughtco.com/spider-mythology-and-folklore-2562730.

Squirrel

"Animals in Myths and Legends," Wildwood Trust (accessed September 14, 2018), http://www.wildwoodtrust.org.uk/files/ks2-myths-legends.pdf.

Alina Bradford. "Squirrels: Diet, Habits and Other Facts," Live Science (June 27, 2014), https://www.livescience.com/28182-squirrels.html.

Jonny Enoch. "Squirrel! Fuzzy Messengers from the Ancient Underworld? The Little-Known Archetype in Mythology," Ancient Origins (November 20, 2017), http://www.ancient-origins.net/opinion-guest-authors/squirrel-fuzzy-messengers-ancient-underworld-little-known-archetype-mythology-021729.

"Native American Squirrel Mythology," Native Languages of the Americas (accessed September 14, 2018), http://www.native-languages.org/legends-squirrel.htm.

"Squirrel Mythology," Bad Witch's Blog (April 4, 2008), http://www.badwitch.co.uk/2008/04/squirrel-mythology.html.

Starfish

"Forty Surprising Starfish Facts," Serious Facts (accessed September 25, 2018), https://www.seriousfacts.com/starfish-facts.

"Native American Starfish Mythology," Native Languages of the Americas (accessed September 25, 2018), http://www.native-languages.org/legends-starfish.htm.

"Starfish," Wikipedia (accessed September 25, 2018), https://en.wikipedia.org/wiki/Starfish.

"*Starfish (Asteroidea)*," Brandon's Wild World (accessed September 25, 2018), http://bransonswildworld.com/starfish-asteroidea.

"Starfish Facts," Soft Schools (accessed September 25, 2018), http://www.softschools.com/facts/animals/starfish_facts/85.

Starling

"European Starling," All About Birds (accessed September 25, 2018), https://www.allaboutbirds.org/guide/European_Starling/overview.

"Murmurations: The Dance of the Starlings," Hertfordshire Life (November 17, 2016), http://www.hertfordshirelife.co.uk/out-about/wildlife/murmurations-the-dance-of-the-starlings-1-4753283.

Gayle Nastasi. "The Truth about Starlings," Gazehound's (June 6, 2015), https://gazehound.com/2015/06/06/the-truth-about-starlings.

"Starlings," Living with Wildlife (accessed September 25, 2018), https://wdfw.wa.gov/living/starlings.html.

"Starlings and Roman Divination," Bird Note (accessed September 25, 2018), https://www.birdnote.org/show/starlings-and-roman-divination.

Stingray

Josh Cassidy, Grace Singer. "How Do Sharks and Rays Use Electricity to Find Hidden Prey?" KQED (August 11, 2015), https://www.kqed.org/science/106591/sharks-and-rays-sense-electricity-fish-cant-hide.

"Common Stingray," British Seafishing (accessed September 25, 2018), http://britishseafishing.co.uk/common-stingray.

"The Cultural Significance of Sharks and Rays in Aboriginal Australia," Marine Education Society of Australasia (accessed September 25, 2018), http://www.mesa.edu.au/seaweek2005/pdf/infosheet08.pdf.

"Freshwater Stingray," Smithsonian National Zoo (accessed September 25, 2018), https://nationalzoo.si.edu/animals/freshwater-stingray.

Te Ahukaram Charles Royal. "Kaitiakitanga—Guardianship and Conservation—Kaitiaki—Guardians," Te Ara, the Encyclopedia of New Zealand (accessed September 26, 2018), http://www.TeAra.govt.nz/en/artwork/11593/whai-stingray.

"Stingray," Bio Expedition (April 13, 2012), https://www.bioexpedition.com/stingray.

"Stingray Facts," Facts (accessed September 25, 2018), http://facts.net/stingray.

Stork

Nancy Maciolek Blake. "Storks in Mythology and Literature," Polish Culture (February 2006), http://culture.polishsite.us/articles/art350.html.

"White Stork Birds," Animal Corner (accessed September 25, 2018), https://animalcorner.co.uk/animals/white-stork-birds.

"White Stork," Animal Spot (accessed September 25, 2018), http://www.animalspot.net/white-stork.html.

Swallow

"Barn Swallow—*Hirundo Rustica*," Nature Works (accessed September 25, 2018), http://www.nhptv.org/natureworks/barnswallow.htm#1.

"Interesting Facts about Swallows," Just Fun Facts (accessed September 25, 2018), http://justfunfacts.com/interesting-facts-about-swallows.

Stephanie. "Barn Swallow," eBestiary (May 29, 2012), http://blogs.evergreen.edu/ebestiary/blog/2012/05/29/barn-swallow.

"Swallow," All about Heaven (accessed September 25, 2018), https://allaboutheaven.org/symbols/845/123/swallow.

"Swallow," Ancient Egypt: The Mythology (accessed September 25, 2018), http://www.egyptianmyths.net/swallow.htm.

"The Swallow: Bird of Freedom," Wonder of Birds (accessed September 25, 2018), http://www.thewonderofbirds.com/swallow.

"The Swallows of Ancient Egypt," Cow of Gold (accessed September 25, 2018), https://cowofgold.wikispaces.com/Swallow.

"Tree Swallow Basics," Tree Swallow Project (accessed September 25, 2018), http://www.treeswallowprojects.com/basics.html.

Swan

"Brunhilde," Norse Gods (accessed September 25, 2018), https://thenorsegods.com/brunhilde.

"Interesting Facts about Swans," Just Fun Facts (accessed September 25, 2018), http://justfunfacts.com/interesting-facts-about-swans.

"List of Celtic Gods and Goddesses," World Mythology (May 28, 2008), http://worldmythology.wikifoundry.com/page/List+of+Celtic+gods+and+goddesses.

"Swans," Domestic Forest (accessed September 25, 2018), https://www.domesticforest.com/swans.

Peter Young. *Swan* (London, UK.: Reaktion Books, 2008).

Tasmanian Devil

Alina Bradford. "Facts about Tasmanian Devils," Live Science (October 23, 2014), https://www.livescience.com/27440-tasmanian-devils.html.

"*Sarcophilus Harrisii*, Tasmanian Devil" Encyclopedia of Life (accessed September 25, 2018), http://eol.org/pages/311781/details.

"Tasmanian Devil," Animal Files (accessed September 25, 2018), http://www.theanimalfiles.com/mammals/marsupials/tasmanian_devil.html.

"Tasmanian Devil," National Geographic Kids (accessed September 25, 2018), https://kids.nationalgeographic.com/animals/tasmanian-devil/#tasmanian-devil-red-ears-log.jpg.

"Truganini," Wikipedia (accessed September 25, 2018), https://en.wikipedia.org/wiki/Truganini.

Maurits Zwankhuizen. "Native Animals Should Be Rechristened with Their Aboriginal Names," *Australian Geographic* (August 15, 2017), https://www.australiangeographic.com.au/topics/wildlife/2017/08/native-animals-should-be-renamed-with-their-aboriginal-names.

Thunderbird

Forsaken Gabriel. "Thunderbird," Mythology and Folklore (March 15, 2018), https://aminoapps.com/c/mythfolklore/page/blog/thunderbird/x8BM_X7u2u3JrmXmL5YpDN4MDmQ61EMQvl.

"The Thunderbird," Native Indian Tribes (accessed September 25, 2018), https://www.warpaths2peacepipes.com/native-american-culture/thunderbird.htm.

"Thunderbird (Mythology)," Wikipedia (accessed September 25, 2018), https://en.wikipedia.org/wiki/Thunderbird_(mythology).

Tracey. "The Return of the Thunder Beings," Prairie Edge (April 4, 2011), http://www.prairieedge.com/tribe-scribe/return-of-thunder-beings.

Tiger

Sharon Guynup. "Why Have Tigers Been Feared and Revered Throughout History?" National Geographic (April 9, 2014), https://blog.nationalgeographic.org/2014/04/09/why-have-tigers-been-feared-and-revered-throughout-history.

Jeffrey Hays. "Tigers: Characteristics and Hunting, Mating and Cub-Raising Behavior," Facts and Details (November 2013), http://factsanddetails.com/asian/cat68/sub432/item2499.html.

Satya Kalra. "What Does Goddess Durga Symbolize?" India Currents (October 18, 2012), https://indiacurrents.com/what-does-goddess-durga-symbolize.

Amelia Meyer. "Tigers in Culture and Folklore," Tigers (accessed November 2, 2018), https://www.tigers.org.za/tigers-in-culture-and-folklore.html.

"The Most Precious Collection of Vietnam's Sacred Animals," Vietnam Net (October 23, 2016), http://english.vietnamnet.vn/fms/special-reports/165358/the-most-precious-collection-of-vietnam-s-sacred-animals.html.

"Tiger Facts," National Geographic (August 2, 2015), http://www.nationalgeographic.com.au/animals/tiger-facts.aspx.

Kate Wan. "Fifty Unusual Facts about Tigers," Listverse (September 10, 2012), https://listverse.com/2012/09/10/50-unusual-facts-about-tigers.

Toucan

Susie Christian. "The Amazing Toucan Bill," Eclectusville (accessed September 25, 2018), http://www.eclectusville.com/2012/toucan_4.html.

Laurie Patsalides. "Study the Toucan: More Than Your Average Cereal Box Character," Bright Hub (September 12, 2012), https://www.brighthub.com/environment/science-environmental/articles/19278.aspx.

"Toucan: Its Oversized Bill Makes It the Rainforest's Most Recognizable Bird," Tambopata Lodge (accessed September 25, 2018), https://www.tambopatalodge.com/en/jungle-blog/toucan-its-oversized-bill-makes-it-the-rainforests-most-recognizable-bird.

"Toco Toucan," Animal Corner (accessed September 25, 2018), https://animalcorner.co.uk/animals/toco-toucan.

"Tucana," Wikipedia (accessed September 25, 2018), https://en.wikipedia.org/wiki/Tucana.

Turkey

Kevin Coyle. "Twelve Unusual and Fascinating Facts about Wild Turkeys," National Wildlife Federation (November 20, 2011), http://blog.nwf.org/2011/11/twelve-unusual-and-fascinating-facts-about-wild-turkeys.

Avery Cullinan. "Nine Fun Facts about Turkeys," Audubon (November 13, 2015) http://www.audubon.org/news/9-fun-facts-about-turkeys

"Domestic Turkey," Wikipedia (accessed September 25, 2018), https://en.wikipedia.org/wiki/Domestic_turkey.

"Native American Turkey Mythology," Native Languages of the Americas (accessed September 25, 2018), http://www.native-languages.org/legends-turkey.htm.

Turtle/Tortoise

"Cultural Depictions of Turtles," Wikipedia (accessed September 26, 2018), https://en.wikipedia.org/wiki/Cultural_depictions_of_turtles.

"Information About Sea Turtles: Green Sea Turtle," Sea Turtle Conservancy (accessed November 13, 2018), https://conserveturtles.org/information-sea-turtles-green-sea-turtle.

"Native American Turtle Mythology," Native Languages of the Americas (accessed September 26, 2018), http://www.native-languages.org/legends-turtle.htm.

Veronica S. Schweitzer. "The Struggle of the Ancients," Coffee Times (accessed September 26, 2018), http://www.coffeetimes.com/aug97.htm.

Unicorn

"Are Unicorns Real?" Unicorn Rules (accessed September 26, 2018), http://www.unicornsrule.com/are-unicorns-real.

Unicorn (cont.)

Jessica Bowe. "Mythical Scotland: Exploring the Legends," Nordic Visitor (accessed September 26, 2018), https://www.nordicvisitor.com/blog/mythical-scotland-exploring-the-legends.

"The Unicorn in Captivity (from the Unicorn Tapestries)," Met Museum (accessed September 26, 2018), https://www.metmuseum.org/art/collection/search/467642.

"Unicorn Mythology," Unicorn Rules (accessed September 26, 2018), http://www.unicornsrule.com/unicorn-mythology.

"Unicorn Myths," Gods and Monsters (accessed September 26, 2018), http://www.gods-and-monsters.com/unicorn-myths.html.

"Unicorn Research," Diana Peterfreud (accessed September 26, 2018), http://dianapeterfreund.com/books/unicorns/research.

Wasp

John Early. "Wasps and Bees: New Zealand's Wasps and Bees," Te Ara, the Encyclopedia of New Zealand (accessed 27 September 2018), http://www.TeAra.govt.nz/en/diagram/11138/features-of-wasps-and-bees.

"Extraction Healing," Shamans Nature (accessed September 26, 2018), https://www.shamansnature.com/article-a.

"Interesting Facts about Wasps," Just Fun Facts (accessed September 26, 2018), http://justfunfacts.com/interesting-facts-about-wasps.

"Wasp," Wikipedia (accessed September 26, 2018), https://en.wikipedia.org/wiki/Was.

"Wasps," Animal Corner (accessed September 26, 2018), https://animalcorner.co.uk/animals/wasps.

Catherine Zuckerman. *Doomsday 2012: The Maya Calendar and the History of the End of the World* (Washington, D.C.: National Geographic Society, 2012).

Weasel/Ferret/Mink

Anja Deli . "History of Ferrets," Friendly Ferret (accessed September 25, 2018), https://www.friendlyferret.com/history-of-ferrets.

Ferret Enrichment: Enriching Your Fuzzbutts Life," Ferret World (accessed July 19, 2018), http://www.ferret-world.com/ferretenrichment.html.

"Least Weasel," International Union for Conservation of Nature Red List (accessed November 13, 2018), https://www.iucnredlist.org/species/70207409/45200499.

"Weasel," Wikipedia (accessed November 13, 2018), https://en.wikipedia.org/wiki/Weasel.

Whale/Beluga/Humpback/Orca

Joslyn C. "Animal Mourning," Interconnectivity: Animals Mourning Together in Modern Stories and Mythology (June 12, 2014), http://scalar.usc.edu/works/chid490animalmourning/animal-mourning.

"Icelandic Myths and Tales of Whales," North Sailing (accessed September 26, 2018), https://www.northsailing.is/2005/03/11/icelandic-myths-and-tales-of-whales.

"Killer Whale," Wikipedia (accessed September 26, 2018), https://en.wikipedia.org/wiki/Killer_whale.

Krista Langlois. "Why Scientists Are Starting to Care About Cultures That Talk to Whales," Smithsonian Magazine (April 3, 2018), https://www.smithsonianmag.com/science/talking-to-whales-180968698/#GPgbfUm4KdUb9tKF.99.

Naomi Millburn. "Meaning of Pacific Northwest Native American Orca Design," Sciencing (April 25, 2017), https://sciencing.com/meaning-pacific-northwest-native-american-orca-design-8139.html.

"Native American Whale Mythology," Native Languages of the Americas (accessed September 26, 2018), http://www.native-languages.org/legends-whale.htm.

"Whales in Art, Literature, and Mythology," Whales Forever (accessed September 26, 2018), https://www.whalesforever.com/whales-in-art-literature-mythology.html.

"Whales in Mythology," Whale Facts (accessed September 26, 2018), http://www.whalefacts.org/whales-in-mythology.

Wolf

"Dire Wolf Mythology," Dire Wolf Project (accessed September 26, 2018), http://www.direwolfproject.com/dire-wolf/dire-wolf-mythology.

Helen Murphy Howell. "The Ancestral Wolf Guardian and Power Spirit," Exemplore (April 17, 2016), https://exemplore.com/spirit-animals/Call-Of-The-Wild-The-Wolf-In-Mythology-Power-Animal.

Karin Lehnardt. "Sixty-Two Interesting Facts about Wolves," Fact Retriever (January 4, 2017), https://www.factretriever.com/wolves-facts.

"Native American Wolf Mythology," Native Languages of the Americas (accessed September 26, 2018), http://www.native-languages.org/legends-wolf.htm.

Wolverine

"Eleven Interesting Facts about Wolverines," IP Factly (July 19, 2016), http://ipfactly.com/11-interesting-facts-wolverines.

"Legendary Native American Figures: Kuekuatsheu (Carcajou)," Native Languages of the Americas (accessed September 26, 2018), http://www.native-languages.org/kuekuatsheu.htm.

Nancy McClure. "The Wolverine, Trickster Hero" Points West (Winter 2011), https://centerofthewest.org/2014/06/11/points-west-online-wolverine-trickster-hero.

Lee Standing Bear Moore and Takatoka. "Spirit Guides," Manataka American Indian Council (accessed September 26, 2018), https://www.manataka.org/page236.html.

Wombat

Mary Bates. "The Creature Feature: 10 Fun Facts about Wombats," Wired (December 4, 2014), https://www.wired.com/2014/12/creature-feature-10-fun-facts-wombats.

"Common Wombat," National Geographic (accessed September 26, 2018), https://www.nationalgeographic.com/animals/mammals/c/common-wombat.

Peter Marinacci. "Wombat Behavior," Wombania (accessed September 26, 2018), http://www.wombania.com/wombats/wombat-behavior.htm.

Ellen Scott. "World Wombat Day: 17 Facts about Wombats You Probably Never Knew," Metro (October 22, 2016), http://metro.co.uk/2016/10/22/international-wombat-day-17-facts-about-wombats-you-probably-never-knew-6207991/?ito=cbshare.

"Wombat Meaning Spiritual," Thrive on News (accessed September 26, 2018), https://thriveonnews.com/wombat-spirit-animal.

Woodpecker/Sapsucker

"Picus," Encyclopedia Britannica (accessed September 26, 2018), https://www.britannica.com/topic/Picus-Roman-mythology.

"Picus," Theodora (accessed September 26, 2018), https://theodora.com/encyclopedia/p/picus.html.

"The Red Headed Woodpecker and Native Americans and More," Redheaded Woodpecker Project (March 22, 2012) http://redheadwoodpecker.blogspot.com/2012/03/red-headed-woodpecker-and-native.html.

"Top 10 Amazing Facts about Woodpeckers," Top 10 Famous (accessed September 26, 2018), http://top10famous.com/top-10-amazing-facts-about-woodpeckers.

"Woodpecker Facts," Soft Schools (accessed September 26, 2018), http://www.softschools.com/facts/animals/woodpecker_facts/323.

Zebra

"About the Plains Zebra of Africa," Prime Safaris (accessed September 26, 2018), https://www.primeugandasafaris.com/blog/about-the-plains-zebra-of-africa.html.

Alina Bradford. "Zebra Facts," Live Science (October 17, 2014,) https://www.livescience.com/27443-zebras.html.

Jade Hillock. "Twenty-Five Amazing Facts about Zebras," Fact Site (accessed September 26, 2016), https://www.thefactsite.com/2015/08/amazing-zebra-facts.html.

Paul Janssen. "Zebra," Out of Africa (accessed September 26, 2018), http://www.outtoafrica.nl/animals/engzebra.html.

Anna Lanning. "Zebra," Hedricks Around the World in One Display (accessed September 26, 2018), http://www.hedricks.com/Promotions/aroundtheworldinonedisplay/zebra.html.

ART CREDITS

Grateful acknowledgement is made for permission to reproduce images from *Animals: 1419 Copyright-Free Illustrations of Mammals, Birds, Fish, Insects, etc.*, selected by Jim Harter (Mineola, NY: Dover Publications, 1979). Copyright © 1979 by Dover Publications, Inc. Specific images are acknowledged below, along with additional credits for other sources.

Aardvark . . . . .Public domain, circa 1894.
Albatross . . . .*Animals.* Dover Publications.
Angelfish. . . . .© Christopher Price. iStock by Getty Images.
Ant. . . . .*Animals.* Dover Publications.
Anteater . . . .*Animals.* Dover Publications
Antelope . . . .© Denisk0. iStock by Getty Images.
Armadillo . . . .© Denisk0. iStock by Getty Images.
Badger . . . .*Animals.* Dover Publications.
Barracuda . . . .© Benoitb. iStock by Getty Images.
Bat . . . .*Animals.* Dover Publications
Bear . . . .© Nicoolay. iStock by Getty Images.
Beaver/Muskrat. . . . .© Graffissimo. iStock by Getty Images.
Bee. . . . .© Graffissimo. iStock by Getty Images.
Beetle . . . .*Animals.* Dover Publications
Blackbird . . . .© Ilbusca. iStock by Getty Images.
Bluebird . . . .*Animals.* Dover Publications
Blue Jay. . . . .*Animals.* Dover Publications
Boar . . . .© Nicoolay. iStock by Getty Images.
Buffalo . . . .*Animals.* Dover Publications.
Butterfly . . . .© Nastasic. iStock by Getty Images.
Camel. . . . .*Animals.* Dover Publications.
Canary . . . .© Morphart Creation. Shutterstock.
Caribou . . . .*Animals.* Dover Publications.
Capybara. . . . .© Hein Nouwens. Shutterstock.
Cardinal . . . .© Ilbusca. iStock by Getty Images.
Carp/Goldfish/Koi . . . .*Animals.* Dover Publications.
Cat . . . .© Hein Nouwens. Shutterstock.
Caterpillar. . . . . .Public domain.Vintage Moth Entomologia.
Catfish . . . .*Animals.* Dover Publications.
Cattle—Bull . . . .*Animals.* Dover Publications.
Cattle—Cow. . . . .*Animals.* Dover Publications.s.
Centipede/Millipede . . . .© Antiquelmgnet. iStock by Getty Images.
Chameleon . . . .*Animals.* Dover Publications..
Cheetah . . . .*Animals.* Dover Publications.
Chickadee. . . . .© Denisk0. iStock by Getty Images.
Chicken—Hen . . . .© Morphart Creation. Shutterstock.
Chicken--Rooster . . . .© Morphart Creation. Shutterstock.
Cicada. . . . .© Natasic. iStock by Getty Images.

Condor . . . . *Animals.* Dover Publications.
Coral . . . . *Animals.* Dover Publications.
Cormorant . . . . *Animals.* Dover Publications.
Cougar . . . . © Benoitb. iStock by Getty Images
Coyote . . . . © Hein Nouwens. Shutterstock
Crab . . . . *Animals.* Dover Publications.
Crane . . . . © Hein Nouwens. Shutterstock.
Carp . . . . *Animals.* Dover Publications.
Cricket . . . . © Ilbusca. iStock by Getty Images.
Crocodile/Alligator . . . . © THEPALMER iStock by Getty Images.
Cuckoo . . . . *Animals.* Dover Publications.
Deer . . . . *Animals.* Dover Publications.
Dog (Domestic) . . . . © Oldies Pixel. Etsy.
Donkey . . . . © Nnehring. iStock by Getty Images.
Dolphin . . . . © Channarong Pherngjanda. Shutterstock.
Dove/Pigeon . . . . © Morphart Creation. Shutterstock.
Dragon . . . . Matthäus Merian *1300 Real and Fanciful Animals: From Seventeenth-Century Engravings* (Mineola, NY: Dover Publications, 1998).
Dragonfly . . . . *Animals.* Dover Publications.
Duck . . . . *Animals.* Dover Publications.
Eagle . . . . *Animals.* Dover Publications.
Earthworm . . . . *Animals.* Dover Publications.
Eel . . . . *Animals.* Dover Publications.
Elephant . . . . *Animals.* Dover Publications.
Elk . . . . © Ilbusca. iStock by Getty Images.
Emu . . . . © Hein Nouwens. Shutterstock.
Falcon . . . . *Animals.* Dover Publications.
Flea . . . . *Animals.* Dover Publications.
Firefly . . . . © Ilbusca. iStock by Getty Images.
Fly . . . . *Animals.* Dover Publications..
Fox . . . . *Animals.* Dover Publications.
Frog . . . . *Animals.* Dover Publications.
Giraffe . . . . *Animals.* Dover Publications.
Goat . . . . *Animals.* Dover Publications.
Goldfinch . . . . © Imagepluss.Vectorstock
Goose . . . . *Animals.* Dover Publications.
Gopher . . . . *Animals.* Dover Publications..
Gorilla . . . . © Nicoolay. iStock by Getty Images.
© Ilbusca. iStock by Getty Images.
Grasshopper . . . . © Ilbusca. iStock by Getty Images.
Grouse . . . . © Natasci. iStock by Getty Images.
Groundhog . . . . © Antiquelmgnet. iStock by Getty Images.
Guinea Pig . . . . © Ivan-96. iStock by Getty Images.
Hawk . . . . © Duncan1890. iStock by Getty Images.
Hedgehog . . . . © Nicoolay. iStock by Getty Images.
Heron . . . . *Animals.* Dover Publications.
Hippopotamus . . . . © Nicoolay. iStock by Getty Images
Horse . . . . © Nnehring. iStock by Getty Images.
Hummingbird . . . . *Animals.* Dover Publications.
Hyena . . . . *Animals.* Dover Publications.

Ibis . . . .© Ilbusca. iStock by Getty Images.
Jackal . . . .*Animals*. Dover Publications.
Jaguar . . . .*Animals*. Dover Publications.
Javelina . . . .© Ilbusca. iStock by Getty Images.
Jellyfish . . . .*Animals*. Dover Publications.
Kangaroo . . . .*Animals*. Dover Publications.
Kingfisher . . . .*Animals*. Dover Publications.
Koala . . . .© Evgeny Turaev. Shutterstock.
Ladybug . . . .© Ilbusca. iStock by Getty Images.
Lark . . . .*Animals*. Dover Publications.
Leech . . . .© Ilbusca. iStock by Getty Images.
Lemur. . . . .© Antiquelmgnet. iStock by Getty Images.
Leopard . . . .*Animals*. Dover Publications.
Lion . . . .*Animals*. Dover Publications.
Lizard . . . .© Benoitb. iStock by Getty Images.
Llama . . . .*Animals*. Dover Publications.
Lynx/Bobcat . . . .*Animals*. Dover Publications.
Manatee . . . .© THEPALMER. iStock by Getty Images.
Meerkat/Mongoose . . . .© THEPALMER. iStock by Getty Images.
Mockingbird . . . .© Nicoolay. iStock by Getty Images
Mole. . . . .© Graffissimo. iStock by Getty Images.
Motmot . . . .© Benoitb. iStock by Getty Images.
Monkey/Baboon/Chimpanzee/Orangutan . . . . . .© Ilbusca. iStock by Getty Images.
Moose. . . . .*Animals*. Dover Publications.
Mosquito . . . .© Ilbusca. iStock by Getty Images.
Moth . . . .© Natasic. iStock by Getty Images.
Mouse. . . . .*Animals*. Dover Publications.
Muskrat. . . . .© Ilbusca. iStock by Getty Images.
Musk Ox . . . .© THEPALMER. iStock by Getty Images.
Nighthawk . . . .© Nnehring. iStock by Getty Images.
Nuthatch. . . . .© Ilbusca. iStock by Getty Images.
Octopus . . . .*Animals*. Dover Publications.
Opossum. . . . .*Animals*. Dover Publications.
Ostrich . . . .*Animals*. Dover Publications.
Otter . . . .© Hein Nouwens. Shutterstock.
Owl . . . .*Animals*. Dover Publications.
Panda . . . .© Evgeny Turaev. Shutterstock.
Parrot . . . .*Animals*. Dover Publications.
Peacock. . . . .*Animals*. Dover Publications.
Pelican . . . .© Ilbusca. iStock by Getty Images.
Penguin. . . . .© Whitemay. iStock by Getty Images.
Pheasant . . . .© Nicoolay. iStock by Getty Images.
Phoenix . . . .© Christos Georghiou. Shutterstock.
Pig . . . .© Andipantz. iStock by Getty Images.
Platypus . . . .*Animals*. Dover Publications.
Porcupine . . . .*Animals*. Dover Publications.
Prairie Dog . . . .© Ilbusca. iStock by Getty Images.
Praying Mantis. . . . .*Animals*. Dover Publications.
Puffin . . . .*Animals*. Dover Publications.
Quail . . . .*Animals*. Dover Publications.
Quetzal. . . . .© Z0_09. iStock by Getty Images.

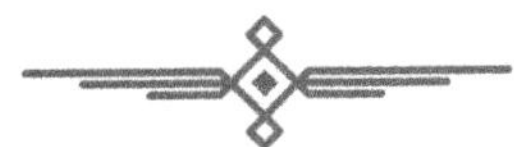

Rabbit . . . .© Retrofutur. iStock by Getty Images.
Raccoon . . . .© THEPALMER. iStock by Getty Images.
Rat. . . . .© Nicoolay. iStock by Getty Images
Raven . . . .© Graffissimo. iStock by Getty Images
Red Panda . . . .© THEPALMER. iStock by Getty Images.
Rhinoceros . . . .*Animals.* Dover Publications.
Roadrunner . . . .© Benoitb. iStock by Getty Images.
Robin. . . . .*Animals.* Dover Publications.
Rooster. . . . .© Iynea. Shutterstock.
Salamander . . . .© Ilbusca. iStock by Getty Images.
Salmon . . . .© Ilbusca. iStock by Getty Images.
Sandpiper . . . .© Benoitb. iStock by Getty Images.
Scorpion . . . .© Ilbusca. iStock by Getty Images.
Seagull . . . .© Natasic. iStock by Getty Images.
Seahorse . . . .© Benoitb. iStock by Getty Images.
Seal. . . . .*Animals.* Dover Publications.
Secretary Bird . . . .*Animals.* Dover Publications.
Shark . . . .*Animals.* Dover Publications.
© Ilbusca. iStock by Getty Images.
Sheep . . . .*Animals.* Dover Publications.
Skunk . . . .*Animals.* Dover Publications.
Sloth. . . . .© Natasic. iStock by Getty Images.
Squirrel. . . . .*Animals.* Dover Publications.
Snail/Slug . . . .*Animals.* Dover Publications.
Snake . . . .*Animals.* Dover Publications.
Sparrow . . . .© Ilbusca. iStock by Getty Images.
Spider . . . .*Animals.* Dover Publications.
Starfish . . . .© Traveler 1116. iStock by Getty Images.
Starling . . . .© Duncan1890. iStock by Getty Images.
Stingray. . . . .*Animals.* Dover Publications.
Stork. . . . .*Animals.* Dover Publications.
Swallow . . . .© Ilbusca. iStock by Getty Images.
Swan. . . . .© Ilbusca. iStock by Getty Images.
Tasmanian Devil . . . .© THEPALMER. iStock by Getty Images.
Thunderbird . . . .© Bosotochka. Shutterstock.
Tiger . . . .© Benoitb. iStock by Getty Images.
Toucan . . . .© Hein Nouwens. Shutterstock.
Tarantula. . . . .*Animals.* Dover Publications.
Turkey . . . .*Animals.* Dover Publications.
Turtle/Tortoise . . . .*Animals.* Dover Publications.
Unicorn . . . .© Barashkova Natalia. Shutterstock.
Wasp. . . . .© Natasic. iStock by Getty Images.
Weasel/Ferret/Mink . . . .© Natasic. iStock by Getty Images.
Whale . . . .© Rawpixel.com. Shutterstock.
Wolf. . . . .© Morphant Creation. Shutterstock.
Wolverine . . . .© Ilbusca. iStock by Getty Images.
Wombat . . . .© Hein Nouwens. Shutterstock.
Woodpecker . . . .© Hein Nouwens. Shutterstock.
Zebra . . . .*Animals.* Dover Publications.

RESOURCES

LORI MORRISON WEBSITE

LoriMorrison.com

You may schedule a private session or an appointment with Lori Morrison online at her website. Also find direct links to attend one of her free live sessions on Facebook, via the "Healing Crystals" page, every Saturday at noon Eastern time, and the other resources below.

CONNECT WITH LORI ON THE SOCIAL NETWORKS

Facebook: facebook.com/LoriMorrisonPowerAnimals

LinkedIn: linkedin.com/in/lori-morrison-9b5a0455

Twitter: twitter.com/lorikmorrison

Instagram: instagram.com/lorikmorrison

FINDING YOUR POWER ANIMAL TOOL

Finding Your Power Animal is a special software program that creates a holographic thumbprint of you through shamanic resonance with your name, birthdate, and place of birth. It searches your energetic field to determine what Power Animal was present with you at birth and then reconnects you with the energy and powers of this Power Animal through your heart chakra. Visit: Clients.LoriMorrison.com/Power-animal.

RECOMMENDED READING

Lori: The Disintegration of My Ordinary Reality by Lori Morrison (Four Jaguars Press)

Shamanism in the New Millennium, compiled by Cate Montana (Elizabeth Chasse)

The Continuum Encyclopedia of Animal Symbolism in Art by Hope B. Werness (Continuum)

The Book of Symbols: Reflections on Archetypal Images, edited by Ami Ronnberg and Kathleen Martin (Taschen)

RECOMMENDED AUDIOS

Tree of Life—Harmony CD (Spirit Concierge), a compelling guided journey through the body's seven primary energy centers, calibrating them with seven frequencies that unravel limiting beliefs and intergenerational obstacles to enlightenment. Available in English and Spanish. Produced by Lori Morrison.

Shamanic Journeying Solo and Double Drumming by Michael Harner (Foundation for Shamanic Studies)

THE TREE OF LIFE COURSE: A JOURNEY TO HUMAN HARMONY

In this course, Lori Morrison takes you beyond the veil of ordinary understanding into the matrix of the soul's journey. She gracefully guides you into alignment with a higher frequency for creating a life of infinite possibilities. By combining Mayan wisdom with cutting-edge technology and the symbolism of the Tree of Life, Lori is able to change the structure of your thoughts and bring you into a balance of mind, body, and soul. By clearing the "lasagna" if the layers and layers of limiting beliefs and cultural conditioning, she guides your soul right smack into the center of your heart. There, through resonance testing, you are guided to align with a higher vibrational frequency, empowering you to create a life of infinite possibilities.

Visit: LoriMorrison.kartra.com/page/join-TOL.

ADDITIONAL RESOURCES

Healing Crystals

HealingCrystals.com

The best place to buy crystals. The reason this site is Lori Morrison's favorite source is that the company clears all of the crystals before they are sold. A portion of their proceeds supports the work of Mayan healers in and around Lake Atitlan, Guatemala. They have a sacred mission and are dedicated to the integrity and knowledge of crystals from around the world.

Four Winds Residential Energy Medicine Training

FourWinds.com

The Foundation for Shamanic Studies
Shamanism.org

Institute of Indigenous Alchemy
Bonesoftheearth.org

Lightsong School
Janengelssmith.com

Gogo Ekhaya Esima
Sangomahealing.com

ABOUT LORI MORRISON

Lori Morrison is a coach, spiritual counselor, medical intuitive, and award-winning author. Her memoir, *Lori: The Disintegration of My Ordinary Reality,* won a Living Now Book Award gold medal, a Non-Fiction Book Award silver medal, and a Book Readers Appreciation Group honor. She was also an Indie Book Award finalist.

Lori has vigorously studied applications of sacred science, shamanic healing, and quantum theory with many of the world's most recognized spiritual teachers. During a career that has spanned the boardrooms of Wall Street and the jungles of Central America, she has developed unique alchemical formulas for living. Through a rare spiritual awakening when she was initiated for two years as a lightning shaman by Mayan ancestral spirits, she was gifted with incredible intuition that she now uses to orchestrate personal transformations. She is capable of dissecting the human experience and helping others to break through the cosmic veil, leading them to higher levels of consciousness. Using her capabilities, Lori has built a successful alternative wellness practice in Sedona, Arizona, working with clients from all over the world. She has had particular success in supporting those who have reached a dead end in finding the underlying causes of their physical and mental health issues. Through the use of cutting-edge technology, sacred science, and shamanic healing practices she is able to go beyond the symptoms and provide successful remedies and awareness needed to resolve chronic conditions and overcome stubborn barriers to health.

Lori has a deep connection to El Salvador and the Mayan world, having spent most of her adult life living in Central America. She is especially proud of her role as a philanthropist for over twenty years as a founder of the Amigos del Lago de Ilopango, an organization that supports the social and environmental needs of wildlife and poverty-stricken families that live in and around Lake Ilopango, El Salvador.

A devotee of creation, she produced a beautiful and transformative album of meditation music, *Harmony: The Tree of Life*, with lyrics recorded in English and Spanish. In addition, she offers a life-changing online course that helps students overcome the limitations of their human experience so that personal freedom can grow.

Lori lives in Sedona in a home that her cat, Tut, allows her and her dog, Gracie, to live in with him. When she is not busy planting the seeds of awakening in others, she enjoys the smell of sweet sage, collecting crystals and stones, kicking fear in the butt, busting beliefs, remaining curious, and hoping that friendly aliens choose to land in her backyard.

Printed in the USA
CPSIA information can be obtained
at www.ICGtesting.com
LVHW082236300924
792599LV00036B/1379